A New Vision, A New Heart, A Renewed Call
Volume Three

Lausanne Occasional Papers
from the 2004 Forum for World Evangelization
hosted by the Lausanne Committee for World Evangelization

Pattaya, Thailand
September 29 – October 5, 2004

A New Vision, A New Heart, A Renewed Call
Volume Three

Lausanne Occasional Papers
from the 2004 Forum for World Evangelization
hosted by the Lausanne Committee for World Evangelization

Pattaya, Thailand
September 29 – October 5, 2004

Edited by

DAVID CLAYDON

*In encouraging the publication and study of the Occasional Papers,
the Lausanne Committee for World Evangelization does not necessarily endorse
every viewpoint expressed in these papers.*

William Carey Library
Pasadena, California
www.WCLBooks.com

A New Vision, A New Heart, A Renewed Call (Volume 3): Lausanne Occasional Papers
from the 2004 Forum for World Evangelization hosted by the Lausanne Committee for
World Evangelization in Pattaya, Thailand, September 29 – October 5, 2004

Scripture taken from the HOLY BIBLE, NEW INTERNATIONAL VERSION.
Copyright © 1973, 1978, 1984 International Bible Society. Used by permission
of Zondervan Bible Publishers.

Cover design: Amanda Valloza

Published by William Carey Library
1605 E. Elizabeth Street
Pasadena, California 91104
www.WCLBooks.com

William Carey Library is a Ministry of the U.S. Center for World Mission, Pasadena.

ISBN 0-87808-365-0

Printed in the United States of America

CONTENTS

CONTENTS

MAKING DISCIPLES OF ORAL LEARNERS

Lausanne Occasional Paper No. 54

This Issue Group on Making Disciples of Oral Learners was Issue Group No. 25

One of the 31 Issues at the Forum focused on "Making Disciples of Oral Learners." Participants in that issue group worked via email for several months in advance of the meeting. We read several papers, offered critique and comment on them, and responded to various questions. We then worked intensively for a week in Pattaya to identify the issues, determine what is already being done, and we now recommend strategies. This document is the product of the group's interactions and reflects a consensus of the participants.

Editorial Committee: Grant Lovejoy - chair, Steve Evans, Annette Hall, David Payne, Sheila Ponraj, Mark Snowden and Avery Willis.

CONTENTS

EXECUTIVE SUMMARY

From the time of the Gutenberg Bible, Christianity "has walked on literate feet" and has directly or indirectly required literacy of others. However, 70% of all people in the world are oral communicators — those who can't, don't, or won't learn through literate means. Four billion in our world are at risk of a Christless eternity unless literate Christians make significant changes in evangelism, discipleship, leader training, and church planting.

Making disciples of oral learners means using communication forms that are familiar within the culture: stories, proverbs, drama, songs, chants, and poetry. Literate approaches rely on lists, outlines, word studies, apologetics, and theological jargon. These literate methods are largely ineffective among two-thirds of the world's peoples. Of necessity, making disciples of oral learners depends on communicating God's word with varied cultures in relevant ways. Only then will the gospel be able to reach to "the uttermost parts of the earth."

Key Issues for the Church to Address:

Five aspects of making disciples of oral learners in the context of the Great Commission must be considered vital to "finishing the task":

1. Make the word of God available to unreached peoples using appropriate oral strategies.

The church is commanded by Christ to "make disciples of all peoples" which certainly includes the vast majority of the yet unreached oral learners. Providing an "oral Bible" allows God's word to be produced accurately from memory for the purpose of re-telling. The "oral Bible" is the singular key to unlocking Church Planting Movements among unreached people groups. However, that "oral Bible" must penetrate the people group to its worldview level belief system. Only then will a Bible become meaningful and useful. The only Bible that will be effective during the lifetime of the vast majority of unreached people is an "oral Bible," probably best presented in narrative form. It is important for the church to understand that a written version of Scripture does not even exist for the majority of languages. Even if literacy were achieved, the Bible would still not exist in some

4,000 languages (see further in Chapter 2).

2. **Use oral communication patterns** that allow the whole community to hear clearly in their mother tongue, to understand, respond, and reproduce the message of the gospel.

Literate church leaders and their missionaries should master new ways of preaching and teaching. Effective ministries among those with an oral learning preference will use communication forms already in place within their own culture. If the gospel is to spread freely and rapidly within an unreached people group, strategists working in that group must do their best to avoid methodology that hinders oral peoples from winning and discipling their own families, friends, and others. Training models will be most effective when they take orality into consideration. Churches will then begin to see training and new leaders emerge from within the oral peoples. These leaders will facilitate church-planting movements to rapidly disciple and equip leaders for the new churches as leaders are raised up by the Holy Spirit.

3. **Avoid syncretism by making disciples of oral learners using oral means.**

If the church is going to avoid syncretism, then the gospel needs to be communicated in the mother tongue of the people we are trying to reach. Both evangelistic as well as discipleship materials cannot be generic but will need to be developed with the worldview of the target people. The stories chosen and the manner in which they are communicated will have to transform the worldview of those who are seeing or hearing the stories. A recorded oral Bible will help serve as a standard to ensure the transmission of the stories remains accurate. These methods will help ensure that the church remains true to the historic beliefs of Christianity and does not mix traditional beliefs in their doctrines or practices.

4. **Equip relational-narrative communicators to make disciples.**

Oral strategies provide multiple ways for effectively engaging a people group to readily involve oral communicators in efforts to reach their own people group and others with the gospel. Storying is one reproducible evangelistic and church-planting approach – new believers can readily share the gospel, plant new churches and disciple new believers in the same way that they themselves were reached and discipled.

5. **Increase Effectiveness among Secondary Oral Learners.**

Oral strategies are also necessary in reaching people whose orality is tied to electronic media. They may be able to read well, but get most of the important information in their lives through stories and music coming through radio, television, film, internet, and other electronic means. We need oral strategies focused on this segment of the world population, too.

How Orality Works on the Local Level

While a storying strategy seems to be one that is particularly appropriate with unreached people groups, many established churches, especially in relational cultures, have found significant benefits to the chronological storying approach.

In evangelism: *One missionary couple cautiously entered a West Africa Muslim village.* My husband and I asked permission of the village chief to live among the people in order to learn more about them. After living among the people, we asked the chief for permission to share God's word in the village. He gave us permission to do whatever we wanted. We did not discuss the religion of Christianity or talk about "the Christian way." We never discussed Islam, Muhammad, or the Quran or the differences between Christianity and Islam. We were there to teach God's word under the leadership of the Holy Spirit. We chose to use only the storying method, to teach the stories of the Bible chronologically and bring out the truths the people needed to know in order to understand the gospel. They began storying in small groups throughout the village and distributed storying cassettes to those who asked. The Imam used some of the stories in his sermons and gave his people permission to listen to the stories. During the next year 20 individuals became followers of Jesus.

In Discipleship: The Puinave people were re-discipled when missionaries discovered syncretism. Although the Puinave had become culturally "Christian" in the 1950s, they mixed magic with Christian do's and don'ts. Many misunderstandings resulted from using the trade language, Spanish. When New Tribes missionaries spent seven years learning the difficult Puinave language in the 1970s, they were surprised at the actual beliefs held among the people. At first, the missionaries tried teaching the Bible using traditional teaching methods. The Puinave nodded their agreement, but obviously missed many of the key points. It was only through a chronological presentation of God's word, Old Testament and on to the Gospels, story by story, that they were able to vividly portray the holy nature and character of God, the sinful condition of man, the grip that Satan has on this world and the redeeming solution to man's predicament found in Jesus Christ. Later, the village elder observed, "I came just this close from going to hell..." holding up his thumb and forefinger. In 1998, New Tribes Mission made this story into a movie titled *Now We See Clearly.*

In Church Leader Training: In a north African Muslim-dominated country, 17 young men (many of whom could barely read and write and some not at all) underwent a two-year leader training program using chronological Bible storying. At the end of two years, students mastered approximately 135 biblical stories in their correct chronological order, spanning from Genesis to Revelation. They were able to tell the stories, compose from one to five songs for each story and enact dramas about each of the stories. A seminary professor gave them a six-hour oral exam. They demonstrated the ability to answer questions about both the facts and theology of the stories and showed an excellent grasp of the gospel message, the nature of God and their new life in Christ. The students quickly and skilfully referred to the stories to answer a variety of theological questions.

In Church Planting: In South America, Jeremy, an IMB worker, joined a larger team that included Wycliffe translation workers. Working with stories adapted from a neighbouring language, Jeremy instilled vision for the storying process in two mother tongue storyers and coached them through learning the stories and telling them to others. Jeremy's two-year involvement has been a significant contributing factor toward a church-planting movement that now has resulted in as many as 20% of the people group becoming believers. In the two years since Jeremy's departure, storyers continue to go to new, unreached villages up and down the river, telling the stories and evangelising.

These are but a few ways that oral strategies are facilitating God's redemptive work among oral peoples on many continents.

Conclusions, Challenge, and Recommendations

The Lausanne Committee on World Evangelization included "Making Disciples of Oral Learners" as an issue group for the first time in 2004. An estimated 90% of the world's Christian workers work among oral peoples using literate communication styles. Orality issues raise an urgent cry for effectiveness.

What a challenge! Yet, more than *four billion* people in our world need a customised strategy delivered in a culturally appropriate manner in order for them to hear, understand, respond to, and reproduce. The church today must embrace oral communicators as partners--together making disciples of all peoples to the glory of God!

Lausanne's orality issue group challenges churches and other Christian organisations to ride the next wave of Kingdom advancement by developing and implementing methods for effective oral strategies. Partners, networks, seminaries, mission agencies, conference, and workshop leaders, as well as other Christian influencers are called upon to recognise the issues of orality in the world around them. We all need to become intentional in making disciples of oral learners. We need to raise awareness, initiate oral communication projects and train missionaries and local leaders in chronological Bible storying as an effective church-planting strategy.

We recommend that:

1. The LCWE highlight this issue as essential for the evangelisation of the world, especially the unreached people groups.

2. The LCWE endorse a "Lausanne Task Force on Making Disciples of Oral Learners" to explore and implement all practical means to advance the cause of making disciples of oral

learners worldwide.

3. The LCWE and others publish material to permeate the missions world with information about oral strategies.

4. Churches and other Christian organisations develop and implement methods, communications and strategies such as:

   a. Local churches to become advocates for specific unreached people groups and promote an engagement with those people groups by using worldview-specific oral methodologies

   b. Seminaries to provide curricula to train pastors and missionaries in oral methodologies

   c. Local churches around the world to utilise oral methodologies as they disciple their own members

   d. Mission agencies to develop strategies for their missionaries and partners to use among oral learners

   e. Regional networks to host conferences in strategic locations around the world for awareness building about oral methodologies

   f. Regional partnerships and agencies to provide training in strategic locations to train local leaders and missionaries in implementing oral strategies among the unreached

   g. Regional partnerships and agencies to develop a network of trainers to train other trainers in oral methodologies

   h. Churches and agencies to record and distribute Bible stories for evangelisation, discipling, and leader training

   i. Broadcast networks and agencies to broadcast chronological Bible stories and recordings of discipleship groups in house church settings - They should include dialogue which reflects culturally appropriate ways of processing the story and interacting with it.

   j. Funding organisations to make resources available for oral methodologies to be implemented with the thousands of language groups, people groups, and segments of societies that are still unreached

With the insights gleaned from research and collaboration, Christians have the opportunity to keep 1.5 billion unreached peoples of the world from a Christless eternity in our generation. Following the examples of Jesus' teaching through parables, primary oral learners who comprise two-thirds of the world can comprehend God's word. The thorough method that oral strategies provide can assist in preventing syncretism. Oral learners can understand at their heart level, within their culture, what it means to follow Jesus. They can be discipled, become leaders, and plant churches. Let us therefore go forth embracing oral communicators as partners, together making disciples of all peoples to the glory of God!

1. A GROWING AWARENESS OF A GLOBAL SITUATION

Pastor Dinanath of India tells his story of ministry among his people:[1]

> I was saved from a Hindu family in 1995 through a cross-cultural missionary. I had a desire to learn more about the word of God and I shared this with the missionary. The missionary sent me to Bible College in 1996. I finished my two years of theological study and came back to my village in 1998. I started sharing the good news in the way as I learnt in the Bible College. To my surprise my people were not able to understand my message. A few people accepted the Lord after much labour. I continued to preach the gospel, but there were little results. I was discouraged and confused and did not know what to do.

But then Pastor Dinanath's story takes a major turn:

> In 1999 I attended a seminar where I learnt how to communicate the gospel using different oral methods. I understood the problem in my communication as I was mostly using a lecture method with printed books, which I learned in the Bible school. After the seminar I went to the village but this time I changed my way of communication. I started using a storytelling method in my native language. I used gospel songs and the traditional music of my people. This time the people in the villages began to understand the gospel in a better way. As a result of it people began to come in large numbers. Many accepted

Christ and took baptism. There was one church with few baptised members in 1999 when I attended the seminar. But now in 2004 we have 75 churches with 1350 baptised members and 100 more people are ready for baptism.

The account described in the first part of Pastor Dinanath's story is not an isolated instance. The gospel is being proclaimed now to more people than at any other time in history, yet many of those are not really *hearing* it. Unfortunately, most evangelical leaders do not realise the magnitude of the problem. Those affected by it include the 4 billion oral communicators of the world: people who can't, don't, or won't take in new information or communicate by literate means. Oral communicators are found in every cultural group in the world and they constitute approximately two-thirds of the world's population! Yet we are not communicating the gospel effectively with them. We will not succeed in reaching the majority of the world unless we make some crucial changes.

Ironically, an estimated 90% of the world's Christian workers presenting the gospel use highly literate communication styles. They use the printed page or expositional, analytical, and logical presentations of God's word--. This makes it difficult, if not impossible, for oral learners to hear and understand the message and communicate it to others. As the ones bringing the message, it is our responsibility to communicate our message in their terms. The pages that follow are intended to help point the way for us to do that.

Current estimates indicate that around two-thirds of the world's population are oral communicators either by necessity or by choice. To effectively communicate with them, we must defer to their oral communication style. Our presentations must match their oral learning styles and preferences. Instead of using outlines, lists, steps, and principles we need to use culturally relevant approaches they would understand. Are we willing to seek God to become better stewards of the Great Commission and address these issues in serving Him in these last days? The Lausanne Forum of 2004 has responded to this challenge in the form of the Issue Group focused on "Making Disciples of Oral Learners."

This terminology, "making disciples" and "oral learners," is a mix of the familiar and unfamiliar. By "making disciples" we mean enabling people to respond in faith to Jesus Christ and to grow in relationship with Him and others with the goal of obeying everything that Jesus commanded (Mt. 28:20). Or as Paul described it in more detail, making disciples involves bringing people to be

> ...filled with the knowledge of [God's] will in all spiritual wisdom and understanding, so that [they] will walk in a manner worthy of the Lord, to please Him in all respects, bearing fruit in every good work and increasing in the knowledge of God; strengthened with all power, according to His glorious might, for the attaining of all steadfastness and patience; joyously giving thanks to the Father, who has qualified us to share in the inheritance of the saints

in light (Col. 1:9b-12, NASB).

Normally discipling takes place in the context of churches that make disciples and plant other churches. By "oral learners" we mean those people who learn best and whose lives are most likely to be transformed when instruction comes in oral forms. Many groups transmit their beliefs, heritage, values and other important information by means of stories, proverbs, poetry, chants, music, dances, ceremonies and rites of passage. The spoken, sung, or chanted word associated with these activities often consists of ornate and elaborate ways to communicate. Those who use these art forms well are highly regarded among their people. Cultures which use these forms of communication are sometimes called "oral cultures."

The members of these societies are referred to as "oral learners" or "oral communicators." In this discussion, we use the terms "oral learner" and "oral communicator" interchangeably at times. With the phrase oral "learner" the focus is more on the receiving act — hearing an oral communication. With the phrase oral "communicator" the focus is more on the act of telling. These societies are relational, group-oriented, face-to-face cultures. Most of the members of these societies learn best through aural means.

Those who have grown up in highly literate societies tend to think of literacy as the norm and oral communication as a deviation. That is not so. All societies, including those having a highly literate segment, have oral communication at their core. Oral communication is the basic function on which writing and literacy is based. When literacy persists in a culture for generations, it begins to change the way people think, act, and communicate — so much so that the members of that literate society may not even realise how their communication styles are different from those of the majority of the world who are oral communicators. These members of a literate society then tend to communicate the gospel in the literate style that speaks to them.

But oral learners find it difficult to follow literate-styled presentations, even if they are made orally. It is not enough to take materials created for literates and simply read them onto a recorded format. Making something audible does not necessarily make it an "oral" style of communication. Not everything on a CD or audiotape is "oral." Some of it is clearly literate in its style even though it is spoken or audible. The same thing is true of other media products created for literate audiences. They may have literate stylistic features that confuse oral learners.

Some people are oral learners because of their limited education. They may not read or write at all, or they may read with difficulty. Many oral learners can read but prefer learning by oral means. If their culture is traditionally oral, they frequently prefer to learn through oral methods even if they are highly educated. When many people in a culture are oral learners, it affects the whole culture and permeates many aspects of people's lives, such as thought processes and decision-making. Scholars call

this whole cluster of characteristics and effects "orality." The Deaf community displays many of these traits that scholars associate with the term orality, though the Deaf cannot properly be called "oral."[2] Likewise, there are literates who demonstrate many characteristics associated with the concept of orality, an effect referred to as "secondary orality." (*Secondary orality* will be addressed in detail in Chapter six.)

In summary, approximately two-thirds of the world's population lives by orality. Many of them have no other choice because they have inadequate literacy skills, but others who are quite literate strongly prefer to learn via oral means. Together they comprise an oral majority who cannot or will not learn well through print-based instruction. This poses a challenge to those who want to communicate effectively with them.

After listening to a speaker discuss the challenge that orality poses, a ministry leader approached the speaker. "If what you say is true," he told the speaker, "we will have to rethink everything we are doing." He was right. Taking orality seriously can revolutionise ministries, and has the potential to greatly increase our effectiveness. But what should we do differently? The following chapters describe specific ways to improve effectiveness in making disciples of oral learners. They describe practical steps that various churches, organisations, and agencies are taking. A number of them share a common vision that addresses the predominance of oral communicators in the world.

That common vision is:
- God's word for every "tribe, tongue, people and nation;
- addressing the issue of orality
- resulting in church planting movements
- providing resources for oral, chronological, narrative presentations of God's word, in order to disciple and equip leaders

To these issues we now turn.

2. GOD'S WORD FOR THE WHOLE WORLD

What is the hope of reaching the four billion persons who are oral learners? What is the hope for getting God's word to the speakers of the four thousand languages still without His word?[3]

The answer comes from Jesus' own model: "...with many similar parables Jesus spoke the word to them, *as much as they could understand*" (Mk. 4:33 NIV, emphasis added). In fact, the passage goes on to say: "He did not say anything to them without using a parable" (Mk. 4:34a NIV). Jesus chose his teaching style to match his listeners' capacities. So should we. Jesus used familiar oral means that they understood. So can we.

One straightforward way to communicate to oral learners in a way they will understand is for them to hear the stories of the Bible in an oral, sequential pattern that they can absorb and remember. The communication of stories in this way has come to be referred to as "chronological Bible storying." It is a proclamation of

God's word in a culturally relevant way that oral learners can understand and respond to.

A "storying" approach to ministry involves selecting and crafting stories that convey the essential biblical message in a way that is sensitive to the worldview of the receptor society. The stories are faithful to the biblical text, and at the same time told in a natural, compelling manner in the heart language. They are expressed in the manner in which that society conveys a treasured, true story. The process also is done in a way that facilitates the hearers in processing the story in a culturally relevant way – normally involving some sort of discussion about or interaction with the story.

Without the presence of God's word there will be no true spiritual movements. Without God's word, an incipient movement will ultimately collapse, splinter, fall prey to cults, or face syncretism with existing local beliefs and practices. Unbelievers need Christians to provide His word in culturally appropriate formats in order for them to understand it and respond to it, but understanding and responding is still not enough for a spiritual movement. Those who respond need to be able to reproduce it — to share it themselves with others who can, in turn, share it with others, with this pattern being repeated many times over. A spiritual movement of this sort can provide a foundation for faith, witness, and church life. For this to happen in an oral society and involve the majority of those oral communicators who will likely remain oral communicators for their lifetime, the process will have to be an oral one for evangelism, discipleship, leader training, and church planting. Because of the communication and learning styles of oral communicators, reflecting their thought and decision-making processes, this should be primarily through narrative presentations of God's word.

This does not mean that we discourage literacy or neglect literates. Experience shows that once oral learners accept the gospel, some will have the desire and persistence to become literate in order to read the Bible for themselves. The development of oral strategies is not a deterrent to translating the Bible into every language. In fact, the opposite is true. These burgeoning church planting movements that result from an oral proclamation will need the whole counsel of God. Requiring non-Christians to learn to read just so that they can consider the Christian faith puts unnecessary obstacles in their path.

We wish all peoples had the written translation of the Scripture in their heart language. But, for the illiterate, written Scripture is not accessible even if it is available in their own language. On the other hand, a Bible translation program that begins with the oral presentation of the Bible through storying and continues with a translation and literacy program is the most comprehensive strategy for communicating the word of God in their heart language. It offers a viable possibility of making disciples of oral learners while at the same time providing the whole counsel of God.

We do not want our call for oral approaches to be seen as setting oral and literate approaches in opposition to one another. It is not a matter of "either-or," but "both-and." Again, the Bible itself gives the model. There are examples throughout the Scriptures where both the written word of God and the spoken word of God are given prominence, often side by side. For example, Moses wrote down the words of the Law (Deut. 31-33). God instructed him to write the words down in a song. God also instructed him to teach the song to the Israelites so that they would always have it in their hearts and on their lips and always remember it.

Similarly in today's world, we envision a systemic approach to evangelism, discipleship, church planting, and leadership development that can involve oral, audio, audio-visual media and print. A systemic, sequential approach with a society of largely oral communicators, for example, might begin with oral Bible storying. It could then possibly begin to involve audio and radio presentations of these same oral stories and other audio and radio products of a broader array based on translated biblical material.[4] In some cases primary visual products may be produced and effectively used.[5] Then the process in some situations may move on to the preparation and distribution of audio-visual products based on translation of further biblical material.[6] Throughout the approach the undergirding process of Bible translation, at first orally and then in a literate manner, provides the entire counsel of God.

In a sequential approach like this, the first biblical stories we use focus very intently on the unique cultural perspective of the people. Specificity to that culture is crucial in order for them to understand the gospel well and embrace Christ. The same will be true of the stories we use in initial discipleship. Later stages in the strategy will give them ever-larger portions of the Bible; at that point our focus will have shifted from cultural specificity to providing complete books of the Bible, a New Testament, and finally the whole Bible.

God's word has transforming impact on people's lives when we present it in ways that they can understand it. For example, missionaries worked for twenty-five years with the Tiv tribe in central Nigeria and saw only twenty-five baptised believers as a result.[7] That is an average of one believer per year of ministry. Their medium of communication was preaching, which they had learned in Bible school was the proper way to evangelise.

Then some young Tiv Christians set the gospel story to musical chants, the indigenous medium of communication. Almost immediately the gospel began to spread like wildfire and soon a quarter million Tivs were worshipping Jesus. The Tivs were not as resistant as the missionaries had thought. A change in method brought abundant fruit. Prior to this the gospel had been "proclaimed," but it had not been heard! The communication strategy chosen had not spoken to the heart of the people. This story underscores that groups may not be necessarily unrespon-sive, but have not yet received the gospel in their learning style. Where traditional literate methods have failed to reach people, appropriate oral strategies have succeeded.

When Christian workers follow these principles, non-Christians are more likely to give the gospel a hearing, more likely to respond in faith to it, and more likely to spread it enthusiastically to their friends, relatives, and neighbours. In the Togolese town of Kpele-Dafo, for instance, the hamlet sprang to life when the message came: "The storyteller is coming!"[8] The sound of drumming announced the coming of the storyteller. Men left their game of *adi*, tailors closed shop, and yawning children roused themselves. The drumming intensified as the storyteller took his place in the centre of the village, where he seated himself on a low, carved bench. The elders of the village arrived in their finery and the animated storyteller, Antoine, exchanged ritual, formalised greetings with his audience. The fetish priestess, clothed in white and wearing her horsehair amulet, stood near, watching intensely.

As night fell and the logs crackled in the fire, Antoine began in melodic, poetic style: "*In the beginning, God created the heavens and the earth...*" When he reached the repeated phrase, "*And God saw that it was good*," he sang a song composed in their familiar call and response style. He sang a line about God's creative work and the villagers sang back, "*And God saw that it was good.*" The villagers quickly memorised their part and sang it enthusiastically. Before long, the villagers began dancing too, to express their delight at this God who created a good world. The village headman joined in the dance, signalling his approval of the story and the event. Antoine continued his story long into the night, accompanied by the sound of drumming and joined in his song by the villagers. When the fire had burned low and the story-song finally ended, no one wanted to leave. The whole experience had engulfed them. A new truth was dawning and their world would never be the same.

Antoine returned many times over the next several weeks, bringing story after story in this way — stories about Abraham and his sons, about the other prophets, about Jesus and God's community. These stories spoke to the villagers' longings, needs, and practices, prompting long conversations with Antoine and among themselves. Gently but firmly the Holy Spirit used the stories to do his transforming work. In time extended families made God's story their own story, the God of the Bible their God. A fetish priest burned his amulets, talismans, and jujus because he no longer needed their protection.

The same storytelling approach was used to bring about the surrender of strongholds and for discipleship. Through Bible storytelling the word of God came to life in the African context. The biblical stories continued as the people of Kpele-Dafo grew in their newfound faith, meeting in house churches and taking this message to neighbouring villages. The same process has now taken place throughout the Volta region of Togo, Benin, and Ghana, resulting in a movement of people to Christ.

Five key principles were at work at Kpele-Dafo.

- The word of God is more effectively communicated through appropriate cultural relationships.
- The word of God will be best heard and understood when we use appropriate oral strategies.
- The word of God is most effectively proclaimed when worldview issues of the unreached are addressed; stories and other cultural forms do this more effectively by inviting listeners to identify with the message.
- The word of God changes individuals, cultures, and worldviews.
- The word of God can be passed along by ordinary Christians if they receive it in appropriate oral forms.

In both these cases the use of familiar, accepted forms of communicating helped to make the biblical message less foreign. People could easily participate in the event. The word became readily available to them. They entered into the stories and the stories entered into them.

In many parts of the unreached world there is open hostility to evangelistic activity. Crusades, mass evangelism, and public preaching are not welcome. Bible studies and open witnessing draw negative responses. In these situations storying can be more fully appreciated. Storying is not confrontational. It is not preaching. It is not overt teaching. It is merely conveying the stories of God's Word, dialoguing about them and leaving the results to God! Most of the time the hearers do not even realise that their values are changing until they can no longer deny the truth. His word says that it will not return void or empty. So, the power of His word, combined with the power of the Holy Spirit, does amazing things! These stories can go where the printed Bible sometimes cannot go. They can cross borders, enter jail cells, even go into the heart of Muslim, Hindu, animist, or socialist homes! They can penetrate the heart of the one listening and change that person's life for eternity.

3. ORAL COMMUNICATORS AND ORAL CULTURES

Developing proficiency in using oral strategies involves several tasks. Literates who want to communicate effectively in oral cultures need to learn about the issue of orality. Walter Ong's book, *Orality and Literacy* (1982) is a respected academic work on the topic. He offers lengthy, technical discussions of the nature of orality and the impact that the development of writing, then typography, had on oral communication and oral cultures. His approach is largely historical.

Another approach to understanding the extent and influence of orality is to consider it in relationship to literacy skills. The reality of low literacy skills even in developed countries has become apparent from a series of surveys, beginning with the National Adult Literacy Survey (NALS) administered by the U. S. Department of Education in the early 1990s.[9]

Researchers found that 48 to 51% of adults in the United States scored at the two lowest levels (out of five levels) of measurable proficiency at a range of literacy skills. While results of the NALS study showed that only 4 to 6% of U. S. adults were totally illiterate, 46 to 53% were identified as unable to function adequately in a highly literate society or process lengthy written information adequately.

It was reported that while many adults at Level 1 (21-23%) could perform tasks involving simple texts and documents, all adults scoring at that level displayed difficulty using certain reading, writing, and computational skills considered necessary for functioning in everyday life. Those at Level 2 could perform simple analysis, but were unable to integrate information from longer texts or documents or carry out mathematical skills when necessary information was contained in the directions. (Interestingly enough, a majority of those at Level 1 and almost all of those at Level 2 described themselves as being able to read English "well" or "very well!")

When the International Adult Literacy Survey (IALS) tested adults in twenty-two countries from 1994-98, similar results emerged in Australia, Canada, Germany, Ireland, the U.K., and elsewhere among developed nations.[10] Although the various governments previously had claimed national literacy rates of 90% or more, the surveys revealed that many people actually had a quite limited range of literacy skills. Such people live day to day largely by oral means even if they are able to read simple, brief materials.

The Bible is certainly not simple, brief material. If half of the population in developed nations, with longstanding literate traditions, is unable to integrate information from a text like the Bible, what is the situation of those in oral cultures with no such tradition when it comes to gaining spiritual truth?

The survey results from NALS and IALS suggest that there is not a simple, black-and-white dichotomy between "literates" and "illiterates." Other studies similarly give more revealing definitions of literacy that characterise it in terms of the different ways people function with literacy in society. One UNESCO document, for example, says:

> A person is functionally literate who can engage in all those activities in which literacy is required for effective function of his or her group and community and also for enabling him or her to continue to use reading, writing, and calculation for his or her own and the community's development.[11]

It is helpful for literate cross-cultural Christian workers to be aware of different degrees of literacy if they are to communicate with people in appropriate ways. These degrees of literacy reflect a continuum. One categorisation of salient points along this continuum is that of James B. Slack, which describes five levels of literacy to be considered in presenting the gospel:

- "Illiterates" cannot read or write.

They have never "seen" a word. In fact, the word for illiteracy in the Indonesia language is *buta huruf*, meaning "blind to letters." For oral communicators, words do not exist as letters, but as sounds related to images of events and to situations that they are seeing or experiencing.

- "Functional illiterates" have been to school but do not continue to read and write regularly after dropping out of school. Within two years, even those who have gone to school for eight years often can read only simple sentences and can no longer receive, recall, or reproduce concepts, ideas, precepts, and principles through literate means. They prefer to get their information orally. Their *functional* level of illiteracy (as opposed to published data) determines how they learn, how they develop their values and beliefs, and how they pass along their culture, including their religious beliefs and practices.

- "Semi-literates" function in a grey transitional area between oral communication and literacy. Even though these individuals have normally gone to school up to 10 years and are classified in every country of the world as literates, they learn primarily by means of narrative presentations.

- "Literate" learners understand and handle information such as ideas, precepts, concepts, and principles by literate means. They tend to rely on printed material as an aid to recall.

- "Highly literate" learners usually have attended college and are often professionals in the liberal arts fields. They are thoroughly print-culture individuals.[12]

Trying to reach the first three categories using customary means presents two major problems: Almost all missionaries and other Christian workers are literate or highly literate, and they communicate primarily by literate means. So they use the method they have mastered to try to communicate with oral learners who do not "hear" them. They think that if they can just simplify their outlines and exposition oral learners can grasp what they are saying. When missionaries try to reach illiterates, they believe that one of their primary tasks is to train a corps of literate nationals (who then face the same problems communicating). For these reasons it is essential that literate church leaders seek to understand orality as the first step in ministering effectively in oral cultures.

Although UNESCO reported in 2003 that almost 80% of adults worldwide can read, that statement is open to challenge. It depends on literacy statistics provided by each member nation of the United Nations. Furthermore, it allows every country's government to decide for itself how to determine who is literate. Malaysia, for instance, counts anyone age 10 or over who has ever enrolled in school as being literate. Other countries simply ask people if they are literate; many people say that they are, even though their reading skills may be too limited to handle text from the Bible. Many people who can write their name and read a simple sentence qualify as literate for census purposes, but they cannot read unfamiliar or lengthy materials with understanding. Their values are not changed by what they read.

In assessing the orality of a people group, it is important to keep in mind that literacy rates often vary greatly from one group to another within a single nation. Minority language groups, many of whom are unreached peoples, are less likely to be literate. Many of them have little interest in becoming literate. Those who intend to work with unreached people groups would be wise to be sceptical of governmental literacy statistics when it comes to functional literacy.

Missions groups such as the International Mission Board (Southern Baptist Convention), Scriptures in Use, and others have developed materials on understanding orality and oral cultures. A selection of these is available at www.chronologicalbiblestorying.com. The annotated bibliography included with this document also suggests a wide array of resources for learning more about orality.

After developing a basic understanding of orality, literate missionaries and ministers then need to learn effective oral communication styles which are culturally relevant. In general, there is a cluster of features that oral learners have in common in processing information — they most readily process information that is concrete and sequential, and which is presented in a highly relational context.

Other aspects of an effective communication style for a particular oral culture may be discovered by careful observation and participation in the life of the community.

Using culturally appropriate oral forms improves the impact of the message. Oral learners "enter" the story and as they absorb sensory data they live the story in the present tense — seeing, hearing, tasting, smelling, and feeling what the persons in the story are experiencing. They hang reality on these sensory experiences. This happened when "Fatima," an immigrant who had never been to school, attended a class to learn French.[13] As a part of the French class, she heard the story of Abraham, Sarah, and Hagar. At the end of the story Fatima said, "That's a true story."

The teacher asked, "What do you mean?"

Fatima replied, "God made Abraham a promise and Abraham didn't have the faith to wait for God. He acted on his own. And look at all the trouble that came to that family. It happens all the time. People don't have the faith to wait for God. They act on their own and they get into trouble just like Abraham did. It's a true story."

Fatima vicariously lived the story. Without prompting from the teacher, she melded the story's experiences with her experiences. The right cultural form enabled the truth to flow unimpeded into her life.

Having identified the communication forms that the culture uses, it is then crucial that ministries use the existing oral communication forms that the culture already uses (i.e.: story, music, drama, poetry, dance, proverbs, etc.) There are many examples of the impact of Bible stories when time and freedom of expression are both given in order to develop a culturally sensitive storying strategy.

One such example of the effectiveness and reproducibility of using music in orality and storying strategies comes from southeastern Africa:

> The ladies gathered on the lawn for their weekly sewing session. They were in a mountain village about forty kilometres from the shores of Lake Malawi. Usually, as the ladies sewed, they sang. I was visiting the house next door as the ladies began to sing. Because I like music, I enjoyed listening to their singing as I talked with my friends. After a while I heard a tune that was vaguely familiar, but I couldn't place it. I listened harder, concentrating on the music rather than my hosts. Then it hit me! The words and tune I was hearing were the same ones I had heard at a Yao music workshop two weeks before and forty kilometres away! In one day, the group developed fourteen Scripture songs focused on essential stories of God's word. In two weeks the song had travelled across the lake and up the mountain to a village forty kilometres away from where the workshop was held! In their own language they were singing:
>
> "In the beginning God created, and it was good!
>
> It was good!

In the beginning God created, and it
was good!

It was good!

It was good!

It was good!

It was good!

It was good!

In the beginning God created, and it
was good!"

The song went on to tell about
God creating the world, then man.
"He made you, He made me," they
sang. Finally the song ended:

"It was good!

It was good!

It was good!

It was good!

All that he had made--yes, it was
good!"[14]

An example of how members of an
oral culture naturally relate to oral forms
of Scripture as their own comes from an
experience of Herbert Klem, doing an academic research project involving various
test groups:

One evening I came to a study
which was crowded out with visitors. I could tell many of the visitors were Muslim elders from the
very community where I was told
so often that people felt too old to
become Christians. I did not want
all those visitors spoiling the structure of my test group, so I politely
asked the visitors to leave these
Christian test lessons. The wise old
elder had a twinkle in his eye as he
gently and politely suggested that
they were having a wonderful time
hearing God speak to them, and that
perhaps I should be the one to
leave. I did not know what to do. I
was thrilled to have a Muslim man

in a Bible study, and he was an
elder leader, but I did not want to
spoil the structure of my test.
When I asked him politely to leave
a second time, he grinned and challenged me to a true test of ownership of the singing Bible tapes. The
one who could sing the least of the
tape from memory would leave, and
the one who could sing the most
could stay. That was the indigenous method of proving cultural
ownership.

Because of the tonal intricacies
of singing oral art in that language,
he knew he had me beat cold — no
contest! The group cheered and
proclaimed him the owner of the
tape. He boasted that only a wise
Yoruba man could compose and
sing this kind of poetry; insiders
loved it and outsiders could admire
from a small distance.

The elder had been warmly attracted to the text because it had
been identified with his culture,
employing art forms that marked it
as his cultural property, even
though it was played on a tape re-
corder supplied by a meddling foreigner. He was pleased with the
form of the message, but he was
also bonding with God's Word from
the book of Hebrews. He was no
longer telling me this was "foreign
religion" but was defending his
right to hear the Scripture. Best of
all, the whole group loved the entire
event.[15]

In addition to the choice of communication form, the choice of what language
to use is crucial. The most effective ministry strategies among oral cultures occur

when the communication is done in the heart language, the mother tongue. It is often easy to overlook the fact that 1.5 billion people speaking over 4,000 different languages are still awaiting God's word in their heart language. Many of these groups have a long history of being a minority people in their own country. When the Bible has come to them in the past, it has often been in a printed form that they cannot read or in a language which does not speak to their heart. In fact, it might be in the language of the very people who they feel have oppressed them for many years.

However, when they hear the stories from God's word in their own language, they are often amazed and have an immediate heart response and cultural identification with that message. They may respond that indeed God has remembered them and He is for them! When they hear the message in their heart language, the words speak to them in an indescribable way. Because it is their own language, it captivates them and they want to hear more.

Stories heard in the mother tongue are easily memorised and retold to others. Oral learners can often recite large portions of scripture when they hear these passages in their mother tongue and packaged in the stories that they can easily learn and reproduce.

Effective ministries among oral cultures should be worldview sensitive in order to build bridges of understanding and confront barriers to the gospel message. Because stories possess the power

to actually change how people think, feel, and behave, and to change the way they see the world, it is important to have a sequential, step-by-step process that leads them to a new, biblical worldview. What is effective in such situations is the oral communication of a set of chronological Bible stories that involve points of similarity between a culture's worldview and a biblical worldview. This incorporates "bridges" from its worldview to the biblical story. It simultaneously confronts "barriers" to the gospel, those elements of the worldview that hinder understanding and acceptance. Over time, confronting worldview barriers with stories of the Bible can lead them to accept a more compelling story than the stories associated with their own worldview.

An example of this account comes from the Asheninka people group in Peru:

> Alejandro, the leader, is doing great in chronological Bible storying and the people understand. He told the story of Jesus calming the waters during the storm and Cladis softly told me that she used to believe that the Owner of the Winds could be stopped by placing your axe in the ground with the blade cutting the wind, but now she knows it is God that created the winds and He is God. Also, she told me that she is not scared of the rainbows anymore because they do not kill you when you walk under them. God created the rainbow to make a promise with us. Alejandro himself came to the understanding that he can baptise the people and the people understand that they can be baptised after

simply believing. So, Alejandro baptised twelve believers last week. It was a week of fiestas. Trip after trip Alejandro tells the stories, *then,* it hits them. It is such an awesome thing to be part of.[16]

Choosing stories that address worldview bridges and barriers of a specific people group or segment of society improves the likelihood that their worldview will be brought into conformity with the biblical pattern, the kingdom of God.

Understanding orality and oral cultures gives us the basis for adopting effective oral communications strategies. These understandings enable us to realise the importance of the word being shared in the mother tongue and in ways that enable the people to embrace the message from God.

4. DISCIPLES TO THE CORE

Syncretism is "the mixing of Christian assumptions with those worldview assumptions that are incompatible with Christianity so that the result is not biblical Christianity."[17] Syncretism weakens the church, warps non-Christians' understanding of Christianity, and withholds from God the full devotion and complete obedience that is rightly due to Him. So the spiritual health and vibrancy of Christian churches depends on developing a faith that is as free from syncretism as possible, a faith that is both biblical and culturally relevant. Several key elements can contribute to discipling oral learners with a minimal amount of syncretism.

The first key element in avoiding

syncretism is communicating with people in their mother tongue — the language in which they learned their religion, values, and cultural identity. They house their innermost thoughts in their mother tongue, so it is the language through which their worldview is most likely to change. They can explain their new faith more readily to others in their people group when they use the mother tongue. In using the mother tongue, one must carefully consider the key biblical terms to use in a language if there is not yet a Bible translation. Concepts like love, grace, and sin, or even the basic notion like the name used for God, the Holy Spirit, or Christ need to be carefully identified. Inadequacies in this area readily lead to syncretism.

When pastors are asked why they preach in a national language or trade language instead of the local language of their congregation, they often respond that they did their theological training in the trade language and that the local language is not rich in theological terms. If the pastor does not know how to express theological terms in the local language, you can be sure that his people are not grasping these important concepts. When the pastor does not preach and teach in the local language, he is leaving the important task of choosing the correct term to interpreters who do not have the benefit of the pastor's theological training. The use of interpreters who are not trained in biblical language can result in wrong words being used for important Christian concepts and this can lead to syncretism or even heresy.

The Puinave people of Colombia were "re-discipled" when missionaries uncovered syncretism.[18] Although the Puinave had become culturally "Christian" in the 1950s, they mixed magic with their understanding of Christianity's behavioural norms. Many misunderstandings resulted from using the national language, Spanish, in their Christian activity. When New Tribes Mission workers spent seven years learning the Puinave language in the 1970s, they were surprised at the syncretistic beliefs held. At first, they tried teaching the Bible using traditional teaching methods. The Puinave nodded their agreement, but missed many of the key points.

It was only through a chronological presentation of God's word, beginning with the Old Testament and on to the Gospels, story by story, that they were able to vividly portray the holy nature and character of God, the sinful condition of man, the grip that Satan has on this world and the redeeming solution to man's predicament found in Jesus Christ. Reflecting on this redemptive panorama of God's provision, the village elder held up his thumb near to his forefinger and observed: "I came just this close from going to hell..."

Consider the example of Jesus. He taught using the common heart language of the people, rather than the trade language. Jesus spoke in the format that the common people understood such as stories, parables, and proverbs. The people who heard were able to understand and apply them, bringing about transformed lives. By communicating in the heart lan-

guage and using the methods that are common in the culture, we can minimise the danger of syncretism and heresy.

A second key element in reducing syncretism is to develop discipling resources that are worldview specific. Generic discipleship materials are insufficient. Certainly there are biblical essentials that every new Christian needs to know, such as prayer, worship, witness, fellowship and ministry. These practices, however, should fit the local culture under the leadership of the Holy Spirit rather than the practices of the host culture of the missionary. Kraft points out that syncretism occurs when the evangelisers impose their cultural values on the new Christians and fail to separate the evangelisers' own culture adequately from the biblical message.[19] If a certain set of discipleship materials worked well with a people group or segment of society, it is because the materials were meaningful to that worldview. The fact that they served so well among one people should serve as a caution that they will not likely meet needs as effectively in a different cultural setting.

The best discipling resource among oral communicators is not a printed booklet but an obedient Christian. Oral communicators learn by observing. Discipleship involves the disciple spending time with the more mature believer learning by following his or her example. The teaching is conducted more by watching and doing rather than just learning facts. Discipling oral learners would best follow the biblical models such as Elijah, Jesus, and Paul. For example, Paul tells the Philippian believers, *"Whatever you have learned or received or heard from me, or seen in me–put it into practice"* (Phil. 4:9 NIV). The goal would be that the disciple would immediately become a discipler. As Paul told Timothy, *". . . the things you have heard me say in the presence of many witnesses entrust to reliable men who will also be qualified to teach others"* (2 Tim. 2:2 NIV).

A third key element in discipling oral learners in order to limit syncretism is to recognise the importance of stories in transforming a person's worldview. N. T. Wright says that stories constitute the core of every culture's worldview. (See the diagram below.) A culture houses its central convictions in its fundamental narrative, whether its narrative is implicit or explicit. The ancient mythologies that we find in cultures around the world are explicit examples of this. Those stories answer four fundamental worldview questions: Who am I? Where am I? What has gone wrong? What can be done about it? Every culture uses stories to tell us what it means to be human, what kind of world we live in, why there is suffering and pain, and what, if anything, we can do to deal with that suffering and pain. Christianity has its own distinctive answers to those worldview questions. In order to influence the worldviews of disciples, we need to tell biblical stories that offer alternative answers to the fundamental worldview questions. The Bible answers these questions with special vividness and power in the opening chapters of Genesis.[20] That is one reason it is so important to include Old Testament stories in discipling. Furthermore, when we tell biblical stories chronologically, we are offering a powerful alternative worldview from the very beginning of our presentation. Biblical stories, and the view of the world embedded in them, can replace or refine the cultural stories and the worldview embedded in them.

Wright argues that this is why Jesus so often told stories, particularly parables. Jesus intended them to challenge the existing Jewish worldview and to provide an alternative picture of reality that Jesus called "the kingdom of God" or "kingdom of heaven." Wright says, *"Stories are, actually, peculiarly good at modifying or subverting other stories and their worldviews. Where head-on attack would certainly fail, the parable hides the wisdom of the serpent behind the innocence of the dove, gaining entrance and favour which can then be used to change assumptions which the hearer would otherwise keep hidden away for safety."*[21]

Wright says stories come into conflict with each other because worldviews and the stories which characterise them represent the realities of one's life. People are threatened by the intrusion of an opposing worldview or story because it challenges their understanding of reality. Wright says, *"The only way of handling the clash between two stories is to tell yet another story explaining how the evidence for the challenging story is in fact deceptive."*[22]

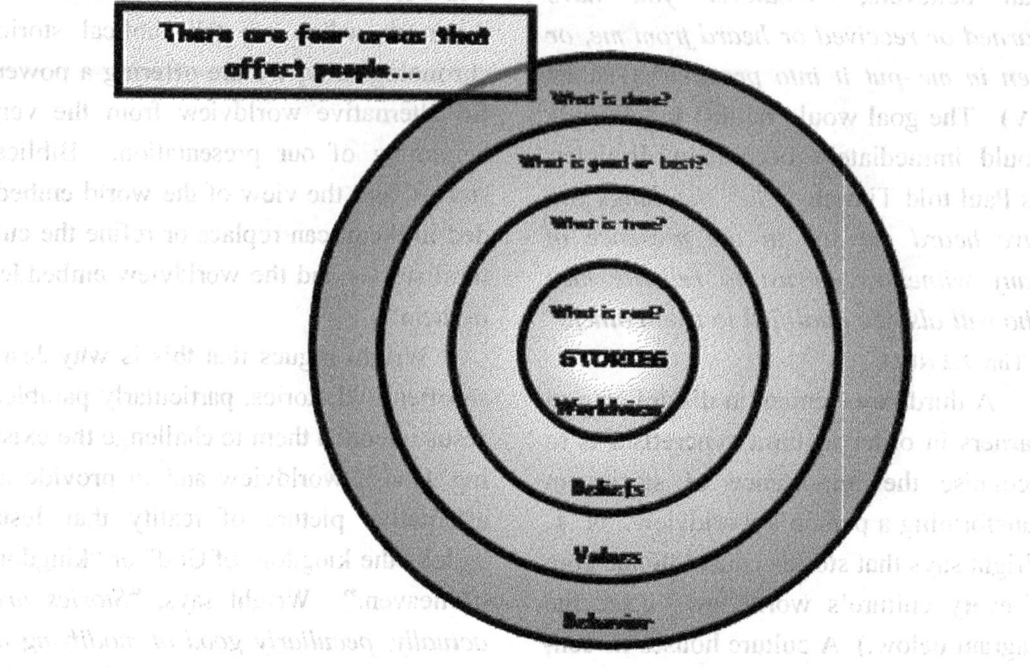

If stories anchor people's existing perspective on the world, then the best thing Christians can do in order to displace that perspective is to tell better stories, and we have them! Our stories must provide biblical answers to the essential questions of life.[23] The more biblical stories people know and can fit into a single comprehensive story of God's saving work, the more completely they are able to embrace a biblical worldview. By changing their fundamental view of the world, we hope to influence a wide array of beliefs and practices which grow out of that fundamental core.

Wright argues that stories lie at the core of a worldview; formal belief statements, including propositional and theological statements, grow out of those stories. Thus discipleship that offers only propositional teaching does not reach to the centre of the worldview. If we give only propositional teaching and do not present biblical *stories* to challenge existing worldview *stories*, we run the risk of syncretism. The cultural stories will continue to comprise the heart of the worldview and discipleship will deal only with the dimensions of the person's life represented in the outer circles in the diagram. Because propositional beliefs are generated by and reflected in the core stories, those cultural stories will continually be challenging the Christian propositional content. We wind up with the tragedy of professing Christians who assent to biblical propositions, but whose essential worldview and value system is deeply tied to worldview stories that have gone unchallenged. That mix of contradictory religious beliefs and practices is the essence of syncretism. It constitutes a failure in discipling.

A careful study of an unreached people group's worldview will reveal common ground, bridges between their worldview and the Bible. On these matters the discipler may simply *reinforce* existing beliefs and practices. Worldview study also will disclose matters on which the people group's worldview is contrary to the biblical ideal; these contrary matters are barriers.[24] In those instances, the discipler guides converts to *replace* the existing belief or practice with the biblical one. In addition, the study may reveal issues in which the existing practices and beliefs can be *revised* into the way of Christ. This approach to discipling aims to minimise the syncretism that comes when people just adopt Christian rituals or practices, but keep intact the mythology that underlies the traditional religion. When their core stories are not challenged and replaced, the traditional mythology will continue and may over time infuse the Christian practices with meanings from the traditional religion.

A fourth key element in order to avoid syncretism is to provide a recorded "oral Bible" for each people group in their language. This is a recorded set of stories, biblically accurate and told in the worldview context. At this point the "oral Bible" may be the only scriptural resource available to oral learners. At some future time, when written Bible translation is completed, then it could be recorded to provide a standard point of reference.

In an "oral Bible," the stories are communicated in natural, live situations by mother tongue "storyers" from the people group, using the mannerisms and storytelling techniques which are appropriate to that people group. The Bible stories are checked to ensure biblical accuracy before recording takes place. By utilising this system that checks the stories as they are told, it will ensure that this recorded "oral Bible" is a plumb line for oral methods such as stories, song, etc.

By telling Bible stories in a straightforward way, we give new converts an opportunity to engage biblical truth directly and discover its message for themselves. This approach is significantly different from the approach that has people read numerous individual verses, sequenced according to the curriculum writer's sense of importance and logic, and largely divorced from their biblical context. Telling a biblical story in an interesting and accurate way is a simple but powerful manner of freeing disciples to process Scripture. They can do it with a minimum of filtering and interpretive baggage coming from the discipler's culture and experience of Christianity. This is especially true when we tell the stories in chronological order, thus putting them in a biblical context.

The practice of keeping the story *pure* (separate from our own comments and interpretive remarks) protects the oral learners from the syncretism that might come from embracing a polished system of ethics, theology, or pastoral philosophy that has a significant dose of European, North American, Korean, Brazilian, or Chinese cultural baggage. Instead they synthesise a biblical theology from the stories and can apply it in all kinds of practical situations with courage.

In summary, those of us who seek to make disciples of oral learners will want them to understand biblical truth and live obedient lives as free from syncretism as possible. We can increase the likelihood of that happening when we disciple in the mother tongue, use worldview-specific approaches instead of generic ones, utilise biblical stories extensively, and work with mother-tongue speakers to produce an "oral Bible" that provides a reliable repository of biblical truth.

5. REPRODUCIBILITY, REPRODUCIBILITY, REPRODUCIBILITY

Many people accept the idea that an oral approach like chronological Bible storying may be appropriate to initial evangelism, but they wonder whether a storying approach is viable for a sustained, indigenous-led church planting movement. Is it adequate for sustained discipleship among second, third, and successive generations and for leadership development in the church? Those working in storying in face-to-face, relational societies assert that not only is it a viable approach to meet these needs—it is the preferred approach to ensure reproducibility and thus sustainability in an emerging, indigenous-led church.

For a spiritual movement to be engaged, we must consciously choose strategies that oral learners can easily reproduce. We must constantly evaluate whether we are modelling the kind of disciples we want the learners to become. This is the most powerful form of discipling. Oral communicators learn best when they pattern themselves after those who led them to Christ. From our first contact with non-Christians, we are modelling how a Christian relates to non-Christians and seeks to introduce them to Jesus Christ. Thus even our evangelism is in this sense a part of discipling.

The first and most basic aspect of ensuring reproducibility in a storying approach is crafting and telling stories in a way that the hearers are able to readily learn and tell themselves and thus effect a reproducing evangelism. This is why we place great importance on the live, natural telling of stories by mother tongue storyers in the common situations where people communicate with one another. When the gospel is communicated to an oral learner in a way that shows dependence on a written or recorded presentation, it inhibits this reproducibility.

A storyer from Senegal reported:
Recently one of the oral learners told all of us the story of Cain and Abel. She was very accurate, animated, and told all of it from memory. She also led the discussion time with questions. The truly amazing part is that she had missed the previous week's lesson and had learned the story at midweek prayer meeting from another woman who had been present for the training. This oral learner had learned the story from one who had herself just learned the story and had learned to tell it. Some of their children who

attend the study with them have prayed: "Thank You that our mother is now able to teach us the Bible."[25]

A similar case is reported among the Santal people of South Asia.[26] Village literacy among this people group was found to be 0.08%. The Santal people have no written history and do not rely on written documents for evidence or for credibility. They rely on what the elders have decided or what the elders say. A Christian outreach effort went to a Santal village and met Marandi, a man who had never been to school. They presented the gospel using oral methods, including stories, visual aids, dramas, songs, dances, and testimonies. Marandi trusted Christ and shared his testimony with his family, who also believed and were baptised. He then went to other relatives and shared his new faith with them, using many of the same oral methods. They also believed and were baptised. He then formed a team of believers, all oral communicators, who went to neighbouring villages using the same combination of stories, dramas, songs, etc. People in those villages accepted Christ, too. Those new believers formed their own teams and they went to yet other villages, still using the same basic strategies that had been introduced in the beginning. Many Santal people believed and they then formed their own outreach teams. The movement continues today among the Santal people.

Other stories and case studies attest that discipling, church planting, and developing leaders are also effectively done by a storying approach. First consider a story that shows effective discipling within an oral, storying approach.

In a dusty village in southwestern Nigeria, "Timothy" serves faithfully as pastor of a young church consisting of Yoruba farmers and their families.[27] Three years into his pastorate, Timothy had the opportunity to attend a short course for pastors on chronological Bible storying. There he learned the ancient way of teaching that was new to him. He was encouraged to tell Bible stories in an accurate and interesting way and then lead the group to retell the story, discuss its meaning, and relate the truths to their lives. Upon arriving home, Timothy decided that on the following Sunday he would try out what he had learned.

Because the conference leader had recommended telling Bible stories in chronological sequence, Timothy decided to begin with the story of the creation of spirit beings. He drew on several biblical passages to formulate this particular story as had been illustrated in the short course. After asking them about their creation stories and getting no response, Timothy told the Yoruba creation story. He used that as a bridge to the biblical narration of the story of the creation of angelic beings. He presented it as a story — without explaining it or exhorting the group. Afterward, he asked for someone to retell the biblical story and someone did. Then he asked them questions and led in a dialogue that helped them understand and apply the story.

"It was thrilling to me that someone was able to tell the story and others made corrections," he later reported. "The people were very eager to hear more of the stories. When they began to ask questions that were beyond the story, I did not answer [their questions] but simply told them, 'as I tell more stories, you will discover that yourself.'"

Timothy explained, "I have come to understand that they are more open to ask questions with this method, unlike when I was using the [denominational] Sunday School book. Even the children were answering questions. So it is good for the children too. I have decided to train someone by sharing the story on Saturday with the person so that he or she can share with the children on Sunday.

"I also discovered as I asked them questions and listened to their questions that they were still holding on to their previous teachings of worshipping angels," Timothy explained. "To them the angels are from heaven and can reach God better, so we can pass through them to God. This session has further taught me that they have not understood my topical sermons. It now gives me the opportunity to explain to them things on this issue which I do not normally preach on."

Timothy used the same approach the next Sunday, telling the story of the creation of the heavens and the earth. After this second storying session with them, he commented, "Some of their questions during the session have made me understand that they have not understood many things from the Bible for these three years [that he had been their pastor]."

Timothy discovered several important lessons about making disciples. He realised that to effectively disciple, one must first determine how one's people learn. Although Timothy had pastored his people for three years, he had not been aware that his preaching style needed to match the people's learning style. They lived in a relational culture with a strong oral tradition. They passed on their history in stories and proverbs. Timothy became conscious of the fact that he was a literate pastor trained in literate teaching methods. The methods he had been taught to use worked well among people highly educated in western schools, but they didn't work well in his situation. He decided to return to his cultural roots as well as model his preaching and teaching after the greatest teacher–Jesus.

Before Timothy changed his teaching methods, he had been frustrated by his people's lack of response. He thought the problem was theirs, that perhaps they were not very intelligent. When Timothy changed his methods the people responded and he discerned that he had been the problem because he had not been communicating effectively. He said, "I have learned to be patient with learners and not to condemn them rashly when they give some 'stupid' answers that are not relevant to what we are discussing. This has encouraged most that didn't use to respond to questions to do so now."

An oral, storying approach can likewise be effective for church planting. A recent church planting movement took place in South Asia among a highly oral people.[28] The oral peoples consisted of various scheduled castes, some of whom were animists while others were of Hindu religious background. From 1997-2003 an agricultural project combined with a chronological Bible storying approach led to approximately two thousand new church starts. An expatriate strategy coordinator worked with two media specialists — one a national and one an expatriate — to develop the biblical stories and the communications strategies. The stories were chosen and crafted with biblical accuracy to engage the people at their worldview values and beliefs level. The stories that were told in the villages were the same stories they heard through the FEBA radio broadcasts. The media specialist and FEBA provided taped recordings that served to improve the hearers' memory of the stories. The local Christian farmers, who were trained in implementing vital agricultural and health technologies, mentored other farmers even on large plantations.

In using those technologies, they told the Bible stories in sequence in the evenings after the agriculture sessions. Those who demonstrated further interest in the Bible stories they heard were invited into Bible story listening groups focused on the radio broadcasts. In the groups they would hear the stories told again but in those groups they were organised to discuss the stories as they heard them. Later the stories were also told face to face by those who became interested in the stories and who embraced Jesus Christ as Lord and Saviour. Again, the stories were circulated on audiocassette. It is important to understand that the stories heard on the radio, the stories told in the fields and villages, and the stories heard on the cassettes were the same stories.

Thousands of believers have come from this wedding of agricultural, health, and storytelling technologies. As this church planting movement continues to escalate through these partner methods, the locals are now addressing aberrant doctrinal beliefs through stories. An independent evaluation of this situation revealed a situation where the lay pastors, discipled and trained by oral methods, maintained essentially correct doctrine, compared to more literate pastors in the same people group, trained by literate means, who exhibited syncretised doctrinal positions. This group dates its origin to a preacher who came in the 1760s. They had about 250 churches when the multiplication of churches began through the storying approaches. Since they began storying, they have gone from a mathematical average of approximately one new church a year to approximately one new church a day.

Another example of church planting using similar storying strategies comes from Romania.[29] Expatriate church planting strategists with the Deaf were involved in a storying approach with associates in planting five Deaf churches. Those among the Romanian Deaf community who became believers through a storying approach in those five church plants went on to plant twenty more Deaf churches. They used the telling of their own testimonies in their heart language, Romanian

Sign Language, coupled with chronological Bible storying.

Deaf communities have many of the features as we have been talking about for oral communicators. In fact, a more comprehensive way of looking at what are called "orality" features is not that they are crucially or exclusively associated with what is spoken by mouth. They are, instead a correlation of ways of processing that are common to face-to-face, highly relational societies. The correlation of ways of processing and communicating involve concrete (rather than abstract) notions; sequential (rather than random) expression of events; and relational (as opposed to individualist) contexts. Both oral cultures and Deaf communities exhibit these characteristics because they are face-to-face, highly relational cultures. Throughout the world Deaf communities are being reached by chronological Bible storying methods. So there is reason to include them in this discussion. (It is in some sense inaccurate to call the Deaf "oral communicators." Furthermore, they dislike the terms "oral," "orality," and "oralism" because they associate the terms with nineteenth and twentieth century efforts to force the Deaf to give up sign language and learn to speak.)

An account of oral, storying strategies that were effective in leadership development comes from North Africa.[30] There 17 young men (many of whom could barely read and write and some not at all) underwent a two-year leader training program using chronological Bible storying. At the end of two years, stu-

dents mastered approximately 135 biblical stories in their correct chronological order, spanning from Genesis to Revelation. They were able to tell the stories, sing from one to five songs for each story, and enact dramas about each of the stories. A seminary professor gave them a six-hour oral exam. They demonstrated the ability to answer questions about both the facts and theology of the stories and showed an excellent grasp of the gospel message, the nature of God, and their new life in Christ. The students quickly and skilfully referred to the stories to answer a variety of theological questions. Given a theological theme, they could accurately name multiple biblical stories in which that theme occurs. If asked, they could tell each story and elaborate on how it addressed the theme.

The professor concluded that "the training process has successfully achieved its goals of enabling students to tell a large number of biblical stories accurately, to have a good understanding of those stories and the theology that they convey and to have an eagerness to share the Christian message. The community received the stories and story-songs enthusiastically and have made them part of the culture and church life alike."

"Various students acknowledged that they entered knowing little of the Old Testament, did not understand the relationship between God and Jesus, did not know the characteristics of God, did not know that God created the angelic beings, had not heard of being born again and did not know that Christians should not seek help from local deities. Upon entering the program these students were unable to communicate the Christian faith to other people, but by the time the training was over, they had dramatically improved their understanding of all of these matters and many more," he said. The songs and stories became so popular that when the students returned to their villages, the local people eagerly gathered to learn the new songs and stories, and frequently sang the Scripture songs and told the stories late into the night, sometimes even until dawn.

The stories and case studies above illustrate various aspects of reproducibility among relational-narrative communicators, both among oral communicators and the Deaf. One important aspect of this involves them telling the story of their own experience of coming to faith in Christ. Those from face-to-face societies readily testify to their personal, daily relationship with Christ. Testimony times in worship services in Western services are limited or non-existent. However, among oral communicators, testimony and prayer times may take up most of the service. When friends and neighbours hear these testimonies and see the change in new converts' lives, they often want to follow the "Jesus road." After they have come to Christ through a process of biblical revelation through stories, the discipler helps them learn an abridged story of the gospel message to use immediately. Disciplers then encourage them to give others the opportunity to hear the biblical stories they heard, in order to consolidate their faith and give these new believers a biblical foundation. Multiple church planting and discipleship efforts from the U. S. to China now incorporate a "my story, your story, God's story, others' stories approach."

Discipling oral communicators involves identifying what the new believers need to know and do and then communicating these truths using appropriate methods. These methods include modelling, telling a Bible story that communicates a truth, discussing it, perhaps memorising a Scripture related to the matter and applying the truth together or individually. Their discipleship is shaped by the modelling of another believer and on-the-job training. This is most effective when the modelling is done by an in-culture or close-culture believer. Discipleship is not just what one does but who one is — a new creature in Christ. Then we must help them understand that discipleship is primarily a matter of obedience to everything Jesus commanded and revealed in Scripture.

Discipling involves having the disciple do all of the preceding plus being held accountable to report back. This model of discipleship emphasises accountability for application in two crucial dimensions: living it and sharing it with others. Oral learners, like all true followers of Jesus, need to practice what Scripture teaches and to pass along to others what they are learning.

Oral communicators are more dependent on relationships in communication than literate learners are. For that reason oral communicators tend to place a higher value on those relationships. They believe persons more than abstract truths. So the spiritual life and modelling of the messenger is crucial. Making disciples of oral communicators requires maintaining a loving relationship with the ones being discipled. Disciplers help oral communicators acquire biblical truth through appropriate oral means and guide them to obey it. Disciplers also teach them to win and disciple others who will in turn disciple others. The new converts join existing churches or form new churches, according to the situation.

Discipling oral communicators should lead directly to church planting as new converts come together in covenant communities of believers to carry out the functions of the church. In many instances, these will be house churches that develop along lines of kinship and friendship. Disciples grow best when, from the beginning of their Christian experience, they take responsibility for evangelising, nurturing new converts, establishing new works, and overseeing the development of their own converts.

Providing orally based leader training for oral learners and equipping them to continue it within their people group is one of the great challenges facing the Church. Those involved in rapidly growing church planting movements must disciple and equip leaders for the new churches as leaders are raised up by the Holy Spirit. If they do not, the expansion of the movement slows or ceases.

A summarisation of the storying approach from the CD series, *Following Jesus: Making Disciples of Oral Learners,* specifies a ten-step process toward making disciples of primary oral learners with reproducibility as the important culminating step:

- *Identify* the biblical principle that you want to communicate–simply and clearly.
- *Evaluate* the worldview issues of the chosen people group.
- *Consider* worldview – the bridges, barriers, and gaps.
- *Select* the biblical stories that are needed to communicate the biblical principle.
- *Plan* (craft) the story and plan the dialogue that is going to follow the story, focusing on the task to be accomplished.
- *Communicate* the story in a culturally appropriate way, using narrative, song, dance, object lessons, and other forms.
- *Apply* the principle by facilitating dialogue with the group, helping them to discover the meaning and application of the story to their own lives.
- *Obey* the discovered principle by implementation steps to be taken by the individuals.
- *Accountability* – establish accountability between group members by mutual and reciprocal commitments to implement the biblical principle in the conduct of their personal lives between members of the group, their families, and other personal relationships.

- *Reproduce* – encourage the group to reproduce the biblical principle, first by demonstrating the principle in their own "witness of life" then in sharing the principle with others.[31]

Bible storying provides a way of engaging a people group that is not highly technological and can readily involve oral communicators in efforts to reach their own people group with the gospel. Storying is thus a reproducible evangelistic and church planting approach — new believers can readily share the gospel, plant new churches, and disciple new believers in the same way that they themselves were reached and discipled.

While a storying strategy seems to be one that is particularly appropriate with unreached people groups, many involved with people groups where there is an established church have found significant benefits to a chronological storying approach in those situations as well. The oral, chronological approach can fill major gaps that literate approaches to evangelism, discipling, church planting, and leadership development have, over the decades, missed.

6. WHEN LITERATES STOP READING

Recall the statement that two-thirds of the world's people can't, won't, or don't read and write. The bulk of this paper has focused on those who can't. This part will focus on those who don't. These are those who choose to learn by oral methods as opposed to literate ones, in spite of their literacy. These people are known as secondary oral learners. James B. Slack defines "secondary oral learners" as "people who have become literate because of their job or schooling, but prefer to be entertained, learn, and communicate by oral means." Walter Ong, father of the modern orality movement, says, "I style the orality of a culture totally untouched by writing or print, 'primary orality.' It is 'primary' by contrast with the 'secondary orality' of present-day high-technology culture, in which a new orality is sustained by telephone, radio, television, and other electronic devices that depend for their existence and functioning on writing and print."[32]

Earlier in this paper we explored the characteristics of oral learners. It is increasingly evident that many of these same characteristics are as descriptive of secondary oral learners as they are of primary oral learners. As such, the effectiveness of our communication is dependent on what we do with this knowledge.

Our purpose is to call missions-minded Christians to explore ways to be more effective in communicating with secondary oral learners–in reaching them for Christ, helping them grow and mobilising them to involvement in ministry.

Why is it important to do this? A 2004 study reported that "literary reading in America is not only declining rapidly among all groups, but the rate of decline has accelerated, especially among the young." This reflects a "massive shift toward electronic media for entertainment and information."[33] Numerous western societies are seeing similar shifts toward electronic media and the accompanying secondary orality.

Consider the following statistics:

- 58% of the U. S. adult population never read another book after high school.
- 42% of U.S. university graduates never read another book.
- Adults in the U.S. spend four hours per day watching TV, three hours listening to the radio and 14 minutes reading magazines.[34]
- British teenagers' pleasure reading declined by about a third from 1991-1998.[35]
- In Denmark one-third of adults do not do any significant amount of reading.[36]
- More than half the adults in the Netherlands hardly ever read a book.[37]
- Dutch 12 year old school children spend, on average, less than half an hour a week reading in their leisure time.

Apparently, related trends are unfolding elsewhere in the world.

"Reading and writing are clearly dying arts," professor Jim Dator of the University of Hawaii said, "something which fewer in the world are doing." More important, he said, is the fact that reading and writing are something fewer and fewer people need to know how to do. "Most people in the world, even most of the literate people in the world in fact, do not get much of their ideas about the world from reading. They get them from watching television, going to the movies, listening to the radio, and other forms of audio-visual communication."[38]

Ravi Zacharias, a Christian apologist, agrees. "More and more we are knowing less and less about the printed tradition," he said. "The ability for abstract reasoning is diminishing in our time, because [people] come to their conclusions on the basis of images. Their capacity for abstract reasoning is gone." Zacharias concludes that we are now in a time where there is a "humiliation of the word" and an "exaltation of the image."[39]

In their book *Church Next: Quantum Changes in Christian Ministry,* Eddie Gibbs and Ian Coffey also conclude that people today are more influenced by audio and visual media than print media. "Theirs is a post-literacy culture for which sound and image have largely replaced the printed word," they claim. The two argue that "instancy" and intimacy are the distinguishing features of today's non-print media, and that seeing, not reading, is the basis for believing.[40]

Pritish Nandi, publisher and television news producer in India, recently wrote an article titled "Will Technology Usher in an Era of Illiteracy?" In it he said, "New technology will no longer divide the world into literate and illiterate people but will bring everyone together in a common platform where the ability to read and write will no longer matter. You will have a new world where people will need an entirely different kind of skills set to succeed."[41]

All of these examples are clear indications of a growing global emergence of secondary orality, or post-literacy as some call it. This phenomenon is causing us to think, communicate, process information, and make decisions more and more like oral peoples. The implications of this have ramifications not only on what we do in evangelism, discipleship, leader training, and church planting, but also on how we do it! We must make adjustments in the way we communicate the message of the gospel, acknowledging that our goal, responsibility, and desire are to communicate truth in the most effective ways possible.

For many of us, it is becoming more and more evident that issues of secondary orality are reaching the very altars of our churches around the world. Christian researcher George Barna said that technology and the mass media have forever changed the ways in which we process information, saying that "the inability to systematically apply scriptural truth produces a spiritual superficiality or immaturity that is reflected in behaviour." He concludes that we must develop new forums and formats through which people will experience, understand, and serve God.[42]

Tommy Jones, author of *Postmodern Youth Ministry,* urges us to tell stories. "Narrative is becoming the primary means of telling beliefs. Since propositional logic has fallen on hard times, stories carry more weight in carrying truths — 'abductive' reasoning. As opposed to deductive or inductive methods, when you tell a story, you 'abduct' listeners from their known worlds into another world."[43]

Rick Durst, academic dean at Golden Gate Seminary in San Francisco, California, agrees. "To be a 'storyteller' is no longer a euphemism for someone with a loose grip on truth," he said. "The storyteller is becoming again the person of wisdom who knows the 'good telling stories' that make and maintain community and meaning." Durst refers to well-known Christian author Leonard Sweet, who sees pastors as "story doctors," who use the "truthing" of biblical stories to heal the dysfunctional stories confining and confounding people's lives, concluding that ministry to the emerging generation will be magnified to the degree that narrative is applied.[44]

How do we get started? First, we need to pray that God will show us how to be more effective. We need to ask for ways to turn what have been barriers into bridges. Second, we need to be observant of what is already proven in how to communicate with literate people who have at least some preference for learning orally. For example, many graduate programs in business administration use case study discussions to teach essential leadership principles. As another example, many of the most effective evangelistic speakers and pastors use stories to illustrate their message points. Dallas Theological Seminary professor Howard Hendricks is quoted as saying that such illustrations are the windows to the soul. As a third example, many who teach the Bible in small groups have discovered that a way to understanding is for the student to see specifically how a Bible truth looks when it is applied. If the leader is able to share his or her own experience (story) with how this works, learning is greatly accelerated.

Summarising this second point, we already know a lot about using oral methods with people who are literate. We just need to surface what we know and become more intentional in using it.

Finally, we must proactively experiment with new ways to be even better in communicating with secondary oral learners. One such experiment is being done in Orlando, Florida, by Campus Crusade for Christ. A group of Christian college students are being taught how to do follow-up and discipleship using storying versus using written materials. Four types of stories are being used by the disciplers:

- God's stories (narratives from Scripture)
- Their stories (stories of the discipler's own experience with God)
- Others' stories (stories from other people's lives and video clips from movies and TV programs)
- Disciples' stories (immediate practical applications of biblical truth so that the new disciple can develop his or her own stories that can be used to minister to others, thus promoting spiritual multiplication)

Similar models are being launched with executives and professionals, as well as with new Christians in Sunday School classes.

These are but a beginning of the kinds of extensive and innovative efforts that will be necessary to learn how to use storying to connect better with secondary oral learners of all educational and socio-economic levels. As lessons are learned, they need to be shared freely to further accelerate the learning process in how to be more effective.

We possess knowledge of the greatest story ever told. We increasingly understand how to communicate that knowledge better with the two-thirds of the population of earth who will receive it best through storying and other oral means. In recent years we have begun to see that storying can greatly increase effectiveness even with literate people, including college students and business and professional people.

Our call to action is simple: Let's do everything we can to set aside any tendencies we might have to ignore or not utilise this fact, and let's pray and take advantage of every effective method so that, in the spirit of the apostle Paul, "by all possible means we might save some."

7. A GROWING ENGAGEMENT

Aspects of the storying approach are still under development and orality is still a relatively young academic discipline. Even so, there is enough confidence in the effectiveness of oral approaches to making disciples that reputable organisations are investing resources in an ever-growing engagement of the approach. Following are several examples reflecting this growing movement.[45]

The International Mission Board (IMB) of the Southern Baptist Convention, the largest denominational international mission agency, is heavily engaged in this approach. IMB has hundreds of field teams using storying as a primary strategy in dozens of countries. In Suriname a storying strategy in one people group enabled Christianity to spread from a handful of known believers to the point of having believers living in every village in that people group in less than five years. Most villages also have a house church.

Scripture In Use (SIU) and local partners, such as Bihar Outreach Network in India and many others around the globe, have trained over 7000 grassroots workers in 50 countries in Communication Bridges to Oral Cultures. This short course equips non-Western workers to understand their own oral cultures and to develop Scripture storying skills and strategies such as story-telling-drama, cultural adaptations of Scripture in song, memorisation, and recitation. SIU focuses on mentoring other agencies through the process of adopting oral methods into their missions programs in order to address orality and the needs of oral cultures within their regions of influence. In one area 75 churches have been planted with 1450 believers, in another area 30 churches were planted in two years; and in another difficult area 22 churches were planted in three years.

Over the past six years, an alliance of international agencies which has come to be known as the Oral Bible Network has sponsored consultations aimed at sharing insights and experiences in orality and storying and promoting the approach. Sponsoring agencies are Campus Crusade for Christ (CCC), Faith Comes by Hearing, IMB, God's Story, Progressive Vision, Scripture In Use, Wycliffe International, Southwestern Baptist Theological Seminary, and Trans World Radio (TWR).

Table 71, a partnership growing out of Amsterdam 2000, involving the leadership of CCC, Discipling A Whole Nation (DAWN), IMB, WorldTeach, Wycliffe and YWAM (Youth With A Mission), has adopted chronological Bible storying as a primary strategy of cooperative efforts.

Progressive Vision has recently produced *Following Jesus: Making Disciples of Oral Learners* (2002), an orally-based discipleship resource. *Following Jesus* models the practice of identifying a biblical truth that should be taught, inquiring how the people group would perceive that truth through their worldview, and then selecting biblical stories that could be used to teach that truth in light of that worldview. It consists of seven modules of 53 audio CDs that teach how to communicate to oral learners. The modules give the format and tell over 400 Bible stories that enable the oral learner to go from being a new Christian to becoming a senior pastor or cross-cultural missionary without having to read.

Epic Partners International, a partnership founded by CCC, IMB, Wycliffe, and YWAM, is engaging a storying approach among unreached peoples. Epic conducts training and workshops and establishes EpiCenters around the world to enable churches or agencies to prepare forty to fifty initial stories in an unreached people's language, equipping mother-tongue storyers to tell the stories and multiply churches. It also makes audio recordings of the stories for archiving and broad sowing by volunteers.

Radio ministries are becoming increasingly involved in supporting oral approaches. FEBA Radio has partnered with other agencies in Central Asia, the Middle East and North Africa in broadcasting stories. TWR has recently identified orality as one of five top strategic initiatives.

A Deaf Bible Network has been formed fostering Deaf nationals recording Bible stories in their native sign languages: *God's Stories in Sign*. Deaf Opportunity Out Reach (DOOR) has four training sites for chronological Bible storying where Deaf leaders from over 25 countries have been trained.

Global Recordings Network (GRN, formerly Gospel Recordings) has produced audio and audio-visual Bible-based evangelism and discipling resources in more than 5500 languages designed specifically for non- and minimally-literate people groups. These resources continue to be refined as GRN develops strategic partnerships with other like-minded organisations to reach the unreached oral communicators of the world.

This growing engagement is not limited to missions agencies. Local churches are getting involved as well. Larry Johnson is a coordinator among pastors in Ellis County, Texas, a rural county south of Dallas.[46] Johnson attended a training event about oral communicators and how to work effectively with them. There he realised that there were many oral communicators in his county and came to understand how the churches could minister to them more effectively. When he returned to Ellis County, he shared his findings with pastors. "They recognised that these are the people they are not reaching through traditional churches," he said. "They may be members, but they are not in positions of leadership and are probably on the fringes."

Johnson then enlisted pastors, interested educators, church members, and other skilled people to identify worldview values and beliefs among Ellis county oral communicators. They then chose biblical stories to speak to the oral peoples' view of the world, crafted them, and set about to test them through telling them to sample groups of oral people in the county. They also selected visual materials to use in conjunction with the stories. They have set a goal of planting 700 churches, most of which will meet in homes.

While making these preparations, Johnson heard through international missions announcements that leaders in Central America needed churches to partner with them in evangelising a specific unreached people group. Today these local churches in Ellis County have gotten additional training in language and worldview issues, and have extended their use of oral strategies to Central America. Johnson comments: "We are now doing overseas among an oral people group what we have been learning to do among our own oral people in Ellis County."

Strategies using oral methods, then, are not unproven theories. They have a proven track record, beginning with biblical times and continuing to the present. Under a wide array of situations, among diverse people groups on virtually every continent, oral strategies have demonstrated their effectiveness in evangelism, discipleship, church planting, and leader development.

What can an individual do to become a part of this growing engagement in making disciples among oral learners? Here are some practical steps: Any individual reading this paper can learn more about the field of orality and storying by reading the books, visiting the websites, or contacting the agencies referenced in this paper. The individual can learn to story passages from the Bible. The individual can identify the nearby oral communicators who are not believers and look for natural opportunities to story the gospel among them and to disciple them with stories. Individuals can share their journey in storying with the local church they are part of, and investigate ways of going global like those in Ellis County have done.

Conclusions

From the time of the Gutenberg Bible, Christianity "has walked on literate feet." Christians have led the literacy movement because of desiring to read the Bible for themselves. Yet Christians increasingly are concerned that hundreds of years have passed without a comprehensive global Kingdom advance. In 2,000 years since Christ's Great Commission, only about 10% of all peoples are evangelical followers of Jesus.

Effective discipling of oral learners allows them to embrace biblical patterns of Christian life and belief and utilise communication forms that are familiar within the culture. Of necessity, discipling oral learners involves communicating the unchanging message of Scripture into varied and ever-changing cultures in worldview-sensitive ways. It means discipling in ways designed to avoid creating dependency on the discipler. It means setting the oral disciples free to evangelise, disciple, plant churches, and train leaders in a never-ceasing pattern. Only then will the message be able to reach to "the uttermost parts of the earth."

So what shall we do with this fresh insight to communicate with oral learners? This is an issue for the Lausanne Committee for World Evangelization (LCWE) and the entire Christian world to investigate, embrace, propagate and utilise in finishing the task of reaching the unreached peoples of the world. Here are proposed actions:

1. The LCWE to highlight this issue as essential for the evangelisation of the world, especially the unreached people groups

2. The LCWE endorse a "Lausanne Task Force on Making Disciples of Oral Learners" to explore and implement all practical means to advance the cause of making disciples of oral learners worldwide

3. The LCWE and others to publish material to permeate the missions world with information about oral strategies

4. Churches and other Christian organisations to develop and implement methods, communications, and strategies such as:

a. Local churches becoming advocates for specific unreached people groups and promoting an engagement with those people groups by using worldview-specific oral methodologies

b. Seminaries providing curricula to train pastors and missionaries in oral methodologies

c. Local churches around the world utilising oral methodologies to disciple their own members as a way of avoiding syncretism

d. Mission agencies developing strategies for their missionaries and partners to use among oral learners

e. Regional networks hosting conferences in strategic locations around the world for awareness building about oral methodologies

f. Regional partnerships and agencies providing training in strategic locations to train local leaders and missionaries in implementing oral strategies among the unreached

g. Regional partnerships and agencies developing a network of trainers to train other trainers in oral methodologies

h. Churches and agencies recording and distributing Bible stories for evangelisation, discipling, and leader training

i. Broadcast networks and agencies broadcasting chronological Bible stories and recordings of a discipleship group in a house church setting, including dialogue reflecting culturally appropriate ways of processing the story and interacting with it

j. Funding organisations making resources available for oral methodologies to be implemented with the thousands of language groups, people groups, and segments of societies that are still unreached

With the insights gleaned from research and collaboration, Christians have the opportunity to reach in our generation the billions of unreached people in the world headed to a Christless eternity. Following the example of Jesus' own witness through parables and proverbs, we can communicate the gospel orally in a way that these unreached people can understand, respond to, and reproduce. Let us therefore go forth embracing oral communicators as partners — together making disciples of all peoples to the glory of God!

8. AN ANNOTATED RESOURCE LIST

In keeping with our interest in assisting churches in ministry, we have listed below a number of resources that churches might use in making disciples of oral learners. This list is representative, not exhaustive. There are doubtless other fine resources not listed here.

In a listing as diverse as this, it is inevitable that some resources will be better suited to a given situation than others. Some of the resources below focus on ministry among unreached peoples having no literacy and no Scripture in their language, while other resources are intended for audiences with significant amounts of literacy. Some of the resources have been carefully tailored for a specific worldview; others have not been. Some resources are free of charge while others involve significant purchases. Some are intensely practical and simple; others are academic and technical in nature. We encourage pastors, churches, missionaries, researchers, and others to discern what resources would best suit their needs.

Resources on Orality, Bible Storying and Audio-Visual Bible Services and Products
Individual Resources

Terry J.O. ed. *Bible Storying: God's Word Story by Story to Empower Every Person Oral or Literate for Witness and Discipling Their Own.*

> *An electronic newsletter on Chronological Bible Storying worldwide. Subscribe free at biblestorying@sbcglobal.net.*

__________. *Journal of Bible Storying.*

> *An electronic journal on the more academic and scholarly side of Chronological Bible Storying. Subscribe free at biblestorying@sbcglobal.net.*

Charlton Heston Presents the Bible. 4 DVDs. GoodTimes DVD. (1993).

> *Shot on location in the Holy Land, this incredible production is more than great literature come to life--it is a walk through history itself. Connect with some of the most beautiful and relevant Bible stories. This is an educational and entertaining family activity, allowing the viewer to experience the power and drama set to rich musical scores. This Bible storytelling resource is in four parts: Genesis, Moses, Jesus, and the Passion. www.hestonbible.com.*

Communication Bridges to Oral Cultures—Master Trainer Series Manuals for Grass Roots Church Planters (80 pp.), *Discipleship through Storytelling* (68 pp.), *Stories and Letters of the Apostles* (34 pp.), accompanied by a 3-DVD set (3 hour video series) available in English, Spanish, French, Hindi, Mandarin, and Amharic (others in progress).

> *These resources are used for a four-day intensive training course for grass roots church planters. Approximately 75-100 training events are given each year in various parts of the world by Scriptures In Use and various partner agencies.*

Evans, Steve. *Communicating Christ in a Cross-Cultural Context: Developing Effective M e d i a and Communication Strategies Leading to Church Planting Movements / The World of Orality.* Workbook/PowerPoint. (2004).

The World of Orality: Limited Edition is a 43-page mini workbook taken from the much larger *Communicating Christ in a Cross-Cultural Context: Developing Effective Media and Communication Strategies Leading to Church Planting Movements.*

It is a good introduction to the world of orality and the development of strategies to reach oral peoples. The accompanying PowerPoint is a general overview of orality and its impact on Christian work around the world. Free download at http://www.communication- strategy.net/ synapse/documents/Files_public.cfm?Website=communication-strategy.net

Willis, Avery. *Following Jesus: Making Disciples of Primary Oral Learners.* Audio CDs. (2003). **Progressive Vision.**

Your answer to critical issues: 1) getting the gospel to all nations; 2) communicating with non-literates; 3) addressing syncretism problems; 4) making disciples of oral learners who comprise 70% of the world's population; 5) the next wave of missions advance. Designed to reach illiterates, functionally illiterates, semi-literates, storying cultures and many others who simply prefer a non-literate approach. Following Jesus consists of seven learning modules that frame this learning experience on audio CD! Designed for translation and cultural adaptation. For information go to http://fjseries.org.

My Place in HIStory. Study Course/Multi-Media. Lifeway Christian Resources. (1999).

A videotape and workbook church training course on how to use Chronological Bible Storying to share the gospel with family, friends and neighbours. https://www.lifeway.com/cgsp/ english/catalog (then do a resource search and indicate My Place in HIStory).

Norwood, Johnny. *Storying for Evangelism and Church Planting (Textbook and Teacher's Manual): For Training Christian Leaders to Teach Both Literate and Oral Oriented Learners How to Do Chronological Bible Storying in Antagonistic as Well as Sympathetic Settings.* Chiang Mai, Thailand (2003).

A step-by-step manual on using pre-selected chronological Bible stories for personal evangelism. For information write jnorwood@gsnconsultants.com.

Tell the Story: A Primer on Chronological Bible Storying. Workbook/Study Course. International Center for Excellence in Leadership, 2003.

Learn how to reach oral communicators effectively with the gospel using this workbook including CD. This workbook consists of 13 lessons, starting with the world of stories to using Chronological Bible Storying for church planting movement strategies. For information go to http://resources.imb.org/index.cfm/fa/prod/ProdID/1140.htm.

Davis, Charlotte ed. *Telling His Story in the Caribbean Basin: Chronological Bible Storying.*

An electronic newsletter sharing the world of Chronological Bible Storying in the Caribbean and South/Central America. Subscribe free at cdavi17@attglobal.net.

The HOPE: The Story of God's Promise for All People. **Mars Hill Productions.**

Created in cooperation with motion picture producers and distributors around the world, The HOPE is a powerful dramatic overview of an incredible story—the Bible—a story many have called the greatest ever told. Designed for cultural adaptation and language translation, *The HOPE* is divided into 12 chapters and 36 events and is available in VHS or DVD format. For information go to http://www.mars-hill.org/media/the_hope_main/the_hope_set.htm.

Organizations, Resources, Services, and Products

The Bible Storytelling Project

The Bible Storytelling Project uses Bible stories in chronological order for the purpose of evangelizing, teaching, preaching, planting new churches and training church leaders. Bible stories in chronological order give a panoramic view of the Bible and an overview of basic Bible doctrine. This project has numerous Bible storytelling resources, including *Storying the Bible: Tools for Bible Storytelling* by Jackson Day. Age-level curriculum is available in English, Spanish, and Portuguese. Contact jackday@pobox.com or http://biblestorytelling.org.

Deaf Church Planting Network

The "Deaf Sign-Bible" visual program is being developed in several sign languages. This includes video, DVD or CD recording accompanied by a set of story cards. The presentation utilizes a system of iconic symbols to aid in memorization and presentation of gospel truths. The presentations provide an overview of the Bible from creation to Christ the way of salvation, the basics of the Christian life, and strategies for church planting. This is an excellent evangelism, discipling, and church planting resource for the Deaf. Also, there are visual recordings of Bible messages in various signed languages. (These are a selection of short Bible stories or messages signed by native Deaf sign users). Go to www.deafchurches.net.

Deaf Opportunity OutReach International (D.O.O.R.)

D.O.O.R. (Deaf Opportunity Out Reach International) uses Chronological Bible Storying in its three regional leadership-training centres: 1) Nairobi, Kenya, 2) San Jose, Costa Rica, and 3) Budapest, Hungary. They have trained 240 Deaf Christians from 44 countries. Go to www.DOORInternational.com.

Faith Comes By Hearing

FCBH has dramatized word-for-word recordings of the entire New Testament in 150 languages, with 50 more in process. They also have training on how to use these recordings to disciple oral people through the formation of Faith Comes By Hearing listening groups. There are 25 national recording teams in 12 Recording Service Centres located throughout the world that are trained to do dramatized recordings including music and sound effects with cutting edge portable digital recording and editing equipment. For more information visit www.fcbh.org.

Global Recordings Network/Gospel Recordings

Global Recordings Network has produced the following resources suitable for use with and by non- or minimally-literate people (oral communicators): *Gospel Messages* in over 5,500 languages. (These are usually a selection of short Bible stories or messages spoken by mother tongue speakers and sometimes incorporate indigenous music); the *Good News* audio-visual program available in over 900 languages (this includes a cassette or CD recording accompanied by a set of 40 pictures giving a brief overview of the Bible from creation to Christ the way of salvation and the basics of the Christian life); the *Look, Listen and Live* audio presentation (available in more than 300 languages, consisting of 8 cassettes with accompanying picture sets: parts 1-5 cover Old Testament stories and themes, parts 6 & 7 cover the four Gospels and part 8 covers the book Acts); *The Living Christ* audio-visual presentation (available in about 30 languages, with 120 loose leaf pictures and commentary on 2 cassettes – the pictures come with a printed script and a set of 20 short lessons for use as a teaching resource). All pictures are also available as black and white line drawings. GRN also offers hand-wind cassette players for use where there is no power and batteries are expensive or not available. For more information, prices and orders go to www.globalrecordings.net/au or www.globalrecordings.net

The God's Story Project

The 80-minute presentation, *God's Story: From Creation To Eternity*, presents the Bible from Genesis to Revelation. Throughout the Old and New Testaments, this panorama of the Scriptures highlights God's plan to rescue fallen mankind. For evangelism and discipling. Available in video, VCD (video CD), audiocassette, audio CD. In total there are over 200 language translations of *God's Story* either finished, in various stages of negotiation or in script translation. This does not include the over one thousand languages that have also been requested. "Our desire is to partner with national Christians, willing to share the workload, to produce a tool for them to use for evangelism and discipleship in their country." TGSP features a village-size backpack containing a VCD player, *God's Story* on Video CD (VCD), a solar panel and a battery power source. These items enable an evangelist to deliver the gospel via *God's Story* to homes and gatherings in remote areas where there is no electricity! Optional PA with wireless mic projects sound clearly to 500 feet. Script, discussion guide and radio script are also available. For information go to www.Gods-Story.org or www.biblevideo.org.

The JESUS Film Project

The *JESUS Film* Project distributes the film "JESUS," a two-hour docudrama about the life of Christ based on the Gospel of Luke. The film has been seen in every country of the world and translated into over 870 languages since its initial release in 1979. The goal is to reach every nation, tribe, people, and tongue, helping them see and hear the story of Jesus in a language they can understand. Through use by The JESUS Film Project, and more than 1,500 Christian agencies, this powerful film has had more than 5 billion viewings worldwide since 1979. As a result, more than 197 million people have indicated decisions to accept Christ as their personal Savior and Lord. The *JESUS* film is available in video, VCD, and DVD formats, as well as in a special children's edition and audio-radio format. Other resources are available as well. Go to
http://www.jesusfilmstore.com/Merchant2/merchant.mvc?Screen=SFNT

MegaVoice

MegaVoice: *The Word in Hand.* "Break the Silence…Finish the Task." A unique application in voice storage and retrieval, designed to dramatically accelerate dissemination of vital information, including God's Word, Chronological Bible Stories, etc. The *MegaVoice Ambassador* is a palm-sized, self-contained digital audio player designed to store up to 160 hours of material and has an internal solar panel for rechargeable batteries. The *MegaVoice Messenger* is a smaller unit, designed to store up to one hour of material, and has been known as the "Talking Tract." For information visit
www.megavoice.com or write info@megavoice.com.

Mission Education Books (MEB)

Mission Education Books is located in Chennai, India and has a wealth of resources on orality, church planting, and Bible storying. They have *Discipleship through Storytelling, Gospel Communication Bridges for Non-Literates* by S. D. Ponraj and Jim Bowman, *Communication Bridges to Oral Cultures II*, and more. Many titles are in languages of India. For information go to
http://www.missionbooks.net/pubtraining.htm.

New Tribes Mission

EE-TAOW!; EE-TAOW! The Next Chapter; and *Now We See Clearly.* Videos/DVDs. New Tribes Mission. Discover the success of chronological presentations of God's Word for effective church planting, discipleship, and correction of syncretism. Go to http://www.ntmbooks.comindex.cfmfuseaction=catalog.shop&shopAction=listCategory&categoryID=5&sr=1. In addition to numerous other resources, NTM offers *Bible Teaching Pictures* on CD. Both in colour and B&W line drawings, this CD contains 105 Bible story pictures to be used in chronological narrative presentations of God's Word. For information go to http://www.ntmbooks.comindex.cfmfuseaction=catalog.shop&shopAction=itemDetail&catalogID=116&categoryid=1&myInventoryID=33

The Radio Bible Project

The Radio Bible Project is a global partnership between Hosanna/Faith Comes By Hearing, the International Bible Society, Trans World Radio, and the United Bible Societies formed to bring the Word of God to oral societies. The Radio Bible consists of 365 fifteen-minute broadcasts of stories from the Old and New Testaments. These programs allow both literate and oral communicators the opportunity to hear the Bible in an engaging fashion. While the core of the Radio Bible is a dramatized Scripture presentation, it also includes background and engagement material so listeners can understand and apply the Scriptural stories to their daily lives. Find more information about this project at www.theradiobible.org

Scriptures In Use

Scriptures In Use specializes in training grass roots church planters to communicate the Oral Bible, guiding and mentoring each church planter to develop a grass roots church planting ministry through simple Bible storytelling and other traditional oral communication media. http://www.siutraining.org. SIU offers *Communication Bridges to Oral Cultures* training course that instils a love for the Scriptures in the mother tongue through a systematic chronological Bible storytelling approach. This 4-day, intensive training teaches the fundamentals of evangelism and discipleship for local leaders or trainers working among non-literate or traditionally oral people groups, and provides: 1) emphasis on church planting through chronological Scripture storytelling in the cultural context of the people group; 2) practical training in effective Scripture storytelling methods; and 3) exploration of stories, adaptations of Scripture in song, dramatization of the parables, audio/video for effective communication to traditional oral cultures. An excellent overview of and tool for the training is *The Ancient Path: Church Planting for Oral Cultures*. DVDs. (2004). Scriptures in Use/Progressive Vision. For more information go to www.siutraining.org/resources.htm.

Vernacular Media Services

VMS brings the Word to the world in a culturally relevant way. "Vernacular" means the local language or mother tongue. "Media" is the path used to bring a message. Vernacular media specialists help Wycliffe Bible translators and national translators use media tools that are culturally appropriate. Scripture may be presented in the local language on video or audiocassette, or in radio programs, dance, or drama. These tools help establish a bridge for oral cultures to understand the Word of God. VMS asks: "What will help to make Scripture a part of these people's lives?" Media options are varied: audio and videocassettes, filmstrips, radio and television, live drama, puppets, and flipcharts. For more information go to http://www.jaars.org/vern.shtml.

Pictures and Related Visual Resources

Bible Pictures. Hong Kong: Hong Kong Baptist Press. A set of 40 traditional colour pictures from
    Noah to Shadrach, Meshach, and Abednego in the Old Testament, 17 on the life and ministry of
    Jesus, and 7 on Acts. Pictures are 12x17 inches on durable card stock.

Biblical Wall-Posters. National Biblical Catechetical and Liturgical Centre, Bangalore, India.
    Large bright colour Indian contextualized biblical posters covering creation to the restoration of
    Israel in 51 pictures and from the annunciation to Elizabeth to a new heaven and new earth in Reve-
    lation for a total of 140 pictures.

Colour It Tell It Bible Stories; Book One: Creation to Moses. Manila: Church Strengthening Min-
    istry, 1992. Projected as a series of five story colouring books for use with children using line
    drawings taken from "Telling the Story..." colour picture set. When completed the series will con-
    tain 103 Bible stories suitable for reading to children, to use in family devotions, or for church-
    centered Bible study or Sunday school. (Book Two: *Moses to Roman Rule*; Book Three: *The Birth
    of Jesus to the Transfiguration*; Book Four: *Jesus and the Children to the Ascension*; and Book
    Five: *the Acts of the Apostles*.) http://csm-publishing.net.

Dawson, David L. *A Visual Survey of the Bible.* Greenville, TX, 1982.
    The Bible's message illustrated in a fifteen foot colour chart showing the panoramic story of re-
    demption from creation to the return of Christ. Also available in Chinese, Korean, Spanish and
    other languages. The chart is also available as a black and white line drawing in which local lan-
    guages could be drawn in and coloured. Accompanying text and choice of end times panels accord-
    ing to theological preference. 4400 Moulton Street, Suite D. Greenville, TX (USA) 75401. Tel
    903-455-3782.

Farris, Mary Lou. *The Adam & Eve Family Tree.* **Norman, OK.**
A helpful colour chart showing the genealogy of Jesus from Adam and Eve. It lists the family lines of the Old Testament along with the names of wives and offspring. It is helpful for sorting out the patriarchal and royal family genealogies.
http://members.aol.com/tmcorner2/a-e_ft.htm.

Good News audiovisual – A set of 40 pictures, available in large (flipchart), medium and small (pocket size) formats, accompanied by a recorded 'commentary'. The story-based programme provides a brief overview of the Bible and then some basic teaching on getting right with God and living as a follower of Jesus. The recorded commentary is available in more than 900 languages. http://globalrecordings.net/au/prod-gn.html

Life of Jesus Mafa. **Versailles, France.** Highly contextualized African teaching pictures with Jesus and all story characters portrayed as African Blacks in typical African village settings. Sixty colour pictures from the Annunciation to **Pentecost.**
http://www.jesusmafa.com/anglais/accueil.htm.

Line Drawings for Bible Stories Asian Style. **Bangkok: New Tribes Mission.** Black and white line drawings lightly contextualized for Southeast Asians in 11x16 inch size supplied as photocopies. A total of 389 pictures divided into 46 "sets" of pictures consisting of 38 Pre-Bible pictures, 193 Old Testament pictures and 158 New Testament pictures. Suggested guide for colouring the pictures locally.

The Living Christ audiovisual – A set of 120 loose leaf, A4 size pictures based on the life of Christ with accompanying recorded commentary, printed script and set of short lesson scripts indicating which pictures to use for the lesson. The recorded commentary is available in about 30 languages. http://globalrecordings.net/au/prod-tlc.html.

Look, Listen & Live **Bible Pictures and Scripts. Global Recordings Network, Inc. (Australia)** An eight-part set of colour Bible pictures (2 formats available: flipcharts [17x13 inches] and picture booklets [5.5x8.5 inches] chronologically arranged with recorded story commentaries. The recorded commentaries are available in more than 200 languages. The first five parts cover Old Testament material while parts 6-8 are based on the Gospels and book of Acts. Printed scripts are available in several languages. The scripts are simple story presentations with Scripture base indicated. Each picture set contains four or five stories with multiple pictures for each story. 24 pictures in each flipchart or booklet. Flip charts are spiral bound at the top; booklets are stapled. http://globalrecordings.net/au/prod-lll.html

Lukens, Betty. *The Bible in Felt.* A three-year cycle of presenting the Bible story chronologically through use of flannel graph pictures. Available in two sizes--classroom size (16x24 inches) and auditorium size (32x48 inches). May be used in place of flat pictures to illustrate, build, or tell the Bible story. Teacher's manual does not contain the stories but suggests background scenes and flannel graph figures to use for each Bible story passage. www.bettylukens.com

Telling the Story. **105 Picture Set. Manila: Church Strengthening Ministry.** A set of 105 individual 17x13 inch colour pictures (103 pictures and 2 maps) jointly developed by Philippine Baptist Mission and New Tribes Mission for use in chronological approaches to teaching. The pictures follow a chronological order and are presented with limited background detail and minimal perspective for use with those of limited visual literacy. Also available in 8.5x11 inch line drawings suitable for photocopy and colouring by local users. http://csm-publishing.net.

Web-Based Resources

http://www.augusthouse.com: August House is an award-winning publisher of children's books, folktale anthologies for all ages and stories for classroom use in book and audio formats. Their books are used in literacy and Title I programs to build language, critical thinking and writing skills even as they entertain. Parents and teachers use August House books, tapes, and CDs in reading comprehension and diversity study, character education, and cross-curriculum lesson plans. Scout leaders and summer camps use their scary story books, world folktales, and trickster tales around the campfire. Sunday School educators use their tales of wisdom and justice as discussion openers. Storytellers use August House storytelling skills handbooks for story resources, for ethnic sourcing, and to prepare for telling stories or public speaking.

http://biblestorytelling.org: The Bible Storytelling Project uses Bible stories in chronological order for the purpose of evangelizing, teaching, preaching, planting new churches, and training church leaders. Bible stories in chronological order give a panoramic view of the Bible and an overview of basic Bible doctrine. This site contains numerous Bible storytelling resources.

http://www.christianstorytelling.com: Their goal is to network Christian storytellers and nurture storytelling in the Christian community. They want to be a resource for churches and Christian organizations. Believing that God has put into each individual a love for hearing a good story, this web site and its creator, John Walsh, encourage storytelling as a powerful way to communicate God's grace to others. John Walsh is dedicated to offering a free story each month, resources for developing storytelling skills, and a growing list of Christian storytellers across the U. S. who are available to perform and to train others in storytelling. Storytelling curriculum and Christian school resources are also available.

http://chronologicalbiblestorying.com: The official Chronological Bible Storying website. Contains training manuals, story sets, advice, research reports, articles, readers, PowerPoint presentations and a number of other helpful training resources.

http://www.communication-strategy.net: The Communication Strategy Network carries a number of articles on Chronological Bible Storying, orality and the use of media for effective church planting strategies; has a number of free downloads; and uses e-newsletter--free by subscription.

http://epicpartners.org: Epic Partners International was founded by four mission-sending organizations: Campus Crusade, International Mission Board, Wycliffe and YWAM. The web site provides information on Quest, Venture, and Journey options. The main goal of Epic is to provide God's Word for oral learners without Bibles and who are lost.

http://www.mediastrategy.org: Mediastrategy is produced by media strategist Dan Henrich of Liberty University; stays current through active blog.

http://newWway.org: Catalytic media use in Church Planting Movements ranging from non-literate methods to media resources and building partners for mission work; sponsored by Mark Snowden, Overseas Communications Director, International Mission Board, SBC; uses e-newsletter--free by subscription.

www.nobs.org: The Network of Biblical Storytellers (NOBS) is an international organization whose mission is to communicate the sacred stories of the biblical tradition. It was formed nearly twenty years ago by people searching for ways to experience and hear anew the word of God as narrative. NOBS develops resources for telling biblical stories through audio, video and computer technologies as well as telling them face-to-face. Members come from the USA, Canada, Australia, Europe, Japan, Singapore, South Africa, the Philippines, and New Zealand. NOBS sponsors the *Journal of Biblical Storytelling* (http://www.nobs.org/journal.htm). P.O. Box 413, Brookville, OH 45309 (USA). TEL 937-833-4141 or 1-800-355-NOBS (from USA); FAX 937-833-5603; nobsint@nobs.org

http://oralbible.com: A network founded by nine missions agencies. The Oral Bible Network has conducted consultations and training workshops for learners and experienced storyers. Member organizations include Campus Crusade, International Mission Board (SBC), Wycliffe, TWR, the JESUS Film Project, Faith Comes By Hearing, Scriptures In Use, The Seed Company, and the God's Story Project.

http://www.stevedenning.com: Steve Denning consults and gives workshops and keynote presentations on topics that include: leadership, innovation, organizational storytelling, business storytelling, springboard storytelling, knowledge management, branding, marketing, values, communication, communities of practice, business performance, collective intelligence, tacit knowledge, business collaboration, knowledge, learning, community, performance improvement, visionary leadership, social potential, institutional community building and internal communications. The site has many storytelling resources.

http://www.storytellingcenter.net: U. S.-based International Storytelling Centre. Inspired by an international renaissance of storytelling, people around the world are turning to the ancient tradition of storytelling to produce positive change in our world. The International Storytelling Center-to further infuse storytelling into the mainstream of our society - is building on its 30-year history to promote the power of storytelling and its creative applications to build a better world. This site is abundant in storytelling resources and activities.

http://www.storynet.org: U.S.-based National Storytellers Network. "Bringing together and nurturing individuals and organizations that use the power of storytelling in all its forms." In addition to numerous resources, NSN features *Storytellers Magazine* and *Storytelling World*. *Storytelling Magazine* is published bimonthly by National Storytelling Network and is available at no charge to NSN Members. Subscriptions only to *Storytelling Magazine* are not available. Single copies, however, may be purchased for $6.50 ($4.95 per issue plus shipping) to U.S. addresses. Storytelling World magazine is now offered as a membership benefit for the National Storytelling Network and is also available via subscription.

http://strategyleader.org: Orville Boyd Jenkins' virtual research centre offers a wide variety of research tools and information about key issues like worldview definition and study, plus people group and ethnicity issues. It is a great resource for learning about the underlying issues of serving oral peoples in a post-literate world. Available resources include up-to-date PowerPoint presentations.

http://www.kn.pacbell.com/wired/fil/pages/liststorytelvi.html: Storytelling--Tales to Tell bills itself as "an internet hotlist on storytelling" and lists dozens of storytelling links.

Bible Software Useful in Story Crafting

BibleWorks 6.0: Computer software contains 93 Bible translations in 29 languages, 12 original language texts with 7 morphology databases, 6 Greek lexicons and dictionaries, 4 Hebrew lexicons and dictionaries, plus 18 practical reference works! While other programs are merely loose collections of books, BibleWorks tightly integrates its databases with the most powerful morphology and analysis tools. Considered a high-end Bible research package competitively priced, BibleWorks has a quality database, permits programming, search   capabilities and customer support. Cost: $299.95. Order info online at www.bibleworks.com or www.discountbible.com (which includes free shipping and a free software package worth $29.95).

Bible Navigator: Computer software offers powerful search features, fast cross-referencing, and an   integrated word processor. This CD-ROM product includes the complete new Holman   Christian   Standard Bible and a library of reference works. Personalization features max-mize its value for reading and study while Internet-enhancements extend your learning. $19.97. Order online at http://www.lifewaystores.com.

iLumina (Gold edition): is the world's first digitally animated Bible and encyclopaedia suite. Carries the full text of the Bible in the New Living Translation and King James Version. The package also includes commentary on every verse and a complete illustrated encyclopaedia. iLumina Gold provides computer animations guided virtual tours of the Holy Land, 20,000 notes and commentaries, and 42 documentary videos on the life of Jesus. Compatible with Windows or Mac OS X. Cost: $89.99 at http://www.iLumina.com or www.Amazon.com .

Logos Bible Series X: Computer software can make your personal Bible study easier and more p r o d u c- tive by giving you access to more content and by acting as an automated "research assistant" that searches, organizes and presents that content in ways that accelerate your study and draw you deeper into the word. Series X lets you have different levels of software - Christian Home Library ($150), Bible Study Library ($250), Pastor's Library ($300), Original Languages Library ($400) and Scholar's Libraries ($600) and Silver Edition ($1,000). The Silver edition contains everything in the X Series; each series builds on the next. (Prices rounded.) The Bible Study Library, for instance, has 115 Bibles, a Greek and Hebrew dictionary, several commentaries, and references that normally cost $2,500 in purchased volumes for $249.95. Order online at http://www.logos.com

9. ENDNOTES

1 The account from Pastor Dinanath is provided by S. D. Ponraj and Sheila Ponraj.

2 Deaf with an upper case "D" by common practice refers to the people group or population segment, in contrast to lower case "deaf" referring to the physical characteristic.

3 Statistics as of Sep. 30, 2004 from Wycliffe International indicate 4558 languages without any of the Bible, out of the 6913 languages currently spoken in the world (see *Ethnologue*, 15th ed.). Dec. 31, 2003 statistics from the United Bible Societies indicate only 2355 languages have some or all of the Bible. Of these, only 414 have an adequate Bible, 1068 have an adequate New Testament, and 873 have at least one book of the Bible [see http://www.biblesociety.org/latestnews/latest273-slr2003stats.html).

4 Examples of some of these sorts of audio and radio presentations in vernacular languages include Global Recordings Network's various Scripture resources; the *JESUS Film* audio versions; *Lives of the Prophets, Life of Jesus* and *Lives of the Apostles* audio versions; Faith Comes by Hearing dramatized recordings of the New Testament; and the Radio Bible, which consists of 365 fifteen-minute broadcasts of stories from the Old and New Testaments. These are described in the Resources section.

5 Examples of primary visual products can include print illustrations and booklets depicting scenes from Bible stories and products like Deaf Missions visual recordings.

6 Examples of audio-visual products are the *JESUS Film* and related Genesis and Luke videos; *God's Story;* and *The Hope.*

7 This story is taken from C. Peter Wagner, *Strategies for Church Growth* (Ventura, California: Regal Books, 1987), 91-92.

8 This story is from Carla Bowman, *Communications Bridges to Oral Cultures* (Tucson AZ, Scriptures in Use, 2004).

9 Irwin S. Kirsch, Ann Jungeblut, Lynn Jenkins and Andrew Kolstad *A First Look at the Findings of the National Adult Literacy Survey,* 3d ed. (Washington: U. S. Department of Education, Office of Educational Research and Improvement, 2002).

10 See http://www.nifl.gov/nifl/facts/IALS.html. See also Albert Tuijnman, *Benchmarking Adult Literacy in America: An International Comparative Study* (Washington, DC: U. S. Department of Education, 2000); also available at http://www.nald.ca/fulltext/Benchmrk/2.htm. This testing has now been conducted in approximately 30 countries, with similar results.

11 http://www.uis.unesco.org/ev.php?ID=5014_201&ID2=DO_TOPIC

12 James B. Slack, "Chronological Bible Storying" unpublished document available at http:///www.chronologicalbiblestorying.com/manuals.

13 This account is from Annette Hall. When a name is introduced within quote marks, this is an indication that this is a pseudonym. In this and some other subsequent instances, names of local workers and in some cases the people group names in the stories and case studies of this paper are not actual names. The names are changed in order to protect the security of these workers. The events told in the stories and case studies are actual events recounted or confirmed by the participants in the 2004 Lausanne Forum Issue Group on "Making Disciples of Oral Learners."

14 This account is from Steve Evans.

15 Herb Klem, "Dependence on Literacy Strategy: Taking a Hard Second Look," *International Journal of Frontier Missions* 12:2 (April-June, 1995) 63-64.

16 This account comes from Pam Ammons, and can be found, along with other examples at: http://www.chronologicalbiblestorying.com/news/newsletters_index.htm.

17 Charles Kraft, "Culture, Worldview and Contextualization," in *Perspectives on the World Christian Movement*, 3d ed., ed. Ralph D. Winter and Steven C. Hawthorne (Pasadena, CA: William Carey Library, 1999), 390.

18 New Tribes Mission, *Now We See Clearly*, video, 1998.

19 Charles Kraft, "Culture, Worldview and Contextualization," 390.

20 What God has done to deal with the problem of sin is revealed much more fully in the Gospels and Epistles, of course, but there are references to God's redemptive plan in the early stories in Genesis.

21 N. T. Wright, *The New Testament and the People of God.* (Minneapolis: Fortress Press, 1992), 40.

22 Wright, 42.

23 Wright, 38-40.

24 Detailed examples and training resources on how to conduct a worldview study can be found on the website www.chronologicalbiblestorying.com

25 From http://www.chronologicalbiblestorying.com/news/newsletters, Oct 2001, Vol. 8, No 4.

26 This account is provided by S. D. Ponraj and Sheila Ponraj

27 This account is provided by Grant Lovejoy.

28 This account is provided by James B. Slack.

29 This account is provided by Mark Sauter and Vesta Sauter.

30 This account is provided by Grant Lovejoy.

31 *Following Jesus: Making Disciples of Primary Oral Learners*, hosted by Avery T. Willis Jr., Progressive Vision, 2002.

31 Ong, Walter J. *Orality & Literacy: The Technologizing of the World* (London and New York: Routledge, 1982).

33 *Reading at Risk: A Survey of Literary Reading in America*, Research Division Report no. 46 (Washington, DC: National Endowment for the Arts, 2004), vii. The term "literary reading" includes books such as romance novels, so these statistics reflect pleasure reading generally, not just the reading of "literary classics." The survey included 17,000 adults and was administered by the U. S. Census Bureau.

34 The first three items are reported by Dan Poynter and cited in http://newwway.org/news/2004/apr_2.htm.

35 *Young People in 1998*, a report compiled from surveys of 18,221 pupils by the Schools Health Education Unit based at Exeter University. Available at http://www.sheu.org.uk/pubs/yp98.htm.

36 Viggo Sogaard, Evangelizing Our World: Insights from Global Inquiry (Pattaya, Thailand: 2004 Forum for World Evangelization, 2004), 11.

37 Both statements about reading in the Netherlands are from Marieke Sanders-ten Holte, "Creating an Optimum Reading Culture in the Low Countries: The Role of Stichting Lezen," a paper presented at the 64th International Federation of Library Associations and Institutions General Conference, Aug.16-21, 1998, Amsterdam, http://www.ifla.org/IV/ifla64/098-80e.htm.

38 Jim Dator, "Families, Communities, and Futures,"http://www.soc.hawaii.edu/future/dator/other/FCF.html

39 Ravi Zacharias, "Mind Games in a World of Images," audiotape.

40 Eddie Gibbs and Ian Coffey, *Church Next: Quantum Changes in Christian Ministry* (Leicester, England: Inter-Varsity Press, 2001), 127.

41 *The International Indian*, 9:4, (August 2001), 22.

42 George Barna, *The Second Coming of the Church: A Blue Print for Survival* (Nashville: Word Publishing, 1998).

43 Tommy Jones, *Postmodern Youth Ministry* (Grand Rapids: Zondervan, 2001), 27.

44 Jones, 27.

45 Many of these ministries produce training and ministry resources. See the Resources section for more information about them and for contact information.

46 This account is provided by James B. Slack.

10. BIBLIOGRAPHY

Orality is a multi-faceted phenomenon that has drawn the attention of writers in many disciplines. Historians, biblical scholars, linguists, psychologists, educators, students of folk tales, communications experts, business consultants, professional storytellers, missionaries, and leaders of emerging churches: all of these and more have written about the phenomenon we refer to as orality. Consequently this bibliography includes a wide variety of books, some of which do not use the term "orality" and many of which have no concern for Christian ministry. Members of the Lausanne special interest group have found useful information in each of them, however. If nothing else, this wide array of books confirms the central role that orality plays in the contemporary world, especially in communication and the shaping of values. Thus far only a few authors have sought to draw on this wide array of scholarship to improve our effectiveness in making disciples of oral learners. But work is in progress that will hopefully meet that need in the years to come.

Books marked with an asterisk (*) in the list below are recommended for Bible college and theological libraries.

Books

Anderson, John R. *Cognitive Psychology and Its Implications.* 4th ed. New York: W. H. Freeman, 1995.
> *In Anderson's discussion of cognitive schemata and worldview, one can understand the importance of story repetition in the avoidance of error.*

Baddeley, A. D. *The Psychology of Memory.* New York: Basic Books, 1976.

Baush, William J. *Storytelling: Imagination and Faith.* Mystic, CT: Twenty-Third Publications, 1984.
> *Bausch refers to a wealth and breadth of stories to capture and pass on from one generation to another the wisdom, imagination, and faith of a people.*

__________. *Storytelling the Word: Homilies & How to Write Them.* Mystic-Connecticut: Twenty-Third Publications, 1996.
> *This book contains 42 homilies and 130 stories used to instruct the reader in the art of storytelling combined with narrative preaching. An appendix correlates the homilies to specific liturgical seasons and a lectionary of readings.*

Bilmes, Jack and Stephen T. Boggs. "Language and Communication: The Foundations of Culture." In *Perspectives on Cross-Cultural Psychology,* ed. Anthony Marsella, Roland Tharp, and Thomas Ciborowski, 47-76. New York: Academic Press, 1979.
> *The authors identify the reality of culture as systems of knowledge in persons' minds.*

Birch, Carol L. and Melissa A.Heckler, eds. Who Says?: Essays on Pivotal Issues in Contemporary Storytelling. Little Rock: August House, 1990.
> *The editors provide ten essays by various writers addressing critical issues in an increasingly potent movement—that of storytelling. They assert that the movement is young and there is no common vocabulary for discussion.*

*Boomershine, Thomas E. *Story Journey. An Invitation to the Gospel as Storytelling.* Nashville: Abingdon Press, 1988.

Using illustrations from the Gospel of Mark, Boomershine makes an excellent case for telling the gospel as stories. He gives practical instruction on learning, remembering, and telling biblical stories for a variety of ministry purposes.

Breech, James. *Jesus and Postmodernism.* Minneapolis: Augsburg Fortress, 1989.

James Breech traces Jesus the storyteller. He looks to the parables of Jesus and their divine uniqueness, their narrative integrity, their truth, and their ethical stance. In this work, the author engages two movements in contemporary theology: postmodernism and narrative theology.

Campbell, Joseph. *The Hero with a Thousand Faces.* New York: Pantheon, 1949.

From the well-known interpreter on mythology, this classic study traces the story of the hero's journey and transformation through virtually all the mythologies of the world, revealing the one archetypal hero in them all.

Carruthers, Mary J. *The Book of Memory: A Study of Memory in Medieval Culture.* New York: Cambridge University Press, 1992.

Cate, Mary Ann and Karol Downey. *From Fear to Faith: Muslim Women and Christian Women.* Pasadena, CA: William Carey Library, 2003.

This is a compendium of messages presented at a conference on reaching Muslim women. The focus is on Muslim women and strategies to lead them to a mature, reproducing faith in Christ. Of particular interest would be the chapters on the Muslim woman's view of God and why Muslim women come to Christ. There is also a chapter describing the use of Chronological Bible Storying as one method of outreach.

Chomsky, Noam. *Language and Mind.* New York: Oxford University Press, 1968.

Cipolla, Carlo M. *Literacy and Development in the West.* New York: Penguin Books. 1969.

This traces the historic emergence of languages, reading, writing, and thus literacy from at least the Classic Greek era to the 1900s. It assists the reader in understanding the historic development of literacy, which is only recent and not that pervasive, even by A.D. 2000.

Clanchy, M. T. *From Memory to Written Record: England, 1066-1307.* London: Edward Arnold, 1979.

Cole, Michael, John Gay, Joseph A. Glick, and Donald W. Sharp. *The Cultural Context of Learning and Thinking.* New York: Basic Books, 1971.

An interesting report of cognitive experiments conducted with non-literates in Africa.

Cole, Michael and Sylvia Scribner. *Culture and Thought.* New York: Wiley, 1974.

Two influential researchers explore the influence of culture on habitual ways of thinking.

Connelly, Bridget. *Arab Folk Epic and Identity.* Berkeley, CA: University of California Press, 1986.

D'Andrade, Roy. "Culture and Human Cognition." In *Cultural Psychology: Essays on Comparative Human Development,* ed. James W. Stigler, Richard A. Shweder, and Gilbert Herdt, 65-129. New York: Cambridge University Press, 1990.

D'Andrade discusses the concept of cognitive schemata and the link between culture, language, and cognition.

Davidson, J. A. *Literature and Literacy in Ancient Greece.* Phoenix 14 (1962), nos. 3-4.

Davis, Donald. *Writing as a Second Language: From Experience to Story to Prose.* Little Rock: August House, 2000.

Davis addresses the issue of language arts in schools, where focus is on reading and writing instead of nourishing the whole oral and kinesthetic realm, that of spoken language. He argues that talking and writing are not to be mutually exclusive in language development and lays out a method to address the issue.

Egan, Kieran. *Teaching as Storytelling: An Alternative Approach to Teaching and Curriculum in the Elementary School.* Chicago: University of Chicago Press, 1986.

> *Egan argues the case for storytelling from an educational perspective, contending that stories are a very sophisticated way of developing both intellect and imagination. He gives special attention to using storytelling across the curriculum.*

*Enyart, David A. *Creative Anticipation: Narrative Sermon Designs for Telling the Story.* N. p.: Xlibris, 2002.

> *Enyart introduces preachers to a variety of ways to preach biblical narratives.*

Finnegan, Ruth. *Limba Stories and Story-telling.* London: Oxford University Press, 1967.

> *This is the best book for looking inside a specific socio-linguistic culture in West Africa to see the issues of orality and literacy as they existed within these people. It is a very scholarly, but practical and easy to read book. An influential study of storytelling practices and their impact in the Limba culture of West Africa, it is widely quoted within the discipline.*

Freidman, Thomas L. *The Lexus and the Olive Tree: Understanding Globalization.* New York: Anchor Books, 1999.

> *This book offers an engrossing look at the international system that is transforming the world today – globalisation. With vivid stories drawn from his extensive travels, Friedman dramatises the conflict between "the Lexus and the olive tree"--the tension between the globalization system and the ancient forces of culture, geography, tradition, and community.*

Gerhardsson, Birger, *Memory and Manuscript: Oral Tradition and Written Transmission in Rabbinic Judaism and Early Christianity.* Copenhagen: Gleerup and Lund, 1961.

> *Gerhardsson deals with the respective roles of memory and manuscripts, orality and literacy from the Abrahamic era to well beyond the New Testament era. He gives a detailed, technical description of the careful, conscious process of transmitting religious instruction during the biblical period and beyond. Frequently dismissed but never refuted, Gerhardsson persisted in setting forth his views and defending his arguments about the relationship of the text to oral and literate religious leaders. Tradition and Transmission in Early Christianity, published in 1964, clarified his views and replied to critics. In 1998 Eerdmans released a single volume combining Memory and Manuscript with Tradition and Transmission and adding new material, including an apology from one of Gerhardsson's early critics, who admits that he and others did not read Gerhardsson's work carefully and thus misrepresented him.*

Gibbs, Eddie and Ian Coffey. *Church Next: Quantum Changes in Christian Ministry.* Downers Grove, IL: Inter Varsity Press, 2001.

> *The authors of this book identify some of the major storm centres through which the church must navigate, not in order to return to a previously more tranquil world, but to enter an entirely new one. The book looks at mission, church structures, developing new leaders and mentoring, worship, spirituality, and evangelism, and asks how ministry must change in order to serve a new generation of Christians.*

Goodwin, Frank J. *A Harmony of the Life of St. Paul.* Baker Book House, 1960.

> *A generally helpful volume for those preparing integrated Acts-Epistles story lessons for advanced tracks of chronological method after the basic evangelism and review tracks. The author integrates the missionary journeys of Paul with the letters written to the churches. May be a bit difficult for the average user, but could be helpful for those preparing lessons for local area use.*

Goody, Jack. *Literacy in Traditional Societies.* Cambridge: Cambridge University Press, 1968.

__________. *The Domestication of the Savage Mind.* Cambridge: Cambridge University Press, 1977. *This is an influential book describing the effects of literacy on non-literate societies and their patterns of thinking.*

Graff, Harvey J. *The Legacies of Literacy: Continuities and Contradictions in Western Culture and Society.* Bloomington: Indiana University Press, 1987.

Graff's work is an outstanding history of the development of literacy in the West and its influence on western culture.

Graham, William A. *Beyond the Written Word: Oral Aspects of Scripture in he History of Religion.* Cambridge: Cambridge UP, 1987.

Graham compares orality and literacy in major religions having both written and oral traditions.

Haaland, Ane. *Pretesting Communication Materials.* Burma: UNICEF Publications, 1984.

This source is helpful in determining whether communication materials will be received and correctly perceived among a specific audience.

Harold, Innis. *The Bias of Communication.* Toronto: University of Toronto Press, 1951.

Harris, Joseph, ed. *The Ballad and Oral Literature.* Cambridge, MA: Harvard University Press, 1991.

Harris, William V. *Ancient Literacy.* Cambridge, MA: Harvard University Press, 1989.

A respected historian explores the nature and extent of literacy in the ancient world. This is a standard work on this topic.

Havelock, Eric. *The Greek Concept of Justice from Its Shadow in Homer to Its Substance in Plato.* Cambridge, MA: Harvard University Press. 1978.

__________. *The Muse Learns to Write: Reflections on Orality and Literacy from Antiquity to the Present.* New Haven: CT: Yale University Press, 1988.

A leading scholar in the historical development of literacy, Havelock presents here the fruit of a lifetime of study on this issue.

Jaffee, Martin S. *Torah in the Mouth: Writing and Oral Tradition in Palestinian Judaism 200 BCE-400 CE.* Oxford: Oxford University Press, 2001.

Jaffee explores the relationship between the written and oral sources in Palestinian Judaism during the era that included the development of Christianity.

Jensen, Richard A. *Thinking in Story: Preaching in a Post-literate Age.* Lima, Ohio: CSS Publishing, 1993.

Poised on the boundary between the print and electronic era, the contemporary church needs to rethink preaching. To this end Jensen offers a strategy for effective communication in this electronic era. Due to present-day media saturation, the author calls for a shift in approaches to gospel proclamation. Jensen argues that trends in western culture make it necessary for Christians to begin thinking in stories and preaching using biblical narratives. He tells how to do this and gives sample sermons.

*Jousse, Marcel. *Le Style Oral Rhythmique et Mnemotechnique Chez les Verbo-moteurs* Paris: G. Beauchesne, 1925; ET, *The Oral Style.* Translated by Edgard Sienaert and Richard Whitaker. New York. Garland, 1990.

One of the early attempts by scholars to describe in detail the methods used by oral communicators.

Kelber, Werner. *The Oral and Written Gospel: The Hermeneutics of Speaking and Writing in the Synoptic Tradition. Mark. Paul and Q.* Philadelphia: Fortress Press, 1983.

Kelber discusses the interplay of oral and written sources with respect to the gospel accounts.

*Klem, Herbert V. *Oral Communication of the Scripture.* Pasadena: William Carey Library, 1982. *The author builds his case for oral communication of the Bible based upon the prevailing literacy situation and oral communication preferences of the African people, and of the situation in Palestine during Jesus' day. He also covers aspects of oral art forms. He includes important concepts for those involved in literacy work as well as evangelising among illiterates. This study is focused primarily on West Africa.*

Levy-Strauss, Claude. *La Pensee Sauvage.* Paris: Plon, 1962; ET, *The Savage Mind.* Chicago: University of Chicago Press, 1966.

Lipman, Doug. *Improving Your Storytelling: Beyond the Basics for All Who Tell Stories in Work or Play.* Little Rock: August House, 1999.

> *This book takes the reader beyond the first, almost natural, steps of storytelling into the world of its more formal contexts. Instead of rules to follow, Lipman provides a series of frameworks that encourages "thinking on your feet." Part of the book looks at the transfer of imagery in a medium that is simultaneously visual, auditory, and kinesthetic.*

Lord, Albert B. *The Singer of Tales.* Harvard Studies in Comparative Literature, vol. 24. 2d ed. Cambridge, MA: Harvard University Press, 2000.

> *This edition of Lord's classic work on Yugoslavian epic poets includes a CD with audio and video recordings of the performances that are the focus of his research. This research, done by Milman Parry and his student, Albert Lord, enabled them to describe how illiterate poets were able to compose monumental epics like the Iliad and Odyssey. This volume established conclusively that oral cultures are capable of producing lengthy, complicated, and beautiful oral art forms without the use of print and reproduce them with accuracy over long periods of time.*

Love, Fran and Jeleta Eckheart. *Ministry to Muslim Women: Longing to Call Them Sisters.* Pasadena, CA: William Carey Library, 2000.

> *This is a compendium of messages presented at a conference on evangelism of Muslim women. It has an extensive section on worldview with several different articles on this subject. The book includes strategies for reaching Muslim women.*

Luria, A. R. *Cognitive Development: Its Cultural and Social Foundations.* Edited by Michael Cole. Translated by Martin Lopez-Morillas and Lynn Solotaroff. Cambridge, MA, and London: Harvard University Press, 1976.

> *Luria's research into peasant life in central Asia had pronounced impact on Walter Ong and the development of later understandings of the impact of literacy on oral peoples, especially in their cognitive development.*

__________. *The Mind of a Mnemonist.* Translated by Lynn Solotaroff. New York: Basic Books, 1968.

> *Luria gives a description of a remarkable journalist who remembered everything that had ever happened to him and explores what that phenomenon reveals about the human memory.*

MacDonald, Margaret Read. *The Storyteller's Start-Up Book: Finding, Learning, Performing and Using Folktales.* Little Rock: August House, 1993.

> *The author believes that every community needs storytellers, actively sharing stories in the classroom, library, recreation centre, and boardroom. MacDonald's step-by-step process is an encouragement for beginners to have confidence in storytelling.*

*McLuhan, Marshall. *The Gutenberg Galaxy: The Making of Typographic Man.* Toronto: University of Toronto Press, 1962.

> *McLuhan was a well-known communications, linguistics, and media specialist. This classic work gave the world the concept of the "global village." It looks back at what the printing revolution did to the world and reflects on what the electronic age will do--creating a totally different world that is almost inconceivable even today. This is an excellent companion book to read along with Cipolla's work.*

Maguire, Jack. *The Power of Personal Storytelling: Spinning Tales to Connect With Others.* New York: Putnam, 1988.

> *Maguire explains how to mine stories buried deep within memory to communicate more effectively, enhance personal and professional relationships, and understand oneself in order to better understand others. Step by step he illustrates how to shape and express true-life stories.*

Malinowski, Bronislaw *The Meaning of Meaning: A Study of the Influence of Language upon Thought and of the Science of Symbolism.* New York: Harcourt, Brace; London: Kegan Paul, Trench, Trubner, 1923.

*Mathewson, Steven D. *The Art of Preaching Old Testament Narrative.* Grand Rapids, MI: Baker Academic, 2002.

Miller, Joseph C. *The African Past Speaks: Essays on Oral Tradition and History.* London: Dawson; Hamden, CT.: Archon, 1980.

Miller, Ted, ed. *The Story.* Carol Stream, IL: Tyndale House, 1986.

> *The Story is an edited version of the Living Bible which presents the Bible story as a continuing and integrated narrative in which individual stories are identified. This volume is of great help in learning how to present the Bible narratively, especially during the time of the kings and prophets and later in the Acts and epistles. While some of the better-known stories are somewhat abridged, enough of the story detail is retained to show the work and purpose of God in carrying out His work of redemption.*

Mooney, Bill and David Holt. *The Storyteller's Guide.* Little Rock, AR: August House, 1996. *Mooney and Holt have collected, edited, and written practical advice from a wide array of professional storytellers. They address issues such as how to create stories from printed texts, how to memorise and rehearse a story, the use of performance techniques, dealing with stage fright, avoiding frequent mistakes made by beginning storytellers, and using stories in a variety of situations.*

Olson, David R. "The Languages of Instruction: The Literate Bias of Schooling." In *Schooling and the Acquisition of Knowledge,* ed. Richard C. Anderson, Rand J. Spiro, and William E. Montague, 65-98. New York: John Wiley & Sons, 1977.

> *Olson discusses how humans acquire knowledge.*

*Ong, Walter J. *Orality and Literacy: The Technologizing of the Word.* London and New York: Routledge, 1982.

> *This is a technical treatise covering the modern discovery of primary oral cultures, some psychodynamics of orality, and oral memory, the story line, and characterisation. It is more suitable for those interested in a deeper study of orality and its role in communication. This is the basic scholarly work in the field to date. No other work has superseded it. Ong takes account of all the major scholarly investigations through 1980.*

Postman, Leo and Geoffrey Keppel, eds. *Verbal Learning and Memory.* Baltimore, Penguin, 1969.

Rosenberg, Bruce A. *Can These Bones Live? The Art of the American Folk Preacher.* Rev. ed. Urbana: University of Illinois Press, 1988.

> *Rosenberg's study focuses on folk preachers, many of them rural pastors, whose sermonic style is influenced by oral traditions of preaching rather than formal academic instruction in preaching. His extensive interviews with the preachers offer insight into oral methods of composition and delivery.*

Rubin, David. *Memory in Oral Traditions: The Cognitive Psychology of Epic, Ballads, and Counting-Out Rhymes.* New York: Oxford University Press, 1995.

Rumelhart, David E. "Schemata: The Building Blocks of Cognition. In *Theoretical Issues in Reading Comprehension,* ed. Rand J. Spiro, Bertram C. Bruce, and William F. Brewer, 33-58. Hillsdale, New Jersey: Lawrence Erlbaum, 1980.

> *This chapter includes a discussion of cognitive schemata and their importance in information processing and memory recall.*

Sample, Tex. *Ministry in an Oral Culture: Living with Will Rogers, Uncle Remus, and Minnie Pearl.* Louisville, KY: John Knox Press, 1994.

> *Sample offers a popularly-written description of traditional oral culture in the United States and its implications for congregational decision making and ethics. This book is very helpful for understanding the unique dynamics of oral-culture churches, whether rural or urban.*

Scribner, Sylvia, and Michael Cole. *The Psychology of Literacy.* Cambridge, MA: Harvard University Press, 1981.

Simons, Annette. *The Story Factor: Inspiration, Influence and Persuasion through the Art of Storytelling.* Cambridge: Perseus, 2001.

Spradley, J. P. *Culture and Cognition: Rule, Maps and Plans.* San Francisco: Chandler, 1972.
A helpful source for envisioning the various aspects of a culture as one seeks to investigate and understand that culture.

*Steffen, Tom A. *Reconnecting God's Story to Ministry: Crosscultural Storytelling at Home and Abroad.* La Habra, CA: Center for Organizational & Ministry Development, 1996.
Steffen draws on a wide array of sources to build a concise but strong case for using Bible storytelling in ministry. He includes a good bibliography of missions-related books and articles related to the topic.

Tannen, Deborah, ed. *Spoken and Written Language: Exploring Orality and Literacy.* Advances in Discourse Processes, vol. 9. Norwood, NJ: Ablex, 1982.
This is a collection of articles on oral and written language including references to Japanese, Chinese, and Javanese, the comparison of comprehension and memory vs. written materials, and literary complexity in everyday storytelling.

Tannen, Deborah. *The Pear Stories: Cultural, Cognitive, and Linguistic Aspects of Narrative Production.* Norwood, NJ: Ablex, 1980.

Tapscott, Don. *Growing Up Digital: The Rise of the Net Generation.* New York: McGraw-Hill, 1998.
The author profiles the rise of the Net Generation, which is using digital technology to change the way individuals and society interact. He makes a distinction between the passive medium of television and the "explosion" of interactive digital media, sparked by the computer and the Internet.

Thomas, Rosalind. *Oral Tradition and Written Record in Classical Athens.* Cambridge: Cambridge University Press, 1989.
A leading researcher explores the relationships of orality and literacy in the first major interaction of the two, in classical Athens. As with many similar historical studies, this one helps the reader understand what preceded literacy and also provides a basis for trying to project what could happen when literacy is introduced into a previously-oral culture.

__________. *Literacy and Orality in Ancient Greece.* Cambridge: Cambridge University Press, 1992.
Thomas extends her research beyond Athens to include ancient Greece as a whole.

UNESCO. *Functional Literacy: Why and How.* Paris: UNESCO, 1971.

UNESCO. *Practical Guide to Functional Literacy.* Paris: UNESCO, 1973.

*Van Rheenen, Gailyn. *Communicating Christ in Animistic Contexts.* Grand Rapids: Baker Book House, 1991.
This is an excellent book about the communication task of the missionary evangelist when facing an animistic worldview. While based on the author's study in Kenya among the Kipsigis people, the book broadly approaches animism in today's world, the process of theological thinking in animistic contexts, and then analyses animistic practices and powers. It concludes with a comparison of sin and salvation in Christianity and animism. One of the best overall texts on looking at spiritual worldviews and how they relate to communication of the gospel.

Van Vleck, Amelia B. *Memory and Re-Creation in Troubadour Lyric.* Berkeley, CA: University of California Press, 1991.

Vansina, *Oral Tradition: A Study of Historical Methodology.* London: Routledge and Kegan Paul, 1961.
Translated from the original in French, this is a somewhat technical treatise on oral tradition as verbal testimony. The chapter on historical knowledge is of interest to the narrative oral storyteller.

*Walsh, John. *The Art of Storytelling*. Chicago: Moody Press, 2003.

> *This book is a practical guide to storytelling written by a storyteller who overcame his stuttering and fear to tell stories professionally. Walsh includes fine learning activities to use alone or with others. He discusses the use of stories both inside church and out.*

*Weber, Hans Rudi. *The Communication of the Gospel to Illiterates*. London: SCM, 1957.

> *This is a case study from Weber's missionary experience among the Luwuk-Banggai people of the Celebes (Indonesia) in 1952. Weber looks at the world of illiterates and how they communicate their ideas. He then proposes using oral and visual means of presenting a holistic historical Bible message. While not a treatise about the use of chronological biblical narratives per se, the book contains many fundamental principles for communicating the gospel to illiterates.*

Willmington, H. L *Willmington's Guide to the Bible*. Carol Stream, IL: Tyndale House Publishers, 1981.

> *A one-volume guide to the Bible in which the Bible story is first presented chronologically. This is followed by a section called "The Theological Method" in which the major doctrines are presented including the doctrines of the Trinity, the Father, the Son, the Spirit, man, the Church, salvation, Satan, angels, the Bible, and prophecy. The last sections include Topical and Historical Study Summaries.*

*Wright, N. T. *The New Testament and the People of God*. Minneapolis: Fortress Press, 1992.

> *This book is a rich and penetrating historical and theological spotlight on first-century Palestinian Judaism, delving into the history, social make-up, worldview, beliefs, and hope of it. One fascinating aspect of the book is how Wright explores worldview and the effect stories have on the shaping of worldview.*

Yates, Francis. *The Art of Memory*. London: Routledge and Kegan Paul; Chicago: University of Chicago Press, 1966.

Articles

Gilbert Ansre, "The Crucial Role of Oral-Scripture: Focus Africa" in *International Journal of Frontier Missions* 12 (Apr.-June 1995), 65-68.

> *Ansre argues that providing Scripture in audio recordings is crucial in reaching both illiterate and post-literate Africans with the gospel.*

Kenneth Bailey, "Informal, Controlled, Oral Tradition and the Synoptic Gospels" in *Asia Journal of Theology* 5 (1991), 34-54.

> *Written by an expert on Middle Eastern peasant society, this is a little-known but crucial study showing that there are distinctly different patterns for oral transmission within a Middle Eastern peasant society. Bailey contends that peasants in upper Egypt carefully transmit valued stories without change while allowing alterations to stories of other kinds. They clearly keep the various kinds of stories separate and transmit them using different guidelines.*

Jim Bowman, "Communicating Christ through Oral Tradition: A Training Model for Grass Roots Church Planters" in *International Journal of Frontier Missions* 20 (Spring 2003), 25-27. *Bowman describes his pilgrimage into training grass roots church planters using oral means.*

Rick Brown, "Communicating God's Message in Oral Cultures" in *International Journal of Frontier Missions* 21 (Fall 2004), 26-32.

> *Brown describes oral cultures in contrast with print cultures and suggests principles and strategies for communicating effectively within oral cultures. He discusses choosing Scripture passages, sequencing them, and determining which medium of communication to use.*

__________. "Selecting and Using Scripture Portions Effectively in Frontier Missions," in International Journal of Frontier Missions 18 (Winter 2001), 10-24.

> *Brown does an excellent job of describing the criteria for selecting biblical stories in working with oral peoples and why sequencing stories chronologically is so effective.*

Paul D. Dyer, "Was Jesus a Zairian?" in *International Journal of Frontier Missions* 12 (Apr.-June 1995), 83-86. *Dyer argues that using the heart language on tape makes "Jesus talk" meaningful and receptor oriented. It is received with positive response and greater receptivity to the gospel.*

Hans Magnus Enzensberger, "In Praise of Illiteracy" in *Harper's* 273 (October 1986), 12-14. *Enzensberger tracks the beginning of the term "illiteracy" to 1876 and notes that the use of the concept is linked to the spread of colonialism.*

Jack Goody, and Ian P. Watt, "The Consequences of Literacy" in *Comparative Studies in History and Society* 5 (1963), 304-345.

Eric Havelock, "*Dikaiosune:* An Essay in Greek Intellectual History," in *Phoenix* 23 (1969), 49-70.

Herbert V. Klem, "Dependence on Literacy Strategy: Taking a Hard Second Look" in *International Journal of Frontier Missions* 12 (Apr.-June 1995), 59-64.

Jean M. Mandler, Sylvia Scribner, Michael Cole, and Marsha DeForest, "Cross-cultural Invariance in Story Recall" in *Child Development* 51 (1980), 19-26. *This article looks at the childhood development of cognitive schemata and the process of schematic activation.*

S. Devasahayam Ponraj, and Chandan K. Sah, "Communication Bridges to Oral Cultures: A Method that Caused a Breakthrough in Starting Several Church Planting Movements in North India" in *International Journal of Frontier Missions* 20 (Spring 2003), 28-31.

Sylvia Scribner and Michael Cole, "Cognitive Consequences of Formal and Informal Education," in Science 9 (November 1973), 553-559. *The authors discuss the different goals of formal (literate) and informal (non-literate) education, noting that non-literate children are sometimes labelled as cognitively deficient when no true deficiency exists.*

Viggo Søgaard, "The Emergence of Audio-Scriptures in Church and Mission" in *International Journal of Frontier Missions* 12 (Apr.-June 1995), 71-75. *A long-time advocate of the use of audio cassettes in Christian ministry explains why that is important and how it is having an impact.*

Tom A. Steffen, "Storying the Storybook to Tribals: A Philippines Perspective of the Chronological Teaching Model," in *International Journal of Frontier Missions* 12 (Apr.-June 1995), 99-105. *Steffen reports on a survey he did to evaluate the effectiveness of the Chronological Teaching method, developed by Trevor McIlwain and used by many groups.*

Paul C. Vitz, "The Use of Stories in Moral Development: New Psychological Reasons for an Old Education Method," *in American Psychologist* 45 (June 1990), 709-720. *Contemporary approaches to moral development and moral education emphasise propositional thinking and verbal discussion of abstract moral dilemmas. In contrast, this article proposes that narratives (stories) are a central factor in a person's moral development. Vitz proposes that narratives and narrative thinking are especially involved in how these processes lead to moral development and therefore that narrative should be rehabilitated as a valuable part of moral education. He includes an extensive bibliography from his discipline.*

Dissertations and Theses

Box, Harry. "Communicating Christianity to Oral, Event-Oriented People." D. Miss., Fuller Theological Seminary, Pasadena, CA, 1992.

Dyer, Paul D. "The Use of Oral Communication Methods (Storytelling, Song/Music, and Drama) in Health Education, Evangelism, and Christian Maturation." D. Min., Bethel Seminary, St. Paul, MN, 1994.

Wilson, John D. "Scripture in an Oral Culture: The Yali of Irian Jaya." Th.M., Faculty of Divinity, University of Edinburgh, Edinburgh, 1988.

11. GLOSSARY FOR *MAKING DISCIPLES OF ORAL LEARNERS*

These terms *and definitions* have been gathered from a variety of sources. This is not an exhaustive list and the definitions are not necessarily universally agreed upon. This is a work in progress. Some definitions will be revised after knowledgeable people continue to make suggestions. *The terms below are part of the larger discussion about "making disciples of oral learners."*

Aliteracy A lack of interest in or enjoyment of reading; characteristic of people who are capable of reading with understanding but do not often read for pleasure. See 'post-literate'.

Barriers The aspects of a culture, circumstances, or religion that hinder a listener in hearing, understanding, or acting upon the message of the Gospel. These are the 'stumbling blocks'. Barriers are discerned by studying the worldview. Barriers are beliefs, practices, or experiences that might keep unbelievers from understanding or accepting spiritual truths. Prior experiences, such as with nominal Christians, may also pose barriers. See 'bridges.'

Basic Bible truths Those biblical truths which are the foundation or essence of truth leading to salvation, the New Testament Church, the discipled life and Christian leadership. The actual body of truths as expressed may vary somewhat for each worldview situation according to prior knowledge and belief. The three terms 'essential Bible Truths', 'Basic Bible Truths' and 'Universal Bible Truths' all describe the generic or basic truths

needed for one of the core objectives such as evangelism, congregationalising a people (or planting a church), discipling, leader training, etc. See 'essential Bible truths', 'universal Bible truths'.

Bible panorama A selection of stories from the Old and New Testaments. A panorama gives a relatively fast opportunity to tell the Old Testament stories, which provide background and a foundation, as well as the New Testament stories. Alternate term for 'mini Bible' or 'panoramic Bible'. See 'fast-tracking', 'mini Bible, 'panoramic Bible'.

Bible storying A generic term which includes the many forms of telling Bible stories, of which Chronological Bible Storying is the main format. Single stories related to ministry needs, thematic story clusters in teaching and preaching, and even storying which begins with the story of Jesus are sometimes used, according to need and strategy.

Bibleless people group A language group or ethnic group which does not yet possess a translation of the Bible, especially the New Testament scriptures.

Bridges The beliefs, practices, or experiences of a culture that can have a beneficial influence upon a person's consideration of the gospel. God-given opportunities for witness, in which needs felt within the culture are met by the Christian faith. Bridges are discerned by studying the 'worldview'. Bridges often provide openings for heightened interest and greater relevancy of the biblical message to a person's worldview. The storyer can intentionally target issues deemed significant to the listener.

CBS See 'Chronological Bible Storying' (acronym)

Chirographic Pertaining to a writing culture.

Chronological Arranged in the order that things happened in time.

Chronological Bible Storying (CBS) A method of sharing biblical truths by telling the stories of the Bible as intact stories in the order that they happened in time. The person using this method leads the hearers to discover the truths in the stories for the purpose of evangelisation, discipleship, church planting, and leader training. Jim Slack and J. O. Terry developed CBS when they saw the need for a purely oral approach to oral peoples. They coined the term *'storying'* to differentiate CBS from Chronological Bible Teaching (see below). CBS is promoted globally by the IMB (the International Mission Board of the Southern Baptist Convention).

Chronological Bible Storytelling The act of presenting biblical truth generally in story format though the story may be deeply paraphrased or may be interrupted for teaching whenever some important issue occurs in the passage. The story may or may not be kept intact as a story. It follows a chronologically organised timeline.

Chronological Bible Teaching The type of chronological Bible instruction used by New Tribes Mission, popularised by Trevor McIl-

wain in the 1970s. It references biblical stories but does not necessarily tell them as intact stories. It uses exposition and explanation as teaching approaches. This presupposes at least semi-literacy on the part of the teacher. CBT methodology reflects NTM's mission of literacy development in conjunction with translation, evangelism, and church planting. See 'New Tribes Mission' and [http://www.ntm.org/].

Church planting movement A rapidly-multiplying increase of indigenous churches planting churches with a given people group or population segment. A Church Planting Movement is not simply an increase in the number of churches, even though this also is positive. A Church Planting Movement occurs when the vision of churches planting churches spreads from the missionary and professional church planter into the churches themselves, so that by their very nature they are winning the lost and reproducing themselves.

Communication The process of giving and understanding a message.

Communication preference The preferred style or method of communication for an individual or group of people. There are two dominant poles in a communication preference continuum – oral and literate. There are major differences between literate or print-oriented communicators and oral communicators in the way they receive information. See 'literate communicator' and 'oral communicator'.

Context "... the whole cognitive environment of the speaker and addressee: their worldview(s), their culture(s), the situation in which they are communicating, their conventions of communication, the immediate context of what they have already said, and any other shared information."

Core story, core story list Core stories are those biblical stories which are so essential to the biblical message and/or so consistently relevant in a variety of cultures that they have been chosen again and again as missionaries put together worldview-specific story sets. A core story list, then, is descriptive rather than prescriptive; it acknowledges the stories that have been used most often in evangelism story sets. It is not intended as a 'universal' list that must always be used, but rather it provides an opportunity to see what other storyers have done. (Initially, the core story list reflected the basic list of stories which included and taught the basic truths leading to evangelism, church planting, discipling, or leader training. The most popular list is that for evangelism.) See 'training story set'.

Crafting a story, story crafting Crafting Bible stories is shaping the stories from a literature format to an oral format and making such changes as needed to maintain a clear focus on the story's main point(s), to give clarity in telling, and to make necessary changes needed for accommodating certain worldview issues and story continuity leading to the storying track objective of evangelism, discipling, leader training, etc. "Crafting Bible Stories for Telling", an unpublished booklet by J. O. Terry, is available in e-format from: biblestorying@sbcglobal.net

Discovery question A question that leads the people to draw a conclusion and discover a biblical truth based on events that occur in a story. Compare 'factual question'.

Discovery time The period after the story when the storyer fixes the story in the people's minds by asking someone from the group to retell the story. The storyer then leads the people to discover biblical truths by asking questions about the story.

Door opener A kind of 'bridge' involving differences which appeal to the audience. Door openers appeal to people and encourage them to open their hearts and minds to hear the message. For example, Joseph forgave his brothers; this is a new value to people who emphasise honour through vengeance. They are also impressed that God was working in Joseph's life to bring good out of the bad things his brothers did; this is a new concept of God for some people. This appeals to them and opens the door to hear more of the Word. See 'bridges'.

Embedded truth Truth that is embedded, retained, situated in, related to, the story and which is evident to the listener without the need to extract the truth in order for the listeners to be aware of its presence and to catch its implication for them. See 'extracted truth'.

Engagement/engaged A people group is engaged when a church planting strategy, consistent with evangelical faith and practice, is under implementation. (In this respect, a people group is not engaged when it has been merely adopted, is the object of focused prayer, or is part of an advocacy strategy.)

Epic, Epic Partners International A partnership founded by IMB, YWAM, Wycliffe, and Campus Crusade. The aim of this partnership is to provide new strategies and resources that will enable the Church to use Chronological Bible Storying as a primary means of reaching the remaining unreached people groups of the world. The vision of Epic is to help reach the remaining unreached people groups with the gospel in the way that best communicates to them. For most, this will require an oral approach. "The ultimate goal is to provide the entire counsel of God in the heart language of every person in a distribution format accessible to all" (from Epic Vision and Priorities document.) An initial outcome of the partnering effort is a three part introductory set of chronological Bible stories, forty to fifty stories, aimed at supporting initial indigenous-led and reproducing churches. There is no standard story set being promoted. Rather the particular set of stories varies for each people group -- a redemptive panorama selected and crafted to best interact with the worldview of each group. This includes stories from the Old Testament, the Gospelss, and Acts and the Epistles. See [http://www.epicpartnersinternational.com].

EpiCenter Resource hub in a strategic location close to population concentration of unreached people groups. Epicenters will provide materials and training for Bible storying. Epicenters will also prepare, duplicate, and distribute recordings and written documents. Part of the Epic strategy.

Epic Quest A two-year internship program specifically devoted to Bible storying for an unreached people group. Entrance to Epic Quest is through Wycliffe, YWAM, Campus Crusade, or the IMB (including the Journeyman/ISC program). An Epic program.

Epic Venture Cooperative project of one year or less in which some short-term helpers come alongside a team in a long-term assignment specifically to further the chronological Bible storying approach. An Epic program.

Essential Bible truths Biblical concepts or teachings that are applicable to all Christians, in all cultures. The biblical 'givens' that must be communicated in ministry because without them Christianity loses its distinctiveness. Sometimes referred to as biblical principles. See 'basic Bible truths', 'universal Bible truths', 'core story'.

Ethnography A description of a culture. A description of the behavior and lifestyle of a people -- a community, society, or ethnic group. The aim in ethnography is to understand another way of life from the 'insider's' point of view. Rather than studying people, ethnography means learning from people. An enquiry into the culture, life, and lifestyles of a specific ethnolinguistic people group. A traditional term for 'worldview'.

Evangelical An evangelical Christian is a person who believes that Jesus Christ is the sole source of salvation through faith in Him, has personal faith and conversion with regeneration by the Holy Spirit, recognises the inspired word of God as the only basis for faith and Christian living, and is committed to <u>biblical</u> preaching and evangelism that brings others to faith in Jesus Christ. Therefore, an evangelical church is a church that is characterised by these same beliefs and principles. Some churches that are not considered evangelical in faith and practice, may contain members who are evangelical.

Evangelism track The first set of stories, taught for the purpose of sharing the gospel with unbelievers or giving believers a firm foundation in God's Word.

Extracted truth Truth that is extracted, that is, drawn out of a story and presented as a list of facts, issues, propositions which comprise the essence of the story. Compare 'embedded truth'.

Factual question A question that can be answered from events that happened in the story without much, if any, interpretive insight. Deals with who, what, when, and where. Compare 'discovery question'.

Fast-tracking The act of telling many biblical stories one after another at a single occasion with little or no opportunity given for discussion of the stories. Used to give a panorama of the biblical story, to test for receptivity, and to give witness when there is a limited window for contact, among other reasons. Formerly called 'mainstreaming'. See 'Bible panorama'.

Functional illiterate/(functional illiteracy) UNESCO has recommended the following definition: "A person is functionally illiterate who cannot engage in all those activities in which literacy is required for effective functioning of his group and community and also for enabling him to continue to use reading, writing and calculation for his own and the community's development." A person who has had some education but does not meet a minimum standard of literacy. To read poorly and without adequate understanding. Lacks sufficient skills in literacy to function as a literate person in his or her society. Some say that statistics indicate that 70% of the world's population who are either illiterate or functionally illiterate. Please see 'illiterate' for comment on usage.

Gaps The difference between potential availability of Scripture and real availability. Language, culture and other barriers and obstacles create a gap between potential and real availability. There are at least four gaps: the translation gap; the distribution gap; the literacy gap; the oral gap. The translation gap includes at least the 2,700 languages with no translation in process and the many languages waiting for Old Testament translation. The distribution gap includes the difference between the number of speakers of languages where a translation has been done and the number of copies of the text which have been printed and distributed. In some major languages there are many more speakers than there are Bibles or New Testaments distributed. The literacy gap exists where a written translated text is available, but speakers of the language are unable to read it. The oral gap exists where there is a translated text, but speakers cannot or will not learn to read it. For such people, audio, video, and radio are possible avenues to access, as well as storytelling.

Grass roots evangelism Evangelism at the grassroots level; done by local believers among local believers. Indigenous evangelism resulting in local believers in indigenous churches.

Grass roots church planting Church planting at the grassroots level; done by local church planters among local believers using reproducible methodology resulting in indigenous local churches.

Gutenberg Galaxy Term coined by Marshall McLuhan in his book by that name. The time, events and people in history when oral communication styles began to move toward literate communication styles in the West. The 'Gutenberg Galaxy', named for Johannes Gutenberg (renowned as the inventor of printing), is the universe of all printed books ever published. One hypothesis is that a post-Gutenberg universe is emerging based on electronic media.

Heart language See 'mother tongue'.

Illiterate Not able to read and write. That person is illiterate who, in a language that he speaks, cannot read and understand anything he would have understood if it had been spoken to him; and who cannot write anything that he can say. Note: Because the word 'illiterate' tends to be accompanied by negative connotations, an alternative term to consider using is 'non-literate'. See 'functional' and 'oral preference'.

IMB/International Mission Board of the Southern Baptist Convention. The International Mission Board is an entity of the Southern Baptist Convention, the nation's largest evangelical denomination, which consists of more than 40,000 churches with nearly 16 million members. The IMB's main objective is to present the gospel of Jesus Christ in order to lead individuals to saving faith in Him and resulting in church-planting movements among all the peoples of the world. IMB is one entrance into the Epic Quest program. Specifically, see [http://imb.org]. More generally, see [http://www.sbc.net/].

Intact narrative Uninterrupted story which is presented as a whole except for a possible aside or two in the story explaining something unfamiliar to the listeners. Compare 'interrupted narrative' and 'interpreted narrative'.

Interpreted narrative The story which is explained, or interpreted, without telling the story. It is talking about the story, telling what is in the story, but never telling the story. Compare 'intact narrative' and 'interrupted narrative'.

Interrupted narrative Telling the story and stopping, periodically, to teach, emphasising themes and issues which occur in the story, then continuing the story until another teaching point is reached. Compare 'intact narrative' and 'interpreted narrative'.

Key terms/key biblical terms A set of basic biblical vocabulary which includes the words for 'God', 'sin', 'punishment', 'sacrifice', 'reconciliation', 'promise', 'Savior' and more. There are not words for these biblical terms in all languages, or there may be words in some languages which could be used but which might carry meanings which will not accurately convey the biblical sense. Determining key terms is an important component of Bible translation.

Learning preference A learning preference is the most common, comfortable and natural way that an individual receives and communicates information. Literate and oral are the two learning preferences discussed in relation to storying. Compare 'communication preference'.

Linking Linking provides connectedness between stories. Carefully spanning time (spacers) and generations (place markers) so that the people know that events happened, but do not have the full details, so that the emotional investment in characters is not lost and the storyer can return to that spot in the future and provide additional stories to fill out the biblical chronology.

Listening task A fact or truth that the storyer asks the people to listen for in a story.

Literate That person is literate who, in a language that he speaks, can read and understand anything he would have understood if it had been spoken to him; and who can write, so that it can be read, anything that he can say.

Literate communicator One whose preferred or most effective communication or learning method is in accordance with literate formats. Literate format or style expresses itself through analytic, sequential, linear, and logical thought patterns. Most missionaries are literate communicators, trying to reach oral communicators. See 'oral communicator'.

Lives of the Prophets and **Lives of the Apostles** A series of booklets prepared for use in the '10/40 Window' consisting of translated biblical passages which present stories of biblical characters and introduce biblical themes. These have been dramatised for audio media and radio broadcast as well.

Lomé 'Y' The Y-shaped diagram which depicts the planning process by which a storyer selects and prepares a set of stories for use in ministry, while keeping in mind the dual concerns of faithfulness to the Bible and meaningfulness to the specific worldview. Named after the place where this was first developed: Lomé, Togo. See 'Ten Step Process' for a later planning model.

Mainstreaming Storying the Bible without discussion. Used to give an overview or when presentation time is limited. The storyer simply goes from story to story with appropriate linking and bridging comments and stories. More recently this term has been replaced by 'fast-tracking' in IMB usage. See 'fast-tracking'.

Mini-Bible A selection of portions from the Old and New Testaments chosen to fit the context and needs of the receptor-language community. Analogous to 'story set' or 'storying track' and 'Bible panorama' or 'panoramic Bible'.

Mother tongue A person's first language; the language of the hearth and home; a person's heart language; the language a person understands best; the language of fear, grief, joy, love, devotion and intimacy; the cherished language learned in infancy between mother and child.

Multi-media 'Multi-media' more commonly refers to a combination of text, graphics, pictures, sound, etc. See 'aliteracy', 'post-literate' and 'secondary oral communicators'.

New Tribes Mission NTM is a missionary organisation that plants churches in tribal communities to reach people who have never had opportunity to hear the gospel. NTM employs a method of Bible instruction called 'Chronological Bible Teaching'. See www.ntm.org.

Non-literate An alternative term for 'illiterate'. See 'illiterate'.

Non-print media Audio and videocassette tapes, disks, film, VCD, DVD, etc. Communications media other than print.

Oral Bible There is no definitive *oral* Bible. The working definition of oral Bible is: 'The accumulated Bible stories that have been told to an oral society.' Typically, this is between 50 and 225 stories. These are usually told in chronological order, though not always, since many times specific problems, concerns, fears etc. may need to be addressed first. So an oral Bible may differ to some extent from one culture to another, depending on felt and/or actual needs, worldview, theology and so forth. Those stories which form the cornerstone of Christian faith will be represented in virtually all oral Bible collections. An oral Bible is the accumulated Bible stories that have been storied to an oral communicator or that can be recalled by memory. "For many oral communicators the only Bible they will have and effectively use is the one they have in their heads and hearts. It is this Bible, an 'oral Bi-ble', that enables them to meditate upon God's Word in their quiet times and devotionals and use it in evangelism, discipleship, church planting, and leadership development. This oral Bible can go where many times the written Bible cannot go. It can cross borders, enter prisons... An oral Bible becomes the permanent possession of an oral communicator and is available for use at all times. Oral communicators are able to retain, recall, and repeat from memory their oral Bible."

Oral Bible network A network of organisations which are all interested in proclaiming the Scriptures through oral methods. Some members are: Campus Crusade for Christ, DAWN, FCBH, Feba Radio, IMB, Global/Network, Gospel Recordings, the JESUS Film Project, New Tribes Mission, Scriptures In Use, Trans World Radio, Vernacular Media Services of JAARS, Wycliffe, and YWAM.

Oral communicator Someone who prefers to learn or process information by oral rather than written means. (Thus, there are literate people whose preferred communication style is oral rather than literate, even though they can read.) Also, someone who cannot read or write. Someone whose preferred or most effective communication and learning format, style, or method is in accordance with oral formats, as contrasted to literate formats.

Oral preference A preference for receiving and processing information in an oral format rather than print. That person may or may not be a reader. See 'oral communicator'.

Orality Almost two-thirds of the world's population is illiterate (non-literate, preliterate) or has an oral preference (can't, won't or don't read and write.) The quality or state of being oral. The constellation of characteristics (cognitive, communicational, and relational) that are typical of cultures that function orally.

See http:// www.chronologicalbiblestorying.com/ MAN-UAL/section_x.htm] for "109 Characteristics of Oral and Literate Communicators".

Oral story models Sets of stories which are determined and agreed upon during a training session and later used by those being trained without having been written down. The outcome, primarily, of story training sessions with oral leaders. Stories are selected through study and suggestion of the trainer and the intuition of those being trained. Critical teaching truths and issues related to understanding and acceptance of the stories is discussed during the training.

Oral tradition Oral traditions are unwritten sources couched in a form suitable for oral transmission. Their preservation depends upon the powers of memory of successive generations of human beings. Oral traditions consist of verbal testimonies which are repeatedly-reported statements, either spoken or sung, concerning the past. Oral tradition is a memory of memories in the most literal way, since the message is learned from what another person recalled and told. "Whenever an African bushman dies, a whole [oral] library goes out of existence." See http:/ /www.chronologicalbiblestorying.com/ MANUAL/section_x.htm for "109 Characteristics of Oral and Literate Communicators"

Panoramic Bible Alternate term for 'mini Bible' or 'Bible panorama'.

People group A significantly large grouping of individuals who perceive themselves to have a common affinity for one another because of their shared language, religion, ethnicity, residence, occupation, class or caste, situation, etc. or combinations of these. For evangelistic purposes: The largest group within which the gospel can spread as a church-planting movement without encountering barriers of understanding or acceptance.

Phase There are phases in the church-planting and evangelism effort, for example, a Church Planting Phase and a Church Strengthening Phase. In CBS, 'storying tracks' are utilised within phases. Within the Church Planting phase there are typically five tracks: Evangelism, Discipleship, Church Planting, Characterisation, and The End Times. Within the Church Strengthening Phase there are an indefinite number of tracks, addressing maturing believers, corrective and instructive themes, church leader training, and other topics, like preaching tracks. See 'story set' and 'storying track'.

Point-of-ministry storying See 'situational storying'.

Post-literate At the close of the 20th century, the phenomenon in which even those who can read and write well are not doing so. The epoch of the audio-visual, termed by some 'the Multi-Media Era', has set in. Some writers also use the term 'aliteracy' to describe this phenomenon. See 'aliteracy', 'multi media,' and 'secondary oral communicators'.

Post-story dialog The teaching/learning time following the told Bible story when a story is retold by listeners, listening tasks are reviewed, or discovery questions and comments are made to draw out and relate story truths to listeners' lives.

Pre-evangelism The process of preparing unbelievers to hear the gospel. This involves choosing a location to hold the storying sessions, building relationships and investigating the people's worldview. This may include the telling of a few topical Bible stories to generate interest in the audience for the evangelism set of stories, such as water stories told during a well drilling project, or grief stories for the bereaved, etc.

Pre-story dialog A time before the Bible story is told when proper cultural greeting, review of previous stories, needed background stories or information, and sensitising questions or comments are made to prepare listeners for the following Bible story.

Primary oral culture Cultures with no knowledge at all of writing

Primary orality The state of persons totally unfamiliar with writing. People who have never 'seen' a word.

Receptor language In translation, this is the language one is translating into, not from. Opposite of source language. 'Receptor' is similar to 'target'.

Reproduce, reproducing, reproducible A Christian, an indigenous church, and/or a strategy of evangelism and church planting able to multiply or affect multiplication without outside help).. Self-replicating, as in 'self-supporting, self-governing, and self-replicating.'

Residual orality This describes those who have been exposed to literacy, even learned to read in school, but who retain a strong preference for learning by oral rather than literate means.

Rhetoric The art of speaking or writing effectively. Specifically, the study of principles and rules of composition formulated by critics of ancient times. Also, the skill of the effective use of speech.

Scripture In Use or **Scripture Use** See SIU or SU below.

Scripture In Use The name of an organisation which specialises in training indigenous church planters in methods of Bible storytelling and other oral communications methods. See http://www.siutraining.org. In addition, please see SIU or SU below.

Secondary oral communicators People who depend on electronic audio and visual communications (multimedia). It is said that in some developing countries people are moving directly from primary orality to secondary orality without passing through an orientation to print. "So as nonprint media become available to them, they move from being primary oral societies to becoming multimedia societies, skipping the stage of literacy." See 'aliteracy', 'post-literate'.

Semi-literate Able to read and write on an elementary level, especially when working with familiar documents and familiar ideas. Able to read but poor in communicating through writing. Students in 10th grade are often characterised as semi-literate, especially if the quality of their schooling is inadequate. If the educational system utilises rote memory as the dominant approach to learning, even high school graduates may test out at semi-literate functionality. This is also true of some high school graduates who spend their final years in a vocational/technical training curriculum instead of a more academic, college preparatory curriculum.

Session See 'story session'.

Shell story models Those model story sets which outline the basic considerations for storying to a given people group and their typical worldview with its barriers and bridges to the gospel. A list of recommended Bible stories and teaching themes are given which relate to the worldview and foundational truths of the gospel the people need to hear. The stories are not fleshed out in their entirety but are given only in a listing or outline with a scripture reference base and possibly a list of the teaching points. The user must complete or fill up the shell in his preparation of the stories in the language to be used in storying.

SIL SIL International is a faith-based organisation that studies, documents and assists in developing the world's lesser-known languages. Its staff shares a Christian commitment to service, academic excellence, and professional engagement through literacy, linguistics, translation, and other disciplines. One aim of SIL is to provide access to the Scriptures in the language and format (media) that best serves the people. SIL is an organisation related to Wycliffe. See [http://www.sil.org].

Situational storying or **point-of-ministry storying** The use of appropriate Bible stories (often those of Jesus' ministry) during a ministry need or opportunity. The primary reason is to lift up Jesus, followed by an invitation to hear more stories. Other story themes may be used appropriate to the ministry activity, such as The Water Stories or The Hope Stories, for disaster relief and ministry.

SIU or **SU** Acronym for 'Scripture in Use'. Generally, 'Scripture in use' or 'Scripture use' refers to varied methods to get the translated Scriptures into use in people's lives other than literacy. These other methods include audio and videocassette recordings, indigenous music, Scripture-in-song and Bible Storying. (SIL has a Scripture Use Coordinator on a par with the Linguistic, Literacy, and Translation Coordinators.) In addition, please see 'Scripture In Use' above. (Note: SU is also the acronym for 'Scripture Union'.)

Source / source language In translation, this is the language one is translating from, not into (for example, New Testament Greek.) Opposite of receptor or target language.

Story crafting See 'crafting'.

Story session/storying session/session The actual time when the storyer uses the storying method. During a session the storyer participates in opening conversation, reads from the Bible, tells the story, and leads discovery (dialog) time.

Story set A collection of biblical stories selected for a specific ministry purpose and usually arranged in chronological order. In an initial CBS strategy, this typically consists of an evangelism story set, discipleship story set, and church-planting story set. The evangelism story set normally contains a series of stories from the Old Testament and the gospels. Church planting story sets draw from the book of Acts. Many evangelism story sets have included 20 to 25 stories that are common to most story sets; this is considered a starting point for adding other stories that present 'bridges' and address 'barriers' specific to the worldview of each people group. The first phase sets the foundation for future phases, including evangelism, church planting, discipleship, leadership development, audio-visual products, radio ministry, and Bible translation. The long-range plan is that someone among those participating in the first phase will catch a vision to continue a longer-term work to see the growth of mature churches within that people group. A story set is the list of crafted (or prepared) stories and suggested teaching/learning activities that compose a track. See 'storying track'.

Storyer The person who uses the storying method to evangelise, disciple or strengthen the church

Storying The term 'storying' is "an attempt to make a strong statement about the value of the intact, uninterrupted Bible narrative as a valuable means of teaching God's Word leading to salvation, church planting, discipling, leader training, and various ministry activities. Storying is not limited in purpose to teaching nonliterates. It is used because it is reproducible by listeners and because the use of story helps to overcome resistance or hostility to traditional Westernised teaching. See 'Chronological Bible Storying' (CBS).

Storying matrix The web or structure of stories that follows the biblical timeline. This is the initial structure given in the first telling of stories or lessons which give an essential biblical framework into which other stories and later truths may be placed.

Storying scarf The Storying Scarf is a cotton scarf designed to put an inexpensive set of durable pictures representing God's Word in the hands of people who could use it to independently share God's word where missionaries cannot go. It is designed to be used in conjunction with a series of 21 chronologically-arranged Bible stories. See http://storyingscarf.com

Storying track The entire series of stories typically arranged in chronological order which have been selected for presentation to a target population for the purpose of evangelism, discipleship or leadership training, whichever the case may be. Some names of tracks are "Evangelism Track", "Review Track", "Last Lessons", or "End Times Track". In CBS, 'storying tracks' are utilised within 'phases'. A 'storying track' is equivalent to a 'story set'. In Chronological Bible Teaching the term 'phase' is used in the same way that 'track' is used to define a set of lessons in CBS. The purpose of the track is to limit the story set to those stories which serve best to accomplish the desired teaching objective. The track is for the benefit of the storyer, but is more or less kept invisible to the listeners. For instance, the storyer does not say, 'Now we will do the Discipleship Track.' See 'story set'.

Table 71 A regular gathering of mission-agency leaders which arose from the Amsterdam 2000 conference. Table 71 has adopted a cooperative strategy centered on orality and Chronological Bible Storying.

Target language See 'receptor language'.

Target population / target people The group the storyer is seeking to reach. Often an 'unreached people group'. The people that have been selected to whom the storyer will story. See 'receptor'.

Ten Step Process Identifies the preparation needed to develop a Bible story set:

Step One: Identify the biblical principle or truth you want to communicate; make it clear and simple. Step Two: Consider the worldview of the chosen people group. Step Three: Identify the bridges, barriers, and gaps in their worldview. Step Four: Select the appropriate Bible story or stories that will communicate the principle considering the worldview issues of the chosen people. Step Five: Craft the story and plan the pre-story and the post-story dialog to emphasise the principle or truth you want to communicate. Step Six: Tell the story in a culturally appropriate way, which will be through narrative and perhaps also through song, dance, drama, or other means. Step Seven: Facilitate the dialogue with the group to help them discover the meaning and the application without your having to tell them. Step Eight: Help the group obey the biblical principle. Step Nine: Establish group accountability. Step Ten: Encourage the group to reproduce this by modeling the principles in their own life and then telling the stories and discipling other people.

The Seed Company (TSC) An organisation devoted to partnering with nationals to plant the seed of God's word; affiliated with Wycliffe. www.theseedcompany.org

Themes Central ideas or truths found in the biblical stories

Track / story track A set of stories joined together by specific themes and told for a particular purpose. That list of stories which address a strategy or teaching objective. See 'storying track'.

Traditional religion and culture The indigenous religion and culture of a local people.

Training story set A redemptive panorama story set that covers the basic elements of a biblical worldview. This consists of the stories found to be common to many storying projects implemented around the world in different contexts in recent years. Compare 'Bible panorama', 'core story list'.

Transition story A brief story told to summarise biblical events that happened between the stories in different lessons. Sometimes called a 'linking story'.

Turning point Factor which is important in decisions to follow Christ in a target or receptor population.

Typographic Of or relating to a print or reading culture.

Unengaged See 'engagement'.

Universal Bible truths See 'basic Bible truths', core story', 'essential Bible truths'.

Unreached people group/ UPG More broadly, an ethnic group which does not possess a church and which does not have the presence of an indigenous Christian witness. A people, usually an ethnolinguistic group, with a historical culture, language and often a geographical place of residence where there is little or no presence of evangelical Christianity, especially in the forms of Bible, Christian gospel presentations, believers, baptisms and churches. A people group within which there is no indigenous community of believing Christians able to evangelise this people group without requiring outside (cross-cultural) assistance. A group is considered 'reached' if it has a viable, indigenous, self-reproducing church movement in its midst. More specifically, a people group in which less than 2% of the population are evangelical Christians.

Visual aid A picture, simple drawing, or object that will help the people remember or understand the story. Considerations: Will some pictures confuse or offend listeners due to cultural considerations? Are contextualised pictures helpful? Will the cost limit wider use?

Worldview The way a specific people view the world around them. Somewhat like wearing tinted lenses, members of a culture look through their worldview, not at it. A worldview is seldom apparent to its adherents unless it comes under question. A worldview consists of fundamental cognitive, affective, and evaluative assumptions about reality. A worldview forms the core of a culture, which guides people in how to act, think, believe, function, and relate. How people look at life and the world around them, a people's view of the world. A profile of the way people within a specified culture live, act, think, and work and relate.

12. PARTICIPANTS

Convener: Avery Willis,   USA
Co-convener: Steve Evans, South Asia
Facilitator: Mark Snowden, USA

Other Participants:
Victor Anderson,   Horn of Africa
Nils Becker,   USA
Jim Bowman,   USA
Graydon Colville,   Australia
Steve Douglass,   USA
Ron Green,   USA
Annette Hall,   North Africa
Morgan Jackson,   USA
Andrew Kanu,   Sierra Leone
Derek Knell,   Cyprus
Grant Lovejoy,   USA
Durk Meijer,   USA
Jay Moon,   West Africa
Ted Olsen,   USA
David Payne,   USA
Roy Peterson,   USA
Sheila Ponraj,   India
Chandan Sah,   India
Vesta Sauter,   Hungary
David Sills,   USA
Jim Slack,   USA
Stephen Stringer,   West Africa
Tom Tatlow,   USA
LaNette Thompson,   West Africa
Bob Varney,   USA

THE NEW PEOPLE NEXT DOOR

Lausanne Occasional Paper No. 55

This Issue Group on Diasporas and International Students
was Issue Group No. 26 A and B

This Occasional Paper was prepared by the whole Issue Group and
the principal writers were Tom Houston, Robin Thomson, Ram Gidoomal,
and Leiton Chinn

CONTENTS

Introduction

INTRODUCTION

This publication is about the opportunities and challenges presented to Christians by the presence of people from different countries who are now living near them. It is written for vicars, pastors, and other leaders of Christian congregations and ministries. It describes the findings of about 50 people who discussed this subject at the Lausanne 2004 Forum on World Evangelization in Thailand in October 2004. They wanted this message to be conveyed to all churches and ministries who are faced with these opportunities and challenges.

The movement of peoples in our world creates many new challenges. The word *"Diaspora"* meaning "a scattering" is used to describe this large-scale movement of people from their homeland to settle permanently or temporarily in other countries. It was first used of the Jewish people scattered in exile from the 6th century BC onwards. The word is also used in the New Testament of God's new people, the followers of Christ, scattered in "exile" (1 Peter 1:1; James 1:1).

There have been many Diasporas over the centuries. However, the 20th and 21st centuries have seen unprecedented movements of peoples, mostly because of war, famine, economic needs, and opportunities. The effects of these migrations are deep and wide-ranging for the Diaspora communities themselves, for their host countries, and for their country of origin.

God controls these movements. The Bible is full of examples, from Genesis to Revelation, of God using them for his purposes. Christ's followers in all countries have great opportunities to engage positively and creatively with these movements, in order to influence them for good and to share the good news of Jesus in ways that are culturally and socially relevant. The overall goal for Christians is to work towards or to seek to influence societies in ways that promote harmony, mutual respect and the celebration of diversity, providing the opportunity for all to explore and discover spiritual truth for themselves and to hear the good news of Jesus.

One of God's commandments to His people is to love the foreigner and stranger in the land and to treat them with respect.

God's command, reflecting His compassion for outsiders, has implications for Diaspora communities, the churches of the countries of origin, and particularly for the receiving churches of the host countries. The church in each of these contexts is challenged to remove negative attitudes and practices and to seize the opportunities.

A limited number of Diasporas are presented in this publication. We tried also to cover others like the Diasporas from English and French speaking Africa, the Arab countries of the Middle East, the countries of the former Soviet Union, Vietnam, Cambodia, and Latin America. We were not able to do this in time for Forum 2004.

We would still like to let the whole church know about the other Diasporas. If representatives from these groups would like to describe their history for a second edition of this book, we would be glad to hear from them. Write to our Chairman, Ram Gidoomal, South Asian Concern, P O Box 43, SUTTON, Surrey SM2 5WL, UK.

For more information about the 2004 Forum, go to the Website www.lausanne.org

1. WE ARE ALL MIGRANTS
The Scope of the Diasporas

Very few people today live in the geographical area where their ancestors originated. Most of us have come from somewhere else even if it was centuries ago.

The movement of peoples has occurred over the centuries for different reasons. In earlier ages, peoples of Asia scattered throughout their hemisphere and even crossed over to North America. South-Sea islanders took sail and inhabited far reaches of the South Pacific.

In the 16th-19th centuries, people moved within the Portuguese, Spanish, French and British Empires to fulfil economic needs. For example, Indian workers went to plantations in Fiji and Central America, or to develop the railways of East Africa. The colonial "motherlands" were also centres of education and culture, attracting the cream of the future leadership of their colonies.

Millions of Europeans migrated in the 19th century to North and South America, Africa, Australia, and New Zealand to escape poverty and make new lives abroad. This proved to be a major factor in the evangelisation of the world even before modern missions.

The 20th and 21st centuries have seen unprecedented movements of peoples. War, famine, and political upheaval were major causes of disruption and displacement in Armenia, Cyprus, Sri Lanka, Vietnam, Somalia, Palestine, and many other places. Post World War II Europe coincided with the end of the colonial era, resulting in an enormous demand for workers, both skilled and unskilled, in the former colonial powers. There was also vast growth in the number of international students from former colonies coming to universities in the West to gain skills to build their countries.

- In 2004: There were an estimated 174 million migrants in the world (reliable statistics are very hard to obtain).
- There were 35 million migrants in sub-Saharan Africa.
- More than 20 million people in Western Europe alone were living in a different country from the one in which they were born.
- In the USA there were 31 million migrants, 85% of these had come from outside Europe, compared to only 38% in 1970.
- In 2003: The 15 countries making up the EU at that time had a net inflow of nearly 1 million migrants.
- In 2001: Some 20 million non-European Union nationals were living in the EU, and this amounted to over 5% of the total population.
- By 2050: One in four people living in the USA are likely to be Hispanic.
- Over 5 million people sought asylum in the EU between 1990 and 2000.

Regional and tribal conflicts in Africa, resulting partly from the colonial divisions of the continent, caused many to be displaced. At the end of the Cold War in 1989 another movement of peoples was triggered within Europe.

At the beginning of the 21st century the flow of peoples is likely to continue and increase for the foreseeable future. *These are factors that will fuel this growth*

- on-going economic inequalities
- the quest for education and economic opportunity
- escape from political and social oppression
- demand for skilled workers
- aging populations in the developed world, in need of personal care and pension support
- religious persecution
- inter-tribal conflict
- students used to receive scholarships, but are now more likely to be funded from families
- urbanisation
- population growth.

Some migrants become *permanent residents* in their host country though they may not have originally intended to stay. Some even become citizens. Others are *temporary migrants* including: international students (see Chapter 7A), contract workers, business people, professionals and entrepreneurs (see Chapter 7F), international bureaucrats and NGO workers, seamen, illegal immigrants, travellers, and military and diplomatic personnel. A third category is displaced people, such as *refugees* or *asylum seekers,* who may be either temporary or permanent (covered by the Lausanne Forum Issue Group focusing on People At Risk)

Examples of Christian activity within Diaspora movements today

Certain ethnic groups have significant population outside of their homeland.

Four of these are the Chinese, South Asians, Filipinos, and Iranians. Essays which include a historical sketch, conditions in host countries and evangelism approaches are found in the Appendices.

2. DIASPORA IN THE BIBLE
What is behind the Diasporas?
The movement of peoples
God controls the movement of peoples

The movement of peoples in our world is part of God's purpose, from the Garden of Eden onwards. Paul told the Athenians that God "determined the times set for [every nation] and the exact places where they should live" so that they would "seek him and perhaps reach out for him and find him" (Acts 17:26-27).

God moves His people in judgment and for redemption

God acted in judgment to expel Adam and Eve from Eden, to send Cain away, and to divide the languages at Babel. But then he began his purpose of redemption through the call of Abram to leave his own country and people for the land of promise, in order to father a nation through which all nations would be blessed. The new nation of Israel began in *Diaspora*, when Jacob and his sons were forced to Egypt (as economic migrants) and then migrated again to inherit the land of promise.

Throughout her history Israel had further experiences of God scattering her in judgment (Leviticus 26:33; Deuteronomy 28:64; Ezekiel 36:19) but also meeting her in the *Diaspora* for renewal and

teaching so that she could communicate God's character to others (Ezekiel 36:23-27).

Diaspora was the place in which Israel learned new things about God, from the wilderness experience of the Pentateuch to the exile under the Babylonian, Persian, Greek and Roman empires.

By the time of Jesus, the Jews were scattered throughout the known world – "from India to Ethiopia" at least (Esther 8:9). Through the network of synagogues around which their communities were organised, first faith in the One Creator God and later the good news of Jesus the Messiah, were transmitted everywhere, to both Jews and Gentiles.

God scattered the early Christian believers from Jerusalem through persecution (Acts 8.1,4). As a result they crossed cultural barriers to share the gospel with the Samaritans and start the first Gentile church (Acts 11:19).

The New Testament writers addressed God's people in *Diaspora*, not only scattered culturally and socially, but spiritual travellers on the way to the homeland, living in two cultures at once (1 Peter 1:1; 2:11-12; James 1:1; Hebrews 11:13-17; 13:14).

God controls the movement of "secular" powers

God's control is not limited to "His" people. It extends to the rise and fall of the world's political and military powers. The vision of the empires in Daniel 2 and 7 demonstrates a philosophy of history: God is in supreme control - morally and spiritually, politically and militarily.

Isaiah and Jeremiah emphasised that Egypt and Assyria, Babylon and Persia were instruments that God used for his purposes, and were themselves subject to his judgment (Isaiah 10:5; 45:1; Jeremiah 25:9-12). He directed the movement not only of Israel but of other nations as well (Amos 9:7).

A vehicle for change

God's people constantly faced the challenge of interacting with alien cultures and traditions.

One response: conformity and compromise

Israel was intended to belong to God and be distinct in every way, a model to the other nations (Exodus 19:4-6; Deuteronomy 4:6-8). The entry into Canaan brought new opportunities, but also brought challenges of alien cultural and religious practices to which Israel was constantly attracted. Israel failed to be distinctive. Instead she followed the other nations into idolatry, injustice, immorality, oppression, and violence. The result was the judgment of the exile.

Another response: separate cultural identity

The small community who returned from exile to Jerusalem faced the old pressures to conform to alien religious practices. **Ezra and Nehemiah** insisted on very strict rules, particularly with regard to the Sabbath and marriage with people of other faiths. This tight control enabled the tiny Jerusalem community to maintain its identity and survive through the following centuries.

The Jewish Diaspora built their community life around the synagogues. It was both a religious and cultural identity. They adapted in one major aspect – by translating their Scriptures from Hebrew into Greek - the Septuagint. This gave access to God's word, not only to their younger generations, but also to the Gentiles.

Many Gentiles were attracted by their faith in the One Creator God and their clear *ethical* teaching. They became known as "god-fearers". But very few were willing to submit to the *cultural* requirements of diet and circumcision, which would cut them off from their Gentile society.

Struggling to adapt

The early church also wrestled with this question of culture. It began by assuming all the cultural requirements of the Jewish law. Even when God scattered the believers through persecution they preached only to Jews (Acts 8:1; 11:19). It took God's direct revelation to Peter and the initiative of *Diaspora* believers to encourage them to cross the cultural barriers and share the good news with Gentiles. The cultural issue almost split the church, as we see from the debate of the Jerusalem Council (Acts 15) and Paul's letters (Galatians 1-2; Romans 14; 1 Corinthians 8-10).

The spiritual opportunities

The good news is for people of all cultures

Paul's theology grappled with the issue of mission to those of other cultures and faiths. How can God's kingdom be truly *universal*, so that people of all cultures can fit in and be truly accessible to all, regardless of their religious and moral achievement?

Paul found the answer to both questions in the gospel of God's grace. All have failed to reach God's standard - religious and non-religious alike - and so God has provided the solution himself in the death and resurrection of Jesus (Romans 3:22-25; 4:25). This sets the gospel free to fit into any culture and background, but the church has to work it out in practice in each generation.

Christ's followers do not belong to any single culture. They are not bound by any form of dress or diet, language or style of worship. But they still have to express their faith and ethics within a particular culture and society. There is no separate "kingdom culture," unconnected with society.

Diaspora followers of Christ can help to develop new forms of cultural expression, with a fusion of different cultures, which will enable people of all backgrounds to draw near to God and follow Christ.

God's people should be faithful and obedient wherever they are placed

The Old Testament gives several positive examples of those who were faithful to God while living in a changed *Diaspora* environment:

Joseph was enabled by God to be faithful and prosper in very difficult *Diaspora* circumstances. As a result he not only influenced Egypt for good but also fulfilled God's purpose of blessing for Israel and through her for the whole world.

Naaman's Israelite servant girl witnessed to the power of the true God in her *Diaspora* location of domestic captivity, while **Ruth**, the foreign widow of an Israelite husband became a witness to God's faithfulness.

Jeremiah wrote to the Jewish exiles in Babylon: "seek the welfare of the city where I have sent you into exile and pray to the Lord on its behalf" (Jeremiah 29:4-7).

Daniel and his friends were outstanding examples of how to live in an alien environment, particularly in the areas of diet and worship (Daniel 1:8; 3:18; 6:10).

Esther remained faithful in her exalted but lonely position and so was used to save God's people.

God's people should welcome all, especially the "alien" and the marginalised

The early church struggled to accept people of different cultural backgrounds, as we have seen (Romans 15:1-7). James challenged his readers about discrimination on the basis of wealth (James 2:1-9), while the Gospel writers showed the example of Jesus who received people of all backgrounds, especially the marginalised (Luke 5:13, 29-32; 7:36-37; 8:2).

The Old Testament witnessed to God's overall purpose, from the beginning, to bless all nations (Genesis 12:1-3; compare Psalm 93:10-13; Isaiah 2:2; 11:10; 49:6; 56:7).

It also gave some specific pointers on welcoming strangers:

- The inclusion of Rahab and Ruth in the genealogies of David and of Jesus showed that Israel was willing (sometimes) to include and honour people of "alien" background (Matthew 1:5-6).
- The special duty of care for the vulnerable and marginalised - widows, orphans, and "strangers" or "resident aliens" (Exodus 23:9; Leviticus 19:33; Deuteronomy 10:19). Israel could understand and empathise with the situation of the "alien" or "stranger," as she had been in that situation in Egypt.

Passages like Acts 6:1-6; 1 Timothy 5:3; James 1:27 show that the early church put this into practice and became known through the 2nd and 3rd centuries for its practical care of the weak and vulnerable. Hospitality - especially to strangers - is not just a Middle Eastern cultural value but a vital spiritual principle (Matthew 25:35; Romans 12:13; 1 Peter 4:9; Hebrews 13:2). (See further *The Biblical Perspective for International Student Ministry - Our Call to Hospitality and Community.)*

God's people should look forward to his ultimate purpose for human society

"The kingdoms of the world have become the kingdom of our Lord and of his Christ" (Revelation 11:15). "Babylon the great city," the icon of global economic activity, has been replaced by "Jerusalem, the heavenly city" (18:2; 21:2) and in that city are "a great number, from every nation, from all tribes and peoples and tongues," worshipping God together (7:9).

The vision of the book of Revelation is one of infinite diversity in perfect unity. The reference to nations, tribes, peoples, tongues is repeated seven times in Revelation, each time in a different order. John wants to make his point absolutely clear.

The "gospel of the kingdom" is to be preached to all nations, before this great vision will be fulfilled (Matthew 24:14). Jesus told his apostles "you will be my witnesses... to the ends of the earth" (Acts 1:8), echoing the words of Isaiah "...that my salvation may reach to the ends of the earth" (Isaiah 49:6; compare Acts 13:47).

So the gospel is to be shared with all, while at the same time we pray that all will live together in peace and harmony, even in a society that does not yet accept the gospel. This leads to some creative tensions, which are all the more obvious and pressing in our global "Diaspora" world, where the cultures and faiths are brought together and combined in new and unexpected ways. Diaspora followers of Christ, along with their brothers and sisters in the host communities, are best placed to work out this challenge, and so fulfil God's ultimate purpose.

3. MELTING POT OR SALAD BOWL?

The Range of Changes

"However you look at it — sooner or later Diaspora brings change."

Diaspora — the movement of people - inevitably stirs things up. It forces cultures and traditions to interact with one another - sometimes unwillingly. Change is inevitable.

A host of relationships are affected; between the host communities and incoming individuals; between the host communities and the Diaspora communities; between the Diaspora communities and their countries of origin; and within the Diaspora communities themselves. They affect those involved mentally, emotionally, and spiritually as well as in practical ways.

Diaspora people, by definition, belong to more than one culture and have to learn to adapt. Some feel that their identity is questioned. They also contribute to changes in the countries and communities in which they live - sometimes welcome, sometimes not. Some "newcomers" arrive into secure situations. For others, it is a sheer matter of survival. This means that they must be continually active, alert to their own interests, protective of their identity, while at the same time under pressure to adapt and integrate.

The host community — including, unfortunately, the Christian community — might feel uncomfortable about the "newcomers," or even see them as a threat. They might be seen as an economic threat — affecting jobs and housing. They might be seen as a cultural threat — changing eating habits, music, traditional customs, etc. They might be seen as a political threat — taking over control of decision making bodies. They might be seen also as a religious and ethical threat — influencing the established concepts of God, male-female status and relationships and family responsibilities.

Change can be painful and the changes brought by the movement of peoples are no exception. While the outcomes may be creative, the process can be long and hard for everybody involved. There is no agreement on how diverse societies should live together. Different models are debated. The American ideal of society was the *Melting Pot* where everything is assimilated in the whole. For some that has been replaced by the Salad Bowl ideal in which each part contributes to the whole whilst maintaining its distinctive form and flavor. Some prioritise *Integration* while others emphasise *Multiculturalism*. Many want *Contact* but fear *Assimilation*, while others desire total *Separation*. Whatever form the interaction may take, the result will still inevitably be change, and the changes have to be coped with.

Personal changes

From simplicity to complexity

The cultural and social interactions between host communities and incoming people are complex. There are countless combinations and patterns of interaction. Boundaries are always under negotiation. Individuals become more than one person and communities are less likely to be monocultural and homogenous and more likely to be bicultural or even multicultural. Sometimes there is more openness to the gospel among the Diaspora because people in transition are receptive to new ideas. (See Enoch Wan, "The Phenomenon of Diaspora: Missiological implications for Christian Missions," in *Scattered: The Filipino Global Presence* [Manila, LifeChange Publishing Inc, 2004].)

From local to global

Culture has become less confined by geography. It is not only manufactured products such as pizzas and cars that can cross national borders - and possibly be re-formed, repackaged, and re-exported from one country to another. Ideas, fashions, and life-styles travel more freely too. They travel faster and reach further than ever before. Through their links with their countries of origin, Diaspora people are a significant channel of cultural extension as well as economic support.

Even though migrants invest socially, economically, and politically in their new society, they may continue to participate in the daily life of the society from which they emigrated but which they did not abandon. Transmigrants are often bilingual, can lead dual lives, move easily between cultures, frequently maintain homes in two countries, and are incorporated as social actors in both (Hanciles 2003:147).

For example, a young Indian student in the UK learns about New Age psychology and takes it back to India, where it is picked up by young Hindus who were not previously interested in their religion.

From isolation to involvement - or the opposite

The Diaspora experience can result in the isolation of individuals and communities, but it can also result in the opposite. Individuals and communities, who previously had lived in comparative isolation, now become more open and contact-seeking. Instead of "going-it-alone" they now look for fellowship.

A woman in Bangladesh secured a tri-band mobile phone from micro-enterprise funding and became the telephone exchange for her remote village. When the phone rang, she would call from her doorway to a neighbour to tell her that her son was calling from San Francisco.

Changes for the worse

Some Diaspora people have to pay a heavy price. They have left behind family, friends, career, and status. Their dreams of the future have been shattered. Their expectations towards their new life have turned out to be mistaken. A Sudanese man in London has two engineering degrees but has to engage in domestic work to support himself because his specialty is not in demand in the UK.

Second and third generation immigrants become disillusioned and frustrated. The influence of the host society widens the gap between generations. Racial, religious, and social discrimination continues despite legislation, public debate, and the efforts of human rights activists. Feelings of exclusion and resentment fester and grow.

> We came to work in your homes as domestic helpers, contractual workers in your farms, factories, and hospitals. We provide the human power for your ships that criss-cross the oceans. Our work is backbreaking, oftentimes dangerous, dirty, degrading, de-skilling, and dehumanising. Many of us are abused mainly because of our being migrants and people of colour.
>
> Poverty, inequality, civil conflicts, persecution, and desire to survive forced us to leave our country and people. Regrettably, we do not feel a "warm Christian welcome." Instead, we are blamed for the crisis of your profit-driven society. We are seen as a wave of plague that must be turned back and controlled. There is now fear and trembling in our midst, not knowing what the future holds for us. What keeps us going is the satisfaction that our euro remittances help our families to survive, that soon we will return home – a dream which is getting to be a myth and illusion. In order to survive and to have hope and meaning in life, we organise "migrant churches" which seem to fascinate some of you for reasons we sometimes cannot understand.
>
> Deep within, we burn with anger, pain and humiliation. Anger at a sense of helplessness, pain in feeling alone and humiliation at the loss of self-respect. Many of us are caught in a cycle of kneeling before the toilet to clean it and kneeling in prayer for strength to do the same.
>
> Cesar Taguba, An Open Letter to Christians in Europe
> Proceeding Documents of the Conference
> ESSERE CHIESA INSIEME / UNITING IN DIVERSITY, Ciampino-Sassone 26-28 March 2004

Changes for the better
Economics

There is no doubt that Diaspora for some has led to great prosperity and growing influence. The contribution to the economies of South East Asia by the Chinese Diaspora has been massive. Many Chinese have become rich in the process.

The Korean Diaspora is not far behind in the West, with a distinctive contribution in the countries of the former Soviet block and Central Asia in particular.

Indians went to East Africa to build the railways and do business. They dominated the local economies, but were then expelled in the 1960/70s. Some stayed on and others have recently returned. Those who were driven out are now prospering in Britain and North America.

The best known example of a prosperous Diaspora is the Jews. There is almost no sphere of life in which they have not excelled and few countries where some of them are not to be found.

The economic impact of these Diaspora groups on their own countries is also a matter of record. The greater part of the investment that has led to the remarkable growth in the economy of mainland China has come from the Chinese Diaspora all over South East Asia.

Liaison between South Asians in Diaspora is a significant factor in some of the successful economic projects in India and Pakistan. (See also the impact of Diaspora remittances on the economy of the

Philippines in Chapter 7C.)

Some people, such as entrepreneurs and professionals, migrate from richer countries to poorer countries in order to maximise their own financial opportunities, and sometimes out of a desire to serve others.

Education

Immigrants are often popularly associated with low-grade workers. Yet in America more than 30% of the members of the country's scientific and engineering workforce are immigrants. And 5% of science and engineering doctorates go to international students.

The National Health Service in UK would collapse if it did not have Diaspora health professionals to serve in it.

Politics

The election of people from other nations to seats in local and national governments is becoming increasingly common. Diaspora Jews returned to Palestine and created a new nation of Israel. They also influence US policy on the Middle East.

Culture

Diaspora people are prominent in the food industry, fashion, entertainment, music, clothing, and dance. (See *The UK Maharajahs* by Ram Gidoomal.)

Changes that are confusing

Religion and ethics

Perhaps the most difficult changes brought by the Diasporas have to do with religion and moral standards. Hindu, Sikh, and Buddhist temples and Muslim mosques are springing up in many cities. Sometimes church buildings are sold and they become mosques. We are experiencing now what other countries experienced when Christian churches began to be built in their cities in earlier centuries.

We may not like this. We may resent the call to prayer from the minaret of a mosque, but we have to adjust to it. It can

---

Immigration and creativity

Creative outputs are "bastards," whose parents may not recognise them... Every situation that increases the possibilities of contaminations   between different cultural formulations potentially heralds creativity...

Countries which are less open to immigration are the ones that should be at the bottom of the creativity, innovation, and development rankings... The way immigrants were welcomed fed the technological boom in areas like San Francisco and Seattle. Almost a third of all the high-tech enterprises in Silicon Valley in the nineties were founded by immigrants from the seventies and eighties...

The cultural scope of the immigrant, whether cultured or living in the street, can be a crucial fact for that recombining of concepts which is at the heart of creativity. Moreover it is above all minorities and not the establishment that push for change...

The need to open borders to immigration is even more urgent when populations are ageing.

Riccardo Viale at a conference on *"The Age of Europe,"* Pontignano, Italy, September 2004 be quite confusing. Sometimes we have more in common with Muslims with regard to prayer and giving and sexual standards than we have with our post-Christian neighbours. People of different religions sometimes unite to fight a common cause.

Christians, like all others, are caught up in this process of interaction and change. We are members of society and therefore part of the ongoing cultural and social change. However, Christians also view society and their fellow citizens – whatever their background - from an additional and overriding perspective that will sometimes be radically different from the prevailing views. They see things in the light of the Kingdom of God.

Recognising that God is in control will enable us to seek how we can contribute in creative ways, whether we are part of Diaspora or host communities. In every situation we will seek God's good purpose for human society, the furtherance of the gospel, and above all God's glory.

4. THE SPIRITUAL OPPORTUNITIES
Where Christians come in

"Impacting the world without having to move; Reaching unreached people groups; Racial reconciliation; Shaping future world leaders"

These are some of the possibilities in the creative ferment of Diaspora. People from all over the world are living just across the street, attending the same schools, working at the same companies.

Those in transition are often more open to the gospel. God's people are called to seize the opportunities for loving service (John 13:35), sharing the good news in season and out of season (1Timothy 4:2; Acts 8:4-5), and making disciples (Acts 11:26; Philippians 4:22; Genesis 39:2; 41; 50:20). This call is to God's people in *Diaspora communities* and in the *host countries*.

Opportunities
Host Christian communities

- *Provide loving hospitality to care for the immediate needs of the "stranger"*

People are most open when they are in transition; they are also the most needy during this time. This presents an opportune time to serve the felt and spiritual needs of their new neighbours, fulfilling the Biblical mandate to care for and welcome newcomers in our midst. In Australia, the Chinese church has found table fellowship and studying the Bible a vital instrument of reaching out to the local Chinese.

- *Break down racial, religious, and cultural barriers before they can be formed*

Misunderstandings between cultures create obstacles. When loving hospitality is given and dialogue is present, these barriers can be prevented and potentially a more peaceful community may result. In a Midwestern city of the USA, there was racial tension against the Indian immigrant community. A church leader suggested a community dinner with the Hindus and Sikhs. This broke down walls of suspicion. It was followed by visits and spiritual dialogue. They now have a high level of trust and mutual respect.

- *Grow in mutual cross-cultural and Biblical values*

  As cultures meet and dialogue, they can grow not only in mutual understanding but also in Christ-likeness. Christians have the opportunity to relate to their new neighbours and gain cultural understanding. On the other hand, the host culture can be influenced by their Diaspora communities. For example, individualistic Western culture may be impacted by an Asian collective culture with its emphasis on family solidarity.

- *Shape leaders from around the world*

  Many international students are educated in foreign countries with the potential of becoming influential leaders in their country of origin. Gandhi and Mandela were both international students.

- *Reach people groups with fewer obstacles to receive the gospel*

  People are more open when they leave countries that are resistant to the gospel. Language and geographical barriers to the gospel are also removed. Mexican immigrants were hosted and prayed for in a Christian woman's living room without her having to leave her home to do foreign missions.

- *Create new relevant forms in expressing Christianity*

  Often Western forms of church are not embraced by other cultures. There are cultural practices which can be transformed into a presentation of the gospel. Diaspora followers of Christ have organised a "Festival of Lights" and an "Alternative Diwali" celebration to share the good news with Hindu and Sikh friends.

- *Provide training for Christian leadership*

  Partnering with Diaspora churches to provide Christian leadership training impacts the leadership of the Diaspora. Some host churches in Finland offer weekly theological education through Evening Bible School for the leaders of Diaspora churches using the Global University curriculum.

Diaspora Christian communities

- *Contribute to the society of their new country*

  "Seek the peace and prosperity of the city to which I have carried you into exile. Pray to the Lord for it, because if it prospers, you too will prosper" (Jeremiah 29:7). In Finland the international Christians filled the Cathedral on the Independence Day, 2004. They wanted to indicate their willingness to seek the welfare of Finland, and proclaim a blessing. The gathering was used to publicly provide the statistics that showed that the majority of migrants are Christian

– not Muslim as the media often portrays.

• *Reach out to others in their own Diaspora through hospitality (Acts 8:4)*

Knowing the struggles and needs of a newcomer is an advantage for those who have already been there. This, coupled with an understanding of culture and language, can greatly minister to a fellow countryman (or woman). A Chinese American Christian professor regularly receives Chinese international students into his home, picking them up from the airport, taking them grocery shopping, and generally orienting them to the culture. Many have come to his Bible study as a result.

• *Reach out to other Diaspora communities (Acts 11:19-20)*

Immigrants and International Students share common concerns of immigration, cross-cultural adjustments, and spiritual needs. This enables them to know how to help each other regardless of country of origin. One Diaspora group may easily identify with the challenges of living in a new environment and may approach other Diaspora communities without a sense of superiority. Diaspora Christian communities are often willing to share facilities with other Diaspora Christian communities. A Chinese church is reaching Hispanic people through meeting felt needs and Asian Indian immigrants through sporting events. Christian international students are well placed to reach other international students.

• *Reach out to the marginalised people in the host country who may not be receptive to those of the host country (2 Samuel 5)*

Marginalised people, who are uncomfortable in their own host culture churches, are often attracted to Diaspora churches. A Filipino American lives in a low income Hispanic neighbourhood to serve to needs of the local children.

• *Be bridges of the gospel to the people in their countries of origin and in other countries (Acts 15:36-41; 8:26-40)*

Since people in the Diasporas are often admired as successful by their own people in their home country, they have opportunities to share their newfound faith when they visit their homeland. A migrant in Australia shared a sermon tape with her parents back home in Hong Kong. After listening to the tape, the father became a Christian. International students who visit or return home have opportunities to tell their families and friends about Jesus.

• *Revitalise the Christian community in their host country*

Migrant Christians and their communities can significantly help established Christianity in the West to renew its mission and evangelism (Matthew 5:13; 13:33, and Jongeneel 2002:33). For example, African churches in London are growing much more rapidly than any other. South East Asians in Sydney changed a dying church to a thriving one. Though actual close co-operation and interaction is still in its infancy, the Diaspora Christians are still having an inspirational effect (See Chapter 7). A similar story about a declining mono-cultural church being significantly revitalised as a growing multi-cultural and multi-national church is recounted in *Where the Nations Meet: The Church in a Multicultural World* by Stephen A Rhodes (InterVarsity Press, 1998).

Considerations

Host Christian community considerations

- Patronising attitudes in the host culture lead to assuming a spiritual and cultural superiority. This in turn marginalises the Diaspora community and church by disempowering the Diaspora leaders. Christians need to be careful not fall into this trap.

- Often the church's attitudes of racial and religious prejudice hinder sharing of the gospel. Black Christians from the Caribbean found coldness instead of welcome when they came to Britain. East African Christians never thought that Asians could follow Christ and so they did not witness to them for many years. International students feel rejected by such a climate, especially in church. Walls were built instead of being torn down. When the church remains silent to the vulnerable, immigrants and international students may face hostility without receiving assistance. Rather than loving and welcoming people of other faiths, Christians often ignore or avoid them.

- Lack of knowledge contributes to fear. The growing number of non-Christian religious buildings, the popularity of Eastern meditation practices and the political agenda of some religious groups can cause Christians to be paralysed rather than seize the opportunities for outreach. Some Christians do not allow or pursue culturally relevant worship forms, dress styles, and practices out of fear of compromising their faith with other religions.

Diaspora Christian communities considerations

- Lack of resources and understanding of their role in evangelism, discipleship, and mission cause barriers. Challenges of Diaspora churches include lack of full-time or trained leaders, lack of cooperation of the church in the host country, lack of facilities, and sustainability.

- Diaspora believers are often a minority within a minority. They are a minority racially, and within their own ethnic group they are a religious minority. As a result, they may feel insecure about sharing their faith with others, especially those of the host culture. Experience with rejection leads to fear of stepping out and more rejection.

- Diaspora communities often are inward looking. Many desire to retain cultural identity to the extreme of forming cultural ghettos. For the Diaspora church, inward looking behaviour creates barriers to reaching out to other ethnic Diasporas, the host culture, and the marginalised.

5. GUIDING PRINCIPLES
Making a Difference
Holding our commitments in creative tension

Increasingly this planet is becoming a "Diaspora" world. This leads to some creative tensions where the cultures and faiths are brought together and combined in new and unexpected ways. In light of this, the following guidelines are relevant:

- **Christians need to combine their commitment to freedom of religion and conscience with the imperative to share the good news.** We have to hold together our absolute commitment to sharing the good news of Jesus along with an equal commitment to freedom of conscience, religion, and speech for all. Though Christians have not always been consistent in this, it is vital that we grasp and practice this truth in today's pluralistic world. One example was when a group of Asian business people of all faiths asked a Christian to organise a conference on "Healing the Wounds," that looked at issues of religious and social justice in Gujarat, India, in 2002. We must not let our commitment to tolerance keep us from finding ways to share our faith.

- **Christians need to stress the need for a personal and relational commitment to Christ that transforms all dimensions of their life individually and as a community.** A growing Christian will increasingly demonstrate Christ-like character, attitudes and goals. People from the background of another religion will be likely to think that being a Christian is just membership of a church or taking the name of Christian. We must present a clear explanation of the gospel.

- **Christians need to hold to their commitment to Christ, while affirming only that which is biblically acceptable in their own heritage, culture, and community.** They also need to value what in other cultures is biblically acceptable.

- **Commitment to Christ is often perceived as identification with Western culture.** People assume that turning to Christ involves leaving one's own community and joining another. We must work actively against this misunderstanding.

- **Christians need to affirm the uniqueness of Christ in ways that welcome those of other faiths.** Christ is unique because he has dealt with the universal problem of sin. Since he died for all, he welcomes all, regardless of background and needs. All come to a saving knowledge of God on the same basis of his free grace. Use of the term "Christian" may have some negative connotations. The use of the terms "follower of Christ" or "disciple of Christ" may be more acceptable. So we need to be sensitive in the way we speak about Christ and our Christian faith.

From across the street to across the world.

The presence of the Diasporas provides exciting opportunities and potential to share the good news. New arrivals may have greater access to the gospel now than they had in their own country. At the same time they may have a greater need for discovery as they redefine their identity. For example, students from restrictive societies studying in New Zealand and Australia often take the opportunity to explore the gospel.

People of very different cultures and faiths from all around the world are living next to each other. As God gives opportunity, we need to seek ways to use this to share the good news, not just with the new neighbours, but, over the longer term, with those they have left behind back home.

> *The traditional distinction between "foreign missions" and "home missions" needs to be replaced by a "multi-directional" concept of "world missions."*

A whole gospel

Our goal in ministry is to bring about through the gospel the transformation of individuals, society, and environment (1 Peter 2:11ff; 1 Timothy 2:1-6). This calls for holistic ministry characterised by the following:

Building bridges

We need to find ways to serve people and care for their felt needs as well as build genuine friendships.

- The Tamil church in East London visited Tamils who were in prison on immigration charges, or who were sick. Their care and prayer had a powerful impact.

- A Chinese congregation in a small city in America connected with illegal immigrants transported from China to the US. Many of the prisoners were unable to speak English and appreciative of the care from the Chinese church. Most came to faith before being deported.

- The Springfield Project in Birmingham works with the families of Mirpuri Muslims from Pakistan, a very tightly closed community. After 7-10 years, trust has been built up and there is a new openness.

- "Operation Friendship" in New Zealand assists students in acculturating to their new society.

- Christians helping Afghani refugee families to adjust to life in Canada have brought some to salvation in Christ.

- An international student minister works with Muslim students in Cambridge through friendship, which has enabled him to be very open and frank. Christian house parties with outdoor activities and food provide a setting for lively evening Bible discussions with international students.

- A missionary teaches English as a Second Language to a Punjabi Christian lady who is married to a Sikh husband. This opened the door to assist this family in moving their residence, which opened another door to meet an entire extended Sikh family, which led to a wonderful opportunity to share the Good News of Salvation in Jesus Christ with them all.

- A former student for the Brahman priesthood teaches Hindi to a local Christian missionary and opens his heart to hear the story of salvation in Christ. He is now attending a church in his language group.

- Visiting summer youth teams join outreach into the South Asian community. Follow-up has led to a church starting to be planted and regular outreach into about 12 families with the desire to lead them all to the Lord.

- Approaching an ethnic community leader with the statement and question: "Hello! I am a Christian in the area. I was wondering what your community needs that I may encourage or help with." This led to a strong children's and youth program being established and around 200 kids being saved. They now live across the country and are raising their own families in the way of the Lord.

- A Punjabi lady who still worships at an altar for her Hindu gods awakened one morning unable to move with excruciating pain in her neck and up-

per back. The missionary was called on to pray which she did. The lady was instantly healed and is increasingly open to hearing the gospel of Christ.

Working to address common concerns

We need to work together with people of all backgrounds on issues of common concern, such as drug abuse, youth issues, unemployment, and racism.

- Masala Bridge Builders are a newly developed resource for groups to meet and discuss issues that concern Diaspora groups.

- A local Diaspora church can seek to reach out to the migrants through an ESL program in conjunction with the program provided by the immigration office. For example, in Australia, immigrants can study English free for over 500 hours. The church can provide facilities and invite the teachers sponsored by the government to conduct English classes. This can be extended to working with other community groups such as art groups, councils, etc.

- International student ministries and Overseas Christian Fellowships can work with the Student Union, International Student Office during orientation, and throughout the semesters to reach out to the international students in seeking to help them to settle and grow in a new country.

Demonstrating mutual respect and celebrating diversity

The gospel demands that we treat people with mutual respect, dignity, and generosity. With Diaspora peoples this includes:

- Serving Diaspora individuals and communities in practical ways, regardless of their faith.
- Opposing racist practices and policies.
- Being advocates for genuine refugees and asylum seekers, when governments are under pressure to restrict their freedoms.
- Allow international students to organise and contribute to cultural events such as having a potluck meal and program that features the food, music, games, and other cultural aspects of a nation or region.
- Speaking out for diversity, when traditional mono-cultural patterns are emphasised.
- Giving our platform to Diaspora people and welcoming them into leadership.

Sharing the good news in ways that are relevant to people's culture

When sharing the gospel with Diaspora people, it is important to be sensitive to the different Diaspora people, their culture, practices, and beliefs. Obviously, there are differences in how one reaches Middle Eastern Muslims from how one reaches Muslims from Indonesia. Or, in how one reaches Chinese people in the West compared to how it is done in China. And even, for example, how the many Asian communities living in London differ from each other.

The local base

The most effective ministries happen through a local Christian fellowship or community, and when possible a local church. A solid ministry has two dimensions:

1. A spiritually nurturing community who worship and learn together, love and serve each other

Peter's letter to the suffering Diaspora believers exhorts them to demonstrate "sincere" and "fervent" love for your brothers'. This love includes hospitality, service, and the ministry of God's word. (1 Peter 1:22; 3:8; 4:8-11). This loving, welcoming community is the essential base for:

2. A witness to the wider community

In the complex social and cultural matrix of our Diaspora society, the church has to reach out to the local community in multiple ways. It will need to:

- Develop new, culturally relevant expressions of church for different groups (this means giving support and space to Diaspora Christians and others to do this)
- Develop links with other Diaspora groups in order to work together to face common challenges and serve their communities
- Develop links with mission agencies and other Christian organisations for mutual learning and sharing of personnel and other needed resources

Diaspora networks

Diaspora is a "network driven phenomenon" (Hanciles) and functions through relationships and contacts around the world. Various kinds of Diaspora networks need to be developed in order to enhance effective ministry. Business and governments recognise the value of networking. For example, India's government and the Federation of Indian Chambers of Commerce and Industry are aggressively networking with successful non-resident Indians to harness their resources and achievements for the uplift of India. See (http://trendwatching.com/trends/2003/03diasporamanagement.html)

In the Christian world, Chinese Diaspora Christians have created a world-wide network for evangelism, as have the Filipino Diaspora Christians (See Chapter 7). The Association of Christian Ministries to Internationals (ACMI) was established in 1981 as a US/Canadian fellowship of international student ministry staff and volunteers to enhance networking, cross training, and cooperation in North America and globally. It is recommended that all Diaspora groups learn from their experiences and explore networking in this way.

The search for partners

As the influence of Christianity declines in the West and turns it into a resistant mission field, the new global order creates new possibilities for Christians from old and new churches to form partnerships (Samuel Escobar, *A Time for Mission: The Challenge for Global Christianity* [InterVarsity Press, 2003], 26-51). These partnerships need to be encouraged and carefully nurtured. Students who return home after graduation create a great network of professionals.

It requires repentance, grace, hu- **mility and the recognition that we all need each other desperately in order to be effective in mission in today's world. Peter's exhortation to love is just as applicable when building relationships between different groups.**

The outcome of partnerships is the sharing of expertise, materials, personnel, prayer, and resources for training. (See Bibliography for lists of resources).

6. OPTIONS
Mobilising Diaspora Communities
This can be achieved by, for example:
Planting churches

National or international networks, such as Lausanne Committee for World Evangelization, CCCOWE, Filipino International Network (FIN), Ethnic America Network, and South Asia Concern may be willing to help mobilise the planting of local churches. There are various approaches:

- Homogeneous Church Planting: those of the same cultural background and language are often in the best position to reach out with the gospel to their own people. This gains from being initiated and funded by the leadership of an established church. The goal is to encourage the Diaspora Christians to form their own churches that enables a sense of belonging.

- Intra-Ethnic Group Church Planting: Established Diaspora Churches may work together by sharing resources for planting new churches for the new immigrants.

- Inter-Ethnic Group Church Planting: Churches of the same denomination but different ethnic backgrounds may pool resources together to plant a new Church for a different Diaspora group. For example, a Chinese speaking Church and an English speaking Church of the same denomination have worked together in the planting of a Filipino Church.
- International Church Planting: churches made up of members from multiple nations.
- Multi-ethnic churches with different congregations offering services in a variety of languages.
- Encourage local churches to allocate special funding for Diaspora ministries.

Instilling a missionary vision in the new church while discipling:

The Diaspora is not only a mission field to be reached, but a group of people with great potential to be mobilised for the Kingdom. In planting a church for Diaspora, there should be the end in mind that it will be a Great Commission Church. The best time to introduce such a concept is during the formative stage of the new church, they should be shaped by a mission driven church growth philosophy. This to be actualised in all ministry aspects: teaching, preaching, planning, and activities in the church. International student churches are being planted with significant growth in discipleship and outreach. Many students utilise the experience of being part of an international stu-

dent church or fellowship when they return home and participate in various kinds of church growth endeavours.

Providing opportunities for implementing The Great Commission

- Foster younger generations in an environment of mission.
- Identify and train leaders.
- Pray for the advance of the gospel by forming mission focused prayer networks.
- Encourage missionary awareness and opportunities such as missions conferences and short term missions.

Working with the church in the host countries

- Encourage the churches in the host countries to break through the ethnic boundary and reach out to the Diaspora. Help them to recognise that Diaspora provides a mission field on their doorstep.
- Encourage the churches to set up International Student Ministries.
- Inform the Church about the current situation of the Diaspora community.
- Build relationships with the Diaspora through cultural festivals, celebrations, special community events.
- Allocate resources to Diaspora ministries.
- Cultivate a friendly atmosphere to welcome members of the Diaspora who come to the church.
- Form networks and partnership with other ethnic Diaspora groups for ministries.
- Maintain relationships with local communities and government

regarding the needs of the Diaspora, e.g. helping with language training, job training, and placement.

- Provide theological training for present and future Diaspora leaders.

Getting support from the church in the countries of origin

Members of the Diaspora often maintain strong ties with their home countries, whose churches may provide ministry support. For example, they may:

- Help the churches and communities of the host countries to understand the cultural and historical background of the Diaspora
- Share training materials so that the church of the host country may understand the Diaspora
- Work together with the Church in the host countries in providing direction and advice for ministries and church planting
- Mobilise prayer support for those who have moved overseas
- Encourage the Diaspora Church to participate in the ministries of their home countries.

For example, for two decades, alumni of the Filipino movement of Inter-Varsity Christian Fellowship living in North America have been conducting an annual Balikatan conference for reunion and fund raising. They have financially supported the work of InterVarsity Philippines and fellow alumni who are in missionary service.

7. CASE STUDIES FROM THE DIASPORA

A. The Formation of Leaders - International Students

For centuries, God has been bringing students to study in other countries. Today, God is moving students and scholars to countries around the world where they can more easily hear and respond to the gospel. Middle Eastern students are in Asian countries, Bhutanese students are in the Philippines, students from the Pacific Rim and Latin America are in Canada, East Asians, Americans, and Africans are in the United Kingdom. This is in fulfilment of Acts 17:26-27. *"From one man he made every nation of men that they should inhabit the whole earth; and he determined the times set for them and the exact places where they should live. God did this so that men would seek him and perhaps reach out for him and find him, though he is not far from each one of us."*

Local churches and student ministries in every nation can share in this strategic opportunity God is giving to them to impact the world for Christ in their own town or city.

An influential, staunch Muslim family from a Middle Eastern country sent their son to study in India. The young man met us and asked for medical help for a long-standing physical problem. Having tried other treatments, all to no avail, we did not know what to do except to look to God. With much hesitation, we prayed over him. For three nights in succession, Jesus revealed Himself in a dream. The ailment disappeared at once. He believed in Jesus and was baptised. Because he faced severe persecution in his home country, he is a church-planter in another Middle Eastern country.

Why is International Student Ministry (ISM) so strategic?

International student ministry can significantly influence the lives of international students, the life and vision of the local Christian community, and the worldwide spread of the gospel.

1. How International Students benefit

- They value the warmth and welcome of a friend, family, and home during a time of loneliness.
- Those from restrictive societies have greater freedom to explore the gospel of Jesus Christ.
- They are often more curious, open, and responsive to the gospel than they would be at home.

  A Chinese woman walked into our discussion group for the first time. When we asked why she came, she shared, "I grew up without any religion. In these past years, the more I talked with my classmates in university, the more we felt an emptiness inside. We have been disillusioned, but we don't know where to turn. I came because I am looking for a guide."

2. How local churches benefit

- Members can develop friendships and communicate the gospel with people from all over the world without knowing a foreign language or leaving home.
- Relationships with international students provide valuable cross-cultural experience for those who wish to serve abroad.
- The church can be involved beyond praying for and giving to mission.
- It is one of the most cost-effective ways of reaching the world for Christ.
- Christian international students contribute to the life of the Christian community in the host country.

3. How the gospel benefits

- Returning Christian graduates often serve in positions of influence that impact their homeland or region in the realm of business, government, education, medicine, technology, etc.
- International students often return home and move into positions of Christian leadership. Returning international students who became church planters include: Bakht Singh of India, John Sung of China, and Kriengsak Chareonwonsak of Thailand.
- Many Christian students return to nations that are home to "unreached people groups" as well as resistant religious groups.
- Returning students who had positive experiences abroad have opened doors for mission projects in their home countries.
- International student ministry often reaches a social class not reached by other mission work in their own country.

  J studied at a university in the Midwest of the United States. He was used of God to influence a whole denomination in Malaysia with the vision of discipleship. Suzy, who studied at the same university, is the director of a Christian school in Indonesia that is leading children and families to Christ.

The biblical perspective on International Student Ministry

1. Our call to mission

Just as God reached out to us, we are commanded to emulate Jesus and "go and make disciples of all nations" (Matthew 28:19). Through the centuries, missions have often focused on going. Today, with increasing numbers of international students coming to us from the ends of the earth, God is presenting us with an opportunity comparable to the day of Pentecost.

The Bible gives several examples of people coming to God's people in search of knowledge about God. The Queen of Sheba, who went to Jerusalem in search of wisdom, had an opportunity to learn more of Jehovah and to eventually come to praise Him (1 Kings 10). Philip was given the responsibility of explaining the gospel to an Ethiopian eunuch on his way back home (Acts 8:26-39). It is believed that the eunuch was one of the key people that contributed to the spread of the gospel to the African continent. In the same way, we are given the responsibility to explain the gospel to internationals who come to us. Perhaps we may be given the privilege to participate in the spread of the gospel in their home country.

2. Our call to hospitality

By virtue of our citizenship in the Kingdom of God, we are now "strangers" although we still live in this world (1 Peter 1:1). Abraham and the other people of faith are models of this dual citizenship (Hebrews 11:13-16). The fact that we feel not entirely at home in our own culture helps us to understand a little of what those who come into our culture feel. This understanding motivates us to give hospitality. *"The alien living with you must be treated as one of your native-born. Love him as yourself..."* is a commandment given with the reminder of the Israelites' own difficulty while living in a foreign land (Leviticus 19:34).

The same call to understand and give hospitality is given to us today. In Matthew 25:31-46, the King Jesus identified with the guest, *"I was a stranger and you invited me in"* and said, *"whatever you did for one of the least of these brothers of mine, you did it for me."* He said that to fail to give hospitality would incur judgment.

Priscilla and Aquila's hospitality towards Apollos helped him to understand God's way more adequately. Later, Apollos contributed to the life of the church where he was welcomed (Acts 18:26-27). In the same way, our care for the international students among us will serve as the bridge over which the gospel travels. In return, our community life is enhanced by their participation.

3. Our call to community

When internationals are welcomed into the local church we are saying to them what God says to us, *"You are no longer foreigners and aliens, but fellow citizens with God's people and member of God's household"* (Ephesians 2:19). God calls us to include people from other cultures into the community of believers. Such an integrated community demonstrates reconciliation and the unity of the people of God in the midst of a world fractured by ethnic and cultural differences.

4. *Our call to God's purpose*

Internationals have often played important roles in God's plan. His position in Egypt enabled Joseph to save the Israelites from famine. Moses grew up in the Egyptian palace and was later called by God to free the Israelites from Egypt. Daniel, an international student in Babylonia became an honoured advisor to several rulers. As individuals and as a community, we are to participate in God's purposes to extend His reign over all the earth. It is God's eternal purpose to have a church for himself from "every nation, tribe, people and language" (Revelation 7:9). International student ministry is a call and an opportunity to partner in reconciling the world to Him and establishing His coming Kingdom. (See chapter 2.)

> M is a graduate student at a university in the United States. At the university's orientation for new international students, M, who is a Christian, was delighted to be invited to a fellowship of Christian international students who are actively involved in a local church. M brings both Christians and non-Christian friends from campus to the fellowship at the church. When a member of the church visited her country, he made a special effort to meet M's parents and family who are believers. The visiting American discovered that M's parents had been cared for by Christians when they had been international students in the U.S. M's father is a government leader in a Muslim county and is an outspoken witness for Christ.

5. *The current scope of International Student Ministry*

Few students studied abroad in the 19th century. The numbers of students increased during the 20th century, especially after World War II. The rate of growth continues to increase dramatically. In 2000 estimated figures worldwide stood at 1.7 million international students at university or tertiary level institutions. According to a report at the 16th annual Australian International Education conference the number of international students worldwide will potentially double by 2015 and double again by 2025. Political, economic, and other factors may alter the flow and destinations of students studying abroad, but growth will continue.

On the next page are two tables showing the increase in the number of International Students in France and their home countries. International Students study all over the world and this is just one example.

Figure 1

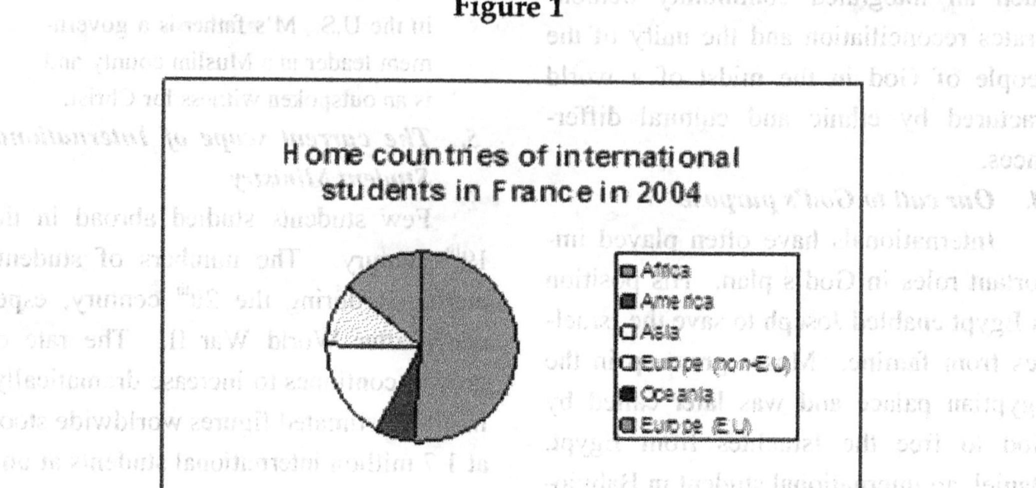

Figure 2

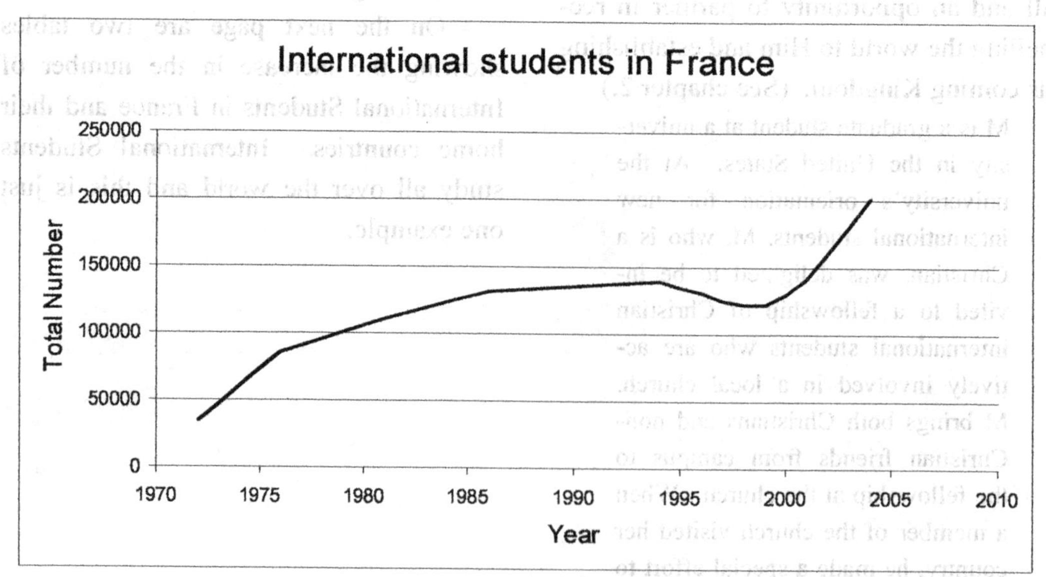

As the number of international students increased in the last half century, more Christians began ministries among these students. Intentional outreach by local congregations and student groups, often in partnership, multiplied. Some examples of this growth are:

Europe:

- ISM began in the United Kingdom in the 1950's with University and Colleges Christian Fellowship (UCCF). When the numbers on international students began to grow in the 1980's, Friends International was founded in order to help churches catch the vision for ISM. Since 1985 it has begun ministries in more than 120 churches in 31 cities.
- God's people in European nations are ministering to internationals through student groups, local churches, and mission agencies.
- In the Ukraine, a new ISM in the Crimea grew to a group of sixty within two years. Around Christmas they bought 100 chocolate bars and hand signed 100 cards, wishing students "Happy New Year" in Russian or in English. Four of them went to visit international students who lived in the dorm of a medical university. Amazingly, the guards let them in, although normally the access to student dorms in the Ukraine is very restricted. They knocked on doors, delivering cards and chocolates, and started conversations with students. Most were suspicious at first. Some asked how much they charged for "this service." But after a bit their suspicion gave way to gratitude. Some invited them to their rooms and even offered them tea.
- The Netherlands and Germany have well established ISMs.
- Believers in Portugal have shared the gospel with North Korean students.

Pacific/Asia:

- Australia's Overseas Christian Fellowship (OCF) was begun by Asian students in the 1960's, and continues to thrive as a student led movement.
- New Zealand has three ISM organisations that have a close working relationship: International Friendship Ministries, Tertiary Students Christian Fellowship, and ISM New Zealand.
- ISM's are growing in the Philippines, Singapore, Malaysia, Korea, Japan, and India. Diliman Bible Church in Manila has ministered to international students at the University of the Philippines for over 25 years.

North America:

- Organised outreach to internationals began in 1911. InterVarsity Christian Fellowship (1944) and International Students, Incorporated (1953) were two early ministries. The growth of ISM in North America has accelerated since the 1980's. Local congregations, campus ministries, denominations, mission agencies, and several new organisations have ISM specialists.

- The (North American) Association of Christians Ministering among Internationals (ACMI) has been a catalyst for further growth through annual conferences and an email network.

Africa

- Organised ministries exist in South Africa and Ivory Coast. Elsewhere both Christian and non-Christian internationals attend local student fellowship meetings.
- Students from some African countries have purposefully gone to study in other countries and pioneered student ministry in their host countries.

Latin America:

- There are emerging ministries in Latin America.
- A Colombian student came to Christ in Brazil, and after returning home became the director of a national student ministry.

Hints and Ideas for International Student Ministry

Additional workers are needed for this strategic mission field. The impact of just one international student returning home as a dedicated disciple of Jesus Christ is enormous. Returning international students have the language, the culture, and no immigration barriers. They are part of the fabric of their society. They can be lifelong missionaries. Consider the example of Bahkt Singh who returned to India, and over his lifetime contributed to the planting of more than 7,000 churches. Imagine the potential missionary force that could result from purposeful witness among the two million international students worldwide. Obviously, the Christian community must be mobilised for this mission opportunity.

1. Some general points

Careful attention to in-depth quality relationships results in evangelising, discipling, and equipping the international students. We must remember that most students will re-enter their home cultures. Our goal is to produce students who walk with Christ, serve in the body, and go on to multiply disciples in and beyond their nations. They need to be taught to feed themselves spiritually, given opportunities to serve in the church, witness effectively, and to disciple others. They must also be prepared to handle transitions, live in a Christ-like manner, be servant leaders, and be lifelong learners.

Over time many returnees grow to be influential in their home country's church. A growing sense of partnership and connection can occur between the former host country church and home country churches. As the returned graduates mature in their ministry, the host church will be encouraged to continue their ministry among international students.

2. When you want to contact students

- Pray for a relationship with key students who can introduce you to their networks of international friends.
- Games and recreational activities and sports, such as a friendly soccer match or volleyball, are natural bridges for getting acquainted.
- Enlist local Christian students to

help develop the ministry to internationals.

- Discover needs and meet them, i.e. friendship and families, hospitality, language conversation partners, admission help, assistance with issues such as accommodation, transportation, and providing information.
- Discover common interests between individual students and believers, encouraging relationships on a basis of mutuality.
- In some settings, internationals may be vulnerable and need special attention:
  - Those dealing with homesickness, isolation, hostility, and cultural adjustments may need someone available to listen, counsel, protect or defend, or include them in a community
  - Those dealing with traumatic issues such as visa problems, imprisonment, hospitalisation due to illness or injury, or automobile accident may need help with legal, bureaucratic, or medical issues, and should be served primarily by the school's International Student office if possible.

On Chinese New Year we invited some students to have a meal with us. Later that evening, we decided to invite these students to visit some of our friends' homes, a part of the Chinese tradition. On the way there, a Chinese woman asked abruptly why I believed in Jesus. We were not talking about any spiritual (religious) matter at that time. This provided an opportunity to share about the gospel with her.

Two models for involvement

Believers of all shades and descriptions, ages and stages can connect with international students in their community and develop a relationship and ministry. Christian students need just to look around the campus to find international students in their classes, labs, library, living, and dining areas. People from the community and churches can inquire at the International Student Office about opportunities to volunteer as hosts, language conversation partners, and other avenues of service.

Choose a model for ministry:

- Local Church Model – mobilising church members to participate in ISM
- Campus Model – mobilising Christian students to reach international students on campus

Combining ministry models often enhances the overall ministry. Partnering between campus ministry where students make contacts, local churches who can offer hospitality, and ethnic churches that offer the gospel in heart languages can be a powerful witness.

Local Church Model

Most Christian communities, irrespective of size, need only to exercise faith to begin an international student ministry that will add a significant dimension to their involvement in world missions. Local churches can adapt these suggestions for beginning a ministry in their own situation:

1. Seek the approval and blessing of church leadership and/or the support of denominational leadership.
2. Identify (lay) leaders to form a ministry team – possibly (but not necessarily) utilising people who already have cross-cultural experience.
3. Recruit volunteers with an appropriate screening process.
4. Provide models of ISM through testimonies, videos, reports from other churches, and input from an ISM specialist.
5. Develop a strategy to connect with international students (friendship partners, teaching English, monthly socials, meeting new arrivals at the airport, visiting ethnic grocery stores, etc.).
6. Teach the team the biblical basis for ISM and the ministry skills relevant to ISM.
7. Provide resources, such as those listed in the bibliography, and regular encouragement to the leadership team & volunteers.
8. Ensure good channels of communication between the team, church leadership, and the congregation.
9. Encourage ISM teams from different churches and ministries to meet together for prayer, encouragement, exchange of ideas, and discussion of possible joint projects.
10. Churches in areas where other ISM's already exist may want to adopt an "unreached" group of students on a given campus.
11. Send ministry team members to an ISM equipping conference.

Our church's international student ministry provides temporary housing to international students who arrive before the dormitories open. One year we housed a Chinese student, C, for almost a week in our home. At dinnertime I would pray before the meal and to my surprise C. began to pray after me, though he was not a believer at the time. After the semester started, he began coming to our international Sunday Fellowship. He also had contact with a local Chinese church. After he decided to make a career shift, he went back to China after one semester. Just before he left, C accepted Christ. We are encouraged that we will see him again in the Kingdom.

A local church can send the believing student as a missionary first to the campus and later to their home country or other place where God calls them. As they are vulnerable in the re-entry process, their host country Christian community should, where possible, help link returning international students to the body of Christ in their home country. Continued prayer, sharing resources, and communication with the returned graduate are important for their encouragement. Websites, phone calls, letters, and visits all help to stimulate encouragement of the returned graduate. The resulting feedback of returnees may stimulate the host Christian community's mission vision and involvement around the world.

Campus Model

Pray to the Lord of the harvest to raise up workers among students (Matthew 9:38).

1. Assess your situation.
2. Find Christian international students to be strategic partners:
   a. If necessary, provide them with discipling and leadership development.
   b. Pray with them for their country of origin and together learn about other countries whose students are present in the university.
   c. Learn from them how best to reach out to their non-Christian peers.
   d. Involve them in training and mentoring, especially about reaching groups such as Muslims, Buddhists, and Hindus.
3. Consider how to best motivate Christian students from the host-country:
   a. For example, today's students may need an experiential approach.
   b. Look for students who already have cross-cultural experience or international friends.
   c. Tell stories of personal experiences that present friendship with internationals as enriching and fun.
   d. Communicate with established Christian student leadership structures so students can be motivated by their leaders who have seen how ISM fits into their existing vision and plans for missions.
4. Provide both Christian internationals and host country students with training in cultural sensitivity, communication, and worldview differences. They may also need help in understanding students from resistant religious groups. Use media appropriate for students from your context.
5. Challenge Christian students (international and host country) to enrol in universities without ISMs in order to start student ministries in those universities. This can be a creative way of spreading ISM in restricted access nations.

German students do most of the international student ministry in Germany. When I was a freshman at university I immediately joined the international bible study group. One year later I became the leader of the group. I asked the staff workers to pray that God would double the number of guests within the next semester. From that day the group started growing. New students came to our group in really strange ways. By the end of the semester the number had almost doubled and we felt that God had heard our prayers. Since that day I know that prayer is what matters most in international student ministry.

Getting started

Prayer should permeate the entire ministry from the beginning and throughout each phase.

- **Profile the campus:**
  - Assess numbers of students, country of origin, services already provided for them.
  - Interview international students to

find out ways and places to meet students.

- **Discover and address the felt needs of students.**

  While visiting our local grocery store, my wife and I saw a Jamaican couple with a fully loaded shopping cart. Since it was near the beginning of the semester, we suspected that they were new students. We offered to drive them to their home (they had come by taxi), had them over for the evening meal, and them helped them with more shopping. They quickly became good friends and involved in our church Bible study. Talk with other Christian ministries and individuals who have contact with international students.

- **Build relationships with students and campus officials, if possible.**
  - Pray for positive relationships with officials.
  - Introduce yourself to the campus official or staff of the International Student Office.
  - Discover existing programs and needs not yet met.
  - Offer volunteer service where possible.

Opening doors to the gospel

Initiate contact through non-religious activities, such as language assistance or sports. This helps build friendships and trust which can lead to openness toward later participation in religious activities. Pray for discernment about students' spiritual openness. An international student's spiritual search can be encouraged in various ways:

- Investigative Bible discussions (one to one or in small groups) Note: Religious discussions with students from restrictive societies are usually best one to one due to peer pressure concerns.
- Large group events (i.e. Christian concert or speaker)
- Language assistance programs, such as tutoring or conversation exchange
- Religious and cultural discussions (e.g. What is the true meaning of Christmas?)
- Friendship dinners
- Mutual sharing of cultures
- Christian literature and media
- Storytelling
- Field trips to sites or natural wonders that spawn spiritual discussions
- Personal testimonies
- Exposing students to justice and reconciliation ministries
- Career mentoring by Christians within the same professional field
  C came to Oxford, England as a visiting academic for six months. He came from a restricted access country in Asia where his grandfather was a Buddhist priest. He was surprised to find that all the people who offered him friendship were Christians. When a member of his department invited C to a bible study in his home, C went "out of intellectual curiosity." Later an ISM worker gave him a Bible in his own language. In a few days, he had read the Scriptures from cover to cover. "God speaks my language!" he cried. Within two weeks he put his faith in Christ and

was baptised. A few days later, C was on a plane home to his country eager to pass on the good news of Jesus to family, friends, and colleagues.

We should always endeavour to present the gospel in a culturally sensitive way with respect for the international student. Before international students become Christians, it will be important for them to compare the assumptions of their world view and the biblical worldview. They may also need to renounce some aspects of their former religious practices. (See Neil Anderson and Daniel Tong material in bibliography.)

Relationships established before a person becomes a Christian are very important for discipling and follow-up. To prepare them for returning home, attention should be given to discipling, especially devotional life, small group Bible study groups, skills and heart for ministry. The ministry responsible for new international believers should take responsibility for their care through re-entry and becoming established at home.

Alfredo put his trust in Jesus Christ while he was a high school exchange student in the United States. Upon returning to his home in Portugal, he went to university and became involved in a Christian ministry on campus. He later became the national director of that ministry. As the director, he developed a partnership with two international missions organisations to pioneer an outreach to international students at two major universities in Portugal. After further studies abroad, Alfredo is now a key leader in the Portuguese Bible Society.

B. The Diaspora of Talent – Business Men and Professionals

There is a Diaspora within the Diasporas. It is the Diaspora of Talent. It is represented in the Bible by Daniel and his three friends and Esther (Daniel 1, Esther 1). From a human point of view it is pragmatic (Daniel 1:3). From God's point of view it is intentional. It is part of his purpose. Scattered through all the Diasporas there are men and women with God-given talent that enables them to make a unique contribution to their new countries. Some of them are godly and their influence is all the greater. Diaspora people everywhere and particularly the business and professional community are wielding an ever-increasing influence. This is true in economics, politics, culture, and spirituality. As with international students, evangelism to this group has to take into account their distinctive profile. Many in this group are multi-lingual, well-educated (often internationally), adaptable, and creative. They are usually members of organised professional networks such as Chambers of Commerce, professional associations, and their own ethnic subgroups. Many of them now live in middle class suburbs, having moved up market from areas of ethnic concentration. While well integrated, many hold tight to their own cultural ways.

However, along with other 2nd and 3rd generation Diaspora communities, although by and large well integrated in the host community, many still struggle between the expectations of their parents and their peer groups. Mixed marriages are increasing. However, many face issues relating to arranged and forced marriages, career choices, and family tensions.

The Economies

The economic strength of Diaspora communities is demonstrated by the fact that they send home almost $62 billion in remittances; in the Philippines it is estimated that remittances amount to 32% of GNP dwarfing both foreign direct investment and aid flow into the country.

Zimbabwean economic migrants in the UK (circa 1 million) are financing a construction boom in the leafy Belgravia suburb of Harare.

Government

The Eritreans with virtually no international support managed to win a protracted 30 year war of independence through the financial support of its widespread Eritrean Diaspora. In foreign policy, Diasporas in their adopted countries have influenced governments to take action affecting the situation in their country of origin; a poor country like Armenia managed to persuade some powerful foreign governments such as France to recognise the 1915 genocide of Armenians in Turkey. They failed to do this in Germany which has a large Turkish Diaspora.

Diaspora communities are able to influence the government on the faith agenda because they are able to say things that the indigenous Christian may not be able to. Diaspora Christians can raise issues highlighting the social consequences

of cultural practices especially where human rights are being violated – forced marriages and honour killings are examples of issues that have been raised in the UK and where government has been forced to take action against these illegal practices. Practices that have hitherto not been openly discussed for fear of offending the "other" and attempting to maintain political correctness.

In another area, Diaspora Christians have engaged with government in speaking out on behalf of persecuted Christians in their countries of origin. They have campaigned for governments not to ignore but to take action against those countries which are violating human rights by persecuting Christians. The major protests in western capitals following Graham Staines tragic murder in India are a case in point.

Media and culture

Diaspora people can also be found in the corridors of power in government and politics; influencing fashion and design; catalysing creativity and innovation; and building their own places of worship. They are seen as a unique resource to both the receiving countries and their countries of origin, something that governments are increasingly recognising and responding to in their policy making. The rapid growth of ethnic media (newspapers, radio & TV stations and the internet) in the Diaspora provides another opportunity for using these channels for evangelism. Many carry regular god slots or religious columns and are open to Christians taking their fair share under broadcasting and licensing rules.

Reconciliation

Diaspora Christians have also been engaged in encouraging reconciliation between different communities affected by violence in their countries of origin. South Asian Christian leaders played a key role in opening dialogue between the leaders of the different faith communities in the United Kingdom following violence between Hindus and Muslims in Gujarat. Even though they had different nationalities when they arrived, common citizenship within the host country provides a unique platform to bring together opposing groups for dialogue, debate and reconciliation.

Opportunities

Another positive outcome from reaching such communities for Christ is the advantage they possess over the indigenous population by virtue of the fact that they have a heritage of networks and special privileges accorded to them. They often have dual citizenship, visa exemptions which can be an important factor in mission to closed countries, and a potential source for future missionaries.

Without these efforts 2nd and 3rd generation Diaspora might gradually disengage from their country of origin and roots - a great loss spiritually as well as culturally, politically, and economically to the nation, the Diaspora, and more importantly, the Kingdom. For a new generation of globally mobile skilled migrants, the danger of disengagement with the homeland is even greater.

The young, professional Diaspora from the "old Commonwealth" and the 10 new EU states assimilate easily in Britain. Latin America and Africa are also haemorrhaging skilled workers and the brain drain has a detrimental impact on both continents so much so that the Mozambique President, Joachim Chissano, in his recent African Union address, appealed to the African Diaspora not to lose their links, but to be "advocates and ambassadors for Africa." Diaspora Christians have a duty to be "advocates and ambassadors" to raise awareness of the prayer needs and need for support for missions in their countries of origin and to see themselves and successive generations as potential sources for leadership and mission.

Witness

Outreach to the business and professional Diaspora communities can have consequences for world evangelism far beyond the size that they represent in terms of world population. The Sindhis are an unreached people group from the 10/40 window. They are business and professional people in the main. A significant percentage of those who have accepted Christ live in the Diaspora. Evangelism to this group represents a significant opportunity for mission at our doorstep, but needs to be approached in an appropriate manner.

The opportunity to build bridges into these communities is much easier as they are more open and prepared to partner across religious divides. On the other hand, many are economically successful and therefore self sufficient - they see no need for God or religion. Others are very spiritual, with tremendous faith in their own gods – all see Christianity as irrelevant. Outreach strategies to these communities that have been tried have included invitations to targeted events such as outreach dinners, professional networks, motivational Christian speakers, and Alpha suppers with special attention being paid to cross-cultural sensitivities in the case of the first generation. Friendship evangelism based on relationships and supported by prayer is one of the critical success factors. In addition, identifying and promoting successful role models from the Diaspora offer further opportunities for outreach.

Resources

Where Diaspora business and professional people have been reached for Christ, there is significant potential that can be unleashed.

The economic impact of the Diaspora especially in developing countries can be dramatic. The impact on funding missions might be even more dramatic. The South Asians in the Diaspora are increasingly playing a catalytic role in the mobilisation of mission movements in South Asia. Diaspora Christians in the UK initiated a creative project that over a seven year period resulted in 50,000 teenagers raising over 10 million dollars for Two-Thirds World relief and development channelled through Christian agencies. Of greater importance, was the raising of the awareness of world mission amongst this youth constituency.

The development of materials for mission, drawing on the experience, resources and expertise of Diaspora Christians is proving invaluable in some cultures. They produce innovative, modern, and culturally relevant materials that appeal particularly to the younger generation in their countries of origin.

Evangelism to this community continues to challenge the local church, and additional resources for research and training are greatly needed.

C. Lords of the Rim – The Chinese Diaspora

Chinese moving overseas has been happening for centuries. One history of it is called "The Lords of the Rim." It can be traced as early as the Tang Dynasty (618-907 AD).[1] In the second half of the 20th Century, movements of Chinese from countries in Southeast Asia, Hong Kong, and China were accelerated by socio-political factors. Though the political situations are relatively stable in many South East Asian countries where the Chinese are staying, considerable numbers of Chinese migrants are still moving to Europe, North America, and Oceania. They do so for family reunions, children's education, and better living conditions.

Present demographics of Chinese Diaspora

"Where there is water, there is Chinese."[2] Following is a table of worldwide distribution of Chinese: the total population of Chinese in Diaspora is estimated to be close to 65 million with 2.77% being Christians.

	Population of Chinese in Diaspora	Population of Chinese Christians in Diaspora	Percentage of Chinese Christians in Diaspora	No. of Overseas Chinese Churches	No. of Overseas Chinese Christians
Asia	58,219,800	1,551,504	2.7%	6,867	1,551,504
North America	3,700,000	208,000	5.62%	1,200	208,000
Europe	1,364,000	13,065	0.96 %	146	13,065
Africa	208,000	570	0.27%	12	570
Latin America	933,600	5,240	0.56%	86	5,240
Oceania	322,900	14,500	4.49%	218	14,500
Overseas Total	64,748,300	1,792,879	2.77%	8,529	1,792,879

The conditions of the Diaspora community in the host countries

The conditions of the Chinese Diaspora communities vary in different host countries. Nowadays, the Chinese at large enjoy a stable and prosperous life in most parts of the world. However, Chinese in some areas have experienced tensions with the people of the host countries. Sometimes, their own behaviour or unprincipled trade cause such tensions.

The unplanned impact of Diaspora on the worldwide Chinese Church[3]

The prophet Isaiah says, "*As the heavens are higher than the earth, so are my ways higher than your ways and my thoughts than your thoughts*" (Isaiah 55:9). Despite the undesirable causes of most of the people movements and the atrocities which many suffered, God has transformed grave human plights into rays of hope for new life. We are awed by God's wisdom when we consider the un-fathomable expansion of the Chinese church outside of China. Very little of this growth was the result of intentional mission projects by mission agencies. Rather, most of the Chinese churches were planted by the Christians in Diaspora (in many cases, with the generous help of Christians in the host countries)! Within the last six decades, thousands of churches were planted (8,600) and over a million (1,800,000) of Chinese were saved.

In addition, creative modes of ministries, Bible colleges, and seminaries, even church leaders and theologians also grew from the Diaspora Christian communities. For example, the formation of CCCOWE is a fruit of the Diaspora Christians.

In spite of noticeable growth, the majority of the people in the Diaspora are still unreached (97%). The goal of evangelism is yet to be achieved. For example, there are more than 10,000 Chinese in North Korea and more than 50,000

Chinese in Saudi Arabia, but there is no established Chinese church in either one of these two countries. It is estimated that nearly a million Chinese will join the Diaspora in the coming decade. The churches in the host countries and the Diaspora should be mobilised to welcome and evangelise the newcomers.

Thankfully, there is renewed momentum in reaching the Diaspora communities. Chinese Christians are very active in sharing the Good News and starting new churches primarily among Chinese people of the host countries.

As the context and situation of the Chinese in Diaspora varies from place to place, no single approach to evangelism is effective in all places. However, some of the proven evangelistic principles are:

- Be culturally sensitive and relevant.
- Develop relational based communities characterised by genuine love and care.
- Present the gospel in the mother tongue.
- Develop leaders from the local Diaspora Christians.
- Engage in networking, partnerships, and strategic alliances.

Potential partners in mission

In retrospect, the Diaspora has been a spiritual blessing to the Chinese. The Lord has blessed the Chinese Diaspora Christians with many gifts. In some countries, statistics showed that the Diaspora have on average a higher level of education than the general population. Many of them are also blessed with financial resources.

Though Chinese moved overseas, the emotional and actual connections with the homeland is strong. In Eastern Malaysia, the Chinese communities have been established for generations. While they acculturated to the Malaysian culture, most of them still keep Chinese names and languages. Mandarin, Fuchow, Hakka, and other dialects are commonly used throughout the Chinese communities.

Many overseas Chinese visit their city or village of origin to maintain the connections and relationship. This provides a background and platform for the Christians in and outside of China to build up networks of fellowship and partnership. There are more and more conferences and visits during the past decades resulting in mutual understanding and sharing of experiences. Some overseas Chinese Christians share the gospel with their relatives when they visit their homeland. Many students became Christians when they studied overseas. Numerous Chinese top level leaders of ministries and churches in Singapore and Malaysia today experienced foundational and formational Christian growth while studying in Australia in the 60's and 70's. By the love and grace of God, these synergies certainly indicate a bright future for the Chinese Church for His glory that will bring blessings to China and other people groups.

Also, owing to new international relationships in the last two decades, Asians are more acceptable to the Muslims. Citizens of Indonesia, Malaysia, and Singapore, for example, are considered as brothers or friends of many Muslim countries. Diaspora Chinese Christians find it relatively easier to approach Muslims and share God's love with them.

Thus, while Diaspora Christians should continue to develop strong local churches, an outward mission focus needs to be fostered. The Diaspora Chinese Church worldwide should call and send missionaries to reach others for Christ. May the Diaspora Churches be a blessing to all nations for the glory of God.

The CCCOWE Story

CCCOWE (Chinese Coordination Centre of World Evangelism) is a spiritual movement that God raised up in the 1970s in the Chinese Church,4 calling the Chinese churches worldwide to unite in spirit and in truth to proclaim the gospel to the world until the Lord returns.

In the second half of the 20th Century, millions of Chinese moved into the worldwide Diaspora for a variety of reasons. CCCOWE is the spiritual movement God raised up for the opportunity of reaching Overseas Chinese and building kingdom minded churches to fulfil His missionary mandate. The core belief of CCCOWE is that the Chinese believers and churches have a responsibility to obey both the Great Commandment of loving one another and the Great Commission of making disciples of all nations. CCCOWE is a catalyst with a global strategy given by God to hasten the growth of the Chinese churches and the expansion of His kingdom through the Chinese Christians in Diaspora.

Chinese churches worldwide have experienced tremendous growth both in number and in every other area since the beginning of CCCOWE in 1976. The increase in blessings is from the Lord as a result of the hard work of many believers and pastors, yet CCCOWE does play a pivotal role as bridge, servant, and a prophet for the Chinese Christian churches in building the kingdom of God.

The Lausanne Movement and the CCCOWE Movement

Like many other Christian movements, CCCOWE began in a prayer meeting and is sustained by the prayers of God's people. CCCOWE is first and foremost a spiritual movement, calling Chinese Christians and churches to prayer and to obedience to our Lord's commandments.

Well before CCCOWE was conceived, God had already raised up other evangelical movements and fellowships of Chinese churches, like NACOCE[5] in North America and Chinese churches networks in other part of the world. However, there was not yet a worldwide network for the coordination and mobilisation of Chinese churches for world evangelism.

It was in 1974, at the "International Congress on World Evangelism" in Lausanne, Switzerland that some seventy Chinese church leaders first shared the vision of convening an international Chinese congress in a prayer meeting. The first "Chinese Congress on World Evangelization" (CCOWE) was thus held in January 1976 in Hong Kong, and The Chinese Coordination Centre of World Evangelism

(CCCOWE) was established to support the movement. Since 1976, CCOWE conference is held every five years in different countries.

Today, CCCOWE has 57 geographic districts each with its own local committee for the promotion of the CCCOWE movement locally. In some regions, like the U.S., Canada, Indonesia etc., the adjacent geographic districts also form a CCCOWE Inter-District office for their regional needs.

CCCOWE is serving the worldwide community of Chinese churches by convening regular and special worldwide and regional conferences, establishing prayer networks, publishing periodicals and literature relevant to the needs Chinese Churches, coordinating resources, both human and material, for the building up of the churches and the kingdom of God among Chinese churches, doing strategic research concerning Chinese churches and world mission, and paying visits to worldwide CCCOWE districts to encourage church leaders and pastors.

The following three important factors contributed to the success of the CCCOWE movement:

1. Networking for a common purpose:

The CCCOWE movement is inclusive, open to all and yet with an explicit goal. It is a fellowship with a common purpose. The explicit purpose of the CCCOWE movement is to advance evangelism both locally and globally for the Chinese people and from the Chinese churches to the ends of the world. The aim of CCCOWE is to encourage the Chinese church worldwide working together for the evangelisation of the Chinese and also mobilise the Chinese churches to be involved in world mission. The CCCOWE movement has always focused on its unique mission.

2. Fellowship without domination:

CCCOWE is a vision driven movement that demands no authority or commitment from the participants other than the same evangelical faith and evangelistic calling. CCCOWE has no membership and thus reserves no privilege for anyone. Everyone joins the movement as an individual and stay-on through participation. This principle created an environment for genuine fellowship in Christ and a unity based on common purpose.

3. A spiritual movement coupled with strategic planning:

In order to serve as a prophet for the Chinese churches, CCCOWE takes upon itself the responsibility of doing research on relevant issues and the overall condition of the worldwide Chinese churches, especially in matters concerning the Chinese in Diaspora and world mission.

In the beginning of the CCCOWE movement, the leaders set forth five 5-year plans for the movement in order to help building up strong, mission-minded churches. They are as following:

- 1976-1981: Renewal of Vision - Rekindle the vision of cooperation and evangelisation
- 1981-1986: Actualisation of Vision - Stimulate efforts in joint ministry and evangelism
- 1986-1991: Focusing on Growth -

Quantitative and qualitative growth in the numbers of Christians, congregations, and workers

- 1991-1996: Evangelism to the Chinese - Evangelisation of the Chinese worldwide
- 1996-2001: World Evangelisation - Cross-cultural evangelisation of all nations and peoples

A renewed vision and re-structuring for a new millennium:

After 25 years of labour and God's blessings, the Chinese Church has grown into adulthood. The number of Chinese churches in Diaspora has grown from around 3,000 to over 8,500 and one third of them have become involved in Mission in meaningful ways. That is a very significant increase from the ten percent involvement in 1978. With the growth of the Chinese churches in a post-modern world, Chinese churches face a new reality and context for ministry and mission.

In order to better serve the Chinese churches in Diaspora, CCCOWE has decided to set a new course for its ministry in the 6th congress held in Kuala Lumpur, Malaysia in 2001. Five principles will guide the future direction of CCCOWE ministries. They are localising ministry functions, building up the team spirit, raising up young leaders, streamlining operation, and focusing on prophetic vision.

Other than the on-going ministries, CCCOWE has added new ministries for the new challenges:

- Up-grading and expanding its ministry on the internet (http://www.cccowe.org)

- Promoting church ministry coordination among Chinese churches worldwide in order to build up local churches and help achieve the ultimate goal of world evangelisation - 18 ministry coordinators were appointed to the task of coordinating different church ministries in four categories: believer's ministry, church ministry, evangelism, and world mission.
- Commission a global research study on the Chinese churches in Diaspora in order to gain understanding and data needed for strategic planning.

CCCOWE will continue to serve faithfully as a servant for the Chinese Churches worldwide, calling them to live up to our Lord's expectation of being light and salt to the world.

D. God's Secret Weapon – The Filipino Diaspora

The migration of people from the Philippines has always existed because of trade within Asia. With the expansion of Spanish (1521–1898) and American (1898–1946) colonisation, Filipinos went as galleon workers to Europe and labourers to North America.

The list of Filipino Exodus by categories chronologically in the last 150 years is as follows:

- The Illustrados (late 1800s) were the so-called cream of the crop of Philippine society during the Spanish colonial era. They were typically mestizos or children of mixed European and local marriages. As the privileged few, they were sent to Europe to further their education. Many of these European trained illustrados returned to lead the revolution against the Spanish rule.

- The Pensionados (early 1900s) were children of influential Filipinos who were friends (with special favour) of the United States. They were sponsored by the American government to study in the United States, and like the illustrados they were mostly mestizos.
- The Sacadas (1906–1940s) were mostly Filipino men who laboured on Hawaiian sugar and pineapple plantations, orchard and vegetable farms on the American mainland, and in the Salmon canneries on the Alaskan coastline.
- The Soldados (1915-present) were volunteers recruited to serve the United States army, navy, and merchant marines during World War I — a trend that continued after World War II. They were given the privilege of staying permanently in their adopted homeland, and eventually allowed to embrace American citizenship.
- The Estudiantes (Post World War II – present) are not only children of the wealthy Filipinos, but include the Filipino state scholars and practitioners who sought further training outside the Philippines. While most of them returned to their homeland to serve their nation, others remained to join the work force in their host nations.

- The Immigrantes (1960–present) were Filipinos who voluntarily left their country to reside mainly in the Western world, particularly in North America, Australia, and Western Europe for greater economic opportunities.
- The Martial Law Exiles (1972 -1986) were victims of martial law declared by then President Ferdinand E. Marcos in 1972. This period consequently resulted in a massive exodus, including wealthy Filipinos. Most of them settled in Western nations.
- The Overseas Filipino Workers [OFWs] (1980s-present) are Filipinos deployed by the Philippine government to work as migrant workers all over the world. They are referred to by their employers as expatriates or temporary workers. The duration of their contracts overseas typically range from one to three years. OFWs are not immigrants nor have acquired permanent resident status in their host countries. OFWs leave the Philippines with the intent of returning. There are two types of OFWs – the sea-based and the land-based. The sea-based OFWs are sailors working on cruise ships, fishing boats, oil tankers, container ships, and oilrigs. The land-based OFWs include medical workers, educators, entertainers, scientists, engineers, construction workers, care givers, bankers, etc.

The following are estimates of the OFWs according to the Philippine Overseas Employment Administration (POEA).
Stock Estimates of OFWs by Major World Group (2001)

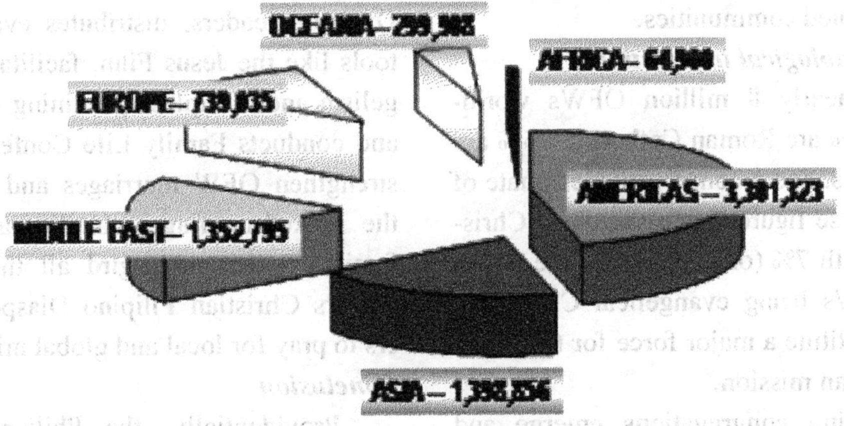

Source: Commission on Filipinos Overseas,
Government of the Philippines, Department of Foreign Affairs

The Filipino Diaspora's global distribution by major world groups is as follows:

- Western World (4 million)
- Buddhist/Hindu World (1.3 million)
- Islamic World (1.7 million)
- Jewish World (30,000)

The socio-economic and missiological implications of Filipino Diaspora

The root cause of the massive Filipino exodus in the past three decades is the high level of unemployment and poverty at home. Moreover, the acceleration of globalisation of trade and labour has lured millions of Filipinos to seek overseas jobs. Approximately 2,800 are deployed for overseas employment each day. The socio-economic and missiological implications of Filipino Diaspora are as follows:

1. Economic implication

Today, there are close to 8 million OFWs deployed in more than 180 countries. They remit back to the Philippines a sizeable part of their income. According to the Philippine government, the remittance of OFWs has become the major avenue of foreign currency (e.g. US$ 7.2 Billion in 2003). Thus, President Gloria Macapagal-Arroyo has hailed OFWs as "the Philippines' modern day heroes."

2. Social implication

Recently deployed OFWs are females who serve as medical professionals, domestic workers, caregivers, and entertainers. There is a gender difference among OFWs: Females are under 35; males, 35 and above. A large number of female OFWs have intermarried with locals. This has resulted in a surge of mestizo children (e.g. Filipino-Japanese, Filipino-Chinese, Filipino-Arab, Filipino-Canadians, Filipino-Italians, etc.). Hence, Filipino blood is now "sprinkled" and "intermingled" across the nations. These OFWs have become an agent of social change in their host nations because they have injected their culture, tradition, and religion into their adopted communities.

3. *Missiological implication*

Of nearly 8 million OFWs worldwide, 80% are Roman Catholics, 15% are protestants, and a conservative estimate of 7% of these figures are evangelical Christians. With 7% (or 560,000) of the 8 million OFWs being evangelical Christians, they constitute a major force for the cause of Christian mission.

Filipino congregations emerge and thrive wherever Filipino diasporas are found, (e.g., Canadian Prairies, the remote Arctic Circle, the oil fields of the Arabian Peninsula, the urban jungles of Singapore, Hong Kong, Taipei, Tokyo, the islands of the Pacific, and in the mega cities of Europe and North America). There are even fellowship groups on cruise ships and fishing vessels. Since Filipinos are adaptable, acceptable, and accessible, they are now involved in cross-cultural ministries as well. In several cities of the world, including Singapore, Hong Kong, London, and Toronto, clusters of Filipino congregations have formed ministerial fellowships for cooperative missions and evangelism initiatives. Innovative evangelic strategies include music concerts, festivals, literature and video distribution, and compassionate work.

In May 1995, the Filipino International Network (FIN) was launched in response to the need for a coordinated global effort to motivate, equip, and mobilise Christian OFWs to help fulfil the Great Commission. To accomplish this objective, FIN coordinates regional and global strategic consultations for Filipino Diaspora leaders, distributes evangelistic tools like the Jesus Film, facilitates evangelism and discipleship training seminars, and conducts Family Life Conferences to strengthen OFW marriages and to reach the mixed-marriage couples and their families. To under-gird all these, FIN gathers Christian Filipino Diaspora leaders to pray for local and global missions.

Conclusion

Providentially, the Philippines became the only Christian nation in Asia due to Spanish colonisation. Similarly, massive exodus of Filipinos driven by economics and politics, God's providence, and sovereignty has overturned the root cause of the Filipino exodus for His glory. The Filipino Diaspora has penetrated the Western World, the Buddhist World, the Islamic World, and the Jewish World.

E. A Sub-continent Abroad – The South Asian Diaspora

South Asians have been on the move as far back as history records. In the centuries just before and after Christ, Buddhist and Hindu missionaries carried their message in all directions, but especially to South East Asia. A Chinese traveller to Cambodia in the 1st century AD saw more than one thousand Brahmins from India living there and teaching the people. The whole region was influenced by Indian trade, colonisation, culture, and religion. The evidence is still there today, in temple architecture and Sanskrit words, especially in the vocabulary of religion, law, and philosophy.

By the 13th century Hindu influence was largely replaced by Islam, at least in Indonesia and the Malay kingdoms, where Gujarati Muslim traders were active. In the 19th and early 20th centuries, the British Empire became the dominant vehicle for spreading Indians abroad, as labour forces for the expanding plantations in Fiji, Malaya, South Africa, and Central America, or to build the railways and run the trade of East and Central Africa. Indians were also going abroad to study, to prepare for careers in law and the public services back home or elsewhere in the Empire, Mahatma Gandhi being the best-known example.

In 1947 the bloody partition of India resulted in hundreds of thousands of people moving within the region and beyond. Later, the need for workers, skilled and unskilled, in Britain and then in the USA, resulted in the movement of thousands more. The expulsion of the East African Asians in the early 1970s brought substantial groups of entrepreneurs and professionals to the West. The end of the 20th century and beginning of the 21st have seen this process continue. South Asians are now in demand as skilled professionals, consultants, entrepreneurs, and traders.

Size and breadth

There are approximately 20 million South Asians outside the sub-continent of South Asia. The figures on the following page give some idea of the numbers across the world at the dawn of the 21st century.

Causative factors

Through the centuries, the causes of movement have been similar, but have varied in importance. The earliest migrants travelled for *trade* and also exported their *culture* and *religion*. The major migrations of the 19th century were driven by the demands of empire for a global *labour force* and the opportunities for *trade*. They took their *culture* with them, and from the end of the 19th century a stream of gurus and teachers disseminated their *religious* teachings, beginning with the arrival of Swami Vivekananda at the Parliament of World Religions in Chicago in 1893. In the 20th and 21st centuries *war* has driven people in fear (Partition in 1947; the Sri Lankan civil war from the 1990s), while the *global market* is calling increasingly for skilled *workers* and *business* entrepreneurs.

The marketplace is not only commercial: *culture, religion,* and *ideas* are still major exports. Hindu and Buddhist concepts and practices, e.g. yoga, have percolated deeply everywhere. South Asian Muslims are the largest and most devoted religious group in the West. "Indian" restaurants rival Chinese as world favorites, while "Bollywood" films and music are becoming the latest craze. *Education* continues to be a major factor - around 200,000 Indians a year apply for student visas to the USA alone.

Diaspora community in the host countries

South Asian Diaspora communities divide along generational lines and the length of time out of contact with the

Australia	1,362,140 'Asians' excluding Chinese
Burma	854,404 Indians
Canada	917,075 South Asians
Denmark	23,287 Pakistani, 14,199 Sri Lankan, 3,996 Indian
Fiji	387,585 Indians
France	60,000 Indian, 30,000 Pakistani, 50,000 Sri Lankan
Germany	7,156 Bangladeshi, 34,709 Indian, 36,924 Pakistani, 54,617 Sri Lankan
Guyana	352,902 Indians
Holland	109,553 Indians (majority from Suriname)
Italy	69,108 South Asians
Kuwait	203,179 South Asians
Malaysia	1,881,799 Indians
Mauritius	829,927 Indo–Mauritians
New Zealand	28,900 Indians
Norway	26,286 Pakistani, 11,918 Sri Lankan, 6,836 Indian, 546 Bangladeshi
Qatar	151,252 Indians, 151,252 Pakistanis
Singapore	343,958 Indians
South Africa RSA	854,371 Indians
East and Central Africa (not RSA)	Approx 1,141,800 South Asians
Suriname	161,666 Indians
Sweden	2628 Bangladeshi, 10377 Indian, 2713 Pakistani, 5700 Sri Lankan
Switzerland	5 151 Indian, 2281 Pakistani, 34, 230 Sri Lankan
Trinidad	444,996 Indians
UAE	1,261,958 South Asians
UK	1,053,411 Indians; 747,285 Pakistanis; 283,063 Bangladeshis; estimated 100,000 Tamils
USA	1,678,765 Asian Indians, 153,533 Pakistanis; 41,280 Bangladeshis (excluding mixed marriages)

Note: It is notoriously difficult to find accurate statistics. This partly reflects the sub-continent's history. Some lists use "Indian" to refer to people originally from undivided India but now from different nations. That's why "Asian" is widely used as a classification. But that can also be confusing: does it include other parts of Asia as well? Details of sources for the figures can be found in *Catalyst for Change: The South Asian Diaspora*, INSADL, 2005.

"mother country". The subculture of Diaspora communities which have been settled abroad for generations are often based on the culture and values of the time they left, with varying degrees of assimilation into the host society.

In the more recent Diaspora settlements, for example in Britain and North America, the divisions between the generations are sharp. First generation individuals regard the sub-continent as "home," while knowing that they made a choice to migrate. Second generations are caught in between two cultures, leading to the acronym ABCD - American Born Confused Deshi - they know they belong to two worlds but sometimes feel neither accepts them. Third generation individuals inhabit a fusion world with confidence, but they risk alienation both from their parents and the larger society, especially if their community is not doing well in education and employment. There are also large disparities between Diaspora communities. Some are very successful in education, business, and professional life while others struggle, with huge unemployment rates, poor education results, and growing drug and gang problems. All communities have faced discrimination, ranging from overt hatred to polite indifference, from obvious exclusion to "glass ceilings" at higher levels.

Percentage of Christians in the movement

It is hard to estimate the number of Christians in the South Asian Diaspora. It is probably less than the 2-3% proportion of Christians in the sub-continent. The majority of South Asian Christians in the Diaspora are from a Christian background in South Asia. In Britain, the South Asians are largely Punjabi, from Pakistan and North India, while in North America there are many more South Indian Christians. Many belong to Asian Christian Fellowships, usually reflecting their regional and language background, worshipping in the same style as they used to "at home." Some professionals, especially those who do not live in a strongly South Asian area, may be part of local churches from the host community, usually in twos or threes. Second and third generation South Asian Christians may join either. Believers from Buddhist, Hindu, Muslim, and Sikh backgrounds are still relatively few. Those that have turned to the Lord in the Diaspora are often from different social and caste backgrounds from the traditional Christian community in South Asia.

Effective evangelism approaches

Effective evangelism approaches among the South Asian Diaspora communities hardly exist. By and large the host country churches have found it difficult to relate to people of a different culture and established faith and have either given up or left them alone. Work with young people, for example Bible clubs, has been fruitful in a number of countries. Several of today's leaders came to Christ as school or university students. However, for the vast majority of South Asians, Christianity is seen as essentially a part of western culture. Jesus (however greatly they respect him) is the god of white and black people.

Effective approaches will require:

- Conviction that Jesus is Saviour and Lord for people of every culture and race, including South Asians from Buddhist, Hindu, Jain, Muslim, Sikh, or any other faith background
- Willingness to build bridges of friendship and trust through loving service, sharing common concerns, and personal relationships - This is necessary to overcome barriers of suspicion or fear (for example with Muslim communities) and to get behind the misperceptions of "Christianity" and focus on following Christ rather than becoming a "Christian"
- Commitment to allow people to follow Christ within their culture and community - This will include awareness of family and community, rather than just individuals. It will be sensitive to forms of worship and religious language. It will consciously seek to develop new forms of church in which people can follow Christ in a way that is open to other members of their community, rather than separating them off. These forms will of course vary greatly.

The number of churches and groups doing this are still a handful. But there is growing evidence that their approach is beginning to bear fruit and will multiply in the next ten years.

The Relationship of Diaspora Christians with host country/countries

Adopting effective approaches of evangelism will require change both from Asian Christians and from the host country churches. They will need to work together in close partnership. A major challenge for South Asian Diaspora followers of Christ will be to engage the larger church in their countries for this task.

Note: South Asians are people living in and originating from Bangladesh, Bhutan, India, Maldive Islands, Nepal, Pakistan, and Sri Lanka.

F. A New Persia? – The Iranian Diaspora

The Iranian Diaspora has existed for centuries; their numbers, however, have dramatically increased in the past 30 years. Near the end of the 1970's, in the midst of secularisation and modernisation, Iran sent more students overseas than any other nation. This was sustained by economic wealth brought in by oil. With the overthrow of the Shah Pahlavi, Iran was proclaimed an Islamic Republic by Ayatollah Khomeini. The regime instantly implemented strict Islamic law and economic policies which curtailed secular influences and Persian/Zoroastrian culture.

The new revolutionary government engaged in an eight year war with Iraq, where 1 million Iranians were killed, injured, or displaced. The loss to the Iranian economy was estimated at one trillion dollars. The regime also imprisoned close to 100,000 people, mainly from oppositional political parties. Subsequently thousands of them were killed. Non-Islamic minority groups, such as Jews, Armenians and Assyrians have faced new pressures and restrictions under the Islamic government, forcing many to leave. Religious anti-conversion laws and persecution of Christian converts also served to frustrate many.

In addition, the political instability contributed to a deteriorating economy, which was caused by the withdrawal of foreign investors. With an unemployment rate over 15%, coupled with the increased cost of living, many found life in Iran nearly impossible and decided to leave.

From 1981 onwards, Iranians began to leave Iran for places of refuge spanning the globe. Initially, Iranians flooded to the United States, Pakistan, and Turkey. A second wave of emigrants went to continental Europe and Canada and the next wave to the United Kingdom. With dete-riorating conditions in Iran, those who were studying abroad chose not to return, but to settle in their respective countries. The Iranian Diaspora currently totals four to five million people, or about 7% of the total Iranian world population.

Iranians Diaspora and their host countries

Turkey has become an important gateway for the Iranian Diaspora. As Iranians do not need visas to enter Turkey, many make Turkey their first stop before continuing on to Europe and beyond. Over the past two decades, Turkey has hosted between half a million to a million Iranians. Table 1 lists some countries with a significant Iranian population.

Table 1 - Number of Iranians per country

Country	Iranian Population (Approx.)
United States	1,000,000
Arabian Gulf States	500,000
Canada	100,000+
Germany	100,000
United Kingdom	100,000
Sweden	60,000
France	30,000
Belgium	30,000
Holland	30,000+
Denmark	10,000
Norway	6000
Finland	2000

Most Iranians living outside of Iran enjoy good living conditions. They are generally not congregated in ghettos, but dispersed in their host communities. Iranians are often successful in their host countries, working in top levels of leadership. Early waves of immigrants to the United States are financially successful and well settled. Iranians in Europe are doing well, although generally less settled and less wealthy. In places like Turkey, because they are not allowed to work, they are economically worse off. Some work illegally and are often taken advantage of by their employers.

Response to the gospel

Iranians are the most receptive Muslim people to the gospel both inside and outside of Iran. More than two decades of strict Islamic rule have served to create disillusionment with Islam, hence openness and receptivity to the gospel is increasing. Although less than 1% (50,000) Iranians in the Diaspora have accepted the Lord, their openness is increasing. It is interesting to note that receptivity to the gospel seems to be inversely proportional to their socioeconomic status. Iranians in America are less open to the gospel than those in Europe. Iranians in Turkey are very open to the gospel, only surpassed by those still in Iran. The openness of Iranians seems to be outstripping personnel and resources, creating a desperate need for trained Farsi speaking Christians to join the work.

Much of the evangelism taking place is done by Iranian believers themselves. They have established churches and house churches in many of their host countries. When Iranian Christians form their own congregations, they tend to be independent and often lack denominational affiliation in their host country. Other Iranians attend local churches and become part of the congregation, which reflects the desire of many Iranians to integrate into their host culture. Iranian Christians are proving to be effective missionaries to countries like Afghanistan.

One caution in reaching out to Iranians is to ensure sincerity in their commitment. Some may profess conversion in order to attain refugee sponsorship. In light of this, baptism should not be rushed into and without proper observation of true heart change. Contact with Persian Christians and resources may be necessary. There is a need for host country churches to partner with Iranian Christians and churches to reach Iranians in the Diaspora.

The openness of Iranians seems to be outstripping personnel and resources, creating a desperate need for trained Farsi speaking Christians to enter the gospel ministry.

Note: Iranians are not Arabs. They are a different people and speak a different language. They are the descendants of the Persians.

G. The Super Salad Bowl – Immigrants in the United States

The United States of America is almost a whole country of immigrants. Apart from the few original inhabitants left, everyone has come from somewhere else over four hundred years. This means that it is too great a task to try and describe the range and complexity of its immigrant character.

USA became Christian by Immigration

This was mainly from Europe between the 16th and the 19th centuries. Millions of English, Scots, Welsh Irish, Swedes, Norwegians, Italians, Poles, Germans, etc. brought with them their Christian faith such as it was and it became a country with a mainly Christian but multinational population. The "melting pot" policy helped them to become "One Nation under God"

USA is still growing by immigration

It is estimated that now the United States is receiving just under 2 million foreign residents annually. Most of American history was about two groups, Black and White, or people of African and European descent. From the 1960s on this changed, largely due to a relaxation of immigration controls. By 2000, the United States was home to 30 million immigrants, about 11 percent of the population. Over 13 million migrants arrived in the 1990s alone. Almost 5 percent of Americans have been in the country for a decade or less.

In 2000, 35 million Americans were counted as Hispanic, almost 60 percent of them of Mexican ancestry. Nearly 12 million more Americans were Asian, of Chinese, Japanese, Filipino, Vietnamese, and Korean stock. Asians and Hispanics combined make up 15 percent of the population today, but this share is projected to grow to almost 25 percent by 2025, and to 33 percent by 2050. By mid-century, 100 million Americans will claim Hispanic origin. They will then constitute one of the world's largest Latino societies, more populous than any actual Hispanic nation with the exception of Mexico or Brazil.

There is a significant Christian presence within all these Diasporas

The number of people in the Diaspora means that in many cities of the USA there may be thousands of Diaspora people but from different Diasporas. The significance of this is not yet appreciated by Christians in the USA or in the rest of the world.

Preoccupied

In the USA, the White churches of European Descent are still preoccupied by their need to send their own missionaries to the rest of the world. They are unaware of the much larger number of Christians who have come to them from the rest of the world who have a better chance of reaching their own countrymen and a contribution to make to their adopted country. They have not yet grasped the significance of Diaspora for the Kingdom.

The Non-white churches tend to be so big that they do not need to think about anyone else. Or they are so small and disconnected that they feel forced to live in isolation. Or they are so recently arrived that language difficulties cut them off from wider fellowship. They too have not yet grasped their significance for the Kingdom.

Two-Thirds World Christians

Christians in the Two-Thirds World fall into two camps. There is a small but energetic number who will move heaven and earth to get to the USA either to study or to stay there permanently. They provide important links between USA and churches in other countries. There is a much larger number who are influenced by the anti-American attitudes of their own secular leaders and write off USA Christianity as rich, self-indulgent, imperialist, and insensitive to the rest of the world.

Europe and the Old Commonwealth

Christians in Europe and the Old Commonwealth countries are also divided. Some have a quiet admiration and real gratitude for the American Churches and what they do for the Kingdom. Many have been influenced by the secular culture's critical, condemnatory, and dismissive attitudes that sometimes go so far as to think that American Churches are sub-Christian.

All of these attitudes have to change if Kingdom priorities are to drive our witness to Christ and the gospel. This is a major shift in our context that holds tremendous promise for the future of the gospel if we can but grasp its significance and act. It will not be difficult to change our attitudes when we understand the realities of the situation.

Whites not the majority for much longer

In the late 1990s California became the nation's first majority-minority state, in which non-Latino whites ceased to form an absolute majority of the population. Within a decade, Latinos alone will constitute a majority of California's people. Latinos also make up one-third of the population of Texas, the second largest state, which could achieve majority-minority status as early as 2005. While the proportion of foreign-born people in Houston was less than 3 percent in 1960, today it is about 25 percent. The white majority, state by state, will over time become the minority. Looking at these changes should make us reconsider our view of American history and its future.

The Latino Christians are bringing youth, enthusiasm, and growth

Latino populations will account for much denominational growth in coming decades. One reason for this is that Latinos are generally much younger than longer-established populations. The national census of 2000 showed that the median age for Hispanics was about 26, younger than that of any other ethnic group and far lower than the median age for Anglo-Whites, which stood at a venerable 38.5. The same proportion of young people is also to be found in the other Diasporas.

Their faith is important to them in their adjustment to the new society and they form enthusiastic congregations. Around half the congregations active today in the Boston-Cambridge area worship in languages other than English. Since immigrant congregations are often small, this does not imply that anything like half of all believers are non-Anglophone, but it does suggest a vigorous growth. When the Greater Boston Baptist Association used posters on subway trains to spread its evangelistic message, the languages used included English, French, Spanish, Portuguese, and Korean. Today, around a third of the Black population of Massachusetts is foreign-born, with roots in the Caribbean or Africa itself, and this influx is suggested by a new wave of Black churches.

Some Diasporas have higher proportions of Christians than exist in their home countries

This is understandable. In situations of instability and persecution like the Middle East, many Christians have felt that the only way to survive was emigrate. Earlier we saw that there is a higher proportion of Christian Chinese in America than in Asia. Also, because the atmosphere is less threatening and hostile, it is easier to become a Japanese Christian in America than in Japan. The Korean community in the United States is deeply imbued with Christian teaching: Christians outnumber Buddhists by ten or twenty to one.

Even the balance between Roman Catholics and Protestants is different from Latin America. Among first-generation Latinos in the United States, Catholics massively outnumber Protestants by 74 to 18 percent, but among the third generation, the Catholic share has shrunk to a 59-32 majority. To try and reduce the continuing haemorrhage of believers, Latino Catholics in the United States have tried very much the same solutions as their counterparts in the Philippines or South America, importing Pentecostal customs like traditional music and instruments during services, and encouraging emotional expres-sions of spontaneous praise and thanksgiving. These tactics may or may not succeed, but in any case the Latino religious scene has been so volatile in recent decades that detailed predictions of any kind are rash. Whatever the exact denominational balance happens to be, the changing racial picture is only going to strengthen overall Christian numbers.

Diaspora Christians believe and practice a biblical gospel

Diaspora Christians from the *South* read the Bible in a way that makes that Christianity look like a wholly different religion from the faith of prosperous advanced societies of Europe or North America. They are quite at home with biblical notions of the supernatural, with ideas like dreams and prophecy. Just as relevant in their eyes are that book's core social and political themes, like martyrdom, oppression, and exile.

Millions of Christians around the world do in fact live in constant danger of persecution or forced conversion, from either governments or local vigilantes. For modern Christians in Nigeria, Egypt, the Sudan, or Indonesia, it is quite conceivable that they might someday find themselves before a tribunal that would demand that they renounce their faith upon pain of death. It is their kin that make up the Diasporas in USA. They provide live links to the poor, the oppressed, and the persecuted Christians around the world.

For Diaspora Christians it has to be the whole gospel

Poverty or the fear of poverty is one of the main driving forces behind the migrations in our time. People recently arrived in our Diasporas have real live memories of that poverty and know its causes. The debate about evangelism versus social concern is an irrelevance to them. Any Gospel that does not address the issues of poverty and discrimination is not good news at all.

Will it be a "melting pot" or a "salad bowl" religiously?

Currently, there is little appreciation of the enormous changes that are coming about because of the demographics in USA. As a consequence, segregation would not be too hard a word to describe the relations between the White and the Non-White Churches. Kingdom of God thinking realises that if this can change, tremendous forces for good could be released in America and in the rest of the world. So what is required to bring about this change?

All Christians need to seek out other Christians who are not like them, "the new people next door," and develop friendships and understanding with them. All congregations need to reach out to other congregations that are not like them and work out how they can affirm their unity with respect for their differences. Within Denominations or people of similar spiritualities, there needs to be formal and informal contacts that will harness all the parts to further the goals of the whole.

This will not be easy. It will encounter resistance. This is understandable because we are all more at home in our own culture than in another. Perhaps it will take a few more trances and sheets let down from heaven (Acts 10). What must not happen is that patronising attitudes or territorial considerations creep in and confound hope and deepen the divisions.

This Study is heavily drawn from the book, *The Next Christendom: The Coming of Global Christianity* by Philip Jenkins (Oxford University Press, 2003) 105, 214-220. The whole book is worth reading.

8. ENDNOTES

1 Danny Wong Tze-Ken, *The Transformation of an Immigrant Society: A Study of the Chinese of Sabah*, London: Asean Academic Press. 1998, 2.

2 *"Worldwide Distribution of Chinese Christians and Chinese Churches"*, compiled by Cyrus Lam, an unpublished paper of the Chinese Coordination Centre of World Evangelism, 2003. Please read the paper for regional breakdown of Chinese population and Chinese churches. A comprehensive research on Chinese churches around the world is being done by CCCOWE. Before the report on that research is done, this is the best data available.

3 For detailed information, please see *"Worldwide Distribution of Chinese Christians and Chinese Churches"*, compiled by Cyrus Lam

4 For the purpose of this paper, "Chinese" means "Chinese living outside of the Mainland China" and the same for "Chinese churches" unless stated otherwise.

5 NACOCE stands for the "North America Congress of Chinese Evangelicals."

9. BIBLIOGRAPHY

** before a title indicates books which are recommended for all College libraries.

International Students

For those just starting

**Halverson, Dean. *Pocket Guide to World Religions,* (Colorado Springs: International Students, Inc)

"Mission and Migration," *Missiology,* 31:1 (2003)

Booklets on witness to people from various cultures

Johnston, Patrick. *Operation World.* OM Publishing.

**Lane, Patty. *A Beginners Guide to Crossing Cultures.* Downers Grove, IL: IVP

Lanier, Sarah A, *Foreign to Familiar: A guide to understanding hot and cold climate cultures.* McDougal
    Publishing Company, 2000.

Lau, Lawson. *God Brings the World to Your Doorstep: Open Your Heart and Home to Welcome the Inter-*
    national. Leadership Publishers, 2005

**Phillips, Tom & Bob Norsworthy. *The World At Your Door.* Bethany.

Sire, James. *The Universe Next Door.* Downers Grove, IL: IVP.
    Non-Christian worldview descriptions.

Storti, Craig. *Figuring Foreigners Out: A Practical Guide.* Intercultural Press.

** ISM training CD. *Touching the Nations.* Friends International, UK.

Weston, Catherine. *Welcoming International Students in Your Church,* Friends International, UK.

Understanding and reaching specific groups

Buddhists

**Thirumalai Madasamy. *Sharing Your Faith with a Buddhist.* Bethany House.

Wagner, Elizabeth. Tearing Down Strongholds: Prayer for Buddhists. Hong Kong Living Books for All.

Weerasinga, Tissa. *The Cross and the Bo Tree.* Taichung, Asia Theological Association.

Chinese

Aikman, David. *Jesus in Beijing: How Christianity is Transforming China and Changing the Global Bal-*
    ance of Power.

Hu, Wenzhong and Cornelius Grove. *Encountering the Chinese: A Guide for Americans* Intercultural
    Press.

**Ling, Samuel & Stacey Bieler, eds. *Chinese Intellectuals and the Gospel.* P. & R. Publishing, 1999.

Tong, Daniel. *"A Biblical Approach to Chinese Traditions and Beliefs"* – www.armourpublishing.com/
    armour/products/product2.jsp?pid=9814045926

Understanding the Chinese Soul, (Lead Consulting) - www.leadconsulting-usa.com

Hindus

**Gidoomal, Ram & Margaret Wardell. *Chapatis for Tea.* Highland Publishing.
    www.southasian.org.uk
**Thirumalai, Madasamy. *Sharing Your Faith with a Hindu.* Bethany House.

Muslims

Accad, Fouad Elias. *Building Bridges: Christianity and Islam.* Nav Press, 1997
**Chapman, Colin. *The Cross and the Crescent,* IVP, UK.
Hoskins, Edward J. *A Muslim's Heart: What Every Christian Needs to Know to Share Christ with Muslims.*
    DawsonMedia, Navigators.
International Journal of Frontier Missions, 17:1 (2000)
McDowell, Bruce A. and Anees Zaka. *Muslims and Christians at the Table.* P. & R. Publishing, 1999.
Muller, Roland. *Honor and Shame: Unlocking the Door.* XLibris Corp.
    Explains how to communicate the gospel from a Western justice/guilt based culture to someone from a non-Western honour/shame based culture

Sikhs

**Gidoomal, Ram & Margaret Wardell. *Lions, Princesses & Gurus.* Highland Publishing -
    www.southasian.org.uk

For Use with International Students

**Anderson, Neil. *The Bondage Breaker.* Freedom in Christ Ministries. www.ficm.org
**Chinn, Lisa E. *Think Home,* ISI. *Re-entry preparation for Christian internationals*
Eaves, John. *Jesus the Liberator* ISI. *See also other Bible studies published by ISI.*
The Parables of Jesus: First Century Illustrations for the World Today. InterFACE Ministries.
McDowell, Bruce A. *The Message of the Holy Book of God Directing One to the True Path.* Tenth International Fellowship, 2003.
    Fifteen studies written for Muslims - www.tifweb.org
**Perry, Bill. *The Storyteller's Bible Study for Internationals.* Multi-Language Media.
    __________. *Crossing Over with Parables.* Multi-Language Media.
Wagner, Fred, ed. *Passport to the Bible: An Explorer's Guide.* Downers Grove, IL:IVP.
    Twenty-four investigative bible discussions covering God, humankind, sin and experiencing God.

A Few Ministry Websites

Association of Christians Ministering Among Internationals www.acmi-network.org Network of international student ministries and volunteers in North America.
Campus Crusade for Christ - www.bridgesinternational.com
European International Student Ministries (EISM) www.eism.penpal4u.net Links to European ministries.
Friends International - www.friendsinternational.org.uk
Institute of Hindu Studies, US Center for World Mission - ihs@uscwm.org
InterFACE Ministries - www.iface.org
International Fellowship of Evangelical Students. www.ifesworld.org Links to student ministries worldwide.
International Students, Inc.-www.isionline.org; (see Resources link);
    www.internationalstudents.org (Website for seekers)
ISM Canada www.ismc.ca
International Student Ministries of New Zealand, Inc. - www.ism.org.nz

InterVarsity Christian Fellowship USA - www.intervarsity.org/ism
> *Articles on ISM, including a more extensive bibliography and links to ISM ministries worldwide.*

Japanese Christian Fellowship Network (JCFN) - www.jcfn.org/englishhome.htm
> *Fellowship and follow-up of returnees to Japan.*

Korean Students Abroad (KOSTA) - www.kosta.ws

Navigators - www.navigators.org/ism

Network of Ministries to Hindus and Sikhs - www.netmhs-subscribe@egroups.com

Sources of Literature and Media

Ambassadors for Christ - www.afcinc.org/afcsite/english/literature/mc-lit/mc_lit.htm
Christian literature for Mainland Chinese.

Apologetics for Muslims - www.answering-islam.org

Chinese spiritual growth materials - www.cbible.net

China Soul for Christ - www.chinasoul.org Evangelistic media by PRC producers.

Fellowship of Faith for Muslims - www.ffm.toronto@sympatico.ca

Innovista - www.innovista.org Apologetics media for Europe and Asia.

International Bible Society www.IBSDirect.com – for orders. Also www.Gospelcom.net/ibs
> *Bibles and passages on line (print and audio) in many languages.*

The JESUS Film. 1-800-432-1997 - Available in over 800 languages

Kitab. - www.kitab.org Evangelistic materials in Asian languages.

Multi-Language Media. - www.multilanguage.com .
> *Christian books and videos in many languages.*

Overseas Campus Magazine - www.oc.org
> *Excellent Chinese magazine for PRC students.*

United Bible Societies - www.biblesociety.org/index2.htm Index listing bible societies worldwide.

The Filipino Diaspora

Manolo, Abella. "Labor Mobility, Trade and Structural Change: The Philippine experience" in *Asian and Pacific Migration Journal*, 2:3 (1993), 249-268

Agoncillo, Teodoro A. *History of the Filipino People,* Quezon City: GAROTECH Publishing, 1993.

Alburo, Florian. "Remittances, Trade and the Philippine Economy" in *Asian and Pacific Migration Journal,* 2:3(1993), 269-284.

Catalan, Daisy C. S. "The Diversity of Filipinos in the United States" - www.yale.edu/ynhti/curriculum/units /1996/4/96.04.05.x.html, (1996)

Catholic Institute for International Relations. *The Labor Trade: Filipino Migrant Workers Around the World,* London: Catholic Institute for International Relations, 1987.

Chant, Sylvia & Cathy McIlwaine. *Women of a Lesser Cost: Female Labour, Foreign Exchange & Philippine Development.* Manila: Ateneo de Manila University Press, 1995.

Commission on Filipinos Overseas (COF). Annual Report 2001, Manila: Department of Foreign Affairs, 2001.

Cruz, Victoria Paz. *Seasonal Orphans and Solo Parents: The Impact of Overseas Migration.* Manila: Scalabrini Migration Center and CBCP Commission on Migration and Tourism, Normine Printing House, 1987.

Kalaw-Tirol, Lorna, ed. *From America to Africa: Voices of Filipino Women Overseas,* Makati City: FAI Resource Management Inc, 2000.

Okamura, Jonathan Y. *Imagining the Filipino American Diaspora: Transnational Relations, Identities, and Communities.* New York and London: Garland Publishing, 1998.

**Pantoja Jr, Luis, Tira, Joy Sadiri & Enoch Wan, eds. *Scattered: The Filipino Global Presence*. Manila: LifeChange Publishing Inc, 2004.

San Juan, Jr, E. *From Exile to Diaspora: Versions of the Filipino Experience in the United States*. Boulder, Westview Press, 1998.

Takaki, Ronald. *In the Heart of America: Immigrants from the Pacific Isles*. Adapted by Rebecca Stefoff with Carol Takaki. New York and Philadelphia, Chelsea Book Publishers, 1995.

The South Asian Diaspora

**Catalyst for Change: The South Asian Diaspora. London, INSADL/South Asian Concern, 2005.

**Chandran, P Emil. "South Asian Diaspora: Challenges and Opportunities" in *Evangelical Missions Quarterly*, October (2004), 450-455

Cumpston, I. M. *Indians Overseas in British Territories*. London: Oxford University Press, 1953.

Gangulee, N. *Indians in the Empire Overseas*. London: New India Publishing House, 1947.

**Gidoomal, Ram, with Mike Fearon. *Sari 'n' Chips*. Tunbridge Wells: MARC, 1993.

**Gidoomal, Ram, with David Porter. *The UK Maharajahs: Inside the South Asian Success Story*. London: Nicholas Brealey, 1997.

Gidoomal, Ram, Deepak Mahtani & David Porter. *The British and How to Deal with Them*. London: Middlesex University Press, 2001.

Gregory, Robert A. *India and East Africa*. Oxford: Clarendon Press, 1971.

James, G. D. *Mobilize To Evangelize*. Singapore, Fellowship of South Asian Christians, 1982.

Morris, H .S. *Indians in Uganda*. London: Weidenfeld and Nicolson, 1968.

Thomas, Chris D. *Diaspora Indians: Church Growth Among Indians In West Malaysia*. Penang, Malaysia Indian Evangelism Council, 1978.

Thomas, Annamma and T.M. Thomas. *Kerala Immigrants In America*. Cochin: Simons Printers and Publishers, 1984.

**Thomson, Robin. *Changing India*. New Delhi: BR Publishing Corporation, 2002.

Tippet, Alan R. *The Fiji Indian Community and its Church*. Eugene OR: Unpublished manuscript.

Immigrants in the United States

Barna, George. "Church Demographics" - www.barna.org, 2004.

Barna, George. "Ethnic Groups Differ Substantially on Matters of Faith" - www.barna.org, 2004.

Barna, George. "Religious Activity Increasing in the West" - www.barna.org, 2004.

Bean, Frank, Jennifer Lee, Jeanne Batalova and Mark Leach. "Immigration and Fading Color Lines in America," Population Reference Bureau, 2004.

Ethnic America Network - www.ethnicamerica.com

Gallegos, Aaron. "Room in the Inn?" in *Sojourner Magazine*, December 1994

Global University. – www.globaluniversity.edu

Gross, Linda. SEAM International Christian Training Center, Artesia, CA - www.seamla.org

**Hanciles, Jehu J. "Migration and Mission, Some Implications for the Twenty-first Century Church" in *International Bulletin of Missionary Research*, 27:4, 2003.

Long, Justin. - www.gem-werc.org/mmrc/mmrc9643.htm.

Martin, Phillip and Elisabeth Midgley. "Immigration: Shaping and Reshaping America" in *IT* June, 2003.

Pluralism Project, Harvard University. - www.pluralismproject.org, 2004.

Population Reference Bureau. *2004 World Population Data Sheet* - www.prb.org.

Warner, R. Stephen and Judith G. Wittner. *Gatherings in Diaspora*. Philadelphia: Temple University Press, 1998.

10. PARTICIPANTS

Ram Gidoomal	Kenya/UK, *Convenor (Diaspora)*
Leiton Chinn	USA, *Convenor (International Students)*
Sik Wah Patrick Tsang	Hong Kong/USA/China, *Co Convenor (Diaspora)*
TV Thomas	Malaysia/Canada, *Facilitator*
Robin Thomson	India/UK, *Theologian*
Tom Houston	UK, *Editorial support*
Sunita Gidoomal	UK, *Editorial support*
Stacey Bieler	USA, *Editorial support*
Nonie Bell	USA, *Editorial support*

Issue Group 26A and 26B Participants

Andrey Bondarenko	Ukraine/USA
Daniel C Brannen	USA
Allen Busenitz	USA
Mavis Chan	Hong Kong/USA
Ei Que Chang	Korea
David Chiu	Canada
Yvonne Choo	Singapore
Yiu Kwai Fun	China
Mark Galpin	UK/Nepal
N Jawahr Gnaniah	USA
Linda Gross	USA
John Kao	Hong Kong/ Canada
Timo Keskitalo	Finland
T E Koshy	India/USA
Vera Kovalova	Ukraine
Ron Landers	USA/Portugal
Christian Lerrahn	Germany
Anita Leung	Hong Kong/Canada
Elaine Lu	Taiwan/USA
Albert Lu	Canada/USA

Michael Marvell	UK/Denmark
Bruce McDowell	Paraguay/USA
Terry McGrath	New Zealand
Beau Miller	USA
Glen Osborn	USA
Arthur Raj	India
Katie J Rawson	USA
Narry Santos	Philippines
Vernon Song	Singapore
Nilo Marcos Sosmena	Philippines
Enoch Wan	China/USA
Richard Weston	UK
Wes & Gayle Wilson	USA
Elaine Yan	Hong Kong/USA
Xiaoli Yang	China/Australia
Sam Yeghnazar	UK
Sadiri Joy Tira	Philippines/Canada

FUNDING FOR EVANGELISM AND MISSION

Lausanne Occasional Paper No. 56

This Issue Group on Funding for Evangelism was Issue Group No.27

This Occasional Paper was prepared by the whole Issue Group and
Dr. Charles Roost and Dr. E. LeBron Fairbanks served as co-editors

CONTENTS

1. **Introduction**

2. **The Challenge**

3. **The Current Scene In Mission Funding**

4. **A New "Mutual Commitment" Model**
   (a) Stewardship
   (b) Relationship
   (c) Accountability
   (d) Interdependence
   (e) Intermediaries

5. **Implementing The "Mutual Commitment" Model**

Conclusion

Participants

1. INTRODUCTION

Lausanne 2004 ... Conference on World Evangelization ... addressed many of the key issues facing the church and its mission in this decade. Participants at the conference were invited to join one of over 30 "Issue Groups," with each group assigned on a specific topic to present a paper reflecting their work. Group #27 was asked to address the issue of "Funding For Evangelism And Mission."

Group #27 consisted of 27 ministry leaders representing several types of ministry and various countries. The majority of the participants lead ministries in what is commonly called "the developing world." The Group was co-led by Dr. E. LeBron Fairbanks (USA) and Dr. Mac-Millan Kiiru (Kenya). Dr. Charles Roost (USA) and Dr. E. LeBron Fairbanks (USA) served as co-editors of this article.

2. THE CHALLENGE

God often chooses to use the resources of this world to accomplish His work. Human resources and financial re-sources seem to be those most significant in the work of the church. History proves that funding for evangelism and mission is very important for the work of the kingdom.

The funding of evangelism and mission has hosted both great achievements for the benefit of the kingdom and significant pain and economic abuse within the body of Christ. As was demonstrated in Christ's ministry and the life of the early church, money is a God-given tool for catalysing mission but when used without integrity and good stewardship it has the potential to create significant harm.

The challenges faced in the funding arena seem to fall into three categories:

- Shortage of funds to accomplish reasonable goals.
- Misuse of funds on the part of ministry personnel and organisations.
- Distortion of biblical principles and standards in fund development.

3. THE CURRENT SCENE IN MISSION FUNDING

The current environment in funding evangelism and mission is generally characterised by a vertical, top/down arrangement where the money from donors "trickles down" to the recipient organisation or ministry. This vertical model, because of its hierarchical nature, has created major problems within the body of Christ. The donor has been reduced to a "source" for funds. The ministry organisation has been reduced to "operators" of fund raising schemes primarily related to organisational budgets. Missing in the model is the character that honours biblical principles for the effective use of God's resources to accomplish His purposes. The top/down relationship within the body of Christ disfigures stewardship and cries out for redemption and transformation.

4. A NEW "MUTUAL COMMITMENT" MODEL

What is required is acceptance of the proper theology of funding and subsequent practices that will point the church to fulfilment of the task of evangelism and mission while affirming the equality of all believers and unity within the body of Christ.

The challenges in funding evangelism and mission in the current environment can be traced back to the lack of an adequate theological framework for the role stewards play as they manage financial resources. In the absence of a comprehensive theology and a reflecting set of principles for financial resources, the world of non-profits has fallen prey to ineffective models and strategies characterised by the following:

1. Lack of a functional theology regard-

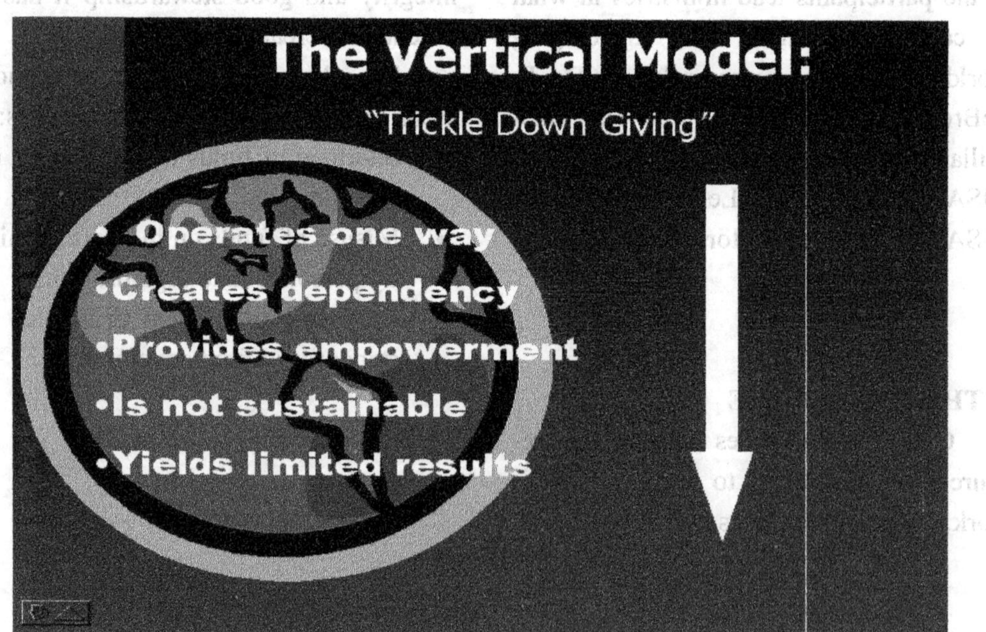

ing fund development and resource management.

2. Lack of mutual understanding, effective strategies and clear funding models concerning the biblical relationship between giver and receiver.

3. An assumption of limited local resources available to the emerging church and the lack of effective leadership in the management of resources.

4. Education and training that is sufficient …

   …in stewardship and fund development at both ministry leadership training institutions and local congregations.

   …for funders in mission strategy.

   …for mission agency executives and their development staffs.

5. Attitudes of dependence on the part of receivers and co-dependence on the part of providers.

The new model, strongly recommended by Lausanne Issue Group #27 "Funding Evangelism and Mission," changes the way giving and receiving is perceived, approached and accomplished. It is recommended with the understanding that such a major paradigm shift will not be easily adopted.

This model, called the "Mutual Commitment" model, is **horizontal** in structure, placing all parties in the fund development effort on an equal plane. In this model, all believers enjoy an equal standing before the throne of Christ. See below.

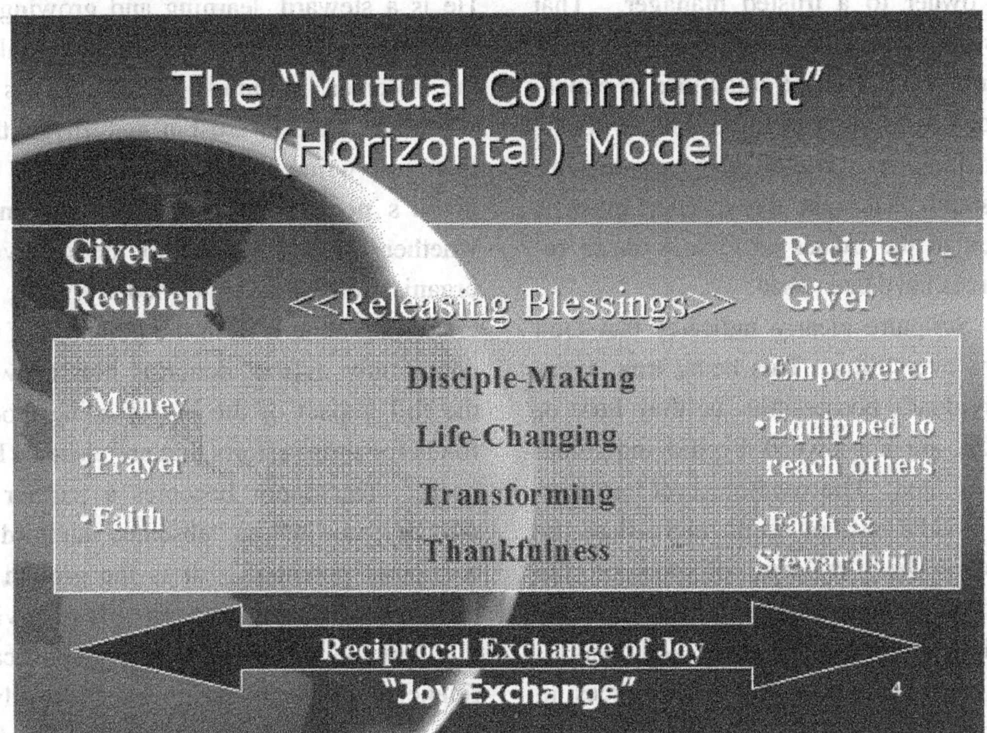

This new model can best be understood in the reorientation of five key concepts within giving and receiving: stewardship, relationship, accountability, dependency and the role of intermediaries.

(a) Stewardship

Unfortunately, most teaching on the subject of stewardship takes place in the church when there is an urgent financial need. "Stewardship" has become the inappropriate synonym for "fund raising." As such, its true impact is lost in the struggle of funding. Closely attached to the fund-raising misconception of stewardship is the assumption that stewardship is only for the "rich."

A steward is anyone who manages resources that are owned by another. Stewardship, then, is the exercise of resource management. It is a trust given by the owner to a trusted manager. That trust includes provision of assets for management and a set of guidelines or expectations as to what is to be done with the owners assets. The effective steward understands that some day a report must be given to the owner as to how those resources have been used.

Scripture clearly indicates that God owns everything. This being true, every individual's possessions, be they little or much, are not owned by the individual but by God. The wealthiest oil barren in the middle east owns no more than the impoverished resident of one of the world's mammoth slums. Every person is simply a manager of what God owns.

Stewardship of God's resources in harmony with His purposes universally runs counter-culture to our humanity. We want to own. Ownership is a highly valued secular economic principle. Yet stewardship, not ownership, is God's design.

How then does one become a mature steward? The biblical record is clear. The workshop in which stewardship, (the management of another's resources) is matured is in the workshop of giving. *"It is better to give than to receive."* Giving, for most people, is a discipline that matures into a grace. For some, it is a gracious gift of God's spirit. The grace and gift of giving have little to do with quantity and everything to do with the steward's effective management of God's resources.

The role of Christian leadership in the fund development journey is greater than meeting the budget. The donor is more than a potential source for more money. He is a steward, learning and growing in the grace of giving. The ultimate goal of the receiver, as funds are sought, is to stimulate that stewardship maturity, rather than just wring another dollar out of the donor's pocket. The solicitor of funds, whether directly related to the receiving organisation or an intermediary, will increasingly benefit from the potential of the donor only as that donor is blessed with the full impact of the joy of using God's funds for those efforts that are close to His heart. The donor becomes a partner in ministry, not just an "absentee landlord of economic potential." It is the growth of the steward in the grace or gift of giving that unlocks his potential for significant financial, prayerful and personal involvement, not the clever manipulation of a message from the receiver.

As the steward grows in stewardship maturity, the desire of that steward will be to more completely understand and identify with the ministry, the receiver. This produces the quality of commitment that unleashes lay energy for expanded ministry. It also opens the ministry leader to a broader responsibility for constructive accountability and communication that feeds stewardship growth.

In the "Mutual Commitment" model for fund development, all parties in the transactions related to God's resources give and receive so that each participant is more qualified than before to manage God's resources in a manner that reflects His value system. In such a commitment, the giving and receiving is elevated to a true spiritual act and freed from the potential of manipulation and abuse.

(b) Relationship

We are members of the Body of Christ and as members we are all interconnected. When one member of the body suffers, the whole body suffers, and when one member of the body succeeds, the whole body succeeds (Romans 12:4ff; 1 Corinthians 12:12ff). It is also imperative for us to remember that the Lord is especially pleased with us when we serve "the least" (cf. Matthew 25:40,45).

As members of the Body we have all been endowed with God-given resources, differently and unequally. God provides differences to require sharing in the Body life of the Church. God's resources are given for a purpose: for the common good, and particularly for the task of the Great Commission.

As members of the Body, we have a horizontal relationship with one another: not of the have and have-nots but as members of the body of Christ; not of the superior to inferior but as brothers and sisters in Christ standing together at the foot of the cross; not of those from the North and those from the South but as citizens of the New Jerusalem. It is in this family relationship that true fellowship in ministry takes place.

The "Mutual Commitment" model dictates that in giving and receiving, relationship must be of utmost importance. In this relationship we are bound by the following:

1. We are to have respect for one another as members of the same family.
2. We are required to work to encourage and support one another.
3. We must celebrate our God-given gifts and share them for evangelism and mission.

Our relationship must never be defined by, nor become limited to, the mechanisms of financial transfers. Relationship value reflects the Body of Christ, not some economic standard or potential.

(c) Accountability

Mutual accountability is one of the most vital elements within the activity of funding mission. Redeemed and transformed accountability has the potential to revolutionise the manner in which funding is accomplished and serves as the strongest vehicle to move funding of mission into a new future.

In the historic "Trickle Down" model with its vertical arrangement, accountability is often sought through a one-way imposition of "rules" from the donor, accompanied often by expectations that particular values will be exhibited in the funded ministry. In the Mutual Commitment model, accountability is first to God and His full design in resource use… for both giver and receiver … and has the purpose of building relationship and trust within the Body. As such, it is multi-directional in concept and function.

The primary corrective task to enhance accountability is to develop a new understanding of individual and corporate stewardship and relationship that emerges out of the practical application of the new theological vision for funding. Included in this new way of thinking are the following concepts:

1. Accountability includes the space for "failure." The relationship which underpins accountability should be capable of dealing with such "failure." This is the case for either side of the relationship. In overseeing the process of funding, both donors and receivers need to manage their expectations in harmony with the redemptive character of God's family.

2. It is vital to create and maintain the fullest mutual level of trust. Such trust can only thrive in an environment of open communication.

3. Good management training is an important element of ensuring faithfulness and good stewardship.

4. There should not be an expectation that funding always produces instant results. In some settings and in some ministries, instant, final results are highly unlikely. Funding produces activity … the Holy Spirit produces results.

5. It is necessary to have mutual clarity, a "code of good practices" that helps define and determine accountability structures before funding/partnership agreements. Models of this mutual understanding must be developed or accumulated from ministries currently practicing them with effective results.

6. Effective accountability can be supported by active research and honest appraisals that serve to strengthen the process of funding and use of funds.

7. Practitioners of mission will implement thoughtful missiology and wise stewardship through integrity and adequate training.

Accountability always requires open and candid relationships. The biblical model of "overseers," instructed in I Timothy and elsewhere, establishes the notion that accountability rests within communal relationships. No individual, regardless of skill or leadership clout, is an island or a sovereign. Each serves in a reporting relationship to the Body.

In the end, the mandate is to "*do what is right not only in the Lord's sight, but also in the eyes of others*" (2 Corinthians 8:21). Those who give and those who receive must be faithful stewards, anticipating that day when all **will** give an account to the Lord for everything He has entrusted to us.

(d) Interdependence

When giving and receiving take place there is always the risk of developing unhealthy dependency. An unfortunate, yet all too often natural consequence, unhealthy dependency is the exclusive expectation that someone external will supply necessary resources.

Such dependency, while born in the economic arena of life, has complications far more widespread than what is happening in the ministry's funding. It often builds into the receiver a set of "needs" and "wants" that stretch the priorities and values of the receiver out of functional form. Concomitantly, this dependency can also develop in the giver a subtle, but real, co-dependency syndrome.

Unhealthy dependency . . .

. . .drains the receiver of initiative. When someone "out there" is financially responsible, personal creativity, drive, and energy soon wane.

. . .creates a one-sided relationship, exacerbating the "haves, have nots" syndrome. This spirit of "unequalness" feeds all that destroys the potential for true relationships and communal oneness.

. . .reduces the self-confidence of the receiver. Leadership thrives on turning a challenge into an opportunity. When that process is short-circuited by dependency, the leader-receiver loses the personal sense of adequacy.

. . .robs the receiver of positive self-image. When one of the two most significant resources for ministry is in the hands of "unknown others," ministry leaders see themselves as handicapped.

. . .may transfer faith and trust in God to the donor. While spiritual language may colour the speech of the receiver, in an unhealthy dependent relationship the receiver can easily have more confidence in special donors than in God. When challenging financial times come, it is the donor who is called upon with a plea for resolution.

. . .distorts the biblical truth of stewardship and the grace of giving. True Christian fund development directly reflects God's purposes for entrusting His people with His financial resources. Dependency causes the receiver to deviate from God's perspective to the temporal science and manipulation of crass fund raising.

. . .fosters the potential for the need to fabricating false reports. When a ministry is totally dependent on an outside source of funds, the need to keep the donor satisfied with positive feedback often leads to reports that are less than honest or truthful. "Stretching the truth" can become a way of life.

...may frequently escalate into a spirit of entitlement. Entitlement is a subtle arrogance built on some admitted need that can, and ought to, be met by someone else. It is the ultimate in loss of responsibility and meaningful self-function.

The receiver is not the only part of the giving-receiving equation that is threatened by unhealthy dependency. Givers also experience counter-productive stewardship attitudes and habits when dependency...

...encourages the development of pride in accomplishment. A distant giver, recognising the significance of the gifts to a ministry, can begin to see her/himself more highly than he/she ought.

...welcomes the exercise of control over the ministry. Control through giving can be experienced as dominance, manipulation, economic motivation, or "spiritual bribery."

...distorts the relationship between receiver and giver. When the mutual relationship of blessing and joy is based on financial potential and need, the mutuality of the relationship suffers the restrictions of limited honesty and vulnerability.

...opens the door for the growth of a superior attitude. The ability to give, while a wonderful grace or gift, does not elevate the giver to a place in God's family above the receiver.

While money is often the key to progress, it is not a replacement for humble participation in God's community.

...fosters co-dependency. When the privilege of giving becomes the major identifier of a person's value and priority system, the giver has become as dependent as the receiver.

The core corrective to this issue of dependency that so often accompanies the giving-receiving transactions is the development of local funding for all ministries. In the environment of local stewards growing in the grace of giving, the need for outside donors will consistently decrease. More importantly, individuals within the local ministry will rise to the full personal and corporate benefits of mature stewardship. This new model goal is interdependence, not dependence or co-dependence.

The new paradigm, The "Mutual Commitment" model, encourages interdependence in that each of the participants in the giving-receiving dynamic is on the same level and understands the mutuality of the process. They may play different roles in the transaction, but each one understands the equality of purpose and ministry that characterises all participants. While the transfer of funds is the temporal content of the relationship, the true significance in the relationship is the common desire to assist each person in growth toward full stewardship maturity. God is not short of funds to accomplish His programs. He is only lacking mature stewards.

(e) Intermediaries

As the world gets more complex, the

fund development process also takes on more complexity. In some cases it is a simple transaction between giver and receiver. In a growing percentage of cases, however, there is an intermediary person or group facilitating the funding relationship between donor and ministry organisation. The intermediary is sometimes a non-programmatic staff member of the receiving organisation, and at other times is an independent broker of available funds from a donor desiring assistance in the giving process.

The role of the intermediary is essentially to bridge the cultural, social, motivational, or geographic gap between giver and receiver. The intermediary becomes the "point person" or the "person of contact" for both the donor and the organisation. If the intermediary is a staff member of the organisation, expectations and supervision come from someone in that organisation. If the intermediary represents a donor or a group of donors, the expectations come from the donor side of the transaction. In either case, the intermediary can become the primary personality in the stewardship transaction. As such, he/she can be a primary determiner of the fund development model utilised. Traditionally it seems easy for intermediaries to exercise the characteristics of the "Trickle Down" model. However, in many cases they hold the key for transition to the "Mutual Commitment" model.

The recommendation of a new fund development model is more likely to receive a casual reception when there is an intermediary who does not understand the "Mutual Commitment" model. If the intermediary is only "dollar conscious" or organisation-budget conscious, facilitating the dynamics of mutual commitment may be seen as too time consuming. The time assumed necessary for mutual benefit is perceived to weaken the potential for economic success. When the receiving organisation and the intermediary are not on the same stewardship page, the "Mutual Commitment" model will likely be distorted and the "Trickle Down" model will naturally take over.

Intermediaries usually reflect the fund development philosophy of the organisation for which they work. If the organisation views fund development only from the perspective of the budget, it is likely the intermediary will exercise the traditional model. If the organisation implements the new mutual benefit model, the intermediary will likely have a greater inclination to be a minister of stewardship, in contrast to a fund raiser.

In either model, the intermediary often orchestrates the style of the relationship between donor and receiver. As the gate-keeper of funds, the intermediary may

1. assume too much power.
2. manipulate board-level control of the use of funds.
3. dictate ministry priorities as a condition of funding.
4. mislead the donor for personal purposes.

The possibility of the intermediary reflecting the new mutual benefit model of fund development will be dependent on:

1. the personal character of the individual
2. the personal and ministerial motivation of the individual
3. the organisational environment in which the person works
4. the nature of the supervision received by the fund broker
5. the level of personal stewardship maturity exercised by the intermediary
6. the history of fund development into which the intermediary fits

Intermediaries are very important considerations in the giver – receiver equation. It is possible they are the only link between donor and receiver. As such, it is imperative that both the donor and the receiver have full confidence and trust in the intermediary. It is equally important for the intermediary to recognise that he/she must fairly and accurately represent both the donor and the receiver in all discussions and transactions. The balance between helping each party grow while at the same time protecting them from misunderstanding or abuse is often a difficult one to maintain.

The intermediary is often the initial voice and sometimes the image of either the donor or the receiver or both. Ultimately the goal of the effective intermediary should be to become transparent in order for a full relationship to develop between the giver and receiver. While the intermediary may facilitate the relationship, he/she must not get in the way of the mutual benefit that should be an ongoing experience between donor and ministry.

5. IMPLEMENTING THE "MUTUAL COMMITMENT" MODEL

A new model, in and of itself, does not a change make. Theory without practice is empty … practice without theory is folly.

The ultimate question asked by the "Funding for Evangelism and Mission" Lausanne Issue Group #27 is, "how does the new model make funding the mission more efficient and effective?" If the theological base for the new model is correct, as those who manage God's resources here on earth mature in stewardship and expand the grace of giving, there will be ample resources for any "project" God desires to see accomplished. He is not short of funds … just short of mature stewards. Humanly, it may seem that His decision to trust His creation to channel His resources into "investments" that accomplish His goals is questionable. That plan, like all of creation, has suffered immensely from the impact of the entry of sin into His creation. Once His creatures became distorted in values and priorities, their use of His creation also suffered. If the management of resources can be redeemed, the use of those resources will be re-channelled into His priorities.

Pragmatically, the questions are as follows: "how does the organisation build a fund development program that accomplishes the 'mutual benefit' design?" "How does the mature donor exercise the grace or gift of giving in such a way that the ministry is moved to the new model?" The crush of ministry budgets and the pressure of general funds war against the transitions necessary to reflect the characteristics of reciprocal blessings between donor and receiver. For decades the donor has been seen as simply the supplier of funds. Furthermore, for decades donors have taken a rather passive attitude toward issues of ministry outside the consistent request for more funds. Out of excess comes that which meets the needs of those in ministry who have no excess. Consequently, there is no mutual growth relationship assumed or generated for the majority of donors other than that reflected in the level of financial participation.

Several steps are to be considered as an organisation makes a commitment to building a mutually benefiting fund development program.

1. Mailing lists, those cold and impersonal lists of names and addresses, may be categorised or stratified differently than by giving experience or potential. If there was a way to identify maturity of giving motivation or level of growth in the grace of giving, those categories would be much more conducive to knowing how best to communicate with mutual blessing than the size of the chequebook. Other categories, such as type of ministry that interests the donor or level of personal involvement with the ministry, would assist in communications more mutually beneficial than the emotive plea for funds.

2. Communications designed specifically for various members of the family may assist in inviting those other than the check-writer. Likewise, specific communications to various professional groupings may provide information useful for stimulating the involvement of those professionals in ministry.

3. Reducing the use of exploitive and emotionally manipulative stories and pictures, without sterilising the message, may over a period of time provide a more accurate picture of ministry than is generated by extreme direct mail. Such a pattern of printed material would help preserve the dignity of those funded in needy parts of the world.

4. Patterns of communication that include more personal interaction, group meetings, conferences, mission trips, etc., will elevate the donor from "source of money" to "partner in ministry."

5. Opportunity for donors to know the challenges as well as the blessings within a ministry will provide a foundation of reality for the donors as they give and pray.

6. Accurate reporting, rather than exaggerated numbers, will encourage respect for and identity with the normal challenges of ministry. A donor funding a "quick fix" to a massive problem will ultimately be

disappointed and cynical about ministry.

7. While an organisation is legally accountable to its Board of Directors, a spirit of accountability to its supporting family would encourage maturity in that family. This is not a simple task. With diverse backgrounds and levels of maturity in the supporting family, the process of being accountable becomes very complex. Yet, the organisation that relates to its constituency in a comprehensive accountability pattern will develop strength in that "family." When members of the supporting family assist in the design of accountability communication, the process becomes less threatening.

8. While the emotive dimension of life opens the door to funding decisions, it is the cognitive that builds maturity in all dimensions of life. The information shared between donor, intermediary and receiver should be structured in such a way that it moves both donor and receiver to a higher level of trust relationship and cognitive connection. The donor needs to be prompted in stewardship growth and ministry awareness. The receiver should consistently refine efforts to both manage and report on the management of God's resources extended to the ministry. Stagnating the donor at the emotive level of involvement is a misuse of the stewardship trust.

Conclusion

The Lausanne Issue Group on Funding recommends a radical shift in the perspective of ministry organisations toward funding principles. A fund development program, principled on biblical truths, has the potential of freeing God's resources from the tyranny of natural human inclination. The issues of funding have more to do with stewards than with money ... more to do with stewardship maturity than matching dollars to budget projections. The ultimate availability of funds to accomplish God's Great Commission is not limited by quantity of resources, but by values and priorities within God's stewards that distort His intentions for effective mobilisation of His wealth.

PARTICIPANTS

E. LeBron Fairbanks, Convener	USA
MacMillan Kiiru, Co-Convener	Kenya
Casey Cobell, Facilitator	USA
George Chavanikamannil, Scribe	India
Charles Roost, Editor	USA
Jay Caven	USA
Gene Davis	India
Lemma Degefa	Ethiopia
Tinshu Genesis Gemuh	Cameroon
Dwight Gibson	USA
Joseph Ikhine	Nigeria
Jerry Lambert	USA
Jean Claude Malanda	Congo
Revocatus Meza	Tanzania
John Rose	United Kingdom
Arndt Schnepper	Germany
Biju Thomas	India
John Thomas	India
Steve Weber	USA
Jonas Yema	Cameroon

EFFECTIVE THEOLOGICAL EDUCATION FOR WORLD EVANGELISATION

Lausanne Occasional Paper No. 57

This Issue Group on this Issue was Issue Group No. 28

This Occasional Paper was prepared by the whole Issue Group and the editors were Pieter Theron and Michael Raiter

CONTENTS

A. Why is effective Education for World Evangelisation Crucial?

    1. Introduction

        1.1 Educating Faith Communities

        1.2 What Kind of Education?

    2. Challenges

        2.1 Contextual and Cultural Issues

            (a) Internal

            (b) External

        2.2 Conclusion

B. What are the Learning Outcomes of Effective Education for World Evangelisation?

    1. What kind of faith communities will effective education for evangelisation produce?

        1.1 School Communities

        1.2 The Church - Greater Commitment to World Evangelisation through a Missionary Lifestyle

            (a) Commitment to Jesus Christ as Lord of Everything and Everywhere

            (b) Christian Discipleship

            (c) Biblical Vision of the Church

            (d) Use of Gifts and Ministries

    2. What kind of persons will it form?

        2.1 Know the Gospel

        2.2 Live and Do the Gospel

        2.3 Tell the Gospel

    3. Christian Leaders of Faith Communities

C. How can Effective Education for World Evangelisation Accomplish This?

1. Biblical and Theological Foundations

    1.1 Basis for Education and Training within the Faith Community

    1.2 A Theology of Theological Education

    1.3 The Implications and Challenges

2. The Model of Jesus

    2.1 Jesus' Strategies and Methods of Teaching

        (a) Concentration on a Small Group

        (b) Life-to-Life Transference / Modelling

        (c) Building a Community

        (d) Use of Stories and Illustrations

        (e) Active Learning / Learning by Doing

        (f) A Holistic and Balanced Approach

    2.2 Jesus' Characteristics as Teacher

        (a) Jesus was a model of what he taught.

        (b) Jesus established relationship with his learners.

        (c) Jesus was comfortable with people of all kinds.

        (d) Jesus was a man on a mission.

        (e) Jesus was prayerful.

    2.3 The Role of the Holy Spirit in Teaching

3. Principles and Strategies for Effective Education

    3.1 Strategic Issues That Must be Addressed in a Training Programme

        (a) Church-Institutional Relationships

        (b) Committed Staff

        (c) Different Levels of Training

        (d) The Role of Mission in Theology

        (e) Economics of Training

    3.2 Overarching Principles for Evangelisation Training Effectiveness:

        (a) Balance between Theory and Practice

        (b) Experiential Learning

        (c) Incarnational and Participatory Learning

        (d). Disciplinary Balance

        (e) Dynamic and Creative

        (f) Evaluative, outcome-focused process

E. Guidelines for Implmentation

1. Implementation Challenges and Issues

2. Key Action Plans

3. Additional Guidelines

3.1 Faculty Development

(a) Faculty Recruitment and Selection

(b) Faculty Awareness of World Mission and Intercultural Exposure

(c) Mentoring and Modelling

3.2 Curriculum Development

3.3. The Local Church and Church Leaders

3.4 Board Members of Training Institutions, Programmes and Local Churches

3.5 Strategic Partnerships

Conclusion

Bibliography

Participants

A. WHY IS EFFECTIVE EDUCATION FOR WORLD EVANGELISATION CRUCIAL?

1. Introduction

When he saw the crowds Jesus had compassion on them, because they were harassed and helpless, like sheep without a shepherd. Then he said to his disciples, "The harvest is plentiful but the workers are few. Ask the Lord of the harvest, therefore, to send out workers into his harvest field" (Matthew 9:37-38).

World evangelisation begins in the heart of the triune God, who sees the people he has created in desperate need. He meets this need in the Good Shepherd who is also paradoxically the Lamb of God who takes away the sins of the world.

God reveals to his people the heart he has for a lost and suffering world and from this revelation a commitment to world evangelisation is born. Jesus himself had to draw the attention of his disciples to the reality that was all around them: "the harvest is plentiful." Although the disciples followed Jesus and listened to him they had never really seen what was staring them in the face. Similarly, today, faith communities of the Lord Jesus gather together in the presence of their risen and ascended Lord, worshipping him and hearing his word, yet many have not *beheld* that "the harvest is plentiful." To see is to observe with one's eyes. To behold is both to see and to understand the significance of that observation. The Lord Jesus calls on his disciples to comprehend the needs of the world around them and then to pray with a view to purposeful action: that workers be sent into the harvest.

The premise of this Issue Group is that there is insufficient commitment on the part of faith communities to world mission. Faith communities need to be educated for world evangelisation.

1.1 Educating Faith Communities

The Issue Group has deliberately chosen the more inclusive term "faith communities" as this embraces the range of groups who we are seeking to educate. In particular, we are addressing churches and educational training institutions. Firstly, churches need to be educated. Many churches have a commitment to local evangelism and yet have not grasped or understood the implications for them of God's global purposes for his creation.

Other churches are so caught up in world mission that they do not see the harvest in their own local contexts. Training institutions vary enormously in their purposes and their methods of teaching. Some adopt a traditionally formal model of education built around imparting the content and skills necessary for the life of faith and works of Christian ministry. Others adopt more non-formal methods of education emphasising, for example, experiential learning or a mentoring approach to education. Whether formal or non-formal, training institutions are critical in infusing the wider faith communities with a vision for, and commitment to, world evangelisation, and the skills and strategies required to implement this vision.

1.2 What kind of Education?

The purpose of this Issue Group is not to report on *how* to do mission. We are not exploring different methods of evangelism. Our focus is on how educational training can build a commitment for world mission and evangelisation.

Education is the vehicle by which institutions and communities convey to their members the attitudes, values, and appropriate behaviours for life within those communities. Necessarily any education must involve the passing on of content. However effective education for world evangelisation must see as its goal the formation of values and attitudes as well as the communication of knowledge and skills. Effective education for evangelisation must, therefore, be transformational.

In summary this Issue Group has given its attention to how a commitment to world evangelisation can be taught and modelled most effectively to Christian faith communities.

2. Challenges

There are a number of challenges to how effective theological education for world evangelisation can be implemented. These challenges are different depending upon the context and the area in which the education is taking place.

Of course, for those theological colleges, Bible schools and church training programmes that have had a strong missional emphasis, the challenges are fewer. They already have an attitude and an approach to training that is already focused on preparing men and women for the Great Commission task. They are showing by the type of leadership that they produce that they are fully engaged as missional institutions. The fruit of their labours is seen in the spread of the Gospel in most areas where they are working. They are equipped, empowered, and intentional in the way in which they evangelise.

However, there are other churches and institutions that are inadequate in their world evangelisation efforts. They may be resistant to change. Sometimes their own traditions are restricting them, or they have lost the vision for this type of work. This results in the failure to allow at least a portion of their best leaders to be free to evangelise. They may have become inward-looking and isolationist.

What are some of the specific challenges that are facing such institutions and communities today?

2.1 Contextual and Cultural Issues

(a) Internal

There appears to be an unhelpful trend in parts of the Christian church where local congregations, denominational boards and leadership, and theological educators do not recognise their missionary calling and have forgotten the imperative of the Great Commission. This failure is the result of several factors.

Firstly, it is possible that the educating institution or church does not have a biblical understanding of the mission of the church. This is particularly true in the West. Many theological colleges and schools are reflecting more and more the secular culture around them. In their interest in being relevant to the needs of those around them, they are making the gospel irrelevant. For example, one disturbing trend is the inclusivism that marks much dialogue between Christians, Muslims, and Jews. A presupposition seems to be that these three monotheistic faiths all worship the same God and this worship, in whatever form it takes, is valid and acceptable. This negates the uniqueness of God's self-revelation in Christ, and must inevitably compromise the truth of the Christ's divinity, dilute the power of the Cross, and render suspect the need of all people for a saving encounter with Jesus Christ Saviour. When such an attitude or belief has infused an educating institution then world evangelisation becomes very difficult.

Secondly, if the leaders are not modelling what it means to be missional, then their students will not be motivated to evangelise. Students study very carefully the walk and witness of their teachers and mentors and learn both good and bad habits from them. A fundamental characteristic of being a Christian is the power of being a witness for Christ. Lack of leadership in this area creates complacency and the absence of an evangelistic ethos within the church of the educating institution. How can students be required to do something that their teachers are not doing?

A third factor is the lack of a comprehensive, integrated training programme that is missional at its core. The gospel needs to be the lens by which theological education takes place. Chris Wright directs us to the Lukan Great Commission (Luke 24:46-47) where, by implication, Jesus tells the disciples that the right way to understand the Old Testament is *messianically* and *missiologically*. The focus of the Old Testament is fundamentally the Messiah and his death and resurrection. Mission to the nations flows from this.[1] If the Bible is being studied, it needs to be studied from the perspective of the mission of Jesus. The church's handbook for mission is the Scriptures. What is the history of the church but the history of mission? Is not the *missio dei* at the core of how Christians are to be obedient? Should not humanity be seen as fallen and in need of a Saviour?

The fourth factor is that in the case of theological colleges and schools, while on the one hand imbibing secular values, on the other hand there is a tendency for them to be isolated from the realities of the world around them. It is possible for the faculty, students, and staff to live in an environment that is protected from the world as they breathe the rarefied air of theological learning and reflection. The obvious danger of such an environment is that it does little to prepare the student for the realities of Christian ministry. Nor does it prepare him or her to be proclaimers of the good news to the lost.

Rather than being isolated and separated from what is going on, theological colleges and schools need to be in constant communication with the local churches. They need, in fact, to see that they are partnering with them in the evangelistic task. The local church is the frontline of ministry. It is where the action is happening, and those involved in the ministry are best qualified to help an educating institution to prepare its students for world evangelisation. If this is not happening, the lack of communication will result in inadequate preparation of future leaders.

A fifth factor could be that the institution does not make sufficient use of missional criteria in the acceptance of new students into their programme or the hiring of faculty and staff. While there are diverse gifts within the body of Christ, those who have a missional and evangelistic orientation will bring a special and much-needed perspective to the school or training centre, that will work to prevent the institution simply perpetuating itself and maintaining the *status quo*. This maintenance approach may appear successful in the beginning as the institution survives on the basis of momentum cre-

ated when it was more missional, but it will eventually run out of energy and die.

(b) External

There are external factors that can also present challenges to effective theological education for world evangelisation.

The first comes from denominations themselves that have lost the fervour to evangelise. Some of the reasons can be inferred from what has already been written. It becomes a challenge for those in the denomination who want to be faithful and obedient, but find that their progress is hindered because of entrenched denominational beliefs and practices that are counter-intuitive to their evangelistic ambitions.

A second challenge is the control that certain accrediting agencies have over the educating institutions. Their requirements for certification or accreditation do not match the educational aspirations and aims of the institution. They can be in conflict because the accrediting agency is working with a different set of parameters and a different definition of what makes an educating institution effective. The result is a continuation of the same downward spiral towards mediocrity and irrelevance.

In areas where Christianity is less established, there are other challenges that can come from governments and societies that are overtly anti-Christian and persecute those who are trying to do gospel ministry. If non-Christian religious fundamentalism is present, open Christian theological education can be prohibited or suppressed, with grave consequences for those who do it.

Poverty can also be a factor that can challenge effective theological education for world evangelisation. Poverty can mean a lack of resources – the inability to have access to books and other teaching materials that would be helpful. The student's own time can be a factor since he or she is not available to study because of the need to work to support a family or even support themselves.

In our day, we are seeing massive movements of people who are leaving their ancestral homes for the urban centres of their various countries. Such movements have created a worldwide population of marginalised people who do not have access to education, employment, and health services. Concentrations of these people in the urban slums have created an environment that is rife with violence, disease, and death. They are in need of a holistic approach to the proclamation of the gospel, but sadly many Christian groups do not recognise their needs and plight. They remain a sea of unreached souls whose spiritual and physical well being has been ignored.

2.2 Conclusion

While there are many challenges that are facing Christian educators today, the mere fact that they are being addressed is a positive step forward. Institutions, churches and individuals do not accept change very quickly. However, the urgency of our present situation demands that these changes do occur as expeditiously as possible so that the whole world can hear the whole gospel.

B. WHAT ARE THE LEARNING OUTCOMES OF EFFECTIVE EDUCATION FOR WORLD EVANGELISATION?

What does effective education for world evangelisation try to achieve? What are the learning outcomes of such education programmes? What kind of faith communities and individuals does it want to produce?

As already explained this report does not deal specifically with the training of evangelists or missionaries but with education and training that would lead to greater commitment to world evangelisation in faith communities as a whole and in the members of such faith communities. Thus, its focus will be the general attitudes, character and spirituality of a community and of individuals who are committed to world evangelisation and who are involved either directly or indirectly. What will such faith communities look like? What will these communities be doing and what will be their attitudes and values regarding mission?

1. What kind of faith communities will effective education for evangelisation produce?

All faith communities – be they local churches, denominations, mission agencies, theological or Christian educational institutions, or training programmes – and their members should be able to know the gospel, live out the gospel, and tell the gospel to others.

All Christian educational and training programmes should actively demonstrate a commitment to a missional framework in theological education. This should especially be the case in formal theological education where mission is frequently an add-on to the school or training programme.

1.1 School Communities

A missional framework for theological education means that mission should form the framework of everything that happens in the school. Many react against a statement like this, and it requires further clarification. This does not mean that mission should be the focus or centrepiece of a training programme. God alone is and should be the centre. The ultimate purpose is to worship and glorify God. But if God is the centre, then God's mission and his purpose also comes into focus, and God's mission, the *missio Dei*, becomes the framework or background against which theological education should take place. Theological education should then develop leaders who will equip God's people for works of service (Ephesians 4:12). These works of service include mission. Furthermore, the works of service are so that the body of Christ may be built up. This body, the faith community, is called by God and sent into the world to participate in and carry out his mission. Thus, a God-centred theological education is by implication missional.

Essentially, the term missional refers to a way of missionary engagement that embraces all of life, and involves both active discipling as well as the conversion to Christ of all the personal, cultural, and social structures of life. According to Robert Banks, for theological education to

be missional means that it is wholly or partly field-based, and that involves some measure of doing what is being studied (life-engaging). It requires observant participation and not merely participant observation. Banks writes,

> "Theological education is a dimension of mission and has a vital missiological content; it is an aspect of the teaching ministry of the church involving specialised testimony to the kingdom. It fulfils this educational service of the faith by (i) forming character, abilities, and thought (ii) informing mind, praxis, and contemplation, and (iii) transforming values, people, and communities. ... Only by maintaining its close link with mission will it remain relevant to changing circumstances, and hold true to the missionary impulse that gave rise to the church and theology."[2]

1.2 The Church - Greater Commitment to World Evangelisation through a Missionary Lifestyle

The church as a missionary church is the agent of God's mission in the world and as such the "agent of spiritual and social transformation in its community."[3] According to Padilla the church that is missionary and practices integral mission has to be an integral church. Such a church has certain characteristics.[4] Effective theological education at all levels, formal and nonformal, within school and church settings, must strife to develop these characteristics in faith communities, and to inculcate a missionary mindset both within the community and in every Christian.

(a) Commitment to Jesus Christ as Lord of Everything and Everywhere

The missional church is committed to Jesus Christ as Lord of everything and everywhere. Padilla writes,

> "… the confession of Jesus Christ – the risen Christ as Lord is essentially a recognition of his sovereignty over the whole of human life and over the whole of creation … The integral church is one which recognises that all spheres of life are "mission fields" and looks for ways of asserting the sovereignty of *Jesus Christ in all of them.* "[5]

(b) Christian Discipleship

The missional church practices Christian discipleship as a missionary lifestyle to which the entire church as a faith community and every member have been called.

(c) Biblical Vision of the Church

The missional church has a vision of the church as the community that confesses Jesus Christ as Lord, and lives in the light of that confession in such a way that in it can be seen the inauguration of a new humanity. In living this confession, the church's witness must be incarnational. In the life, ministry, death, resurrection, and exaltation of Jesus Christ a new era has been inaugurated in salvation history. In this era the church has been called and given the mission to make disciples of all peoples. The church is empowered for this mission by the Holy Spirit and is therefore also a community of the Spirit. The Holy Spirit makes possible the existence of the church and the success of its mission.

(d) Use of Gifts and Ministries

The missional church recognises "the use of gifts and ministries as instruments that the Spirit of God uses to prepare the church and all its members to fulfil their vocation as God's co-workers in the world."[6] Gifts and ministries are the means used by the Spirit of God to equip the church as an agent of mission, an agent of change in society – change that reflects God's plan for human life and the whole of creation. This is how the Spirit empowers the church for its mission and witness.[7] The whole church with every member as an agent of integral mission, engaged in all areas of human life and creation, is the vision that theological education for world evangelisation should instil in all church leaders and church members. Every Christian, by the simple fact of being a disciple of Christ, shares in the commission to go into the world in the name of Jesus Christ as his witnesses, and to make disciples of all peoples. Some will do so directly as full-time missionaries and evangelists. Others will do so by living a missionary lifestyle and being witnesses wherever they are, in the market or workplace, at home, or at play. Others again will do so by being involved in supporting the intentional missionary activities of the church and full-time missionaries through prayer and giving.

2. What kind of persons will it form?

2.1 Know the gospel

Every Christian should know the basic message and contents of the gospel. They should be growing in this knowledge through regular Bible study and meditation on God's word. They should be able to explain and defend their faith and continue to grow both in their confidence in sharing Christ, and their ability to do so. Every Christian should have grasped the truth of God's desire for all nations and peoples to worship and glorify him. They should understand the biblical imperatives for mission: the amazing love of God for lost sinners, the imperative of the Great Commission, and the uniqueness of Christ in a pluralistic world. All these truths motivate every believer to be involved in mission and live a missionary lifestyle.

2.2 Live and do the gospel

In order to live out the gospel and to live a missionary lifestyle, Christians need to know how to integrate their faith with their daily lives and practice, and apply it to their contexts. A missionary lifestyle requires Christ-like character, holy living, personal integrity, servanthood, and compassion for other people. Effective education for world evangelisation should enable and facilitate continuous growth in these areas. It should facilitate self-awareness, develop a healthy self-concept and identity of being in Christ and created in the image of God. It should also enable Christians to identify and develop their God-given gifts and potential, so that they can be involved in the "works of service" and participate in God's mission wherever they are.

2.3 Tell the gospel

Every Christian is to be a disciple and witness of Jesus Christ. All of us are called to obey the Great Commission: to make disciples of all peoples. This does not imply that everyone must become a fulltime evangelist or missionary. Not everyone is called to that or has the gift of the evangelist, but everyone is called to be a witness to Jesus Christ, and to communicate the gospel message wherever they are. Every time and in every place where Christians interact or intersect with the unbelieving world and peoples they are to communicate the gospel in word and in deed. Every Christian should be involved in praying for, supporting, and giving to mission.

3. Christian leaders of faith communities

Christian leaders play a key role in developing a greater commitment to world evangelisation. Faith communities are influenced and shaped by their leaders. If leaders do not have this commitment, the community will not have it, or it will have to depend for this commitment on the small majority of committed individuals and volunteers who are involved in mission. The problem is that in such cases mission becomes just one more activity of the church, and must compete for attention and resources with other programmes, instead of being the focus and framework of what the church is doing, of being a missionary church. Thus, the leaders of faith communities, pastors of local churches, denominational leaders, mission leaders, heads of schools, teachers, and faculty should all demonstrate commitment to God's mission in their lives and ministry. They should demonstrate a commitment to and exhibit a missionary lifestyle. They should set an example and model this to their communities. Theological education for world mission should equip them with the necessary knowledge, attitudes, spirituality and skills to accomplish this. It should ensure that all their graduates enter their ministries with a passion and vision for world evangelisation and with the necessary competencies to lead their faith communities in this mission.

C. HOW CAN EFFECTIVE EDUCATION FOR WORLD EVANGELISATION ACCOMPLISH THIS?

1. Biblical and theological foundations

We will now identify biblical and theological foundations of training for world evangelisation in three respects.

1.1 Basis for Education and Training within the Faith Community

The basis for missions in the church is grounded in God the Father, who himself is the Missionary par excellence. From the beginning God sought out runaway humanity (Genesis 3), and in the fullness of time sent his Son to redeem a lost world. Jesus in turn sends his church: *"As the Father has sent me, so send I you"* (John 20:21). This is why the church's mission is in fact God's mission, or *missio Dei.* However, God enlists redeemed humanity to join Him in *missio Dei,* as fellow-workers in the task of reconciling a lost world to Himself (2 Corinthians 5:18-20). The faith community is called, therefore, to serve as witness

through the enabling power of the Holy Spirit (Acts 1:8). However, mission entails disciple-making — *"As you go, make disciples of all nations..."* (Matthew 28:19). The task of disciple-making underscores the educational basis of the commission given to the faith community. It is discipleship unto life transformation — a process of growth and development of the total person, spiritual, intellectual, volitional, and emotional – to the end that the disciple is made fit for life here and in the hereafter.

1.2 A Theology of Theological Education

A theology of theological education must be grounded in *missio Dei* and in a proper understanding of the church (this faith community), her purpose and mission in the world. This is important as we encounter what we might call "the changing faces of the church" today. The church is "called out" by God as the new humanity, whose purpose, *inter alia,* is to glorify God by participating with Him in the ministry of reconciliation, as mentioned already. The church has a missional purpose, which is enhanced through education, both of her leadership and of the generality of her membership.

A theology of theological education must be grounded in a proper understanding of the central role of the Holy Spirit and of the grace gifts (*charismata*) with which the enabling Holy Spirit endows every genuine member of this faith community as well as the cultivation of these gifts through training. It is the Holy Spirit who equips with gifts – both in terms of offices or leadership of the faith community (Ephesians 4:7-13), and in terms of individual endowments which enable those so endowed to function in the task of disciple-making (Romans 12; 1Corinthians 12). However, the gifts still have to be cultivated and developed through training (2 Timothy 1:6). Thus we see a justification for the training and equipping of both the church leadership and the members of the faith community.

1.3 The Implications and Challenges

The following conclusions are therefore in order:

- Those who educate others for ministry must target training in the grace gifts for *both* leadership and laity within the faith community. They must take seriously Harvie Conn's observation concerning the historical marginalisation of the laity. Conn noted that "this occurred when ordination began to shift from its biblical function as the church's affirmation of gifts of the Spirit to the institutionalised imprimatur of salaried status, ranks, authority."[8] This observation does not diminish in any way the place for providing specialised training for the leadership of the faith community. Instead it warns against neglecting, and failing to encourage and develop, the many grace gifts made available to the faith community by the enabling Holy Spirit.

- The end to which training must be directed is the promotion of the *missio Dei*, to which the church is called of God to participate. Unfortunately, mission has tended to be peripheral to theological education because it has equally been peripheral to the church, whereas mission should be at the very centre of the entire theological enterprise.[9] The traditional four-fold disciplines of Biblical Studies, Theology, Church History, and Practical Theology so prevalent in our institutions of training are challenged to discern their missiological and missional roles.[10] Specifically this involves both the call for specific missiological studies in our curriculum of training, as well as the intentional teaching of the four-fold disciplines from a missiological perspective.

- The purely academic pursuit of theology is a misdirection and a distortion of the purpose of equipping of the saints for ministry. We do well to heed Robert Ferris' call to move away from "theology-as-science," a legacy of the Enlightenment, to "theology-as-engagement."[11]

- The central unifier of theological education, or what makes it coherent, is not just *theologia*, understood as divine wisdom and the cognitive disposition towards the acquiring of the knowledge of divine things in all areas of life.[12] Neither is it just *missiologia*, which entails an understanding of the *missio Dei* to include work done across cultures, in pastoral, educational and diaconal settings, in scholarly pursuits and everything done in "taking captive diverse human thoughts so they will be obedient to Christ."[13] It is also "missional," which goes beyond mere academic discipline that is devoid of *active* discipling and converting cultural structures into Christ in a life-engaging mission.[14] All three must be held in a balance in our educational endeavours, in light of what God is doing today to transform the world.

2. The Model of Jesus

What methods and strategies would effectively equip people for world evangelisation? In teaching his disciples, what methods did Jesus use? What characteristics did he display? What principles did he espouse? Jesus serves as the best role model for all theological educators in educating Christians for evangelism and missions.

2.1 Jesus' Strategies and Methods of Teaching

Jesus taught in such a way that his disciples could replicate what he was doing and eventually become leaders and teachers of others. The following are some of the strategies used by Jesus.

(a) Concentration on a Small Group

Jesus taught the crowd, but He regularly taught the twelve in a small group setting. Sometimes He only took Peter, James, and John. He had very little time (three years), but He never seemed to think that teaching such a small group was a waste of time! Jesus concentrated on building up the twelve disciples. Jesus illustrated a fundamental principle of teaching: that other things being equal, the more concentrated the size of the group being taught, the greater the opportunity for effective instruction.[15] Learners feel

secure with each other. It encourages freedom to ask questions and interact. This method not only enhances students' participation and discussions, it also helps teachers know the students individually. Today's institutions often contain classes of several hundred. Even knowing the names of the students, let alone their life situations, becomes almost impossible.

(b) Life-to-Life Transference/Modelling

Jesus' approach to discipleship was life-oriented. He took the disciples with Him in the various circumstances of life that He encountered on a daily basis. The disciples walked with Jesus in the real world.[16]

Jesus did not just teach from mouth to ear but from heart-to-heart. His goal was not simply "getting the lessons across" but transforming students toward Christlikeness.[17] For this to happen, proximity and intimacy is necessary. Thus, Jesus stayed with his disciples. Robert Coleman comments: *"amazing as it may seem, all Jesus did to teach those men his way was to draw them close to himself. He was his own school and curriculum."*[18] Jesus used the principle of life-to-life transference. This required that He spend an enormous amount of time with His disciples. Jesus poured out His life into the lives of His disciples.

Learning occurs in structured situations, but more so in informal situations during normal everyday living. Most people learn more effectively when they both hear and see a particular truth applied in a real life-situation. The principle of life transference is based on the concept of "modelling."[19] Jesus taught and lived truth before His disciples. He demonstrated what He expected them to learn. Jesus did not ask anyone to do or be anything which He had not first demonstrated in His own life.[20]

Juan Carlos Ortiz stresses that discipleship is not a communication of knowledge, but a communication of life. In a discipleship relationship we do not teach the other person to know what we know but to become what we are. So we teach more by living than by talking.[21] The quality of life is caught, rather than taught.[22]

(c) Building a Community

Jesus brought the disciples together as a community. They shared the same money bag, used the same boat and ate from the same communion table! He built a community of learners, a team that fellowshipped and shared dreams together. Jesus did not encourage "competition," but rather "companionship" as fellow-followers of Christ. After the ascension of Christ, they stood firm together for the resurrected Lord. Learners need to belong to each other, so they can learn from each other. This is especially true as adult learners, for their vast life experiences comprise a huge resource for the community to which they belong.

Community life is crucial to our maturing process. As David Watson says: "Christianity is all about relationships: our relationship with God and our relationship with others."[23] Michael Wilkins emphasises that growth in our developing walk with Jesus will be, in part, proportional to our accountability to others.[24]

(d) Use of Stories and Illustrations

Jesus used many parables, drawing object lessons from life. He frequently combined them with his miracles. Indeed, many of his miracles may be considered acted parables. In the book of John, each miracle is followed by a discourse. For examples, after the feeding of the five thousands, the discourse was on "I am the Bread of Life" (John 5); after the healing of the blind, his teaching was on "I am the Light of the World" (John 9). Thus his teaching was interesting, memorable, and life-oriented. Using all teachable moments, He helped students visualise. When asked, "Who is the greatest in the kingdom of heaven?" He picked up a child (Matthew 18:1-9). His teaching was set in the context of the learners.

(e) Active Learning/Learning by Doing

Jesus engaged his learners with questions and actions. One time he asked, "Who do people say the Son of Man is?" and later He asked, "But what about you? Who do you say I am?" He would not give them a straight-forward answer; He engaged their minds. He also engaged them in action by sending them out two-by-two, by twelve and by seventy.

The disciples had to put into actual practice what they had seen and learned from their master. So Jesus sent them forth. He first gave them some briefing instructions on their mission (Mark 6:7-11; Matthew 10:5-42; Luke 9:1-6; Luke 10:1-16). When the disciples got back they reported to Jesus all that they had done and taught (Mark 6:30; Luke 9:10; 10:17).

Jesus trained the disciples to take over the tasks that he was doing. Their responsibilities grew as their maturity developed. He sent them out on their own, then gently correcting them, instructing them still more (e.g. Mark 9:17-29), until the time when he could leave them altogether.[25]

Learning by doing is the most effective way of learning. Accountable, supervised internship or field-education is often lacking in today's theological institutions. What is taught is not put into practice. Reading a motorcar's maintenance manual does not qualify a mechanic. In the same way, knowing just the Bible and theology does not qualify us as pastors, teachers, evangelists, or missionaries.

(f) A Holistic and Balanced Approach

Jesus used an integrated approach to teaching. He did not only focus on the lesson content but also on the disciples' character and conduct. He expected his disciples not just to understand but also to value and actually do what they were taught.[26] He was concerned with the development of the *head* (cognitive), the *heart* (affective), and the *hands* (skill) or the knowing, being and doing. His educational approach equipped the disciples in theological reflection, spiritual formation and ministry skills.

2.2 Jesus' Characteristics as Teacher

Effective education requires certain type of teachers. The kind of teachers we have in theological education will greatly affect the kind of training we provide and the kind of people we graduate. The teachers are the lifeblood of any training

institution.

Who was Jesus as teacher? What made him effective as a teacher?

(a) Jesus was a model of what he taught.

It is said that "what we are" speaks more loudly than "what we say." Lesson is more "caught from" than "taught by" a teacher. Jesus lived what He taught. What He taught flowed out of who He was. His words and actions reinforced each other.

Jesus intentionally modelled to his disciples all He wanted them to know, be, and do. People need concrete examples, both in private life and public ministry. The educator must not just teach the skills of evangelism in the classroom, but model them in the world. The teacher cannot just speak about compassion for the poor, or express a concern for social injustice, but be seen to be putting the words into concrete actions. Without concrete examples, learning is impaired.

(b) Jesus established relationship with his learners.

Jesus knew his learners and had a warm positive relationship with them. He was interested in their personal lives. Jesus was not just a teacher to them but also a mentor and a friend, helping them process their life and ministry experiences.

Another weakness in our training nowadays is the lack of proximity between the teacher and the students. Their contact time is confined to the classroom. We have already seen that the smaller the group the more effective the education is likely to be. One of the most encouraging trends in education today has been the development of the mentoring model. Mentoring is building relationships and investing time and energy in the transfer of values, skills, and attitudes.[27] Of course, this is time consuming and often time is a scarce commodity in the training institution. Schools must be encouraged to look carefully at issues such as class sizes and teaching load in order to maximise opportunities for the development of meaningful teacher/student relationships.

(c) Jesus was comfortable with people of all kinds.

Jesus was able to connect with a wide range of people – rich or poor, Jew or Gentile, male or female. He surrounded himself with people of all kinds. He knew how to relate with people of different race, language, or age bracket.

A teacher who can build bridges to all people will be the most effective. We need teachers who have rapport with learners of different backgrounds. This requires an extra degree of energy and commitment, but this is important if we want our students to have the ability to communicate to all kinds of people and be effective agents for world evangelisation.

(d) Jesus was a man on a mission.

Jesus knew His mission. He was focused on His mission and He fulfilled His mission. Knowing what He came to do gave Him power to teach with authority. He called people to follow Him and be committed to His mission.

We have a mission to perform. Jesus has commissioned us to *"go and make disciples of all nations teaching them to observe everything that I have com-*manded you..."* (Matthew 28:19). We are to stay focused and committed to this mission. We need teachers who are passionate about fulfilling the Great Commission.

(e) Jesus was prayerful.

Jesus was dependent on the Father for His work and teaching. He maintained connection with him through prayer. Prayer was an essential part of Jesus' life and ministry. His regular communion with the Father was His source of strength and power, enabling Him to overcome temptation and fulfil the will of the Father.

We could only be effective in our task as we depend on God and appropriate His power for ministry. If Jesus needed time alone in prayer, how much more do we? We need to spend more time being with the Lord rather than being too preoccupied with doing things for Him. Focusing on productivity to the neglect of prayer and meditation is one reason why our training programmes may be ineffective.

2.3 The Role of the Holy Spirit in Teaching

Teaching is a spiritual task, involving spiritual truths to meet spiritual needs. This requires spiritual power. The Holy Spirit is the source of this power.

The Bible emphasises the role of the Holy Spirit as teacher. It is only through the Holy Spirit that a person can receive spiritual truth (1 Corinthians 2:12, 14). Without the illuminating power of the Holy Spirit the word of God will not be able to penetrate and transform the human heart.

As teachers we must acknowledge the help of the Holy Spirit who stands right beside us, teaching and encouraging us. "The Holy spirit works in the learning process by helping teachers understand the content, the learner and the appropriate methods. Most importantly, the Spirit helps the teacher to walk a Christ-like life."[28]

Appropriate methods and strategies are important to facilitate effective education for evangelisation. However, Daryl Eldridge reminds us that "the success of the teaching ministry of the church is not dependent upon efficient organisation, new programmes, modern teaching methods, or the latest technology. The power of the teaching ministry is dependent upon our faithful obedience to the teaching of the Holy Spirit."[29]

3. Principles and strategies for effective education

Our Issue Group discussed the following questions:

- What are principles and strategies for developing greater commitment to world evangelisation?
- What are the normative principles for educational strategies which will lead to a greater commitment to world evangelisation by churches, theological institutions of learning, other training programmes, Christian organisations and individual Christians?
- What are principles and strategies for building faith communities for the task of world evangelisation?

In other words, what are the key principles and strategies that are useful for evangelisation training programmes at all levels in order to increase the ability and motivation of faith communities for the task of world evangelisation?

This discussion yielded input of three main types.

3.1 *Strategic Issues That Must be Addressed in a Training Programme*

(a) Church-Institutional Relationships

Questions need to be asked regarding the nature of the relationship between the local church and the training institution, whether it is church or school-based. These questions should include, but not be limited to, the nature of financial support and the degree to which both serve the other. It would be good if this relationship could be governed by a solid understanding of the most current thinking regarding strategic partnerships.

(b) Committed Staff

A training institution with a commitment to mission will have on its staff those who share this same commitment. We have already acknowledged that not all are gifted evangelists, but the staff, both teaching and administrative, ought to be men and women themselves committed to the gospel of Jesus Christ. The more convergence there is between the various academic and professional skills a person brings to the school and their commitment to world evangelisation, then the more effective a training programme will be in building faith communities for world evangelisation.

(c) Different Levels of Training

World evangelisation is the responsibility of every Christian no matter their age or location in life. Therefore, evangelisation training should be available at multiple levels that fit the age, gifting, experience, and professions represented by the students. Training often overlooks certain groups of people or special needs of people, for example, children, people with disabilities, and oral learners. Particular emphasis on training these groups or people who will work with them should be considered. Training should then be contextualised to fit these factors as closely as possible, in order to ensure relevance of the training offered. Also, at some of the higher levels, a reasonable principle of selectivity should be exercised in order to ensure that advanced training efforts are offered to those who are both personally gifted and interested and whose faith communities have recognised their effectiveness as an evangeliser.

(d) The Role of Mission in Theology

In every context, the prior question of the role of mission in theology must be addressed. Consensus must be found as to whether world evangelisation is the ultimate purpose of the faith community, or whether world evangelisation is only one among many manifestations of a life maturing in Christ, but which is ultimately lived for the more ultimate purpose of giving glory to God. This question will have great significance not just for the place that evangelisation finds in the overall curriculum of the training programme, but also the relationship between trainers particular to this programme and other theologians.

(e) Economics of Training

The economic implications of evangelisation should not be overlooked. The most effective evangelisation training programmes have taken into account that effective ministry costs money and students have to find some means of support both while they are receiving training, and once their time of training has ended. Therefore, creative means should be employed to offer cost-effective training as well as consideration of vocational or employment options during and after the programme.

3.2 Overarching Principles for Evangelisation Training Effectiveness:

(a) Balance between Theory and Practice

Good training includes elements of both theory and practice, and is able to keep both of these elements in tension. A programme too theoretical may train effective thinkers on evangelisation, but is unlikely to equip students with the skills to actually engage in the task. Similarly, a programme based too strongly in practice may not enable students to become reflective practitioners or to function as effective evangelisers in any context other than the one in which they were trained. Furthermore, the decision of how to appropriately strike this balance should be significantly informed by the issue of different levels of training (see paragraph 3.1 (c) above), student and cultural learning styles, and other contextual factors such as the prevalence of post-modern or modern perspectives, or the realities of students' economic situations.

(b) Experiential Learning

Related to the practical component of training addressed above, students also need the opportunity to put their new skills, attitudes, and understandings to work in real-life settings. They then need the opportunity for mature theological reflection upon these experiences, guided by a teacher or mentor. The most effective experiential learning takes place when an appropriate level of oversight and support is offered and the experience is reasonably similar to the context in which the student is expected to eventually put their new learning into practice.

Good balance needs to also be found between learning alone or one-on-one, and group learning opportunities. Certainly, students need time to acquire knowledge and reflect for themselves how it can best be applied in their own lives. However, students also need the opportunity to benefit from the co-learning experience, allowing their peers and mentors to refine their thinking and choices through constructive criticism.

(c) Incarnational and Participatory Learning

One of the challenges of education for evangelisation is helping students understand the relationships between what they are learning and their everyday lives. One of the best ways to do this is by taking an incarnational approach to ministry, that is, one where the instructor tries as much as possible to become familiar with the lives of the people they are teaching, and to share as much of his/her life with their students as is feasible. The primary purpose of such an engagement, whether it is termed mentoring or modelling, is to demonstrate how what is being taught can be lived out on a moment by moment basis. Along with this comes the reciprocal need to allow students' prior and current experiences to affect the content and style of teaching, even offering students the opportunity to share their relevant experiences or unique understandings with others. Following Jesus' model, however, training at this depth cannot be offered to everyone – rather this should be a trainer's investment in only a few – around twelve at a time at the most, and often fewer depending on the level of investment being offered.

(d) Disciplinary Balance

Good evangelisation education is always interdisciplinary, often drawing on theology, cross- cultural studies, communication theory, etc.

(e) Dynamic and Creative

Flexibility in the training task is key, as is openness to new approaches, models and forms of training. Good trainers are able to change their plans and lecture materials on the spot, and able to identify and make use of serendipitous circumstances. Furthermore, part of excellence in training is the ability to change course content and approaches over time to fit the needs of different audiences based on contextual factors and individual student variation.

(f) Evaluative, outcome-focused process

By setting and working towards outcomes in training, instructors can have ways to easily identify the value of different approaches and content. Experience also tends to show that training that regularly seeks feedback from students and then makes appropriate changes based on that input is more effective than training that does not.

3.3 Four Steps for Fostering Commitment to World Evangelisation

These insights are probably more relevant to a discussion of effective content, but have been organised according to the model proposed for encouraging the involvement of faith communities in the task of world evangelisation both locally and globally. Obviously the delivery and format of this content would be organised and adjusted according to the issues and principles identified above.

(a) Exposure to Biblical Mandate (in the context of the whole counsel of God)

Students must be exposed to the various biblical and theological themes that undergird and inform evangelisation. Although this will ideally take place in the context of a larger discipling process, the themes that our group particularly identified as crucially important are:

- Vision of God for Humanity
- Vision of God for the Church
- Vision of God for the World
- Holistic understanding of the gospel – especially its spiritual and social dimensions

(b) Learn and Become Skilled in Methods and Strategy

Students need to acquire skills and understandings for the actual task of evangelisation, including:

- Skill of communication – knowing what to communicate and how to do it
- Skill of confrontation – both other people and spiritual powers
- Skill of contextualisation – being able to explain the gospel in different cultural contexts
- Networking and partnerships – how to strategically work with others towards the task of world evangelisation
- Health concerns – part of a holistic gospel, both for self and others

All of these things need to be delivered in a way that is informed by the missiological desideratum

(c) Experience the Need for Salvation

More than understanding the theological imperative, this step has to do with experiencing the spiritual and physical neediness of people for the gospel. It will include such content as:

- An engagement with the local and global context – understanding the needs of the world
- Partnering with the local church

(d) Be Given, or Learn to Recognise Opportunities for Evangelisation

This component is about getting people to take concrete steps and seize upon their opportunities. It might include:

- Mentoring
- Short term missions opportunities

4. Learning content/areas

Organisations such as commercial companies, government bodies, and peak bodies make commitments to personnel and set aside financial resources for training and development. Through this commitment they acknowledge that people are their best assets, that training gives them the competitive edge and that tangible benefits are achieved.[30]

National military forces spend millions of dollars on training their armed personnel in preparation for battle. Armies need to be ready for front-line action when required. They spend time in the classroom in addition to spending many hours in mock battle conditions and on practice ranges/fields.

A similar attitude and commitment to educating and equipping the Christian community for world evangelisation is required. God desires the people of God to be equipped with the required knowledge, skills, and attitudes that will enhance the plans and purposes He has for the world. Training at various levels (church-based, non-formal and formal) is vital. Strategic planning must incorporate a training dimension.

In addition to the principles and strategies, the content must be considered and not ignored. The content of training programmes must be evaluated. If the content is not applicable or relevant, then the programme will not enable learners to use the material in the field after the training programme.

Training programmes must be continuously evaluated to reflect the context. As the context changes so should the training. Missiological and Christian educators must have the capacity to reflect and evaluate for this to occur. How flexible is an educational system to adapt to changing times?

The context for today's world has shifted from Christendom to the post-Christendom era and from a modern era to post-modernity. The characteristics of this age have to be considered. If education is going to be effective for world evangelisation, the pedagogical methodology of the nature of training and its associated curricula should be preparing workers to be competent to operate in a pluralistic environment.[31]

The world context is crying out for missiological reflective practitioners, a term coined by Bill Taylor from WEA, even more so post-9/11 September.[32] Missiology is not determined by human events but is shaped and informed by them. This discipline can help in the interpretation of events and provides guidance to the missional church. We need to avoid the dangers of oversimplifying the complex assignment which has been given to us. Too often serious missiological reflection has been hampered by an overemphasis on the pragmatic, and by reductionist thinking. Therefore, there needs to be the releasing of **reflective practitioners** within the global body (self-missiologising, in regards to the message and the method/medium, and self-evaluating).

4.1 Core Learning Areas

Neither curriculum content nor detailed descriptions of courses can be discussed here. Broad areas of learning that should be addressed in effective education programmes for world evangelisation will be discussed. The nature of the audience will determine content. Two groups should be targeted.

Firstly, there are those that will be training to be short-term or long-term cross-cultural evangelists, either within their own country or in another country. Local evangelists could be included in this group. This group would be in the minority within the Christian community. A missiological oriented theological framework would prepare such workers. Some of the significant areas for understanding the cultural encounter that occurs include:

i. Cross-cultural communication

ii. The process of contextualisation and associated skills: Contextualisation is a vital component in the communication process for the orator as the message and methods are influenced by the context.[33] If the receptors can understand the message and the cultural distance is reduced or minimalised, the acceptance of the message is enhanced. Bruce Nicholls writes that *"contextualisation is a dynamic process of the church's reflection on the interaction of the text as word of God and the context as a specific human situation in obedience to Christ and His mission in the world."*[34] Dean Gilliland adds that the process is guided by the Holy Spirit and all elements must be brought under the Lordship of Christ. It has been applied to a number of areas of church life such as church leadership structure, theology, theological education, the gospel presentation/evangelistic message, Bible translation, missiology and music and art.[35] Much has been written in the past 20 years on contextualisation, its functions, the reasons for its necessity and its value.[36] The Biblical foundation is seen in God's dealings with Israel, Jesus and His mission and the early church's reaction to the expansion of the gospel into the Roman Empire is also well documented.[37]

iii. Holistic understanding of mission

iv. Theology of religion

v. Dialogue

vi. Cultural perspectives

vii. Religious worldviews

viii. The process of building strong cross-cultural relationships

Secondly, there are those who remain at home within the church and who would fall within the category of sender. These people use their resources and skills to support the world evangelisation tasks and activities at home and abroad. Most senders would be primarily equipped through their local church and a para-church organisation rather than in a formal theological environment. For this group the learning would not have the same intensity and depth as for those being "goers."

The variations of courses entitled *"Perspectives on the World Christian Movement"* provide a potential foundation for this group.

4.2 New Challenges and Issues

A number of challenges and issues arise in responding to these two groups.

(a) Missiology and Course Content/Curriculum

The question then arises whether missiology should be the dominant framework by which all theological education is based.[38] The debate has only increased in intensity over the last decade.

T. Steffen asks the question "Which Discipline is the Fairest of Them All?"[39] He claims that missiology is multi-disciplinary in nature and holistic. It integrates history, theology, the social sciences, and mission strategy.

The challenge in this area impacts more on the theological colleges, particularly in the western world, many of which are focused on church maintenance rather than church expansion. This means that the emphasis is more on pastoral care and leadership rather than missional preparation. Too often denominations service their own needs rather than carry a kingdom perspective. The curricula reflect this emphasis. Missions and evangelism are relegated to elective status in general pastor training, and mission training is often confined to optional annual mission trips.

(b) Contextualisation and Training

The challenge of world evangelisation has been well documented, especially in the concepts and principles of unreached people groups and the 10/40 Window. The Muslim, Hindu, and Buddhist blocs pose stretching and difficult challenges for the western missionary force.

Much research continues to be done into why progress has been difficult and slow. One of the primary causes is the fact that Christianity was seen to be a foreign religion. Eminent Hindu, Muslim, and Buddhist leaders have often reinforced this belief publicly and through various media. The message was origi-nally delivered by western missionaries, who were often not culturally sensitive and some times driven by inappropriate motives. The original planting did not show respect for the traditional cultural and religious contexts. The western style architecture of the churches planted was foreign and so different from traditional architecture.

Even in today's pluralistic, post-modern Western cultures Christianity is increasingly perceived to be alien to the culture and out of touch with an evolving society. The traditional denominations are struggling to be seen as culturally relevant as the empire of Christendom collapses. This is evident in Australia, for example. Those people attending churches on a regular basis are declining. An increasing number of congregations are being closed due to insufficient numbers and for not being financially viable. Regular church attendees are predominantly the aging Baby Builders and Boomers. The younger generations are tending to avoid the church. There is a growth of interest in non-Christian religions and new kinds of spirituality, while secularism continues to win many adherents. The number of those in the five-yearly Australian Census claiming to be Christian is declining. The percentage is now around 60%. The spread of globalisation has led to an increase in what has been termed "tribalisation," or the creation of many sub-cultural groups, many of which are not connected to each other. In many Western countries today the Christian community is just one other tribe, another sub-cultural group.

Formal education institutions, in both the western world and the two-thirds world must address the perception of the foreignness of Christianity and provide ways for trainees to overcome this perception for education to be effective for world evangelisation. This can be achieved through courses (macro-level) and/or individual subjects/modules (micro-level). Future workers must understand the causes and results of this perception and be equipped to respond proactively and in a manner that expresses culturally sensitive and relevant Christianity.

Therefore the focus of such training must be missional and contextual. The fundamental need is to prepare workers with the capacity and skills to be able to be effective in their particular context. As these contexts are so varied, we need to be developing potential gospel ambassadors into missiological reflective practitioners.

4.3 Conclusion

For effective education for world evangelisation to occur, particularly within formal institutions, a greater emphasis on missiology, applied anthropology and contextualisation must be apparent in training. If not, the consequences are potentially great for global Christianity and its mission. The perception of the foreignness of Christianity will only continue as God's people become more isolated and removed from the societies in which they are living.

D. EXAMPLES OF EFFECTIVE EDUCATION FOR WORLD EVANGELISATION

In this section we will present reports from various members of the Issue Group, which will describe, from their own context, different models of effective education for evangelisation. We have sought to present a variety of models, formal and non-formal, institutional and communal.

1. Discipleship training for unlikely heroes – Operation Mobilization, Adelaide, Australia

Para-church organisations can provide a model for missional focused discipleship training programmes. Discipleship Training for Unlikely Heroes (nicknamed D2) has been developed and operated by Operation Mobilization in Adelaide, Australia and several other centres in Oceania. Dr Yi-An Neoh, the State Director, seeking a way to connect with young people, established the first course in July 2001. D2 aims to be a catalyst for spiritual growth in the lives of youth aged 15–25.

The objectives are:
1. To initiate radical spiritual growth in the lives of youth
2. To mobilise youth for service within and outside of their church
3. To help youth recognise their responsibility to be Global Christians
4. To encourage youth to use the gifts God has given them
5. To develop youth physically as well as spiritually

Two programmes are held each year. Each programme is launched with a

"Bootcamp" with a speaker and physical training, and followed by 8 or 9 weekly 4-hour community times between 6am and 10am on a Saturday morning. The standard morning routine involves physical training, breakfast, spiritual disciplines, country focus, prayer in pairs for the country and personal issues, and two hours of teaching by pastors, Christian workers, and Bible College lecturers. Following D2 is an optional café meeting, which allows people to relax and catch up. Also there are leadership training days on any public holidays that fall during the course and a dinner at the conclusion.

Within each programme there are three streams or courses offered. Some students later repeat courses as a way to participate. The courses are oriented around the ethos and the values of Operation Mobilization in regards to discipleship and mobilising for mission. There are three packaged courses that are modified each time they are delivered.

1. The first course is a basic discipleship programme that endeavours to cover the basics of spiritual disciplines, biblical approaches to issues of life like finance and fostering a heart for the nations.

2. The second course is entitled "The Next Challenge: Exploring God's World." This is a no-holds barred eight-week missions course that explores the biblical, historical, strategic, cultural, and personal aspects of cross-cultural mission.

3. The third course is entitled "Outside the Box: Reaching the World Next Door." This is an evangelism course which incorporates Wycliffe's 4-week applied anthropological course "Operation Encounter".

The first strength of the programme is its dual emphasis on both the local and global dimensions of mission.

The second strength is the balance between teaching and cognitive input, and practical experience. Along with weekly Scripture memorisation, there is the encouragement to participate in evangelistic activities outside the hours of the programme. Fundraising activities help those from the group fund short-term mission trips.

Another strength is the desire to work in partnership. Teams from the programme visit the local churches of the participants. The relationship between the organising group and the pastors of these churches is further fostered through a number of activities, functions, and visits.

There have been over 300 participants in the three years the programme has run. At least three people are serving with mission agencies as a result. Over 20 have taken part on a short-term trip or attended an OM MAP programme in Sydney. Several churches are being transformed by the impact of the missional focus developed in D2, particularly amongst the youth.

For more information consult *www.D2.om.org*.

2. Victory Leadership Institute

Victory Christian Fellowship (VCF) began in the Philippines in 1984 as a ministry primarily geared to evangelising university students and planting churches on or near university campuses. Since its beginnings the Victory movement in the Philippines currently has 44 churches with some 25,000 members. In addition, the VCF movement has sent out university-based church planting teams to 14 nations spread throughout Southeast Asia and the world.

The training arm of the movement, Victory Leadership Institute (VLI), began in June of 1993. The VLI motto is "Making Disciples, Training Leaders, Planting Churches." This missional motto is at the heart of all that VLI teachers seek to accomplish in each VLI class. The leaders of VLI resolutely believe that God has called them to make disciples and followers of Jesus, not just converts. It will be these disciples who, when properly trained and equipped, will take the gospel into the ends of the earth and enhance his Kingdom by planting churches. Furthermore, VLI's approach to teaching is from the local church context. The programmes are designed to be practical and readily applicable in the local church. Most of the illustrations, problems, and cases that are used in the classroom are from actual pastoring and church planting experiences. The interaction and dynamics of the school is such that it is really an extension of the local church.

VLI has a two-tiered approach to training: church members and church planting pastors and missionaries. All church members receive two years of training, attending one three-hour class session each week throughout the year, for a total of 39 weeks each year. Year one follows the emphasis of Ephesians 4:12: equipping church members for the work of ministry. During this year they receive teaching on discipleship, evangelism, spiritual gifts, the life of faith, as well as theology and the Bible. Year two emphasises leadership training, with continuing courses on discipleship, theology, and the Bible. Also covered during this second year are courses on world missions, church history, and worldview. The end goal of these two years is that these church members will be able to competently lead cell groups and other ministries related to the local church. VLI has trained approximately 6,500 VCF church members using this curriculum.

After completing the above two-year sequence, those VCF church members who exhibit evidence of a calling to church planting — either in the Philippines or abroad — are selected to attend an intensive one-year full-time study programme in VLI's School of World Missions. These third-year VLI students must be university graduates, have the recommendation of their local VCF pastor and be capable of doing graduate-level course work. The School of World Missions programme consists of two 18-week semesters offering 15 course units per semester. These courses are specifically geared to equipping these future VCF church planters in the theoretical and practical "how to" of evangelising, discipling, and planting churches, especially in multi-cultural and cross-cultural contexts. The curriculum consists of courses in World

Missions, Bible Interpretation, Cultural Anthropology, Biblical Theology of Missions, Missionary Spirituality, Contextualisation, Urban Ministry, Cross-Cultural Evangelism, and Church Planting. Interspersed within many of these courses are significant field work components, as well as practical church experiences: leading weekly cell group meetings, significant ministry involvement in Sunday ministry opportunities, and three hours of campus ministry each week. Furthermore, each student must take part in a three-week cross-cultural ministry internship. All of these third year courses are credited by Asian Theological Seminary (ATS) and most VLI third-year graduates receive graduate diplomas from ATS as well. VLI has given this advanced ministry training to approximately 400 VCF church planting pastors and missionaries.

3. Diploma in theological education programme (DTE) at the Hindustan Bible Institute and College (HBI), Chennai, India

3.1 Brief Background and History of HBI

Hindustan Bible Institute and College (HBI) located in the city of Chennai, India, came into existence in the context of nationalisation. It was established in 1952 with a vision to "Train one Indian to reach another Indian." This vision was born out of the conviction that in the changing political climate it would become exceedingly difficult for "missionaries" to find open doors in the sub-continent leading to the need to train Indian leadership for the mission of the church in India.

HBI, however, has not succumbed to the pressure to remain traditional in its outlook and approach to theological education. Consistent evaluation and reflection on the nature of theological education has prompted the leadership to experiment with different approaches and methods in order to produce effective leaders for the church and her mission in the Indian context. This case study is about one such attempt to make theological education more accessible and meaningful to a particular group of young people.

3.2 The DTE Programme

The purpose of the Diploma in Theological Education programme is to train emerging young leaders for the church in their various walks of life. The programme is designed, over the period of a year, to provide foundational theological training alongside equipping in skills of evangelism and discipleship.

(a) The Rationale for the Experiment

In 1999, an experiment to make this programme more effective was implemented. Initially, this programme was set up to be a one-year residential programme, with the students attending regular class hours like the other seminary students. It quickly became clear however that this approach was not fulfilling the purpose of the programme. To remain mission-focused and society-centred it was imperative that the approach and methodology had to undergo a radical change.

(b) The Experiment Itself

The first step was to clearly define the target group. Clearly, if this programme was to provide training for young emerging leaders for the church in its mission in society, the class had to consist of individuals who were not considering the traditional ministry callings as their vocation. Rather, the focus had to be on young Christians who were called to be "salt" and "light" in the "marketplace." Such a focus obviously meant that the whole programme needed radical restructuring. The approach had to be one that moved away from a traditional understanding of theological education as it applied to the training of clergy and full time missionaries.

Second, a new approach obviously required a new methodology, which laid equal emphasis on reflection and practice. The focus had to be on training the participants as they went about their normal, everyday life. More attention had to be given to reflection in the midst of engagement, as well as mentoring.

(c) The Implementation

Applications were invited from young believers who had been admitted into Madras University and other affiliated undergraduate colleges in the city. Those admitted into the DTE programme could avail themselves of the hostel facilities on the HBI campus while at the same time pursuing their course of secular study in the university. Such an arrangement would also enable rich interaction with those being trained for "full-time" ministry. Three evenings a week were devoted to "classes" during which time they engaged in critical reflection on issues concerning faith and witness in their univer-

sity context. During the course of study, the small group of 10 or 12 students was under the mentorship and close guidance of the dean of the programme. This provided the avenue for significant input into their lives.

Upon completing the DTE programme the students had the option of staying on and enrolling in a Master of Biblical Studies, a two-year programme geared towards equipping lay people in the city of Madras. This degree would be awarded once they passed their undergraduate programme in the university.

3.3 Some Key Features

a. *Praxis driven* – The DTE programme forced the leadership of HBI to endeavour to seek a right balance between theory and practice. Since the aim was to train individuals who would be effective in their witness and engagement in the Indian context, it was important that this balance be maintained.

b. *Mission driven* – A clear mission focus, where engaging their context was a significant part of the training was a distinct move away from the regular residential programmes where training takes place in isolation.

c. *Mentor driven* – The role of the teacher/mentor reaches its pinnacle in this process. Discipling and modelling takes on greater importance in this method, where the ministry and lifestyle of the teacher/mentor are closely watched and scrutinised.

d. *Student driven* – The learner becomes the central figure in this process. Spiritual formation, character development, skill enhancement and knowledge building all take place with the learners' needs and context in mind.

4. The Anglican presence in Honduras: 1862 to present

4.1 Historical Background

During the administration of President José Santos Guardiola in 1862, the United Kingdom offered Honduras several small islands some thirty to fifty kilometres off the north coast of the Central American republic. One of the requirements in the deed of gift was that Honduras would need to allow the "Protestant Religion" amongst the inhabitants of the islands. The settlers there were mostly descendents of English corsairs who had taken refuge in the islands in the previous century to avoid capture. They spoke English and were either Methodists or Anglicans. Up to that time, Honduran citizens were required by law to be Roman Catholic.

In the following decades, Anglican Church work was limited to English-speaking chaplaincies primarily in the banana growing areas of the country. English and American employees would worship in churches that were built by the fruit companies for their benefit. There was no consideration of doing any missionary work or evangelistic outreach to the Spanish-speaking inhabitants.

The Anglican Churches in the country remained under the jurisdiction of the Church of England until 1956 when they became part of the Episcopal Church in the United States. In 1967, Honduras was one of five Central American districts and in 1975 became a diocese in its own right that elected its first Bishop in 1977.

There were only a handful of congregations that were all English-speaking.

4.2 Initiation of Work in Spanish

In 1974, the Rev. James H. Douglass, who was serving as the Vicar of St. John the Baptist Church in Puerto Cortés, Honduras, was approached by some residents of a small village twenty kilometres to the west of the port city. They wanted a "Misa en español" – a Mass in Spanish and were hoping that the Rev. Douglass could help them.

He initiated services there and shortly afterwards Hurricane Fifi hit the western part of Honduras and killed nearly 10,000 people. During the rescue and relief efforts afterwards, the Episcopal Church was particularly involved, acting as a conduit for food, clothing and other supplies, and building houses for those who had lost their homes. The Rev. Douglass increased the number of congregations on the north coast to seven.

At the same time, the new Bishop of Honduras, Hugo Pina, began to establish small congregations in rural areas around the city of San Pedro Sula. Similar work began in other parts of the country. There was an acute shortage of ordained clergy, so Bishop Pina began to ordain former Roman Catholic seminarians and priests to fill the void.

The model for "evangelisation" during this period was based on the premise that since they were working in a primarily Roman Catholic culture, the worship style, appearance, and approach to ministry should parallel that of the Roman Catholic Church. A former Nicaraguan Roman Catholic seminarian, who had been ordained in the Episcopal Church, actually published a brochure that stated, "There is no difference between the Episcopal Church and the Roman Catholic Church."

This model was flawed and while the church actually continued to grow, the retention rate of members was limited and the percentage of genuine conversions was low.

4.3 Missionary Intervention

In 1981, the first missionaries of the South American Missionary Society (SAMS) of the Episcopal Church arrived in the country at the invitation of Bishop Pina. SAMS is an evangelical missionary society in the Anglican tradition that has had a long history of missionary work in Latin America.

Over the years the SAMS missionaries had a profound impact on the country. Instead of imitating the Roman Catholic Church, the missionaries were active leading people to a saving relationship in Jesus Christ. Small group Bible studies were begun. Missionaries were given the opportunity to preach in Sunday worship, and one-on-one witnessing and sharing of the gospel took place.

The missionaries had a strong impact on one young Honduran of West Indian descent, who became a strong, committed Christian as a result. This young man was eventually elected the first Honduran Bishop of the Diocese of Honduras in 2001. The SAMS missionaries introduced Evangelism Explosion into the Episcopal Church and this evangelistic method bore much fruit.

They also utilised a church planting strategy that had been developed by the Christian and Missionary Alliance Church in South America called "Encounter with God." This resulted in the founding of a congregation in the capital city that served as a model for other church planting activity in the country. The strategy is heavily dependent on campaign evangelism, personal evangelism, discipleship and leadership development.

The church continued to grow, but many of the new congregations were nothing more than "sacramental stations", where baptisms, confirmations, burials, and the Eucharist took place.

In 1994, the second Bishop of Honduras, Leo Frade, placed a SAMS missionary in charge of developing a national evangelistic strategy. This missionary formed an Evangelism Commission and trained them in the work of evangelism.

Over the next three years the Commission alternated between offering regional evangelism workshops with open air campaigns in villages and provincial capitals around the country. The training workshops had a strong practical component, for the participants were sent out to do door-to-door evangelism — a methodology that worked well in rural areas especially. The open air events were large events with music and evangelistic sermons. They were held in the main squares of the towns or, in some cases, in the middle of the road. Preaching events also took place in local Episcopal Churches.

A national training event was held as the focus of the annual Diocesan Convention (Synod), so that the leaders of all the parishes – lay and clergy both – could be trained in evangelism. This evangelism training complemented the theological education programmeme in the Diocese, which by the end of the 1990's had abandoned the previous curriculum and was teaching more biblically orthodox courses. The number of Honduran pastors increased during this time, most of which were charged with the responsibility of founding new churches in addition to serving existing congregations. Even with all of this evangelistic activity, there still remained an element within the Diocese that was resistant to evangelisation. This group insisted on maintaining its catholic identity and felt that evangelism was not appropriate for the Episcopal Church; that the strength of the Episcopal Church was its ability to differentiate itself from the scores of evangelical and Pentecostal churches that were being founded all over the country.

However, when the Rev. Lloyd Allen was elected Bishop in 2001, he immediately encouraged the continuing work of evangelism and evangelism training. While maintaining the Episcopal Church's denominational distinctiveness, he has gradually moved the Diocese into a much stronger evangelical position. In 1998, the Episcopal Church in Honduras had 52 congregations with about 17,000 baptised members.

By 2004, the number of congregations had grown to over 150. There are forty-seven clergy in the Diocese and over 30,000 baptised members. Bishop Allen credits the evangelistic ministry of the clergy and Diocese with this growth. Alpha, Evangelism Explosion, and the Cursillo movement have been very effective tools. Experiencing God is used for both evangelistic and discipling purposes. Youth evangelism is also taking place through a ministry called "Happening."

A missional ethos is beginning to permeate the Diocese and one former SAMS missionary is actually training Hondurans for overseas missionary service. There are still a number of obstacles and some of the earlier tensions have not been resolved, but the Diocese is moving forward and serving as a model for ministry throughout Central America and the Caribbean.

5. Mission as the integrating focus at Tyndale Seminary

Since 1996, Tyndale Seminary in Toronto has intentionally organised its programmes around a missional paradigm of education. This approach affirms that the Triune God is, by nature, a missionary God who calls, equips, and sends his people to participate in God's mission to the world as witnesses to Christ in the power of the Spirit. The church is, by nature, a missionary people who are called to engage their various contexts, through word and deed, as representatives of the Kingdom of God. Given this understanding, we assume that theological education should be concerned, first and foremost, with holistic formation for holistic mission that engages the world.

Our first step toward embracing a missional focus began in 1996 with the introduction of an experimental stream within the Master of Theological Studies degree known as the M.T.S. Modular Program. It is aimed at working laypeople seeking to integrate their faith with their work and everyday life, rather than those preparing for professional ministry. This is a cohort programme completed in three years. Students take classes one night per week, while retaining their jobs. The curriculum offers one course at a time, in six-week intensive blocks. Spiritual formation and mentoring experiences are balanced with classical theological disciplines. Courses in biblical, theological, and historical studies are taught with an emphasis on personal and communal engagement with the world, alongside courses whose subject matter naturally turns students outward toward the world (for example, on work and vocation, ethics, apologetics, mission, and evangelism). The programme offers a cohesive, integrative experience that equips lay leaders to engage the world — their workplaces, neighbourhoods and communities — for Christ.

Building upon the insights gained in the M.T.S. Modular Program, a comprehensive curriculum revision for the remaining degree programmes was undertaken during 1999-2001. In this revision

process, we began by developing missionally-based, outcomes-oriented competencies for each degree programme and for each major within each degree (for example, a major in Christian Education within the M.Div. degree). The new curriculum introduced three new courses required for all students: "Gospel, Church and Culture," "Spiritual Formation" and "Leadership Development." These "signature courses" present key themes in the missional paradigm that informs the whole curriculum, and fosters faithful and creative ways of forming individuals and communities for mission. Classical theological disciplines such as biblical studies, systematic theology and church history are increasingly taught with special attention to missional themes.

Finally, in 2004 the seminary introduced an experimental programme within the Master of Divinity degree known as the "MDiv In-Ministry Program." This is another cohort programme, with classes one day per week, for students preparing for congregational leadership roles. Because students are employed in various forms of pastoral ministry while they study, their actual congregations become learning laboratories. Pedagogically, this is achieved through assignments which require students to integrate biblical-theological learning by implementing practical initiatives within their ministries. The programme also features multi-layered mentoring, involving peer friendships, counsellors, spiritual directors, ministry support groups in their churches and relationships with faculty. Its integrative focus is exemplified in its experimental approach to teaching homiletics. There is no course on preaching, but preaching is explored as a unit within each of the 19 courses in their sequence. Students preach in the context of weekly chapel services, and receive individualised feedback from faculty.

Student reaction to these initiatives has been strongly positive. Some important challenges remain. This is an ongoing transformation process that involves substantially rethinking inherited seminary approaches that have favoured maintenance of church programmes rather than formation for mission, and that have been oriented primary by the perspectives of scholarly guilds rather than the church's agenda of equipping disciples. New ways of teaching, new approaches to student assessment and new levels of professional development for faculty are required.

6. Asian Theological Seminary

Asian Theological Seminary (ATS), founded in 1969, is one of the largest non-denominational evangelical seminaries in Asia, serving approximately one hundred different denominations and para-church organisations in the Philippines and throughout Asia. Its 21 programmes – which range from programmes for lay people to doctoral candidates - service approximately 1,000 students each year, with Certificate programmes and masters-level Graduate Diploma, M.A., M.Div. and doctoral degrees. Every year 40-50 international students from 12-14 different nations study at the seminary. Some 25 full-time faculty-mostly Filipinos and other Asians-teach at ATS, the majority with earned doctorates. To date there have been over 1,300 masters-level graduates from the seminary.

ATS's vision through the years is reflected in its motto: "Committed to the Word, Caring for the World." The seminary's six core values reflect that motto with the core value on "Community" especially emphasising the missional commitment of the school: "...as an Asian seminary, we seek to be aware of the needs of our continent and to equip students in their particular contexts. The Philippine context in which we are located provides the basic concrete situation within which we do theology, while also providing strong motivation for cross-cultural ministry (missions)." ATS is passionate about discovering how to incarnate Christ in the diverse contexts of Asia and training workers who can minister the transforming Gospel in such contexts.

A formal missions programme was begun at the seminary in 1983 when a missions major was added to the basic M.Div. curriculum, followed in 1984 with a two-year "Master of Missions" degree. From 1984 through 1992 there were 16 missions graduates, though many M.Div. graduates also took several missions-related courses. The missions programme was totally revamped in the years 1993 and 1994 with the addition of Graduate Diploma and M.A. degrees in missions. The new missions curriculum was designed to be much more relevant to the Asian situation. This refocusing helped to greatly increase the number of missions' graduates. In the ten years from 1994 to 2003 there were over 150 masters-level missions graduates.

The innovative missions curriculum of ATS offers a three-tiered approach to formal graduate-level missionary training. The foundational year (Graduate Diploma level) is mainly filled with core missiological coursework: Cultural Anthropology, Missionary Life and Spirituality, Theory and Practice of Urban Ministry, World Missions, Biblical Theology of Missions, Cross-Cultural Evangelism and Church Planting, and Doing Theology in Context. Additional courses on Bible Introduction, Hermeneutics and basic Theology round out the first year. Even more Bible and theology courses are added during the second year (M.A. level) for additional grounding of missions students in the Scriptures. The M.Div. degree with a missions major includes the core missiological coursework scattered over the typical three years of study along with the standard courses required for this more "professional" ministerial degree. Students have the choice of going one step at a time, from Graduate Diploma level first, then on to the M.A. level and finally to the M.Div. level, or to mix up the coursework somewhat and apply for the M.A. or M.Div. degree. Most missions students choose to terminate their studies with the M.A. degree.

The missions programme of ATS is designed to improve the qualifications and skills of pastors, evangelists, church planters, church workers, mission administrators, missionaries, and missionary candidates who desire training at the graduate level. Key objectives of this programme include holistic formation (academic, spiritual, and professional) and the integration of theory and praxis. The programme aims to develop Christian practitioners who are able to initiate and sustain evangelism, discipleship, and church planting efforts in culturally sensitive, holistic, and transformational ways, as well as to be more effective communicators of the gospel in both multi-cultural and cross-cultural contexts, particularly in Asian and 10/40 window countries and urban centres.

The missions programme emphasises the practical dimensions of ministry with many of the courses requiring out-of-classroom exposure and research trips for "hands-on" ministry involvement to supplement the background theory of the classroom. Besides this, all missions students are required to do an intensive three-week cross-cultural exposure trip to a Muslim or Buddhist context as a part of their internship requirements.

Two courses are foundational to both the ATS missions programme as well as to the entire seminary. The first is the required World Missions course, which is an adapted "Perspectives" course using materials originally developed and contextualised for Latin America. This is a multi-faceted course focusing on the biblical, historical, cultural, and strategic dimensions of the task of world missions. Particular focus is placed upon "unreached peoples": God's concern for them, who they are, how to locate and identify them, and how to reach them. The second foundational required course is entitled "Transformational Theology." This is a multi-disciplinary course that reflects the basic ethos of ATS: attempting to explore the biblical, theological, missiological, and practical dimensions of what it means to transform individuals, cultures, and nations with the whole gospel of Jesus Christ.

7. St. Paul's Evangelical Lutheran Church, Minneapolis, MN., USA

Since 1990, Minneapolis and St. Paul – the Twin Cities – have seen a massive influx of refugees and immigrants from around the world. A cultural transformation is taking place as neighbourhoods are filled by the sights, sounds, and smells of other countries. The Twin Cities metro area boasts the largest Hmong, Somali, Oromo, and Tibetan populations in North America, and large Liberian and Sudanese populations. Approximately 90,000 Hmong, 50,000 Somali, and 17,000 Oromo and Ethiopians now live in the metro area - two-thirds of whom have arrived within the past five years. In addition, the University of Minnesota is home to the largest Chinese student population in the United States. Further, during the past decade the Twin Cities have become the eighth fastest growing Latino area in the U.S. Recent census figures show that this represents a 231.7 % increase in the diversity of its peoples in ten years![40] The Twin Cities is now one of the most culturally diverse metropolitan communities in the U.S. All this adds up to over half a million internationals, speaking more than 140 different languages!

This not only reflects a significant cultural shift, but also introduces a new world religious demographic to the Twin Cities. In 1990 there were just four mosques; today there are over sixty. In 1999, for the first time in the history of the Twin Cities, Islam surpassed Judaism as the religion with the largest number of adherents after Christianity. Since 1999 the Muslim population has more than doubled and more than tripled since 1995. East African immigration has accounted for a large percentage of the growth of Islam. Over 95% of East African immigrants are Muslim and 50% of the Twin Cities Muslim population is Somali.[41]

God is bringing the world, the mission field, to the doorstep of every Christian church in the Twin Cities! The church is responding, with over 300 churches planted in the past three years. This is one new church every three days. More churches are taking seriously the need to demonstrate the love of Christ in their communities.

When Roland Wells arrived in 1988 as pastor of St. Paul's Evangelical Lutheran Church in the shadow of the skyscrapers of downtown Minneapolis, he found himself in a quandary. St. Paul's 130-year-old congregation was a small gathering of suburbanites committed to making a difference in its urban neighbourhood. Members had remained at the distinctly inner-city church because they viewed their membership as a matter of mission. "Our people wanted to do significant things in the city," Wells remembers, "but didn't know how to go about it."

Enter CitySpirit Ministries and the School of Urban Ministry (SUM). St. Paul's launched these two initiatives in 1991. CitySpirit builds partnerships with suburban congregations by bringing them into the city and providing cross-cultural mission opportunities. SUM is a training school for members of St. Paul's and other inner city churches and suburban partners. The vision of these two ministries is "to develop a congregation-based, low-cost model of starting new ministries to un-reached people groups through training and linking city and suburban congrega-tions in order to strengthen both." The key goal of CitySpirit and SUM is to equip churches and their members for ministry.

Every Monday evening, "students" gather to learn from practitioners from around the Twin Cities about how to "do" urban ministry. The first semester begins with a strong emphasis on prayer and bib-lical and cross-cultural studies. Students not only make use of books and study ma-terials, but they are engaged in mission in the city. Through field trips, service-learning projects and studying successful ministries, they learn to minister to people from other cultures. The second semester includes a study of world religions and their access points for Christian witness, a course on grant writing for non-profit or-ganisations, and an overview of chal-lenges facing the city, such as chemical dependency, homelessness and the short-age of affordable housing, prostitution, gangs, mental illness, refugee resettle-ment, political structures, church planting,

etc. The focus of the second semester is on experiential learning and mentorship from urban "missionaries." Throughout the semester, students work together and serve community ministries to research a specific "mission field" in the Twin Cities. They investigate the felt needs of this community, engage in service-learning, and create detailed project reports on how to be effective missionaries to a specific people group. Reports addressing sched-uling, publicity, fund raising, vision im-plementation, staying on task, staff train-ing, effective team management, etc., are prepared.

The impact of the SUM strategy has been felt in the Twin Cities. Several new ministries have been started and inner city churches planted. Some graduates work with a faith-based chemical dependency treatment programme. Others are engaged in planting and supporting new ethnic churches. One graduate has planted an inner city church that reaches out to the homeless, prostitutes, drug addicts, and dealers and provides an intense mentor-ship community for men. Another gradu-ate organised a cross-cultural ministry for African-American single mothers in an apartment complex near St. Paul's Church. Other graduates work for social service agencies, serve as nurses in com-munity clinics and hospitals, provide legal aid for the poor, teach in local public schools, manage affordable housing pro-jects, work in city government, and a few have started small businesses.

The SUM model is now in the proc-ess of expanding to provide intentional, experiential, and missional education to college students. A partnership of seven Christian colleges in the Twin Cities has formed the Urban College Cross-Cultural Coalition – U4C. Students with a passion for urban mission, regardless of their major - whether education, business, nursing, sociology, religion, political science, etc. – will live together in the city, partner with community churches, ministries, and service organisations to learn… and be engaged in God's mission of love and care.

E. GUIDELINES FOR IMPLEMENTATION

This section does not deal with curriculum development or the development of training programmes, but with how training programmes can implement or bring about the changes – the principles and strategies we identified above in Section C.3. How can they bring about the changes that will enable effective education for world evangelisation?

The target audiences of these recommendations and guidelines are the local churches and all theological training institutions and programmes. It is aimed especially at the leaders of institutions like the board members, the chairperson of the board, the heads or leaders of training programmes, the faculty or teachers of these training programmes, the heads of mission agencies, the heads of mission departments in schools. It is also aimed at denominational leaders and the leaders or pastors of local churches, and finally also the church members and lay leaders.

1. Implementation challenges and issues

Any change process involves challenges and encounters resistance. In trying to implement these principles and strategies, leaders of faith communities and training programmes will encounter several challenges. Our group identified some of these challenges that they may face. Of course, different contexts will present different challenges. The aim is not to propose precise solutions or to give ideas on how to deal with these challenges. Space does not allow that. Some of the action plans proposed below may help in dealing with the challenges. Every training programme should seek creative ways appropriate to their own contexts to deal with these and other challenges they may face.

- **Resistance to change** – In any organisation there is always, to varying degrees, resistance to change. Leaders should be aware of these and of the reasons for the resistance. They should equip themselves with the necessary knowledge and skills to become effective managers of change, enabling them to move their programmes or schools from the traditional to a new mindset.

- **Accrediting agencies and government regulations for recognition** – Training programmes or schools that seek accreditation with agencies or government recognition or approval may deal with requirements that make it very difficult for them to implement the principles, strategies and action plans proposed in this report.

- **Financial resources** – Some of the required changes and implementation of the proposed action plans and strategies will require additional financial resources which may be difficult for training programmes, especially in the majority world, to obtain. Are the proposed strategies and action plans viable financially?
- **Market economy and competition** – Closely related to financial challenges is the impact of a market economy on our schools. Many programmes are tuition driven and depend on high enrolment numbers, which may not be conducive for implementing effective education strategies for world evangelisation. Theological education is being influenced by the creation of a "consumer driven" training market. There is increasing competition between theological schools and a growing number of training programmes. These impact the number of students, quality of training, availability of financial resources and faculty. The commoditisation of training and presenting it as a packaged product is detrimental to character formation, spirituality, and a missional approach to theological education.
- **Faculty challenges** – Implementation will face several challenges related to the academic staff or trainers in training programmes.
  - ◆ *Teaching methodologies and educational philosophies* – Many training programmes and faculty

exhibit inflexibility by adhering to traditional pedagogies. Often the cause for this is that they are unaware of newer or more effective learning strategies. Most faculty teach as they themselves were taught and were trained only in their respective disciplines, not in educational methodologies and principles. Schools may not be providing the necessary professional development for their faculty in these areas. Some faculty may not be convinced of the validity of relational, nonformal and community learning strategies.

  - ◆ *Lack of training* – Faculty and trainers may be ill-equipped or have little experience in some of the strategies proposed here, for example mentoring. Some may feel inadequate to do this, or feel that this is not their area or gift.
  - ◆ *Faculty recruitment and development* – How to find a best fit between the school's mission, vision, core values, and the faculty it seeks to appoint? Faculty may not agree with the missional purpose of training programmes. They may not have the necessary qualifications – professional, personality, spirituality, experience, relationally – to be involved in the kind of education envisioned here.
  - ◆ *Workload of faculty* – In many training programmes faculty are overburdened. This is especially the case in contexts where

financial resources are a serious problem, and faculty have to take on additional teaching or administrative loads. This leaves very little additional time and energy for more involvement in ministry or intensive interactions with students as some of these strategies may require.

♦ *"Publish or perish" mentality* – In many formal training programmes there is a strong emphasis on research and publication. Faculty are expected, in many cases required, to publish. This leaves very little time for the time-intensive and personalised strategies proposed here. It also contributes to the pressure to specialise in focused areas, which in turn contributes to the fragmentation we experience in theological education.

- **Gap between the church and formal training programmes** – There is an apparent disconnect between the church and formal theological training programmes. There seems to be a lack of communication between them. They have different expectations of each other, or their expectations are not always clearly communicated to each other. Schools are not always aware of the real needs of the church and its context, and seem not to really attempt to listen to discover those needs.

- **Governance challenges** – The boards of training programmes may not share the same vision and values in terms of world mission and the need for a missional framework for theological education. Many boards are too uninvolved, and others again are guilty of micromanagement in their schools. Board and governance support for the changes proposed here will be crucial.

2. Key action plans

Our Issue Group explored action plans or action ideas for leaders of training programmes that may help them to implement the principles and strategies for effective theological education for world evangelisation. We identified many creative and useful ideas. However, in our discussion we concluded that there are four key action plans that should be implemented first before attempting some of the other action ideas. Here we present these key action plans and under the heading of *Additional Guidelines* we offer some of the other action ideas that leaders could consider to help them to implement and move toward effective theological education for world mission.

The conviction of this Issue Group is that there is insufficient commitment on the part of faith communities to world mission. Faith communities need to be educated for world evangelisation. Therefore:

1. Schools and churches should be intentional about their missional commitment, especially as expressed in:

a. Faculty and support staff selection

b. Professional development of faculty and support

   c. Curriculum review and development
   d. Student assessment
   e. Board selection
   f. Linking to other similar groups and training programmes internationally

2. Leaders of institutions and programmes should have an understanding of world mission and therefore insure that those who work in the training programmes share that understanding. How can any faith community become truly missional when there are key staff who are indifferent to God's saving purposes for his creation? In particular, we commend *Perspectives* or other equivalent world mission courses or seminars as very helpful in developing a mission-mindedness amongst people.

3. School personnel and key church leaders ought to be exposed to the realities of human needs and cross-cultural ministry and have the ability to transmit this concern for world mission to others through teaching, training, and discipling.

4. We encourage closer and strategic partnerships between all entities invested and involved in education for world evangelisation: schools, churches, mission organisations, and mission-minded individuals.

3. Additional guidelines

Here we briefly discuss more action plans and guidelines that may enable training programme leaders to implement the effective theological education for world evangelisation. The following serves as a resource for training programmes. We realise that training programmes may not be able to use all of these, and not all may be applicable or appropriate to all contexts.

3.1 Faculty Development

- **Experiential learning** - Faculty, teachers, and trainers in training programmes should recognise the value of experiential learning and be given opportunities to develop their teaching skills and expertise in experiential learning as well as their mentoring skills. We are aware that mentoring is a complex issue and that it is not always viable and an option for all faculty. It is not possible for teachers to mentor the whole class, but they can use experiential learning techniques in class and mentor a selected few. Faculty involvement in ministry practice should become a priority. There is a need to be actively involved with the students in field-based learning.

- **Professional development:**
  - ◆ Training programmes should consider professional development programmes for all their staff that will have as its outcome a missional paradigm. It should enable them to understand the importance of a missional framework for everything they do and to embrace such a missional framework.
  - ◆ Professional development should help faculty to explore and embrace different teaching styles,

methodologies, and to use various types of media to facilitate quality learning. It should expose them to different educational approaches and philosophies.

- It should also help them to teach their subjects from an intercultural perspective and missional framework.
- It should enable faculty to become life-long learners and reflective practitioners who are continuously learning and growing in all areas — professional, personal, character, and spirituality.

(a) Faculty Recruitment and Selection

Recruitment of faculty becomes crucial in developing effective theological education for world evangelisation. We should select the right faculty. During the selection process we should choose faculty with world mission and a missional framework in mind. The criteria for faculty recruitment should include a demonstrable missional perspective and passion for mission. Some experience in evangelistic, discipleship, or church planting ministries, and considerable other ministry experience should be a requirement.

(b) Faculty Awareness of World Mission and Intercultural Exposure

To develop a missional awareness faculty would greatly benefit from involvement in a missions practice or ministry on a regular basis. They should be encouraged to join with students on short-term missions exposure experiences and be involved in practical mission projects with students. Some could be involved in actual evangelism and church planting projects. For these they can determine learning outcomes with the students and assess the achievement of these with them in class or back at the school.

Schools should seek partnerships with schools from other countries and exchange faculty. Student exchanges can also contribute to this awareness and exposure, not only of the faculty but also of other staff and the student body. Scholarships and grants could be established for such faculty and student exchanges.

Missionaries on home assignment can serve as a resident missionary or missiologist and be involved in the school community. Active missionaries could be guests of the training programmes to tell their story, teach by example and experience, interface, and interact with the faculty and students. This could happen also in the local congregation who should take advantage of the missionary's presence.

Faculty could establish links and network with mission agencies, individual missionaries, and churches in the mission field or majority world. This should facilitate and develop an interest in a missional mindset. Schools should plan to send faculty, not only the missions faculty, to missions conferences.

The leadership, values, and practices of schools should encourage the faculty toward and hold them accountable for an evangelistic lifestyle.

(c) Mentoring and Modelling

Mentoring is talked about much these days. There is no question about the effectiveness of mentoring if it is done well. Mentoring as a training tool and the concept of "journeying together" should be recaptured or reinstalled as an approach in education.

However, mentoring can take various forms, and it can achieve different outcomes. There are many issues involved in mentoring and, just as with teaching, you can have effective and ineffective mentoring, and good and bad mentors. Of course, it would be simplistic to suggest that mentoring is the panacea for all problems faced in effective education for evangelism.

If we consider mentoring as part of our curriculum, we must first clarify what we mean by the term and then clarify what outcomes we want to achieve through mentoring. What purposes will mentoring serve in our curriculum? Furthermore, faculty would need training in mentoring since it involves very specific attitudes, values and skills. We also need to ask whether effective mentoring in theological education with its current structures and approaches is realistic. A faculty member can effectively mentor only so many students. Who will be mentored and who will not be mentored would become an issue. Many people are "mentored" through the models of others without entering into a formal and intentional mentoring relationship with those persons.

For effective education for world evangelisation the whole Christian community needs to be involved in the education process. Community leaders should model Christlikeness and equip others to model Christlikeness. This Christlikeness should be seen in character, mission mindedness, an evangelistic lifestyle and an involvement in the community where Christians are effective as the light and salt of the world.

3.2 Curriculum Development

Training programmes should implement a review of curriculum to incorporate a missional paradigm, experiential learning and exposure to human needs in both local and broader contexts. They should assess educational process and methodology in order to determine the extent to which the programme is truly missional. They should asses programmes, curricula and syllabi to see the extent to which these approximate or divert from a missional orientation. In their assessment they should get feedback from their students, graduates, church leaders and lay members on the training and their understanding of mission.

The curriculum development process should identify the resources (personnel, information, materials, time, and funds) available that can assist the achievement and implementation of a training programme that has a missional orientation. There would be considerable value in developing an action plan that will incorporate this objective, a missional framework in the institution. Every subject should echo a missional dimension. It would also be beneficial if materials could be produced that suggest ways in which missions can be integrated into the whole of the curriculum. The following ideas may be worth consideration:

- Incorporate in the curriculum and the library bibliographies and materials from the majority world, and make greater use of their resources.
- Include practical assignments that would enable students to do something with a missional dimension or intention.
- Offer specialised courses on evangelisation, church planting, theology of mission, and the current trends in missiology.

3.3. *The Local Church and Church Leaders*

All church leaders – denominational leaders, pastors of local congregations, lay leaders – must have a passion and vision for world mission. They must lead their churches in this vision and into an involvement in world mission. They must equip them to be faith communities that live a missionary lifestyle in the world.

They should teach and expose their churches and members to missions. There are many good programmes and resources available for missions mobilisation that can be used effectively. They should conduct seminars and workshops on mobilising the whole church for evangelism. A major component of this should be the real going out, being involved in missions, and then evaluating and learning from the experience.

Churches should consider retreats for all their staff or workers, but particularly those lay leaders, pastors, denominational leaders, teachers and staff who are involved in Christian education. Such a retreat would focus on mission and aim at developing a missional framework and missionary lifestyle.

There would be tremendous benefit in pastors and their lay leaders taking regular short-term mission exposure trips. Mission agencies could help to facilitate such trips.

Pulpit ministry - Pastors are also teachers in the pulpit and they should use the pulpit ministry to educate and challenge believers to go into the world, and to be witnesses in the marketplace or wherever they are.

The Family - Parents should teach their children how to witness and reach their friends. Churches could help to develop family projects connected to world evangelisation. They could equip families to open up their homes for prayer, healing, counselling, and to witness for Christ. Churches should have actual programmes or activities that can bring the families closer to the mission fields or mission projects. They should equip and facilitate families to pray for and support mission. The natural locus for this kind of training is the local church. One component of theological education should be the equipping of pastors to, in turn, equip the families in their churches for missionary engagement.

3.4 *Board Members of Training Institutions, Programmes, and Local Churches*

An understanding of, and a vision and passion for, mission should be part of the selection criteria for all board members of churches, schools, and training programmes. They should have a commitment to world evangelisation. Board members should understand the institution's mission and vision. They are the custodians of the mission statement.

3.5 Strategic Partnerships

We should develop strategic partnerships between the schools, training programmes, churches, mission agencies, specific people and organisations in the wider society. Formal training institutions should implement a programme of regular contact and dialogue with local churches and denominations to build relationships for training and to gain an understanding of their training needs. It should help them to discover how they can serve the church better. A further benefit of such a symbiotic relationship is that it might ensure that there is no disjunction between theological and missiological education in any of the faith communities.

Through formal and non-formal networks, there should be interaction between educational institutions and churches of the western world and the majority world. The benefits of such interactions are obvious as they would facilitate learning from each other and mutual enrichment.

This Issue Group recommends more intentional times of dialogue between the church and theological faculty, thereby linking the church's mission directly with training. We encourage theological schools in their training programmes to use resource people from churches, para-church organisations, and mission agencies, as well as Christians in the market place, and other Christian professionals.

Partnerships between churches and schools/training programmes should not be limited to administrative matters with little dialogue or input regarding vision, curriculum and student selection.

Pastors and church leaders should seek intentional relationships with missions (local, national, global). In the face of a world of overwhelming spiritual and physical needs, churches are often simply reactive to the multitude of human needs, rather than carefully assessing in an informed way how they can best contribute to the task of world evangelisation. Local churches can help training programmes to restructure by appealing to accreditation bodies to adapt their requirements and standards in such a way that they address the training needs of the churches as they seek to minister in a given local context, and as they seek to inform and equip their members for world evangelisation. Such bodies of accreditation could revisit their own standards to ensure that they are serving and not hindering the development of effective theological education for world evangelisation.

Conclusion

What is the place of God in our theological education, and in doing theology? God alone is, and should be, the centre of theological education. Growing in the knowledge of God and in His purposes for His world must be the ultimate purpose of all theological education. Integral to God's purpose for His creation is the drawing to Himself of a people, from every tribe, nation and tongue, who will live holy lives to the praise of His glory.

Consequently, a missional approach to theological education is vital. No longer can missiology remain on the margins of the theological curriculum like some "lost sheep…scattered among the folds of history, theology, comparative religions, and education, wandering from the theological field to the practical and back again" (in the colourful words of J.L. Dunstan). God's mission is done in partnership with the church. The church is sent by Jesus Christ to continue and sustain his mission, which is the annunciation and restitution of God's kingdom and the salvation which has been made available to all. Theological education plays a key role in preparing God's servant people to fulfil this missionary calling by their life and by their words. Thus, theological education must be done within a missional framework and serve to develop mission-minded servant leaders.

The other Issue Groups of the 2004 Lausanne Congress on World Evangelization have reminded us that there are many challenges facing us as we seek to proclaim Christ in the twenty-first century.

Just to mention a few: the evangelisation of children; the youth; non-traditional families; the great majority of the world's population who are oral learners; people with disabilities; the poor; AIDS sufferers; the challenge of a Christian witness in the marketplace; religious and non-religious spirituality in the postmodern world; reconciliation and peace in a world full of conflicts; religious fundamentalism; globalisation; urbanisation; the crucial need for partnerships in ministry and mission; and many others. We who are involved in theological education are called to address these issues.

What is theological education for world mission doing to prepare the church and faith communities to deal with these challenges effectively? There is a real need for theological education to re-envision and restructure itself. We pray that this paper and its recommendations may encourage leaders of theological training programmes to be innovative, and restructure theological education so that it develops greater commitment to world evangelisation in faith communities.

ENDNOTES

1 Chris Wright, *Truth With a Mission: Towards a Missiological Hermeneutic of the Bible.* (Leicester: RTSF, 2002).

2 Banks, Robert, *Reenvisioning Theological Education: Exploring a Missional Alternative to Current Models,* (Grand Rapids: William B. Eerdmans, 1999), 131-132.

3 Padilla, C. René, "Introduction: An Ecclesiology for Integral Mission" in Tetsunao Yamamori and C. René Padilla, (Buenos Aires: Ediciones Kairos 2004), 19.

4 The following is a summary of the characteristics as explained by C.R. Padilla 2004, 20-49.

5 C.R. Padilla 2004, 23, 27.

6 C.R. Padilla 2004, 20.

7 C.R. Padilla 2004, 43.

8 Conn Harvie M., "Theological Education and the Search for Excellence" in *Westminster Theological Journal* 41:2 (1979), 331.

9 Rowen, Samuel, "Missiology and the Coherence of Theological Education" in Duane Elmer and Lois McKinney, eds. *With An Eye on the Future: Development and Mission in the 21st Century* (Monrovia, CA.: MARC, 1996), 96.

10 S. Rowen 1996, 98-99.

11 Ferris, Robert, "The Role of Theology in Theological Education" in Duane Elmer and Lois McKinney eds. *With An Eye on the Future: Development and Mission in the 21st Century* (Monrovia, CA.: MARC, 1996), 103-05.

12 Farley, Edward. *Theologia: The Fragmentation and Unity of Theological Education* (Philadelphia: Fortress Press, 1983) 43f.

13 S. Rowen 1996, 96f.

14 R. Banks 1999.

15 Robert Coleman, *The Master Plan of Evangelism,* (Manila: O.M.F. Literature, 1975), 19.

16 Michael J. Wilkins, *Following the Master: Discipleship in the Steps of Jesus,* (Grand Rapids: Zondervan, 1992), 142.

17 Rick Yount, "Jesus the Master Teacher" in D. Eldridge ed. *The Teaching Ministry of the Church.* (Nashville, Tennessee: Broadman & Holman, 1995), 33.

18 R. Coleman, 1975, 28.

19 Allan Coppedge, *The Biblical Principles of Discipleship,* (Grand Rapids: Zondervan, 1989), 61.

20 R. Coleman 1975, 61, 63.

21 Juan Carlos Ortiz, *Call to Discipleship,* (New Jersey: Logos International, 1975), 67, 68.

22 David Watson, *Discipleship,* (Great Britain: Hodder and Stoughton, 1981), 83.

23 D. Watson 1981, 50.

24 M.J. Wilkins 1992, 143.

25 D. Watson 1981, 83.

26 R. Yount 1995, 35, 39.

27 Ted Engstrom, *The Fine Art of Mentoring*, (Tennessee: Wolgemuth and Hyatt 1989), 20.

28 D. Eldridge 1995, 48.

29 D. Eldridge 1995, 57.

30 Business Council of Australia, *Training Australians: A Better Way of Working: 27 case studies from leading Australian organizations of their best training strategies* (Melbourne: Business Council of Australia, 1990), 10-11.

31 M. Stackhouse, *Apologia: Contextualization, Globalization and Mission in Theological Education* (Grand Rapids, MI: William B Eerdmans, 1988), 167.

32 W.D. Taylor, "From Iguassu to the reflective practitioners of the global family of Christ" in W.D. Taylor ed., *Global Missiology for the 21st Century: The Iguassu Dialogue* (Grand Rapids, MI: Baker Academic, 2000), 3-12.

33 R. Kinsler,, 'Mission and Context: the current debate about Contextualisation' in *Evangelical Missions Quarterly* (January 1978), 23-29.

34 B. Nicholls, "Doing Theology in Context" in *Evangelical Review of Theology* (July 1987), 101-106.

35 D. Gilliland, ed., *The Word Among Us: Contextualizing Theology for Mission Today* (Dallas: Word, 1989), 28.

36 D. Whiteman, "Contextualisation: The Theory, the Gap, the Challenge" in *International Bulletin of Missionary Research* (January 1997), 2-7.

37 J.R. Davies, "Biblical Precedence for Contextualisation" in *Evangelical Review of Theology* (1997), 197-214; D. Gilliland, ed., *The Word Among Us*, chs. 2 and 3; A. Glasser, "Help from an Unexpected Quarter or, the Old Testament and Contextualisation" in *Missiology* October 1979, 403-410; D.J. Hesselgrave, and E. Rommen, *Contextualisation: Meanings, Methods and Model* (Grand Rapids, MI: Baker Books, 1989), ch.1.

38 Missiology is a difficult word to define. Alternative definitions are legion. See Michael D. Raiter, "Sent for this Purpose' Mission and Missiology and their Search for Meaning" in *Ripe for Harvest: Christian Mission in the NT and in Our World* (Carlisle: Paternoster, 2000), 106-150, and T. Steffen, "Missiology's Journey for Acceptance in the Educational World" in *Missiology: An International Review* 31:2 (April 2003), 131-153.

39 Steffen, 2003, 139ff.

40 It should also be noted that many immigrants did not take part in the US Census for fear of eviction (overcrowding in apartments), or because they are undocumented.

41 Research and surveys conducted by Religious Information Resources in *City Scope Report – Twin Cities*, 2003: Census Updates, Minneapolis Star Tribune, St Paul's Pioneer Press, *Operation World.* 21st Century Edition, ed. Patrick Johnstone and Jason Mandryk (Waynesboro: Paternoster, 2001), The Catholic Spirit, Cedar-Riverside Neighbourhood Action Plan, and a *Directory of Non Profit Organizations in Minnesota* (4th Edition, 2000).

BIBLIOGRAPHY

Adeyemo, T. "The Renewal of Evangelical Theological Education." *Evangelical Theological Education To-day-II: Agenda for Renewal.* (1982), 5-12.

Banks, Robert. *Reenvisioning Theological Education: Exploring a Missional Alternative to Current Model.* Grand Rapids, MI: William B. Eerdmans, 1999.

Baumohl, Anton. *Making Adults Disciples.* London: Scripture Union, 1984.

Berry, Howard A., and Linda A. Chisholm. *Understanding the Education – And Through It the Culture – in Education Abroad.* New York: The International Partnership for Service-Learning, 2002.

__________. *Service-Learning in Higher Education Around the World.* New York: The International Partnership for Service-Learning, 1999.

__________. *How to Serve and Learn Abroad Effectively: Students Tell Students.* New York: The Partnership for Service-Learning, 1992.

Biehl, Bobb. *Mentoring.* Nashville, TN: Broadman & Holman Publishers, 1996.

Bowen, Earle, and Eleanor. *Contextualization of Teaching Methodology in Theological Education in Africa.* ERIC Document Reproduction Service No. ED 315 382, 1988.

Brookfield, S.D. *Understanding and Facilitating Adult Learning.* San Francisco: Jossey-Bass, 1987.

__________. *Developing Critical Thinkers: Challenging Adults to Explore Alternative Ways of Thinking and Acting.* San Francisco: Jossey-Bass, 1987.

Brooking Stuart, et al. *A Missional Resource Book for Theological Teachers.* Draft title - Yet to be published.
> *Growing out of the 2004 Forum for World Evangelization the need for resources to assist theological teachers to think missionally was clearly perceived. A group from the theological education issue group is working towards publishing such a resource book with illustrations of key theological concepts from around the world.*

Brown, Keith E. *Missions in the Local Asian Church: Examples of Local Asian Churches Which Have Successful Missions Program.* (1987).

Bruce, A.B. *The Training of the Twelve.* Grand Rapids, MI: Kregel Publications, 1988.

Buchanan, Edward A. "Virtual Theological Education: Cybertraining for Evangelization and Discipleship." *Faith and Mission.* 14 (1997) 28-45.

Cantor, Jeffrey A. *Experiential Learning in Higher Education: Linking Classroom and Community,* Washington, DC: The George Washington University, 1995.
> *This book provides a review of the literature focusing on the experiential learner; forms of experiential learning, administrative issues, learning theories and cognitive development, learning styles and needs of non-traditional learners, learning through service, evaluation of the learning process, etc.*

Chew, Jim. *When You Cross Cultures: Vital Issues Facing Christian Missions.* Singapore: The Navigators, 1990.

Chopp, Rebecca. *Saving Work: Feminist Practices of Theological Education.* Louisville: Westminster/John Knox, 1995.

Cobb, John B., and J.C. Hough, *Christian Identity and Theological Education.* Chico, CA: Scholars Press, 1985.

Coleman, Robert E. *The Mind of The Master.* Old Tappan, New Jersey: Fleming H. Revell, 1977.

__________. *The Master Plan of Evangelism.* Tarrytown, NY: Fleming H. Revell, 1963.

Connell, Christopher. "Eastern Mennonite University: From Bible School to 'Global Village' University." *Internationalizing the Campus: Profiles of Success at Colleges and Universities.* 2003, 25-32.

Conn, Harvie M. "Theological Education and the Search for Excellence." *Westminster Theological Journal.* 41:2 (1979), 311-363.

Coppedge, Allan. *The Biblical Principles of Discipleship.* Grand Rapids: Zondervan, 1989.

Costas, Orlando. "Theological Education and Mission." *New Alternatives in Theological Education.* Oxford: Regnum, 1986.

Cross, P. *Adults as Learners: Increasing Participation and Facilitating Learning.* San Francisco: Jossey-Bass, 1981.

Cunningham, Jack R. "Theological Education and the Lay Person." *Review and Expositor.* 93 (1996) 7-76.

Daloz, L. *Effective Teaching as Mentoring.* San Francisco: Jossey-Bass, 1987.

Davis, Ron Lee. *Mentoring The Strategy of The Master.* Nashville, TN: Thomas Nelson Publisher, 1991.

Dewey, John. *Experience and Education.* New York: Simon and Schuster, 1997.

Eims, Leroy. *The Lost Art of Disciple Making.* Colorado Springs: CO: NavPress, 1981.

Eldridge, Daryl. "The Role of the Holy Spirit in Teaching" in D. Eldridge, ed. *The Teaching Ministry of the Church.* Nashville, Tennessee: Broadman & Holman, 1999, 43-58.

Elmer, Duane and Lois McKinney, eds. *With an Eye on the Future: Development and Mission in the 21st Century.* Monrovia, CA.: MARC, 1996.

Engstrom, Ted. *The Fine Art of Mentoring.* Tennessee: Wolgemuth and Hyatt, 1989.

Farley, Edward. *Theologia: The Fragmentation and Unity of Theological Education.* Philadelphia: Fortress Press, 1983, 43f.

Ferris, Robert. "The Role of Theology in Theological Education" in Duane Elmer and Lois McKinney, eds., *With An Eye on the Future: Development and Mission in the 21st Century.* Monrovia, CA.: MARC, 1996, 101-111.

Ferris, Robert W. *Renewal in Theological Education: Strategies for Change.* Wheaton, IL: The Billy Graham Center, 1990.

Ford, LeRoy. *Design for Teaching and Training.* Nashville, TN: Broadman & Holman Publishers, 1978.

Freire, Paulo. *Pedagogy of Hope.* New York: The Continuum Publishing Company, 1999.

__________. *Teachers as Cultural Workers: Letters to Those Who Dare to Teach.* Boulder, CO: Westview Press, 1998.

__________. *Pedagogy of the Oppressed.* New York: The Continuum Publishing Company, 1970.

Frost, Michael and Alan Hirsch. *The Shaping of Things to Come.* Peabody, MA: Hendrickson Publishers, 2003.

> *This book is a "must-read" for anyone that is serious about advancing the gospel in the 21st century. The basic thesis of the authors, an Australian and a South African who are planting churches in Australia, is that Christendom is rapidly dying in the Western world. By "Christendom," they mean the dominance of the church in Western culture from the fourth century, when Constantine proclaimed Christianity the religion of the Roman Empire, until recently.*

Furey, Patricia. "A Framework for Cross-Cultural Analysis of Teaching Methods." *Teaching across Cultures in the University.* Washington, DC: NAFSA- Association of International Educators, 1986.

Gochenour, Theodore, ed. *Beyond Experience: An Experiential Approach to Cross-Cultural Education.* Yarmouth, ME: Intercultural Press, 1993.

Goldsmith, Marshall and L. Lyons, A. Freas, eds. *Coaching For Leadership.* San Francisco, CA: Jossey-Bass Pfeiffer, 2000.

Green, Michael. *Evangelism Now and Then.* London, UK: Darton, Longman and Todd, 1992.

__________. *Evangelism through the Local Church.* Nashville, TN: Oliver Nelson, 1992.

__________. *Freed To Serve.* London, UK: Hodder and Stoughton, 1983.

Griffiths, Michael. *The Example of Jesus.* Leicester, UK: InterVarsity Press, 1985.

__________. *Get Your Church Involved in World Mission.* Singapore: OMF Books, 1972.

Harley, David C. *Preparing to Serve: Training for Cross-cultural Mission.* Pasadena, California: William Carey Library, 1995.

Harner, Nevin C. and David D. Baker. *Missionary Education in Your Church.* New York. Friendship Press, 1950.

Harris, Stephen. *Culture and Learning.* Canberra, Australia: Institute for Aboriginal Studies, 1984.

Harris, Roger; Hugh Guthrie, Barry Hobart, and David Lundberg. *Competency-Based Education and Training: Between a Rock and a Whirlpool.* MacMillan Education, 1995.

> *These practitioners discuss critically a number of significant key issues raised by Competency-Based Education and Training. Due to application being difficult, some practical applicatory material for education and training programmes is supplied.*

Heisey, Nancy R., and Daniel S. Schipani. *Theological Education on Five Continents: Anabaptist Perspectives.* Elkhart, IN: Institute of Mennonite Studies, 1997.

Hilgard, Ernest, and Gordon Bower. *Theories of Learning.* 5th ed, Englewood Cliffs, NJ: Prentice Hall, 1981.

Johnstone, P. *The Church is Bigger Than You Think: The Unfinished Task of World Evangelization.* Fearn, UK/Gerrards Cross, UK: Christian Focus Publications/WEC, 1998.

> *The church is growing but many challenges remain. In meeting these challenges the author explores practical ways in which local churches, training institutions and mission agencies can break down the barriers that abound between them and which have had a strong historical legacy. The challenge is for training institutions is to be more mission minded and more church minded.*

Kelsey, David H. "Reflections on Theological Education as Character Formation." *Theological Education.* 25:1 (Autumn 1988), 62-75.

Kohl, Manfred W. and A.N. Lal Senanayake, eds. *Educating for Tomorrow: Theological Leadership for the Asian Context.* SAIACS Press and Overseas Council International, 2002.

Kolb, David. *Experiential Learning.* Englewood Cliffs, NJ: Prentice Hall, 1984.

Kraft, Charles H. *Communication Theory for Christian Witness.* Nashville: Abingdon, 1983.

__________. *Communicating Jesus' Way.* rev. ed. Pasadena, CA: William Carey Library, 1999.

Krallmann, Günter. *Mentoring for Mission: A Handbook on Leadership Principles Exemplified by Jesus Christ.* Waynesboro, GA: Gabriel Publishing, 2002.

> *An excellent in-depth analysis of Jesus' approach to mentoring with the primary purpose of mission.*

Kridel, Craig, Robert V. Bullough Jr., and Paul Shaker, eds. *Teachers and Mentors: Profiles of Distinguished Twentieth Century Professors of Education.* New York and London: Garland Publishing, Inc., 1996.

> *This book offers perspectives on the management of learning that incorporate formal education with valuable learning outside the educational system.*

Lefever, Marlene D. *Learning Styles: Reaching Everyone God Gave You to Teach.* Paris, Ontario: David C. Cook Publishing Co, 1995.

George Lindbeck, "Spiritual Formation and Theological Education" in *Theological Education.* 24: Supplement 1 (1988) 10-32.

Lingenfelter, Judith E., and Sherwood G. Lingenfelter. *Teaching Cross-Culturally: An Incarnational Model for Learning and Teaching.* Grand Rapids, MI: Baker Academic, 2003.

Ann Lutterman-Aguilar and Orval Gingerich. "Experiential Pedagogy for Study Abroad: Educating for Global Citizenship." *Frontiers: The Interdisciplinary Journal of Study Abroad.* (Winter 2002), 41-82.

Martin, Alvin, ed. *The Means of World Evangelization: Missiological Education at Fuller School of World Mission.* South Pasadena, CA: William Carey Library, 1974.

Martinson, Paul Varo, ed. *Mission at the Dawn of the 21st Century: A Vision for the Church.* Minneapolis: Kirk House Publishers, 1999.

Ortiz, Juan Carlos. *Call to Discipleship.* New Jersey: Logos International, 1975.

Ott, Bernhard. "Mission Oriented Theological Education: Moving beyond Traditional Models of Theological Education." *Transformation* 18: 2 (2001), 74-86.

Padilla, C. Rene, ed. *New Alternative in Theological Education.* Oxford: Regnum, 1986.

Page, Michael R., Andrew C. Cohen, Barbara Kappler, Julie Chi and James Lassegard, eds. *Maximizing Study Abroad.* Minneapolis: University of Minnesota, 2002.

Palmer, Parker J. *To Know As We Are Known: Education as a Spiritual Journey.* San Francisco: Harper and Row, 1993.

Perry, Dwight. "Ministerial Formation in the African-American Church." *A Heart for the City: Effective Ministries to the Urban Community.* Chicago: Moody Bible Institute, 1999.

Peterson, Chip F. "Preparing Engaged Citizens: Three Models of Experiential Education for Social Justice." *Frontiers: The Interdisciplinary Journal of Study Abroad.* (Winter 2002), 41-82.

Petersen, Jim and Mike Shamy. *The Insider: Bringing the Kingdom of God into Your Everyday World.* Colorado Springs, CO: NavPress, 2003.

Petersen, Jim. *Living Proof: Sharing the Gospel Naturally.* Colorado Springs, CO: NavPress, 1989.

Pollard, Mike.   *Cultivating a Missions-Active Church.* Peachtree City, GA: ACMC, 1988.

Pusch, Margaret D. ed. *Multicultural Education: A Cross Cultural Training Approach.* Yarmouth, ME: Intercultural Press, 1984.

Raiter, Michael D. "Sent for this Purpose: Mission and Missiology and their Search for Meaning." R.J. Gibson ed. *Ripe for Harvest: Christian Mission in the NT and in our World.* Carlisle: Paternoster, 2000, 106-150.

Reed, Layman E. *Preparing Missionaries for Intercultural Communication/Bi-cultural Approach.* Pasadena, California: William Carey Library, 1988.

Reid, Alvin. *Introduction To Evangelism.* Nashville, TN: Broadman & Holman Publishers, 1998.

Rowen, Samuel. "Missiology and the Coherence of Theological Education." Duane Elmer and Lois McKinney eds. *With An Eye on the Future: Development and Mission in the 21st Centur.* Monrovia, CA.: MARC, 1996, 93-100.

Seelye, H. Ned. *Experiential Activities for Intercultural Learning.* Yarmouth, ME: Intercultural Press, 1996.

Shor, Ira. *Empowering Education: Critical Teaching for Social Change.* Chicago: University of Chicago Press, 1992.

Shor, Ira. ed. *Freire for the Classroom: A Source Book for Liberating Teaching.* Portsmouth, NH: Boyton/Cook Publishers, 1987.

Smite, Robert C. "Training College Students for Urban Ministry." *A Heart for the City: Effective Ministries to the Urban Community.* Chicago: Moody Bible Institute, 1999.

Spencer, Daniel. "Experiential Education: A Method for Transformation and Liberation." *Global Perspectives* 6. (Spring, 1989), Minneapolis: Center for Global Education.

Stackhouse, Max L., Tim Dearbon and Scott Paeth, eds. *The Local Church in Global Era: Reflection for a New Century.* 2000.

Stanley, Paul, D. Clinton and J. Robert. *Connecting.* Colorado Springs, CO: NavPress, 1992.

Telford, T. *Missions in the 21st Century: Getting Your Church into the Game.* Wheaton, IL: Harold Shaw Publishers, 1998.

> This former baseball umpire draws upon baseball analogies to assist and inspire local churches to be active in world evangelisation.

Thomas, Alan M. *Beyond Education: A New Perspective on Society's Management of Learning.* San Francisco: Jossey-Bass Publishers, 1991.

> This book provides heroes in the educational fields, who consistently mentor others.

Tobia, Cynthia. *The Way They Learn.* Wheaton, IL: Tyndale, 1994.

Van Engen, C., J.D. Woodberry and E.J. Elliston, eds. *Missiological Education for the 21st Century: The Book, the Circle, and the Sandals.* Maryknoll, NY: Orbis Books, 1996.

Watson, David. *Discipleship.* Sevenoaks, UK: Hodder and Stoughton, 1981.

Wheeler, Barbara, and Edward Farley. *Shifting Boundaries: Contextual Approaches to the Structure of Theological Education.* Louisville, KY: Westminster/John Knox, 1991.

Wilkins, Michael J. *Following the Master: Discipleship in the Steps of Jesus.* Grand Rapids: Zondervan, 1992.

Winter, Ralph D. and Steven C. Hawthorne, eds. *Perspectives on the World Christian Movement.* 3d ed. Pasadena: William Carey Library, 1999.

Woodberry, J. Dudley, Charles Van Engen and Edgar J. Elliston. *Missiological Education for the 21st Century: The Book, the Circle and the Sandals.* Maryknoll, NY: Orbis Books, 1997.

Yount, William R. *Called to Teach: An Introduction to the Ministry of Teaching.* Nashville, Tennessee: Broadman and Holman Publishers, 1999.

> An exellent source to understand Biblical-based education with practical spiritual insight.

Yount, Rick. "Jesus the Master Teacher." D. Eldridge, ed. *The Teaching Ministry of the Church.* Nashville, Tennessee: Broadman & Holman, 1995.

Zachary, Lois J. *The Mentor's Guide.* San Francisco, CA: Jossey-Bass, 2000.

Zahniser, A.H. Mathias. *Symbol and Ceremony: Making Disciples Across Cultures.* Monrovia, CA: MARC, 1997.

PARTICIPANTS

This report is the collaborative outcome of the members of Issue Group 28: Effective Theological Education for World Evangelisation. The following are the members of this group who attended the 2004 Forum as well as those who were not able to attend, but participated actively and contributed to the discussions before the Forum.

Pieter F. Theron (editor and convenor),	South Africa/ Philippines
Wafik Wahba (co-convenor),	Canada
Theresa Lua (facilitator),	Philippines
Victor Babajide Cole (theologian),	Kenya
Michael Raiter (co-editor and theologian)	Australia
Kumar Abraham	Sri Lanka /Philippines
Stuart Brooking	Australia
Larry Caldwell	U.S.A. /Philippines
Ebenezer Samuel Chelladurai	India
V.C. George Cherian	India
Jim Chew	New Zealand
Paul Cornelius	India
Les Crawford	U.S.A.
David Fenrick	U.S.A.
Mark Grace	New Zealand
Brian Harris	New Zealand
Laura Humphries	U.K.
Dusan Jaura	Slovakia
Jesudason Jeyaraj	India
John Macdonald	U.S.A.
Dieumeme Noelliste	Jamaica
Brainerd Prince	India
Wolfgang Schulze	Germany
David Scott	U.S.A.
Kwai Lin Stephens	Mongolia
Andrzej Turkanik	Austria

David Turnbull   Australia
Colleen Yim   India
Barnabas Chelliah   India

Not at forum but contributed
Alfred Itiowe   Nigeria
Esther J. Kibor   Kenya
Michal Klus   Czech Republic
Iman Iragaba Mushishi   South Africa

BIOETHICS: OBSTACLE OR OPPORTUNITY FOR THE GOSPEL?

Lausanne Occasional Paper No. 58

This Issue Group on this topic was Issue Group No. 29

The content of this Occasional Paper was prepared by the whole Issue Group, with special drafting responsibilities handled by Dr Roland Chia and Dr Denise Cooper (with Dr James Thobaben for Story/Commentary #7) and special editorial responsibilities handled by Dr Andrew Fergusson and Dr John Kilner

CONTENTS

Introduction

Part I. Theological Foundations for Bioethics
1. What Does it Mean to be Human?
2. The Value of Human Life
3. Suffering and Death
4. Health, Healing, and Hope
5. Stewardship
6. Justice
7. Science, Medicine and the Christian Faith
8. The Church

Part II. Opportunities for the Gospel
Generic Strategies
1. Justice in Health Care
2. Caregiver-Patient Relationships
3. End-of-Life Care
4. Abortion
5. Reproductive Technologies
6. Stem-Cell Research
7. Genetic Modification in Agriculture
8. Human Enhancement

Participants

INTRODUCTION

Two questions faced the bioethics group at the 2004 World Evangelisation Forum. First, many were asking "What is bioethics?" and second, "What on earth has it got to do with evangelisation?"

The first is easier. For the purposes of this paper, **bioethics is the study of ethical issues relating to the provision of health care, to emerging biotechnologies, and to biomedical research.** We live in an age of phenomenal advances in life sciences and their attendant technologies. From the mapping of the human genome, to successful cloning of mammals and the harvesting of human stem cells, these advances present both great promise for new medical treatments and profound concerns about the harm they may do to society. Genetics, cybernetics and nanotechnology, for instance, which promise to reverse or eliminate diseases, could also be used to engineer "better" humans, or even "trans-humans" or "post-humans" that render the humans of today obsolete.

The second question is the focus of this paper. How does bioethics present both obstacles and opportunities for the gospel? Bioethics certainly represents a major challenge to Christian witness. On the one hand, secular bioethics often present a narrow biological view of health and an instrumental view of human life, such that human beings who have limited capacities are assigned a lesser value. This outlook seems to leave little space for the psychological and social dimensions of human life, let alone its spiritual dimension. In addition, especially in some Western societies, bioethics tends to be dominated by concern for individuals and their rights, while neglecting an understanding of the common good and our mutual responsibilities. However, the obstacles are not all generated from outside the community of faith. Christians are often perceived and portrayed as unreasonably conservative, and may in fact be so. They appear opposed to technological progress, and rigid, uncaring and legalistic when they speak against technologies and research that offer hope and relief to suffering people.

Bioethics also provides special opportunities for the gospel. When people encounter infertility, illness, and the fragility of their own bodies, and when they confront their own mortality as they observe or experience the dying process, the illusion of control over their lives is threatened, or even shattered. Where will such people turn for help with their questions and the decisions they must make about medical treatments? If Christians become known as reliable and thoughtful sources of information and counsel about these issues, opportunities to present a Christian view of life, meaning, suffering, and death will arise. The questions at the heart of bioethics are also at the heart of the gospel.

Biotechnologies relating to nonhuman life also raise profound questions about our relationship with the world around us, and as in health care, about the nature of justice. By engaging in these issues, Christians can challenge others to consider what a "good society" looks like, and what nourishes such a society. Again, the gospel provides a radical and credible alternative to prevailing worldviews.

Finally, the way we "do" Christian bioethics should witness to God's grace and love towards sinners. Love, acceptance, and the offer of forgiveness ought to characterise our discussions, rather than laying down rules and condemning those who break them. We are called to "live a life worthy of the gospel" as a response to God's grace, but God's grace is open to all. The gospel is good news, perhaps especially for those who have made bad decisions about their lives.

Part I of this paper examines those central themes which provide a theological framework for Christian bioethics. Part II examines bioethical decision-making in the context of Christian ministry, using eight stories. The issues involved in each are analysed briefly, specific strategies are suggested that a Christian community might use as opportunities to commend the gospel, and resources for further information are mentioned.

PART I
THEOLOGICAL FOUNDATIONS FOR BIOETHICS

Christian bioethics is based on the self-revelation of God in Jesus Christ, witnessed to by the Old and New Testaments. The community of faith transmits the tradition of God's saving acts in history, culminating in the story of the life, death, resurrection, and ascension of Jesus of Nazareth. This story provides the framework within which Christians interpret the world and their relationship to it. As the church remembers, retells, and reflects on this story, she allows herself to be actively shaped by the Holy Spirit. Christians should not only look at the world differently, but also conduct themselves differently.

1. What Does it Mean to be Human?

The creation narrative is foundational to understanding what it means to be human. Like other animals and plants, human beings are creatures, not gods or demi-gods. We are made from the dust of the earth. We are dependent on God for our very being. Yet humans are distinguished from the rest of creation in that

we are charged with exercising stewardship of the earth's resources, we have the
breath (or spirit) of God breathed into us,
and uniquely we are made in the image of
God:

> *Then God said, 'Let us make hu-*
> *mankind in our image, according to*
> *our likeness, and let them have do-*
> *minion over the fish of the sea and*
> *over the birds of the air, and over*
> *the cattle, and over all the wild ani-*
> *mals of the earth, and over every*
> *creeping thing that creeps upon the*
> *earth. So God created humankind*
> *in his own image, in the image of*
> *God he created them; male and*
> *female he created them.'* (Genesis
> 1:26-27)

> *'Then the Lord God formed man*
> *from the dust of the ground, and*
> *breathed into his nostrils the breath*
> *of life, and the man became a living*
> *being'* (Genesis 2:7)

Although the concept of the image of
God is widely considered definitive of
human nature, it is difficult to know precisely what it means. The different interpretations broadly fall into three categories: substantial, relational, and functional.
The *substantial* view of the image has a
long history in Christian theology while
the *relational* view is perhaps more
prominent now. These two categories correspond roughly to the two different kinds
of "image" one can picture. The first is the
one inscribed upon an object, such as the
sovereign's image on a coin. The other is
the more intangible kind one sees in a mirror. A third category views the image as
functional and holds that the image of God

is found in the exercise of "dominion" and
"stewardship" of the rest of creation
(Genesis 1:28).

All three views shed light on what
the Bible means and implies by the image
of God in humans. If only one view is
considered, our understanding of this important biblical concept is impoverished.

Understanding the image as *substan-*
tial implies that the image of God is im-
printed on the person as an image is impressed on a coin. Human beings are created in a particular way and possess a nature distinct from the other animals that
gives them the capacity to reflect God.
The substantial view draws attention to
the species distinction between human
beings and the animal kingdom, and it
affirms that the image of God must be
found whenever the human species is
found. It is thus intrinsic to who we are.
Some have wondered if the image is a particular human characteristic, such as our
personality, creativity, rationality, spirituality, or something else. However, no such
characteristic is identified in Scripture as
defining what the image is, though such
characteristics may well result from being
created in God's image. If this substantial
approach is taken, the image is generally
connected to a strong theology of *crea-*
tion. The image is the way that God has
made humanity and, by implication, it
ought not to be changed. This view therefore limits any attempt to modify human
nature, and historically this kind of approach has been most influential.

A recent trend is to view the image as
something more dynamic and intangible.

The *relational* view holds that the image of God is defined by relationships. Genesis 1:27, with its reference to humanity being made as male and female is taken by some to make the image of God equivalent to being made male and female. However, as with the functional "dominion" idea, similarly linked with the image in the previous verse, so the relational idea here may well more be a result of being created in God's image rather than a definition of what the image as such.

The *relational* implications of the image of God include the truth that among all God's creatures, human beings alone know God and are consciously related to him. Further included is the emphasis that the divine intention behind the creation of humankind is fellowship and communion. But in this dynamic, understanding the future dimension of the image also becomes much more important. That is, it includes the notion of *the image as a future possibility*. The image is what is *to be* formed in us; it is the goal. As Paul says in Romans 8:29 we are to be conformed to the image of the Christ Jesus.

These more relational implications of the image are grounded not so much in a theology of *creation* as in a theology of *redemption*. They suggest that the difficulty in determining which human characteristic is *the* defining aspect of the image of God in us arises precisely because the image is not something to be defined in terms of any one aspect of humanity. The image is not a past tense, but a dynamic and future element, and is formed in us in our becoming human—in being all that we are. No one specific characteristic makes us human; rather, God is found in us in the whole of our being. The image is a destiny, a direction, and a destination, rather than merely a statement about our origin.

Of course, the two perspectives, the *substantial and creational* on the one hand and the *dynamic and future-oriented* on the other, are not necessarily to be set against each other. A conflict arises only if an emphasis on the image as dynamic, associated with a strong theology about the future, becomes an argument for looking for great changes in human nature itself as people move towards God's goal for human life. That strong a relational emphasis may well encourage people to see justification for enhancing, developing, and changing human nature in a way that more conservative, creational theology would typically not allow.

In secular bioethics, the emphasis has moved from what it means to be human to what it means to be a "person." The criteria for personhood are variously defined, but usually relate to the capacities of the being in question, such as intellectual or decision making capacity. Using these criteria, some humans may not qualify as persons, whereas some non-human animals might. Against this, the substantial view of the image of God affirms that all humans bear the image simply as humans and independent of their individual qualities. Even the poorest functioning human being has a different status from the most intelligent animal. It is important to maintain this, since one interpretation of the relational view of the image of God may also exclude some humans from being image bearers, namely those who seem incapable of relationships (e.g. the very young, the demented, the severely intellectually disabled). It needs to be emphasized that these humans can be known and loved by others, and are so by God, so that they are indeed "in relationship" by virtue of being human.

Another problem with the concept of personhood is that it tends to separate the "person" from his or her body. Especially in the West, Christian theology also has for too long neglected the body in favour of the soul. The Bible presents a unitary view of the person. God created human beings as a psychosomatic unity of body and soul, and we will be resurrected as a body-soul unity. While a human cannot be simply reduced to his or her body and its functions, neither should the body be despised or neglected.

Ultimately, the story of the Fall brings us face to face with the stark reality that ours is a sin-marred world in need of God's salvation. It helps us not just to understand the presence of evil and suffering in our world, but also to acknowledge the nature of human rebellion, which extends into all human cultural enterprises, including science and medicine. Part of what it means to be human is to live in a fragmented world, with perverted reason, desires, and relationships.

2. The Value of Human Life

The biblical description of human beings as created in the image of God points to the value that God accords to human life, and murder is prohibited for this very reason:

> *Whoever sheds the blood of a human, by a human shall that person's blood be shed; for in his own image God created humankind.*
> (Genesis 9:6)

The special significance God assigns to human life is often described in terms of the sanctity of human life. Life is a freely bestowed gift from God and therefore is to be welcomed with joy and thanksgiving, as a testimony to God's grace. Human life must also be cherished and protected because it is an expression of the creative love of God, who has brought us into being not merely for biological existence but for fellowship and communion with him. Further, God values us so much that he sent his Son to die on the cross so that we might receive the gift of eternal life (Colossians 1:12; Ephesians 1:18).

That the Bible is unequivocal, that innocent human life may not be destroyed, is clearly evident in the commandment: "You shall not murder" (Exodus 20:13; Deuteronomy 5:17) and the sanction against those who take a human life:

> *And for your own lifeblood I will surely require a reckoning: from every animal I will require it and from human beings, each one for the blood of another, I will require a reckoning for human life.*
> (Genesis 9:5)

The value accorded to human life is also seen in the biblical portrayal of a God who protects the weak and the vulnerable.

The psalmist speaks of the care God shows to unborn children in their mothers' wombs (Psalm 139:13-16). This recognition ought to inform our attitudes to the sick, the disabled, the very young, and the aged.

Some human individuals, patients in a permanent vegetative state for instance, are physically alive, but cannot be said to have those qualities or experiences that are normally associated with "being alive." Some bioethicists argue that the value of a human life is dependent on the "quality of life," the condition, and the capacities of the individual, and therefore varies. The life of a foetus, or someone who is demented or severely disabled, is thus of lesser value and under some circumstances may be taken. Christians, however, maintain that all human lives are of equal worth, yet we recognise that modern medical decisions cannot avoid some "quality of life" considerations. For example, judgments that the burden of a treatment outweighs its benefits for a particular patient involve an evaluation of the patient's quality of life. There is no obligation to extend human life by the maximum amount of time if the patient will die soon regardless of treatment and treatment will add burden to the dying process. Both "sanctity of life" and "quality of life" considerations are legitimate and important, with the proviso that for Christians, quality considerations cannot justify overriding the sanctity of human life.

3. Suffering and Death

A Christian understanding of human suffering and death has profound implications for the way we view the practice of medicine. Suffering and death are the consequences of sin – not necessarily individual *sins*, but sin. They entered the world through the disobedience of the first humans, Adam and Eve. The Fall not only affects human will and dispositions, it disrupts the very structures of reality, the fabric of the created order, so that they now appear incomprehensible and arbitrary.

The reality of suffering, and indeed the presence of evil in the world, pose serious challenges to Christian theology. On the one hand, God is full of mercy and compassion, and it would be incongruous to think that He would want to cause suffering. On the other, God is sovereign and nothing occurs apart from His will. To explain this apparent contradiction we may postulate a distinction between what God wills and what He desires, between what He intends and what He permits. God does not desire that a child should be born with cystic fibrosis or that a young adult should develop a malignant brain tumour. Nevertheless, God sometimes allows these things to occur as the consequence of the fallen reality to which human beings belong and for which they are responsible. God does not desire or intend that His rebellious creatures should suffer, but He *allows* it. It is only in this sense that suffering may be said to be part of the divine (permissive) will.

Human suffering must also be viewed from the perspective of the cross of Christ. God has, through the mystery of the suffering and death of His incarnate Son, reversed the effects of sin and delivered humankind from death. Of course, human suffering continues to be a reality in our world even after the death and resurrection of Jesus Christ some two thousand years ago. Although these events signalled the ultimate victory of God over sin, death, and evil, this victory will not be fully and universally realised until the consummation of the kingdom of God. Only then will this sin-marred world be transformed and transfigured into the new heavens and the new earth.

Yet the suffering of Christ brings a different perspective to suffering. It demonstrates that not all suffering is due to the personal sin of the individual sufferer, since Christ is without sin. We also see that on the cross, God Himself participates in human suffering. Furthermore, the New Testament introduces another dimension to human suffering when it speaks of believers sharing in Christ's suffering when they suffer (Philippians 3:10). Seen in this light, Christ's death gives meaning to human suffering, such that some Christians speak of "redemptive suffering." This concept must be properly understood if we are to avoid either of two false conclusions. First, to say that some suffering can be redemptive does not mean that suffering should be morbidly sought for its own sake. To do this would be to ignore the fact that God sent His Son to deliver us from sin and death, and therefore from suffering. Secondly, the concept of redemptive suffering does not imply that all suffering is redemptive. Suffering can be so intense and so dehumanising that it overwhelms sufferers with their own mis-

ery and causes them to give up on life itself.

Yet some physical and mental suffering can be "redemptive" in that it furthers spiritual growth by forcing us to come to terms with the reality of our own sinfulness and frailty. Suffering is an evil to be resisted, but God can use even the evil of human suffering and pain to benefit the sufferer. Suffering can help us to come to the realisation of our total dependence on the mercy of God. It can heighten our understanding of our own limitations and help us to accept that there are many aspects of life beyond our control. Suffering can purify us from the passions that corrupt our relationships with God, others, and ourselves. It forces us to reconsider and reorder our priorities so that we will seek above all what is ultimately most important (Luke 10:42). Suffering also offers the possibility of a closer relationship with Jesus. Suffering and pain are inevitable in this fallen and fractured world, but we can and should look ahead to the eradication of evil and suffering in the transfigured creation. In the meantime, we are obliged sometimes to accept suffering and to seek spiritual healing through it.

We turn now to a biblical understanding of death. The Genesis account introduces the reality of death when God reminds Adam

You [shall] return to the ground for
out of it you were taken; you are
dust, and to dust you shall return.
(Genesis 3:19)

Paul also teaches that sin and death entered into the world because of the rebellion of Adam (Romans 5:12). Death is a universal human experience, the great equaliser in that it is the end of all regardless of race, status, wealth or influence (Ecclesiastes 2:15-16, 3:19-21, 5:15-16, 9:1-6). The Good News, however, is that God has sent His Son to overcome death and to grant eternal life to all who believe. Jesus offers the hope of eternal life (John 5:24; Luke 14:14; Matthew 22:31). Paul speaks about the victory over death that Jesus has made possible. Death does not have the last word, because it is defeated by the sacrificial death and glorious resurrection of Christ.

'Where, O death, is your victory?
Where, O death, is your sting?'
The sting of death is sin, and the power of sin is the law. But thanks be to God! He gives us victory through our Lord Jesus Christ..
(1 Corinthians 15:55-57)

There is therefore now an ambiguity about death for Christians. As an enemy (1 Corinthians 15:26), it should be resisted. Aggressive life-saving or life-prolonging treatment is often justified. That is what medicine is generally about. Neither should death be invited or taken hold of (as in suicide or euthanasia). Yet as a defeated enemy, which now serves as the necessary gateway to eternal life, death need not be resisted at every turn. There comes a point for each of us when death should be accepted as inevitable, even appropriate. To discern when this point is reached is not always simple; there are cases in which the line that sepa-

rates beneficial and futile treatment is not clear. However, doing everything necessary to delay death is not required when someone is unavoidably dying, since the sting of death is removed and it does not have the final word. It is not part of good medicine to prolong the dying process: "A dying man needs to die as a sleepy man needs to sleep, and there comes a time when it is wrong, as well as useless, to resist" (Steward Alsop). As ethicist Daniel Callahan puts it:

Of each serious illness, especially with the elderly, a question should be asked and a possibility entertained: could it be that this illness is the one that either will be fatal, or since some disease must be fatal, should soon be allowed to be fatal? If so, then a different strategy toward it should come into play, an effort to work toward a peaceful death rather than fight for a cure.

4. Health, Healing and Hope

The Christian doctrine of the resurrection of the dead means that our hope has to do with death's undoing, not with its mitigation or evasion. Further, this doctrine stresses that it is not just some essential part of the human being that survives, but that the whole person will be raised. Perhaps most significantly for bioethics, the doctrine implies that sickness and death are enemies that ultimately only God can conquer; that perfect health and healing will only be experienced in the consummated kingdom of God.

The concept of resurrection is present in the Old Testament (Isaiah 26:19; Daniel 12:2; Psalm 49:15; Psalm 17:15), but it is taught most explicitly in the New Testament, both by Jesus (Matthew 22:29-32; Mark 12:24-27; Luke 20:34-38; John 5:25, 28-29) and by Paul. The general resurrection is grounded in the resurrection of Christ (1 Corinthians 15:12-14). While emphasising the discontinuities between this life and the resurrected life (1 Corinthians 15:42-44), Paul also stresses the corporeal or bodily nature of the resurrection life.

Resurrection is not merely bringing dead bodies back to life, but a *new* creation, which nevertheless guarantees the identity of the individual, in that it is the same person who has died who is raised. There is healing, transformation, and completion (Philippians 3:21). In the resurrection, everything that is bound up with the person is preserved; our whole history is present, but as healed and reconciled with God and others.

What can we conclude about our attitudes to sickness, death and medical science? On the one hand, sickness and death must be strenuously resisted since they do not represent the original divine intention for humans, but its subversion. This provides a powerful justification for efforts to treat, eradicate, and prevent diseases. Following the example of the healing ministry of Jesus, we see sickness as an evil to be driven out. On the other hand, since only God can bring about health and human perfection in the end, we must reject attempts to arrogate that function to ourselves, believing that our science and technology (which is another way of saying we ourselves) can achieve it.

5. Stewardship

We turn now to the question of human responsibility in medicine and biotechnology, and the boundaries beyond which we should not venture. Boundaries here refer not to technological or scientific limits but to *moral* limits to the scientific enterprise. The cultural mandate of Genesis 1:28 sanctions the scientific enterprise, and we understand that science, as made possible by the grace of God, should be directed towards the preservation and care of God's creatures, including humans. The command to fill and subdue the earth and to rule over the living creatures can be applied generally, although not exclusively, to science and technology, including biotechnology. Human beings have been given the task of superintending God's good creation and are therefore *response-able* beings before God. In the Genesis narrative God delegated this cultural task to human beings *before* the Fall, thereby emphasising that it was God's original purpose for humankind.

Although human rebelliousness and sin did not nullify the divine cultural mandate, it distorts humankind's perception and perverts its attitude towards it. Humans now assert their own resourcefulness in creating and fashioning their own lives, wanting to become their own creators. They have ceased to recognise their own creatureliness because of their refusal to acknowledge God. Because sinfulness is inextricably bound up with human nature, it is present in everything that human beings do and touches every aspect of the human cultural enterprise. The story of the tower of Babel (Genesis 11:1-9) illustrates the attempt to "reach the heavens" and achieve a reputation through technology.

This brings us to the problematic concept of "playing God." This phrase might be understood simply to reflect what humans should legitimately do as God's stewards – to imitate his character (as much as we are able) and to act in the world according to his purposes. Nevertheless, the concept is more commonly understood to invoke a perspective that on the one hand renders God superfluous, and on the other elevates human scientific and technological skill to a status that does not belong to it. Where the idea of God is deemed superfluous, human beings accord themselves the status of "maker."

> *The fundamental perspective ... with which (to) contrast 'playing God' is to view the world ... as if God were given..... That means, among other things, that the end of all things may be left to God. ... From this perspective, our responsibilities, while great, will not be regarded as being of messianic proportion. There will be some room, then, for an ethics of means as well as the consideration of consequences, for reflection about the kind of behaviour which is worthy of human nature as created by God, as embodied and interdependent, for example.* (Allen Verhey)

The fundamental concern in the warning against "playing God" is the fact that there are broader theological ramifications to certain actions than what is included in an ethic defined by narrow humanitarian considerations. As Christians,

particularly Christian scientists, doctors, and policymakers, faithfulness to God must be our first priority, above worldly success, and even above the quest for scientific progress. While Christian stewardship compels us to work hard to alleviate the suffering of our fellow human beings, it also warns us against the self-idolatry that causes us to think that we can usurp the place of God.

> *We would do well to tackle such issues in the ways God directs, rather than developing our own strategies – perhaps following worldly techniques – in a vain attempt to improve on God's abilities or timing. It does not matter where in the lifespan a bioethical issue arises ... God's way is the best way, and it is our task to learn as much about it as we can.* (John Kilner)

6. Justice

In pluralistic, post-Enlightenment cultures we tend to understand justice in a minimalist way, reduced to the protection of personal autonomy – providing the space for individuals to act according to their own preferences as long as they do not violate the autonomy of another. The strength of such a view of justice is that it can provide a basis for conversation between people of different cultures and religions. But it also has serious weaknesses.

One significant weakness is that such a notion of justice enables us only to see the constraints to exercise in seeking goods, without telling us which goods to seek. The emphasis on personal autonomy and "rights" pushes substantive moral issues and questions to the margin. It allows for space for autonomous action, without indicating how that space is to be filled. Further, the overriding emphasis on the prohibition against violating another's autonomy tends to reduce covenantal relationships, like the doctor-patient relationship, to matters of contract. There is no room for a genuinely mutual decision-making, a partnership with reciprocal responsibilities and mutual trust.

Christian bioethics looks to a much richer concept of justice, based on the story of God and his dealings with his people. It is a story of a God who hears the cries of his people and delivers them from the bondage of slavery in Egypt. It is a story of salvation and covenant, which culminates in Jesus Christ, the incarnate Son of God, who not only came to announce and demonstrate the justice of God, but also to inaugurate the kingdom of God, which is His just reign. From it we come to understand the true meaning of justice and the demands it places on us.

Such justice tells us something of the goods to seek, life and human flourishing among them. Such justice exercises some constraints besides respect for the sometimes-arbitrary preferences of another, constraints that include the prohibition against the destruction of an embodied image of God. Such justice will nurture covenantal relations, not reduce them to contractual or instrumental relationships. It will defend the weak and advocate for the powerless against the powers that resist God's cause. Such [merciful justice will] ... visit

the sick (Matthew 25:36,43), not abandon or eliminate them. Indeed, it will discover in 'the least of these' and in their vulnerability the very image of Christ (Matthew 25:40,45). (Allen Verhey)

Biblical justice directs special attention to those who have less, because there is a basic equality of every human being, created alike in God's image, which requires that the basic life-sustaining needs of all alike be met (eg, 2 Corinthians 8:13-14).

7. Science, Medicine and the Christian faith

The scientific enterprise is an exercise of stewardship – a responsibility entrusted to humankind by its Creator – and should be directed towards the betterment of individuals as well as society. Medical science and practice are ways in which sickness and disease are resisted and the Christian ethic of love compels us to engage thus with the world. Throughout its history, the Church has played a significant role in the establishment of hospitals and other health-care institutions. Insofar as health care sciences are directed towards compassionate healing, they must be understood as God's gift to humankind, an aspect of his common grace.

We are also profoundly aware of the gravity of sin that touches every aspect of human culture. Science in general, and medical science in particular, can either be channels of divine grace or vehicles of human sinfulness. They can be employed to harm and destroy rather than to heal and restore, as is evident in history. The scientific and technological enterprise can also be tainted by sinful aspirations for glory and economic gain. When both are relentlessly pursued, science and technology can bring harm not just to individuals, but also to society. Even when its goals are noble, science may be conducted in an inhumane manner when the ends of science are said to justify the means it uses. The "greater good" argument is often used to justify ethically dubious scientific research or therapeutic procedures, but despite its strong humanitarian overtones, this argument is abstract and superficial. Christian ethics, and even conventional wisdom, insist that certain procedures must not be allowed, whatever the promise of therapeutic benefit. In the shadow of Nazism, the Nuremberg Code declared, "no experiment should be conducted where there is an *a priori* reason to believe that death or disabling injury will occur."

Regarding the goals of medicine, there has since the work of Alasdair MacIntyre been a renewed interest in virtue ethics, centred on the particular internal goods or goals of specific moral practices. The Hippocratic Oath arguably represents the most ancient medical expression of such an outlook. The writer(s) of the *Oath* did not merely apply a general moral theory to a medicine conceived as morally neutral, but tried to draw out the moral significance inherent in the practice itself and "the standards coherent with the good of the craft."

In another Hippocratic work, *The Art*, the proper goals of medicine are defined: doing away with the sufferings of the sick, lessening the violence of their diseases, and refusing to treat those who are overmastered by their diseases, realising that in such cases medicine is powerless.

Similarly, Stanley Hauerwas claims that medicine in itself represents a sectarian commitment about how to care for the ill. The Oath did not reflect the broad consensus of society but only the convictions of a small group of physicians in the late 4th Century BC. The Oath's prohibitions were rooted in a practice, the purpose of which is to benefit the sick. Such a purpose puts limits on the use to which medical skills can be put -- they cannot be used for alien ends, such as the destruction of human life or health. Hauerwas says the Oath is a form of "natural morality" in which Christians rightly believe they continue to have a stake. As Leon Kass says:

> *'(The Oath) might still be right if, as I believe, the essential activity of healing the sick is still the same, despite all the enormous changes in medical practice. That is, if to be healthy or whole still means largely what it did in ancient Greece, if the desire of the ill to be whole is no different, and if the healing relation between the physician and the one to be healed is in essence the same.'*

8. The Church

As a distinctive event, community, and institution, the church has its origins in God, but it exists with and in view of the world. The church is called and sent by God to the world to bear witness to God's reconciliation, healing, and transformation of the creation in Jesus Christ. In its ministry of proclamation and service, and in its stewardship of the creation, the church participates in, as well as points to the reality of the kingdom of God.

Christian witness comes out of the church's profound solidarity with the world. The human struggles "outside of the church" for justice, peace, liberation, and for healing, are not alien to the people of God; they are also the struggles of that human community we call the church. It must also be stressed that even as it serves as the instrument of divine grace, the church very much shares in the brokenness and struggles of the world.

Christian witness, however, is not just solidarity with the world. If it is an authentic application of God's saving acts, then it is also a prophetic judgement of the world. In particular, the church must stand in opposition to the belief in self-righteousness, in humanity's inherent natural goodness, and moral perfectibility.

The profound tension between solidarity and opposition characterises the relationship between the church and the world. In order for the church to fulfil its task, it must be true to itself and to its own calling, yet it is not called to withdraw from the world, but rather is sent to the world to proclaim the messages of grace and forgiveness, as well as prophetic judgment.

Worship

Worship is the central activity of the church, in which the people assemble to hear, reflect on, and perhaps discuss God's word, and then praise God with song and prayer. As revelation and response, worship provides a perspective that informs and shapes our perception of the world and our responsibilities.

Worship forces us to confront the world as it is – fallen, fragmented, terrifying, and yet beautiful and mysterious. The words of the liturgy – "deliver us from evil," "help," "save," "defend us" – point to the enormity of human suffering caused either by human wickedness or the capricious forces of nature. In worship we are confronted by the stark reality of evil as we pray "Lord, have mercy," but worship also helps us to see the beauty of God's creation and appreciate the sheer wonder of life.

Worship involves the deep pathos of the memory of God and the pathos of hoping that the promises of God will be fulfilled in our sin-scarred world. It therefore opens us to the reality of the eternal and enables us to recognise the future that has already dawned upon us. Christian worship comprises praise, thanksgiving, confession, and prayer. Praise is focused on who God *is*, thanksgiving is a response to what God *does*, and *has done*. As we recognise the holiness of God, we are led into confession of our own sin and prayer for forgiveness. As we also acknowledge our total dependence on God, so we come to God in petition (prayer for our own needs) and intercession (prayer for the needs of others, including the suffering and the sick).

Praise, thanksgiving, and confession in congregational worship rarely have much connection with bioethical challenges such as biotechnologies threatening unborn human life or the prolonged dying of elderly people, but that need not be the case. Praising God for His creativity in crafting human life in all of its genetic complexity is perfectly appropriate. So is thanking God for defeating death on the cross so that we need not fear dying. Confessing our self-centered disinterest in helping others who have chosen to keep, rather than abort a disabled child is appropriate as well. By confining our attention to bioethics to educational classrooms, we miss a huge opportunity not only to educate people but also to help them connect bioethics to their life of faith in Christ.

The ministry of prayer in the church is particularly vital to those who are struggling with issues related to bioethics – the childless couple considering artificial reproductive technology, the pregnant single mother considering abortion, and the terminally ill patient contemplating suicide. Although prayer may not always change their situation, it may give them the wisdom and the moral courage to choose obedience.

Music and singing are an important part of the worship tradition in many churches. From joyful and exuberant praise to awe-filled wonder, from confident declaration of God's mighty acts to the anguished cry of the desperate in the tradition of the lament psalms, songs are a powerful way of both expressing and evoking an emotional response that goes beyond words. There are numerous hymns and contemporary songs that focus on bioethically significant themes.

Teaching

In order for Christians to be God's witnesses in this age of rapid developments in biotechnology, the church must continuously strengthen its teaching ministry. Teaching is inextricably bound to the Church's mission: "Therefore go and make disciples of all nations, baptising them in the name of the Father and of the Son and of the Holy Spirit, and *teaching* them to obey everything I have commanded you" (Matthew 28:19-20). Elders or pastors are not just required to "oversee" but also to instruct their flock (1 Timothy 3:2-3). In the New Testament and the early church, teaching has not only to do with doctrine but also with moral instruction, that is, with practical application.

Yet the pressing demands of ministry sometimes make it difficult for clergy to keep abreast with the most recent developments in biotechnology, such as cloning or stem cell research. Church leaders and teachers will therefore often need to rely on the work of theologians and Christian bioethicists.

Leaders cannot assume that Christian health professionals and bioscientists are aware of the ethical issues in their profession, but must encourage them to be involved in Christian professional associations such as the various Christian Medical Fellowships and Christian bioethics centres that have developed teaching and training resources. Christian health professionals and bioscientists need to be challenged to a discipleship that counts the costs and to be supported in it. They are under pressure from their profession to conform; indeed their careers may be at stake. This is especially so for those working in ethically controversial areas like stem cell research or cloning.

Lay Christians should be encouraged to be examples and witnesses when confronted with bioethical decisions. Many bioethical issues, such as abortion and euthanasia, are not technically difficult to understand, but their pastoral sensitivity, or perhaps their controversial nature seems to render them too hot to handle for many preachers. Christians need thoughtful teaching on issues that profoundly impact so many lives. In most locations there are individuals in the congregation or in the larger community that can provide such teaching. Church leaders themselves should be receiving some bioethics training as part of the ongoing education and nurture they receive from their denominations or clergy associations.

Pastoral Ministry

In the Christian context, pastoral ministry is part of discipleship and includes practical care, prayer, emotional support, and counselling. It is the function not only of the pastor, but of the whole Christian community. We are to correct each other, to "bear one another's burdens," (Galatians 6:2) and to admonish, encourage, and pray for each other. When caring for or counselling those who are not members of the Christian community, there is an additional apologetic and evangelistic opportunity. The counsellor, pastor, or social worker comes alongside those whom he or she is seeking to help and aids them in their search for meaning. But this requires sensitivity and respect.

The gospel is not served through manipulating the suffering and vulnerable.

Churches need to become known as the places in the community where their members and all others can go to get the information they need in order to understand which reproductive technologies, genetic tests, stem cell treatments, or alternative medicines they can use without violating important ethical standards. Unless churches have ample information available on such bioethical challenges, and counsellors to help people apply that information to their own situations, churches are missing a huge opportunity to connect with people at the very times when they are most open to the gospel. Church leaders would do well to identify, or develop, if necessary, gifted and informed health care professionals, scientists, educators, and others in their congregation with whom the primary counsellors can share the counselling load.

Outreach

The outreach ministry of the church is its sharing of the gospel to those outside the church. Although verbal proclamation is an essential aspect, evangelism is not confined to that because there are other ways in which the gospel can be shared. The ministry of Jesus, who came not only to proclaim the word of God but also to perform the works of God, demonstrates that the gospel must be shared in word and deed, by verbal proclamation and visible demonstration. Proclamation and social action are inseparable, though they are not to be equated. Failure to distinguish between them often leads to neglecting proclamation, which is essential to the New Testament concept of evangelism. On the other hand, modern evangelicals, perhaps forgetting the historical emphasis of early evangelicalism on social reforms, often have a narrow focus on verbal proclamation, considering people's material and social needs of secondary or little importance. The Lausanne movement aims to hold the two elements together: "The whole church taking the whole gospel to the whole world."

When we care for people in need in the name of Jesus, we also open their hearts to the gospel. However, we must be careful to ensure that our social action does not become a gimmick to entice people to become Christians. Social action, as a response to the divine call, has its own integrity and vitality. At the same time, we rejoice when our genuine acts of compassion open the door to evangelism. It is with this understanding and motivation that we reach out to people encountering bioethical challenges.

Service

One way in which the church can serve society is by providing examples of sound bioethical decision-making. Individual Christians can demonstrate their commitment to the faith by refusing options that would violate the will of God as revealed in Scripture. Beyond these individual efforts, the church can also "incarnate" its values in institutions such as hospices and crisis pregnancy counselling centres, which serve as a prophetic witness to society of the deeper meaning of human existence.

Apologetics

Another way in which the church can reach out is to challenge popular views on bioethical issues. There are important points of contact between secular and Christian bioethics, and these provide the basis for Christian apologetics. Apologetics is the defence of the truth-claims of the Christian faith. This is possible because all truth comes from God, and God has created the world to bear witness to Him. There is a need in the evangelistic work of the church for responsible and serious justifications for the main themes of the Christian faith. Apologetics aims to lend intellectual integrity and depth to evangelism, ensuring that faith remains rooted in the head, as well as in the heart.

Human reason provides an important point of contact for the gospel. Christianity is not irrational; neither is the rationality of the Christian faith so discontinuous with secular rationality that there is no point of contact whatsoever between the two. Many Christian arguments about bioethical issues can be expressed in a way that resonates with the values and concerns of non-believers.

Advocacy/Political Engagement

Social action is part of the Church's mission simply because there is no disjunction between faith and life, belief and action. As Arthur Simon puts it, "To take major areas of life, those having to do with social and economic decisions that vitally affect all of us, and to put them into a compartment carefully separated from faith is to turn much of life over to the devil." The church, as Marsha Fowler puts it, is a body that acts – with voice. The church ought to speak prophetically against injustice, and on behalf of those without a voice.

The church therefore ought to be involved in bioethical decision-making not just at an individual level, but at a political and social level as well, by formulating and promoting a social ethic. According to Marsha Fowler, the process includes:

- Examining Scripture and tradition for Christian understanding and guidance
- Gaining insights from people who are directly affected by the problem or issue
- Gaining insights from experts who have studied the issue or worked in the field
- Being sensitive to the broader social context relevant to the issue
- Prayer
- Proclaiming the Christian perspective and working towards its realisation.

In democratic societies, the church has the opportunity to influence governmental policies and laws, not through coercion or manipulation, or imposition of the will of the minority who may be in power, but through persuasion and enlisting the support of non-believers. Individual local congregations may lack the expertise or resources to tackle the more complex technological issues, but they can interact at a denominational level, or in partnership with specialised groups such as Christian ethics centres and health care professionals' associations. As when believers draw alongside of unbelievers who are personally wres-

tling with bioethical challenges, so when believers draw alongside unbelievers to engage burning bioethical issues, there are ample opportunities to discuss what it is that makes sense of the life and dignity that all are striving to protect (i.e., to discuss the gospel).

PART II
OPPORTUNITIES FOR THE GOSPEL
Generic Strategies

Before considering eight stories about specific bioethical decision-making in the context of ministry, there are some strategies for using bioethics as an opportunity for the gospel that could apply in all cases.

The church ought to provide useful information and support to people confronted by difficult bioethical choices. Christians should also present a challenging and attractive alternative to prevailing secular attitudes. There is a wide range of activities that could be conducted in order to do this, but as not every local church has the resources to conduct all these activities, each should work closely with appropriate parachurch organisations and denominational structures. Various denominations could share their resources in developing programmes and events.

Church congregations are encouraged to undertake activities, such as the following:

Worship

(1) Conduct rituals such as funeral services in a way that provides opportunities to comfort those who mourn, explore the mystery of suffering, present the hope of the gospel sensitively, and challenge non-believers to consider their own mortality. Non-verbal communication through music, poetry, drama, and liturgy is especially powerful.

(2) Develop liturgies and worship materials for deaths through miscarriages and stillbirth.

(3) Create a special service commemorating the deaths of unborn children through abortion. This could be conducted on St. Luke's Day, as part of a Health Care Sunday or Sanctity of Life Sunday, or as a specially advertised mid-week service. Consider writing or using music specifically on this theme (Graham Kendrick wrote a song to commemorate the 1967 UK Abortion Act). Include prayers of confession for those who may have been involved in abortion (both men and women) and prayers for their healing.

(4) Hold dedication services for graduating medical students and other health care professionals. Invite representatives from students' local churches. Use an oath/declaration such as the Christian version of the Hippocratic Oath or a version designed by the students.

Teaching

(1) Encourage congregational teaching through sermons, Bible studies, and courses to equip church members for discussions with friends and work mates.

(2) Organise public events on topical bio-ethical issues. These could be seminars or talks by expert, engaging speakers (e.g., invite someone from a Christian bioethics centre or ethics lecturer from a theological college) or even a series of talks/seminars. They would preferably be at a neutral public venue such as the local school, or a café. Such programmes should be widely publicised (e.g., letterbox drops, posters in local shopping centres) because they are meant primarily for unbelievers. Church members should invite friends.

(3) Arrange a lecture or meeting at a local university or secondary school, possibly through a student Christian group.

(4) Identify congregation members (possibly health care professionals) to do further study in bioethics and act as resource people. For example, a masters degree in bioethics can now be undertaken, without re-locating, from Trinity International University (www.tiu.edu).

(5) Set up a bioethics resource centre, with:

- Resources about commonly encountered bioethics issues such as end-of-life care and reproductive technologies, which can be discussed with neighbours and friends;
- Summary sheets of issues, for example, those prepared by The Center for Bioethics and Human Dignity (CBHD—www.cbhd.org);
- The international Christian bioethics journal *Ethics and Medicine;*
- Newsletters and other communications from Christian bioethics centres such as those in your own area or those sponsoring the *Ethics and*

Medicine journal: England's The Centre for Bioethics and Public Policy (www.cbpp.ac.uk), The Netherlands' Lindeboom Instituut (www.lindeboominstituut.nl), and The Center for Bioethics and Human Dignity (see above);

- Books in simple language specifically for a broad public, for example, CBHD's BioBasics series, which exists in multiple languages and is published in various parts of the world.

(6) Publicise relevant internet sites, for example:

- Overtly Christian sites such as www.cbhd.org, www.pfm.org, w w w . c m d a h o m e . o r g , w w w . c m f . o r g . u k and www.thecbc.org;
- Sites not using explicitly theological language, yet in harmony with biblical world view, such as www.bioethics.com.

Pastoral Ministry

(1) Establish a pregnancy crisis/antenatal testing counselling centre.

(2) Work alongside hospital chaplaincy. Chaplains who work in hospitals should be equipped to provide basic counselling on a range of bioethical issues. Chaplains should also be able to help patients and family members to get in touch with Christian counselling agencies or specialist organisations.

(3) Work with hospitals to establish hospital-based support groups for patients and their families that are open to all.

(4) Offer and promote counselling services to help congregational members and

the community at large deal with bioethical challenges in their lives.

Outreach Strategies

Service

(1) Participate on hospital/university clinical and research ethics committees.

(2) Establish or be involved in a hospice to care for dying persons.

(3) Establish or be involved in an AIDS orphanage.

(4) Establish or be involved in a crisis pregnancy counselling centre.

Apologetics

(1) Write letters to the press.

(2) Make media appearances and give interviews; be available and capable.

(3) Encourage health care and other professionals to attend secular professional meetings and be involved in secular organisations.

Advocacy/Political Engagement

(1) Make written and oral submissions to governmental enquiries/hearings.

(2) Be involved in public discussions held by other organizations.

(3) Lobby politicians through letters and visits.

(4) Write letters to the press addressing proposed laws and policies.

(5) Participate in demonstrations and marches.

1. Justice in Health Care

An urban congregation in sub-Saharan Africa has very positive experiences with *Mercy Ships* and other short-term medical outreach programmes. They approach a mission agency staffed by Europeans, Americans and local health professionals. It is funded by Korean Christians and they plan to establish a permanent clinic. The local congregation argue this is one of their most powerful evangelistic tools.

'The government provides only the bare minimum when it comes to health care' says one of the elders. 'If someone is very sick, they may get treatment at a public hospital for a reduced fee, but often there is no opportunity to access medical services. It's not so bad here as in rural areas, but even here in the city there are not enough facilities. So people with "connections" get served in the hospital sooner, even before people who may be very sick and have waited a long time, but don't know the "right" people.' He goes on: 'Western and Asian churches who are economically strong but don't help their poorer brothers and sisters, never mind those who might be evangelised, are really no different than the rest of the world. Christians who have much have a duty to help believers who have little.'

Another influential church leader takes a different view. She claims the local congregation should instead put their efforts into expanding local services. 'Health care is a right and the government should provide it. When the church steps in all it does is supply a quick fix, like putting a plaster or bandaid on a gaping wound. Both the local people and the mission agencies should try to get the laws changed to provide adequate national health-care services.'

What Issues Does This Story Raise?

One issue concerns definitions of health and health care. Health can be defined very broadly, as by the World Health Organisation (1948): "Health is a state of complete physical, mental and social well being, and not merely the absence of disease or infirmity." But this definition is unhelpful, as health in this sense cannot be measured and the standard is unachievable this side of heaven.

A more modest definition as "the absence of disease" is more useful. Health care is then anything aimed at reducing or eliminating disease. Sometimes people speak of basic health care, which includes elements such as clean water, sanitation, and access to adequate nutrition. These basic and most important determinants of health are not normally seen as the responsibility of health professionals. In fact, poverty is the most powerful determinant of ill health in all societies. Similarly, health education programmes have greater impact on community health than on treating sick individuals. Regarding conventional health services, preventive measures like immunization are arguably the most strategic and cost effective.

To claim health care is a "right" implies someone has a moral duty to provide it, but who has this duty? It is often assumed to be government, but we each belong to a community where all are vulnerable to disease or injury and therefore the community has the primary responsibility to care. For practical reasons, much of this task is assigned to government on behalf of the community, but this does not absolve the community of all responsibility. Family, home, or community based care may be the most appropriate kind. If government and/or community fail to provide health care, does the church have a duty to step in? This raises the issues of the relationship between political advocacy, the church's works of service, and evangelism.

Then there are questions of how much health care, or exactly which services ought to be provided, and whether this varies with available resources of money, technology, and expertise. For example, is anything resembling comprehensive health care economically possible in nations with high HIV infection rates? Furthermore, if nations cannot fund their own health care, what responsibilities do other nations or the worldwide church have to assist? So the major issue here is justice. How should scarce health care resources be distributed within a country? On the basis of "connections?" Ability to pay? And what about the injustice in the global distribution of health care resources?

What Does the Bible Say?

Distributive justice is a major issue in bioethics: not only for medical treatment and health services, but also for the benefits of research. That every person ought to have access to appropriate (at least basic) health care is an assumption shared by both Christian and secular bioethics. For the Christian, this is established on the premise that all humans are created in the image of God and therefore deserve equal respect and access to what is essential in order to live. Health care is not only the privilege of those able to pay, but should be accessible to everyone regardless of their financial or social status. The emergence of managed care medicine, where for-profit organizations run health care institutions, has raised legitimate concerns about the commodification of medical treatment. Will such companies choose t h e i n t e r e s t s o f t h e i r "customers" (patients) when these conflict with the interests of shareholders? Although investors could choose fewer returns in exchange for the company conducting itself responsibly, this seems unlikely.

It may be argued that because rich nations have the *capacity*, both in medical knowledge and economic resources, to defend the right to a decent minimum of good health care for every citizen, we can claim this as society's *obligation*. However, while it may be possible to provide a "decent minimum" (whatever that is) to every citizen, specialised and high technology treatments are usually expensive and not accessible to all, even in wealthy nations. Several criteria have been proposed for treatment allocation:

- *Need*: Who has the greatest need?
- *Ability to pay*: Who has the resources to buy treatment?
- *Merit*: Who, because of their past contribution to society, most warrants it?
- *Social value*: Who has the greatest potential to contribute to society in the future?

- *Desert*: Who is disqualified from treatment because of past actions? For example: Does a person with liver destruction from alcohol abuse *deserve* a liver transplant? Or a smoker a lung transplant?
- *Age:* In some countries, patients over 65 automatically no longer qualify for certain expensive treatments.
- *Type of disease:* The state will allocate resources for the treatment of certain diseases but not others.
- *Equality:* Equal persons are to be treated equally in health care, that is, persons with similar conditions must be treated in the same way.

Though sometimes difficult to implement, *equality* best corresponds to the Christian emphasis on equal human worth. Biblical emphasis on *need* is seen in the imperative to care for the poor (Proverbs 14:31; Isaiah 58:6-7; James 2:1-4). The poor include not only the economically deprived, but the weak, sick, and very vulnerable – those who are unable to support or help themselves. As 2 Corinthians 8:13-14 makes clear, the aim of giving special attention to the poor and weak is because they fall short of the equality they ought to enjoy as created in the image of God. With regard to *desert*, the Bible teaches that those who are able to work must do so. Conversely, those who are able but unwilling to work do not merit a share in society's resources (1 Thessalonians 5:12-14; 2 Thessalonians 3:6-10). In theory, one could also forfeit a claim on society's resources by knowingly causing one's own disease. However, to be fair,

such a standard would need to be applied to all unhealthy behaviours (over-working, over-eating, etc.), which seems unlikely to happen since it would both be difficult to implement and result in a culture of control and blame.

Biblical teaching on distributive justice has shaped Western health care: "The churches took it upon themselves to provide out of their resources for their brothers and sisters in other churches who were less fortunate (Acts 2:44-45, 4:32-35, 11:27-30; 2 Corinthians 8-9), and this pattern continued in much of the Western world until this century, when governments took over the responsibility of caring for the poor from the churches and forcibly redistributed society's goods from the prosperous to the poor" (Scott Rae).

Principles of justice need to be applied not only nationally but globally, since in the global economy, a nation's responsibilities are not limited to the good of its own citizens. It is disappointing, for example, that of the billions of US dollars spent on medical research, 90% is directed towards conditions causing only 10% of global disease.

The church has a special calling to care for the sick wherever it is located and regardless of how governments fulfil their duty. Wealthy Christians should, as an issue of justice, contribute generously to the health care of less fortunate neighbours. But a medical clinic may not be the best way to achieve the greatest health improvement for our sub-Saharan community. Alternative models, such as community nurse practitioners and health care educators, or using funds for public health measures such as clean water, sanitation, and food supplies might be more effective.

Our African church leaders who want health care partnership with an overseas church are correct about the duty of wealthy Christians to help in this way. They are right about the connection with evangelism. Can Christians evangelise with integrity in nations enduring major health care crises such as AIDS without acting to help the sick and their families? Words and action go together. The gospel must be shown as well as spoken.

Nevertheless, the church leader who wants to lobby and change the law is correct as well. Political engagement and advocacy for the poor and powerless are also part of mission. It is not "either-or" as implied in this story. It is unlikely that any one church or agency has the financial resources to meet the broad health needs of any African nation!

What Opportunities for the Gospel are There?

[*See also "Generic Strategies" above*]

When the church meets human needs, we encounter people at a time when they have been sensitised to their lack of control, and perhaps to their need for God. So this creates an opportunity for evangelism, though it should be handled with respect for people's vulnerability. Equally, the church engaging politically and in advocacy speaks powerfully to the world of God's love for the world.

This story offers a more personal opportunity for the gospel to be proclaimed.

How will these two groups of leaders resolve their disagreement? Will they show respectful listening and a willingness to submit to the other? Will they demonstrate grace and forbearance? Will there be forgiveness for harsh or hurtful words? Will they be able to move forward working together, learning from each other, and recognizing each has different but necessary contributions to make to the church and its work? Will there be reconciliation despite differences? What a testimony that would be!

Further Resources

Bruce Birch. *Let Justice Roll Down*. Philadelphia, PA: Westminster/John Knox, 1991.

Evvy Hay Campbell, ed. *Ethical Issues in Health-Related Missions*. Bannockburn, IL: CBHD, 1997.

John Kilner, et al., eds. *The Changing Face of Health Care*. Grand Rapids, MI: William B. Eerdmans and Cambridge, UK: Paternoster; 1998.

John Kilner. *Life on the Line*. Bannockburn, IL: CBHD, 1992.

Donal O'Mathuna, et al. *Basic Questions on Healthcare*. Grand Rapids, MI: Kregel, 2004.

Johan J Polder, Henk Jochemsen. "Professional autonomy and the health care system." *Theoretical Medicine and Bioethics* 21 (2000) No.5, 477-491.

2. Caregiver-Patient Relationships

Señor Gomez visits his local doctor because he has lost a lot of weight over the last five months. The doctor orders an X-ray that shows a shadow and he suspects lung cancer because his patient smokes heavily. He sends him to the regional hospital without much explanation, but with a letter for the specialist.

A month later, Señor Gomez returns to his local doctor, who asks him: "What did the other place say?"

"They didn't say much, because they were too busy," he answers. But he hands over a letter from the specialist:

Dear Dr.,

Señor Gomez has lung cancer.

Suggest pain relief.

Yours etc

The local doctor provides some pain-relieving medicine and sends Señor Gomez home. Three months later, the family brings him back unconscious. The emergency doctor on duty breaks the bad news to the family, and advises them to take him home, call a priest, and allow him to die in peace.

What Issues Does This Story Raise?

The issues cluster around two broad areas. The first is the nature of the relationship between caregiver and patient and the role and responsibility of each. The second is how we deal with approaching death and how we care for dying people and their families. In addition, there is the issue of justice, since it seems treatments for lung cancer that would generally be available in wealthy countries were either unavailable or not offered to Señor Gomez. This might be due to inadequate resources, unfair discrimination against him, or simply his inability to pay.

The first area includes such questions as how caregivers treat their patients, whether they accord them dignity and respect, what information they should convey to them, and how they do this. There are also the questions of involving the patient in the medical decision-making process, and the further possible role of family or community in this. Neither Señor Gomez nor his family were given any information about his condition, or what the future might hold, or any opportunity to be involved in decisions. The first two doctors seemed distant and uncaring. They are classic examples of "paternalism" (where doctors treat patients like children, making important decisions on their behalf) except that paternalism implies a certain benevolence, with the doctor acting in the perceived best interests of the patient. Yet these doctors seemed to care very little for their patient's interests at all. Indeed, it seems odd even to speak of the doctor-patient "relationship" in this case, since it barely seems to exist (the final doctor appears to show more concern, at least telling the family what is going on). A poor doctor-patient relationship is a serious problem, since the quality of this relationship is known to be very important for the outcome of treatment.

Paternalism was the dominant model of the doctor-patient relationship until the modern discipline of bioethics introduced the principle of respect for patient autonomy. Autonomy is the freedom to exercise self-determination, without external restraint. In the medical context, it means that doctors recognise the patient's body is his or her own, and that medical procedures cannot be conducted without the patient's consent. This is important because doctors exercise considerable power and authority over their patients. But for patient consent to be meaningful, the patient must be well-informed about risks and benefits, possible alternatives, and so on. Even if there are no treatment decisions to be made, the principle of respect for autonomy requires disclosure of health information because it is of vital interest to the patient. We might say Señor Gomez had a "right" to know he had an illness that would kill him. This knowledge was essential to his life plans, relationships, self-understanding and possibly to his spiritual well-being. Whether Señor Gomez himself would make the health care and other decisions that would depend upon such information - or those decisions would be more of a communal process involving family members and others - would depend on his particular cultural setting. But complete information would be needed in any case.

We might ask whether the doctors fulfilled their obligations as doctors to Señor Gomez, whether or not he was content to be treated like this? Were they able to realize the goals of medical practice in their dealings with him? Did they demonstrate the kind of character traits (virtues) that we associate with being a good doctor? Or would Señor Gomez and his family rightly have felt let down by them, even if they provided the "correct" treatment?

The second cluster of issues deals with how we treat those who are dying. In spite of all the advances of modern medicine, every one of us will die, and likely spend some time in a health care system before we do. It used to be considered a necessary skill for doctors to keep from patients the knowledge that they were seriously ill, or likely to die. Today, at least in Western cultures, the trend is to keep the patient fully informed. However, apart from the specialist discipline of palliative care, medicine often seems focused on avoiding death, and many doctors are uncomfortable talking about death. Señor Gomez's doctors may have wanted to avoid a painful scene and distressing questions. Breaking bad news is difficult; it reminds us only too painfully of our own mortality. Perhaps they simply wanted to avoid admitting they could not cure him. He may have represented a failure to them.

Probably Señor Gomez knew the truth or guessed it. But because he was not given permission to speak of it, he was left to deal with it utterly alone. He was deprived of the opportunity to ask questions about his future, to share his fears, and to prepare for death. The suffering associated with facing death is often intense, and many people today think of the ideal death as one that is sudden — one that they are unaware of and unprepared for, such as dying in their sleep. But previous generations of Christians used to pray to be delivered from such a sudden death. The *ars moriendi* (art of dying) meant a careful working through of emotional, relational, and especially spiritual issues as one prepared for death. The need to prepare for death spiritually is recognised by our last doctor, when he advises the family to call a priest, but by then it is too late for the patient.

Two important goals of healthcare are healing and the alleviation of suffering. Señor Gomez was apparently beyond a cure, and although his physical pain was addressed through medication, it seems his suffering was not fully addressed. Further discussion of death and dying issues and biblical counsel related to them, will be saved until the next story about end-of-life care.

What Does the Bible Say?

Respect for Persons

The Christian ethic of care includes treating each patient with dignity and respect, as one created in the image of God. This entails honouring patients as individuals by including them as far as possible in the decision-making process, and acknowledging their individual preferences and values. Speaking theologically, only God has an absolute prerogative over the life of the patient, not the health care professional. Any decisions the physician makes regarding the invasion or hurting of the patient must be made in light of this exclusively divine prerogative. Just as God permits each of us to make our own decisions, even foolish ones, so we need to give people the freedom to make their own choices, in consultation with whomever they wish. We can advise, we can try to persuade, but we ought not and usually cannot force them to agree. We are not free to act paternalistically in the sense of doing good to competent people against their expressed will.

Autonomy

Yet the Christian faith also introduces significant qualifications to the concept of human autonomy. For instance, we cannot affirm certain secular understandings of autonomy that give little weight to claims of relationships and responsibility to other human beings. The liberal ideal of the unencumbered, freely- choosing individual who acts solely in accord with his or her own life plans is not only unrealistic, it is contrary to the biblical picture of humans created for interdependent relationship with others, and a dependent submission to the authority of God. Insistence on being in charge of one's own life is not consistent with looking to the interests of others (Philippians 2:3-4), or the many New Testament "one another" exhortations (e.g. 1 Corinthians 12:25; Galatians 5:13; Ephesians 5:21; Colossians 3:16; 1 Thessalonians 5:11). Being fully human does not consist of being utterly independent and setting one's own course, as we see from the fully human Christ, who gave His life for others and submitted to the will of his heavenly Father. Yet He freely chose to do this, so that his autonomy was not compromised. The principle of autonomy should not be used in a way that ignores people's connections and relationships, or implies complete freedom from responsibility to others.

The Caregiver-Patient Relationship

The caregiver-patient relationship cannot be abstracted from the social and cultural context in which health care is actually practised. In many places, and often with older patients, paternalism is still accepted, even expected, by patients. They are happy to hand over decisions about their future because "doctor knows best." In some cultures, individual autonomy gives way to the patient's family making medical decisions on their behalf. The family may direct the doctor not to tell the patient details, especially of a terminal illness, in order to avoid distressing him or her. At the other extreme, in Western cultures consumerism and materialism have elevated autonomy to the point where patients may be understood not only to have the right to refuse treatment, but even to demand the treatment of their choice. Patients become *customers*, or health care consumers. *Patient* from the Latin simply means 'the one who suffers." Patients are people who are sick and often in pain, vulnerable, and fearful. They often do not have the understanding, the training, and perhaps even the energy to take complete control of crucial medical decisions. The image of a customer, when applied to many patients, fails truly to reflect their condition, especially in emergencies and with severely ill or intellectually or psychologically compromised patients.

Looking at the doctor-patient relationship as a commercial contract is supposed to empower the patient by turning the doctor into a service provider (like a vending machine) who carries out the patient's will, but the reality of the inequality of knowledge and power between the parties actually leaves most patients more vulnerable to exploitation. In a contractual relationship, responsibility is limited to what is specified. The doctor's responsibility to exercise beneficence (to act for the patient's good) and to be trustworthy in caring for the patient beyond what is specified in the contract, is minimized or eliminated. This has led some writers to suggest that a better model for the doctor-patient relationship is a covenant. Indeed, the earliest record of a code of medical ethics, the Hippocratic Oath, takes such a form.

The biblical notion of covenant centres on God's covenants with individuals and with his people, but covenants are also made between people (e.g., Jonathan and David). By comparing the marriage relationship to that between Christ and the church, Paul implies that this also is a covenant relationship. A covenant is characterised by several elements: a gift, a promise, commitment, a comprehensive fidelity that extends beyond particulars to unforeseen and unforeseeable contingencies, and a set of specific moral obligations. Contracts are designed to protect the self-interest of each party, but a covenant involves commitment to look out for the interests of the other, and thus protects the more vulnerable partner. Yet, a covenant also recognizes that the gift element of the relationship is not purely one-sided or philanthropic: caregivers receive from their patients as well as give.

Compared to a contract, which is of limited duration and imposes only external obligations, a covenant effects internal changes that apply to all of life. Covenantal obligations may even be inconsistent with entering certain contracts, such as a "marriage" contract that stipulates freedom for one or both partners to have sexual relationships with others. An example of covenant medicine would be the surgeon who refuses to perform disfiguring or unnecessary surgery, even when this is what a competent patient, exercising his or her autonomy, asks for. The covenantal model of the caregiver–patient relationship implies that doctors (and other health care professionals) have moral obligations simply as doctors, which arise from the nature of their practice, and which are particular to their role. In order to practise well, they need to cultivate certain virtues to achieve the goals of their profession.

Professional Virtues

The concept of virtue pervades the scriptures, and is especially seen in the New Testament emphasis on the heart as of primary importance and the internal source of external behaviour (Matthew 15:10-20, 23:25-26) and the need for transformation of the inner being by the Holy Spirit (Romans 12:2; Galatians 5:22-23; Ephesians 4: 23-24). Virtues are acquired human qualities, which when practised, enable us to flourish as human beings. In the Christian context, this means becoming more Christ-like in our character and behaviour.

However, certain roles and relationships also entail particular responsibilities and virtues. When we think of someone as a good mother, a good husband, a good teacher, or a good politician, we acknowledge that they have the qualities to do that job well, in a moral as well as a technical sense. Health care professionals also require certain moral virtues to do their job well. Conversely, certain vices prevent this. Aristotle envisaged the virtues as means between two extremes (vices), and this is well illustrated by certain medical virtues. On the one hand, doctors need to have compassion, and they need to be moved to action by suffering; on the other, they need to be able to remain detached enough from human suffering to make careful reasoned decisions. They need to be empathetic in order to understand patients' concerns, but not so identified with them that they lose the capacity for independent judgment. In other words, they need to appreciate the patient's helplessness and hopelessness without sharing it or being overwhelmed by it. Doctors need to be open and honest in breaking bad news, and yet they also need to be sensitive and responsive to how much the patient can take in, not 'brutally' honest. They need to have courage both in attempting difficult procedures and talking about difficult issues, without being reckless or unthinking. They need to be confident and assertive, without being arrogant or aggressive. Above all, health care professionals need what we all need -- the wisdom to see situations as they really are, and to apply ethical principles to that particular context. Such wisdom cannot simply be taught in text books, but also requires experience, reflection and role models, and the work of the Holy Spirit.

What Opportunities for the Gospel are There?

[See also "Generic Strategies" above]

The character and quality of health care Christians provide ought to commend the gospel through demonstrating the love of Christ. Birth and death are particular times when a window is opened to the transcendent, and patients and their families may be more open then to thinking about spiritual issues. Many patients also seek forgiveness for past wrongs and reconciliation with estranged family members or friends. Christian health professionals, chaplains, and hospital visitors have the opportunity to raise these issues and share the gospel when appropriate in their care of those who are dying. And Christian patients can witness to their caregivers in the grace, acceptance, hope, and peace they display.

The church can minister to dying people and their families through services for healing and reconciliation, through hospital and home visiting, and through hospice care. Christians have no need to participate in the denial of suffering and death which characterises secular culture. Over the centuries, Christians have developed rich resources to help them through times of darkness or even despair. The gospel provides a way to understand death that robs it of its terror and absurdity. Funerals ought not to be the only time we talk about dying!

Further Resources

Paul Brand and Philip Yancey. *The Gift of Pain.* Grand Rapids, MI: Zondervan, 1997.

John Kilner, et al., eds. *The Changing Face of Health Care.* Grand Rapids, MI: William B. Eerdmans and Cambridge, UK: Paternoster; 1998.

Hippocratic Oath. For example, in Kilner et al. 172-173.

Alasdair MacIntyre. *After Virtue.* 2nd ed. Notre Dame, IN: University of Notre Dame Press, 1984.

William F May. *The Physician's Covenant: Images of the Healer in Medical Ethics.* Philadelphia, PA: The Westminster Press, 1983.

Edmund Pellegrino and David Thomasma. *The Christian Virtues in Medical Practice.* Washington, DC: Georgetown Univ. Press, 1996.

Philip Yancey. *Where is God When It Hurts?.* Grand Rapids, MI: Zondervan, 1997.

3. End-of-Life Care

Mrs Milowicz is a 60 year old widow who had a severe stroke eight months ago, which left her bed bound and unable to swallow. She has gone into a nursing (caring) home, but her only daughter, Anna, is not satisfied with the conditions there. It is understaffed and those who are there seem poorly trained. Anna visits her mother every day, carrying out many of the nursing tasks herself, but this is difficult for her as she lives on the other side of town, with her husband who is unemployed and two children who are at school. She relies on the bus service and the trip to the nursing home takes up to two hours.

Mrs Milowicz has now been sent to the hospital, because her nasogastric feeding tube (a tube inserted through the nose which goes into the stomach) has come out, and the staff are unable to replace it. Anna arrives with her, and explains the situation in the nursing home. She also tells the doctor that her mother has progressively deteriorated over the months and no longer communicates.

The doctor notes the daughter's good care for her mother, since there are no bed sores. But Anna admits she is finding the daily visits very tiring and she is upset because her mother doesn't even talk to her any more. 'It's such a strain, doctor' she says, 'I don't know how much longer I can keep doing it. I've had to give up my job, and we can't keep up with the bills.'

The doctor tells her that putting the feeding tube back would not benefit her mother who is in the process of dying. The doctor also tells her 'I see the love you have for your mother, but it looks like it is now time for God to take care of her'.

'Do you mean we will just let her starve to death?' Anna asks. Then after a moment's reflection she adds: 'Isn't there anything else you could do to make it easier?'

What Issues Does This Story Raise?

The first is the difficult question of knowing when it is time to stop efforts to fight disease and stop interventions that prolong life, recognising that the time has come for the patient to die. This is often referred to as "letting nature take its course," but how do we know when this time has come? In the secular context, this is generally through assessments that continuing treatment would be futile, or that it would impose an unreasonable burden on the patient relative to the benefit to be gained.

Futility is a notion frequently invoked, but much contested. A task is futile if the goals at which it is aimed cannot be achieved whatever efforts are made. Whether a particular treatment is futile will depend on how the goals of treatment are defined. When a patient is severely and permanently brain damaged, treatment such as artificial ventilation will not be deemed futile if the goal is simply to keep the patient alive -- this may be done for many years. However, if the goal is restoration of consciousness or the ability to communicate, it will be deemed futile. Artificial feeding also may keep an unconscious person alive for many years, but it too will be judged futile if the goal is to restore consciousness. What is the goal of the feeding in this case? Quality of life considerations are commonly included here. Mrs. Milowicz is not unconscious; she has awareness, but is unable to do anything for herself and now appears unable to communicate (though her lack of communication may be due to a treatable cause such as depression).

The role of quality-of-life assessment is at least as controversial as futility considerations, whether carried out by the patient, the patient's family, or the medical team. Because such assessment involves weighing up the benefits of a particular treatment against the burden it imposes, it begs the question of whether a life not considered to be particularly "beneficial" should therefore not continue. Benefits include both prolonging life and improving how the patient feels and/or functions. What sort of benefit to the patient, or to anyone else, is unconscious life on a life support system with only a tiny chance of recovery? The burdens of the treatment include possible side effects, pain, and discomfort. This is not an issue for unconscious patients, but may be for Mrs Milowicz; some patients pull their nasogastric tubes out because they are uncomfortable. Burdens also include the cost of the treatment, including financial cost, to the patient and the family. In this case Anna and her family are bearing a large burden.

In the case of artificial feeding, there is an added issue. Most people would see artificial respiration (being on a ventilator, which generally requires being in an intensive care unit) as a high technology intervention that is clearly medical treatment. As such, it may be refused by patients or by someone acting as their decision-maker if they are incompetent to decide, or the medical team may withdraw it if they consider it inappropriate. However, is feeding by a nasogastric tube, or else by a PEG-tube inserted surgically into the patient's stomach, a medical treatment, or is it simply an alternative way of providing food and water, part of the basic care we owe all people? Legally, it has been deemed the former by courts in the UK, USA and Australia. But Christians continue to be divided over the question, and in 2004 Pope John Paul II declared at a conference that it is ordinary care that is required to be given to patients in the "persistent vegetative state." He said withdrawing artificial feeding is equivalent to euthanasia, it is "euthanasia by omission."

Mrs. Milowicz, however, is neither comatose, nor in a persistent vegetative state, so we might ask whether, apart from the nasogastric feeding, there is other treatment or rehabilitation she might receive that would offer real hope for improvement in her condition. It seems she is not receiving any physiotherapy, occupational therapy, or specialised nursing care. At 60 years of age, she might have a good chance of recovering some function and many years of life ahead of her. This raises the issue, one of justice, about the allocation of funding to programmes and therapies for disabled persons, and may reflect discrimination against people with disability. But possibly Mrs Milowicz would have received much better care if she had lived elsewhere, particularly if she had private health insurance.

So it is not altogether clear that it is time to "hand over her care to God," as advocated by the doctor. Whose decision should this be? If, as in the case of Mrs. Milowicz, the patient is unable to participate in the process, should it be the health care team, the family, or a joint decision? Conflicts between these two groups, or within families, are legal minefields that in some countries often end up in court. It is frequently recommended patients make their wishes known in writing in advance through so-called "advance directives," in case they end up in such a situation. However, if they do not, how should the family members decide on their behalf? Will a sense of guilt on Anna's part that she is failing to do her duty to her mother affect her decision? Or her weariness and love for her own family? Can she disentangle her mother's interests from her own? Should she?

Finally, there is the issue of euthanasia. Instead of removing the feeding tube and allowing the patient to die – which might take weeks, and in a conscious patient be distressing for the patient and those who care for her – some might prefer an alternative. They might think it more compassionate, having decided that it is time for Mrs. Milowicz to die, to end her life quickly and painlessly. This seems to be what Anna is hinting at. The American Medical Association's Council on Ethical and Judicial Affairs defines euthanasia as "the act of bringing about the death of a hopelessly ill and suffering person in a relatively quick and painless way for reasons of mercy." Sometimes medical involvement is assumed, as in John Keown's definition: "doctors making decisions which have the effect of shortening a patient's life (that) are based on the belief that the patient would be better off dead." If Mrs. Milowicz's doctor had given her a lethal injection, it would have been a case of *non-voluntary* euthanasia: the provision of euthanasia to an incompetent person without the explicit consent of the patient. *Voluntary* euthanasia is euthanasia that is provided for a competent person with his or her informed consent. If the person is able to cause the death (e.g., by swallowing pills), albeit with help, then it is also commonly called assisted suicide. *Involuntary* euthanasia is euthanasia performed without a competent person's consent.

Advocates of euthanasia present three main moral justifications for it. The first is respect for autonomy. In voluntary euthanasia, the patient exercises his or her right to self-determination, in this case the "right-to-die" (which is really a claimed right to be killed). However, euthanasia supporters usually limit this right to people who are suffering greatly. Logically, if the right to self-determination applies to all, then why should the "right-to-die" be limited only to those who are terminally ill and/or in great pain? What about others (assuming they are of sound mind) who find their lives meaningless or intolerable? Yet most people object to the thought of a healthy young person being killed simply because they freely choose it.

The second justification will perhaps appear more acceptable to Christians. It is argued that euthanasia provides compassionate relief from suffering. Isn't the alleviation of human suffering surely part of what the love of one's neighbour entails? It is certainly one of the goals of health care. In certain circumstances, could the obligation to relieve suffering outweigh the general prohibition against killing? One of the problems with this argument is that it would apply equally to non-voluntary as to voluntary euthanasia. As a matter of justice, why should not the suffering of incompetent patients be relieved as well as that of competent patients? Both the autonomy and the compassion arguments prove too much, unless one envisages a broader programme of euthanasia than is generally advocated by its supporters (at least in public).

The third justification, like the second, is particularly appealing to those with a utilitarian perspective, for whom the only morally relevant factor in assessing an action is whether its consequences are good. They argue that there is nothing morally significant in the bare difference between "killing" and "letting die;" these are simply different ways of achieving a certain outcome and whether they are right or not depends on whether the outcome is desirable or not. We already permit letting die under certain circumstances, they note, so logically we should permit euthanasia under the same circumstances. In fact, a painless injection might be preferable to being "starved to death."

Others, including most Christians, argue that there is a difference between these, because while letting die may be right under some circumstances, killing the innocent is always wrong. Usually the difference is expressed in terms of the intention of the action (or omission) and of causality. If the intention of withdrawing treatment is to remove unreasonable or futile treatment, for instance, then it is permissible or even obligatory. Death may be foreseen as a likely outcome (though not absolutely inevitable) without being intended or aimed at and will essentially be caused by the disease. If the intention of removing treatment is to end the patient's life, it is morally equivalent to killing by an act such as a lethal injection.

What Does the Bible Say?

When is it right to stop fighting death and let go of life?

The Bible does not explicitly address the array of technology that can be used today to prolong life in the face of injury or disease that would once have been uniformly fatal, but it does give us some broad principles about the value of human life, and an understanding of disease and death.

We saw in Part 1 that it is appropriate to promote health and healing, as suffering and death are evils to be opposed. Nevertheless, Christians understand death as an inevitable end to life, and for the believer, the gateway to resurrected life, so that it need not and should not be resisted at all costs. It is an enemy, but a defeated enemy. Christians may use carefully-defined criteria of futility and the weighing up of burdens and benefit, in prayer, to discern when God is calling a person home. What ought to be avoided, though, are decisions based on an assessment that someone's life is worth less than another's (because they function at a lower level or have pain or suffering). We may decide that a treatment is not worthwhile, but not that a person's life is not worthwhile, since all humans are made in the image of God and share the same value.

In deciding whether a treatment is appropriate, it is reasonable to take into account the cost of the treatment — again if rightly considered. Some treatments such as artificial feeding, which are readily available in wealthy Western countries, are simply not available or would be prohibitively expensive, in many other places. It is hardly life-affirming to use all of a family's resources to extend the life of one member, at the cost of subjecting all other family members to life-threatening poverty. On the other hand, no patients should be deprived of the opportunity to take food by mouth if they can (in many conditions, the inability to swallow does indicate that a person is dying).

There is no indication in the Bible of an obligation to prolong every life as long as possible. Once a person is dying and nothing will change this, it seems better to allow this to happen as naturally, though comfortably, as possible. Fighting death to the very end does not allow the patient or family to prepare spiritually for death, and may actually add burden to the dying process.

Since disease is a universal human problem, the responsibility of caring for the sick ought to be shared by the whole community (see 'Justice' in Part I above). It is often anxiety about being a burden to loved ones that prompts requests for euthanasia, but if this burden were shared it would be much easier for all to bear. Here the church can and should provide help.

Euthanasia

A biblical understanding of the exercise of autonomy does not mean that people are morally free to do whatever they choose. Certain choices represent disobedience to God's moral law, which protects innocent human life. This protection even extends to suicide and giving someone else permission to kill you. Life should be received moment by moment as a gift from the Creator, and never be seen as one's own possession that can be disposed of as one wishes. Suicide is basically a contradiction of our nature as creatures, because it expresses our unwillingness to see life as God's gift. It is true that emotionally ill persons and those suffering from depression can irrationally resort to taking their own lives. In such cases, the person cannot be seen as a responsible or culpable agent. There are cases when suicide is the deliberate decision of a morally responsible agent. If suicide must be rejected, both physician-assisted-suicide and euthanasia must also be rejected because no human being (including a doctor) has authority over the life of another human being.

Suffering is of course to be resisted, but this resistance is informed by the understanding that its final eradication lies in the hands of God. In the area of medical ethics, the principle that governs Christian compassion is "maximise care," not "minimise suffering." If it is the latter, then there is a sense in which the elimination of *sufferers* can be justified, but the duty of the doctor is "always to care, and never to kill." This has been embedded in the tradition of Western medicine for over two millennia, and is given clear expression in the Hippocratic Oath's injunction not to "give a deadly drug to anybody if asked for it, nor ... make suggestion to this effect." Even human beings with the poorest quality of life in terms of disfigurement, loss of function, or pain, are made in the image of God, and therefore the sanctity of their life cannot be overridden by quality of life considerations.

In fact, modern palliative medicine can deal with almost all physical pain and many other distressing symptoms at the end of life, such as nausea and breathlessness. Yet the most profound suffering at the end of life is existential, which is not amenable to purely medical treatment. That is why palliative care is multidisciplinary and includes pastoral care, and why it deals not only with patients as individuals, but in the context of their family and other close relationships. Inducing a hasty death denies the patient and their family the opportunity to do the work of dying, which can ultimately be deeply satisfying. There is something profoundly inappropriate about providing a medical "solution" to suffering that is not basically a medical problem.

What Opportunities for the Gospel are There?
[See also "Generic Strategies" above]

Decisions about stopping life-prolonging treatment bring patients and their families face to face with mortality and questions regarding the meaning of life and death. Discussions about "letting nature take its course" may lead to an exploration of the spiritual realities and forces that govern life and are ultimately beyond human control. Christian health care workers, counsellors, chaplains, and hospital visitors may contribute to these discussions, both with patients and families, and in health care team meetings.

A request for euthanasia from a patient is often an opportunity to discuss the underlying sources of the patient's pain and hopelessness. Especially for lonely patients without close family or friends, the church can provide the caring community which reconnects the patient in relationships and provides the meaning their lives seem to lack. Of course, this is also a powerful witness to the love of Jesus, and may provide an opening for talking about the hope for life beyond death.

Euthanasia is a topic of general interest both within and outside the church. Ministers should ensure members of their congregation are equipped to discuss it intelligently with neighbours and work colleagues. Public seminars, debates, or panel discussions create apologetic opportunities since the Christian arguments against euthanasia often resonate with people who have no faith commitment.

The church can play a special role in affirming the lives of disabled people, or of anyone with a supposedly low quality of life, through providing or participating in programmes of respite care, through welcoming such people at services and events, and through advocating for government services and facilities for them. Opposing the legalization of assisted suicide or euthanasia is itself a wonderful affirmation of those typically judged to be lowest on the "quality of life scale." Such affirmations can readily lead to opportunities to explain the reasons underlying them - i.e., the gospel.

Further Resources

The Center for Bioethics and Human Dignity. *Advance Directive Kit.* Bannockburn, IL: www.cbhd.org, 2004.

James H. Casson. *Dying: the Greatest Adventure of My Life.* 5th ed, published with Peter Casson, *My Cancer.* England, UK: Christian Medical Fellowship, 1999.

Arthur Dyck. *Life's Worth*. Grand Rapids, MI: William B. Eerdmans, 2002.

John Keown. *Euthanasia, Ethics and Public Policy*. Cambridge, UK: Cambridge Univ. Press, 2002.

John Kilner, et al., eds. *Dignity and Dying*. Grand Rapids, MI: William B. Eerdmans and Cambridge, UK: Paternoster, 1996.

C. Ben Mitchell, et al. eds. *Aging, Death, and the Quest for Immortality*. Grand Rapids, MI: William B. Eerdmans, 2004.

Gary Stewart, et al. *Basic Questions on End of Life Decisions*. Grand Rapids, MI: Kregel, 1998.

-----.*Basic Questions on Suicide and Euthanasia*. Grand Rapids, MI: Kregel, 1998.

Joni Eareckson Tada. *The Life and Death Dilemma*. Grand Rapids, MI: Zondervan, 1995.

4. Abortion

Katia is a 17-year-old Russian student who lives with her divorced mother. Her mother has to work two jobs to pay for ballet lessons for Katia, who has won many competitions and dreams of becoming an international star. One of her fellow dancers is Ivan and through spending time with him, they have grown closer, to the point where they have begun to sleep together. They have talked about getting married one day, but both have many goals to achieve before then.

Just a few months before the national competitions, Katia misses her menstrual period. At first she thinks this might be due to stress or her strenuous training regime, but after another month, she starts to panic, and visits her doctor. She is stunned to learn she is pregnant and calls Ivan in tears. He is also shocked and asks her what she is going to do about it. He says, "Neither of us is ready for a baby now. Why don't you visit one of those clinics?"

Katia doesn't know what to do. She is too ashamed to tell her mother, so she makes an appointment at a pregnancy counselling service. Here she is told by a very kind nurse she should not worry and that a simple procedure will solve her problem for her. So, even though she is upset about what she is doing, she makes an appointment for a termination of pregnancy and this is performed the following week.

Ten years later, Katia has moved to the USA to pursue her ballet career and has started to attend a church. There she meets Todd, a committed Christian who is active in the pro-life movement. He strongly believes that abortion under any circumstances is wrong. They begin dating and things progress rapidly. Todd thanks God for sending him this wonderful woman as a friend and potential wife. He thinks about Katia constantly and daydreams about their future together as missionaries in Russia.

When Todd asks Katia to marry him, she begins to cry. "Oh, Todd," she sobs, "I love you so much. But there's something I have to tell you." When she tells him about her abortion, Todd feels as if his whole world has fallen apart. How could he ever forgive her? Why has God allowed him to fall in love with a woman who has killed her own baby?

Over time, and with counselling from their pastor, Todd is able to forgive Katia, and they get married the next year. They are thrilled when two years later Katia discovers she is pregnant. But, on antenatal testing, the foetus is discovered to have Down syndrome. Their doctor encourages them to consider aborting.

What Issues Does This Story Raise?

In considering abortion, many Christian writers focus exclusively on the moral status of the foetus. But though very important, this is only one of several issues raised by this story in particular and abortion more generally. The language used by various people in this story indicates what kind of being they think the unborn child is -- to Ivan it is not yet a baby, the clinic nurse talks about termination of pregnancy, Todd thinks Katia has killed her baby, and to the doctor who does the antenatal test, it is a foetus.

Not all women who have abortions are single, but the trend for greater numbers of young people to be sexually active, and at an earlier age, has greatly increased the number of unplanned and often unwanted pregnancies. This is associated in the West with the decline of Christian and other traditional moral values, the promotion through global media of recreational and casual sexual experience, and a decreasing emphasis on marriage and child rearing. Sex education, as early as primary school, and the easy availability of contraception in many places, have not prevented many teenage pregnancies.

Pregnancy is often presented as a woman's responsibility, an individual choice. But at least one other person is involved. In fact, all of society bears some responsibility for our sex-saturated culture and the difficulties single women face bringing up children. Although two people are involved in conceiving a child, the biological facts mean that an unfair burden of responsibility falls on the woman compared to the man. It is she who experiences bodily changes, sickness, and the risks of pregnancy and childbirth. Generally, if she keeps the child, she will bear a greater share of the nurturing task, perhaps all of it if her partner abandons her. Ironically, the emphasis that has been placed on abortion being a woman's choice has meant women must bear alone a burden they ought to be able to share. If she chooses not to abort, she may be held solely responsible for the resulting child simply because she made a choice to keep it. A man may feel that offering to pay for an abortion is the beginning and end of his responsibility.

Despite having a "choice," many women feel coerced into decisions they would rather not make; they in fact feel they have "no choice." This helplessness may be exacerbated in the case of young women who are minors and may not be considered competent to make other major medical decisions, but who are generally held to be able to make this decision alone. It is at least open to doubt whether they, and indeed other women, always receive and understand sufficient information about the nature of the procedure, the nature of the foetus (e.g., looking at ultrasound pictures), or the possible negative consequences of the procedure, in order to give fully informed consent.

The other important factor in the social context of abortion today is the changed role of women. In many societies, women expect to participate in work or careers alongside men. Childbearing, if it figures in their life plans at all, is only one part of it. The community's expectations reinforce this view. While much of the social stigma of bearing a child out of wedlock has gone (at least outside the Christian and some other religious communities), women may be made to feel guilty for not fulfilling their academic or earning potential, or for bringing a child into a less than ideal situation. Motherhood is accorded relatively little value in many communities today. Many women need a great deal of courage, as well as emotional and practical support, if they are to continue with an "unwanted" pregnancy in the face of all these social pressures.

In contrast to the general acceptance of abortion in secular society, abortion is singled out in some sections of the church as a particularly heinous sin. Todd illustrates this attitude. Yet, is having or procuring an abortion so much worse than other sins, and is it an unforgivable sin?

Todd and Katia's dilemma also raises the issue of the quality of life of people with disabilities. Do some conditions mean that a child would be better off never being born? Would this be the case with Down syndrome? Is it reasonable to take into account the burden on the parents, other family members, and the community of caring for such a child? Or is aborting children with disabilities fundamentally unjust, since it discriminates against them solely on the basis of their disability and deprives them of opportunities, in this case life itself, which would not be lawful or condoned once the child was born? A further issue is that of the purpose of antenatal testing and whether the results can or should be used to pressure a woman into an abortion.

Finally, this case confronts us with the mystery and uncertainty of our lives. Both Katia and Todd, for different reasons, may have wondered why their child had Down syndrome. Was it a punishment for a previous abortion, or for marrying a woman who had had an abortion? What was God doing in all of this?

What Does the Bible Say?

Neither Old nor New Testament directly addresses the question of the morality of abortion. Yet it was practised in the ancient world, including the Graeco-Roman culture of New Testament times. There were many folk remedies and physical techniques of varying effectiveness, but without anaesthetics, antibiotics, or blood transfusion, the more effective methods were also riskier to the life of the mother. The Hippocratic Oath prohibited medical abortion, but the Bible is silent. One passage is sometimes cited, by both supporters and opponents of abortion, namely, Exodus 21:22-25, which deals with spontaneous abortion (miscarriage) as a result of accidental injury to a pregnant woman during a fight. There is difficulty with the translation of this passage. The NRSV translation indicates that if the woman is killed or injured, then *lex talionis* applies, i.e., the penalty matches the injury to the woman, but if the only mishap is miscarriage, the penalty is a fine. Nevertheless, the NIV translation indicates that if as a result of the injury the child is born prematurely but otherwise unharmed, a fine applies. If, however, either the mother or child suffers serious injury or death, *lex talionis* applies. The first translation implies that the life of the foetus does not have the same status as a woman, the second that it does. Both translations have scholarly support and which is preferred will probably depend on the presuppositions of the reader.

However, as we have seen, the Bible does teach that each human being is created in the image of God and his or her life, therefore, should not be violated (this applies to the life of abortionists too, as extremists who attempt to kill them need to remember). But is human life before birth such a human being, and so entitled to this protection?

The Bible does not explicitly tell us when the life of a human individual begins, but it certainly speaks of life in the womb as continuous with and equivalent to life after birth in respect of relationship to God. Psalm 139 brings this out clearly:

> *You* ... created *my* inmost self, and
> put *me* together ... *You* know *me*
> through and through, from having
> watched *my* bones take shape when
> *I* was being formed in secret.

In the womb, the foetus is already an *I* who is addressed by God, and according to Christian tradition, the incarnation did not take place when the baby Jesus was born, but in the virgin's womb. Mary was in the earliest stage of pregnancy when Jesus was recognized by his cousin John, himself a six-month foetus (Luke 1: 39-45). Therefore it seems that abortion is the wilful killing of an innocent human being. This view of the foetus profoundly shaped the early Church's attitude towards abortion. For instance, the mid-second century document the *Didache* declares "do not murder a child by abortion" (2:2) and this has generally been the position of the church ever since. There have been some exceptions, such as life-saving surgery that removes a pregnant woman's uterus (say for cancer) and may result in the death of the foetus, other cases of pregnancy–related danger to the mother's life, and more controversially, cases of rape or incest.

Most abortions these days, however, are for social or emotional reasons that do not seem to provide sufficient moral justification for such a serious action. Nevertheless, the church needs to do more than simply prohibit or condemn abortion in these circumstances. It also needs to challenge the assumptions that undergird its justification by society and the law, as exemplified by the US Supreme Court's 1973 *Roe v. Wade* decision. The argument based on privacy and autonomy is expressed as "I can do with my body as I wish." It assumes that we only have obligations to others if we choose to, and neglects the real bonds that exist between people, especially the parent-child bond.

Humans are made for relationships and find their identity in relationships with God and with each other (Genesis 1, 2). We have obligations to our neighbours, even to strangers and enemies, as shown in the parable of the Good Samaritan. How much more ought parents to protect and care for their children, and especially vulnerable children, such as those who are disabled and who call for special care and protection. However, the trend towards antenatal testing and abortion of foetuses with any disability, or even undesirable characteristics, represents a quite different attitude to one's children: they are seen as commodities, objects of quality control. Abortion is the means by which the inferior or disappointing product is rejected (see the next story's consideration of pro-creation versus reproduction).

If we reject the individualism that makes abortion a woman's personal choice, we also need to reject the individualism that it makes it her sole responsibility. There is solidarity in sin, and whole communities may be held responsible for the sins of individuals, as seen when Israel was punished collectively as a nation. As has been said, many people contribute to abortion decisions apart from the woman herself: the woman's partner, her family, friends, abortion counsellors and health care workers, and society itself. The church can demonstrate its acknowledgement of this communal responsibility by offering practical assistance and support to women during pregnancy and in raising their children. "Unwanted" children, or the children of mothers without the resources to care for them, ought to be welcomed and cared for by the church community.

In the case of a foetus diagnosed with a disability, this community responsibility to share the burden is especially important. It must be acknowledged that the care of such children is often too much for a single individual or family to cope with

alone. We have seen that disabilities, even if profound, do not change the worth of an individual's life or mean that they can therefore be killed, either before or after birth, as they too are made in God's image. We have seen that God's justice is especially concerned with the most vulnerable and needy in our midst. But justice also demands that we share the burden of care.

Todd's dilemma raises the issue of whether some sins are worse than others. Perhaps he secretly wondered whether Katia could really be forgiven by God for doing such a thing. Perhaps Katia also wondered, especially when their child was diagnosed with Down syndrome. We need to make clear that God's forgiveness won through the death of Christ and accepted through faith extends to all sins. We are told to be similarly gracious and forgiving, as we have experienced the grace and forgiveness of God ourselves and know ourselves to be sinners too (Matthew 6:9-15, 18:21-35). Disease and disability are a result of living in a sinful, fallen world. To assume automatically that they are a punishment for sin in a particular situation is wrong. When Jesus was asked whose sin was responsible for a man being born blind, he replied "Neither this man nor his parents sinned, he was born blind so that God's works might be revealed in him" (John 9:1ff).

What opportunities for the gospel are there?

[*See also "Generic Strategies" above*]

The church has the opportunity to bring the message of grace to people before, during, and after decisions about abortion.

Before such situations arise, the church has a role in sex education – both in providing it directly and, even better, in teaching families to educate their children. Such education should promote abstinence as God's design for unmarried people, to avoid unwanted pregnancy and sexually transmitted disease. Premarital counselling can help couples explore their attitudes to the value of human life and their attitudes to children, especially disabled ones, and how they might respond to unplanned pregnancy.

During the period right after a woman learns she is pregnant, the church can provide crisis pregnancy counselling, and in particular, offer resources to enable people to continue with pregnancy. The church should also demonstrate grace to those who choose to abort. Church members can offer adoption, especially for disabled children, as an alternative to abortion.

After abortion decisions, the church can offer counselling to both women and men who experience guilt through the establishment of post-abortion syndrome groups and the public proclamation of forgiveness of sins for those who repent. The church can also present an alternative to abortion of disabled children in offering practical support to parents. This could include provision of respite care, and running programmes for disabled people that affirm their dignity as children of God. Such programmes may attract unbelievers with disabled children to the church.

When Christians engage in political action against abortion, it is important they are consistent in affirming the value of human life. There is no place for violence or hatred, even against those who promote abortions and perform them. In all its activities and liturgy, the church should aim to celebrate human life in all its diversity.

Further Resources

Randy Alcorn. *Pro-Life Answers to Pro-Choice Arguments*. Sisters, OR: Multnomah, 1992.

Frank Beckwith. *Politically Correct Death*. Grand Rapids, MI: Baker Book House, 1994.

Crisis pregnancy information:

www.care-net.org

www.cpworld.org

http://covenantnews.com/pregnant

Scott Klusendorf. *Pro-Life 101*. Signal Hill, CA: Stand to Reason, 2002.

Norma McCorvey and Gary Thomas. *Won By Love*. Nashville, TN: Thomas Nelson, 1998.

Paul Stallsworth (ed), *The Church and Abortion* (Nashville, TN, USA: Abingdon, 1993)

5. Reproductive technologies

Evening is falling when Suzanne finds William. The doctor has just told her she is not pregnant and, indeed, could not become pregnant. Something is wrong with her body. She has been told her womb is fine, but she has no eggs that could live. A tear is in her eye as she says to William having children is natural. It is what all couples should do. It is what God wanted when he said "Be fruitful and multiply." William says "I love you no matter what. We'll see what options there are."

After three weeks, at the recommendation of their family doctor, William and Suzanne visit a specialist at a city clinic. The specialist offers several options. "You can, of course, go home and accept this is nature's way. Or you could adopt. Though this would not be your child genetically, no doubt you would grow to love the baby. Or we could try an assisted reproductive technique. We'd take eggs from a donor and fertilize them with William's sperm. At that stage you could choose the sex of your child too, if you want. We would then pick the best few embryos and insert them into Suzanne. The ones that grow best will be kept in the womb."

On the ride home, the couple decide they should go ahead. Suzanne says "At least our baby will have part of our genes and I will be able to feel him grow in me. That way he is part of both of us."

"Let's pray about it, but I think this is a good idea," William responds, "and if you want, we can talk it over with the pastor."

"No, not yet. Let's keep this to ourselves, at least for now," she replies.

After eight months, though still not pregnant, the couple has an argument about who should know what. William says

"Sweetheart, this is simply how some people have children nowadays. Of course we can tell your parents and mine...and, of course, we will tell the baby when he – and the doctor said we could select the sperm so our child should be male – when he is old enough."

Suzanne replies, "There is no way we are going to tell anyone about this. It is between us and the doctor."

It is two years later, driving home from the specialist, having been told once again that the procedure has failed, that William asks

Suzanne if this is not God telling them the whole thing is wrong. They have spent a lot of money and have even been told by the doctor that he could allow them only one more try. Once again Suzanne is crying. "Should we adopt? There are babies in our country and throughout the world who need parents. We could love a baby, I know." They drive home in silence.

What Issues Does This Story Raise?

Infertility affects at least one in ten couples, and any discussion of it must acknowledge the pain it involves. As having children is seen to be normal and natural, the inability to have them may cause profound grief, and raise the question "Why me?" Sometimes women's inability to conceive may be associated with past induced abortions, or with sexually transmitted pelvic inflammatory disease, but often there is no obvious medical cause. Infertility may threaten one's sense of identity as a woman if femininity is identified with motherhood, or as a man if fertility is confused with sexual potency.

There are several different medical techniques, often called forms of assisted reproductive technology (ART), designed to overcome infertility. *In vitro fertilisation* (IVF) uses a combination of fertility drugs and egg transfer techniques. *In vitro* is Latin for "in glass," referring to the glass dish used in the lab. First, a woman takes hormonal drugs to hyperstimulate her ovaries to produce a large number of eggs. These are then removed from her ovaries using a laparoscope (a tube inserted through a small opening in the abdominal wall) and mixed with sperm in a culture dish. At the appropriate stage of growth -- usually 36 to 48 hours after fusion (fertilisation), when 8 to 16 cells have resulted from cell growth and division -- the resulting embryo or several embryos are transferred into a woman's uterus (the term "embryo" will be used here, as it most commonly is, to refer to a human during the first eight weeks after conception takes place through fertilisation, cloning, etc.). A more technically complex form of IVF is *intra-cytoplasmic sperm injection* (ICSI), in which a single sperm is injected into the cytoplasm of the egg to fertilise it.

In *gamete intra-fallopian transfer* (GIFT), eggs are retrieved and placed into a catheter with an air bubble and sperm, then inserted into the fallopian tube (which must be functioning properly) where fertilisation is expected to take place. The average success rate of ART in terms of live births is somewhat less than 20% per treatment cycle. There are also risks, especially to women from whom eggs are harvested. The hormones used to hyperstimulate the ovary may cause it to rupture, and the anaesthetic has its own risks. The procedure may accidentally result in an ectopic pregnancy (in the fallopian tube rather than the uterus), which is not viable and threatens the life of the mother through rupture of the tube. Women may accept these risks for the sake of becoming pregnant themselves, but it becomes more problematic when eggs are donated to a third party. If donors are paid, could poor women become "human hens?" Another concern is whether women participating in ART will feel pressured to donate "spare eggs" to another couple?

The possibility of using ART raises big questions about the nature of the family and childbearing. Is inability to have a child a disease? Do people have a "right" to children genetically related to them? Who should be allowed to use ART – unmarried couples, singles, homosexual couples? Should William and Suzanne accept that it is God's will for them not to have their "own" children, or should they see ART as God's provision for them? There are also questions regarding the relationship between marriage and childbearing. In some ART, a third party is involved in the process, as when the sperm or eggs come from donors. Will Suzanne fully think of herself as the mother if the child results from a donor egg? Could William be committing the reproductive equivalent of adultery with the egg donor? Furthermore, the woman who has the embryo implanted may not be the biological mother (source of the eggs) but a surrogate. Who will the child think is his or her "real" mother? Partly for these reasons, particularly if donor sperm or eggs are involved, ART is often perceived as crossing a moral boundary, as "tinkering with nature," or "playing God."

In addition, the actual techniques may be morally problematic. Because of the low success rate of the procedure and the difficulties in harvesting eggs, many embryos are often created at a time and those not transferred to the uterus are stored (frozen) for repeated attempts. At the conclusion of the treatment, any unwanted embryos may be donated to other couples, destroyed, or used for research, and this raises the issue of the moral status of the embryo. Furthermore, to increase the chance of a viable pregnancy, usually several embryos are implanted, which may result in multiple pregnancy. Selective abortion, where one or more of the foetuses are removed, may then be considered.

Then there are questions about whether donors of sperm or eggs should remain anonymous. How much should children born as a result of ART be told about their parentage? The story also raises justice issues. First, these technologies are expensive, either to the user or the taxpayer. Some would argue that their limited success rates mean they are not cost effective, or a good choice relative to other health expenditures. Second, it could be argued it would be more morally just for childless couples to adopt embryos, orphaned, or unwanted children -- especially from poorer countries -- than to put scarce resources into having children of their own. After all, should we have children to meet our own needs and fulfil our expectations, or to demonstrate God's unconditional love?

This last question raises the issue of discrimination. In choosing to select a male child, William and Suzanne are being sexist. They may also reject adoption for racist reasons, or may be discriminating against persons with disabilities, as babies available for adoption often are either from ethnic minorities or have a disability.

Finally what is the role of the church in these decisions? Are reproductive issues simply the concern of the couple involved, or should these difficult questions be shared with their pastor and wise Christian friends?

What Does the Bible Say?
Procreation and Reproduction

There is a subtle but significant change in perspective when the language for having children shifts from procreation to reproduction. The Nicene Creed's reference to Jesus being *begotten*, not *made*, may indicate a difference that is also morally relevant for ART. "Reproduction" evokes the concepts of commodities, the production line, quality control, and rejection of inferior products. The shift from "procreation" to "reproduction" in the wake of ART points to the basic desire of human beings to master the world by exercising their freedom.

The biblical idea of procreation (or begetting) is quite different. In begetting, the life resulting is the outcome of the mutual love of husband and wife. Procreation cannot be the sole aim of their love because love is not utilitarian. Neither should procreation be separated from the love relationship between husband and wife. The child is not the product of the will of a husband and wife, but God's gift to their mutual self-giving, the embodiment of the union of his or her parents (c.f. Genesis 33:5; Joshua 24:3-4; Psalm 127:3; Isaiah 8:18). The biological facts of conception and birth as the result of the sexual union between a man and a woman must not detract from the "given-ness" of the child.

ART potentially allows a complete separation of procreation from its proper context of marriage. This is evident in the move to change the definition of infertility from the inability of a specific couple to conceive, to the inability of a woman to conceive for any reason, including that she does not have a male partner ("social infertility"). Procreation is taken out of the family into the laboratory, whereas according to the Christian tradition, God is the Creator and parents are the only legitimate "*pro*creators." ART also opens the door to the commodification of human bodies and bodily products, as when direct or indirect payments are made to egg or sperm donors or to surrogate mothers. This is an affront to the dignity of a human being made in the image of God. As Edwin Hui has observed, *"[A] person is first constituted by the loving relationship of God whose love is marked by its gratuitousness in creation, providence and in redemption, all gratis."* Much is lost if all this becomes reduced to merchandise for sale.

Procreation is neither the exercise of a right nor merely a means of self-fulfilment. While children are clearly a blessing from God, the ability to have them must be seen in light of the mystery of God's providence. This outlook does not rule out all medical assistance in cases of infertility, but indicates the need for caution.

Infertility

Infertility is but one of the many results of the Fall, although Genesis 3:16 seems to single out difficulties in childbearing for women. Throughout the Old Testament, barrenness is regarded as a curse or punishment from God, often seen in terms of God closing the womb (e.g., Genesis 16:2, 30:2; 2 Samuel 6:23). In a world where women's most important role was bearing sons to continue the family name, childless women despaired, even those such as Rachel and Hannah who were greatly loved by their husbands. Their stories demonstrate two possible responses. One is to take matters into one's own hands — the earliest forms of "assisted reproduction" involved surrogacy, with Sarah and later Rachel using their maidservants to bear their husbands' children for them. Although not explicitly condemned in the text, it is clear from the way things turn out that the better response is prayer and continued faith in God, as demonstrated by Hannah (1 Samuel 1).

The New Testament introduces a very different understanding of family. Instead of being based on blood relationships, it is based on faith in God as heavenly Father, and we are adopted into a new family (John 1:12, Galatians 4:5, Ephesians 1:5). So singleness and celibacy are now an option, as demonstrated by Jesus and Paul. Children are still to be welcomed, but there is no duty to have them. As with illness, infertility is no longer seen as attributable to an individual's sin. Infertile couples must not consider themselves second-class, and infertility must not be seen as God's disfavour.

Although even for Christians, infertility is often full of anguish, the infertile couple may trust that God will fulfil his purposes through their union in other ways, and they may seek to be available for tasks not open to those with children.

Destruction of Embryos and Foetuses

Although it is a natural human desire to have children, the desire to have them at all costs is idolatrous. Such costs are financial and emotional, but also the cost of the lives of human embryos. Some Christians argue that even in the "natural" process of procreation, there is wastage of embryos that either fail to implant or are spontaneously aborted and therefore a similar level of wastage is acceptable in ART. However, almost all would agree there are significant moral problems with techniques that deliberately create far more embryos than will be required, so that they will likely be destroyed or used for research. Understanding the magnitude of these problems requires a clear view of the humanity of early embryos — a matter to be considered in the next story. We have already considered, in relation to the abortion story, the significant moral problems with selective abortion -- also called foetal reduction when multiple pregnancy results from ART. A good consequence, such as having a child, cannot justify wrong means to accomplish it (the "greater good" argument is considered in the next story).

Choosing the Attributes of Our Offspring

Because children are a gift from God and not the direct result of human willing, it seems incongruous to demand certain attributes, such as gender. Genetic screening before birth and allowing only the best to live will be discussed in Story 8 below. Children are also treated as commodities rather than gifts when potential sperm or egg donors are selected on the basis of intelligence, race, height, and other characteristics.

Donor Sperm and Eggs

There are strong reasons why Christians might reject ART involving sperm and eggs from a third party. Such an approach breaks the connection between marriage, sexual intercourse, and procreation; instead efforts are made to ensure a "product." Lines of kinship are blurred and confused, and a third party intrudes into the procreative relationship. This applies to creating a child through sperm or egg donation or insemination, and surrogacy arrangements (whether commercial or altruistic). These practices also present difficulties to the resulting children in terms of "genetic bewilderment."

What Opportunities for the Gospel are There?

[*See also "Generic Strategies" above*]

The pain of infertility and/or the stress of ART may well bring people into contact with the church for counselling and prayer. The church could be more intentional about this by running support groups for childless couples, to which non-believers are welcome. Couples could be encouraged to trust God for the future, assured that their problems are not a punishment for sin, and helped to find the meaning and value of their lives in God rather than merely in human achievement.

The gospel can free people to be confident of their identity in Christ and their place in his family, and this may be especially important for women.

The church has a role to play in education about ART and its implications, so that people understand the deeper issues involved and are helped to explore all their options. In particular, Christians who adopt children, especially disabled children or those of a different race, offer a tangible witness to a just alternative to ART and to God's unconditional love and acceptance. The church needs to provide them every support possible, ranging from a welcoming attitude to respite care as needed.

Further Resources

Linda Bevington and Russell DiSilvestro, eds. *The Pill.* Bannockburn, IL: CBHD/www.cbhd.org, 2003.

Debra Evans. *Without Moral Limits: Women, Reproduction, and Medical Technology.* updated edition. Wheaton, IL: Crossway, 2000.

Edwin Hui. *At the Beginning of Life.* Downers Grove, IL: InterVarsity, 2002.

John Kilner, et al., eds. *The Reproduction Revolution.* Grand Rapids, MI: William B. Eerdmans, 2000.

Scott Rae. *Brave New Families.* Grand Rapids, MI: Baker Book House, 1996.

Gary Stewart, et al. *Basic Questions on Reproductive Technologies.* Grand Rapids, MI: Kregel, 1998.

6. Stem Cell Research

Mary and Theng Huat have been undergoing treatment for infertility for over a year. Recently, they went through a round of in vitro fertilization (IVF). Mary's fertility doctor retrieved 12 eggs and fertilised them with Theng Huat's sperm, which resulted in ten embryos. Three were transferred to Mary's uterus: the other seven were frozen in the clinic for later use.

None of the first three embryos implanted resulted in a pregnancy, but on the second cycle of treatment Mary became pregnant with twins. A year or so after the birth of a healthy girl and boy, Mary's gynaecologist sent a letter asking whether or not she and her husband had decided what they wanted to do with their four frozen embryos. The letter indicated that if they no longer wanted them stored, they should call Mr Tan at the clinic.

'What do you think?' Mary asks Theng Huat after opening the letter. They haven't made up their minds whether they want any more children, but they are also unsure about what happens to the embryos if they say they don't want them. So Mary calls Mr Tan and asks him about this. 'If you remember, we discussed this when you signed the consent form for the treatment' he replies. 'Of course, you can simply have us throw the frozen embryos away, if you no longer need them, but it would be much more sensible for you to donate them for embryonic stem cell research.' 'What's that?' Mary asks. Mr Tan explains, 'It is research that uses embryos to develop new medical treatments. We think this research holds tremendous promise for treating conditions like diabetes, heart disease, Alzheimer's and Parkinson's.'

That evening Mary discusses donation with her husband over dinner. Theng Huat observes that his father has already benefited from experimental stem cell treatment for his heart disease, so donating their embryos for further stem cell research would probably be a good idea. 'I would agree with you' says Mary 'but I seem to recall they used your father's own cells to develop the treatment for his heart condition. We would be letting them use embryos instead. Is that really the same thing?'

What Issues Does This Story Raise?

The issues of the moral status of human embryos and what we do with them come to the fore here. Parents may no longer need embryos frozen for them during the course of IVF. By law in many countries they must be defrosted and so die, after a certain period of time. Or they may be donated to other childless couples (an option sometimes offered) or, as often suggested, used for research since "they are going to die anyway." One major research use they are often used for is to provide a source of embryonic stem cells, which were first isolated and grown in 1998.

Stem cells (SCs) are cells that produce other cells, tissues, and organs, somewhat like the way that the stem of a plant is the source from which branches, leaves, and flowers develop. They may be derived from a number of sources. Adult SCs are commonly confused or conflated with embryonic SCs, as in our story. Up until the 16-cell stage, all the cells of an embryo are *totipotent* -- they have the ability to give rise to every cell type in the body, as well as to a new individual. During the first week of development, the embryo forms a cluster of cells called an "inner cell mass" and these cells — called embryonic SCs — are *pluripotent*: they can give rise to every cell type but not a new individual. They are obtained for research purposes by removing them from the embryo, causing the death of the embryo in the process. Pluripotent SCs can also be derived from five to ten week foetuses, obtained from either spontaneous or induced abortions, or the surgical removal of an ectopic pregnancy. SCs taken from the bodies of adults or children, or from umbilical cord blood, are less versatile (less plastic) and can therefore give rise to only a limited number of cells and tissues; they are *multipotent*.

SCs other than embryonic SCs, are generally referred to under the single heading of "adult" SCs since, unlike in the case of embryonic SCs, they do not require destroying the source from which they are taken and they most often come from adults. While a term like "non-embryonic" would be more accurate, the familiar term "adult" SCs will be used here. There is still scientific disagreement as to whether adult SCs of one type (e.g., blood, muscle, or nerve SCs) can produce cells of a different type. Early studies, which indicated they could, have not been replicated. However, if it turns out that they can, or they can stimulate other cells to develop through some other mechanism, then all the therapeutic benefits of stem cell research may be achievable without embryonic SCs. As of this writing, all 60 or so of the medical conditions helped by SC treatments in human beings have involved adult SCs rather than embryonic SCs.

Every SC has the capacity to produce millions of cells, but only embryonic SCs have been successfully propagated and maintained in the laboratory. Moreover, adult SCs in tissue are in limited supply and sometimes difficult to locate, except in bone marrow and blood. Nevertheless, at present they appear to be safer to use, in that embryonic SCs are more likely to produce tumors. A major challenge in all SC research is delivering SCs to the target location in the body. Nevertheless, it is considered to have enormous potential in treating conditions such as Parkinson's Disease, insulin dependent diabetes, spinal cord damage, autoimmune diseases, and some genetic disorders. Adult SC therapies have been used for some time, with bone marrow transplants being the best-known example.

To prevent the recipient from rejecting donor cells, those cells probably must either be genetically "matched" to the recipient or come from the recipient (as happens now with bone marrow taken from a patient before chemotherapy, which is then returned to the patient to replenish marrow damaged by the chemotherapy). In the case of embryonic SCs, probably the surest way to achieve the best genetic match with the recipient would be through a cloning process. In cloning, which was used to produce Dolly the sheep, an ordinary cell would be taken, say from the skin of the patient, and its nucleus placed into a human egg cell whose nucleus had been removed. After stimulation, this cell would start dividing like a regular embryo,

though one virtually identical genetically to the patient, like an identical twin. This technique would therefore create a source of tailor-made SCs for the patient that could potentially become any tissue type and would cause no problems with rejection. One common name for this technique, "therapeutic cloning," is misleading because the process is fatal rather than therapeutic (healing) for a subject involved in the research, the embryo. "Research cloning" is a better term, sometimes used to distinguish it from "reproductive cloning," where a clone implanted in the uterus leads to the birth of a new individual who is genetically identical to another. Both are forms of cloning — it's just that the intention for how the embryo is to be treated after the cloning (nuclear transfer) has been completed is different. Many people feel that research cloning is an inevitable consequence of embryonic SC research.

Even some who do not object to destroying existing embryos find it morally problematic to create embryos deliberately in order to destroy them for their SCs. They also argue that once research cloning is performed, it is only a matter of time before reproductive cloning will occur. It is hard to imagine prohibiting only reproductive cloning and therefore *forcing* anyone pregnant with a cloned child to abort. There are many misgivings about reproductive cloning, especially about the uses it might be put to, about physical and psychological risks for the child and about the impact on the family. One potential use would be the creation of "saviour siblings" as sources of tissue donation for diseased children. This raises questions about whether such children are being used as a means to an end, rather than valued in their own right.

What Does the Bible Say?
The Moral Status of the Human Embryo

In considering research involving human embryonic SCs, much depends on the moral status of the human embryo. If this embryo is nothing more than human tissue, then even research that destroys embryos does not pose any insurmountable ethical problems. If, however, even the early embryo has the full moral status of a human person, made in the image of God, then the destruction of embryos in research should never be allowed. Discussing the status of the embryo brings us back to the debate on when human life begins (see story 4 on abortion).

Although, as we have seen, the Bible does not explicitly tell us when the life of a new human individual begins, it is reasonable to argue from both philosophical and scientific perspectives that this is at conception. Neither scientists nor philosophers are agreed on when human life begins, in the sense of when the embryo or foetus acquires significant moral status and thus a "right to life" with protection from being killed. So-called "scientific" conclusions about the emergence of human life are typically also informed by philosophical presuppositions about what it means to be human, or to be a "person" who, as such, ought to be protected.

Some take the view that a human person does not exist until the baby is metab-

olically independent from the mother, at birth. This was Plato's position, but generally it is held to be too arbitrary a point to have moral significance. Peter Singer's position is even more radical: he claims that even a human infant has no right to protection from being killed until it attains the capacity for self-awareness and preference formation and thus becomes a "person," around the age of two.

Another view is that before the foetus is sentient – i.e., able to experience sensations, particularly pain -- it does not have full moral status. Sentience is certainly present around 26 weeks of pregnancy, but may occur earlier. However, using this criterion would also exclude even temporarily unconscious adults from the right not to be killed.

A third view, related to developments in neuroscience, is that moral status is acquired when the human-specific electroencephalogram (E.E.G., or "brain waves") is detected at around six weeks. Proponents of this view argue that since the discontinuation of brain waves is a definition of death, so the beginning of brain waves must be an indication of the beginning of a human life. Nevertheless, there is a profound difference between a dead person who permanently lacks brain activity and a foetus who lacks it only temporarily until it develops later in the process of normal growth.

Another view is that personhood emerges with individuation, at the decisive moment when the embryo is implanted into the womb. Proponents of this view distinguish between the embryo (after implantation) and the pre-embryo (before implantation) and offer two main reasons. The first is that 20-50% of embryos spontaneously miscarry before implantation and they consider it obvious that so many human beings are not dying. But such a view does not sufficiently appreciate the tragedy of the Fall, which has wreaked havoc with the natural order, including human reproduction (see Genesis 3:16; c.f. Romans 8:22). While it would be wonderful to be able to prevent these embryonic deaths, we have a much greater ability and obligation to avoid actually killing embryos and especially to avoid creating them with the intention of destroying them.

The second reason is the phenomenon of "twinning," which only occurs before implantation. If a new human individual begins at conception, how can one then become two? It seems strange to think that scientists have the ability to control or confer personhood since they can delay implantation and can also induce twinning. But if personhood begins at conception, then there are at least two possibilities. There may be more than one person present at conception, or there may be one person present at that time, with another person coming into being when twinning occurs. In either case, there is not *less than* one person present at conception.

Finally, the "genetic" hypothesis maintains that a new human individual begins at conception. In normal reproduction, that means at fertilisation when the egg and sperm nuclei fuse. As Ronan O'Rahilly and Fabiola Muller explain in their embryology textbook, *'Fertilisation is a critical landmark because, under ordinary circumstances, a new genetically human organism is thereby formed.... The embryo now exists as a genetic unity.'* The argument for personhood at conception is philosophically very compelling indeed. At this point, the early embryo, called a zygote, is endowed with a unique genetic code enabling this new human being to develop and mature into a complete human adult. The argument of some, that the zygote is not a human being because the zygote does not look like one, is very weak. A zygote is exactly what you looked like at that stage of development, along with everyone else alive today. The philosophical argument (like the theological one) is based on the nature of the object in question. A zygote of human parentage cannot become a dog or a cat. Just as the zygote of a horse bears the nature of its parents, so the zygote of human parentage shares the parents' nature.

Fertilisation represents a distinct point where the new individual is formed. Implantation, on the other hand, merely changes the source of the individual's nurture, rather than the essence of the individual's nature. The distinction between "pre-embryo" and (implanted) embryo, while made by many members of the scientific community, appears to be an arbitrary one from this perspective. Implantation relates to *where* the embryo is, not *what* the embryo is.

Doubt and disagreement will likely continue among Christians regarding the moral status of the early human embryo, but in the face of such doubt, we should err on the side of caution, because what is at stake, the image of God, is so important. Even if we concluded there were only a small chance that the early embryo has full moral status and the right to protection, we ought to act as if such is the case. No one reverses a car who recognizes there is even a small chance a child is behind it on the driveway.

The Greater Good Argument

The most powerful argument in favour of human embryonic SC research is the "greater good argument." Scientists and policy makers base their advocacy of this research on its enormous therapeutic potential. The argument is compelling and emotive simply because the motivation is to alleviate or eradicate the suffering of so many people. So those who express caution or think that embryonic SC research should not be allowed are sometimes viewed not only as being anti-progress or anti-science, but lacking in compassion. A Christian response must take into consideration the therapeutic promise of this research. Healing and the alleviation of suffering have always been an integral part of the Christian tradition. Yet we must consider the means as well as the ends. Good ends should never be achieved by evil means. The argument that the end justifies the means is based on *utilitarianism*. This form of philosophy, whose most famous contemporary advocate is Peter Singer, holds that no acts are intrinsically wrong, but that their morality is determined solely by their consequences. Sufficiently good

consequences (or the promise of them) can justify any action. Christian ethics, however, maintains that certain acts are wrong in themselves and cannot be justified even by wonderful consequences. The use and subsequent destruction of any bearer of God's image, regardless of how old or well-formed, should never be permitted, even in the name of scientific research and for the benefit of the common good. In the shadow of Nazism, the Nuremberg Code declared that "no experiment should be conducted where there is an *a priori* reason to believe that death or disabling injury will occur." Similarly, the 1975 Helsinki Declaration of the World Medical Association asserts that "concern for the interests of the subject must always prevail over the interest of science and society."

Nevertheless, we may welcome medical or scientific research — including SC research — that promises therapeutic applications but does not harm or destroy human beings in the process. We ought to support and encourage research conducted on non-embryonic SCs such as those obtained from adult tissue or umbilical cord blood. This research holds great therapeutic potential, as studies are already documenting.

What Opportunities for the gospel are There?

[*See also "Generic Strategies" above*]

The church has a role to play in informing its members and the community at large about the nature and implications of SC research. This issue opens up the question "Is there anything you wouldn't do (to find a cure for a disease that affects you or someone you love)?" This leads on to the more general discussion about reasons for ethical judgments. Considering the value and meaning of human life can lead to thinking about the source of that value and meaning.

Christians who are well informed can take opportunities to serve on research ethics committees and commend a Christian approach to these and similar issues. Christian researchers can witness to their beliefs through refusing to participate in unethical research projects. If in the future therapies become available based on embryonic SCs, believers may be called to demonstrate their obedience to God and their faith in him by refusing such treatments, even at great personal cost. Caring for other believers therefore joins the list of reasons to advocate actively now for the funding of adult SC research. As with any bioethical issue, Christians should be as well known for what they support as for what they oppose.

Further Resources

Linda Bevington, et al. *Basic Questions on Genetics, Stem Cell Research, and Cloning.* Grand Rapids, MI: Kregel, 2004.

The Center for Bioethics and Human Dignity, two-sided Q/A flier on "Therapeutic Cloning and Stem Cell Research." Bannockburn, IL: www.cbhd.org, 2005.

Henk Jochemsen, ed. *Human Stem Cells: Source of Hope and of Controversy.* Ede, The Netherlands: The Prof dr G A Lindeboom Institute;

and Jerusalem, Israel: Business Ethics Centre of Jerusalem, 2003.

John Kilner and C. Ben Mitchell. *Does God Need Our Help?* Wheaton, IL: Tyndale, 2003.

www.stemcellresearch.org

7. Genetic Modification in Agriculture

A Western laboratory has been working to develop a plant resistant to an insect that periodically devastates regions in certain tropical developing nations. The insects impact the population in two ways: first, locals are deprived of an important food source, and second, they lose a primary source of income. As a farmer says "Because of these insects and what they did to my crop last year, I can hardly feed my kids, let alone afford to send them to high school." The corporation working on this new plant, or genetically modified organism (GMO), claims to be acting charitably, since the crop is not frequently grown for use in the West.

Some local leaders are attempting to work with the Western corporation to bring this GMO into production. They claim the GMO will allow people using traditional agricultural techniques to overcome the continuing problem with the insects. The plants will have higher resistance and higher yield. A corporation representative claims "In the future, we will also be able to make this variety more nutritious and taste better." Local leaders who support the project argue the choice should be in the hands of local producers, not paternalistic "green" politicians overseas: "This will help feed our families and raise our standard of living. And if we're healthier and better off, we won't need to move into the overcrowded cities."

Yet not everyone is happy. "This is no more than a new form of colonialism" says a spokesperson for locals opposed to genetically modified crops. "They're really just experimenting – economically, biologically, socially – on vulnerable people like us. Our farmers will depend on the multinational company for seed. There may be great damage to our fragile ecosystem if the GMO becomes a weed or hybridises local plants." He also points out the slight possibility that farmers and their families will become ill from eating or growing the plant, and notes that their concept of traditional farming will be irrevocably damaged. Those opposed to GMOs are taking the "precautionary" approach.

The situation is further complicated because various environmental groups in the West are protesting against GMOs and rightly or wrongly, this corporation has been branded as greedy, callous, and short-sighted. Local church leaders have been drawn into the debate too, because some local farmers and some local politicians are Christians. To make matters worse, two mission representatives, one from the USA and one from Germany, take exactly opposite positions. The American claims this is simply a matter of justice: people need to be fed. The German suggests precaution does make sense and further states that Christians should not support any research that might later be used to alter human beings.

What Issues Does This Story Raise?

First, the fact is that humans have been altering plants and animals for agricultural purposes for millennia. This has been done by selective breeding, producing hybrid plants, and transporting species into new ecosystems. Corn, wheat, horses, and cattle are a few examples. But biotechnology has brought new issues.

To understand them, we need to con-sider the motivations of the various groups. A corporation wanting to introduce a GMO may be acting in a colonialist manner. Their executives may genuinely believe they are "helping," but if they have not involved the people of the communities where the technology will be applied, they are using their power inappropriately. Similarly, environmentalists from the West will frequently use their interpretive framework without proper consideration or involvement of the people. In this case the locals may be more concerned with food than hypothetical and perhaps even unlikely environmental consequences. It is an abuse of power to ignore what the local communities are actually saying, or even worse to dismiss them as "ignorant," just to appeal to political constituencies back in the West.

Who may benefit and who may be hurt by specific decisions should be considered. Groups involved in genetic modification (GM) include:

- Scientists and other supportive academics with technical knowledge.
- Processors/seed companies with economic clout.
- Farmers who control the planting of GMOs and raising of animal GMOs.
- Consumers who have choices in the market.
- Governments who are supposed to protect members of "social contracts."
- Advocacy groups (especially environmental, anti-globalisation, and community development groups) and international organisations like the

United Nations, who see themselves, rightly or wrongly, as protectors of the commons.

- Local inhabitants, including those who have developed particular plant and animal lines over centuries.

Issues of potential danger can be classified in a variety of ways. Simply for convenience here they are listed by the dangers (and later benefits) to humans and to nature. While humans are distinct from the rest of nature, they are simultaneously a part of nature. So this distinction in the lists is for analysis only, as humans are ecologically connected with whatever happens to the rest of the created order. These lists do not include weighting or probability of occurrence.

Dangers to Humans

- Excessive use of pesticides may occur, since some GMOs are not affected by them.
- GMOs could create health problems in individuals allergic to inserted genes.
- A genetic modification that causes disease may accidentally occur.
- Developing the technology makes it possible for those with terrorist intentions to mount bio-warfare.
- Governments may currently be developing bio-warfare technologies using the skills developed in GM research.
- As with other modern forms of agriculture, a "monoculture" (a plant or animal with very little genetic variation, which is not the normal state in nature) will produce very well, but may then be vulnerable to a disease

that will wipe out the entire crop.

- Corporations that produce GMOs may attempt "vertical integration" — they will try to have a monopoly by controlling planting, growth (including which fertilisers and pesticides are used), harvesting, storage, and value addition through processing, marketing, and distribution — thus depriving growers and others of access to markets.
- Corporations may attempt to "own" the genetic information, and thus control distribution of plant and animal lines that have been developed over centuries (a form of economic colonialism).
- GM products may accidentally contaminate other products, thus lowering their value.

Dangers to Nature

- A GMO might become an invasive species with no natural predators or other controls, and force out native species.
- Unpredictable changes might occur that cannot be stopped, since introducing GMOs into nature will be irreversible.
- Especially in crossing species lines, humans are violating the integrity of species.
- Genetic modifications may "jump" (outcross) to related species in the ecosystem.
- GMOs may control pests, but also unintentionally hurt beneficial species.

- Pests will grow that are resistant to genetic modifications and then attack all similar crops.
- Animal genetic modification, as with much industrial farming, can be cruel to the animals by creating animals fit only to sit in growing facilities until slaughtered.

Potential benefits include:

Benefits to Humans

- More reliable yields for farmers through control of the impact of insects, disease, drought, frost, etc.
- Less damage to farmers' health through less use of pesticide, since GMs will control pests.
- Possibly less hard work for farmers.
- Ability to add nutrients to plants to improve nutrition in a population.
- Higher production/yield for farmers.
- Easier and more reliable processing.
- Value can be added to products.

Benefits to Nature

- Less use of pesticides, thus killing fewer harmless and beneficial species living in the same fields as the pests.
- Possible genetic "banking" and subsequent protection of endangered species.
- More reliable crops leading to less acreage in production, thus protecting ecosystems.
- Development of pollution-controlling microbes.

Of course, simple lists do not adequately present the relative weight that should be given to these various benefits and risks, nor the probability of something occurring. The best that we can do is turn

to experts for information, seeking the least biased among them and using at least two or three different sources of information.

Those who oppose GMOs often invoke the precautionary principle, that the application of a technology should be prohibited when the outcomes are both unpredictable and potentially catastrophic. This is helpful, but not if it leads to stopping all applications of technologies because there is "some" chance something might go wrong. Risk is a comparative concept, and the risk of doing something must be compared to the risks of alternatives, including not doing anything.

Those who favour technologies sometimes choose to minimise risk, or not take into account the catastrophic nature of a possible incident because the probability seems relatively low. There is a long tradition of corporations, Western nations, and indigenous political leaders not taking into account "externalities" -- costs to the environment and community that are ignored by the people who create them because those costs are not readily observed or are rapidly diffused. Air pollution is an example of an externality; it is a real cost for those who get sick, but the polluters rarely pay. Also, those with a strong bent toward finding technical solutions to problems may disregard other options. For instance, sometimes returning to traditional farming methods or traditional crops rather than cash crops might be as effective as any GMO.

The implications of genetic modification remain uncertain, even though some risks once associated with the technologies seem to have been addressed. Precaution is important when outcomes are unknown, but precaution is not the same as a technological freeze. Genetic modification in agriculture is a technology about which Christian believers may honestly disagree. It is reasonable and consistent with Scripture either to proceed cautiously with some GMOs or to ask for a few more years of strictly controlled research.

What Does The Bible Say?
Stewardship

Christians believe and must proclaim that humans are a genuinely distinct species, created by God in his image, and as his servants. With this in view, humans have both the stewardship opportunity to use the earth for their needs and the stewardship obligation to protect the earth that does not belong to them, but to God. The remaining two-fold question is "How shall we be stewards of nature, and how shall we take care of humans in desperate need?"

Christians must reject any radical environmental argument that declares humans to be of no more significance than any other creature or even (the most extreme view) that humans are weeds that should be allowed to die out. Jesus asked, *'Are not five sparrows sold for two pennies? Yet not one of them is forgotten in God's sight. But even the hairs of your head are all counted. Do not be afraid; you are of more value than many sparrows'* (Luke 12:6-7). Genetic modification is one possible means of addressing the need for justice for the oppressed and

mercy for the hungry. It is far too easy for those in so-called developed countries to dismiss desperate needs. Though environmentalism is fundamentally a concern for all peoples, the comfort of the "developed" often allows them to make pronouncements that sound, at best, like one more extension of paternalism.

Yet those who are faithful to the Creator must recognize that humans are stewards who may use, but not abuse, that which God has created. Nature is the Lord's, and praises his name (Psalm 66, 69, 89, 103, 104, 145, and in particular 148). Nature and the individual "members" of the natural world have intrinsic value, for the Lord declared they were "good" at their creation. Each person is loved by the Lord and of special concern to him, yet this does not mean that the sparrows (or the lions, or the frogs, or the grasses, or the trees) are of no concern to the Lord God who made them all and declared them good. In addition, protecting nature sometimes directly serves the needs of human beings, such as when vulnerable communities confront the unjust, abusive appropriation of natural resources, or their use as "test sites." Christians must recognise who has power and what kind of power (political, military, economic, etc.) and who is vulnerable and to what extent. Power is not intrinsically evil, but unrecognised power is readily abused.

Why Does God Allow Suffering?

In this case, some people are blaming the insect infestations on sin. Certainly, all suffering is finally attributable to sin – but not always to the specific sins of those who are actually faced with tragedy. Certainly, if a people "build their house on the sand" they should not be surprised when the floods rise and sweep the building away (Matthew 7:24 ff). Yet, the Scripture is clear – from Job through the teachings of Christ – that the suffering of individuals or people groups cannot always be attributed to their own sin. To the contrary, sometimes people suffer at the hands of others, and sometimes simply because they/we live in a fallen world.

Are the people of the community doing whatever they can to prevent infestations, including altering agricultural techniques? Have the problems been worsened by trade systems that shift agriculture away from holistic, balanced rotations to planting for a world market? Is the developed world responsible for helping peoples in the developing world, or is such assistance viewed as "charity" from the greater to the lesser? Then, beyond the question of blame lies a more basic question for the faithful: how can and how should the believers help needy humans – especially fellow believers (Galatians 6:10) – while also being respectful of God's creation?

What Opportunities for the gospel are There?
[See also "Generic Strategies" above]

It is more in understanding the tragedy and being willing to help, than in the specific technology applied, that the greatest evangelistic opportunity exists. Christians can use service to others as a means of declaring the reality of God's service to us in Jesus Christ. Indeed, God understands human need and human suffering because he took upon himself the mantle of human frailty (Hebrews 4:14 ff). Of course, this has no evangelistic significance unless the faithful do something to demonstrate that God's redemption of the lost allows those who follow Him to also serve those who stand in need – be the need spiritual or physical (James 2:16).

It is reasonable and moral that the missionaries, in humble conversation with the local people, respond to the need with immediate assistance and long term agricultural assistance, whether using GMOs or not. It may be that using genetically modified plants and animals is deemed beneficial, or it may be that it is seen as being too risky, both to ecosystems and to the social and economic well-being of local communities. While the GMO decision is an important one, and one that remains open to reasonable debate, the commitment on the part of the faithful to do *something* significant for other believers in need, for unbelievers in need, and for nature itself, is undeniable.

Further Resources
These sources represent material from across the spectrum on genetic modification of non-human life, since there is not a lot of up-to-date biblical-Christian analysis available. The web sites in particular will make it easier to stay current on rapidly changing technology.

Committee on Environmental Impacts Associated with Commercialization of Transgenic Plants, Board on Agriculture and Natural

Resources, National Research Council, *Environmental Effects of Transgenic Plants: The Scope and Adequacy of Regulation*. Washington, DC: National Academies Press, 2002.

Gary Comstock. *Vexing Nature: On the Ethical Case Against Agricultural Biotechnology*. Boston, MA: Kluwer Academic Publishers, 2000.

David Evans, et al., eds. *Biblical Holism and Agriculture*. Pasadena, CA: William Carey Library, 2003.

Vandana Shiva. *Stolen Harvest: The Hijacking of the Global Food Supply*. Cambridge MA: South End Press, 2000.

Web sites:

AgBioForum: www.agbioforum.org

AgBioTech website: www.biotech-info.net/index.html

Glossary of biotechnology terms: ***www.biotechterms.org***

Intellectual property and genetic ownership. www.intelliwareint.com/R E L A T E D % 2 0 B I O - LINKS.htm#INTELLECTUAL% 20PROPERTY

Transgenic Plants and World Agriculture. Report prepared under the auspices of the Royal Society of London, the US National Academy of Sciences, the Brazilian Academy of Sciences, the Chinese Academy of Sciences, the Indian National Science Academy, the Mexican Academy of Sciences and the Third World Academy of Sci-ences. (July 2000): www.nap.edu/html/transgenic

US government website with numerous links, including international: w w w . n a l . u s d a . g o v / b i c / Education_res

Wingspread Declaration: http://www.johnsonfdn.org/ whatsnew/conferences'99/ july19_21'99.html

8. Human Enhancement

It is the year 2020. Darren and Kylie are a young couple married for two years. Darren works for a large insurance company in Sydney, Australia and Kylie is a kindergarten teacher. They attend an independent evangelical community church, where they lead a Bible study and fellowship group.

Kylie and Darren have decided it is time to start a family, so they visit their local Reproductive Clinic for the preliminary tests, which routinely include genetic testing. At their interview with the doctor, she tells them that if any genetically transmitted disease is found in either of them, pre-implantation genetic diagnosis (PGD) will enable them to make sure they do not pass the disease on to their children. This technique involves producing a number of embryos in the laboratory using their own sperm and eggs. The embryos are then tested to identify whether or not they carry the disease gene and only disease-free ones are implanted.

The doctor also mentions that if they wish, they can select either male or female embryos for implantation. In addition (since they have private health insurance) they could use gene modification on their selected embryo to enhance qualities such as intelligence or athletic ability. "For instance," she says, "I couldn't help noticing both of you are on the short side and a bit overweight. Why not help your children avoid these challenges?"

Darren and Kylie go home with lots of thoughts and questions, as well as some worries about what they might be doing. The next evening Kylie raises the topic of sex selection and genetic enhancement at her book club group. Most are very enthusiastic and encourage them to "do the best for your children."

But they are still confused and doubtful whether this is the sort of thing Christians should do. They visit their pastor, but when they explain the situation, he admits it is not an issue he knows anything about and he has no idea where they can get any material from a Christian perspective. "Why doesn't the church have any resources about this?" they ask.

What Issues Does This Story Raise?

In this futuristic, but by no means fantastic scenario, we see some consequences of current trends in biotechnology. First, comprehensive screening of prospective parents to see if they carry genetic disease has become routine, as has pre-implantation diagnosis. Embryos are created using IVF technology, with cells removed from each for analysis. Only one or two embryos free of disease and perhaps also with desirable characteristics will be implanted, the rest discarded.

There are serious questions here about consent to such procedures, what information is provided before people give this consent, and whether they have real choices once the results are known. If Darren or Kylie were diagnosed with a genetic disease, or perhaps simply a genetic predisposition to a disease, would they be able to choose not to use IVF tech-

nology and PGD if they had moral problems with the techniques, or if they were simply prepared to take the risk? If they did go for PGD, who would make the decisions about which genetic conditions would disqualify embryos? Should they take the opportunity to select the sex of their child when it is offered? How would they decide which sex? This last issue indicates that more than healing treatment (therapy) is involved here. Also in view is human enhancement — "improving" human beings beyond what medical need requires.

Currently, most genetic screening before birth involves testing the foetus in the womb. In amniocentesis, some of the fluid surrounding the foetus is removed, cultured, and then tested. Other technologies include chorionic villus sampling (CVS), alpha-fetoprotein testing (AFT) and fluorescent *in situ* hybridisation (FISH). Such tests are performed more and more frequently, yet the old questions remain: What are we to do with the knowledge we have attained? What does the genetic anomaly mean? Is it possible to predict its consequences? Is a cure available?

A problem confronting genetic screening of any kind is that we can diagnose more than we can interpret. We do not know the implications of the genetic variations we are able to detect. Further, we can diagnose more anomalies than we can cure or ameliorate. If Darren or Kylie is discovered to be a disease carrier, they are confronted with very difficult choices.

They can:

- Avoid pregnancy completely
- Use IVF and PGD
- Use IVF with a donor sperm or egg to replace the one carrying the disease
- Risk a natural pregnancy and either have antenatal screening or not
- If antenatal screening reveals the foetus has the disease, either abort the foetus or continue with the pregnancy.

Choosing this last option and continuing the pregnancy would mean giving birth to a baby with the genetic disease, which in turn may mean expensive long-term therapy and possibly poor quality of life. Parents may feel guilty whatever they choose. They may find it especially difficult to deal with an ambiguous diagnosis or a situation in which the consequences of a genetic anomaly are uncertain.

Then there is the use of gene technology to alter human genes, whether to treat genetic disease, or as in this case, to "enhance" certain desirable qualities. Many people feel that as long as genes are altered for therapeutic purposes and not to "design" individuals by altering their traits, the technology is acceptable. Yet further reflection shows that therapy and enhancement cannot always be clearly distinguished. On the one hand, the technology can be intended to correct a defective gene that would cause a fatal disease. On the other, that same technology can potentially be used to "correct" a physical trait, such as hair or eye colour, that is perceived as a "defect," though associated

with psychological rather than physical problems. "Correcting" such a gene would then be therapeutic psychologically, and any distinction between therapy and enhancement becomes ambiguous. For many physical characteristics, such as height, the distinction between normal and abnormal is arbitrary and largely defined socially. How short (or tall) do people have to be before they could be said to have a condition requiring therapy?

Engaging in genetic therapy with an adult who can assess and consent to the risks involved is one thing, but subjecting endless future generations to such risks without their consent is another. Some people are very averse to risk, and it simply is not honest to assume that all people would willingly accept genetic alterations that would significantly affect them — whether intended for therapy or enhancement — until the procedure is demonstrably safe. Not only individuals, but also the future of the human race is on the line, and it is not clear how the first experiments genetically shaping future generations could ethically take place, in light of the dangers involved. In particular, it would seem presumptuous to engage in such experiments without having the ability to reverse any genetic problems created, rather than discarding the human "mistakes."

The problem only becomes worse when the intention is not therapy, but enhancement. This again raises the issue of the commodification of children — producing them as means to suit the priorities and preferences of others. Moreover, the widespread use of genetic enhancement techniques would eventually change the characteristics of the whole population, raising the spectre of eugenics.

The concept of designer babies also raises the question of how realistic expectations are that gene technology will produce a perfect child. Genetic determinism is the view that every aspect of human beings is determined by their genes. Yet, clearly environmental factors and human choices are extremely important.

Some argue that to single out genetic enhancement for disapproval is inconsistent, because humans constantly use all sorts of means to enhance their appearance and performance, such as diet, exercise, hairdressing, cosmetics, drugs, and surgery. However, the difference between making such decisions for oneself and making them for future generations must not be forgotten here. Even where people are making decisions for themselves, a number of other questions arise. People are already living longer, partly through medical intervention, so why not delay aging and death by decades through gene therapy? What of other new technologies that promise human enhancement, such as artificial organs or robotic limbs? What about the possibility of human-computer hybrids? Could we be heading toward a radical transformation of our species — a post-human future?

We must consider the justice implications of these technologies. Most likely, those who have access to them will be those already privileged economically and socially, thus increasing the gap between themselves and the less privileged. Then there is the question of whether genetic enhancement of, say, athletic ability represents an unfair advantage, similar to performance-enhancing drugs. Large corporations are investing in these technologies, expecting to reap huge financial rewards. Should they be available equally to all, or not at all? Should public funding be allocated to gene therapies or enhancement, and is this the best use of health money?

What Does The Bible Say?
Pre-Birth Screening and PGD

As discussed in Story 6, reproductive technologies distance parents from their offspring. Rather than being seen as a gift of grace, children are increasingly seen as commodities, objects of quality control. Thinkers like law professor John Robertson have employed terms like "procreative liberty" to speak of the right of parents to decide their "reproductive goals." Pre-birth screening keeps open the possibility of the woman "walking away" from the pregnancy and the child, up until birth, and encourages the outlook that a close relationship or "bonding" does not begin until the child is born. As Gilbert Meilaender puts it:

> *. . . we deceive ourselves if we suppose that, as a routine feature of medical practice, [screening] can simply assist a couple to prepare themselves for their child's birth. It does exactly the opposite. It sets our foot on a path that is difficult to exit. We may tell ourselves that we only want health for the foe-*

tus, that abortion is not a possible end in view, but for the most part I think, we thereby deceive ourselves. The technology carries its own momentum, which, if not irresistible, is nevertheless very powerful. It prepares us not for the kind of commitment that parenthood requires, an unconditional commitment, but a kind of responsibility that finite beings ought to reject. The time of pregnancy will be better spent learning to love the child we have been given before we begin to evaluate and assess that child's capacities. Christians could do the world a considerable favour and could bear substantial witness to the meaning of God's own love for the world if they would simply say 'no' to routinised prenatal screening — thereby saying to their children and, by implication to others: 'It's good that you exist.'

Peter Singer and other bioethicists consider it appropriate to deem the lives of severely disabled unborn infants "not worth living." But we have seen that all humans bear the image of God; they are not possessions to be disposed of because they do not meet our criteria of normalcy.

Genetic Enhancement

As a result of the ambiguity between genetic therapy and enhancement, we might think genetic intervention is an activity where science should not venture at all, that it is "playing God." But there are at least two theological reasons why Christians should support gene therapy for already-existing individuals. First, like all medical technology, genetic technology can be seen as a gift from God to be used to alleviate human suffering — part of the exercise of human dominion. Second, genetic technology is a means by which humankind can combat the consequences of sin. Scripture clearly establishes the relationship between sin and the disruption of nature (which includes genetic disorder). As noted previously, therapeutic interventions focused on changing the genetics of all future generations is ethically problematic because of the potential harms and lack of consent involved. But in such cases, the problem is not with the therapeutic intent itself.

When using genetic technology for enhancement, however, even the therapeutic intent is missing. Behind the use of genetic technology for physical enhancement is the view that certain traits (like black hair or dark skin) are inferior to other traits (like blond hair and fair skin), and that people who possess these traits are less valued by society. Such a view is not Christian; indeed it would imply God made a mistake by including such diverse traits in the human race.

Therefore, we ought to affirm the work of geneticists whose aim is to treat genetic disease in those who have it, but we should resist the lure of a secular utopianism based on genetic modification. There is much more to humans than their genes. While genetic science may be able to correct certain genetic disorders that are the consequence of sin, it has no power to entirely remove sin itself, or its consequences. Humanity's dilemma is much more profound than can be solved with any medical therapy, no matter how sophisticated. A society made up of "designed" genetic disease-free individuals would have its own problems, particularly related to the commodification of humans, the marginalisation of the disabled or different, and the emotional disconnection between parents and their children.

What Opportunities for the gospel are There?

[*See also "Generic Strategies" above*]

Kylie's book club gives her a wonderful opportunity to talk about several important matters: what it really means to do the best for your children, the value of human life, the meaning of procreation, and unconditional love. She can then be ready to give the reasons for her views, which will likely resonate with some members of the group.

Christians may witness to their faith in God's goodness and care, and their commitment to biblical values by refusing to participate in antenatal screening or PGD, or at least making it clear that abortion and discarding embryos are not options for them. Similarly they may reject opportunities for enhancing their offspring, which may well become a sacrificial act as more and more people pursue enhancement and those who do not become disadvantaged.

Meanwhile, church leaders need to have at hand the resources that can help people understand and address these immensely important issues!

Further Resources

Linda Bevington, et al. *Genetics, Stem Cell Research, and Cloning.* Grand Rapids, MI: Kregel, 2004.

Charles Colson and Nigel Cameron. *Human Dignity in the Biotech Century.* Downers Grove, IL: InterVarsity, 2004.

Timothy Demy and Gary Stewart, eds. *Genetic Engineering.* Grand Rapids, MI: Kregel, 1999.

Films and Plays: *Bicentennial Man, Frankenstein, Gattaca, I Robot, RUR.*

John Kilner, et al., eds. *Cutting-Edge Bioethics.* Grand Rapids, MI: William B. Eerdmans, 2002.

------ . *Genetic Ethics.* Grand Rapids, MI: William B. Eerdmans and Cambridge, UK: Paternoster; 1997.

C. Ben Mitchell, et al., eds. *Aging, Death, and the Quest for Immortality.* Grand Rapids, MI: William B. Eerdmans, 2004.

PARTICIPANTS

Ghislain Agbede	Central African Republic
Roland Chia	Singapore (Theologian)
Denise Cooper	Australia (Co-Convenor)
Brian Edgar	Australia
Antonio da Silva	Norway
Andrew Fergusson	UK (Convenor)
Henk Jochemsen	The Netherlands
John Kilner	USA (Facilitator)
Jan Kunene	Republic of South Africa
James Thobaben	USA

BUSINESS AS MISSION

Lausanne Occasional Paper No. 59

This Issue Group on Business as mission was Issue Group No.30

This Occasional Paper was prepared by the whole Issue Group and the Editors are Mats Tunehag, Wayne McGee and Josie Plummer

CONTENTS

FOREWORD

INTRODUCTION
Part I: Setting the Scene
WHAT IS BUSINESS AS MISSION? *Clarifying Terms*
THE WORD AND THE MISSION: *Biblical Foundations for Business as Mission*
THE WORLD AND THE MARKETPLACE: *The Present Context for Business as Mission, Opportunities and Challenges*

Part II: Business as Mission in Practice
THE ESSENTIALS OF GOOD BUSINESS AS MISSION: *10 Guiding Principles*
STORIES OF BUSINESS AS MISSION: *Case Studies*

Part III: Enabling the Body
MOBILISING FOR BUSINESS AS MISSION: *Releasing Untapped Resources in the Global Church*
PARTNERSHIP: *The Vital Role of Mission Agencies and the Church*

Part IV: Looking Forward
STRATEGIC RECOMMENDATIONS: *Specific Steps for Action*
THE BUSINESS AS MISSION MANIFESTO

APPENDICES

Appendix A: Participants

Appendix B: Assignment and Process

Appendix C: Additional General Case Studies

Appendix D: Obstacles and Solutions to Business and Church Partnership

Appendix E: Case Study of Mission Agency Involvement in Business as mission

Appendix F: Endnotes

Appendix G: Resource Directory

    Books

    Articles and Papers

    Organisations, Networks and Web Links

    Training Institutions

    Additional Tools

Appendix H: Endorsements

NOTE: All unattributed quotes represent comments written by individual members of the Business as mission Issue Group during the course of work on this document.

FOREWORD

We believe we are experiencing a movement of God among His people. As we have engaged in **business as mission** over the last ten years, we have increasingly experienced God at work in a **new way, all over the world**, both in the **marketplace** and in the **Church**. This dynamic movement within the Body of Christ is based on God's love for the world and His call to His Church. It is a new wave of activity that is closely linked with the work of the Holy Spirit throughout history. It is a relevant strategy for the 21st century. God is raising up a new work force of men and women from around the world. These men and women are on a mission for God's glory in and through business. Christian leaders in business, church, missions and beyond have all concurred that God is at work and business as mission is dynamically meeting the various needs of a world in desperate need of the whole Gospel! Just listen to what a few have to say:

True to God's Calling

Rene Padilla is a prominent Argentinean theologian, missiologist, and author, who enthusiastically endorses business as mission, and says that it is "closely related to Jesus' call to His disciples—to be the salt of the earth."

God at Work Yesterday, Today, & Tomorrow

Both business and church leaders recognise the historical dimension of business as mission as is evident in the following quotes:

> "New leadership is needed in the 21st century, as we look at effective and holistic mission strategies. Business has historically been a key frontier in extending the Kingdom."
> Stuart McGreevy , Chairman, TBN Transformational Business Network

> "In the earliest history of the Christian mission, the saving news of Christ was often carried to new places by those who were seeking to do business."
> Harry Goodhew, Retired Anglican Archbishop of Sydney, Australia

A Relevant Strategy for the 21st Century

Business as mission is not simply a fundraising tactic or a visa platform, but a relevant strategy for the 21st century – especially in the 10/40 Window:

> "The use of business in global outreach is a strategy of choice for

the context of the 21st century mission." Ted Yamamori, International Director of the Lausanne movement, LCWE.

"Economic-based mission will bring a major change to the face of Christian missions, and it is more than just a new strategy—there is a promise connected to it: He who lends to the poor lends to the Lord, and he will reward him for what he has done. (Proverbs 19:17)" Jürg Opprecht, Founder and President, BPN Business and Professional Network

"Business as mission is a relevant strategy to meet the challenges in the 10/40-window and beyond." Luis Bush, USA/Argentina, Founder of the AD2000 Movement

The Body of Christ at Work

"Businessmen and women are being called to embrace a new responsibility under God to transform the societies of the world at large through creative acts of love." J. Gunnar Olson, Chairman and Founder of ICCC, International Christian Chamber of Commerce

It is with great joy and expectation that we submit this report to the Church worldwide.

Mats Tunehag, Wayne McGee and
Josie Plummer

INTRODUCTION
A World in Need

The world holds fresh opportunities and challenges for the global Church. In regions where Islam, Hinduism, and Buddhism are dominant and where 90% of the world's unreached peoples live, you also find 80% of the world's poorest populations. Unemployment in these countries ranges from 30% to 80% and it is even higher among Christian minorities. Furthermore, many Christians and others in Sub-Saharan Africa and Latin America are living in poverty because of lack of jobs and unjust economic systems.

Over the next 20 years, more than 2 billion people will enter societies where there are few churches and very few jobs.

What should be the response of the Church and particularly Christian business people to such challenges?

> *What the poor want is not aid, but jobs – real jobs, not subsidised ones. This is the dignity and self-reliance they deserve.*

Business as Mission – a Renewed Call

There is a wave of thousands of Christian business people from all continents who are experiencing a dynamic move of God as part of a renewed call to His kingdom work. God is on the move in Latin America, Asia, Europe, North America, Africa, and the Pacific regions, calling His global church to rediscover His heart and intention for business.

God established the institution and practice of business as a means of fulfilling His **creation mandate** to steward and care for all of creation. He is releasing the power of business to aid in the task of fulfilling the **great commission**, making disciples of all nations. God longs to be glorified through our business activities.

Business people are being challenged to look anew at their business activities as an expression of their calling and service to God. They are being affirmed in their vocation as business people and used as instruments for extending God's kingdom. God has led a growing number of business people to think strategically about how they can integrate their skills and experience in business with the task of world mission. God is calling many more business people, from all nations to go to all nations, in this new paradigm of mission.

> *"God has gifted some with the resources of mind and spirit to be businessmen and women. Business-as-mission seeks to support and encourage those who are gifted by God in this way. It aims to stimulate interest in, and commitment to, doing business as unto the Lord. Its desire is to assist business people to see the opportunities that exist, to use their skills and talents to bless those in the poorest and most needy parts of the world, and to provide in those contexts credible opportunities to demonstrate and proclaim Christ."*
>
> Harry Goodhew, Retired Anglican Archbishop of Sydney, Australia

One term being used for this new mission movement is **"business as mission."** Business, in and of itself, is the ministry and instrument of mission. It is about releasing the entrepreneurs and business professionals within the church in order to transform the world through their business activities.

The implication of "the whole church taking the whole gospel to the whole world" includes affirming and mobilising the business people in the Body of Christ. It means releasing them to use their gifts in business to lift the oppression of the poor through business, to transform their own communities and nations through business, and to carry the good news to the "ends of the earth" through business.

Breaking New Ground

Kingdom focused business has been called a strategy of choice for the 21st century mission. In many countries where the name of Christ is least often heard or understood, Christians are better welcomed as business people, not "missionaries." Business is about relationships in the context of everyday life, and provides numerous ways to bless individuals, communities, and nations.

This blessing is already a growing reality in places like Asia and can be illustrated by these two examples:

1) A Christian in Central Asia tried to witness to his people, a Muslim community with very few believers, but he was seen as a "professional Christian," not real to them, and probably paid by Westerners to proselytise. He experienced open hostility and alienation. Later he started a small cattle business. His lifestyle became understandable and natural to them. Even though they knew he was still a follower of Isa/Jesus, he

was now acceptable. He was one of them, perceived as dealing with real life issues and meeting real needs. He has since been invited to sit on the council of elders for his community.

2) An IT-company exists in India among a major unreached people with the intention to make Christ known among these people. Through the many natural opportunities that business provides, the founder can share his faith in word and deed. The company's strategic plan reads: "Our purpose is to serve:

1. *Our **Customers** with creative, innovative, reliable, top-quality solutions;*

2. *Our **Employees** with meaningful and challenging work, stability, good salaries, development, and a p l e a s a n t w o r k - environment;*

3. *Our other **Stakeholders** by providing attractive returns on their investments;*

4. *The **Country** by creating knowledge and wealth and contributing to local concerns;*

5. *__Society__ by showing that success and high moral standards can co-exist; and*

6. *Ultimately **God** by being faithful and good stewards."*

After centuries of Christian work among unemployed Muslims and among poor Buddhists and Hindus, we have seen only limited progress. The Church should recognise the need for renewed thinking and application of being and doing church and missions; as more of the same thing will not result in a better harvest.

Breaking new ground in the task of global evangelisation requires new methods and strategies. There is a growing need to provide models for mission that are financially sustainable and will strengthen local churches and national missionary movements. Business as mission is one response. It is crucial that Christian business people are equipped and supported to take up their key role in transforming their own nation and beyond.

At a meeting of Christian leaders from Eastern European countries, leader after leader from different denominations echoed, *"Do not send us money, it only creates division; send us business people who can create jobs for us, that we can build ourselves up. A leader from Croatia went so far to say, 'Sending us missionaries is good, but we'd prefer that you send us godly businessmen, who can teach us and help us to start businesses and create jobs in a Christ-like way.*[1]

A Christian businesswoman from Central Asia said: *"There are many seminars and teachings on how to start a business. There are business schools with local and foreign teachers. But there are few resources to get **practical** help in starting a real business not just hearing about how to start a business."*

Our desire is to acknowledge the ways that business can and does glorify God. Business can be used for good, and to help grow His kingdom. There are unique and wonderful opportunities that God is calling us to through business, businesses that help restore human dignity and hope as well as provide a context for sharing the gospel of the Kingdom. We dream of seeing the Church, as the whole Body of Christ, taking the whole Gospel to the whole world. Our prayer is that God's kingdom would come in all spheres of society within every nation. Our goal is to see people and communities transformed by the power of the gospel. Business as mission is about affirming, mobilising, equipping and deploying business people to this end.

> *The business of 'business as mission' is to reveal Christ through business. When this is done effectively, the outcome is transformational.*

To the greater Glory of God!

Part I: Setting the Scene
1. WHAT IS BUSINESS AS MISSION?
Clarifying Terms
Introduction

The purpose of this chapter is to briefly clarify a few key terms and expressions. The descriptions used here are simply to aid us to communicate clearly and consistently. It is *not* our aim to create a "Business as mission orthodoxy" or terminology, or to exclude groups or initiatives that prefer other terms and definitions. Other expressions commonly used in the movement include "transformational business," "great commission companies" and "kingdom business." The authors recognise that in some contexts "Business as mission" is not the most helpful or preferred term. The expression "Business as mission" itself can be considered a fairly broad term that encompasses various areas where business and missions connect.

Our terms here are further limited both culturally and linguistically, since this paper was prepared in English. We expect alternative expressions to be developed which communicate meaningfully in other languages, and other religious, political and cultural settings. The parameters outlined in this document should be considered as a "dotted line" that allows for future change and for anomalies, which will force us to reconsider and revise according to the situation and its specific needs.

Business as mission is based on the principle of . . . HOLISTIC MISSION

Holistic mission attempts to bring all aspects of life and godliness into an organic biblical whole. This includes God's concerns for such business related issues as economic development, employment and unemployment, economic justice, and the use and distribution of natural and creative resources among the human family. These are aspects of God's redemptive work through Jesus Christ and the Church.

Evangelism and social concerns are often still addressed as though they were separate and unrelated from each other. This assumes a divide between what we consider "sacred" or "spiritual" and what we consider "secular" or "physical." The biblical worldview rather is one that promotes an integrated and seamless holistic view of life. Ministry should not be compartmentalised or fragmented into the spiritual and the physical. Business as mission is an expression of this truly holistic paradigm.

> *Business is a mission, a calling, a ministry in its own right. Human activity reflects our divine origin, having been created to be creative, to create good things by good processes, for us to enjoy – with others.*

Business as mission has a Kingdom of God perspective . . . . . *KINGDOM BUSINESS*

Kingdom businesses start from the theological premise that all Christians have a calling to love and serve God with all of their heart, soul, strength, and mind, as well as to love and serve their neighbours. God calls people to work for His kingdom in business just as certainly as He calls people to work in other kinds of ministry or mission ventures.

In this paper, we will often use the term "kingdom business" rather than "Business as mission-business." We recognise the importance of extending God's kingdom through business in any context. However, we want to highlight the biblical mandate to serve the poor and oppressed, in particular in those areas where the gospel has yet to be received. This will lead us to a focus on cross-cultural activity, and should draw our attention to areas of endemic poverty and/or unevangelised communities. We acknowledge that this does not automatically suppose the crossing of international borders and will be necessary within culturally "near" communities as well.

A function of Business as mission is to act as a catalyst, to inspire and encourage people to get into business and to stay in business, especially in the developing world.

Business as mission is different from but related to . . . . . *WORKPLACE MINISTRIES*

Workplace Ministries are primarily focused on taking the gospel to people where they work, preferably through the witness of co-workers and professional colleagues. These ministries encourage the integration of biblical principles into every aspect of business practice, to the glory of God. Business as mission naturally includes these elements of workplace ministry.

When a workplace ministry is initiated in a business owned by believers to intentionally advance the kingdom of God, there will be substantial overlap. Workplace ministry can choose to limit its focus solely "within" the business context itself. Business as mission is focused both "within" and "through" the business. It seeks to harness the power and resource of business for intentional mission impact in the community or nation at large. Workplace ministry may occur in any setting. However, Business as mission is intentional about the "to all peoples" mandate, and seeks out areas with the greatest spiritual and physical needs.

Business as mission is different from but related to . . . TENTMAKING

"Tentmaking" refers principally to the practice of Christian professionals, who support themselves financially by working as employees or by engaging in business. In this way they are able to conduct their ministries without depending upon donors and without burdening the people they serve. Tentmaking connotes the integration of work and witness, with an emphasis on encouraging evangelism by lay Christians rather than clergy and ministry professionals.

Where tentmakers are part of business ventures that facilitate their mission goals, there is substantial overlap with Business as mission. However, although a tentmaker might be a part of a business, the business itself might not be an integral part of the ministry, as it is with Business as mission. Business as mission sees business both as the medium and the message.

Business as mission most often involves "job-making" as an integral part of its mission. Tentmaking may involve this, but is more often simply about "job-taking" — taking up employment somewhere in order to facilitate ministry.

Business as mission is different from . . . BUSINESS FOR MISSIONS

Profits from business can be donated to support missions and ministries. This is different from Business as mission. One might call this business *for* missions, using business ventures to fund other kinds of ministry. We recognise that profit from a business can be used to support "missions" and that this is good and valid. Likewise, employees can use some of their salary to give to charitable causes. While this should be encouraged, none of us would like to be operated on by a surgeon whose only ambition is to make money to give to the church! Instead we expect he has the right skills and drive to operate with excellence, doing his job with full professional integrity. Likewise, a Business as mission-business must produce more than goods and services in order to generate new wealth. It seeks to fulfil God's kingdom purposes and values through every aspect of its operations. A "business for mission" concept can limit business and business people to a role of funding the "real ministry." While funding is an important function, Business as mission is about for-profit businesses that have a kingdom focus.

Business as mission does not condone . . . . . NON-BUSINESSES AND NON-MISSIONS

Two approaches to business that do not come within the scope of "Business as mission" by any definition are: (1) fake businesses that are not actually functioning businesses, but exist solely to provide visas for missionaries to enter countries otherwise closed to them. (2) Businesses that purport to have Christian motivations, but which operate only for private economic advantage and not for the kingdom of God. Neither do we mean businesses run by Christians with no clear and defined kingdom strategy in place.

Business as mission pursues . . . PROFIT

Business must be financially sustainable, producing goods or services that people are willing to pay for. Sustainability implies that the activity is profitable. Profits are an essential element of all businesses, in all cultures. Without profit the business cannot survive and fulfil its purpose. Accordingly, Business as mission -- businesses are *real* business that genuinely exist to generate wealth and profits. Business as mission does not view profits as inherently evil, bad, or unbiblical. Quite the contrary, profits are good, desired, and beneficial to God and His purposes, as long as they are not oppressive or derived from gouging customers or selling products and services that do not honour Christ and His gospel.

Temporary subsidies may be utilised to establish a Business as mission initiative. Permanent subsidies or financial support without expectation of ultimate prof-itability are closer to charitable or donor-based ministries than Business as mission based ministries.

> *The business of business is business. And the business of business as mission is business with a kingdom of God purpose and perspective.*

Business as mission comes in all . . . SHAPES AND SIZES

The methodologies, as well as the business and ministry strategies used, will be creatively diverse, just as God created us in infinite variety. Does the size of the business matter? Yes and No! Christian micro-enterprise programmes exist that help provide necessary income for families and individuals resulting in community development, churches being planted, and discipleship taking place. In short, Christian micro-enterprise development has been well accepted and is highly effective for the kingdom. A significant body of work already exists dedicated to it. It has a legitimate place in the broader definition and practice of Business as mission.

However, our focus will be on larger scale business, where there has been a comparative lack of attention. If we are to tackle the enormity of the challenge before us we need to think and act bigger, beyond micro to small, medium and large size businesses.

Business as mission is not about . . . . JOBS AND MONEY PER-SE

The Russian Mafia also creates jobs and gives people a chance to earn money.

Creating jobs and earning money is not an end in itself. Work and business are ordained by God. Work is a human and divine activity providing a means to support our families and to contribute to the positive development of our communities and countries. However, Business as mission is not a Christianised job-creation scheme. The goal is not simply about making people materially better off. Business as mission is actively praying and incarnating Jesus' prayer: "May your kingdom come, may your will be done," even in the marketplace.

The real bottom line of Business as mission is *"ad maiorem Dei gloriam,"* for the greater glory of God.

2. THE WORD AND THE MISSION
Biblical Foundations for Business as Mission

God's Purpose for Business in the Work of Creation

(a) The Purpose and Nature of God

We cannot understand our purpose and mission in life unless we understand what God's purpose and mission is. God acts for His glory. He created the cosmos that reflects His glory and goodness (Psalm 8, 19). Although this creation has been marred by sin and its consequences (Genesis 3), God continues a redemptive relationship with creation through ongoing creativity and the sustaining of all things. God the Father has made men and women in His image (Genesis 1:27). He embraces His children in loving-kindness, and is concerned with our holistic redemption.

God the King is in a kingdom relationship with all humanity as individuals and as nations (peoples). God's purpose is to receive glory from among every people (nation/ethnic group) by holistically redeeming those who know, love and worship him (Psalm 64, 1Timothy 1:15-17).

Business as mission keeps four things in mind: a) God is at the centre; b) the scope is global; c) peoples (nations, ethnic groups) and people (individuals) are the focus; d) His glory is the outcome.

God is Spirit. Yet God's creative acts are perceived most clearly in physical form. We experience this dramatically in the diversity of the vast stellar expanse, to the intimate uniqueness of our own molecular weave of a DNA. God's nature is inherently creative. He has created all things, physical and spiritual. Thus we read in Scripture that He created heaven and earth, sun and moon, water and trees, animals and human beings. His nature reveals an inherent evaluation, innovation, and delight in the creation.

God enjoys His creation. His initial satisfaction is indicated by His repeated appraisal of it as "good." He walked daily in the garden and met with His people as a sign of His pleasure in His creation. His love for His creation is evident in that He continues to creatively sustain all things.

(b) Human Co-creativity and Work

Theology is inter-related to anthropology. Understanding who God is leads us to a deeper understanding of who we are.

God is continually active in creation, working to bring goodness, enjoying the fruit of His labour, and sharing it with others. Created in God's image, humanity is also capable of creating, unashamedly enjoying, and sharing the fruit of our labours with others. As God delighted in that which He created, so He is concerned for its maintenance and fruitfulness. Man is to co-labour with God in this work, as seen in the first blessings and commandments given to Adam and Eve: "be fruitful," "multiply," "fill the earth," and "subdue it" (Genesis 1:28).

There is an implicit invitation to enjoy the creation, as well as a responsibility for creation's care and well being. We are to care for God's creation as beneficent overseers. We have the responsibility to respect and care for each other and the natural ongoing processes of the creation of which we are stewards.

God gives us the capacity we need to fulfil the task. Adam and Eve were to be involved in the added value processes that create wealth! Work enables the translation of raw resources into food, goods, and services. Work creates wealth (a surplus) and this in turn creates more work (employment).

Work is an act of worship. Remember the story of Cain and Abel in Genesis Chapter 4. Abel's offering came out of the fruit of his labour. In contrast, Cain's offering was the result of the natural agricultural process. In other words, Cain's offering was a fruit of the earth and not a fruit of his own labour. The concept in Hebrew culture was that Cain was not fully "involved" in what he was offering to God. Cain's offering lacked any redemptive action that would have been the result of his own work.

Work is something that is simultaneously both deeply divine and deeply human. It is a tangible act that reveals a human-divine partnership in creation. Work is not to be understood as a curse or consequence of the fall. Rather, it was a blessing and commandment given to Adam and Eve before the fall. Work is a human activity that flows from God's delegated mandate of stewardship over creation. God gives us the creative capacity, wisdom, and tools (gifts/talents) to do it. God took pleasure in the physical aspect of His creation. We too can delight in creating useful and excellent products and services.

(c) Business and the Cultural Mandate of Stewardship

Economic activity is rooted in the creation story. Business and enterprise form the institution that creates and sustains wealth for a just society. In the same way, government is designed to create and sustain an organised society. Family is designed to create and sustain well-adjusted individuals. This is God's ordained order.

The Bible has much to say about ethical and fair dealing in work and business. It has instructional texts on what is pleasing to God in relationship to business relationships, employment, trading, using money, lending, and so on. In business these can be practically applied in areas such as quality control, fair wages, good working conditions, reasonable return on investments, corporate social responsibility, etc.

The biblical idea of stewardship not only encompasses the care of creation, but the responsibility of personal stewardship of both talents and wealth as well. Business provides an opportunity for those talented in enterprise (entrepreneurs) and others (employees) to use their particular gifts in service to others as unto to the Lord. In its capacity to provide employment, business sustains not only those who establish enterprises, but also those who are employed or benefit from the goods and/or services provided. Business enables needs to be met, and to bless others as a consequence. Business conducted in accord with biblical principles of stewardship offers numerous opportunities to glorify God. For a Christian, business is a vocation, to be conducted in the spirit of the kingdom of God.

> *"The biblical worldview provides a framework for work being sacred, for labour having dignity. This concept of work is that it is a vocation—one's calling. ... This biblical concept understands that God is at work in the world building His Kingdom, and that, among other things, He calls us to participate in the building of His Kingdom through our work."*
>
> *- Darrow L. Miller - Developing a Biblical Theology of Vocation, 2002*

(d) The Fall and its Negative Consequences for Business

After sin came into the world, good things were distorted and disrupted (Genesis 3). The fall also affected work and creativity. Work continues to be a divine command to us, but we must now contest with considerable challenges and problems posed by sinful people doing business in a fallen world. As with everything else in the world, the whole process of creativity and work has been affected by sin.

Work and business offer many opportunities for sin. Exploitation of the poor, greed, dishonesty, and idolatry are just a few examples. But this does not mean that Christians should not engage in business. It is equally true that there are also many opportunities to glorify God.

Productive work and co-creation with God confer dignity and purpose to the individual. Lack of work, or work that degrades the individual, has a dehumanising effect. The loss of ability to support oneself and to contribute to others (family, community, etc.) represents a loss of dignity and is far from God's original design.

After the fall, a focus on community was shattered by selfishness and greed. This resulted in an attitude that says; "This is mine; I made it for me and me alone." The fall has led to numerous systems whereby people are exploited or enslaved economically while a few have been unjustly made rich.

But God prepared for a restoration of creation, including work and creativity, through Jesus Christ. Our mandate continues to be stewards of creation and of our personal talents and the wealth our talents generate. We are called to play a role in God's restoration process by helping to restore the inherent dignity and value of work. We are to be ambassadors of God's kingdom in the market place, to be salt and light in and through business. As salt and light, we are to bless peoples from every culture, through God-honouring business enterprise and the reformation of unjust economic systems.

Before we consider more deeply the redemptive potential of Business as mission, we will briefly explore some examples of business within the history and mission of Israel, as well as look at the relevance of business in relation to the message of the New Testament.

Business and the History and Mission of Israel

(a) Joseph the Business Administrator

One of the clearest examples of God's purpose for business can be seen in the life of Joseph (Genesis 47 to 50). Joseph had experienced the negative side of life, having been sold into slavery and later placed in prison in Egypt. Nevertheless, God freed him and placed him at the head of Pharaoh's agro-business with authority through government. His management skills are apparent. He knew that seven years of bountiful harvests would be followed by seven years of scarcity. Joseph ordered that a large percentage of the bountiful harvests be set aside for the lean years. Here we see one of God's major purposes for business highlighted: God wants the resources of creation to be harnessed (through business skills) so that all of humanity would have its needs met.

(b) Israel Models Economic Principles for the Nations

Four hundred years later, the Israelites were still in Egypt, although now as slaves. God saw the horrific conditions of His people and heard their cries (Exodus 1 to 3). He saw that they were not receiving the just reward or fruit of their labours. As He freed His people and led them towards the Promised Land, He established the social and economic (business) conditions necessary for a godly society. God knew that some might want to change the godly vocation of work into an idolatrous pursuit of money and possessions. Therefore, for the well-being of His people, the Lord established statutes related to property, work, and business (Ezekiel 21 to 23, Leviticus 25). For example, the Israelites were to keep the Sabbath as a special day and to abstain from business pursuits in order to enjoy the rest and restoration that God desired. They were to leave part of their fields un-harvested so that the orphans, widows, and foreigners among them might have access to God's goodness by gleaning from the excess of an abundant harvest. They were not to charge undue interest from the poor of their country. In short, they were to honour God in the midst of their labour and fruitfulness, obeying the limits and ordinances He established. In so doing, they would continue to be blessed by Him as a testament to the nations (Deuteronomy 26-28).

> *God's promises to Israel as they left slavery in Egypt were not isolated to blessings of an unseen nature. He promised He would bless them in every area of life including their crops, livestock and business.... What the Bible emphasises for the poor is opportunity versus aid. Aid is reserved for those who have absolutely no way of providing for themselves and will die without*

> *assistance. Israel is certainly in this kind of circumstance in the wilderness. And God provides for the Israelites, however...the day they had the feasibility to provide for themselves the manna was withdrawn... God does not want to create a dependent people but a people who drew on the gifts, talents and resources He had given to see them provide for themselves.*
>
> *- Landa Cope – Old Testament Template www.ottemplate.org*

(c) The Dynamic of Jubilee

Especially significant to this discussion is the biblical legislation regarding Jubilee (Leviticus 25, Deuteronomy 15). In the natural course of life, some people would become richer and some poorer. The poverty of some would lead them to borrow money and acquire devastating debts. Others would even be forced to sell themselves into slavery. God had a radical solution for this poverty. At the end of seven years all debts would be forgiven and the slaves should be set free. Deuteronomy 15 explains in detail how godly values should be practised concerning labour and economics, and how this would offer relief for the poor. God promised Israel that "there will be no poor among you" (15:4) if Israel would publicly and privately put into practice God's principles of Jubilee. God prescribes what must be done "If there is a poor man with you" (15:7-10). This demonstrates that poverty can not be abolished by a sudden intervention of God alone, but by right practice and obedience by God's people to God's commands.

More powerful legislation would be enacted every fiftieth year. Some people might become so poor that they would have to sell off their property in order to feed their families. To remedy this extreme poverty, God declared that every fifty years there would be a Jubilee. The land would be returned to the original families and their descendants. Thus, each family was given the means to start their own family businesses over again through the reallocation of property. All would have a fresh start. Redemption was to be demonstrated tangibly in the social and economic spheres of life.

(d) The Prophets and a Call to do Business God's Way

God's Spirit spoke through the prophet Amos to correct abuses in businesses of his day. Workers had become so undervalued that poor people were sold for a pair of shoes (Amos 2.6). Amos raised his prophetic voice to condemn this abominable practice. We also see the damaging effects of structural sin or indirect sin through unjust systems. Amos directed part of his message to some of the married women of Israel, whom he denounced as cows of Bashan (Amos 4:1). The women demanded that their husbands provide them with more and more luxuries. The husbands carried out their wives' wishes. In God's sight, both husbands and wives were guilty of exploitation and oppression of poor workers. God's concern with economic justice and business practice is emphasised by the way He addresses them through His prophets, including, for example, Jeremiah (Jeremiah 5:24-29, 6:12-13,

22:13-17), Ezekiel (Ezekiel 18 and 22:12-13), Micah (Micah 2:6,10-15) and Habakkuk (Habakkuk 2:6-9).

(e) The Hebrew Vision of Shalom

The overarching biblical idea of shalom is that of wholeness and peace in our relationship with God, with self, with each other, and with creation. Shalom is God's intention for His creation and is encompassed in our creation mandate to tend the earth and to one another. It embodied the Hebrew aspiration and vision of peace, wholeness, and well-being (1 Kings 4:25, Psalm 85:10-13). Throughout the Old Testament, God's promise of favour and restoration always included both material and immaterial blessing. Having enough to eat and a secure shelter is to be understood as a direct sign of God's goodness and affirmation (Deuteronomy 8, Ezekiel 34:25-31, Isaiah 49:60-61).

Justice and righteousness are closely linked to shalom. The primary application of the word justice (or righteousness) in the bible refers to corporate or social holiness and the relief of oppression. This embraces the whole of creation and is not merely limited to personal responsibility and ethics.

The Gospel – Good News for Rich and Poor

(a) The Kingdom of God and the Great Commission

In the Lord's Prayer, Jesus taught believers to pray "Thy kingdom come," and "For Thine is the kingdom" (Matthew 6:10, 13). This prayer compels us to acknowledge that the kingdom of God is both present as well as future. From the beginning of Jesus ministry He preached that the kingdom of God had come ("The time is fulfilled, and the kingdom of God is at hand." Mark 1:15). He also demonstrated that the gospel of the kingdom of God is "good news to the poor."

"The Spirit of the Lord is on me, b+ecause he has anointed me to preach good news to the poor. He has sent me to proclaim freedom for the prisoners and recovery of sight for the blind, to release the oppressed, to proclaim the year of the Lord's favour. "(Luke 4.18-19, NIV).

The gospel of eternal salvation through Jesus Christ is good news for everyone, rich and poor alike. Without the final work of the cross and spiritual new birth in Jesus, we have no hope (John 3:16-17, Romans 6:4-11, 1 Corinthians 15:12-19). The gospel of God's grace and mercy is very good news for the "poor in spirit, for theirs is the kingdom of heaven" (Matthew 5:3). But the gospel of the kingdom is intended to be especially good news for the materially and financially poor of this present world. This is because individuals, families, businesses, and societies that live by biblical principles of work, stewardship, faithfulness, and justice will alleviate most causes of human suffering and poverty.

Jesus proclaimed and brought in His person the rule of God. The promised deliverance had come. Representatives from all nations are invited to come within His realm and under His authority and grace.

The mandate that the King gave to His followers was to *"make disciples of all nations,"* (Matthew 28:18-20). We are to have a transforming impact in the world. How are we to do this? By taking the gospel, the good news about the Glorious King and His kingdom, to the nations (*"baptising them in the name of the Father and of the Son and of the Holy Spirit"* 28:19) and teaching them to obey everything He had commanded (28:20). We should understand this "Great Commission" as an incredible responsibility to utterly revolutionise all aspects of life and society. The nations are to reflect His kingdom principles and His glory. But this transformation will only be realised when the nations have been discipled, as a result of His people living out His "Great Commandment" to *"love the Lord your God with all your heart and with all your soul and with all your mind"* and to *"love your neighbour as yourself"* (Matthew 22:36-39, NIV).

(b) The Holistic Gospel in Church History

Only when we understand the enormity of the Great Commission and the Great Commandment together, will we fully appreciate how much we needed to hear Him say, "I am with you in this always!" (Matthew 28:20).

In Luke 4, Jesus clearly defined His mission as evangelism, social holiness, and justice. This is Jesus' holistic mission to a broken world. It is a mix of spiritual, political, social, as well as economic objectives. This is a gospel that would have been more readily grasped by Jesus' Hebrew audience and the early Church, with their built-in understanding of shalom, than by sections of the church today that has been influenced by other worldviews.

The apostle Paul says that we are saved by grace, not by our own effort (Ephesians 2:8-10). Then he follows up saying that we have been created for good deeds, which God had already prepared for us to do. The word translated "deeds" is *ergon* in Greek which means work, craft, business, art, good work, etc. It is the root of the word *ergate,* which means worker, employee, and entrepreneur. There has never been a separation between the grace of God and practical, tangible, real actions experienced in the physical realm here on the earth.

Work ethics and social sensitivity were both contributors to early Church growth, providing respect for the Christian community within the greater society at large (Acts 4:32-35). But it was not long before the Church was influenced by Greek philosophy (Gnosticism and Plato), political structures (Constantinian religious nationalism), and a social class system. This negatively influenced the Christian concept of work and wealth in the wider context of society and the gospel.

These and other unbiblical perspectives inherited from outside the biblical worldview have resulted in:

1. Dichotomising life into separate compartments, which accommodates a dualistic view putting a divide between the sacred and the secular. This exalts the "spiritual" at the expense of the "physical," and the clergy at the expense of the laity.
2. Spiritualising our faith when we

should not. We often spiritualise Jesus' and the Old Testament's teaching about wealth, the poor, and peace making.

3. Individualising our faith at the expense of thinking corporately and collectively. We emphasise personal holiness and individual transformation, rather than social holiness and societal transformation.

The Reformation of the 16th century recovered the doctrine of the priesthood of all believers. This included labour as being a Christian calling to glorify God. The great revival movements of the 18th and 19th centuries promoted holiness and Christian service in all areas of life, including business and the work place. The movement of God's spirit during these last decades has been towards a truer integration of evangelism, social concern, work, and faith by evangelicals.

Application: The Redemptive Potential of Business as Mission

Poverty is holistic in nature and consists of not only economic poverty but social, political, and spiritual poverty as well. The solution to holistic poverty must be the holistic and transforming message of shalom. Business as mission is a response both to the mandate of stewardship over creation, as well as the mandate of the great commission to all nations. It is a response to the immense spiritual and physical needs of the world, and its application is displayed on many levels:

(a) Business Restores Dignity and Empowers

Business restores dignity through creating employment, through righteous and equal treatment in relationships, and through empowerment.

God intends that none of His creation be idle (unemployed) and unproductive. To **not** be able to work, to not be creative, and to be unable to help and support oneself and one's family leads to a loss of dignity as a human being. Businesses that create employment are part of God's redemptive plan and process. However, employment should not be the sole target. We need to empower people through training, mentorship, personal development, and ownership, so that people can improve themselves, their communities, and their societies. This will in turn lead to better jobs, and the starting of their own businesses. This is in line with God's purpose and our mission to restore human dignity, to create jobs, and to start and develop businesses. Christian entrepreneurs from every church, city, and nation must be affirmed in this task.

God also expects fair treatment to be modelled in our businesses; He rejects underpayment, harsh treatment, and poor working conditions. He rejects unfair wages to workers and exorbitant prices to consumers. God rejects any form of exploitation and unjust treatment of one social group by another and/or one individual by another.

Business can empower and set people free economically, socially, and politically; economic transformation is about people having relative abundance and participating in wealth generation. Social transformation is about having enough income to acquire goods and services through exchange, and to have access to and adequate means for food, housing, education, water, health, transportation, etc. People who are both economically and socially strong in turn tend to be politically stronger. Work and business enables dignity, self-confidence, production, wealth generation, and increase, which are the keys to social transformation.

(b) Business Provides the Context for Discipleship

Business is about relationships with others: employers and employees, buyers and sellers, producers and consumers, suppliers and distributors. This creates a whole arena where those who know Christ can share their faith and witness to those who do not know Him. Christians in business become "salt and light" to people in their workplaces since discipleship is demonstrating the ways of God through the course of every day relationships. God is glorified when Christian business people work as unto the Lord, fearing God by hating dishonest gain, corruption, and nepotism; love and respect others, and demonstrate Christian values (showing integrity, stewardship, accountability etc.), by sharing the gospel in word and deed.

Business is a recognised institution in society that brings credibility to relationships with the community as a whole. Thus business brings opportunities to influence and disciple the wider society through the relationships it brings. The individual or company becomes "salt and light" to the community (or nation) in the marketplace.

(c) Business Promotes Environmental Stewardship

Business can also intentionally promote better environmental stewardship. Business continually involves different relationships with nature. Business relates to stewardship through decisions regarding the types and locations of products fabricated and services rendered, of production methods, of types of resources used, and of the disposal of waste.

(d) Business is Able to Reinforce Peace and Community

Businesses contribute to society in three distinct ways: through their primary business activities, their community or social investment activities, and in their participation in public policy discourse. Engaging in any of these three functions can contribute to community stability and conflict prevention. A business might also promote peace and community by having workers from different backgrounds working together for a common purpose.

The private business community in general is a potential resource that could be enlisted to reduce the incidence, severity, frequency, and effects of conflict. The idea of peace and community should permeate all business activity.

(e) Business Can Strengthen the Church

Business strengthens the Church in general. The more people are engaged in productive work, the more the local church is strengthened to do its work. Increased revenue and organisational capacity enable the church to broaden its role and strengthen its relevance and impact, both in the community and globally.

Believers living in poverty or in areas of endemic unemployment especially need businesses. Otherwise, they are excluded from economic and social opportunities. They become bereft of influence or the ability to be salt and light in their community. They become salt that has lost its saltiness, offering little or no good news in societies that are already cold or hostile to Christian faith.

(f) Business Facilitates Going "To All Peoples"

Christians are welcomed into even hostile or closed communities/countries when they bring the prospect of business and economic advantage. This must be done honestly, and not just as an entry strategy to do "real spiritual ministry," or as a clandestine cover for unlawful evangelisation. By being salt and light, and ambassadors of the blessings of Christ through business and its positive impact on society, Christian business people will ultimately lead people to seek God.

The Glory of God Through Business as Mission

In his theological reflections on business, Wayne Grudem[2] begins by explaining how business has been neglected as a way to glorify God:

When people hear the phrase "glorifying God," it probably first implies worship -- singing praise to God and giving thanks to him. Then it might suggest evangelism -- glorifying God by telling others about him. It might even suggest giving -- glorifying God by contributing money to evangelism, to building up the church, and to the needs of the poor. Or it might suggest moral living -- acting in a way that honours God. Finally, [it] might suggest a life of faith -- depending on God in prayer and in our daily attitudes of heart. These five...are certainly appropriate ways to glorify God. But they are not my focus in this book. Instead of these things, I want to look at business in itself -- not just the ways business can contribute to work the church is already doing.

Grudem then goes on to highlight how various aspects of business can glorify God, such as ownership, employment, profit, commercial transactions, and the effect of business on world poverty.

Our conclusion is that business can glorify God in numerous ways, both directly (of itself), as particularly highlighted by Wayne Grudem, and indirectly, as highlighted in the section above. Our specific task here is to show how business is part of the *missio Dei,* and therefore a full and valid expression of the mission of the Body of Christ to the ends of the earth.

In Jesus' parable of the talents, the servants were commended for investing their financial "talents" and receiving back an honest return for their Master and His domain (Matthew 25.14-30). Today, Christians with business talents are called to invest their assets and abilities into the kingdom of God. By giving finances to missions and charities, of course, but more so by giving themselves, their experience, their know-how, their business acumen, etc. to establish the kingdom of God both locally in their own region and nation, but also to the remotest parts of the earth (Acts 1.8).

Business as mission is an act of co-creation in imitation of God, and hence a response to the Creation Mandate. It is Good News in itself, and hence an inseparable part of the Great Commission. Kingdom building is about wealth generation and spiritual transformation. As such, Business as mission should be viewed not only within the narrow church-mission-business perspective, but also within the wider macro- perspective of sustainable, transformational development consisting of abundance, empowerment, character, and service in which people break loose from the shackles of a world bound by abject poverty.

3. THE WORLD AND THE MARKETPLACE
The Present Context for Business Mission, Opportunities and Challenges
A Global Movement Gathering Momentum

Business as mission does not represent a new paradigm in itself, but is part of a broader paradigm shift that recognises the holistic nature of *missio Dei*, and affirms all vocations. The evangelical church is learning how to more effectively declare the Gospel in its fullness.

We are recapturing the biblical vision of the Body of Christ, breaking through doctrinal errors and historical barriers that have resulted in the false dichotomies that have stifled the Church's full impact in society. These dichotomies of the sacred versus the secular and the role of the clergy at the exclusion of the laity are being dismantled. Luther and Calvin helped us understand that every believer's vocation is means of glorifying God. But it is only in more recent years that we have begun to understand the full potential and value of this doctrine as it relates to cross-cultural mission.

At the Lausanne Congress held in 1974, several emerging world church leaders sounded the cry for the evangelical church to engage in more than mere proclamation of the gospel. They called for a fully-orbed demonstration of the Gospel. Statements from Congresses in Lausanne in 1974 and Pattaya in 1980 reflect this clarion call. By this reckoning we are about one generation into the needed worldview shift. Many activities have gained full acceptance by the evangelical community, including relief and development, workplace ministries, micro-finance efforts, business training, and so forth. But these have typically been carried out as non-profit activities.

Since the early 1990's there has been a growing "Business as mission" movement among the laity that is being expressed in various ways. There have been many international, regional, and national Business as mission gatherings. Articles and books are being published, websites have developed, and academic institutions are including Business as mission courses in their curricula.

However, for-profit businesses, *especially* those that are multinational in scope, are still treated with a high degree of ambivalence, scepticism and even hostility within the church at large. This explains why many feel that the Business as mission movement is at the very beginning of a paradigm shift. It is more accurate to say that Business as mission is at the tail end of a broader shift taking place within the church as a fuller understanding of holistic mission matures.

There is obvious potential for business people to play a more active role in taking the gospel cross-culturally. We cannot ignore the global reality and the need to release kingdom business strategies that have power to bring about deep and lasting spiritual, social, and economic transformation. We are faced with both significant opportunities, as well as challenges.

> *"The Spirit of the Lord is on me, because he has anointed me to preach good news to the poor, He has sent me to proclaim freedom for the prisoners and recovery of sight for the blind, to release the oppressed, to proclaim the year of the Lord's favour."*
> Luke 4.18-19, NIV

Opportunities for Business as Mission
(a) A World in Need

About 50% of the world's population lives on less than two U.S. dollars a day. That represents a staggering number -- over 2.8 billion people. Of these, 1.2 billion live on *one* U.S. dollar a day. Imagine a population twice the size of the USA, Canada, Mexico and Brazil combined, where each person exists on $1 a day. In addition to poverty, there are the devastating effects of disease that plague the poorest nations. At the end of 2002, an estimated 42 million people around the world were living with HIV/AIDS. 30 million of these people live in Sub Saharan Africa. This is further aggravated by a disparity whereby the richest 20% of the world's population own approximately 80% of the world's wealth; whilst the poorest 20% own approximately 1%. There is a tragic correlation between poverty, disease, and unemployment.

There is also a devastating link between lack of jobs and a variety of social ills. Human trafficking stands out as one of the most heinous. Trafficking is the term used for modern-day slavery, and describes the act of the enslavement of a man, woman, or child. Traffickers use force, fraud, or coercion to hold their victims against their will. Women and children are often trafficked and forced into prostitution. A root cause of trafficking is unemployment. Christians in business can and must address this.

30 years ago, the South East Asian countries were economic nobodies. Their economies were based on low-priced commodities. Japanese companies started setting up manufacturing plants that were welcomed with open arms by the Asian governments. Why? Because jobs and training were provided for the population, and new technologies were shared that

allowed these nations to compete at a global level.

Within a few years, enterprising Asians, trained by the Japanese, began starting their own plants. Today the largest chip manufacturers are in Taiwan, Singapore, and Malaysia, and are all locally owned. While Japanese companies did not have a social transformational agenda when they invested in Asia, nevertheless it demonstrates powerfully how enterprise can alleviate poverty.

> *I believe the only long-term solution to world poverty is business. That is because businesses produce goods, and businesses produce jobs. And businesses continue producing goods year after year, and continue providing jobs and paying wages year after year. Therefore if we are ever going to see long-term solutions to world poverty, I believe it will come through starting and maintaining productive, profitable business.*
>
> - Wayne Grudem -- *Business for the Glory of God*, Crossway 2003

(b) The Limitations of Aid and Development Strategies

Traditionally development agencies have focussed on providing aid to poor countries as a means of tackling poverty. While aid and disaster relief remain important, governments and NGO's have recognised that aid alone is insufficient to alleviate the problem of endemic poverty. Development projects have an important role to play in education, caring for the vulnerable, skills training, and community-based enterprise such as handicraft development and subsistence farming. But these are rarely self-sustaining projects. Many such projects run out of support after a while. One of the problems with aid is the need to keep asking donors for repeated support. In many cases, donor fatigue eventually sets in. When funding is withdrawn, the "false market" that the local population depended upon is exposed when it disappears. This is tragic and creates more problems than were solved.

Investing in sustainable businesses creates employment, and therefore true economic development for these countries. Real employment gives people dignity and a self-determination that can transform their community. This is in contrast to the dependency culture that is often engendered by aid. To alleviate poverty, people need a "hand-up, not a hand-out." The poor want real jobs, not subsidised ones. This is the cry for dignity and self-reliance that they deserve.

> *We should develop a kind of work and production – intellectual or physical – whose aim is "to become profitable" in order to serve human life.*

(c) A Holistic Development Approach

There is an increasing recognition of the need for and benefits of a sustainable holistic approach by mission agencies, development agencies, and businesses. Christians can participate and should contribute in these arenas. We should set the trends and standards by further developing the concepts and practical applications of Business as mission. We should aim at working with "all people of good will."

Henry Ford once said: "A business that only makes money is a poor kind of business." Most businesses exist solely to make a profit for their shareholders. That is what is referred to as the financial bottom line. Business as mission looks beyond a financial bottom line to a "multiple bottom line," taking into account financial, social, spiritual, and environmental returns.

> *Economics is a fundamental sphere in the process of social development and without it human existence could not be feasible. From a scriptural perspective, human life should be orientated by specific values, the values of the kingdom of God. Therefore, any aspect of social life must be evaluated in the light of such criteria.*

(d) Globalisation

The world is changing. Our way of being and doing church and missions needs to change as well.

During the past 2000 years, many Christians have sought effective means and opportunities to glorify God among all peoples. During the past 200 years, areas such as health and education have opened doors to serve in various communities. The uniting of business with missions is nothing new. The Nestorians, the Moravians, William Carey, the Basel Mission, various Catholic and monastic orders, have all used business in various ways for the expansion of Christianity, albeit not without complications.

However, due to unprecedented changes resulting from rapid globalisation, business (as in the "Business as mission" concept) is primed to take centre stage in the evangelisation and discipleship of the peoples of the world. Just as the Pax Romana created a favourable environment for the rapid expansion of the early Church, so globalisation has done so today. We need to recognise that globalisation has two sides; it can be used for benevolent economic development, but it can also be used for exploitation.

Business is globalising. It extends from international financial transactions to the availability of real-time information and branded products, anywhere, anytime. We buy American products made in the Philippines. We call a local number and speak to a call centre across the world. Culture is also becoming globalised. You see Coca-Cola bill boards in the jungles of Africa and Latin-America. CNN brings fragmented news-bites to every corner of the world. In a distant corner of Siberia you can watch MTV while drinking Swedish vodka.

The church is also experiencing the effects of globalisation through multidimensional missions; the church from everywhere going to everywhere.

The increasingly easy transfer of, and access to, finance, technology, and information offers the Church an unprecedented opportunity to disciple the nations through starting new businesses. With the collapse of communism, almost all governments are seeking business development and inward investment since they are in need of these resources for economic growth.

(e) Business is Welcome

There are many doors that are closed to "professional" Christians, traditional missionaries, and Christian workers, but there is not a single country in the world that would not welcome business and investment. It meets real needs. It provides job opportunities as well as training. It helps countries to develop not only economically, but also in other ways through the development of a middle class, increased tax revenue, more skilled labour force, and so forth. In traditional missions, one talks about "closed countries" and "restricted access countries," but there are no closed doors for real business people doing real business. Governments around the world welcome real business!

(f) Business is Influential

We must not underestimate the power of business. Its potential to have a major impact both on individuals and communities is huge. This potential can be positive or negative.

There is a wonderful web of relationships that comes with business and enterprise. This is a gift that should not be despised. Christians who enter business have the unique opportunity to positively touch and impact the lives of influential people who can leverage resources.

A key Christian leader in a major Muslim country said: "The modus operandi of professional Christians (e.g. missionaries) is not culturally natural, and certainly not sustainable or reproducible. Business as mission is about being real and having natural relationships, participating in peoples' lives through work and business, being salt and light."

Especially in Muslim countries, there is an ever growing suspicion of foreigners who seem to be "in country" without a legitimate purpose. This makes building even the most casual relationships strained because of an insufficient answer to the question, "What do you do?"

Business as mission can be the platform to foster a workplace environment where Christian principles and ethics can be introduced and demonstrated as the standard. In Uganda, a management consulting company, founded on biblical principles and truths, seeks to develop leadership and management skills in the arenas of both business and government. In the nine years the company has been in existence, it has established influence with business leaders, not only in Uganda, but in 12 other African countries.

When Jesus gave the Great Commission, He said "as you are in the process of going – disciple." This grammatical construction implies that as you are in the process of your normal (business) life, you should naturally disciple the nations. It is true that a fully devoted businessperson has time constraints, but then so do the people we are seeking to influence.

(g) Business Releases Untapped Resources for Building the Church

The task before us is quite challenging, and includes the need to create jobs, new business start ups, access venture capital, business know-how, access to markets, and clear business ethics. Drawing on the same existing resources for traditional missions will not be enough.

However, there are thousands of people in churches world-wide, with the right skillsets, experiences, and contacts that can make a significant difference cross-culturally through Business as mission. Mobilising, deploying, equipping, and supporting them effectively will release untapped resources for the mission of the Church.

All countries and cultures have entrepreneurial people. These business people (or potential ones) hold some of the most critical keys to practically demonstrate the kingdom of God. This is most essential in areas of the world where the name of Jesus is rarely heard, and if heard often misunderstood. Christians with a calling and gifting for business should be affirmed and encouraged.

Where there is no indigenous church, Business as mission can be a powerful part of the strategic plan for church planting. Church planting and business planting can go together hand in hand.

Kingdom businesses provide the local church and new disciples with models that they can easily understand and replicate. A new believer can relate to and learn from someone who is working out their Christianity in daily work life just like them. To the local church, the principles of empowerment, sustainability, and multiplication are modelled, rather than dependency. In turn, new Christian business people are affirmed, strengthened, and released to serve God and His kingdom through business.

Challenges to Business as Mission
(a) A Slow Paradigm Shift in Worldview Among Christians

We are in the midst of a significant paradigm shift in the thinking of the evangelical Christian community. Paradigm shifts do NOT happen over night; it is a long process, usually taking a generation or more.

The issue of the sacred-secular dichotomy has surfaced again and again in our research and discussions. It is a major internal challenge that the Church and the Business as mission movement must face.

> *In order to begin to understand the hindrances that may deter the effectiveness of the business-as-mission model in Africa, one needs to appreciate the way Christianity was initially introduced to Africa. Early missionaries presented Christianity to Africans as a great dichotomy between the 'spiritual' and 'secular'.*

Every paradigm is developed and upheld by a certain terminology. This applies to the thinking behind the sacred – secular dichotomy. It is seen in phrases like "full time ministry" and "real ministry." It is very easy to profess a belief in a new paradigm (such as a seamlessly integrated holistic worldview) but then continue to use old paradigm language, or misapply new terms to an old paradigm.

The word "holistic" may be used, but dichotomised thinking may be the underlying foundation. This results in pseudo-holism. In the bible, we see an integrated holism, and not two parts (physical and spiritual) awkwardly tacked together. There is no hierarchy with spiritual things at the top and physical things at the bottom. They are not separated realms with different values attached.

We do not want to simply add "business" to the social action agenda of the church. We cannot simply regard business as a useful tool for meeting people's physical needs. There is a deeper need for a paradigm shift where the sacred and secular become integrated as in the biblical worldview. Discipleship and transformation should address the whole person seeking practical applications in the market place.

There are already many Christian organisations that are working in the area of community development. In some cases, this has involved establishing programmes of micro finance, co-operative societies, etcetera. All these, without a doubt, contribute significantly to sustainable development in poor communities. However, in a few cases this has become an 'end' in itself. The danger is that a reluctance sometimes develops to fully share the Christian faith, and the social activity alone is considered a sufficient testimony of faith. The result can be a suc-

cessful programme, business or organisation, but one which is not focused on making the gospel of Christ fully known. We must be aware of similar pitfalls in the practice of business as mission and take steps to avoid them.

(b) The Stigma of Business and the Passivity of the Laity

In many parts of the global church, the vocation of business has a real stigma. This is largely a result of the pervasive Christian worldview that elevates the "spiritual" realm above the material realm.

In many church bodies, the Christian business community has been effectively minimised, or even marginalised, by what Dr. R. Paul Stevens has described as the unbiblical spiritual hierarchy of vocations.[3] Diagram 1 represents the pyramid that so many in the church are seeking to climb. Each step of the way supposedly gets you closer to becoming more spiritual. Subconsciously, many believe that God is more pleased or satisfied with the service of those in the upper sections, those known as "professional" clergy. Unfortunately, for many, lawyers and politicians don't seem to even make the chart!

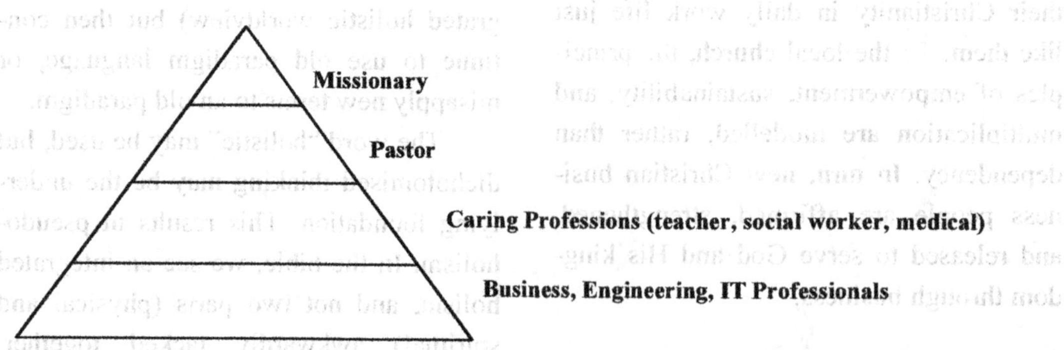

A closely related problem to this ingrained church culture is the underlying assumption that the clergy are the ones that minister, and the laity are relatively passive. Pastors may find it difficult to affirm and release (or even relate to!) leaders in other spheres of "real" life.

Many today hold the traditional mission paradigm as sacred because it is the ultimate demonstration of devotion! I mean really, if you are a "missionary" in a remote part of the world you must have made the ultimate sacrifice and your entire life is given to the spiritual pursuit of God and the proclamation of the Gospel. However, when I read about many pioneer missionaries, most believed in a holistic approach and made incredible strides to bring about economic development to the communities where they served. At some point the shift was made and those who were sent to the field only had the background of a Bible school education instead of any other kind of work skills. That instilled into the life of the new convert that the most 'spiritual' people were not found in the business world, but rather were full time professional Christians

This false hierarchy can be reinforced by different cultural factors around the globe. For instance, in some cultures hard work is frequently seen as a punishment from God as a result of the fall. Therefore the underlying theological framework does little to challenge this misconception, and there is little effort made to address the value of work, productivity, or sustainability.

Making a profit or taking an income from business activity is also regarded with widespread suspicion in the mission community and in many churches. Money is seen as a necessary evil, and one should not try to make more of it than necessary. As a result, business is often regarded as corrupt and evil at worst, and at best, a necessary but distasteful activity (made more acceptable if you are known by the clergy to tithe regularly or to contribute substantially to the building campaign).

In India the perception towards business is often negative in the Christian community. So when a business person becomes a Christian, often the person quits their job to be considered 'more spiritual'.

How then, will business people be affirmed in their vocation to integrate their faith with their daily working life? How will they believe that their gifts and experience have potential to make a powerful impact on their communities, nations, and to the ends of the earth? This is particularly crucial in nations where Christian entrepreneurs and business people are most needed because of rampant unemployment and the existence of corrupt and unjust cultural systems and institutions in need of reform.

> *In Latin America, there is an issue when talking about ascribing the same value for all vocations. I still see a sort of discrimination against those with skill/training in business and management taking leadership within Christian ministries and the Church. For instance, the seminaries are reluctant to accept those with MBAs to take leadership posts in administration. We still see theologians doing that. It reminds me of the time the pastors wouldn't accept a Christian psychologist to serve in Christian counselling. Praise the Lord, those years are gone, and now we need to accept that those skilled in business and management should lead and use their gifts in ministries of every kind.*

(c) Tensions in Coupling Business and Mission

There are inherent tensions when you couple together business goals and "mission" goals. Some of these we will explore in later chapters. However, it is worth mentioning that historic examples exist where enterprise has been closely associated with the advancement of the gospel, but has resulted in confusion and exploitation. These are reasons why some express mistrust and reservation.

We need to have a healthy critique of past and present practices, without discarding the fact that business has potential power for good. We need to recognise the dangers and pitfalls and examine how to avoid them.

(d) Protectionism

We must not be naïve regarding the drawbacks of globalisation and the flip side of unrestricted capitalism. Trade barriers set up by the US, EU, and Japan (to name but a few) represent major hindrances for fair and free trade. The West professes free trade, but practises a form of protectionism. Examples of this can be seen in the form of the farm subsidies of the EU and Canada, as well as steel tariffs of the USA. A level playing field in the area of international trade is a mirage. Business as mission does not operate in a vacuum, and there is a need for Christians in law and politics, as well as business, to address these issues.

(e) Lack of Affirmation and Equipping

It is doubtful if a reform of international trading laws on its own will automatically stimulate fair and free trade. Unless local people are effectively trained, encouraged, and supported to get into business, they will be unable to benefit from the immense potential that domestic and foreign trade has to offer. One of the biggest needs is to impart the Business as mission vision with practical support and training.

In some regions there may be a lack of involvement in business by Christians, or at best hesitant involvement, due to the stigma attached to business already described. However, there are often other reasons why people fail to be involved. These include: the lack of good models, lack of a business driven mind within the culture, inadequate awareness of sound business principles, lack of professional proposals for the development of viable projects, lack of access to adequate capital and investment, lack of good networks and support, and so on.

One of the reasons for these factors is the immaturity of the Business as mission movement. There is a felt need for developing support networks, disseminating good models, learning and moving on from past failures, making good business training available, developing funding, accountability and mentoring mechanisms, and in general enabling the entrepreneurs in each nation.

(f) Spiritual Opposition

Business people should not automatically blame their failure on Satan if they have neglected to apply sound business practice or failed to factor in the normal vagaries of business life. One hindrance to starting sustainable kingdom businesses has been the over-spiritualization of business operations so that good business principles are too often ignored.

> *From personal experience and from the experience of about ten other business-as-mission - business owners I work with on a regular basis, we know that the spiritual warfare is serious. We know that the redemption of souls and resources at the same time is something the enemy will not allow to happen without trying to deal a few serious blows.*

However, we should not ignore that any disciple walking in his or her true calling walks into battle on a spiritual plane. The full armour of God and a spiritual alertness "with all prayer and petition" (Ephesians 6:18) are basic requirements for the kingdom business person.

(g) Difficult Conditions for Business

Many countries that are in the greatest need of transformation also represent hostile environments for business. Corruption, intimidation, and economic or political instability make it challenging for any business to survive.

Most business investors would normally not invest in some of the places that Jesus has called us to venture. That is why it is even more important that we provide those called to start businesses in these difficult places with the support that they need. We need to look at creative solutions to the fact that low returns on investment are inherent in these difficult places. To create a better business environment in these challenging locations, it is crucial that we work with those called to transform legal, political, and educational spheres, and with those relief and development entities that form the vanguard.

It takes time to lay a solid Business as mission foundation, but its importance must not be neglected. There is a tremendous opportunity to reach into hostile or "closed countries" and to minister to those most in need through Business as mission. It requires more than simply sending skilled, equipped, and devoted business-men and women to these places. It requires more than simply affirming national entrepreneurs that God will use to transform their communities. It will require ongoing partnering, support, and encouragement until there is a sustainable and profitable business venture. Even then, our "kingdom goal" is not simply that these new businesses grow, become profitable, and reproduce, but that they have a lasting impact on the social, spiritual, material, and environmental aspects of their society.

Part II: Business as Mission in Practice
4. THE ESSENTIALS OF GOOD BUSINESS AS MISSION
Ten Guiding Principles
Introduction

Having identified Business as mission (BAM) as an integral and vital part of the overall mission of the Church, it is important to identify those things that set Business as mission apart from "business as normal" (BAN). As the illustration below demonstrates, there are some complementary areas of overlap between the two. For example, a good Business as mission business will, by definition, have many of the characteristics of any well-run business. A kingdom business must be profitable and sustainable just as any other business. Integrity, fairness and excellent customer service are characteristics of any good business, not just a Business as mission venture. As such, those characteristics will not by themselves necessarily point people to Christ. A kingdom business begins with the foundation of any good business, but takes its stewardship responsibilities even further.

This chapter will highlight the overarching principles that distinguish Business as mission from business as normal. It is important to note that the *application* of a principle will vary from context to context. For example, for spiritual guidance and accountability, some companies have found it useful to have formal contractual relationships with churches or mission agencies. While this approach has merit, it is merely one of many ways to seek prayer support (Principle #8) and to maintain spiritual accountability (Principle #3). Thus we are intentionally avoiding the term "best practices." The actual practices can vary according to the specific social, cultural, religious, or economic

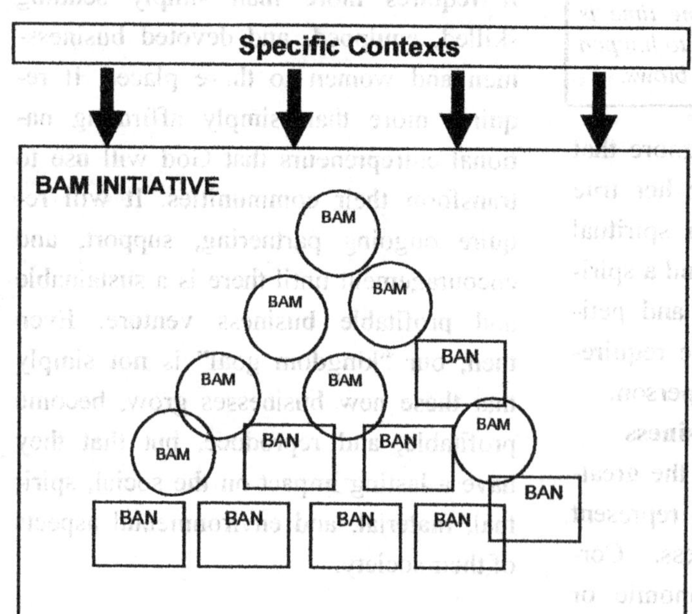

BUILDING BLOCKS OF A BUSINESS AS MISSION INITIATIVE/ COMPANY

BAN = "Business as Normal" i.e. foundational business principles which apply to all business initiatives.

BAM = "Business as mission" i.e. essential distinctives of a BAM initiative.

Specific contexts will dictate how the business is built in practice.

context, but the "guiding principle" is the same.

In addition, the *depth* to which each principle is applied and its *focus* will vary from business to business. For example, one business might emphasise the need to create jobs in areas of endemic unemployment (related to Principle #3 & #4), whereas another might place more emphasis on coupling the business with a church planting strategy (also Principle #3 & #4).

What follows is a list of principles that should underpin a Business as mission business. This is divided into two sections. First we list the basic foundational principles that must exist in any good business. Following that are the principles that distinguish a good Business as mission business.

Foundational Business Principles

1. Strives to be profitable and sustainable in the long term.

Profit is an indication that resources are being used wisely. It indicates that the product or service being produced and sold does so at a price that covers the cost of the resources, including the cost of capital. For most businesses, profits are fleeting, and never a sure thing. It is common for businesses to experience periods of low profit, and even negative profit. Thus it is important to take a long-term view of profitability. Occasional windfalls are often what will sustain a company through periods of financial losses. For that reason, a well-managed business will use extreme care when considering whether and when to distribute profits. Thus, profit, and its retention, is not nec-

essarily an indication of greed.

2. Strives for excellence, operates with integrity, and has a system of accountability.

While it is possible for a disreputable business to make money by cutting corners, this is not a viable long-term business strategy. People eventually wise up, bad reputation spreads, and the company eventually goes out of business. Long term viability and success requires an unflinching commitment to excellence and a reputation for hard work, honesty, and fairness. This is a basic law of economics, and holds true regardless of whether the company is owned by a Christian. There are standard business practices and benchmarks of excellence that no business, including a kingdom business, can afford to neglect. Furthermore, companies that are committed to doing business with excellence are transparent, and encourage criticism, feedback, and accountability from employees and the local community.

Business as Mission Distinctives

3. Has a kingdom motivation, purpose, and plan that is shared and embraced by the senior management and owners.

Good business practice alone will not by itself point people to Jesus. For that to happen the company must be more intentional. This begins with a plan, preferably a written one, which reflects the kingdom motivation and purpose of the business. By "kingdom motivation and purpose" we mean a desire to have a positive and lasting impact in the local community, as well as the local church. The owners and managers are mindful of the fact that, while the business itself may not last indefinitely, the impact can be a lasting one. Furthermore, the spiritual priorities of the company are regularly communicated to employees and customers in a culturally sensitive way.

Example: The founder of a company established in Turkey left the multinational world to focus on developing a "Great Commission Company." He wanted to do world-class business while facilitating church planting work in the 10-40 Window. He deliberately focused on Turkey as one of the "largest unreached nations on earth" and intentionally moved to a small city in a region of Turkey with 1.5 million people and no church. His business and community involvement have given him the opportunity to speak the good news to his employees and others in the community that might never have otherwise heard the gospel.

Example: The initial goal of Evangelistic Commerce was to generate funds for mission agencies. It was soon realised that much more could be done to spread the gospel. Now, with over 60 employees, the company holds daily prayers attended by Christians, Hindus, and Muslims, and has bi-weekly Bible studies. The company is able to emphasise personal care for employees and actively demonstrate the love of Jesus through the leadership of Christian managers. Beyond being salt and light within the company, management has helped form two churches and a Christian elementary school.

4. Aims at holistic transformation of individuals and communities.

In line with its kingdom motivation, the business will leverage every opportunity to bring spiritual, social, economic, or environmental benefits to the community at large. The company is a relevant force within the community, and respected by the local leaders. It seeks to be, if at all possible, at peace with all stakeholders and conducts itself in a socially responsible, culturally appropriate way. The company sets a high moral standard for itself, and is not content merely adhering to the minimum requirements of the law. It also avoids producing products or services that are harmful, or are perceived as harmful or sinful in some cultures.

Example: A company in Asia has found that through its business activities, the majority of employees in the business have accepted Christ and many local people have been influenced by the gospel. New companies have been started in remote places and resulted in new churches being established as well. In addition, many employees are actively investing time to influence their communities. The government has given the business awards for their activities, and as a consequence, those in the business have had a chance to model right living before officials and become a positive influence in their region.

Example: A successful Costa Rican healthcare enterprise, Clínica Bíblica, has partnered with other ministries with similar objectives. It works in strategic partnership with Roblealto Children's Ministry, whose mission is to minister to the spiritual and physical needs of Costa Rican children from difficult situations. This mission is closely aligned with its own healing ministry through business. Clínica Bíblica uses its medical expertise to meet the medical needs of Roblealto children and benefits by ministering to children they would not otherwise meet.

5. Seeks the holistic welfare of employees.

The company sets a high standard in the way it treats its employees. An ongoing effort is made to make the work and working conditions as safe and pleasant as possible. Employees are treated with dignity, and are given opportunities for personal and professional growth. The value of the family is upheld.

Example: Being able to work at home provides weavers in the "D company" with the flexibility to attend to other responsibilities such as family, field work, and other jobs. Women, often excluded from many aspects of business life, can freely and equally participate in making rugs.

Example: After experiencing periods of neglecting both God and family because of business pressures, TRP Limited instituted a plan and accountability structures for rest and renewal. Current practices include one day per week to pray and plan for business, church, and family needs.

6. Seeks to maximise the kingdom impact of its financial and non-financial resources.

The managers and owners recognise that God is ultimately the owner of the company. As such, they focus on how to maximise the kingdom impact of the company. For some companies, they donate money to other ministries. Other companies may have less financial freedom, but will contribute to the advancement of God's kingdom in other ways, such as through employee development programs, the management of its supply chain, and so forth. A word of caution is appropriate here. Some people feel strongly that corporations should tithe from their profits. We prefer a less legalistic approach for two reasons. First, as pointed out in Principle #1, it is sometimes more appropriate to retain profits. Second, some people will be tempted to think that tithing fulfils their Business as mission obligation, and they will not aggressively seek other ways to use their company for Christ. Generosity is good, but more importantly, the managers and owners should take a holistic view of Business as mission, and how to integrate a business *and* mission strategy.

Example: The D weaving company started as a job creation project, targeting the economic, spiritual, and personal welfare of the villages in which it works. More than a decade after its founding, this commitment had outgrown the initial project and produced an additional commitment to founding schools. Today D company supports more than ten schools, which have impacted over 600 families in 100 villages. It has also helped finance the construction of several churches in the surrounding villages.

Example: Clínica Bíblica uses its surplus income to support its many dependent community ministries. The network to which it belongs uses its combined income to subsidise the medical care of all needy patients. They divide income into three: one third towards building and maintenance costs, one third towards medical equipment and one third to fund other medical or social action ministries.

7. Models Christ-like, servant leadership, and develops it in others.

Managers of Business as mission businesses lead by example, and reflect Christ by serving others. Furthermore, they mentor and disciple others through word and deed. Questions about faith and its relevance are encouraged and handled in a contextually appropriate way. Decisions are checked against the question of "What would Jesus do in this situation?" Managers meet regularly for prayer, and employees are encouraged to do the same. Employees, customers, and other stakeholders are prayed for by name on a regular basis. In some cases, a spiritual mentor (such as a local pastor) is retained by the company for the purpose of emotional and spiritual care of employees.

Example: The founder of a company in Asia shares: "Our employees learn from us that service to our customers is the foundation of our business. In fact, being willing to serve is an eternal value. Business is God's training ground to teach us to serve."

Example: In the BA company in South East Asia, they have been learning about living the Gospel. John relates: "The Lord was showing me the power of disci-

pling people in the workplace. Where do Christians spend most time? Where will character flaws show up? Is this in church on Sunday, or in the weekday workplace? Therefore, where should people be discipled? In many church meetings the Word is only spoken. In the workplace, it must be lived and Christian discipleship modelled in response to real challenges."

8. Intentionally implements ethical Christ-honouring practice that does not conflict with the gospel.

Kingdom businesses operate on moral and ethical principles of the Bible. These can be followed by all business people to their benefit. Kingdom businesses are enterprises whose purpose is to produce goods and to perform services that accomplish God's will on earth as revealed and proclaimed in the Bible. They intentionally apply Christ's teaching to their business life and practice. They ensure accountability systems that address areas of ethics and Christ-likeness. They carefully evaluate their goods and services to ensure they do not conflict with the message of the gospel.

Example: Adhering to Christ-honouring business ethics has limited some financially profitable business opportunities for TRP Limited in Central Asia. Fluctuating bureaucratic and economic conditions and instances of corruption have added to the challenges of doing profitable business in an ethical manner. The founder has support from a Christian mentor and a network of like-minded business people in Central Asia. He also understands that an abundant prayer life and deep knowledge of God and His word are *NOT* optional if one wants to do effective spiritual work in the business world.

9. Is pro-active in intercession and seeks the prayer support of others.

Managers and owners seek prayer support from others and maintain open lines of communication with those prayer supporters. Satan will do everything possible to sabotage the kingdom goals of the company, so specific attention must be given to spiritual warfare. Pro-active intercession for the business is integral to the leadership of the company.

Example: In the beginning of the business, the founder of a company in Asia was not prepared for the degree of spiritual warfare he encountered. He didn't intentionally focus on prayer, either by himself or with the few believers he knew. As time went on, he determined that "prayer is work," and through prayer, as well as organising others to join him, he began to see results. He has found that systematically having someone praying for each employee each day was the best investment that he could have ever made.

10. Seeks to harness the power of networking with like-minded organisations.

As the proverb states: two are better than one and a three-strand cord is not easily broken (Ecclesiastes 4:12). Companies that are networked can be a powerful force. Often, multiple organisations (for-profit or non-profit) can accomplish more for the Kingdom by working together than by working separately. Good Kingdom businesses seek out those relationships and are open to serving other organisations that have similar goals.

Example: The founder of TRP Limited has been involved in setting up a loose network of about 200 people within a Central Asian country, and another 50 outside of the country, who are interested in pursuing kingdom business in that country. A web site is being set up to facilitate networking and to encourage **believers doing business in that nation.**

Example: From 1991 to 1993, AMI averaged sales of over $10 million per year, and currently has equity in nine operations in East Asia. From this position of strength, AMI has established strategic alliances with more than 15 non-profit agencies to do education, development, and church-planting work among local East Asian and Muslim communities. In each company the Great Commission (GC) strategy co-ordinator, networks with local church leaders and creates strategies related to evangelism, discipleship, and church planting. Expatriates are spiritually accountable to a church or mission agency, and have contracts that describe and specify their job descriptions and working terms.

Our aim here has been to offer a set of guiding principles for those who wish to put Business as mission into practice. This is not a definitive list, and will no doubt be refined through collective experience; however, these points offer a starting point. The principles were drawn out from the Issue Group's own knowledge and experience of best practices. Case studies submitted especially for this paper as well as other existing literature were also used. Case studies that most fully reflected the principles were then chosen as examples. Some of these can be found in full in Chapter 5 and Appendix C. For further reading on existing Business as mission ventures, as well as other examples of best practice, please see the Resource Directory in Appendix F. In particular the books: *On Kingdom Business*, by Yamamori & Eldred, *Great Commission Companies*, by Rundle & Steffen, and *Transform the World* by Swarr & Nordstrom are especially helpful and instructive in this regard.

5. STORIES OF BUSINESS AS MISSION
Case Studies
Introduction

The purpose of this chapter is to tell some Business as mission stories. These cases will give the reader an idea of what Business as mission really looks like in practice.

The style and depth of application of the key Business as mission principles will vary, sometimes dramatically, from context to context. The particular methods and strategies used must be diverse and creative depending on each business, its primary focus, and context. These short stories show how these principles can manifest themselves in different practices and priorities of the business. They show how often the principles were learned by trial and error. They show that principles were sometimes applied intentionally and were sometimes applied intentionally and in other cases unintentionally.

These stories are included to give the reader a taste of the different "flavours" of Business as mission that we can learn from and be inspired by. Two additional cases can be found in Appendix C.

TRP Limited
(a) Company Background

"Michael," the founder of "TRP Limited," moved to a Central Asian Republic in 1997 after working 13 years in the medical sector. He was motivated by his passion to see a reproducing and self-sustaining church movement there. The prayer guide *Operation World* calls this country the "largest unreached nation" on earth. In a population of 71 million, there are only about 2,400 national Christians in about 75 small congregations.

Michael first opened a liaison office for medical equipment imports. Then in 2000, while on a trip to his home country, he met the owners of a large, global, food trading company. The CEO was sympathetic to Michael's Christian vision, and because the company wanted to expand its business, agreed to train and mentor him as a food and agricultural products buying agent. Using $110,000 in private capital, Michael and his wife established TRP Limited in 2001 as a trading and consulting company.

The learning curve was very steep, but Michael was able to find a Christian mentor who had extensive international business and trade experience.

In only their first season, TRP Limited accounted for over 20% of the bottled extra virgin olive oil exports to the U.S., sold in some 7,000 stores in 30 states. They have developed their own brand that with a distinct "natural, healthy, and fair-trade" emphasis. TRP Limited's other work includes having a consulting role with a large importer of edible nuts into China, negotiating a contract with a Fortune 500 company in the area of renewable energy, as well as other food and agricultural projects.

(b) Description of Specific Business as mission Practices

Michael was the only foreign speaker at a national Food Symposium in his sector. His work has given him the opportunity to speak on television, and to be written up in the most popular national business newspapers. His role in the business community led to Michael being asked to serve as the secretary of a national Community Association in his city.

Michael's business and community involvement have given him the opportunity to share the good news with his employees and others in the community. His real life experience in the business world has enabled him to have more empathy and authority in counselling work with those in the small church where he serves with two others as a non-paid pastor.

Michael is passionate to see more business people who are walking with Christ share the vision and play an active role in his and similar countries. On a voluntary basis, he has been involved in setting up a loose network of about 200 believers and another 50 outside of the country, who are interested in pursuing business in that country. Business educators

and students, as well as experienced business people, have made short term visits to assist. Several "Business Consultations" have been held. A web site is being set up to facilitate networking and to encourage believers doing business.

(c) Analysis of Company and Practices

The company is self-supporting, but the start up capital has not yet been repatriated.

Adhering to Christ-honouring business ethics has limited some opportunities for financially profitable business. Fluctuating bureaucratic and economic conditions and instances of corruption have added to the challenges of doing profitable business in an ethical manner. Michael hopes that recent reforms will improve the business environment as the country applies for EU membership.

(d) Lessons Learned

Be Customer and Market Centred: Without customers and effective ways to get the product to the market, no company can survive. Marketing means "loving your customer as yourself."

Sometimes Free Advice Can Be Valuable: Government, academic experts, and mentors from the Christian business world will sometime give gratis assistance. Mentors can turn out to be people that we already know but whose business skills we have not previously valued.

Get Professional Help: Attorneys, accountants, and consultants can be costly, but the mistakes that are made by not using them can be deadly.

Balance & Rest: After periodic times of neglecting God and family because of the demands of the business, the need for accountability and a plan for rest and renewal became evident. Current practices include one day per week to walk in the hills or at the coast to listen to God, pray and plan for the business, as well as church and family needs. An abundant prayer life and deep knowledge of God and His word are NOT optional if one wants to do effective spiritual work in the business world.

D Company

D. is a Farstan weaving project providing jobs in villages around the second largest city in Farstan. It strives to empower the poor through village ownership of production assets, and to provide education by supporting the development of schools in the villages.

Weaving is a traditional skill, but villagers wanting to work with D are trained in order to guarantee quality designs and workmanship. D provided looms for participating villagers to use in their homes. D also provides the raw materials for the artisans. Completing a weaving project might take several months, so D makes partial payments to the producers to provide operating capital and family resources during the production process.

D is essentially a marketing organisation for the artisans, targeting an international market and utilising an alternative trade organisation. This marketing strategy enables D to pay artisans effective wages significantly above the going market wage.

The enterprise has had multifaceted impact on the villages. In addition to more than doubling the income of the artisans, the company has helped to establish several schools. One school has 750 students, of which over half are females. With sustainable income, many are making long-lasting commitments to the village and doctors have returned to the villages they once abandoned, in the hope of making a lasting difference.

The enterprise also supports families. The flexibility afforded by placing the weaving looms in the artisans' home allows villagers to attend to other responsibilities, including family and field work. Women, often excluded from many aspects of business life, can now freely and equally participate in weaving.

Each village elects a head supervisor from among the workers. The supervisor is a resource to other weavers in the village. The village will collectively identify the specific needs of the community.

The weavers and supervisors find they relate to each other in ways they might never have experienced otherwise. A Muslim supervisor to a Christian worker ceases to be identified as Muslim; instead, they are friends and partners working for a common goal and the welfare of the entire village.

Evangelistic Commerce

(a) Background

Tom Sudyk worked for 12 years in the law-enforcement field before beginning his career in business, starting and selling over 20 companies. In 1999, he went on a trip to India to assist a mission agency with a financial integrity issue. He became aware of the Indian government's restrictions on foreign funds entering India, particularly for Christian missions. Sudyk saw the opportunity to start a company in India to create funds for missions.

(b) Company Formation

After identifying an industry (medical transcription) and hiring a Christian Indian manager, Sudyk started a company in Chennai, India. He then secured a US medical transcription company as a customer and the business started operations in early 2000. The company's initial capitalisation was approximately $150,000 with the business becoming profitable after two years. It has since expanded to include software development, data conversion, and CAD (architectural drafting) design, as well as a medical transcription training school.

(c) Company Ministry

The initial goal for the company was to generate funds for mission agencies. It was soon realised that much more could be done to spread the gospel. Now, with over 60 employees, the company holds daily prayers attended by Christians, Hindus, and Muslims, and has bi-weekly Bible studies. The company is able to emphasise personal care for employees and actively demonstrate the love of Jesus through the leadership of Christian managers. Beyond being salt and light within the company, the company's management has helped form two churches and a Christian elementary school.

The company has provided technical and financial assistance to a computer-training school for physically disabled individuals and hired several of their students.

(d) Replication – Next Generation

Sudyk recognised that American business students who felt called to Christian service/missions were encouraged to leave business school and enter theological training. He formed an NGO and began a college internship program to encourage business students to use the vehicle of global business for the spread of the gospel into countries that are closed to traditional mission work. Currently the NGO works with over 200 Christian colleges, and through an alliance with Intervarsity Christian Fellowship, a significant number of secular universities and MBA programs.

(e) Lessons Learned

It is easier to teach ministry to a businessperson than business to a mission person. They focus on good business practice and integrating ministry into the business, rather than starting a mission and trying to posture it as a business. If the business thrives, so does ministry to its employees and community, all without foreign funding or donations.

AM International

In 1989 "Bob," the company's founder, left the multinational corporate world to focus on developing Great Commission companies. He wanted to do world-class business while facilitating church-planting work in the 10-40 Window.

Bob bought a controlling interest in AMI, a consulting and manufacturing firm specialising in the technology sector. Within a few months, they had four employees. From 1991 to 1993, the company averaged sales of over $10 million per year in turn-key technologies in lighting and other high-automation manufacturing. They currently have equity in nine operations in East Asia.

The company has managed new factories in East Asia on behalf of publicly traded American companies, and has smaller manufacturing and representation offices in the Middle East and North Africa. The capitalisation for these manufacturing ventures is generally US $1-10 million, with AMI holding between 15 and 100 percent. They have established strategic alliances with more than 15 non-profit agencies to do education, development, and church-planting work among local East Asian and in some sensitive communities.

The large investment of money and high technology gives them strong political leverage. East Asian governments generally welcome foreign manufacturers, especially those with larger capitalisation. When a company makes money and provides jobs for the local people, the government will not interfere unless the business is openly breaking the law or embarrassing the government (causing it to "lose face").

Each of AMI's operations has a Great Commission (GC) strategy co-ordinator, a spiritual entrepreneur, and consultant who networks with local church leaders and creates strategies related to evangelism, discipleship, and church planting. GCs are on the local company's board of directors to ensure the presence of annual GC plans

that are ambitious but culturally achievable. Such plans set goals, define purpose, and create synergy for maximum kingdom effectiveness.

AMI emphasises church-planting or ministry teams focused on cities or people groups. Expatriates are spiritually accountable to a church or mission agency, and have contracts that describe and specify their job descriptions and working terms.

Normally, the team leader is not the general manager. Bob has found that stand-alone kingdom entrepreneurs are limited both in terms of finances and effectiveness. They need to be part of a team for accountability and encouragement. When AMI started working in a certain Central Asian Republic during the early 1990's, the number of Muslims who were followers of Christ was fewer than 10. Within a few years, however, many employees were meeting for discipleship on a weekly basis with more than 80 people of the majority faith who are now followers of Jesus. This demonstrates the effectiveness of a team of kingdom professionals.

The management teams are multiethnic and multinational. This gives companies a broader network and provides more specialisation in skills to meet targets. In companies with only national employees, workers may struggle to communicate with multinational companies and have a limited business perspective.

Not all the managers are Christians, but most are GC-committed Christians and no key managers are antagonistic to the GC goals of the company. Salaries are based primarily on performance, and not donor support. It is difficult for a manager to make good decisions not tied to his or her compensation. They do allow part-time non-nationals to receive compensation via non-profit groups.

AMI companies have significant export markets, which help to insulate against local corruption. They also provide political leverage as the government recognises that the companies bring profits from external markets that stimulate local economic growth.

Bob shares: "We are God's fellow workers. We plant the seeds by using business, but God gives the growth."

Asian Company

A manufacturing enterprise in Asia was started in 1988 with an idea, 5 employees, and $10,000 in capital. Within 15 years, the enterprise had grown to 350 employees, exports of $3,000,000 and $400,000 in profits.

(a) Early misunderstandings

The founder, "Jim," had some early misunderstandings regarding the purpose of his business and good business practices. He thought that because he was doing "God's work" that God would cut him some slack and not make him adhere to normal business laws that other successful business people follow. It took time for Jim to understand that business is a system that God has ordered by His laws and ordained in creation. To redeem it, we must understand and operate within its "natural law."

Jim assumed that the business was only a vehicle for something more impor-

tant. He didn't realise that people would connect his authenticity in business with authenticity in other things, including his words.

Pressures in the business that should have caused Jim to trust God more wore him down instead. He expected ministry to happen after work, rather than through opportunities in business. He did not look to daily normal business activities as a means to disciple people. He missed opportunities. Jim admits he wasn't prepared for the spiritual warfare he encountered. He didn't do the work of praying well, either by himself, or with the few believers he knew.

(b) Lessons learned through experience

Jim learned that the system of "business" is another of God's creations. Learning the system is like getting to know Him. It is honourable, not worldly. The "world's ways" are attempts to short-circuit His system. Business was never meant to result in temporary reward, but always intended to create money and develop eternally valuable skills, which gives us the chance to invest in other eternal things.

Prayer is important work, and is the key to seeing results. Jim found that praying for people BY NAME, not by group, gave the most visible results. He mobilised many to join the prayer effort. Jim found that systematically having someone praying for each employee each day was the best investment he ever made.

Business is God's training ground to teach us to serve. Look at management books and see what they say about serving. Service is a skill we will need to be able to put on our employment application in the New Jerusalem. Business allows us to practice it now! Jim realised that the events of the business day were the best place to disciple people. It is possible to see hundreds of people and their relatives impacted by the gospel while running a business.

(c) Bearing Fruit

Jim learned that successful business can holistically transform both individuals and communities. The majority of employees in the business have now accepted Christ. Christ's name has been lifted up in hundreds of ways and events. The influence of the gospel has been extended to many people beyond the business itself. In addition, Jim and his team have been able to start new companies in remote places, which have resulted in new churches. A fellowship of newly employed beggars has emerged. In addition, many employees are actively investing time to influence their communities. Believers are trying to establish Christ's kingdom in an area known to be in the control of many witches.

Business creates opportunities. Governments recognise an entity positively when it has benefited its people. The government has given the business awards for their activities. As a consequence, Jim and others in the business have had a chance to model Christ and witness to local government officials.

Money is being put back into society and the church, rather than taken from them for support (millions of dollars in salaries). Many "missionaries" have been on the field for many years without need of any external financial support.

Jim is aware of all that could be done better and his own incredible weaknesses. However, he hopes that his lessons learned will be able to encourage others -- to God's Glory.

Part III: Enabling the Body
6. MOBILISING FOR BUSINESS AS MISSION
Releasing Untapped Resources in the Global Church
Introduction

Business as mission is a part of a wider movement that is emerging. This is the result of entrenched barriers within Christian thought and church culture being broken down. These barriers relate most strongly to the sacred-secular divide, which by extension has produced a clergy-laity division.

In evangelical language, the term "full-time ministry" has meant serving as a "professional Christian" in the role of Pastor, Missionary, or Evangelist. However, we must acknowledge the ministry of the laity, that is, every member of the Body of Christ serving God, 24 hours a day, 7 days a week, in every arena. In business and the marketplace, Christian business people are called and gifted to live and operate in Christ-honouring ways. They are to be "salt and light" through business.

This is foundational for Business as mission, which affirms, equips, and deploys Christians to make a transforming impact for God's kingdom in and through business. We need to mobilise business people to take up their vital role in fulfilling the Great Commission. This is especially true in places where the name of Jesus is rarely heard or understood, and where His care and compassion is rarely experienced.

We must think in terms of mobilisation of business people from all nations, going to all nations in cross-cultural expressions of Business as mission. However, we should not neglect same and near-culture expressions of Business as mission. It is vital that we affirm and equip Christian business people in close proximity to the areas of need and mobilise them for this cause. They are the ones who can most readily make a lasting transformational impact in their own communities and nations. They are usually struggling for support in Christian cultures that often regard business with suspicion and often even hostility.

Whether ministering cross-culturally or within their own culture, Christian business people must be encouraged in their calling and vocation of business. If they feel called to serve Christ, they should no longer be automatically directed to give up their business life and minister in the pattern of a traditional "pastor" or "missionary" (which is often wrongly held up as a "higher calling"). Business people have unique skills and experience that the world needs in order to experience the full good news of the gospel.

> *As for the relationship of business to serving God, when people ask how their lives can "glorify God", they are not usually told, "Go into business."... When students ask, "How can I serve God with my life?" they don't often hear the answer, "Go into business."*
>
> - Wayne Grudem – *Business for the Glory of God*, Crossway 2003

There is a role for church leaders to affirm and help to mobilise business professionals and entrepreneurs. The result would be that business people are liberated to recognise their workplace or business as their primary arena of ministry and then intentionally consider how they could be ambassadors for God's kingdom both locally and globally.

Steps for Mobilisation

1. Imparting Vision

Mobilising for Business as mission begins with vision impartation. Essential messages to convey are God's view on creation, work, and business, His calling to minister holistically, to manifest His kingdom in the marketplace, and to pray and work for transformed lives and societies among all peoples.

2. Identification

Who has the entrepreneurial gift? Who has a calling to business? Who is equipped? We must avoid the danger of thinking that the only Western business people can do Business as mission. All countries have entrepreneurs and business people. Those with a business gifting need to be identified and encouraged. In some cases, business people will leave a country to go to another. An effective Business as mission strategy will include the identification of key business people in their own culture or country, who can be affirmed, trained, equipped, and deployed. Mobilisation will always include this identification process.

3. Affirmation

One of the most essential elements in mobilisation is that Christians in business are affirmed in their calling. Christian business people should be released into service in the marketplace. They need ongoing affirmation as they remain in business. Church leaders should consider laying hands and praying for business people on a Sunday morning. This is important for others like teachers, social workers, engineers, and lawyers as well.

4. Recruitment

Mobilising for Business as mission goes beyond affirming Christians who are in business. Business as mission poses questions such as: How can you make an intentional impact for God's kingdom in and through your business? In Business as mission, the business is both the medium and the message. If God has called a person to business, the next question is: Where should they do it? Where the gospel need is greatest, or its message weakest? We need to be proactively recruiting for strategic deployment and help business people to develop their place in the mission of the church.

5. Screening

Successful Business as mission implementation pre-supposes that the right people are used for the right activities. If there is a cross-cultural element to a Business as mission initiative, it becomes even more important that people with the right skill sets are being recruited and deployed. Each business, organisation, and network involved in Business as mission should develop criteria and qualifications required for successful implementation.

6. Training & Equipping

This step could involve a variety of content or format, from basic business training to learning cross-cultural communication skills. A critical success factor is for experienced business leaders to provide hands-on mentoring to new recruits.

7. Mobilisation of Resources

Additional resources are required for Business as mission and include access to networks and contacts, to develop markets, to match opportunities with personnel, etc. Without these, the resource of capital alone is insufficient. However, the mobilisation of capital is in itself a vital component. There is sufficient potential capital that could be available from investors with a "kingdom perspective" if they were made aware of these strategic investment opportunities that have eternal value. New human resources are required and may come from a new generation of young entrepreneurs, educated in business schools and trained in real marketplace companies. They could be partnered with business leaders who provide experience and financial capital for these young leaders.

8. Deployment

Business as mission takes a global view. It is an integral part of the whole church taking the whole gospel to the whole world. Business as mission is about going from everywhere to anywhere, affirming, enabling, and deploying business people from east and west, from south and north. Part of the mobilisation process must include getting help from and being connected with strategic opportunities to serve in other countries.

Problems and Barriers

Many major barriers have already been touched upon. A key barrier that has reoccurred throughout the preparations of this paper has been the reality of the sacred-secular divide and the clergy-laity division. These barriers must be overcome to effectively mobilise for Business as mission.

Other hindrances include instances when a congregational leader understands the issues and strives to be supportive, but is often limited by the demands and responsibilities of running the local church. We must also be open to learning from other members of the Body of Christ. For instance, there is much to learn from the Reformed and Catholic traditions that have done significant work on the theology of work, on being good stewards of creation, and participating in God's redemptive work in the world.

Specific barriers include the fact that business people have often been under-utilised, misused, or looked down upon. Additional problems that were recognised encompass the influence of prosperity theology, confusion with other related but different strategies, the need for consistent quality control, and guarding against fraud and the level of risk taking and work involved.

(a) Under-utilised

There is a widespread failure to realise the potential and calling that business people have as agents of God's kingdom. There can be a sense of passivity and a vague feeling of guilt when business people resign themselves to simply filling church pews and writing checks to "redeem their wealth." Others are frustrated in roles that do not suit them, instead of finding acceptance and pleasure in being used by God in the way he has shaped and gifted them as business people.

(b) Misused

Many business people find themselves treated as cash cows. They are only approached for their money by the church or Christian organisations. In some cultures, profits of a business owned by a Christian are to be given to support their church without question. However, being in business does not necessarily mean that there is a lot of personal or company money available. They may be in dire financial need, perhaps making less money than their employees, or struggling to capitalise the business or meet cash flow demands. There is a danger of seeing business from a mere utilitarian perspective. Business is not simply a source of funding for "spiritual ministries." Instead, business can be a ministry in itself, and the use of profits or personal giving should be complimentary to that.

(c) Looked Down Upon

The Church is still struggling to understand God's view on work, business, wealth creation, and money. All too often business people are looked down upon because they are "dealing with mammon," since they are operating in difficult arenas prone to corruption. However, money is not evil in itself. The Bible says that the love of money is a root of all kinds of evil (1 Timothy 6:10). This misunderstanding creates a sense of distance and rejection for many business people, causing an unnecessary rift between church and business. This must be overcome as we are mobilising for Business as mission.

> *I think that negative attitudes toward business in itself is ultimately a lie of the enemy who wants to keep God's people from fulfilling His purposes.*

(d) Prosperity Theology

The other extreme of those who are suspicious about money or seeking a profit, are those who have been strongly influenced by prosperity theology that advocates abundant material provision as a sign of God's blessing. We must ask, "Why did God give us money?" The Bible teaches a balanced view, where God blesses us with material goods, but they are to be both enjoyed AND used for His purposes. The teaching of stewardship is required, with an emphasis on eternal investment.

(e) A Distinct Strategy

Business as mission is a distinct strategy to create profitable commercial enterprises with an intentional kingdom purpose. A challenge will be to prevent confusion that it is merely a new donor strategy repackaged or renamed to enhance fundraising. Business as mission is an emerging strategy that is complimentary to, but distinct from, other economic development programs or mission endeavours.

(f) Ensuring Quality Control and Guarding From Fraud

As Business as mission grows and develops, we need to increasingly consider how to avoid fraud, uphold ethical standards, as well as develop and encourage quality control and integrity checks. Not everything calling itself Business as mission will necessarily be what we define here as Business as mission. Sin and wrong motivation will result in the distortion or counterfeiting of something that has tremendous potential for good. Sometimes lack of quality will come from bad practice rather than from malicious fraud. Not everyone seeking investments will have good accountability systems.

(g) The Level of Risk-Taking and Commitment Required

Mobilising for Business as mission requires a different approach to other forms of mission. Business involves a different level of risk taking. There are issues related to personal financial equity and welfare of employees. Other issues impact on family, finances, time schedule, church ministry, community, and how people are viewed in the workplace. It is necessary to develop a strong Christ-like perspective of persons and material things.

It is important to recognise that starting up a business in one's own country is very difficult, and the reality is that the vast majority of new businesses do not last five years. Adding a cross-cultural dimension adds to the complexity and level of risk. This is because of other issues such as corruption, the lack of a conducive environment for business, and the challenge of cultural sensitivity. The level of hard work, focus, and commitment that is required should not be underestimated. There is the potential to put extra strain on other relationships, and not be understood by people whose world has been framed by an 8 hour a day job.

Existing Resources

There is an increasing number of resources and initiatives for Business as mission mobilisation. The Resource Directory in Appendix F provides a comprehensive list. It is worth highlighting some categories of mobilisation tools and models that exist and are working. Articles, books, and websites are important in the mobilisation process. So are Christian business people with exposure to Business as mission that are able to envision and enthuse others. Several organisations and groups around the world are organising vision trips, field trips, and exposure trips to give people a personal motivational experience. These and other groups provide opportunities to donate to or invest in Business as mission initiatives.

There are Business as mission meetings and consultations. These have been at local, national, and regional levels. In the UK there are local Business as mission groups, in Uganda there is a nation-wide network, and in Central Asia there is a regular regional consultation.

There are many mission agencies that are supportive of or engaging in Business

as mission strategies. Business as mission is presented as an opportunity for service alongside other ministry opportunities. These agencies are developing new policy and structures for partnership with, and the mobilisation of new Business as mission initiatives.

This Lausanne Occasional Paper on Business as mission is in itself intended to be an instrument to be used in mobilisation.

Final Comments

As business people are mobilised, we do not want to create a separate "business track," a Business as mission movement disconnected from the broader mission efforts of the church. It is important that we do not settle simply for a horizontal partnership or network of "Business as mission" practitioners and initiatives. Business people must ask themselves how they will fit into the whole, both in terms of broad vision, and in real partnership. How will "Business as mission" connect with other Christians exercising their gifts and callings, whether in Law-as-Mission, Medicine-as-Mission, Education-as-Mission, Bible-Translation-as-Mission, Radio-as-Mission, and others? Together we can have a greater impact. Vertically linked, we are more likely to see holistic transformation of people and communities. In our reflections, strategies, and implementation, we need to constantly consider the whole the Body of Christ at work.

Given the enormity of the task and the huge potential in the body of Christ, there will always be a great need for more and better mobilisation. There is a great deal more that could be done; more comprehensive suggestions for strategy are made in Chapter 8: Strategic Recommendations.

7. PARTNERSHIP
The Vital Role of Mission Agencies and the Church
Introduction

In this chapter, we want to explore the importance of partnership, helping churches and mission agencies relate to Business as mission. We will tackle philosophical and operational considerations that commonly arise in response to Business as mission.

We recognise many changes are taking place in the church and missions arena. We affirm that the Body of Christ has many expressions. There are individual entrepreneurs, businesses, Business as mission networks, marketplace ministries, sending and supporting churches, local churches on the "receiving end," emerging churches, denominationally linked agencies, and inter-denominational mission agencies. These all come in various sizes, shapes, and forms.

In practice, Business as mission can connect with different kinds of church and mission entities, as the diagram below shows. Ultimately churches, mission agencies, and kingdom businesses have the same purpose: to bring glory to God's name among all nations. Partnership and unity between different entities and initiatives working towards this common end will only strengthen God's people and make kingdom endeavours more effective.

During our consultation process,

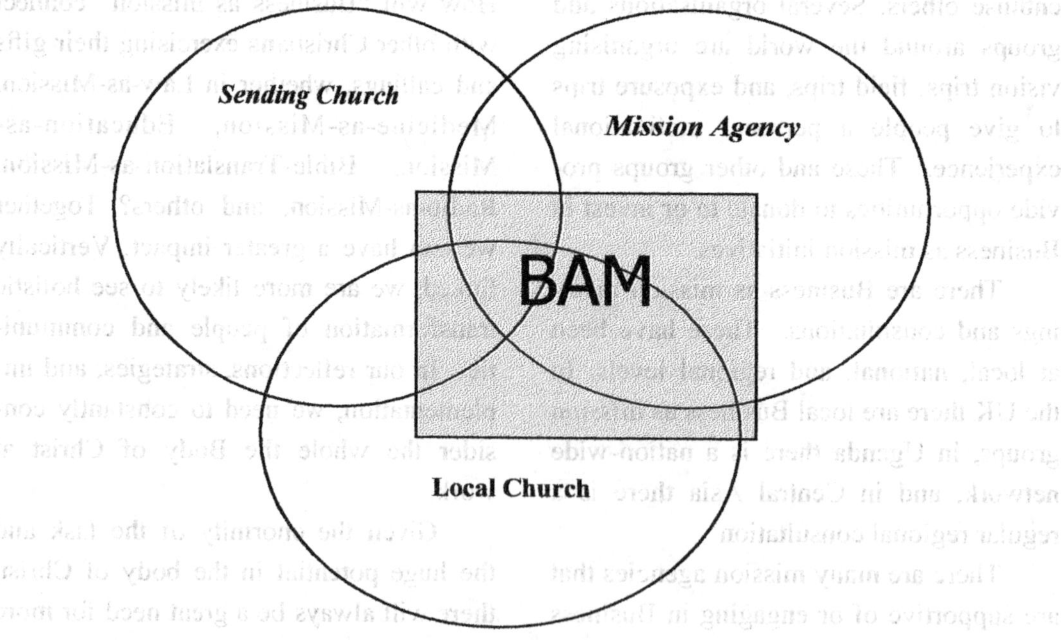

business people as well as church and mission leaders identified obstacles to effective partnership, and together looked at solutions. A summary of these obstacles and solutions can be found in Appendix D.

The Context for Partnership with the Church

The Church has a vital role to play in affirming and equipping business people in their Great Commission mandate.

There are various contexts through which a relationship between Business as mission and the church can manifest itself. These contexts often overlap with each other.

(a) Business as Mission and the Local Church

It is crucial that any kingdom business initiative works in partnership with the local church(es) in close proximity to the business wherever possible. Otherwise, the danger is that new initiatives will disenfranchise the church, instead of strengthening it. Strengthening the local church must be an aim of every kingdom business.

Any partnership between Business as mission and the local church must strive for a win-win situation, where each party benefits and affirms the other. This is possible where the same vision for God's kingdom is shared. Churches provide fellowship for business people, ideally equipping and energising them for their vocational ministry. Churches and pastors can provide teaching, training, and pastoral support for business owners and pro-

fessionals. Business people can bring their management and other skills as a contribution to body life. Kingdom businesses might provide employment for some church members, which is vital in areas where unemployment significantly weakens the church.

There is a need for partnership through prayer, mutual encouragement, and in ministry projects together in the community. A local church might initiate new Business as mission ventures as part of its own outreach, or it might encourage its members to launch and support new Business as mission leaders who are gifted entrepreneurs.

(b) Business as Mission and the Sending Church

Church leaders and congregations play a vital part in facilitating Christian business people to take up their role in building God's kingdom. Churches can affirm, help recruit, and equip those being sent out for Business as mission work. Organising short-term teams of business professionals to use their education and expertise in a cross-cultural mission setting has proven highly effective. Business people bring their gifts and entrepreneurial ideas and can release creativity and resources for the church's mission strategy.

(c) Business as Mission Where There is Little or No Local Church Presence

Business as mission is a strategy that can give access to places where there is no public expression of the local church. Business planting and church planting can go hand in hand. (Although a distinction between the roles of spiritual leadership and employer might be helpful to avoid conflicts of interest.) In this context, Business as mission can model partnership from the initial stages of local church growth, despite a hostile environment. It can open doors for transformational ministry where traditional mission models and other expressions of the church are forbidden.

For example, in a Middle Eastern country, an Arab tribal leader is the local owner of a Business as mission business. He has excellent connections with the local government and is the only believer in the community. The community respects him because he has shown genuine concern for the physical needs of his people. An agreed portion of the profits of the company are invested in development projects in his area. It is expected that a church will emerge in this area in the next generation.

In some parts of the world, such as the Arabian Peninsula, there is a significant expatriate community. A variety of international expatriate churches exist where there is no indigenous church. This presents an opportunity for expatriate Christian business people to use their business skills to encourage the expatriate and persecuted church in the community. For example, an Arab expatriate church felt intimidated in an Islamic country. A vision was born encouraging the church to make a difference in their community, sharing the love of Christ. The pastor of the church initiated a school project that employs members of his congregation. The quality of education attracts children from the local upper class. As a result the church can touch and influence the local community while at the same time running a for-profit business.

Missions Organisations and Business as Mission

Business as mission is a strategy that is gaining momentum in both mission and Christian business communities. While there is a marked distinction between these two communities at present, new "bizzionaries"[4] are being mobilised that have a more integrated approach. The distinction will diminish in future generations. We very much encourage the multiplication of such initiatives. New mission support mechanisms and sending entities that are focused on the special nature and needs of Business as mission are required. For-profit business can adapt to some kinds of cultures, methods, and structures better than some other types of mission activity. Therefore, whilst not drawing a false barrier between business and "mission," it is important to look at how these different mission approaches and structures might work together.

There are several levels on which mission organisations can engage with Business as mission:

- Mission organisations can affirm and

> *"Mission agencies and businesses might use different structures and methods to reach the same goal. However, honouring the integrity and uniqueness of both in form and function will allow each part to serve the other and the whole body together."*
>
> - Swarr & Nordstrom – *Transform the World,* 1999

endorse Business as mission as a strategy. Capacity can be increased through acceptance and openness.

- Mission organisations can offer their experience and resources in informal or formal collaboration with kingdom businesses.
- Mission organisations can be a vessel through which kingdom businesses can be born, nurtured, and multiplied.

(a) Affirmation

Mission pastors, mission executives, and field leaders should advocate for Business as mission through their organisation even if close collaboration is not possible. This increases the opportunity for Business as mission practitioners to work on good terms with other local ministry ventures. This encourages healthy support of one another in the field.

We suggest that all mission executives and leaders should grapple with the concept of Business as mission so that they are able to affirm in principle the idea that business can be a powerful strategy to disciple nations.

> *To "get it" in our experience, does not happen overnight. It requires patience and consistent communication. We must model business-as-mission, not simply lecture to the field and home offices on the concepts. Doors of understanding are cracking open as men and women begin to see examples of businesses that are not simply financial generators for "the real work", but are ministries in and of themselves.*

(b) Collaboration

Mission agencies can be vital partners to help business set appropriate mission (kingdom) goals. They can help with issues of accountability through ongoing input. Mission personnel can help evaluate whether a business venture is suitable for the local context or culture. Mission agencies can give input on the bigger picture, helping to strategically deploy a business. They can help link the business with the wider work of God in a nation or particular community.

Mission agencies have local knowledge, support networks, contacts, training tools, cross-cultural and language skills, appropriate literature and evangelistic tools, etc. that can benefit Business as mission initiatives. Mission personnel can be seconded to help the business with pastoral support or spiritual mentoring for their staff. Mission agencies and businesses can work on joint projects in the community. They can work together to disciple new believers within the business. Mission organisations can help mobilise interest, prayer support, short-term teams, or personnel for the business through their more extensive networks.

(c) Starting Business as mission Initiatives

Many mission personnel are already among the Business as mission pioneers. They are confronted daily with the needs of the communities they serve. They have seen how Business as mission is an appropriate and effective response to those needs. A major asset possessed by such pioneers is a deeply felt compassion for the people they serve. Some of these Business as mission practitioners have led certain organisations to thoroughly evaluate Business as mission as a strategy. Those agencies have either embraced business ventures as part of their own outreach or have entered into strategic partnership with kingdom businesses closely related to them.

There are philosophical and operational considerations related to the integration of business and mission in partnership. The strengths of each can be combined to produce increased fruitfulness. However, there is a potential for tension as these traditionally different entities meet. There are inherent dangers as each represents a different culture. We hope this section will assist agencies and churches to grapple with the implications of this new movement in mission.[5]

Philosophical Considerations and Differences in Approach

(a) Doubt about for-profit activity or the close association of economic and mission activity

For centuries the predominant view has been that missionaries should be donor-supported within a not-for-profit context. The prevailing view has been that one can either serve God or make money. Only recently, some activities such as microfinance have gained acceptance. However, overtly for-profit models still attract suspicion. Why do we assume that non-profit organisations are better for society than for-profit business? What makes small business morally superior to big business?

Our organisation is working with former Tibetan-Buddhists that are passionate about planting churches in their homeland. Security issues make traditional church planting work prohibitive. These young men are purchasing yaks, goods, and other materials, travelling into villages with no known witness, selling their goods, signing contracts for future goods and services, developing relationships, as a result small groups of believers have spring up. The in-country director is a former owner of an auto parts store from the US, who "gets it". His mission agency doesn't. In addition to running this project, which has seen 20 small businesses launched, he runs a couple of small companies of his own in order to maintain his visa status. The agency has asked that some of these companies close, as they are becoming profitable. He, on the other hand, challenges the new small business owners to be as profitable as possible, in order to grow, maintain legitimacy in the eyes of the villages, and employ others

Historical examples exist where economic power has resulted in distortion of mission objectives and actually harmed the gospel. We must acknowledge this and learn from these mistakes. However, this does not mean that we should totally dismiss the potential for good that business represents. Rather, organisational safeguards and careful evaluation of the implications of our activities on future generations are in order.[6]

(b) Fears that business attitudes and culture will alter the ethos of the organisation

For obvious reasons, there are likely to be differences in priorities, expectations, and approach between a business entity and a mission agency. Business culture is different from the culture of a typical mission organisation. There is a need to look at policies, procedures, and strategies to discover how to make room for the business strategy without causing undue tension. Careful examination of the "DNA" of the organisation, along with ongoing evaluation and clear communication are necessary. Keeping the business structure somewhat distinct from the mission structure is likely to be beneficial.

(c) Fear of focusing only on physical/ economic transformation that does not extend to spiritual transformation

There is a concern among many that business activity can overshadow evangelistic proclamation, spiritual transformation, or church planting. Good cases of Business as mission, with holistic kingdom goals, have proved that this does not have to happen. Business as mission should always seek to practice and proclaim the fullness of the kingdom of God in a sensitive manner. Kingdom business people realise they cannot simply allow people to go hell wealthier than they were before. Business provides a credible basis for being present while demonstrating a concern for the whole life of the men and women they seek to lead to Christ.

(d) Fear that the mission force will be eroded or corrupted through business

Another concern is that Business as mission efforts may cause a conflict of interest. There is a danger that mission personnel might jump on the business

> *Working in the wealthy and sophisticated and wealthy country means that our business does not contribute to the overall economic development of the country. However, our business is more than an entry strategy. A valid reason for being here in this capacity is that it is a holistic approach. We are placing ourselves in this arena and running our business in a Christ-like manner. Our actions speak louder than our words!*

bandwagon without a workable plan. This would lead to failure of both business and ministry objectives. Others might view business as an easy means to an end (visa, financial income, access strategy, etc.) and find themselves so distracted by the demands of the "means" that their original "end" is never reached. Thorough policy development by mission agencies, including clear leadership and accountability structures for Business as mission, is necessary to prevent this from happening. Business expertise, a solid business plan, adequate capitalisation, and the formation of clear kingdom goals are essential. Fraudulent business must be avoided through a thorough assessment of each opportunity.

The demands or even the success of the business, could lead some to stray from their original mission goals. Thought must be given to ownership structure and the use of profit in order to provide adequate accountability and to guard against falling prey to the love of money. These are dangers for any Christian in any business. It is easy to be seduced by worldly values and ambition (2 Corinthians 1:12). But this also applies to all types of ministry. The key to prevention is to nurture a godly personal motivation. This is a matter of personal discipleship and accountability. Spiritual oversight and evaluation processes can help to keep biblical values at the forefront. Context is a factor since corruption and unethical practice is more accepted in some societies. Training in Christian business and financial ethics appropriate to the cultural context is required.

> *In China, there is saying "bu jian bu shang", which when translated means "one cannot be successful in business without first being cunning". We are sad to see Christian businesses, founded with the aim of glorifying the name of God, fall prey to worldliness. I know of a Chinese Christian brother who uses his business premises to disciple young believers and serves as an underground church for regular meetings He is able to contribute substantially to the mission work in that region. But when I casually asked him for advice on a business problem, his solution was simple – do it the way any Chinese businessman would. I was particularly disappointed that the missionary organisation that received his donations did not raise an eyebrow over his actions.*

(e) Doubts about whether missionaries should get involved in business – or business people in missions

Being an effective mission leader does not imply that a person will make a successful businessperson. Just as a businessperson needs to understand good mission practice, a person with a missionary background needs to understand and respect good business principles. Understanding, openness to learn, and above all, practical experience are the best indicators of future success. There is a clear need for people to be teamed with others with complementary skills. Working alongside established entrepreneurs (or missionary veterans, as applicable) is essential.

In the business world, outsourcing and strategic partnerships are the norm. There should be openness to providing expertise to one another. There is no need for kingdom business to automatically bypass traditional missionary structures and organisations. In order to be effective, synergy is needed. Affirmation of each other and the right application of complimentary gifts and abilities is of primary importance.

> *Many mission people who have tried to make the transition from 'full time ministry' to holistic ministry through business-as-mission have often been idealistic. They often discover that business-as-mission is even more full time than 'full time ministry'! They have been ill equipped, or given their 'blessing' before a serious assessment was made of the feasibility of the project or of the ability of the person who carried the vision. In our part of the world I see a lot of mission people with great potential to be successful in the transition to business-as-mission. We are entering an era where they can make the transition because support structures and the expertise needed for accountability and evaluation are coming into being.*

Operational Considerations for Business as mission

What follows is an outline of some operational considerations that arise when mission agencies incorporate into their organisation a Business as mission strategy. These are mostly questions that organisations will have to answer for themselves depending on their situation.

(a) Legal and Structural Issues

Structural and legal boundaries must exist between business and charitable or not-for-profit organisations. These are fundamentally important issues that must be acknowledged and will require policy. The term "Business as mission" does not mean a business masquerading in a charitable structure. There must be no confusion between the mission entity and the business entity in legal terms. Legal and revenue related issues arise that are related to the tax-exempt status of the charitable organisation. Being open and accountable about sources of funding or donations is essential. In the eyes of the government these boundaries exist to prevent not-for-profit entities competing unfairly with businesses. Great care must be taken when positioning any new business entity with regard to an existing not-for-profit organisation. Professional expertise must be sought.

> *In BA Company, we believe that a business should be both excellent in whatever business it is doing, and at the same time be excellent in the ways of the Lord. They are not mutually exclusive. The mission community must not assume that a business will be excellent simply through much prayer and perseverance. It cannot simply assume that every unqualified person with a mission calling will do excellent business so long as he entrusts himself to the Lord. In other words, not every missionary should be given the money to start a business just because he has the vision. He needs to be equipped, not only spiritually but also technically, or he must have access to people who are.*

(b) Funding and Salary Issues

Questions arise over whether a Business as mission worker should receive a salary through the business if they are also part of a mission agency. Or should they maintain an income from the agency or through donor support? Mission personnel pursuing a business strategy may have to combine sources of income to minimise the negative aspects of relying on either one or the other. In some cases in the initial stages, the business may only be able to support a minimum salary, or none at all. Will prayer and support networks be maintained? What will the supporting churches think? What is an "appropriate" level of income or standard of living and lifestyle? Should income be supplemented by business revenues? Will this create tension within the organisation? What should the accountability structure look like?

The issue of financial control might arise. A comment made by Indonesian mission leaders highlights this: "How will we control them (the ministry workers) if they have their own income, and are not looking to us to meet their needs?"

(c) Recruiting and Training

A special recruiting and training strategy is needed. Areas such as biblical knowledge, cultural awareness, language training (if necessary), and spiritual maturity will need to be assessed. It is likely that kingdom business initiatives will require skill sets that may not naturally be found through the organisation's normal recruiting procedures.

> *In our business we have made it a policy to take on potential BAM-ers and given them a "safer" environment to learn and develop. On the field we have laid down a number of training criteria for both the "stout business person" who feels God is calling them to take their business into an unreached situation, as well as for the "stout missions person" who feels God is calling them to walk the Business as mission route. When it comes to people who have been in missions for a long time, there is a need for serious soul searching and good business coaching by people IN THE FIELD. For business people, our initial list of required training included the "Personal Financial Freedom" course,[7] the World Perspectives course,[8] helping them understand the spiritual dynamics of doing business for the kingdom together with an awareness of the spiritual warfare involved. For all potential BAM-ers we asked them to do a business feasibility study and a ministry feasibility study.*

(d) Pastoral Care and Accountability Structures

Systems for accountability must address business and financial goals, kingdom goals for the business, and community and personal growth and development goals. It might be appropriate for different people or entities to hold the Business as

mission initiative accountable in each of these different areas. For example, a board of directors should monitor the financial/business decisions. A Great Commission Coordinator (GCC) or spiritual overseer should monitor the company's Great Commission goals. The mission agency could help in that arena, as well as help monitor goals for personal growth and development of personnel. There can be significant overlap between these different areas so integration may be appropriate.

An agreement about pastoral care should be reached. Pastoral care should be made available outside the leadership structure of the business itself. Resource sharing across organisations is often a good strategy.

> *Our mission has a team of counsellors in three locations across our region. They are made available to the wider mission community, including the BAMers for pastoral care, training (preventive counselling!), crises management and regular counselling.*

(e) Staffing and Resource Issues

There must be a realistic assessment about what resources can be released to support Business as mission initiatives and how support services will be administrated. Where kingdom businesses operate in close proximity to other ministry activities, an understanding should be established (even written) on how resources and personnel (staff time, facilities, and so on) will be shared. A clear distinction must be made between which financial resources are allocated to which entity. This will usually be a legal requirement.

> *I have been in the home offices of many organisations across the globe and have actively advocated business-as-mission as a concept. I usually get an enthusiastic response from home office folks when I share the potential for business to be a catalyst for holistic church planting efforts. But home office people have full plates. They are often suspicious or threatened by anything that smells of 'more work'. The big challenge we have faced is finding implementers that are actually able to serve the strategy that they endorse in principle.*

Partnership Examples

(a) Christian Missionary Fellowship (CMF) International

CMF International is a mission agency that has added Business as mission to its overall mission strategy. They have formed a separate, but linked not-for-profit agency. They did legal research into the question of taxation of for-profit ventures within the non-profit realm. They make capital investments into businesses that allow them to place personnel on the field, often among an unreached people group. The mission organisation is involved in recruiting, training, accountability, and pastoral care for Business as mission personnel. Start-up capital is raised through both venture capitalists and churches that want to donate funds where they see a mission purpose. Financial sustainability is a key marker for success. Two businesses are already profitable. The have established a policy related to "excess profits" that ties profits back into related ministry activities. Each venture has a culturally relevant ministry plan that is as important as its business plan. For a fuller case study on CMF – see Appendix E.

(b) J Organisation

J. Organisation takes indigenous evangelicals who reside in unreached environments and who have a passion for the gospel and gives them small business training. They focus on market-driven concepts and biblical foundations for enterprise. They help these people get started in their own small business via a loan. The purpose is always to aid in expanding the kingdom among their own people. J Organisation actively partners with agencies on the field who oversee the local program. Churches based in the USA supply short-term teams of business professionals and funding.

One successful example is the organisation's work with former Ethiopian Orthodox Priests that are passionate about planting churches in northern Ethiopia. There is little gospel activity present in that region. These church planters work closely with and under the spiritual authority of an international mission agency. They are trained in biblical story telling as part of the kingdom strategy. They are starting small companies primarily using irrigation pumps. They travel to different villages and use the pumps to take water from rivers to irrigate farmers' fields. There is a charge for providing this service. This business activity creates the opportunity for relationships, which opens doors for sharing the gospel. Each church planter has four villages that are visited twice a month. He is able to do business to meet his personal needs, and while doing that he can encourage small groups of believers in each village. One of these groups is made up entirely of "customers."

(c) Kuzoko Game Reserve

Kuzoko represents a major business investment in the Blue Crane Municipality of the Eastern Cape Province in South Africa. It is in one of the poorest provinces in the country, with 87% unemployment and an HIV infection rate of 20%. Given the high unemployment in the region, the strategy was to make an initial investment that would then stimulate other economic activity. The game reserve is projected to create over one hundred jobs on a sustainable basis. The management of Kuzuko Game Reserve is also encouraging the employees to set up their own enterprises. One such business is a fencing company that employs 70 people. The Kuzuko Game Reserve management has assisted the new company in drawing up a business plan, raising capital, and contract negotiation. The creation of jobs makes a significant impact on unemployment and poverty in the area.

As employers, they believe that they should not also play the role of the pastor, so they invite other agencies to come and run mission and church programs. They encourage staff to attend services, but there is no coercion or discrimination. Spiritual transformation is taking place through Kuzuko as they facilitate missions. The result has been that almost 50% of their employees have come to faith in Christ.

Part IV: Looking Forward
8.STRATEGIC RECOMMENDATIONS
Specific Steps for Action
General Observations

We recognise that the Holy Spirit is awakening and restoring the business community to use its skills and resources for building the kingdom of God. In alignment with the strong emphasis of Lausanne Forum 2004, we recognise mission as holistic transformation. Transformational, kingdom focused business is therefore part of our mission. In order to realise the potential of this movement and following God's leading, it is our imperative to take strategic action.

First, we identify some general areas around which we should give prayerful consideration for the development and implementation of strategy. This will be followed by some specific recommendations and a call to action directed to key parts of the Body of Christ.

(a) Imparting Vision and Mobilisation

The concept of business as a kingdom building resource and its strategic nature is still fairly new, and sometimes even foreign to many. As outlined more fully in Chapter 6, there is a critical need to impart vision for transforming business and for the development of numerous mobilisation tools and programmes.

(b) Significant Release of Capital

Adequate capital will be required to

implement successful Business as mission initiatives, especially on a larger scale. In order to enable the generation, release, and appropriate use of significant wealth to meet the needs of the Business as mission movement and the communities that are to be targeted, a "framework of leverage" is needed. This would involve bringing together of venture capital, merchant banking and other relevant business skills. Those who have experience and competencies in these domains need to intentionally and creatively engage with Business as mission. It is imagined that this will include using the skills, resources, networks, etc. of transnational corporations and government agencies as well.

(c) Matchmaking Both People and Capital

Both people and capital exist "out there" in the Christian business community and beyond. Mobilising these resources is the first step. However, many viable Business as mission opportunities have suffered as a result of not making the right connections. A major challenge is to proactively develop matchmaking processes. This will take people and resources. Facilitators are needed, together with an adequate support and accountability structure.

In order to support and multiply the development of new and existing kingdom businesses, there is also a great need for mentors. Those with the relevant experience, networks, intellectual capital, and technology need to be intentionally seeking to develop business-to-business mentoring models.

(d) Capacity Building

Once we have begun effectively mobilising and matchmaking new resources in terms of people and capital, do we have the capacity to handle them and offer effective deployment and support services? At the sending end, do we have the capacity to accommodate and train people? In the field, is there a receptivity to accept and integrate these strategies? We need to ensure that we have functional entities on both ends that can effectively handle people and money and make strategic decisions. We need effective cross-cultural communication, and to build understanding, both between sending and in-field locations, and between those from a business culture and those from a mission culture.

(e) Capturing Intellectual Capital

There is a need for good theology and research, and for relevant strategy, reflection, and action. We need to further develop the theology of work and business in conjunction with field-based strategies and practice. There are lessons to be learned from the history of missions and from Business as mission initiatives that have had a transformational impact.

(f) Case Studies

A crucial facet of capturing intellectual capital is the gathering of case studies. Case studies need to be researched, documented and evaluated. Telling inspiring stories, sharing good practice, and learning from experience will assist in all the other areas of strategic action.

There needs to be a commitment on the part of kingdom businesses themselves to consistently document sector-specific case studies of cutting-edge business initiatives and enterprise. This should be done through analysis and the application of thorough reviews generated by adequate evaluation mechanisms.

(g) Macro Level Thinking

We want to effect radical, holistic transformation of society's economic systems and structures. The reality of globalisation is increasingly having direct impact on people of all nations and cultures everywhere. As Christians we must intentionally seek to align business with kingdom of God purposes at a macro- level.

We must focus strategic thinking on the equipping and enabling of kingdom businesses that can competitively operate in a global market. This should include taking into account emerging markets and global trends. By capitalising on emerging opportunities, there is the potential to put kingdom businesses in the best position to set the pace and industry standards, and as market leaders, to command significant market share on a global level. For example, emerging issues include the movement of human and intellectual capital, technology transfer, and outsourcing to emerging markets. Another important area requiring consideration is how to respond to the global implications related to changes in access to and the use of essential natural resources such as water and energy.

(h) Building of Strategic Alliances

In business it is important to always look for leverage points and alliances that can create synergy. There are churches, mission agencies, and marketplace ministries involved in or exploring Business as mission. Where there is a felt need, it is important to explore the benefit of creating national, regional, and international strategic alliances with others that share values and purpose.

We also need cross-discipline partnerships between business and areas such as politics, education, healthcare, and other relevant areas. There needs to be an emphasis on the development of strategic partnerships and alliances that can leverage political influence at local, national, regional, and global levels. This could include engaging government at both the local and national levels, as has been the case in areas of Central Asia.

(i) Consultations, Events, and Facilitators

To be able to empower and support the Business as mission movement, people are needed to serve as facilitators. There is a need for regional and national Business as mission consultations, facilitators and equipping events. Funding is needed to further these.

> *"Holy people must stop going into "church work" as their natural course of action and take up holy orders of farming, industry, law education, banking and journalism with the same zeal previously given to traditional evangelism, pastoral or missionary work."*
>
> - Dallas Willard – The Spirit of the Disciplines

Specific Strategic Recommendations

(a) To the Church World-Wide

There is a need for the church to recognise that the Holy Spirit is restoring the role of business in the mobilisation of resources for mission and the extension of God's kingdom. The following are strategic recommendations:

1. All churches and Christian organisations, on every continent, must closely examine beliefs and practices with regards to:
   - the sacred-secular dichotomised worldview
   - the clergy-laity concept and divide.
2. To develop concepts of a biblical holistic worldview, that positively restores the role of business into the church at large.
3. To catalyse and mobilise the business community through affirming, equipping, and releasing business people for their kingdom building vocational role.
4. To endorse and promote the Lausanne Business as mission Manifesto on the role of kingdom business and Christian business people.

Practical tip: *give a sermon (or two!) on Business as mission, using the material provided in this report!*

(b) To Christians in Business

Business in itself is an activity that can glorify God. In addition, it is a strategic means by which the great commission and the great commandment can be fulfilled. Considering this, the following recommendations are given:

1. Receive the affirmation of the vocational calling of business. Strive to further understand the theological basis of how business practices and profits can be something good and gifted by God.
2. Discover God's specific purpose for your business. Strive to identify kingdom returns as well as financial returns. Identify the impacts of the business on the local economy and environment and how the business can work with the local church and the church at large.
3. Establish a clear accountability and support framework for the business in terms of the economic, social, environmental, and spiritual impacts.
4. Identify potential mentors and leadership development relationships.

And if God has called and equipped you to do business, ask yourself:

1. Where shall I do business? Maybe you are called to an area of the world where the name of Jesus is rarely heard, or in the most poor and needy communities or nations?
2. How can I do business in such a way that God is being glorified? How can the kingdom of God be demonstrated and manifested in and through my business? Do I have a kingdom of God plan for my business as well as a business plan? Should I invite someone to be the "kingdom auditor" of my business?
3. Can I assist by being a mentor to someone in my country or in other countries?

4. What other Christians in business can I link up with, others who also have a vision for business as mission?

Practical Tip: Use the Resource Directory accompanying this report to find relevant books and websites to help you explore these issues.

(c) To Workplace and Marketplace Ministries

There are numerous workplace (or marketplace) organisations and ministries around the world. They have different purposes and agendas. We recommend that these groups:

1. Learn about business as mission and transformational business and prayerfully consider embracing and incorporating business as mission into their ministries.
2. Develop partnerships with others that are working on business as mission, whether churches, missions agencies, or other workplace ministries.
3. Sponsor and facilitate national and regional business as mission consultations and joint collaboration and learning.
4. Mobilize your constituencies to participate in business as mission initiatives.

Practical tip: Include business as mission in the program in one of your meetings!

(d) To Mission Agencies and Executives

Mission agencies are key partners and need to develop a framework for engaging with the work of kingdom businesses. It is recommended that they:

1. Develop a kingdom business perspec-

tive by utilising current and future programs of learning, applicable to both short and long term personnel.
2. Encourage and facilitate research and case studies for specific enterprises and their kingdom impact.
3. Create collaboration between mission agencies and businesses in order to further mutual objectives and release resources.
4. Develop wider and more creative recruitment campaigns for those with business skills, including the creation of opportunities for business people through the church.
5. Develop long term business as mission strategies within the organisation — this would include undertaking surveys and audits on business as mission activities.

Practical tip: Write about business as mission in your newsletter, magazine, website, etc.

(e) To Christian Training Institutions

The changing face of missions and the decreasing number of people entering Christian training institutions needs to be addressed. The following recommendations are applied to Bible Colleges, Seminaries, Christian Universities, and other centres of Christian learning:

1. Incorporate a kingdom business perspectives course into current and future programs of learning, for both short and long term programs.
2. In order to enrich the above recommendation, encourage and facilitate current research and case studies on specific enterprises and their kingdom impact.

3. Develop and run courses encompassing a biblically integrated holistic worldview. Develop and run courses on business as mission. These courses could also be offered and made available to MBA and Economics students in other academic institutions.

4. Create internship programs with kingdom-focused companies and encourage collaboration of these companies in joint learning.

5. Encourage the creation of kingdom business alumni networks and kingdom focused business-angel and venture capital networks.

Practical tip: Run a one-day seminar on business as mission. See Resource Directory for further tips.

(f) To the Christian Media

The rise of new multimedia technology provides an opportunity for the expansion of kingdom business initiatives. In order to achieve this, the following actions are recommended:

1. Help facilitate the use of all media available to promote business as mission activities and materials such as case studies, articles, and regular feature columns that promote transformational business awareness through examples.

2. Use of multimedia and on-line technology for kingdom business training, development, and guidance

3. Encourage closer working relationships between business and the media in developing media strategies and policies, taking into account issues of sensitivity and risk.

9. THE BUSINESS AS MISSION MANIFESTO

The Lausanne (LCWE)[9] 2004 Forum Business as Mission Issue Group worked for a year, addressing issues relating to God's purposes for work and business, the role of business people in church and missions, the needs of the world, and the potential response of business. The group consisted of more than 70 people from all continents. Most came from a business background, but there were also church and mission leaders, educators, theologians, lawyers, and researchers. The collaboration process included 60 papers, 25 cases studies, several national and regional business as mission consultations, and email-based discussions, culminating in a week of face to face dialogue and work. These are **some** of our observations.

Affirmations

- We believe that **God** has created all men and women in His image with the ability to be creative, creating good things for themselves and for others -- this includes business.

- We believe in following in the footsteps of **Jesus**, who constantly and consistently met the needs of the people He encountered, thus demonstrating the love of God and the rule of His kingdom.

- We believe that the **Holy Spirit** empowers all members of the **Body of Christ** to serve, and to meet the real spiritual and physical needs of others, demonstrating the kingdom of God.

- We believe that God has called and equipped business people to make a

Kingdom difference in and through their businesses.

- We believe that the **gospel** has the power to transform individuals, communities and societies. Christians in business should therefore be a part of this holistic transformation through business.
- We recognise the fact that poverty and unemployment are often rampant in areas where the name of Jesus is rarely heard and understood.
- We recognise both the dire need for and the importance of business development. However, it is more than just business per se. **Business as mission** is about business with a Kingdom of God perspective, purpose, and impact.
- We recognise that there is a need for job creation and for multiplication of businesses all over the world, aiming at the quadruple bottom line: spiritual, economical, social and environmental transformation.
- We recognise the fact that the church has a huge and largely untapped resource in the Christian business community to meet needs of the world — in and through business — and bring glory to God in the market place and beyond.

Recommendations

We call upon the Church worldwide to identify, affirm, pray for, commission, and release business people and entrepreneurs to exercise their gifts and calling as business people in the world — among all peoples and to the ends of the earth.

We call upon business people globally to receive this affirmation and to consider how their gifts and experience might be used to help meet the world's most pressing spiritual and physical needs through Business as mission.

Conclusion

The real bottom line of business as mission is **AMDG - *ad maiorem Dei gloriam*** — for the greater glory of God.

Business as Mission Issue Group
October 2004

APPENDICES
APPENDIX A PARTICIPANTS

Convening Team
Mats Tunehag, Sweden – Convenor
Wayne McGee, USA/Africa/UK – Co-convenor
Josie Plummer, UK – Facilitator

Issue Group Members

Crystal Alman, Colombia/USA
Etienne Atger, France
D Batchelder, USA
Alan Bergstedt, USA
Branko Bjelajac, Serbia & Montenegro
Mark Boyce, USA
H.Fernando Bullon, Costa Rica
David Bussau, Australia
Joao Mordomo, Brazil
Julie Chambliss, USA
Chuck Chan, China
David de Groen, Australia
Miguel Angel De Marco, Argentina/USA
Hartwig Eitzen, Paraguay
Norm Ewert, USA
Dan Fredericks, USA
Hans Udo Fuchs, Brazil/Angola
Edward S. Gaamuwa, Uganda
Zack Gakunju, Kenya
Ricky Gnanakan, India
Harry Goodhew, Australia
Paul Heiss, USA
Kent Humphreys, USA

Neal Johnson, USA
Isaac Kasana, Uganda
Dibinga Kashale, Cote d'Ivoire
Victor Kathramalla, India
Jorg Knoblauch, Germany
Sergey Lisunov, Kyrgyzstan
David Llewellyn, USA
Adrian McComb, Australia
Stuart McGreevy, UK
Roweena Mendoza, Philippines
Alfred Neufeld, Paraguay
Jorge Nunez, Argentina
Flavio Jason Orr, Brazil
Mike Perreau, UK
Doug Priest, USA
Bill Rigden UK/South Asia
Steve Rundle, USA
Lindy Scott, USA
Tom Sudyk, USA
Lynda Sudyk, USA
Daron Tan, Malaysia
Eric Tan NH, Singapore
Dennis Tongoi, Kenya
Tim Waddell, USA

John Warton, USA
Jane Wathome, Kenya
Cade Willis, USA/Singapore
Galina Zhanbekova, Kazakhstan
Craig, Canada
DMM, Turkey
Kay, Turkey

Additional Issue Group Members
(Contributing by email but not at Forum)
Mike Baer, USA
Steve Beck, USA
W Chan, Hong Kong
M G, India
Makonen Getu, UK
Martien Kelderman, New Zealand
Scott McFarlane, USA
Xavier Molinari, France
Dwight Nordstrom, USA
John Ong, Singapore
M Stoltz, USA
Kim Tan, UK
Jonathan Thornton, UK
Dag Wilund, Sweden

APPENDIX B
ASSIGNMENT AND PROCESS
Forum Brief

The Forum 2004 was convened by the Lausanne Committee for World Evangelization (LCWE) with the vision to examine through unprecedented global inquiry, the trends and needs in evangelism and in response, develop specific action plans for Church leaders to use in addressing our most difficult local and global evangelism issues.

The brief from LCWE to each Issue Group was to create a well researched paper on the assigned issue which would be presented at the Forum and consequently published as a Lausanne Occasional Paper. The paper was to:

- Identify the questions that are involved in the topic and outline the obstacles to breakthroughs in global evangelism directly related to the issue.
- Consider the theological underpinnings of the issue.
- Collect some of the best case studies that will help others to understand the issue and ways of responding to it.
- Develop specific and pragmatic strategies that will stimulate the Church to action, encompassing recommendations that could be implemented globally, nationally, and locally.

Purpose and Objectives of the Business as Mission Issue Group

The business as mission Issue Group first examined this task as it related to business as mission identifying their main purpose and primary objectives:

Purpose

To examine the obstacles, challenges, and opportunities to glorify God globally by furthering His kingdom through the strategy of business as mission, and through our deliberations and findings to bring strategic recommendations to the Church world-wide on ways to respond to these opportunities and challenges.

Objective 1

To examine God's purposes for business and to develop a biblical perspective on stewardship, work, and business as it relates to the holistic mission of the Church in the world.

Objective 2

Learn from examples of Christians who have made strategic differences in societies through business, especially on the mission field, seeing the kingdom of God impact peoples lives spiritually, socially, and economically.

Objective 3

Explore ways to mobilise the Christian business community, impart a vision for business as mission, affirm them in their calling, and provide connection for practical application for their ministry in mission settings.

Objective 4

Explore business as mission's potential impact and implications on existing mission and development paradigms and practices, theologically and operationally.

Objective 5

Identify national, regional, and global business as mission networks and initiatives, and support them by producing a comprehensive list of available resources including published materials, training programmes, web based resources, and others.

Working Groups were formed to tackle each objective with each Issue Group member contributing to one or two of the Working Groups. Discussion and writing papers on various critical issues for each objective took place by email in preparation for the Forum. Before the Forum in September 2004, the Convening Team prepared a draft document based on the sum of the preliminary work. The majority of the Issue Group members gathered together during the Forum for vital discussion and further editing work, as well as for strategic planning for the future. The authorship of the paper is therefore rightly attributed to all of the business as mission Issue Group contributors listed in Appendix A. The final editing, however, was carried out by the Convening Team, who assume full responsibility for any errors and omissions in the finished document.

Business as Mission Issue Group
Convening Team

Mats Tunehag, Convenor
Wayne McGee, Co-convenor
Josie Plummer, Facilitator

APPENDIX C
ADDITIONAL GENERAL CASE STUDIES

BA Company

In Singapore in 1991, John, who was a career missionary, was given a consultancy by a local Christian business man. The business man would continue as Principal Consultant and make the money; John would disburse it. Sensing that there was something more, they set up BA as a limited liability company to own the consultancy and other businesses that the Lord might give them. John understood that BA was to establish righteous, redemptive businesses, dedicated to the Lord and operating on kingdom principles.

John shares, "There is power in discipling in the workplace, where most Christians spend much of their time and where their character flaws will be exposed. In church the Word may only be spoken, in the workplace it must be lived, and Christian responses modelled in real (e.g. ethical) challenges. It is better to teach a man to fish than to give him a fish, but it is better still to teach a suitable man to manage a fish farm. Then he will learn not just a practical skill, but character and ethical skills."

BA now operates in Southeast Asia, East Asia, and the Middle East. BAX (in a less-reached Southeast Asian nation) was established in 1995 as an investment company, with seed funding from BA Singapore. Later, an import-export company was added. The companies now employ expatriates from several nations and numerous nationals. Business activities have included rural craft, tile-making, and sewing projects, an art and design studio, a coffee shop employing ex-prostitutes, a metalwork business employing youths from squatter communities, and a website design business. Garment inspection and palm sugar export are being investigated. Each project has its own rationale. Some have been small, replicable, village-based, and people-intensive. They have enabled preaching points and churches to be set up and people have come to Christ. Others reflect BA's concern for the very poor and disadvantaged, and some of these run with associated small-business loans. We are now developing projects to employ more educated urban nationals in whose hands the future of the nation rests.

BAX has spun off a local NGO that now involves around 150 nationals and has become the main ministry arm. It incorporates a small children's home and job creation projects.

Since 1995, a BA representative office has provided a ministry platform in a large, less open nation. This has enabled the presence of a language translation business whose primary objective is to disciple young nationals. More recently a restaurant has been set up, to employ nationals with a wider range of skills. BA does not run these businesses.

Underlying values of the in-field businesses are to model righteous business with redemptive purpose, provide independence, dignity, and discipleship through employment, and give legitimate identity to foreign professionals and local church leaders.

Those involved view the Lord as the owner of BA. Equity holders sign a declaration that they are acting only as stewards, and have no beneficial interest. Business and Great Commission (GC) oversight are kept separate. The GC Overseer sits on the Board, but has minimal operational function.

The idea is not to build a BA empire. They have avoided a business conglomerate approach. The companies are linked relationally but not legally. Oversight operates through servant leadership, spiritual authority, and fellowship. They accept the risk of possible abuse of the BA name. The prayer is that BA businesses will spin off indigenous movements amongst the target peoples. These may be businesses, local NGOs, churches, or new business as mission movements!

John has no interest in business for business' sake, he says, "To chop down a tree, we use the best available tool, whether a sharp axe or chain saw. For world evangelisation, the best tool may often be business. I soon discovered that carrying a business card is a conversation starter, whereas saying "I am a missionary" is a conversation-ender! Our Gospel is too powerful to lock up in traditional concepts of mission, church buildings, and activities."

BA Singapore has released some US $200,000 to support missions and missionaries globally. The investments prioritise business as mission start-ups with people whom their staff know and can relate to. These projects must have GC oversight and short-term initial support for missionaries from the developing world.

John concludes, "Our in-field companies have been only marginally profitable, and have not usually financially supported the field missionaries who have set them up. Viewed as business this is not great -- but neither is the performance of many other businesses in our operating environments. The most important thing is that a range of ministries have been established without creating dependency or the need of donor funding."

Clínica Bíblica: The Business of Healthcare, the Ministry of Healing
(a) Purpose, History, and Structural Overview

The Clínica Bíblica Hospital and Medical Centre in San José, Costa Rica, has grown and adapted over 75 years to boldly proclaim the kingdom of God through improving the medical and spiritual well-being of a community in need. Clínica Bíblica (literally, "Bible-Based Clinic") is a Christian ministry-become-enterprise that was originally founded 1921, by British missionary couple Harry and Susan Strachan. The Strachan's arrived in San José to focus on evangelizing a largely godless population. What they encountered was an infant mortality rate of 1 in 3 and a hungry and chronically ill child population in desperate need of medical care. Their vision soon expanded to improving the physical wellbeing of the population, especially its children.

Since it opened its doors in July 1929, the Clínica Bíblica has committed itself to bringing medical care to the Costa

Rican population regardless of race, religion, or ability to pay. Today, the original two-story building still stands in the shadows of the five story hospital, a twelve-story medical office complex and a 180,000 square foot addition that will triple the size of the hospital when it is finished. This mammoth campus, in the centre of what is quickly becoming San José's official medical district, is today's Clínica Bíblica.

From day one the clinic encountered what many organisations with similar goals encounters: exponential demand versus limited resources. During the 1940's and 50's, Clínica Bíblica was able to play a key role, through the generosity of many Americans and the heart of many local professionals, in the expansion of medical availability in Costa Rica.

Additionally, the quality of the medical services at the clinic attracted even the wealthiest citizens in need of emergency procedures and routine care. For the first time, the doctors were able to charge a fee for services provided, and the ministry was no longer so largely dependent on donations. This would prove to be crucial in later years. Even today, Christian or non-Christian, wealthy or poor, residents from anywhere in the country will tell you that Clínica Bíblica is simply the best medical care there is in Costa Rica.

During the early years, the operations and finances depended largely on one woman from Winnipeg, Canada. Dr. Marie C. Cameron, who served as chief surgeon at the hospital for thirty-six years. Her decision to retire in 1968 left a seemingly bottomless hole. Faced with financial and missiological crisis, the decision was made by the largely North American leadership to close the hospital in one month. It was at this crossroads that a crucial decision had to be made that would affect the hospital for decades to come. The question was: Is the quality medical care and excellent medical training that Clínica Bíblica provides so valuable to Costa Rica that the local community will be willing to direct as well as fund the clinic themselves? The answer: Yes, it was.

The funds were raised in under thirty days, and with great reservation, the hospital was turned over for the first time to Costa Rican ownership. In 1968, Clínica Bíblica came under the direction of the newly formed ASEMECO (Costa Rican Medical Services Association). The board of volunteers is largely Costa Rican and is responsible for all ASEMECO decisions. It exists to grow and sustain the hospital and all its other ministries to meet the medical and spiritual needs of Costa Rican citizens.

Today, the majority of patients arrive not in taxis or luxury cars at the front doors of the hospital, but by public buses coming from the various neighbourhoods and slums surrounding the city. These poor (and often refugees from nearby countries) who fall through the cracks of the national Social Security system, enter Clínica Bíblica's doors to receive the medical care they are prevented from receiving at a state hospital. Quite simply, Clínica Bíblica's policy is not to deny medical care to anyone, regardless of citizenship or financial ability.

The hospital is open twenty-four hours a day, filling prescriptions, performing surgery, or fighting cancer. This kingdom work expands beyond the borders of medicine. On the second story of the hospital is the chaplain's office, who leads staff Bible studies and makes daily visits to patients' rooms for prayer. There is also an in-house beauty salon. The clinic believes that those who look good, feel good, and it strives to meet *all* physical needs of the person during their stay in the hospital.

With so much "charity," how does Clínica Bíblica remain financially sustainable? This is the key: Those who *can* pay for the medical services and medication they receive *do* pay. They will pay, because they want the best. From there, people pay on a sliding scale according to ability. The combined income from every department, laboratory and *farmacia* in the ASEMECO network, as well as reimbursements from the Social Security department of the Costa Rican government, are enough to subsidise the medical care of all needy patients. One third of income goes towards building and maintenance costs, one third goes towards medical equipment, and one third goes to fund other medical or social action ministries throughout the community directed or supported by ASEMECO. As an example, during the Fiscal Year 2003, ASEMECO generated $20.6 million. The five year average had been $15.7 million. After supporting its many dependent community ministries and subsidising thousands of patients, ASEMECO earned nearly $1.6 million in profits.

(b) Lessons to learn from Clinica Biblica

1. Unashamed presentation of the gospel — proclaiming the Kingdom of God — will be accepted (tolerated at least) if the product or service provided is the best available.

Several years ago, at the groundbreaking ceremony for the new hospital expansion, the President of Costa Rica turned over one shovel of dirt. Gospel tracts produced by the clinic are displayed prominently at every admissions desk, yet over one hundred non-believing doctors still come to work each day. Why? Because Clínica Bíblica offers the best medical care available. Much of this case study comes back to this reality, but it cannot be overstated for the simple reason that being the best in an industry opens financial, governmental and influential doors that few other attributes can.

2. Incorporating non-Christian workers into an evangelical Christian enterprise environment can maximize performance and create internal witnessing opportunities.

Surprisingly, only half of the medical staff employed by the clinic profess to be evangelical. Faith is not the deciding factor for employment. For Clínica Bíblica to hire only evangelicals would compromise the quality of their service and eliminate a key ministry to many of Costa Rica's most successful medical professionals. The desire of ADEMESCO is to hire the best professionals available and to integrate them into an overtly evangelical environment. This is, in itself, an internal ministry of the hospital.

Roblealto chicken farm and children's ministry in San José, closely linked with Clínica Bíblica in community outreach efforts, also employs hard-working believers and non-believers alike. Roblealto invites them into a Christian environment where they are exposed to weekly Bible studies, daily prayer, and the personal witness of dozens of co-workers who view their jobs as their ministries. Obviously, there are some positions in these ministries — especially Roblealto children's ministry, for example, where evangelical Christian workers are essential to the mission of the enterprise.

3. Implement local leadership at all levels of the organisation and intentionally transition to local leadership over a period of time.

From the outset, local Costa Rican women with hearts for the mission of the clinic volunteered their time and services to assist as nurses especially in the areas of surgery and gynaecology. Taking advantage of this willing workforce, but very aware of its narrow skills base, the hospital opened a nursing school less than ten years after the inauguration of their first facility. As the hospital has grown, so has the nursing school. Today, the school is looked upon as Clínica Bíblica's greatest contribution to Costa Rican healthcare. Numerous other medical missions around the world have failed or dropped into obscurity over the decades as the stream of

North American medical professionals has dried up. Graduating and employing a constant supply of new Costa Rican nurses ensures a workforce that, by the nature of their education, is equipped to meet the high standards of the clinic. This educational opportunity alone is a kingdom-building activity and is beneficial to the longevity of the hospital.

Despite early reliance on foreign leadership, the hospital has empowered Costa Ricans in key professional positions within the organisation, and it so commended itself to influential figures in the local community that these individuals felt comfortable *asking* for control of the enterprise when the crisis came in 1968. Without the Strachans, Cameron, or other early professionals, the Costa Ricans would never have learned the skills they needed to be able to practice excellent medicine and to earn money in the process.

4. Subsidising goods and services for those who do not need a subsidy is not always appropriate.

If Christian enterprises are going to enter a community with the intention of offering goods or services at a subsidised rate, they must carefully consider where that subsidy will come from. If it cannot come in part, from other members of the local population, the enterprise may need to be re-evaluated. The litmus test for Clínica Bíblica's price list is whether the highest rates charged for medical care are still reasonable. The popularity of the hospital among Costa Rica's wealthy and the loyalty of patients, even with the existence of the other private hospitals, indicates that they are.

5. A Christian business can remain true to its original mission without compromising its growth, and vice versa.

The original mission of the Strachans has been carefully and prayerfully maintained over seventy-five years. Clínica Bíblica's desire to minister to the spiritual and medical needs of the Costa Rican community, without access to medicine, children especially, remains uncompromised to this day. That does not mean, however, that the clinic ministers *only* to this population. In 1968, part of the reasoning behind the initial decision to close the clinic was that the majority of Costa Ricans without access to medical care were living in the rural areas and mountains outside the city. The clinic, it was thought, should relocate to a rural area to avoid mission drift.

Rather, thanks to the last-minute financial support and united leadership of local medical professionals (the first ASEMECO board) the hospital found a different solution. Remaining in the city and ministering to the medical and spiritual needs of the urban population would sustain a stream of income that could be used to fund new and expanded medical ministries in the rural areas. Trying to fund a rural medical enterprise without income from the main downtown facility would have been nearly impossible. Since that critical year, ASEMECO uses one third of its income to support ministries of social action, rural medical assistance and training, children's health, and evangelism --

all Kingdom activities done in the name of Christ. Mission growth and mission drift are two different things. Often, mission growth may provide the capital and influence necessary to ensure that the original mission is met for years to come.

6. Interest for the Kingdom of God at large demands that Christian enterprises partner with others of similar objectives whenever appropriate.

The first and best example is ASEMECO's partnership with Roblealto Children's Ministry. Again, Roblealto's mission is to minister to the spiritual and physical needs of Costa Rican children from broken homes or abusive situations. While not entirely self-sustaining and dependent upon large sums of donor support, much of Roblealto's income comes from profits of a chicken-hatching operation under the same name that meets 85 percent of the Costa Rican demand for egg-laying chickens. How do these two Christian ministry-businesses work together?

Clínica Bíblica uses its medical expertise to meet the medical needs of Roblealto children and benefits by ministering to children they would not otherwise meet. Roblealto is able to more fully fulfil its mission by meeting immediate medical and nutritional needs of its children. For both of these organizations to refrain from cooperation would compromise the breadth of Clínica Bíblica's ministry and the depth of Roblealto's.

Conclusion

The biblical principles found in the literature of Clínica Bíblica are the same ones that are encountered in practice.

They are able, while fully embraced by a modern secular society and government, to successfully and sustainably proclaim the Kingdom of God through economic and ministry activities that meet the very real spiritual and medical needs of their own people.

APPENDIX D
OBSTACLES AND SOLUTIONS TO BUSINESS AND CHURCH/MISSION PARTNERSHIP

In this exercise we were looking at barriers in terms of both perception and reality. We initially divided the Issue Group into 1) business people; and 2) church/mission people to discuss obstacles and concerns from both sides of the existing sacred/secular divide. For some, the distinction was false because they would have described themselves as either, but we asked them to choose which they most related to for the purpose of the discussion. We then mixed the groups and discussed solutions.

Obstacles Perceived by Business People:
What are the **obstacles** and **concerns** to partnership between missions, churches and business?

- Lack of clear lines of demarcation between what is business and what is church, including lines of responsibility, accountability, and expectations up front. Conflicts of interest of personnel involved in business between activities in church/ministry and time/money allocated to what they do.

- Control of the assets and operations of the business by the local church in the partnership.

- Misunderstanding of business concepts, especially profit, which is perceived as bad or unholy. A feeling that money and profit are dirty, and that money is the root of all evil (instead of the *love of* money), especially in an ex-communist society.

- Each side is intimidated by the other; business is intimidated by the spirituality of the church people.

- Different language, culture, and work ethic, and a misconception that missionaries spend time praying and relating, and will forgive if they are cheated, while business people are tougher and want things done.

- High expectations on the business as mission person by the church that he should give away all his profits, as opposed to recognizing it as a ministry in itself.

- Misconception of business by the church in terms of being seen as only providing finances, serving on committees, or merely providing free services to the church, etc.

- In some countries, business people are using their status in the church for their own commercial purposes instead of spiritual purposes.

- Business and church would each want the best people, giving rise to competition for personnel.

- Potential conflicts related to mixing of money from non-profit/church with business. Jeopardizing tax-free status of the non-profit will complicate matters.

- Pressure of needing to be accountable for how many souls are saved as business as mission company reports to the home or local church.
- Holistic mission is not readily understood among the clergy; dualism is ingrained and perpetuated by pastors in their seminary training, and clergy may be too busy to try to understand holistic mission concepts.

Obstacles Perceived by Church/Mission People

What are the **obstacles** and **concerns** to partnership between missions/churches and business?

- Seminaries reinforce the sacred-secular and clergy-laity dichotomy.
- Spirituality and poverty in some places are closely associated (e.g. Latin America), so poverty may be spiritualized.
- Tendency towards "independent types" running business (entrepreneurial spirit) can often result in the lack of association, affiliation, and partnership, or a sense of belonging to a bigger movement or a church, church planting movement, mission agency, etc.
- Business people in other nations tend to go to international churches rather than local churches.
- Business people do not learn the local language or the cultural context at a deeper level.
- Whoever has the money holds the power, exhibited in cases of pastors

not challenging morality or ethics of business people, projects standing or falling with the nod of a businessperson, and board members who do not know missiological issues, but have the money-take-project decisions.

- Mutual lack of respect for each others gifting.
- Discrepancies of lifestyle between pastors and business people.
- Business people don't tend to talk about structural sin very much. Latin American churches see structural sin challenged in the Bible and talk about it; there is a "disconnect" between first world business people and this perspective in the developing world.
- Dilemma of whether an economic solution should be used for a "biblical" problem.
- Church has little business experience.
- Business is essentially "survival of the fittest" and individualistic, and this is opposed to the faith, which is inclusive.
- Bad experiences of the wrong mixing of church and business matters have soured things. This is a historical fact.
- A need not to polarize pastors and business people, because there are pastors who are both business people and also pastors. We need to acknowledge this. There are models of this in Africa.
- Mission agencies and churches feel it is their responsibility to do mission, so there can be an obstacle in seeing a businessman with a different lifestyle doing mission.

Suggested Solutions to the Obstacles and Concerns

From mixed groups of business people and church/mission people:

- Just as we pray for regular missionaries, we should pray collectively for successful Business as mission efforts.
- Make it clear who determines which ministries are blessed by profits of a business as mission company. Should the church of the business person be involved in determining where the money goes?
- Need to build bridges between churches and businesses; start at the local church level within congregations.
- Examine the areas where both groups can help each other. Run a business as mission course in seminaries and at the local church level. Teach about God's word in the marketplace and its applications.
- Secular – spiritual dichotomy can be addressed at the grassroots level. Business as mission business people have to disciple other business as mission business people.
- Need for one-on-one dialogue between business people and church and mission people, rather than organization to organization. Not a debate but a dialogue.
- The money that the church wants should be addressed up front by the business. Business never asks money from the church so it should be same vice versa.

- It is a good idea for the church to validate that the business can use its profits for good works in the community, and that this is an appropriate use of the profits. This does not refer to tithing.
- Seminaries have addressed business as mission -- setting models, training individuals, and in some countries, having teachers/leaders partially or fully supported by business.
- In seminaries, successful business people who have seen business as mission working should teach it.
- At the mission agency level, business as mission should be taught by practitioners.
- Recognize that there are two cultures – business and mission. We should be applying the cross-cultural missiological methods that we know!
- Take business as mission people, pastors, and theologians to business schools to help them understand the ethical issues. Help business people catch a vision for the need.
- In the seminary or business school, you should have a business as mission practitioner and a theology teacher teaching side by side.
- Business as mission people and other lay people should teach – empower laity.
- Money be given anonymously so no one feels they have the right to pull strings and exert authority.
- Business people should assimilate themselves into the local community so they are accepted by the local

church. For example, in some contexts, local churches have to invite you to attend. A business person has a good opportunity to be invited by a local church because they are assimilated into the community and they relate with the locals.

- Rather than follow the Western church model of full time ministry as an ideal, look for leadership in the local church to model Ephesians 4:12.
- Training programs, case studies, and demonstrations of appropriate use and levels of profit.
- Pastors could go to businessmen asking how they could help them fulfil their ministry or add to their business as mission ministry instead of businesspeople fulfilling a role in the church.
- Integration, accountability, and the need for transparency. The need for team building where business people and mission people work together to encourage integration between the two.

APPENDIX E
CASE STUDY OF MISSION AGENCY INVOLVEMENT IN BUSINESS AS MISSION
Christian Missionary Fellowship International

CMF International, which is fifty-five years old, became involved in what we called "bi-vocational missions" a dozen years ago. Admittedly, we knew very little about business when we started,

and our earliest adventures included subsidised employment opportunities (teaching English) as a visa platform involving a valid and easily understood way to link with people for witness in restricted access nations. Our personnel had ESL certification at the college level and held down real jobs.

We determined to form a separate, but closely linked, not-for-profit agency whose name did not include any Christian terminology. Since a major purpose of this agency would involve business, we did legal research on the question of taxation of for- profit ventures within the non-profit realm. The new agency has its own headquarters, has a separate slate of officers, receives funding from donors, and we have included staff at the new agency who have successful business experience, (i.e. volunteers who had opted for early retirement or who do not need full time jobs).

Our staff have taken the business as mission message to the churches that support our agency. Business people have responded with enthusiasm. We have scheduled short-term trips with these people to lecture in national universities and other settings, to evaluate business opportunities, and to help us partner with and establish several businesses. Others with business experience have helped us write or evaluate business plans.

We have forged a link with a strong campus ministry at a US technology-based university from which we recruit people to work in our businesses overseas. Some of our traditional missionaries have been "re-tooled" and now function in established business as mission roles. One dentist with African missionary experience now runs a profitable and government approved dental clinic on another continent, with proceeds from the business used to aid the persecuted church.

One of the businesses with which we are involved is a chemical processing venture. Our capital outlay is but a small portion of this multi-million dollar facility, but this investment allows us to place personnel in the facility to be directly involved with the local workers, their families, and their communities. Another business just starting is a physical fitness and learning centre in an urban city in Asia. We also have a specialised rock-crushing venture that links an indigenous church, a well-established overseas company, and foreign mission personnel who are focused on an unreached Muslim people group.

Our personnel overseas are members of teams and are linked with team leaders for member care (in country if possible, otherwise via regular personal visits). Supervision comes from their team leader or an appointed work supervisor. Our home-based staff are involved in recruiting, screening, training, and supporting personnel. Accountability and operations are shared by the traditional mission agency staff and the business as mission staff. We have not written new policies and procedures for our business as mission efforts, but we do revise our traditional missionary procedures to fit our business as mission personnel.

One of the markers of a business as mission project is financial viability over time. In most of our business ventures, we are at the front end of the process. These businesses are only in the first couple of years of operation. Two are already profitable. Our Board has developed an "excess profits" policy that ties such profit directly to related ministry efforts. Indeed, each venture has a culturally relevant ministry plan that is equally as important as its business plan.

(a) Barriers

Not every traditional mission agency should become involved in business as mission, whether for reasons of divine call, resistance from staff or donors, ability to undertake business ventures, or experience. Within our mission, we have encountered some resistance from Board members, missionaries, churches, and home staff. However, we have persevered by including the business as mission strategy along with the other mission strategies.

Our Board of Directors, together with spouses and agency staff, scheduled a Board meeting in a "closed-country" specifically to try to understand some of the challenges that exist in a context where business as mission is the strategy of choice. We heard reports from our various business partners, as well as case studies from other business as mission efforts. Following the meeting, on-site visits were made to our business as mission projects. Business as mission is but one approach to countries inaccessible to traditional missionary methods. There are opportunities for linking with the local church and partnering with local believers. Our mission's strategy in such contexts has involved ministry through humanitarian, educational and business spheres.

(b) What Next?

Initial start-up capital for business efforts need not only come from venture capitalists. We have found that churches, usually larger churches, become energized about business as mission and are willing to contribute funds if they can see a missional purpose. There is much than can be done.

We need time to demonstrate the on-going financial viability of our ventures, and we need to more fully develop the policies and procedures that relate to profit in the not for profit sector. We need to recruit additional professional people with mission interest who will live in cross-cultural settings and to evaluate their effectiveness in the holistic integration of business and mission.

In business as mission efforts, business people may need to be reminded to seek interaction with traditional mission personnel.

APPENDIX F
ENDNOTES

1 Extract from an unpublished newsletter by Patrick Lai

2 Wayne Grudem, *Business for the Glory of God: The Bible's Teaching on the Moral Goodness of Business* (Crossway, 2003), 12.

3 R. Paul Stevens, "The Other Six Days: Vocations, Work and Ministry," in *Biblical Perspectives*, 1999.

4 A business person with a kingdom mission, a word coined to demonstrate the hybrid nature of this new breed of missionary combining the attributes of a businessperson and missionary.

5 The following discussion represents a brief overview of the key issues. For an example of how one mission organisation has handled these and other considerations please visit: www.businessasmission.com 'Guidelines' for Youth With a Mission. Also see other mission agencies listed in the Resource Directory.

6 For a thorough examination of these issues, see William J. Danker, *Profit for the Lord: Economic Activities in Moravian Missions and the Basel Mission Trading Company*, (William B. Eerdmans, 1971, Wipf & Stock, 2002)

7 Earl Pitts, *Walking in Financial Freedom* and other resources, see www.wealthrichesmoney.org

8 Ralph D. Winter and Steven C. Hawthorn, ed. *Perspectives on the World Christian Movement*, (more info from www. perspectives.org)

9 Lausanne Committee for World Evangelization

APPENDIX G
RESOURCE DIRECTORY

The resources compiled in this document are classified in the following categories.

I. **Books**
II. **Articles and Papers**
III. **Organisations, Networks, and Web Links**
IV. **Training Institutions**
V. **Additional Tools**

I. Books

Befus, David R. *Kingdom Business: The Ministry of Promoting Economic Development.* Miami:Latin America Mission, 2002.

> *Befus writes from his experience in integrating ministry with economic activity and presents five models of integration. Spanish and English translations.*

Burkett, Larry. *Business by the Book: The Complete Guide of Biblical Principles for the Workplace.* Nashville, TN: Thomas Nelson, 1998.

> *Practical advice for how to apply biblical principles to business operation and management.*

Bussau, David, and Russell Mask. *Christian Micro enterprise Development: An Introduction.* Regnum Books, 2003.

> *A handbook to equip practitioners and donors to build Christ's Kingdom   through Christian MED. Compares Christian MED case studies to secular practices.*

Cleveland, Paul, Gregory Gronbacher, Gary Quinlivan, and Michel Therrien. *A Catholic Response to Economic Globalization: Applications of Catholic Social Teaching.* Grand Rapids, MI.: Acton Institute, 2001.

> *Gives a Catholic perspective on globalisation and a Christians responsibility in today's global marketplace.*

Chan, Kim-kwong, and Tetsunao Yamamori. *Holistice Entrepreneurs in China: A Handbook on the World Trade Organization and New Opportunities for Christians.* Pasadena, CA.: William Carey International University Press, 2002.

> *Practical information on the economic changes taking place in China and the   opportunities for Christian business entrepreneurs being created.*

Danker, William. *Profit for the Lord.* Eugene, Oreg.: Wipf & Stock, 2002, originally published by Eerdmans, 1971).

> *Economic activities of the Moravian Mission movement and the Basel Mission Trading Company, gives a comprehensive history and draws conclusions to learn from for today's business-as-mission activities.*

de Soto, Hernando. *The Mystery of Capital, Why Capitalism Triumphs in the West and Fails Everywhere Else.* New York, NY: Basic Books, 2000.

> *Examines the problem of why some countries succeed at capitalism and others fail.   He finds a link to the legal structure of property and property rights of each nation.*

Gibson, Dan. *Avoiding the Tentmaker Trap.* Ontario, Canada: WEC International, 1997.

> *Practical guidance for the prospective tentmaker, including a comprehensive   resource list of books and organisations.*

Gnanakan, Richard S. *Work in God's World: Insights into a Theology of Work.* Bangalore, India: Theological Book Trust, 2003.

> *Theological reflections on work from an Indian perspective.*

Greene, Mark. *Supporting Christians at Work: A Practical Guide for Busy Pastors.* London: London Institute for Contemporary Christianity, 2001.

Grudem, Wayne *Business for the Glory of God: The Bibles Teaching on the Moral Goodness of Business.* Wheaton, IL: Crossway, 2003.

> *Examines how business, in particular ownership, employment, profit, money, inequality of possessions, competition etc. may glorify God.*

Hamilton, Don. *Tentmakers Speak: Practical Advice from Over 400 Missionary Tentmakers.* Duarte, CA.: TMQ Research, 1987.

> *Research led book sharing insights from tentmakers' real life experiences. Available at www.intent.org*

Hammond, Pete, R. Paul Stevens and Todd Svanoe. *Marketplace Annotated Bibliography: A Christian Guide to Books on Work, Business and Vocation.* Downers Grove, IL: InterVarsity Press, 2002.

> *Comprehensive listing of 1200 books on marketplace-faith integration. The authors include a historical survey of the marketplace-faith movement and a variety of thematic indexes.*

Hill, Dr. Alexander. *Just Business - Christian Ethics for the Marketplace.* Downers Grove, IL.: InterVarsity Press, 1997.

> *An introduction to business ethics and help for examining ethical issues that arise in any business development context.*

Humphreys, Kent. *Lasting Investments: A Pastor's Guide for Equipping Workplace Leaders to Leave a Spiritual Legacy.* Colorado Springs, CO: NavPress, 2004.

> *Rediscovering the common goals and visions that pastors and workplace leaders share. Steps for establishing and maintaining fruitful and powerful relationships.*

Knoblauch, Dr. Jorg and Jurg Opprecht. *Kingdom Companies: How 24 Executives Around the Globe Serve Jesus Christ Through Their Businesses.* Self published, 2004.

> *Introduces kingdom companies - those businesses that operate on biblical values and as a means of spreading the gospel. Highlights principles for kingdom companies   through short company profiles. (Contact:knoblauch@tempus.de)*

Lai, Patrick. *Window Businesses: Doing Tentmaking in the 10/40 Window.* Pasadena, CA:William Carey International University Press, 2003.

> *Practical guide for starting businesses as a tentmaker in countries at various   economic stages.*

Lewis, Jonathan, ed. *Working Your Way to the Nations: A Guide to Effective Tentmaking.* Downers Grove, IL.: InterVarsity Press, 1997.

> *A study guide and handbook on tentmaking, with a series of practical essays by experienced specialists. Available at www.tentmakernet.com — free to download in English, Spanish, Portuguese, Korean and Arabic.*

Myers, Bryant *Walking with the Poor: Principles and Practices of Transformational Development.* Maryknoll, N.Y.: Orbis, 1999.

> *Theological basis for economic development and holistic mission, with discussion on the application of these principles.*

Nash, Laura, Ken Blanchard and Scotty McLennan. *Church on Sunday, Work on Monday: The Challenge of Fusing Christian Values with Business Life.* San Francisco, CA: Jossey-Bass, 2001.

> *A guide to improving communication between the worlds of church and business. They draw on extensive research including case studies and interviews, and define the obstacles to such communication..*

Novak, Michael. *Business as a Calling: Work and the Examined Life.* New York, NY: The Free Press, 1996.

> *Examines the interplay between religion and business and the effect on the moral and social condition of a nation.*

Ogden, Greg *Unfinished Business: Returning the Ministry to the People of God.* Grand Rapids, MI: Zondervan, 2003.

> *Advocating a lay driven model of ministry, he sets out important movements for the church to be able to her to place ministry back in the hands of the people: Passive to active · Maintenance to mission · Clergy to people of God Teacher/caregiver to equipping enabler.*

Olsen, J. Gunnar. *Business Unlimited: Memories of the Coming Kingdom.* ICCC, 2002, Scandanavia Publishing House, 2004.

> *The autobiography of Gunnar Olson, founder of the International Christian Chamber of Commerce. A story of an intimate walk with God which has led to the author being used to influ ence nations. Available at www.iccc.net.*

Prahalad, C.K. *The Fortune at the Bottom of the Pyramid: Eradicating Poverty Through Profits.* Upper Saddle River, NJ: Wharton School Publishing, 2005.

> *The relationship between business and development in developing nations. Examining the entrepreneurial ability and buying power of the poor.*

Rundle, Steve, and Tom Steffen *Great Commission Companies: The Emerging Role of Business in Missions.* Downers Grove, IL.: InterVarsity Press, 2003.

> *Introduces principles for Great Commission Companies in the context of globalisation. Provides five case studies from businesses involved in mission.*

Sherman, Doug, and William Hendricks. *Your Work Matters to God.* Colorado Springs: NavPress, 1987.

> *Clearly sets out theological basis for work having intrinsic value in itself and in contrast to the "sacred-secular dichotomy."*

Silvoso, Ed. *Anointed for Business: How Christians Can Use Their Influence in the Marketplace to Change the World.* Ventura, CA.: Regal, 2002.

> *Silvoso shows how ministry in the marketplace should go hand in hand with building God's kingdom and transforming society. He urges the church to overcome the barriers that remain to integrating business and ministry.*

Schlossberg, Herbert, Ronald J. Sider and Vinay Samuel, eds. *Christianity and Economics in the Post-Cold War Era.* Grand Rapids, MI: William B. Eerdmans, 1994.

> *Developed from the second Oxford Conference on Christian Faith and Economics, this book reproduces the 1990 Oxford Declaration itself and eleven critical responses on the subject of Christian faith and economics.*

Stevens, R. Paul. *The Other Six Days: Vocation, Work, and Ministry in Biblical Perspectives.* Grand Rapids, MI: William B. Eerdmans, 1999.

Explores the theological, structural and cultural reasons for the divide between those who "do" ministry and those to whom it is "done". Stevens shows that the clergy-laity division has no basis in the New Testament and challenges all Christians to rediscover what it means to live daily as God's people.

Suter, Heinz and Dr. Marco Gmur. *Business Power for God's Purpose.* Greng, Switz.:VKG Publishing, 1997.

Introduction to the role of business in the task of world evangelisation, including history and ethics and some cases. Concludes with some principles for application.

Swarr, Sharon B. and Dwight Nordstrom. *Transform the World: Biblical Vison and Purpose for Business.* Center for Entrepreunership and Economic Development, 1999.

A Biblical introduction to the domain of business followed by some practical guides and principles for developing "Great Commission businesses."Available at www.ceed-uofn.org.

Tongoi, Dennis. *Mixing God with Money: Strategies for Living in an Uncertain Economy.* Nairobi: Bezelel, 2002.

Examines the biblical view of money, taking into consideration some of the unique dynamics of managing finances in the Third World. Tongoi considers the socio-economic context of Africa, such as demands of the extended family and the lack of access to credit. Available at www.harvestfoundation.org/kenya.htm.

Tsukahira, Peter. *My Father's Business.* Self-published, 2000.

Guidelines for ministry in the marketplace, drawing from authors experience as both a pastor and business leader.

Willard, Dallas. *The Spirit of the Disciplines.* New York, NY: HarperCollins, 1991.

The application of the spiritual discipline for the Christian disciple. Includes a chapter on the question 'Is Poverty Spiritual?'.

Wilson, J. Christy, Jr. *Today's Tentmakers.* Wheaton, IL: Tyndale, 1979.

Introduction to the idea of tentmaking from one of the founding fathers of the modern tentmaking movement.

Yamamori, Tetsunao. *Penetrating Missions' Final Frontier: A New Strategy for Unreached People.* Downers Grove, IL: InterVarsity Press, 1993.

Yamamori presents a challenge for tentmakers to go out into places other missionaries cannot, all in the light of the remaining task of world missions.

Yamamori, Tetsunao, and Kenneth A. Eldred, eds. *On Kingdom Business: Transforming Missions Through Entrepreneurial Strategies.* Wheaton, IL: Crossway Books, 2003.

Divided into three parts: casestudies, essays and conclusions, this is a thorough introduction to the concept of kingdom business from a broad range of experienced contributors.

II. Articles and Papers

Baker, Dwight. "William Carey and the Business Model for Missions." Unpublished manuscript (2001). Available at www.globalconnections.co.uk/pdfs/careybusinessbaker.pdf.

Chan, K.C. and Scott McFarlane. "Business-as-missions: Stewardship and Leadership development in a global economy" at Christian Business Faculty Association annual conference, Northwest Nazarene University (October, 2002). Available at info@ec-i.org.

Christensen, Derek. "Training Endurance Food for Serious Tentmakers." in *International Journal of Frontier Missions* 14:3 (1997)133-138. Available at www.ijfm.org

Cope, Landa. "Economics: Old Testament Template" Unpublished manuscript. Available at www.ottemplate.org.

Cox, John. "The Tentmaking Movement in Historical Perspective." in *International Journal of Frontier Missions* 14:3 (1997) 111-117. Available at www.ijfm.org

Daniels, Denise, Tim Dearborn, Randel S. Franz, Gary L. Karns, Jeff Van Duzer and Kenman L. Wong. "Toward a Theology of Business" at The Fifth International Symposium on Catholic Social and Management Education, Bilbao, Spain (July, 2003) Available at The Center for Integrity in Business, Seattle Pacific University - www.spu.edu/depts/sbe/cib/scholarship_cib.htm#papers

Dean, Judith. "Why Trade Matters for the Poor" at 20th Anniversary Conference Association of Christian Economists, Washington, DC (January, 2003). Available at www.ec-i.org/articles.htm

English, David. "Paul's Secret: A First-Century Strategy for a Twenty-first-century World" *World Christian* 14:3 (2001) 22-26.

Ewert, Norm. "The Role of Business Enterprise in Christian Mission" in *Transformation* 9 (1992) 7-14.

Grenz, Stanley J. "God's Business: A Foundation for Christian Mission in the Marketplace" in *Crux* 35:1 (1999) 19-25. Available from Regent College publications: www.gospelcom.net/regent/regentnew/crux/

Hagan, David. "Strategic Impact Through Multiplying Modular Business" in *International Journal of Frontier Missions* 15:1 (1998): 27-28, 46. Available at www.ijfm.org.

Hock, Ronald F. "The Workshop as a Social Setting for Paul's Missionary Preaching." in *The Catholic Biblical Quarterly* 14:3 (1979) 439-450.

Lai, Patrick. "Starting a Business in a Restricted Access Nation" in *International Journal of Frontier Missions* 15:1 (1998) 41-46. Available at www.ijfm.org.

———. "Tentmaking: In Search of a Workable Definition" Unpublished manuscript (2000). Available at www.tentmakernet.com/articles.

Lupton, Bob. "Markets and Missions" at EC Institute (August, 2003). Available at www.ec-i.org/articles.htm.

Markiewicz, Mark. "Business-as-mission, or How two Grocers changed the course of a Nation" at Central Asia Business Consultation (1999). Published by Business Professional Network info@bpn.org or excerpts at www.tentmakernet.com/articles.

McLoughlin, Michael. "Back to the Future of Missions: The Case for Marketplace Ministry" in *Vocatio* (2000)1-6.

Llewellyn, David. "The Witness of Work: Business-as-mission" Unpublished manuscript (2004). Available at www.businessasmission.com/pages/papers_articles

McFarlane, Scott. Six Ways to get involved in the Business-as-missions Movement" in *Regent Business Review* 11 (2004). Available at www.regent.edu/acad/schbus/maz/busreview/articlesindex.html

Morris, Robert. "Shrewd Yet Innocent: Thoughts on Tentmaking Integrity" *International Journal of Frontier Missions* 15:1 (1998) 5-8. Available at www.ijfm.org.

Nordstrom, Dwight and Jim Nielsen. "How Business Is Integral to Tentmaking" in *International Journal of Frontier Missions* 15:1 (1998) 15-18. Available at www.ijfm.org.

Norrish, Howard. "Lone Ranger: Yes or No?" in *Evangelical Missions Quarterly* 26 (1990) 6-14. Available at www.wheaton.edu/bgc/EMIS/1990/loneranger.html

Packer, J.I. "The Christian's Purpose in Business" in Richard C. Chewning, ed. *Biblical Principles and Business: The Practice*. Colorado Springs: NavPress, 1990, 16-25.

Reapsome, Jim. "Paul: The Nonprofessional Missionary" *Occasional Bulletin*. (1997). Available at www.missiology.org/EMS/bulletins/reapsome.htm

Rundle, Steve. "Ministry, Profits and the Schizophrenic Tentmaker." *Evangelical Missions Quarterly* 36:3 (2000) 292-300. Available at www.wheaton.edu/bgc/EMIS/2000/ministryprofits.html

Rundle, Steve and Tom Steffen. "Building a Great Commission Company" *Regent Business Review* 11 (2004). Available at www.regent.edu/acad/schbus/maz/busreview/articlesindex.html

Seibert, Dr. Kent W. and Scott McFarlane. "For the Love of Business: Demonstrating the Reality of God Through the Practice of Business" at The 20th Annual Christian Business Faculty Association Conference (October, 2004). Available at: www.ec-i.org/cbfapaper.pdf

Siemens, Ruth E. "Why Did Paul Make Tents? A Biblical Basis for Tentmaking" in *GO Paper* A-1 (1998). Available at www.globalopps.org/materials.htm.

-----. "The Tentmakers and Their Churches: Mutual Responsibility" *GO Paper* A-9 (1997). Available at www.globalopps.org/materials.htm.

-----. "The Tentmaker's Preparation for Work and Witness." in *GO Paper* A-5 (1997). Available at www.globalopps.org/materials.htm.

Schmidt, Karen. "Versatile Vocation – Using Marketplace Skills to Reach the World for Christ" in *World Christian* (1999) 31-33.

Stevens, R. Paul "The Marketplace: Mission Field or Mission?" in *Crux* 37:3 (2001) 7-16. Available from Regent College publications:www.gospelcom.net/regent/regentnew/crux/

Swarr, Sharon B. and Dwight Nordstrom. "Best Practice for Business-as-missions" abbreviated from 'Transform the World (1999). Available at www.tentmakernet.com/articles/bestpractise.htm

Taylor, Gary. "Don't Call Me a Tentmaker" in *International Journal of Frontier Missions* 15:1 (1998) 23-24. Available at www.ijfm.org.

Tsukahira, Peter. "The Business of the Kingdom" Unpublished manuscript. Available at www.tentmakernet.com/articles.

Tunehag, Mats. "Business-as-mission" Unpublished manuscript (2001). Available at www.globalconnections.co.uk/pdfs/businessasmissiontunehag.pdf.

Warton, John H. Jr. "Employment and the Dignity of Life – the Economic Agenda of the Church" at Convention of Christian Businessmen in Panama (2002), and Argentina, (2003).

J. Christy Jr. "Successful Tentmaking Depends on Mission Agencies" in *International Journal of Frontier Missions* 14:3 (1997) 141-143. Available at www.ijfm.org.

III. Organisations, Networks and Web Links
Classification:

M = Mobilisation   N = Networking / Connecting

R = Resource Site   B = Have Businesses or Projects

T = Offers Training   S = Offers Services (other than educational)

MM = Marketplace /Workplace Ministry Site   MED = Christian Micro Economic Development Site

Advancing Churches in Missions Commitment – Business as mission – M / N / T
> www.acmc.org/bam
>
> *ACMC – Business as mission provides training and resources to equip mission pastors with the Biblical understanding that business people have a calling to their workplace both locally and globally. ACMC – Business as mission will work with mission committees and mission pastors to establish BAM programs in the local church*

Bridge Builders International – M / N / B
> www.bridgebuildersint.com
>
> *A core ministry of BBI is Economic Development projects in the Baltic region.*

Business as Mission Resource Centre – Youth With A Mission – N / R
> www.businessasmission.com
>
> *Collection of resources for all those interested in Business-as-mission. Home to comprehensive lists of books, articles, web links and toolboxes. Also contains Guidelines for YWAM staff for business projects. A regularly updated copy of this paper and resource directory will be available at this site.*

Business Professional Network – M / N / B

> www.bpn.org
>
> *Seeks ways to encourage and support others in the task of "missions through business." Connects western world business resources with needs and opportunities in the developing world. See also BPN AG.*

Centre for Entrepreneurship and Economic Development – T / R

> www.ceed-uofn.org
>
> *CEED has resources for people who have a call to disciple nations through the sphere of business. CEED offers 'Frontier Business Creation' seminars.*

Christian Transformation Resource Centre – N / R / S / MED

> www.ctrc-cmed.org
>
> *Comprehensive resources for equipping Christians in the strategy of Christian micro enterprise development. Lists of organisations, networks, articles and resources.*

Christian Missionary Fellowship International – M / B

> www.cmfi.org
>
> *Uses business development as a mission's strategy.*

EC Institute – M / N / T / R / S

> www.ec-i.org
>
> *EC Institute seeks to educate, equip, mobilise and connect Christian business owners, professionals and business/engineering students for business as mission. EC Institute does this through written resources, vision trips, training programs, conferences/ seminars/ workshops, internships and semester programs.*

Ethnic International / Ethnic US – M / N / B / T

> etienneatger@club-internet.fr; xavier.molinari@wanadoo.fr or wmcgee@compuserve.com
>
> *Ethnic International and Ethnic US exist to assist in economic development in emerging nations through the creation of businesses. They offer training with a special focus on French speaking countries.*

Equip – M / T / S

> www.repurposing.biz
>
> *They equip believers to transform societies, primarily by working with mid-market companies. Equip offers opportunities to become involved, including training, to go on consultancy trips.*

Evangelistic Commerce – N / B

> www.evangelisticcommerce.org
>
> *Evangelistic Commerce works at bridging the gap between business and mission by using commerce to establish value added, large scale businesses that are blessing an economy through wealth creation, thereby creating a sustainable witness for Christ.*

Fellowship of Companies for Christ International – Christ@Work - N / R / MM

> www.fcci.org
>
> Christ@work equips and encourages company leaders to operate their businesses and conduct their personal lives according to biblical principles.

Global Disciples Network – Creative Access Associates – N / M / R

> www.globaldisciples.org
>
> Brings together churches, mission agencies, businesses and concerned individuals to find ways for Christians to access restricted areas using economic development opportunities. Categorised list of weblinks to country, people group and mission research information.

Global Hand – S / N

  www.globalhand.org

  Redistributes goods that are no longer needed by their original owners. Hold inventory list of equipment that may be of benefit to those starting businesses to save capital.

Global Opportunities – N / M / T / R

  www.globalopps.org

  Helping Tentmakers disciple the Nations. GO has free Tentmakers Training and Articles available on it's site, plus tentmaking stories, news, events and other resources.

IMPACT Center – M / N / T

  www.impact-center.org/business.htm

  IMPACT Center has a vision for mobilising business people - by networking with the global body of Christ and helping people to bring societal change in the nations. Yearly business seminar, with teaching and opportunities for trips.

Integra Venture – B / S / MED

  www.integra.sk

  Integra is a Central and Eastern European co-operative initiative which helps grow small businesses. They help local entrepreneurs succeed, enabling them to become agents of community transformation.

Intent – N / R / MM / S

  www.intent.org

  Intent's vision is to network kingdom professionals for global impact. Resources for kingdom professionals serving at tentmakers. List of links to organisations and tentmaking opportunities.

International Christian Chamber of Commerce – N / T

  www.iccc.net

  The vision of ICCC calls for a world-wide network of committed businesspeople in contact with each other, exchanging ideas, products and services; and thereby, proclaiming the rightful authority of Christ to the world at large.

International Coalition of Workplace Ministries – R / T / N / S / MM

  www.icwm.net

  ICWM is a network of workplace ministries with one common goal – to transform the workplace for Christ. Comprehensive directory of organisations, events, articles and publications related to integrating faith in the marketplace.

InterVarsity Ministry in Daily Life – R / MM

  www.ivmdl.org

  IVMDL Resource Group exists to help the church recover the biblical truth that God calls all Christians to minister daily in the places they live and work. Contains directories, bible studies, book lists, articles, casestudies.

Jubilee Action – N / B

  www.jubileeaction.co.uk

  Jubilee Action's work includes the Business Partnerships concept - Jubilee Action is re-defining how charities tackle poverty by using effective business partnerships with local people, to develop significant commercial ventures that will transform poor communities.

Kenya Investment Trust – N / S

  kit@africaonline.co.ke

  KIT seeks to reduce poverty among Kenyans through access to business credit, provision of business training, counselling, mentoring, lobbying and advocacy for an enabling environment and facilitating networking of local and international businesses guided by the principles of Jesus Christ.

Kingdom Business Forum – M / N

www.kingdombusinessforum.org

KBF exists to advance the concept of kingdom business. Through KBF, investors, entrepreneurs, business professors and students, and mission leaders can come together to share information. Regular teaching and equipping events.

Leaders GIFTS – T

www.leadersgifts.com

Leaders GIFTS produces specialised media training resources for leadership development and services in all spheres of society.

Marketplace Leaders – R / S / MM

www.marketplaceleaders.org

Marketplace Leader's *purpose is to help men and women fulfil their God-given calling in and through their work life. They offer teaching, equipping services and resources.*

Mennonite Economic Development Associates – B / M / S / MED

www.meda.org

MEDA is an association of Christians in business and the professions committed to addressing human needs around the world through business-oriented economic development programs, and to applying biblical teachings in the marketplace.

OPEN Networkers – N / T / S / R

www.opennetworkers.net

OPEN exists to upgrade, serve and facilitate tentmakers who are currently on the field working among the least reached peoples of the world. OPEN provides a network for servicing and coaching tentmakers through relationships built on trust.

Partners Worldwide – M / B / N / T

www.partnersworldwide.org

PCD encourages and equips Christian business people to help the poor and each other in partnerships. List of opportunities to get involved.

Scruples – MM / N / R

www.scruples.net

Online marketplace community with numerous discussion forums and resources, including business-as-mission.

Strategic Christian Services – T / N

www.gostrategic.org

Strategic Christian Services seeks to educate, train, and work with people who want to see transformation take place. They offer correspondence schools, seminars, educational products, and consulting services to churches, businesses, and governments.

Tentmakernet – N / R / M / S

www.tentmakernet.com/index.html

Network of tentmaker mobilisers supporting national representatives. Tentmakernet has resources, articles, details of events and a links list of most Tentmaking organisations.

Tentmakers International Exchange – N / M / T

www.tieinfo.org

TIE's aim is to be a service organisation for tentmakers, they mobilise, train and support Christians to use their vocations in ministry. They send a monthly email-newsletter.

Transformational Business Network – M / N / B / S

www.tbnetwork.org

TBN is for those with a heart for using their business skills for God's Kingdom - to bring spiritual and physical transformation where it is most needed. They offer short Exposure Trips on the field to link-up with projects. Annual impact conference.

Turkey Business Network – N / S

Contact: tr@Trbiz.org

Connecting kingdom companies in Turkey.

Uganda Bizzionary Network - M / N / S

Contact: ikasana@ids-Ug.com

Connecting kingdom minded business people in Uganda.

World Partners – B / S

www.worldpartners.org

World Partners supports local initiatives in developing countries through entrepreneurial ventures with a Christian element. Assists national entrepreneurs who have a workable business plan with mentoring and capital.

IV. Training Institutions

ACTS Institute, India

Contact: actsinst@blr.vsnl.net.in or ricky@gnanakan.com

Biola University, USA

www.biola.edu

Offers business-as-mission course modules.

Chalmers Center for Economic Development at Covenant College, USA

www.chalmers.org

Resources and training courses for micro-enterprise and small business development.

Eastern University, USA

www.eastern.edu

EC Institute, USA

www.ec-i.org

Offers Global Business training and internship programs for senior and graduate level university students. Many participants receive college credit for programs.

The Macquarie Christian Studies Institute, Australia

www.mcsi.edu.au

MCSI offers programs in Market Place Theology.

Regent College, Canada

www.regent-college.edu

Offers Marketplace Ministries courses at the Marketplace Institute.

Regent University, USA

www.regent.edu

Singapore Bible College

www.sbc.edu.sg

Wheaton College, USA

www.wheaton.edu

Business-as-mission research focus with collaboration of missions and economics faculties. Also Centre for Applied Christian Ethics.

Whitworth College, USA
>	www.whitworth.edu
>	See School of Global Commerce and Management.

V. Additional Tools

Bi-Lingual Pro-Forma Business Plan in outline form for teaching and training purposes; available in English- Russian, English-Spanish from the Business Professional Network. www.bpn.org

Crown Financial Resources – online and training resources. Equipping people worldwide to learn, apply and teach God's financial principles so they may know Christ more intimately, be free to serve Him, and help fund the Great Commission. www.crown.org

Dieu, L'argent, le Business et Nous (translated: God, Money, Business and Us): A series of seminars on cassette tape consisting of 3 sets in French from Ethnic International - Etienne Atger, Xavier Molinari and Wayne McGee. Contact: Ethnic International; c/o Xavier Molinari; 4, rue derriere les murs; 02570 Chezy sur Marne or xavier.molinari@wanadoo.fr

Perspectives on the World Christian Movement – foundational training course introducing biblical basis for on world missions and what God is doing around the world. www.perspectives.org

Planning a Successful Small Business Seminar - A full outline of seminar can be found at the Scruples website. www.scruples.org/web/seminars/pssb.htm

Walking in Financial Freedom training course and other training resources by Earl Pitts. www.wealthrichesmoney.org

APPENDIX H
ENDORSEMENTS

"New leadership is needed in the 21st century, as we look at effective and holistic mission strategies. Business has historically been a key frontier in extending the Kingdom. The Lausanne think-tank has the potential of making a significant contribution to the churches rediscovery of empowering its business community to engage enthusiastically and proactively with its role in establishing the Kingdom of God on Earth!"

Stuart McGreevy, Chairman, TBN Transformational Business Network

"The use of business in global outreach is a strategy of choice for the context of the 21st century mission. People involved in entrepreneurial tentmaking, kingdom business, and transformational development through business, should partner with Mats Tunehag — a respected global mission leader — and his colleagues, as they are leading & organising a Lausanne think tank on Business as mission."

Ted Yamamori, Lausanne International Director and Co-editor of On Kingdom Business: Transforming Missions Through Entrepreneurial Strategies

"Economic-based mission will bring a major change to the face of Christian missions, and it is more than just a new strategy—there is a promise connected to it: He who lends to the poor lends to the Lord, and he will reward him for what he has done (Proverbs 19:17). The Lausanne Think Tank will serve as a platform of mutual encouragement and inspiration. I am looking forward to be part of it."

Jürg Opprecht, Founder & President BPN Business and Professional Network

"The Business as mission think tank is providing a wonderful opportunity for reflection on and inspiration for the creation and use of money (and "secular" work!) in the service of God. I enthusiastically endorse this project closely related to Jesus' call to His disciples—to be "the salt of the earth".

Rene Padilla, Argentinean theologian, missiologist, author and International President of Tearfund UK

"Business as mission is a relevant strategy to meet the challenges in the 10/40-window and beyond. The Lausanne think tank on Business as mission has significant potential of formulating practical approaches in support of God's mission for the global church in the 21st century."

Luis Bush, USA/Argentina Director, World Inquiry, founder of the AD2000 Movement

"As the market place is to the nations what the blood stream is to the body, created for its support and growth, businessmen and women are being called to embrace a new responsibility under God to transform the societies in world at large through creative acts of love. It is a call to fruitfulness and multiplication for the purposes of the Kingdom of God, and it is time for the poor and needy of the world to experience God's love through business. This requires a release into a new dimension in our business experience in which corporate goals, strategies and plans become the outward manifestation of an inward walk of faith. Therefore, I warmly support Mats Tunehag and his colleagues, all respected global mission leaders, in their efforts in organising a Lausanne Think Tank on Business as mission."

J. Gunnar Olson, Chairman and Founder of ICCC, International Christian Chamber of Commerce

"God has gifted some with the resources of mind and spirit to be businessmen and women. Business as mission seeks to support and encourage those who are gifted by God in this way. It aims to stimulate interest in, and commitment to, doing business as unto the Lord. Its desire is to assist business people to see the opportunities that exist, to use their skills and talents to bless those in the poorest and most needy parts of the world and to provide in those context credible opportunities to demonstrate and proclaim Christ. I warmly support this endeavour and the global think tank, recalling that in the earliest history of the Christian mission the saving news of Christ was often carried to new places by those who were seeking to do business."

Harry Goodhew, Retired Anglican Archbishop of Sydney, Australia

JEWISH EVANGELISM:
A CALL TO THE CHURCH

Lausanne Occasional Paper No. 60

This Occasional Paper was prepared by Issue Group No. 31, "Reaching Jewish People with the Gospel." It was the smallest of the Issue Groups at the 2004 Forum. This report is the combined effort of the seven-member team that referred to itself as the Jewish Evangelism Working Session (JEWS), all long-time members of the Lausanne Consultation on Jewish Evangelism (LCJE), a network that formed out of the 1980 LCWE meeting also at Pattaya (see Appendix A). As a group, they speak for themselves in this report. LCJE's *Rules and Procedures* give them no mandate to speak on behalf of the entire LCJE network.

The seven-member team consisted of:

Tuvya Zaretsky (Editor),

Kai Kjær-Hansen (Convenor)

Ole Chr. Kvarme (Theological Consultant)

Bodil F. Skjøtt (Facilitator)

Richard Harvey

Theresa Newell

Susan Perlman.

This report is released with our prayers and the hope that it will stimulate our brothers and sisters in the body of Christ to a new vision, heart, and call for Jewish evangelism.

Correspondence can be directed to:

Dr. Kai Kjær-Hansen, International Co-ordinator

Lausanne Consultation on Jewish Evangelism

Ellebækvej 5, Box 11

DK-8520 Lystrup, Denmark

E-mail: lcje-int@skjern-net.dk

CONTENTS

WE ARE NOT ASHAMED OF THE GOSPEL

Jewish evangelism means to share the gospel with Jewish people. Jesus did it and the apostles did it. The first communities of Jewish believers in Jerusalem and Galilee did it. The early church took shape through Paul's evangelistic ministry to Jewish communities around the Mediterranean. Sharing the gospel with Jewish people was the beginning of world evangelism.

In every generation throughout Christian history, Jewish believers in Jesus have been part of the church. However, that history has at times been difficult and the experience of Jewish people with the church has, during various periods, been characterised by suffering. Today the church is called upon to welcome and appreciate the renewed presence of Jewish believers in Jesus within the body of Christ – both in Israel and in other countries around the world.

The theme of the 2004 Forum was "A New Heart, a New Vision, a Renewed Call." The Jewish Evangelism Working Session (JEWS) of the Forum wants to challenge the church:

- To develop a new heart for the Jewish people

- To acquire a new vision of the church that is composed of the Jewish people along with all the nations of the earth

- To demonstrate a renewed call to share the good news with Jewish people everywhere

A New Heart

In an era of global pluralism and terrorism it is time for the church to develop a new heart for the Jewish people. The history of the wrongdoings by the church against the people of Israel throughout the ages cannot be unwritten. This record, as evidenced by the Holocaust of the last century, has been so difficult that many Christians are of the opinion that the church has forfeited its credibility and its right to share the gospel with Jewish people. In this regard we state:

We are ashamed of the church's atrocities against the Jewish people and the teaching of contempt that has taken place through the history of the church, and we denounce it.

We pledge ourselves to remember the misdeeds of the church against Jewish people. Only with this memory in mind can Christians develop a new heart for the Jewish people. Such tragic history should also be a mirror through which evangelistic efforts today may be critically analysed – for Jews first and also for non-Jews.

A New Vision

In this age of globalisation, the church needs to acquire a new vision for the salvation of the Jewish people and of all nations of the earth. When Jewish people today, together with the other nations, confess faith in Jesus as their Saviour, it is a sign of hope for the church and for the world. Therefore, we also state:

We are not ashamed of the gospel. In the words of the Jewish apostle Paul, the gospel is "the power of God for the salvation of everyone who believes: first for the Jew, then for the Gentile" (Romans 1:16).

We therefore also pledge ourselves to uphold such a vision for the church that affirms that in Christ we are one, Jew and gentile, and that in Christ alone is the hope of salvation for both Israel and the nations.

A Renewed Call

As those who maintain that in the gospel of Jesus alone is salvation for both Jews and gentiles, we realise that we also make ourselves vulnerable to accusations of spiritual arrogance, religious imperialism, and supersessionism vis-à-vis the synagogue.

Yet, we affirm that Jewish evangelism, and world evangelism, is not triumphalistic. Genuine evangelisation of Jews and non-Jews is accomplished only by the victory of God, who raised Jesus from the dead and calls all people to Him through faith in the crucified and resurrected Saviour. The evangelist who brings the good news to others needs to receive the same gospel just as much.

We therefore pledge ourselves to encourage the worldwide church to demonstrate a renewed call to share the grace and the truth of the Lord with Jewish people everywhere, and to realise afresh the importance of Jewish evangelism.

Much is at stake when some in the church denounce Jewish evangelism. Many do so today without realising the theological and missiological implications of their position. This report will describe some of the most important implications of any failure to evangelise the Jewish people. It will briefly describe the Jewish world, some of the issues facing Jewish believers in Jesus, and a variety of current practices in the field of Jewish evangelism.

For what is at stake?

If Jesus is not the Messiah for the Jewish people then neither is He the Christ for the nations.

1. GOD'S COVENANT WITH THE JEWISH PEOPLE AND JEWISH EVANGELISM

Jewish evangelism is happening today, but is under severe attack. Many Christians question the need and the legitimacy of sharing the gospel with Jewish people. This chapter will attempt to show that, from a New Testament perspective, Jewish evangelism is most appropriate.

Those who oppose it are therefore out of step with the biblical understanding of mission.

(a) The Jew Jesus and the First Recipients of the Gospel

Historically speaking, Christianity began as a Jewish phenomenon. The first to believe Jesus to be the Messiah were Jews. According to their understanding, *the place* of revelation was the land of the Jews, *the source* of revelation was the God of Israel, *the first recipients* of revelation were the Jews, and *the main character* of revelation was the Jew Jesus. This Jesus was born to a Jewish mother, and was given a good and normal Jewish name, Yeshua, "the Lord's salvation." According to Matthew 1:21, the significance of what Jesus did is understood from His name: He came to save – to save His people – from their sins. The *kind* of salvation this Jesus/Yeshua offered His people is here made clear. This is the theme that runs through all of the New Testament.

After the disciples of Jesus had experienced that the God of Israel had raised Him from the dead and they had received the Holy Spirit, they preached the gospel – to Jews first. The first Jesus-movement was made up of Jews, and these Jewish believers saw Jesus as the fulfilment of God's promises to Israel. God revealed and poured out His love for Israel and the world through Jesus. The Lord made known His providential and saving love for all those who believe in Him.

Salvation came to Israel through Jesus. This meant good news also for the gentiles. The nations could likewise obtain adoption through him. Together, Jews and gentiles call upon the one same God of Israel, addressing Him as *Abba*, Father, in the name of Jesus and by the Holy Spirit (cf. Galatians 4:6-7).

This fundamental New Testament perspective is critical. If we lose sight of the first recipients of the gospel, its significance is diminished for all peoples. So how can it be that anyone would withhold the revelation and the outpouring of the saving love of the God of Israel from Jewish people or from anyone else?

(b) Jewish-Christian Dialogue after the Holocaust

The Holocaust has become the decisive turning point in Jewish-Christian dialogue. This dialogue has to a large extent influenced views within the church regarding the legitimacy of Jewish evangelism.

Jewish-Christian dialogue after the Second World War produced positive results in many areas. It is a dialogue that *had* to occur and which *had* to lead the church to a reconsideration of its own theology and practice with regard to the Jewish people. Numerous conferences have been held, and the documents produced as a result are numbered in the hundreds.[1] Some of the key issues dealt with in past Jewish-Christian dialogues are:

- The Holocaust and the role of the church - recognition of its guilt.
- Anti-Semitism and anti-Judaism within the church - recognition of its sinfulness.
- The establishment of the State of

Israel - willingness to consider this as a sign of God's faithfulness towards His Jewish people.

- The God of Israel as the father of Jesus Christ - renunciation of Marcionism (the heretical position that God as revealed in the OT was not the Father of Jesus).
- The Jewish roots of the church – recognition that the New Testament can only be understood against the background of the Hebrew scriptures (which the church calls the Old Testament).
- Israel's permanent election and God's enduring covenant with His people – denouncement of the view that the church is the new Israel or has replaced Israel in God's history of salvation.

These and similar issues deserve a renewed and intensified reflection by the church (see below discussion in chapter 4). Dialogue to create understanding between different faith communities is valuable, especially between adherents of Judaism and Christianity. Preconceptions need to be avoided and misconceptions overcome. Dialogue can help both communities to observe the commandment "You shall not give false testimony against your neighbour." Such goals are positive and make important contributions to improved understanding.

Yet difficult questions remain. If God has not annulled His covenant with the people of Israel, do Jews then still need Jesus for salvation? This simple, yet complex question can not be avoided.

From a New Testament perspective, God's enduring covenant with the people of Israel does not make Jewish evangelism unnecessary. Those who insist otherwise not only oversimplify theologically, but undermine the very essence of the new covenant.

(c) Jewish Evangelism since World War II

At the first Assembly of the World Council of Churches (WCC) in 1948, anti-Semitism was defined as sin against God and man. The many failures of the church towards the Jewish people were acknowledged. At the same time, it was maintained that Jews are included in the evangelistic work of the church. Today the WCC, along with some other church bodies, question as to whether the gospel needs to be shared with the Jewish people. During the course of Jewish-Christian dialogues, Jewish evangelism has been denounced frequently, although some have attempted to maintain the position that the church still has an obligation to witness to the Jewish people. Nevertheless, over the years it has become more and more difficult to see what is the nature of this witness.

Not everybody will express it as categorically as a German theologian did in 1979, when he wrote that Jewish evangelism is the "Endlösung der Judenfrage mit anderen Mitteln" – the final solution to the Jewish question by other means. Nevertheless, the rejection of Jewish evangelism has been strengthened in the last decades. Some have suggested that Israel and the church both belong to the one people of

God. Therefore, goes this reasoning, neither of them can proselytise the other. Hence, they conclude, Jewish evangelism is an anachronism.

Today it is an exception when larger Christian denominations give their unreserved support to Jewish evangelism. Many denominational and independent Christian mission organisations to the Jews have ceased to exist, while others have redefined their purpose to accomplish something other than evangelism. The majority of the forums in which Jewish-Christian dialogue takes place today reject direct Jewish evangelism and regard it with contempt (see chapter 4). Jewish resistance to evangelisation is to be expected, but it is puzzling that Christians would deprive Jews of the gospel of Jesus. He is, after all, the very best gift of God, and gentiles have received Him from the Jews.

It is apparent that some of the major obstacles to Jewish evangelism today come not from outside the church, but from within it.

(d) Documents in Favour of Jewish Evangelism

Although the majority of recent Christian statements either speak vaguely or directly reject Jewish evangelism, there are some exceptions. We will mention three statements which clearly give an unambiguous "yes" to Jewish evangelism and which are all endorsed by LCWE (see Appendix B):

(1) *Christian Witness to the Jewish People* (1980)

(2) *The Willowbank Declaration on the Christian Gospel and the Jewish People* (1989)

(3) *Manila Manifesto* (1989)

These documents affirm that the people of Israel remain God's covenant people, and as such have a continued role to play within God's salvation history. These statements also reject the idea that God's enduring covenant with Israel renders faith in Jesus unnecessary. The obligation to share the gospel with Jewish people remains. That responsibility abides, even after the Holocaust.

It is understandable that Jews disagree with such a positive view of evangelism. Their disagreement has been expressed in such sharp terms that are usually avoided in Jewish-Christian relations. In reaction to *The Willowbank Declaration* the then National Director of Inter-Religious Affairs for the American Jewish Committee called it a "blueprint for spiritual genocide that is shot through with the ancient Christian 'teaching of contempt' for Jews and Judaism." Elsewhere he referred to the Declaration as "wrongheaded" and "arrogant." The President of the Union of American Hebrew Congregations at the time described the Declaration as "retrograde and primitive," and "the worst kind of Christian religious imperialism."[2] Such language does not create a constructive atmosphere for the discussion of different opinions.

(e) Dabru Emet: Against Jewish Evangelism

At the beginning of the third millennium we note a radical change of position. It can best be illustrated by considering a

Jewish document entitled *Dabru Emet: A Jewish Statement on Christians and Christianity*. It was published by a small inter-denominational group of Jewish scholars in the year 2000.[3] *Dabru Emet* is the Hebrew for "Speak the Truth" (cf. Zechariah 8:18).

Dabru Emet contains the following eight theses:

1. Jews and Christians worship the same God.
2. Jews and Christians seek authority from the same book – the Bible (what Jews call *Tanakh* and Christians call the Old Testament).
3. Christians can respect the claim of the Jewish people upon the land of Israel.
4. Jews and Christians accept the moral principles of Torah.
5. Nazism was not a Christian phenomenon.
6. The humanly irreconcilable difference between Jews and Christians will not be settled until God redeems the entire world as promised in Scripture.
7. A new relationship between Jews and Christians will not weaken Jewish practice.
8. Jews and Christians must work together for justice and peace.

An introduction to the statement asserts that recent years have witnessed "a dramatic and unprecedented shift in Jewish and Christian relations." The transformation is attributed to Christians who no longer characterise "Judaism as a failed religion, or, at best, a religion that pre-pared the way and is completed in Christianity." It rightly maintains that an "increasing number of church bodies, both Roman Catholic and Protestant, have made public statements of their remorse about Christian mistreatment of Jews and Judaism." In these statements Christians have acknowledged "God's enduring covenant with the Jewish people and celebrate the contribution of Judaism to world civilisation and to Christian faith itself."

Dabru Emet further maintains that the time has therefore come for Jews to be taught about "the efforts of Christians to honour Judaism." Since Christianity has changed its view on Judaism, goes the reasoning, the time has come for Jews to reflect on "what Judaism may now say about Christianity."

Dabru Emet takes the position that "Christian worship is not a viable religious choice for Jews." With that core assumption the document continues, "as Jewish theologians, we rejoice that, through Christianity, hundreds of millions of people have entered into relationship with the God of Israel." It further maintains the mutually contradictory positions that "Christians know and serve God through Jesus Christ and the Christian tradition. Jews know and serve God through Torah and the Jewish tradition."

Does such sentiment sound promising for Jewish-gentile relations? Some Christians feel a great temptation to agree with the *Dabru Emet* document. However, the greater obligation of all Christians is to the one who is the *Truth*. That commitment should prevent Christian believers from following the way that *Dabru Emet* proposes. Jesus said, "I am the way, and the truth and the life. No one comes to the Father except through me" (John 14:6). The following sections explain further.

(f) God's Covenant with His People

"Covenant" and "election" are key terms in the Old Testament and are of the utmost importance for an understanding of Jewish identity today. In a similar way, "covenant" and "election" are central concepts in the New Testament and of the utmost importance for Christian identity and a correct understanding of the church.

The God of Israel has not annulled the unconditional election of His people Israel. That simple statement is contrary to what has often been held by the church through the ages. However, it does correspond with biblical thought and the understanding found among most of those involved in Jewish evangelism over the last two centuries.

God called Abraham from among the nations to establish a universal covenant with the patriarch and his seed to be a blessing to all peoples of the earth (Genesis 12:1-3). This promise includes the everlasting preservation of Israel in order to carry out God's purpose (see Jeremiah 31:35-37). Paul echoes the promise in Romans 11:1, *"Did God reject his people? By no means!"* and again in Romans 11:28-29, *"...but as far as election is concerned, they are loved on account of the patriarchs, for God's gifts and his call are irrevocable."* God has therefore preserved Israel and He has not finished with the Jewish people in His redemptive plan.

When Christ came to die for the just forgiveness of sin and then rose again, He fulfilled the promise of the new covenant (Jeremiah 31:33-34) and also what was promised to Abraham (Galatians 3:15-29). After Christ ascended to heaven, the Holy Spirit was poured out on His disciples at the Jewish feast of Pentecost. They received the Spirit of God as the affirming sign and the signature of the new covenant (Acts 2:32-36). In the days of the apostles, a remnant of Jewish people recognised this unique prophetic fulfilment and received the Messiah in faith. In the same manner, a remnant has always belonged to the new covenant in the one body of Christ. While a portion of Israel continues not to believe in God's Messiah, it remains God's will that the church reach the remnant of Israel in every generation until the day when *"all Israel will be saved"* (Romans 11:26).

Paul did not describe the church as having replaced Israel in God's salvation history. Neither did he exclude the people of Israel from needing the gospel of Christ for salvation. Paul makes it clear in Romans 10:9, *"That if you confess with your mouth, 'Jesus is Lord,' and believe in your heart that God raised Him from the dead, you shall be saved."* Regarding the *way* of salvation there is *"no difference between Jew and Gentile"* (Romans 10:12).

Contemporary thinking on covenant, which has dominated recent Jewish-Christian dialogue, wrongly places Jews and gentiles in different positions for receiving salvation. When the significance of the unique person of Jesus for the salvation of all people is rejected or diminished, then Christian theology and mission suffer irreparably.

(g) Contemporary Thinking on Covenant

The covenant thinking, which has dominated Jewish-Christian dialogue, is often described as a *two-covenant theology* or a *double/dual-covenant theology*. Such a description is not accurate. There is also sometimes presented a *single-covenant theology* in which Christianity is seen as a kind of Judaism for gentiles. Furthermore, some two-covenant theologians really subscribe to a multi-covenant theology or a covenantal pluralism, where the God of Israel has a covenant relationship with all people and with all religions. These notions did not just arise in the modern era.

During the early Middle Ages Jewish scholars considered Christians to be idol worshippers. From the late thirteenth century onward an accommodation was reached. If gentiles wanted to believe in Jesus as the Messiah, in His divinity, and the tri-unity of God, this should not be challenged, but Jews who held such beliefs were still be considered idol worshippers.

Only in the beginning of the twentieth century does a systematic theology – or rather philosophy – actually teach the notion of the two ways of salvation. The German-Jewish philosopher of religion, Franz Rosenzweig (1886-1929), played an important role in this matter. He came very close to embracing Christianity, but then reconsidered. The following is a famous quote by Rosenzweig from 1913 in which he refers to John 14:6 and Luke 15:31. It reads

> We are wholly agreed as to what Christ and his Church mean to the world: no one can reach the Father save through him. No one can reach the Father! But the situation is quite different for one who does not have to reach the Father because he is already with him. And this is true of the people of Israel...[4]

This poor exegesis of John 14:6 and of the parable regarding the prodigal son in Luke 15 still served an apologetic purpose. According to Rosenzweig, the Jewish people need no mediator. The Jew is already with God. Gentiles, however, need a mediator, the Jew Jesus. According to Rosenzweig Jews and gentiles, therefore, complement each other. Both have a God-given role to play in the world. Until Rosenzweig, no Jewish thinker had spoken so positively about Christianity. The tone is similarly positive in current covenant thinking. The arguments can vary, but the main conclusions are the same. They are, first, that God has an enduring covenant with the people of Israel that has not been annulled. Second, this covenant renders faith in Jesus unnecessary for Jews, and third, that faith in Jesus has brought gentiles into a covenant relationship with the God of Israel.

Many people find that this modern covenant thinking, and its variations, has an almost "evangelical" ring to it. An illusion is created that a solution has been found to the difficult relationship between Judaism and Christianity. Both are viewed as equal, and desired by the same God. Both have a divine assignment in this world. There is no competition with each other about Jewish or gentile souls. Therefore, Christian mission to the Jewish people should come to an end. It is offered that the Christian church no longer needs to have a bad conscience over its failure to bring the gospel to the Jewish people. The church, then, has been released from what it previously considered a God-given missionary obligation. This has happened, so it is said, not because of a negative prohibition, but because of a positive theological reason. But is it really that simple?

Indeed, God does have an enduring covenant with His people Israel. Yes, gentiles have found a covenant relationship with the God of Israel through faith in Jesus. However, Jews and gentiles can only enjoy the promised blessing of this enduring covenant through faith in Jesus. The reality of that relationship is confirmed by the gift of the Holy Spirit.

(h) Regarding Truth Claims - As if Judaism and Christianity Make no Truth Claims!

Dabru Emet tries to make it sound simple when it maintains that "*Jews can respect Christians' faithfulness to their revelation just as we expect Christians to respect our faithfulness to our revelation.*" However, this is an oversimplification of what is at stake. The matter is far more complex. A Jewish scholar, critical of *Dabru Emet*, has defined what is at stake for both Judaism and Christianity. He wrote, "*Dabru Emet* is not wrong to draw attention to common scriptures and 'similar lessons.' The problem is that it reduces what is not common to mere differences of opinion — as if the two traditions make no truth claims."[5]

It is indeed easy to "respect" each other when what separates is reduced to mere difference of opinion and matters of little importance. Genuine "respect" for the revelation of the other is necessary. The problem is, however, that it is the focal point of Christian revelation that the God of Israel speaks and acts in and through Jesus and that He does so out of love for the people of Israel. If this aspect of Christian revelation is ignored, then it is emptied of its real content.

It is appropriate to ask where did the claim that Jewish people need the gospel for salvation first come from? Did a later triumphalistic gentile church invent it? No! It originated when *Jewish* disciples of Jesus first preached the gospel to Jewish pilgrims at the Jewish feast of Pentecost. Regarding Jesus, they claimed that "Salvation is found in no one else, for there is no other name under heaven given to men by which we must be saved" (Acts 4:12).

The New Testament itself makes the exclusive claim that salvation can only be found through faith in Jesus. Non-Jewish Christians who joined the church subsequently can take neither honour nor blame for the declaration. Hence, Jewish evangelism cannot rightly be labelled as anti-Semitism, anti-Judaism, or supersessionism (i.e. replacing the Jewish faith).

(i) Theological Inconsistencies

It is beyond doubt that the New Testament witness presents Jesus as the Messiah for the Jewish people. Yet, acceptance of His Messiahship can only be given through faith. Some may hold the view that Jesus was a false Messiah or a failed Messiah. To claim that Jesus is irrelevant for the salvation of the Jewish people whilst being relevant for the salvation of the gentiles is unbiblical and illogical.

The two-covenant theory and its recent expressions seem a natural solution to the relationship between Judaism and Christianity from a modern Jewish perspective. It is not easy to understand how Christian theologians can advocate it in light of the self-defeating logic on which it rests.

How can the same Jesus be the Saviour for the entire world, on the one hand, and not be the Saviour for the Jewish people of that world, on the other? How can the Jesus who met first His own Jewish people with the radical invitation to receive God's saving love, and with the equally radical call to follow Him in obedience, be no longer relevant for that same Jewish people? Unless God is inconsistent and partisan, how can He provide a means of salvation that is no longer available or relevant for Jews, but only for gentiles?

Jesus is not an irrelevant Jew, nor is He a Jewish irrelevance. If He is not Messiah for Israel, then He is not Christ for the nations.

Jesus is either the Messiah for all, or He is not the Messiah at all.

(j) Other Forms of Replacement

Based on the New Testament, Jews need the gospel for salvation as much as anyone else does. However, it is puzzling that there are bible-believing Christians who are eager to proclaim the gospel to all other peoples, but who would exclude the people of Israel from evangelistic mission, replacing gospel proclamation with acts of charity. How is it that some Christians even leave the door ajar for a salvation to Israel that is *without* Jesus? A few examples follow.

Christian dialogue with Jewish people can be beneficial. However, dialogue that becomes a replacement for mission does not live up to the command to make disciples.

Christians who aid in the return of Jewish people to the State of Israel show genuine care and compassion. However, if aid and compassion become a replacement for or a hindrance to the preaching of Jesus here and now, then it does not live up to the command to make disciples of all nations.

Christians can lend political and financial support to the State of Israel. However, if such support becomes a replacement for evangelistic mission among Jews, then it does not live up to the command to make disciples of all nations including the nation of Israel.

Eschatological beliefs about the future of Israel in God's plan of salvation are important. However, if such thinking concerning God's future for Israel becomes a replacement for Jewish evangelism here and now, something is wrong. Regardless of how the future of Israel might develop in God's plans, the time for

Jewish people to hear of salvation is today.

A false alternative to organised Christian missionary activity is found in the claim that Christian witness to Jews consists only in the loving quality of communal life. But one does not preclude the other. The loving manner of Christian life is a proper discipline, but faith comes by hearing the gospel (Romans 10:17). The church was not birthed solely through the apostles' communal life, but also through their public proclamation of the gospel and their missionary activity.

These evangelical forms of "replacement theology" are obstructions to the advance of the gospel among the Jewish people. They are just as harmful to the cause of Christian outreach to Jewish people as other forms of replacement theology have been for the church's appreciation of Israel's place in salvation history.

(k) The Test of Tolerance

Without doubt, the accusations of supersessionism and religious triumphalism will continue to be raised against those who subscribe to Jewish evangelism. Christians, among whom are Jewish believers in Jesus, who have met the grace of God and are committed to *the Truth* in the gospel, can live with such an accusation.

Religious pluralists advocate tolerance towards others, but are often intolerant of those who believe in the revelation of absolute truth. Both Judaism and Christianity do that, and members of those faith communities should take note. It is worth reflecting on the statement of a Jewish thinker, the late Arthur A. Cohen. He said,

"The test of tolerance is where men combat for truth but honour persons." As those called to a ministry of Jewish evangelism, we must accept this test and, with God's help, pass it.

Whilst Cohen cannot be viewed as supportive of Jewish evangelism, it is worth noting that he added:

> I cannot, in conscience, oppose missionary activity to the Jews, and I endorse missionary witness to Christians. It is an activity I find ultimately unrewarding, for the activity is designed more to enable the missioner to witness to himself than to bring the unbeliever to believe. Needless to say, where the special psychology of the aggressor is self-vindication, the temptation to misrepresent, to connive and insinuate, to deceive and to trick is often too great. But if to missionize is to bear witness, not to one's self but to the truth and it is in the discourse of truth that the missionary confronts the missionized, it is justified.[6]

All involved in world evangelisation should heed this warning, as missionaries must avoid the danger of self-promotion. There must be guidelines for ethical conduct in evangelism, and appropriate self-examination and reflection on motives.

Contemporary covenant thinkers should take the divergent truth claims of the respective faith communities more seriously, as should all that are engaged in Jewish-Christian dialogue. It is a loss to both Judaism and Christianity that too many theological concessions are made on critical issues in the interests of mutual acceptance.

Those committed to Jewish evangelism are not about to give up the conviction that Jews need Jesus, despite the fact that some representatives of contemporary Judaism are willing to recognise Christians as a people who have a covenant relationship with the God of Israel. It is strange that such Jews would depart from the fundamental given of the Hebrew scriptures that Israel is *the* chosen people, to replace it with the idea that Israel is only one among many other chosen peoples.

Christians need to recognise Israel as the chosen people in order to understand correctly their own relationship with the God of Israel through Jesus the Messiah — God's chosen one. A biblically consistent theology prioritises truth over mere tolerance.

(I) Jewish Evangelism – for the Sake of Whom?

For whom is Jewish evangelism undertaken? Five summary points are outlined:

1. For the sake of the Jews

God's continued covenant with the Jewish people does not annul their need of Jesus for salvation. Neither does the covenant imply that they are saved in a manner that differs from non-Jews. Faith comes through the proclamation of the gospel and therefore the gospel needs to be proclaimed to the Jewish people. A "yes" to Jewish evangelism insures that Jewish people are not deprived of the possibility of salvation through faith in Jesus. There is no basis in the New Testament for saying that Israel has any qualification that provides forgiveness of sins other than through faith in Jesus.

2. For the sake of the church

Jewish evangelism leads the church into a close contact with the Jewish people. This is important for the church itself. It forces the church to denounce any form of Marcionism (see below in chapter 4). A close contact with the Jewish people sharpens the church's understanding of its biblical roots. The roots of the church are to be found in Israel's salvation history. The structure of the church is built upon Israel and the hope of the church is closely connected with Israel. The church has an incomplete self-understanding without Israel. A "yes" to Jewish evangelism presents the church with a challenge to understand its bonds to Israel and the God of Israel. The fact that these matters are discussed within the Jewish-Christian dialogue does not exempt the church as such from dealing with them.

3. For the sake of world evangelism

Jewish evangelism is not a higher calling or more important in God's sight than evangelisation of other peoples. However, theologically and missiologically, Jewish evangelism has a unique role to play. Jewish evangelism has maintained that if the people who have been historically closest to God need the gospel for salvation, then all other peoples need the gospel as well.

When the legitimacy and the necessity of Jewish evangelism are questioned, then the door is open to religious universalism. The uniqueness of Jesus would be denied.

4. For the sake of Jewish believers in Jesus

Jewish believers in Jesus are often ostracised by their own people for their faith in Jesus. They need understanding and support from the rest of the church. A "no" to Jewish evangelism leaves Jewish believers in Jesus isolated. They would be affirmed by neither the Jewish community nor by the church (see chapter 4).

5. For the sake of God's love and glory.

Finally and fundamentally, Jewish evangelism is necessary for the sake of God's love and His glory. A "no" to Jewish evangelism implies that the death of Jesus for sin was insignificant, and would lead to a great omission from the Great Commission. A "no" to Jewish evangelism withholds God's saving love from the people of Israel. A "yes" to Jewish evangelism opens the door for Jewish people to share in God's glory as revealed in the new covenant or "testament."

The church must consider these matters and again endorse and commit itself to Jewish evangelism.

Much is at stake.

If Jesus is not the Messiah for the Jewish people, then neither is He Christ for the nations.

Either Jesus is the Messiah for all, or He is not the Messiah at all.

2. THE JEWISH COMMUNITY AND JEWISH EVANGELISM

C.S. Lewis wrote in the introduction to Joy Davidman's book, *Smoke on the Mountain*:

> In a sense, the converted Jew is the only normal human being in the world. To him, in the first instance, the promises were made, and he has availed himself of them. He calls Abraham his father by hereditary right as well as by divine courtesy. He has taken the whole syllabus in order, as it was set; eaten the dinner according to the menu. Everyone else is, from one point of view, a special case, dealt with under emergency regulations.

Today there are less than 14 million Jews in a world of 6.4 billion people. Jews comprise a mere one fourth of one percent of the world's population. Residing in over 130 countries, Jewish population by region breaks down as follows: North America (6 million), Israel (5.2 million), Europe (2 million), Latin America (500,000), Australasia (100,000) and South Africa (90,000). See Appendix C for further details.

The Jewish world today is filled with paradoxes: diversity and commonality, secularism and spirituality, rigidity and mobility. Following is a snapshot of that world, a brief glimpse of Jewish missions in the past, what the field looks like today, and why there is so much of an uproar over what should be normal in God's economy.

(a) A Diverse Community

A common Jewish adage is that if

you ask two Jews one question, you will get three opinions. Jews are a diverse people in thought, culture, religious expression, and self-identification.

There are diverse cultural differences among Jews who come from Ashkenazi and Sephardi backgrounds. They include food, music, and how one observes holiday and life cycle events. Ashkenazi Jews descend from German, Polish, Austrian, and Eastern European Jews. A large proportion of North American Jewry is of this background. Sephardi Jews are descended from the Jews of Spain and Portugal who settled in North Africa and Southern Europe. In modern Israel, Sephardi also refers to Jews of Near Eastern descent.

There is a diversity of religious expressions amongst Jews. Some follow Orthodox, Conservative, Liberal [Reform] and Reconstructionist, Humanistic, or Hassidic forms of Judaism while others identify as secularists, agnostics, or atheists. Contemporary Jewry has also embraced alternative religious forms in Kabbalah (mystical Judaism), New Age, a form of Jewish Buddhism, and Jewish Hinduism.

Self-identification among Jews is a reflection of their geography. Israeli and Diaspora Jews live out a respective Jewishness with differing perspectives. A majority of Israeli Jews are secular without a need for religious affiliation. They speak a Jewish language, Hebrew. They defend the Jewish State by service in the Israeli military. Their calendar includes Jewish festivals and their children study the Bible in schools as part of their history. On the other hand, Diaspora Jews live as a minority presence in the diverse countries they inhabit outside of Israel. They often define themselves by what they are not (e.g. "We Jews don't believe in Jesus").

(b) Commonalities

While the Jewish people are not monolithic, there is much that they hold in common.

1). Suffering and victimisation: Anti-Semitism transcends the divergent cultures, religious expressions, and self-identification of Jewish people. Anti-Semitism is an ideology that blames Jewish people for the evils of the world. It is often politically linked with opposition to the State of Israel. It is prevalent today. The language of anti-Semitism proliferates on the Internet. International anti-Semitic hatred has recently been seen in the form of synagogue bombings, desecration of Jewish cemeteries, attacks on Jewish tourists, and the various forms of terrorist attacks on Israelis at home and abroad. Jews feel the sting of anti-Semitic hatred whether they live in Jerusalem, Paris, Wellington, or Northridge. One result is a Jewish mistrust of a perceived hostile gentile world. The call to the church includes making a change in that perception.

2) Identification with Israel: The fulfilment of God's promised land to Abraham, the father of the Jewish people, holds a special place for many Jews today. Modern Israel was created as a safe home for Jewish refugees. Any threat to Israel's security is perceived as a threat to Jews around the world. Jewish survival is linked to the homeland security of Israel today. Therefore, Israel is inextricably a part of the Jew psyche everywhere.

3) Thirst for spirituality: Spirituality in the Jewish context is bound up with becoming a better, more knowledgeable, Jew. The meaning of Jewishness is sought in historical roots and the biblical meaning of being chosen by God. The quest for that meaning is sought in Jewish mysticism, Torah study or Law-keeping, the pursuit of justice and social causes, and higher learning in all disciplines.

4) A community on the move: Emigration of Jews from Arab countries in the 1950s was a significant population shift. Fifty years later Jews from the former Soviet Union are on the move again. Figures on this emigration from 1990 to the present include roughly 875,000 to Israel, 200,000 to New York, and 200,000 to Germany. These newcomers are more open to the gospel than are the Jews who are already entrenched in society. Other movements include shifts within geographic regions. For example, in the US, Jewish people are moving out of eastern seaboard cities to growing centres like Phoenix, Las Vegas, and south Florida. Israeli population continues to grow. It is projected that by the year 2020 the Israeli Jewish population will be the largest in the world. These shifts have major implications for Jewish evangelism strategy.

5) A changing generation: World Jewry is changing. Most of the 400,000 American Jewish university students avoid campus Jewish institutions. American Jewish divorce rates have increased, rivalled only by the intermarriage rates. Recent surveys indicate an 80 percent intermarriage rate among Russian and Ukrainian Jewry. German and Hungarian Jewish communities follow with 60 percent intermarriage rates. Jews in the United States intermarry at a 54 percent rate; Jews from France, Britain, and Argentina follow at 45 percent. Canadian Jews intermarry at a rate of 35 percent, Australians at 22 percent, South Africans 20 percent, and Mexicans 10 percent. In Israel, the rate of intermarriage is only five percent, with most intermarried families coming from the former Soviet Union.[7]

These factors provide opportunities for the practitioners of Jewish evangelism. They are the grounds for potential new initiatives to reach a diverse Jewish world with the gospel.

(c) Jewish Mission through the Ages

The Jewish community at the time of the second Temple was just as diverse as the Jewish community is today. The disciples of Jesus came from different cultural backgrounds within diverse Jewish societies, and they held a variety of religious and political views. Their mutual response to the teaching of Jesus is what united them.

The Acts of the Apostles tells how they first proclaimed the gospel among the Jewish pilgrims in Jerusalem during the festival days of *Shavuot* (Pentecost). There have always been Jewish members in the body of Christ ever since. Jewish believers in Jesus were the first missionaries, church planters, and martyrs. They were the first to spread the good news of the Messiah throughout the Greco-Roman world.

Jewish believers in Jesus have been identified throughout the ages since. Whole groups of Jews are recognisable in the church, living out expressions of Jewish identity and Christian faith even at the end of the fourth century. Around that time, the separation between church and synagogue had become complete. Jews in churches were forbidden to maintain their Jewishness, and Christians were forbidden in the synagogues. Jewish believers in Jesus became a marginalised group, seen as neither fish nor fowl. They were regarded as a threat to the integrity of both Judaism and the Christian church. Even so, in every century there have been Jewish people represented within the church. Some came by forced conversions, which is a tragic part of church history. Others in every era became followers of Jesus out of genuine belief.

Beginning in the seventeenth century, pietistic and evangelical movements found a renewed interest in the Jewish people and their continuing role within salvation history. At that time, trained missionaries were sent out to work amongst Jewish people, particularly in Eastern Europe.

The Evangelical Awakening in Great Britain and North America in the nineteenth century saw the establishment of modern Jewish missionary societies. Many of the missionaries were Jewish believers, reaching out to their own people in the name of Jesus. Jewish believers have contributed significantly to the mission of the church even into our present times.

In the nineteenth century Jewish believers began to challenge the historical notion among the church and Jewish communities that held Jewishness and Jesus as mutually exclusive. By the end of the twentieth century, a revitalised movement of Jewish followers of Jesus was growing rapidly and internationally. A new day has dawned in Jewish history when once again Jews are proclaiming the gospel of Jesus the Messiah in Jerusalem and in other parts of the world.

(d) Jewish Believers and Jewish Evangelism

Estimates of the number of Jewish believers in Jesus worldwide vary greatly. Christian researcher Patrick Johnstone offers the international figure of 332,000.[8] Anti-missionary organisations have speculated 275,000 as their number.[9]

Jewish evangelism mission workers would certainly be encouraged by either of the above. However, Jewish missionary statesman Moishe Rosen addressed the issue of exaggeration at the 2003 LCJE international conference in Helsinki, Finland, "…when I look for them [Jewish believers] I don't find them, and I'm sure the reason I don't find them is because they are not there. At least not in the huge numbers we are given."[10]

In Israel, there are more non-Jews converting to Judaism each year than there are Jews coming to Christ. It has been said that in the US alone there are 200,000 "Jews by choice" who identify as coming from a non-Jewish background.[11] A conservative estimate of the number of Jewish believers in the world today is 50,000 to 90,000. It is difficult to be more precise.

Below is a representative look at some of the areas where Jewish believers in Jesus live. Their Messianic Jewish identity is diverse, yet provides a clear testimony of faith in Jesus for their non-believing Jewish counterparts.[12]

Israel

A 1999 survey of Messianic congregations in Israel found about 5000 believers attending Messianic congregations. That figure includes non-Jewish spouses, their children, and some gentiles.[13] Since that time, the number of Jewish believers in the land has increased.

Most are part of the approximately 100 congregations or independent small groups. However, there are national structures for them to network together under a leadership conference, a national evangelism committee, and through children, youth, and camping programmes. These serve to bind the movement together. Independent mission agencies operate in Israel working in co-operation with local congregations as well. With the arrival of Russian-speaking Jewish believers, new congregations have sprung up. Likewise, the Ethiopian Jewish believers in Jesus have also established congregations.

Theological and practical training is now available in country at accredited bible schools like Israel College of the Bible. Founded in 1990, ICB provides undergraduate education for Israelis who previously had to leave the country for an equivalent course of study. The Caspari Center for Biblical and Jewish Studies was established in 1983. It offers classes in leadership and children's work for local congregations and individuals. Both are situated in Jerusalem.

It is a myth that evangelism is illegal in Israel. Under Israeli law, believers in Jesus are free to express and share their faith with the adult population. Evangelistic literature, books, and videos are distributed. Personal evangelistic visits are conducted and gospel outreach is done at public events like the New Age festivals. Organised evangelistic campaigns are held and evangelism among Israeli Jewish and Arab students takes place on university campuses in Israel throughout the year. Youth and children's ministry is conducted through bible clubs, humanitarian aid, youth camps, and conferences. Evangelism efforts have not been free of harassment. Some Jewish believers face negative reaction, polarising newspaper coverage, and physical harassment.

A significant number of the Israelis who come to faith in Christ do so while travelling abroad. Some suggestions for evangelistic strategy can be found in the final section of this paper.

Russia and the Former Soviet Union

A significant demographic shift has occurred, though there is still a large number of Russian speaking Jews in the former Soviet Union (FSU). A major evangelistic effort continues, even while the degree of openness has decreased. Jewish people continue coming to faith in Christ. Dozens of mission works are reaching out to the Jews in nine provinces, Ukraine, Russia, Byelorussia, Moldova,

Estonia, Kazakhstan, Kirghizstan, Turkmenistan, and Uzbekistan.

These ministries include street evangelism and literature distribution, personal visits and outreach concerts along with music and dance festivals. They have been planting congregations of Jewish believers in Jesus, conducting public holiday celebrations, holding small group bible studies, engaging in discipleship, offering children's ministries, using radio broadcasts and internet evangelism. They do prison outreach, Messianic conferences, literature distribution, bible translation, humanitarian aid, and medical assistance along with bible education and training in Jewish evangelism.

There are many challenges facing Jewish evangelism in the FSU at this time:

Rise of anti-Semitism: Random acts of violence against Jewish institutions and Messianic events alike. Missionaries to the Jews are physically and verbally abused by nationalists who dislike them simply because they are Jews.

Return of Soviet-era restrictions: Restrictions are most prevalent in the central Asian republics. Registration laws are restrictive, and visas for new workers are limited. Laws are pending which would threaten the current legality of street proclamation.

Rise of organised anti-missionary activity: The anti-missionary Magen League engages in counter-leafleting, destruction of personal property, verbal abuse and physical attacks. They also file false accusations in the press and with local police authorities.

Despite the rise of religious opposition and political restrictions, the gospel is going forth. The best evidence of this can be seen not only in the FSU, but also by implication in the rest of the world. Russian Jewish believers in Jesus, who first heard the gospel in the FSU, are currently witnessing in Israel, the US, Canada, and Germany.

Germany

In contrast to the devastation of Germany's Jewish community (population was 565,000 in 1933 but only 20,000 in mid-1960s) there is a brighter picture today. Since 1990, Germany has become the fastest growing Jewish population in Europe. Of the approximately 200,000 Jews in Germany, 80 percent are Jewish immigrants from the FSU. Several hundred have come to faith in Jesus.

Messianic congregations are found in key centres of the country. Russian-language evangelistic literature is produced and distributed. Jewish evangelism training materials are available in German.

Russian Jewish believers in Jesus have some unique characteristics. They possess a strong Jewish identity, yet lack knowledge of Judaism and Jewish traditions. Most would consider themselves atheists and humanists. They are well-educated professionals, yet many are unemployed. Most of the young people are university students. They are open to ideas and to conversation. They have a deep respect for Germans, yet have a difficult time adjusting to their new culture.

The challenges to reach this community are great. Jewish mission agencies from the US and Western Europe have directed resources to ministry in Germany. These ministries include direct evangelism through literature distribution, one-on-one discipleship, public outreach events, planting congregations, Bible translation, Internet, radio broadcasts, and humanitarian aid.

North America

Canada: There are three main centres for Jewish life, and therefore mission, in Canada. Toronto has a high number of Holocaust survivors residing there. Montreal has a significant Hassidic community. Vancouver is a university city with its highest Jewish concentration on the campus. About a dozen Jewish mission agencies and more than a dozen Messianic congregations span the country.

United States: The number of US Jewish believers is estimated between 40,000 and 60,000. Many are part of mainline churches. However, there are 400 Messianic congregations and fellowship groups covering most of the fifty states where a significant number of Jewish believers in Jesus worship. Jewish evangelism agencies field approximately 150 full time missionaries to minister in the US. They are doing direct evangelism, literature distribution, personal visits, door to door, campus outreach, camps and youth work, planting Messianic congregations, holy days events, public meetings, music concerts, drama, debates, film screenings, evangelistic advertising, evangelistic web-sites, chat room ministry, Jewish evangelism seminars, radio and television programmes, and relief work.

Some agencies are very specialised and are structured to reach one segment of the American Jewish population, such as Israelis living in Los Angeles or Hassidic Jews in New York. Some focus on one methodology, such as church planting or radio ministry. Others work broadly, doing direct outreach and educating churches in Jewish evangelism. The theological spectrum is diverse, although most are able to subscribe to the Lausanne Covenant.

(e) Opposition to Jewish Evangelism

Opposition to Jewish Evangelism is not new. It has roots in the spiritual realm. God chose to convey His truth to the world through the Jewish people. "Salvation is of the Jews" (John 4:22). God's character, the trustworthiness of the Bible, and the promises concerning future world redemption will be demonstrated through the survival of the Jewish people and in their salvation through Christ (Romans 11:12 & 15). Therefore, spiritual forces are arrayed against God and His chosen people.

One of the most significant aspects of Jewish evangelism is the organisations that have formed with the sole purpose of combating the missionary "threat." Such groups are found as Yad L'Achim in Israel, Magen League in the FSU, and Jews for Judaism in North America.

Other agencies like the network of Jewish Federations in North America, Jewish Boards of Deputies in the UK, Australia, and South Africa, and various rabbinical associations also engage in anti-missionary activity as just one item on their agendas. All of these various groups are considered opposition, not the enemy. They are also Jewish people, for whom the Messiah died.

(f) Opposition Strategies

Educational: Opposition groups have produced apologetic literature, videos, and audio tapes attempting to contradict New Testament Messianic claims fulfilled in Jesus. Such materials also present the historic persecution of Jews at the hands of Christians as the case upon which it is claimed that Jewish faith in Christ is allegedly tantamount to disloyalty to the Jewish people and to joining their persecutors. They have developed seminars to instruct Jewish individuals on how to respond to missionaries.

Sociological: Opposition agencies work to create an inflammatory climate where Jews who consider the claims of Christ fear being regarded as outcasts. The authenticity of the Jewish identity of Jesus' followers is questioned. Their loyalty to the Jewish people is challenged. Their access to the Jewish community networks is jeopardised by being barred from traditional synagogue life or burial in Jewish cemeteries.

Situational: These organisations also seek to shut down Jewish evangelistic efforts by putting pressure on both governmental authorities and private sector groups. They utilise letter writing and phone campaigns, expressions of offence that are orchestrated to get radio stations to drop ad campaigns, and bring pressure to bear on private establishments to break contracts for hosting evangelistic events.

Dialogue: The ostensible goal of Jewish-Christian dialogue is better mutual understanding. True dialogue is worthwhile. However, the Jewish dialogue partners want Christians to understand that Jews do not need Jesus. Thus, dialogues become one-sided propaganda opportunities. Evidence for this is the Jewish ground rule that Jewish believers in Jesus not be allowed to take part in any of the dialogues.

Organizational: Some opposition efforts aim at effecting change in denominational and church mission policies. The goal is to marginalise Jewish evangelism or eliminate it completely from the church mandate to make disciples of *all* nations. Under the guise of "interfaith understanding," full-time Jewish professionals are employed to lobby church bodies to forgo forthright evangelism to the Jewish people. For example, US Jewish leaders, in consultation with a subcommittee of national Catholic Bishops, helped prepare a major document labelling the conversion of Jews to Christianity as no longer theologically acceptable in the Catholic Church.[14]

Methodological: Evangelicals are hard pressed to recant the need for gospel witness to all peoples of the earth. When opposition to Jewish evangelism fails to gain the exclusion of Jewish people from the great commission, they attack the motives and methodology of Jewish mission efforts. False and unsubstantiated charges of unethical tactics, misleading, deceptive, cult-like, exploitative, insensitive practices, and of preying on vulnerable people are levelled against the practitioners of Jewish evangelism. Pressure is brought to bear on evangelical Christians to disassociate from Jewish mission efforts and agencies. They are expected to respond to the demands of "offended" Jewish community leaders, by choosing to affirm the traditional faith of Judaism without need for Jesus. This is sometimes attempted through well-publicised statements asking evangelicals not to single out Jews for evangelism. They are urged to "sign on" in order to distance their churches from "inappropriate" Jewish mission efforts. Some evangelical leaders have capitulated, fearing that their support of Jewish evangelism might jeopardise their friendship with Jewish community leaders. The cost of such "friendship," at the sacrificial price of Jewish evangelism, is the jeopardy of Jewish souls.

(g) Summary

Jewish evangelism is one of the more difficult fields of Christian mission. However, opposition to the gospel is to be expected and those who labour in this field are not discouraged by it. Many look for a potential "Apostle Paul" among those who care enough to oppose so vigorously. The large majority of the Jewish people are not involved in the types of opposition listed above. Most would defend the right of Jewish missions to exist and to freely present the message of Jesus for consideration by Jews and gentiles.

3. JEWISH BELIEVERS IN THE CHURCH

This section considers the role of Jewish believers in Jesus in the church. What are the theological issues and practical concerns they bring? How does their presence in the body of Christ point towards the future in-gathering of Israel and the nations? How do they identify themselves? What forms of worship and ecclesiology do they adopt? How do they express their faith in Yeshua (Jesus) in the light of Jewish culture, tradition and religious thought? How do they see the political realities and prophetic significance of the Middle East conflict, and what are they doing practically to seek peace, justice and reconciliation with their Arab Christian brothers and sisters? These matters of contextual theology challenge not only Messianic Jews but also all Christians who wish to understand the significance of the Jewish roots of their faith and the nature of the people of God. How they are resolved will have a significant effect on Jewish evangelism.

(a) Messianic Jewish Thought

Here is some reflection on theology by and about Jewish Believers in Jesus. The fact that Jewish believers in Jesus still exist after 2000 years has theological significance. It is a matter upon which all Christians are called to reflect. Jewish believers in Jesus represent the remnant of Israel saved by grace, the re-grafted natural olive branches, and the token of the continuing election of Israel. They want their lives to demonstrate these fundamental truths and they invite both Jew and Christian to witness the resurgence of a Jewish expression of New Testament faith. Messianic Jews contribute to the character and work of the whole body of Christ. They bear witness to their biblical heritage as children of Abraham and its fulfilment in the Messiah. Their presence inspires the church in its mission. They challenge the church to a deeper understanding of the purposes of God and to echo Paul's heartfelt concern that all Israel might be saved.

The Scriptures are the starting point for this theological reflection. Messianic Jews read the Scriptures through the dual hermeneutical frameworks of Jewish and Christian interpretative traditions. The life, teaching, and ministry of Jesus and the early church is their model and is normative for their belief and practice.

Messianic Jews see themselves as belonging to both the Jewish people and the body of Christ. They construct their identities by negotiating within the boundary lines of both communities. Messianic Judaism can be defined as a Christian form of Judaism and a Jewish form of Christianity. It sets the agenda for full discussion of the problematic issues raised by such a paradoxical formulation.

Messianic Jews have sometimes been accused of "going back under the law" from a Christian perspective, and of producing a "false and deceptive form of Christianity masquerading as Judaism" by the Jewish community. So it is necessary for them to reflect theologically on their beliefs and explain their position. Just as the first believers in the book of Acts were summoned before the bar of public opinion, religious leadership and political authority, so too today Messianic Jews are called to account before Jew, Christian, and state.

(b) The Need for Theology

In the last thirty years, many Jewish people have come to believe in Jesus, bringing out the need and opportunity for theological reflection on the significance of a growing Jewish presence within the body of Christ. Attention has focused on evangelism, congregational planting, and pastoral ministry, often in circumstances where misunderstanding and opposition have been the main challenges. Consequently few theologians have emerged from within the movement. The modern expression of Jewish believers in Jesus is barely one generation old, although their illustrious forbears such as the nineteenth-century Joseph Rabinowitz outlined important theological concerns on ecclesiology, contextualisation, and spirituality. Few present-day leaders have had theological training in Jewish or Christian seminaries or academic theology departments. Nevertheless, their practical wisdom derived from the thirty years' hands-on experience in evangelism and pastoral ministry has brought invaluable resources from which to construct such a local theology, or "ethno-theology."

Another challenge to theological reflection is that Jewish tradition has criticised the discipline of theology, regarding it as abstract, cerebral, and overly systematised, whereas Jewish thought claims a more holistic, eclectic, and pragmatic orientation. Whilst the church has a long tradition of creeds and statements of faith, in Judaism this has been the exception rather than the rule. Some Jewish believers are reluctant to draw up or sign up to statements of belief. Such reluctance can be addressed sensitively yet firmly, recalling the scriptural mandate to hold fast the teachings of the Lord and his disciples. This will lead to a firm and confident acclamation of faith.

Messianic Jews are faced with many questions arising from the combination of their background as Jews and their belief in Jesus. They also have rich possibilities for the integration of Jewish and Christian life and faith. Celebration of Jewish festivals and observance of Jewish practices such as circumcision and *bar mitzvah* (coming of age), allow Jewish believers to promote Jewish life and culture whilst demonstrating the Messianic fulfilment that Jesus brings. Both in Israel and the Diaspora they seek to integrate their faith with their membership of the Jewish community, adopting, adapting, or where necessary, abandoning aspects of their Jewishness depending on how this affects their Christian testimony. How they process these questions is the task of Messianic thought and calls for the prayers, support, and empathetic engagement of the wider Christian community.

(c) Messianic Jewish Identity

Just as the Jewish community continues to wrestle with the questions "Who is a Jew?" and "What shapes Jewish identity?" Also Messianic Jews are concerned with identity issues. What they are called

prioritises these concerns and raises important theological and personal considerations. A variety of terms are used to describe Jewish believers in Jesus, and each can have a range of meanings.

"Jews for Jesus" can apply broadly to all Jews who believe in Jesus, and this is the name of one of the best-known mission agencies. "Messianic Jew/Judaism" is now the most commonly used term (Hebrew: *Yehudi Meshichi)*. It may refer to all Jewish believers in Jesus, the majority of whom worship in mainstream denominational churches, or specifically those who belong to Messianic congregations and synagogues. The earlier term "Hebrew Christian/Christianity" identifies those worshipping in mainstream denominational churches but can also have a wider application.

Some prefer "Messianic Jewishness" to "Messianic Judaism" because the term "Jewishness" appears more focused on ethnic and cultural rather than religious issues or "Judaism." Both signal a change in orientation. The primary loyalty of a "Messianic Jew" is to believe in Jesus as Messiah. Others in the Jewish community have objected that all Jews are "Messianic" in that they await the coming of the Messiah. The term "Messianic Jew" has also been used to describe religiously motivated political supporters of Zionism. Whilst this has led to some confusion in the Jewish community about Messianic Jews, it has been of strategic value in raising the question of the identity of Israel's Messiah and stating clearly that Jewish people who believe in Jesus are still Jews.

"Jewish Christian/Christianity" focuses on the primary identity of a "Christian" who comes from an ethnic and cultural Jewish background. Some use the more neutral "Jewish Believer in Jesus" or "Jewish believer." In Israel a popular term is "Jewish Believer in Yeshua" (*Yehudi Ma'amin b'Yeshua*).

Whilst this debate on terminology has yet to reach a conclusion, Messianic Jews must focus on the real issues underlying such discussion, namely the Messiahship of Jesus and the rightness of following Him. It is unrealistic to think that the terms themselves will make any difference to one's self-perception or the views of others, when the key question is not one of personal identity but of divinely revealed truth about the Messiah.

(d) A Theology of Cultural Identity

The Bible has divine authority for Messianic Jews and is the key resource for them. Yet there are different understandings of how to interpret Scripture in the light of Jewish tradition. This can become the controlling hermeneutical factor in biblical interpretation, leading to an over-emphasis on the "Jewishness" of Messianic Jewish identity, at the expense of the Christ-event. Alternatively, it is possible to read Scripture with an over-emphasis on the divine aspects of Christ's nature whilst not always appreciating how the incarnation took place in a particular human culture and Jewish context. A helpful balance to this is the theological teaching about creation that places high value on the goodness of the created order. Ethnic, cultural, and gender differentiations are part of the purposes of God for humanity, but there should be no sense of ethnic, national, or racial pride that makes one group feel superior to another. Messianic Jews, alongside their sisters and brothers in Christ, must think through these issues carefully and clearly in order to formulate a theology of culture from which a mature evaluation of Jewish identity fulfilled in the Messiah may emerge.

Jewish community concerns over identity and survival in the light of the threats of assimilation, secularisation, and anti-Semitism are reflected in the lives of Messianic Jews concerned for an abiding testimony to their people. The additional factors of belief in Jesus and membership of the body of Christ present big challenges to the nature of Jewish identity, and Messianic Jews are well aware of the difficulties they face as they define and construct an "authentic Messianic Jewish identity."

(e) Authentic Messianic Jewish Identity

Religious Jews define Jewishness as primarily a religious identity resulting from the religion of Judaism (as practised by the Orthodox and other denominational varieties of Judaism). However, the majority of Jews do not have a religiously defined identity, preferring to see "Jewishness" as a complex of factors that combine to create ethnic and cultural identity. These include language, history, culture, territory, religion, politics, humour, and demographic factors.

How do Messianic Jews put their religious identity in practice? Their ecclesiology expresses their debt to the historic

Christian denominations and the work of the mission agencies that came from them, and their own desire to integrate and incorporate aspects of synagogue worship and Jewish traditional elements. The use of the *siddur* (Jewish prayer book), celebration of the Jewish festivals and life cycle, are held in tension with the pattern of Christian worship, its creeds, and festivals. There are a considerable variety of practices found throughout the Messianic congregations and among those in mainstream churches.

(f) Messianic Identity in Israel

Jewish believers in Jesus reflect the diversity of the global Jewish community. In Israel, Messianic Jews feel under pressure from the orthodox rabbinical establishment that is influential on matters of immigration, citizenship, and religious freedom. Whilst the majority of Israelis are secular and have little objection to Messianic Jews, the orthodox groupings have challenged their right of return to the land.

Within Israel the mix of immigrants from the former Soviet Union, the US, Ethiopia, alongside native born *sabras*, leads to a diversity of practices, styles of worship, congregational leadership and some tensions. There are also contrasts between the older and younger generations of Jewish believers. The youth movement in Israel is finding ways to relate to the pluralistic and postmodern culture around them whilst affirming the truths they have received through the relatively conservative congregational structures of their parents. The Israeli congre-gations exhibit the same breadth of belief and practice that is found in the worldwide church. Denominational links, the charismatic movement, evangelistic strategy, and the role of women in ministry are issues on which there is much diversity, in addition to the particular issues that concern Jewish believers in Jesus.

Messianic Jews need to be particularly concerned about issues of peace, justice, and reconciliation. The ongoing quest to develop a distinctive Jewish identity highlights the need for right relationships with Arab brothers and sisters in Christ. Many have views on prophecy that leave little room for negotiation over territory and little confidence in the peace process. Nevertheless, at the practical and personal level, initiatives have been taken to bring Jewish and Arab believers together to experience the reconciling love of the Messiah across the boundaries of ethnicity. Regular meetings for pastors, young people, and women in formal and informal contexts are a vital demonstration of the difference that Jesus makes. There are encouraging signs challenging the *status quo* of cultural myopia, political intransigence, and the cycles of violence and hatred. Such activities take place at great personal cost to those involved, and Christians should support these initiatives with prayerful concern, refusing to allow themselves to be polarised into a simplistic allegiance to one side against the other.

(g) Evangelism and Gentiles in Jewish Evangelism

Messianic Jews are divided on the role of gentiles in Jewish evangelism. Whilst some resent the interference of the so-called "gentile church" and mission agencies in Jewish evangelism, others welcome this. They point to their own coming to faith as the fruit of the efforts of mainstream churches and Christians, and to the evidence that most Jewish people who come to faith in Jesus do so through the witness of Christian friends. However, some Messianic Jews argue for a "Post-Missionary Messianic Judaism" (the title of a forthcoming book by a Messianic leader in the US) which specifically disassociates itself from the missionary enterprise. Their concern to "have Jewish grandchildren" leads to an antipathy to involvement in the wider church, including support for mission agencies. Others argue that all missionaries should leave the land of Israel and leave evangelism to the local believers. Such a view is extreme, impractical, and falls short of the biblical model of the church's united worldwide mission of God to the world -- reflecting *missio Dei*.

A small but vocal minority would seek to delegitimise and neutralise the effects of Jewish evangelism. However, the majority of Jewish believers, longing for their families to receive the good news, are grateful that Christians care enough to pray and to witness. They are unconcerned whether Jewish or non-Jewish friends present the gospel. There is a great need for Jewish believers to be called into ministry among their own people, in addition to the many who are already involved.

The relationship between missions and Messianic congregations reflects the church/parachurch tensions commonly found in missionary contexts, with the activities of the historic denominations in Israel posing the dangers of "empire building" but allowing for the possibility of handing over responsibility and leadership to truly indigenous local believers. There are numerous examples of both practices and the more forward-looking expatriate agencies have focused on the training and empowering of local leaders wherever possible.

(h) What about the Law?

The term *torah* means more than just law. It includes teaching, instruction, and revelation. It is used to refer both to the Pentateuch and Mosaic Law, the Hebrew scriptures of the Old Testament, the Jewish religious tradition (the Mishnah, Talmud, and later Rabbinic writings) and as a general term for revelation or teaching. The intended sense of *Torah* is not always clear.

Jewish religious groupings interpret Torah differently. Orthodox Jews are strict in their observance of the laws of the Pentateuch, which are further expanded, interpreted, and applied by Rabbinic tradition. Conservative Jews modify this traditional observance in the light of modernity. Reform, Liberal, and Reconstructionist Jews adopt a humanist, postmodern position that looks to the *Torah* for moral principles and cultural norms, but these may be re-negotiated, and there are few absolutes. Most Jewish people observe some aspects of the Mosaic Law as customary and traditional, rather than out of the conviction that God commands them.

Messianic Jews believe that the Law has been fulfilled by Jesus (Matthew 5:17) and that He is the goal of the Law (Romans 10:4). Just as there are different understandings of the relationship between law and grace in the church and different Christian evaluations of the law, so there are different views among Messianic Jews. Some see the Law of Moses as obsolete. Jesus has inaugurated the new covenant. The old has gone. The laws of sacrifice have been fulfilled in Christ. The civil laws were only relevant to ancient Israel. Only the universal moral law as exemplified in the Ten Commandments is still applicable. It is therefore misguided to observe aspects of the Mosaic Law and leads back to bondage in legalism. If Messianic Jews observe the Mosaic Law, they are denying the grace of God and justification by faith alone. They rebuild the middle wall of partition, attempting to justify themselves by works of the law.

A second view affirms the cultural and social practices of the Mosaic Law, yet this is not for religious reasons. Customs that make up Jewish identity have been incorporated into Jewish life by tradition over the centuries, such as the calendar, circumcision, and the food laws. These are still normative for ethnic, cultural, and national identity, but have no theological merit and do not add to righteousness. Consequently, they are not prescriptive on Jewish believers in Jesus, who are free to observe them if they choose.

A third approach recognises the continuing validity of Jewish tradition as the interpretative context for understanding the biblical *Torah* of the Old and New Testaments. Jesus in his teaching and example, and the practice of the early church, defined a new *halacha* (rule of conduct) for the new covenant community. This *halacha* is developed today following the first Christians' example in the book of Acts. They observed Jewish lifestyle and practices, adapted some, abandoned others, and applied only a few to the nations. Messianic Jews who observe *Torah* in this way both acknowledge its value, but challenge its interpretation by the main branches of Judaism. They propose a new interpretation of *Torah* based on the teaching and practice of Jesus and the first disciples.

A final and controversial position argues that Messianic Jews should in general observe the *Torah* according to Orthodox or Conservative tradition, with only a few exceptions. This will enable them to develop their "primary identity" within the Jewish community rather than the "mainstream church." They should see themselves as members of the community of Israel and as part of the synagogue, even if others do not accept them. This challenges Messianic Jews to identify fully with their cultural and religious heritage rather than deny, ignore, or approach it in an adversarial manner.

The great danger of this last approach is a compromise on the uniqueness of

Christ and the freedom the gospel brings. Whilst such an option may be attractive for those wishing to receive a validation of their identity from the Jewish community, it can lead to a diminishment of effective testimony. The self-understanding that may be gained from such an approach leads to isolation from other believers. *Torah* observance at the cost of the visible unity of the body of Christ can only result in loss of fellowship and faith.

The outworking of the above-mentioned positions is seen in the way Messianic Jews worship. Some follow the liturgy of the synagogue, using the *siddur* (Jewish Prayer Book) and Jewish liturgy. Others produce contextualised liturgies that combine elements of Jewish and Christian worship. This can result in a creative, holistic liturgy reflecting the worship-styles and backgrounds of its participants in a way that is relevant and expressive to Jewish visitors, but at worst, it leads to an undignified and irreverent mess. Some attempt to have no liturgy at all. Most Messianic Jews are happily integrated in mainstream churches where they follow the liturgies of the denominations to which they belong. Many appreciate additional opportunities to celebrate Jewish festivals such as Passover and the Jewish New Year, with other Jewish believers, acknowledging how such festivals point to Jesus and are fulfilled in Him.

These understandings of *Torah* impact on Jewish life and lifestyle. Many Jewish believers observe Jewish holidays and life cycle events (circumcision, *bar mitzvah*, etc.), using them as opportunities to witness to the Jewishness of Jesus and his own teaching at such events. Some go further, observing various degrees of *kashrut* (the kosher food laws), the Sabbath. A few consciously seek to fulfil the requirements of Orthodox and Conservative Jewish observance. One community of Messianic congregations is developing its own *halachic* formulation (Jewish religious law). While there is no broadly recognised authority in the Messianic Jewish community, there are ongoing discussions on the need for a Messianic *beth din* (legal council) that will have authority to rule on disputed religious issues.

(i) Messianic Jews and Prophecy

Many Messianic Jews understand the return of their people to the land of Israel as a fulfilment of biblical prophecy. They hold different views on how the state of Israel should respond in the Middle East conflict. They see Israel's survival as God's providential purpose in bringing His people back to the land and giving them renewed sovereignty. Whether they live in Israel or in the Diaspora, they have strong attachment to Israel and long for peace and security in the region. Messianic Jews serve in the army, put their children through the Israeli school system, and contribute as good citizens to the life of the country. They share the passion and the pain of Zion, and they pray for a solution.

Among some there is a "millennial fever," which does not always promote sympathy with those who suffer now. Others are deeply involved in the ministry of reconciliation. Many, whilst sympathetic to the Zionist position, are cautious in expressing political and prophetic views. For them, a healthy emphasis on evangelism and unity in the body of Messiah overrides political and prophetic opinions. A variety of prophetic expectations and political opinions are found, but there is no united view on the principles of biblical interpretation, let alone how the biblical data meshes with contemporary events.

Among Jewish believers in the Diaspora there is a small but steady flow of those becoming Israeli citizens. The majority of Jewish believers in Jesus still live outside the land and do not believe they are called to immigrate to Israel. Whilst the majority of Jewish believers in the land would be unwilling to concede territory to the Palestinians, there have been several initiatives at local level for reconciliation with Arab Christians. These operate under the difficult circumstances of the *Intifada*. Arab and Jewish pastors, young people, and women meet regularly for prayer and the sharing of their lives together. Friendships made across the political divide are a powerful expression of the reconciling love of the Messiah.

(j) The Unity of God and the Uniqueness of Christ

Messianic Jews formulate the doctrines of the trinity and incarnation in Jewish terms. The majority hold firmly to these truths. Yet Jewish tradition denies the divinity of Christ and the plural unity of the Godhead, and these issues are frequently debated. Messianic Jews have a vital contribution to make in this discussion. The challenge for apologetics is to express Christian truth in Jewish terms with biblical integrity, theological accuracy, and intercultural sensitivity. The same issues occur in witness to Muslims, and the two ministries have much to learn from one another in these areas.

One helpful approach expresses the historic creeds in terms and thought-forms of Jewish discourse. The challenge here is to correctly articulate the complex understandings of the nature of Christ and the trinity. The scriptures are the basis for the creeds and the appropriate means of explaining them to Jewish enquirers. Discussion of key passages focuses on the evidence for the plural unity of the Godhead, the divine/human characteristics of the "Angel of the LORD," and the role of the Messiah.

Some Messianic Jews also use Rabbinic tradition and *midrash* (Jewish commentary on scripture) to explain these truths. This provides useful illustrative material, but care must be taken not to over-interpret these extra-biblical texts or rely too heavily upon them. The New Testament shows a more developed understanding of the Messiah in the light of Jesus' death, resurrection, and ascension. Rabbinic tradition speculates on these issues, but does not provide a definitive formulation of what is clearly revealed in Christ and made known by the illumination of the Holy Spirit.

Some express their understanding of the trinity and the incarnation using the terms and conceptual framework of the Jewish mystical tradition, the Kabbalah. In its complex literature is found the plural nature of the Godhead, and the Messiah as divine intermediary and emanation of the Divinity. There is some apologetic value in showing how ideas of the plural nature of God and the divinity of the Messiah are not completely alien to Judaism. In fact the subject has been a matter of speculation in some Jewish circles for many centuries, expressive of the longing for true redemption. There are many analogies between the Messianic idea in kabbalistic thought and the New Testament presentation of Jesus, such as His pre-existence, agency in creation, incarnation, suffering, atonement and resurrection. However, the Jewish mystical tradition compromises on the nature and being of God, using a gnostic and dualistic understanding of the immanence of the good Creator within an evil creation that awaits redemption. Such parallels in Jewish tradition should not be pressed too far, as they lead to a defective cosmology and Christology.

Others search for a post-modern formulation of the trinity. This reflects on the work of some Jewish thinkers who acknowledge the possibility of God's incarnation in the people of Israel, but have difficulty relating this understanding of incarnation to Jesus.

A small minority have acknowledged Jesus as human Messiah but denied his divine eternal nature. They see this as incompatible with the strict monotheism of Jewish tradition, which affirms the singularity and indivisibility of God. There are some Messianic Jews who deny the divinity of Christ, choosing Arian and Adoptionist Christologies and a Unitarian view

of the nature of God. Their desire is to set the Messiahship of Jesus within traditional Jewish categories, which regard worship of any being other than the invisible God, as idolatry. This is a minority position held by less than 5%, but is indicative of the seriousness of the problem.[15]

(k) The Future of Messianic Jews

In church history, a distinction was made between the heretical "Ebionites" and the orthodox "Nazarenes" by the early church fathers. This generalisation reflected the perspective of non-Jewish Christians on their Jewish brethren, and was not entirely accurate or charitable. Yet there are some similarities with present-day Jewish believers in Jesus. Various outcomes are possible for the movement. With many thousands in the worldwide church, there are signs of healthy growth and development, in personal discipleship, leadership training, congregational maturity, youth movements, and theological reflection.

For Messianic groups some important principles apply. Efforts at contextualisation must be faithful to Scripture and cannot include anti-Christian elements that might be common Jewish understandings. These include prayers for forgiveness without substitutionary atonement, or what is commonly understood as prayers for the dead. Messianic Jewish worship practices and retention of Jewish customs must be authentic expressions of individuals and members of the group. Care should be taken to affirm the unity of the body of Christ, both in the Diaspora with all Christians and particularly with Arab Christians in Israel.

It is to be hoped that engagement with these issues will produce an informed and theologically mature next generation. If the Messianic movement can retain the supremacy of the Messiah and the authority of Scripture in its faith and practice, it will avoid a pride and parochialism that could threaten its well-being. If it can deepen its understanding and love for the Messiah and walk in his path of humility and servanthood, it will continue to grow, bearing effective testimony to the Jewish people about her Messiah, and bearing light to the nations as the saved remnant of Israel.

Christians who are concerned for the salvation and welfare of the Jewish people can rejoice at the increasing number of Jewish people coming to know their Messiah. They exist as a renewed expression of God's faithfulness to his ancient people. We pray that they will fulfil the vision of their destiny, commit their lives to loving service, and respond to the Lord's call to be a light to the nations as they bear witness to the Messiah of Israel. May they benefit from the theological resources, pastoral support and loving encouragement of their wider Christian family.

4. CHALLENGES FACING JEWISH EVANGELISM

As the church renews its vision for Jewish evangelism, it must face several challenges associated with this difficult task. This section outlines these for consideration, in the hope that deeper understanding of and engagement in Jewish evangelism will result.

(a) Irreconcilable Truth Claims

Some Christians argue that dialogue is all that Christian mission to the Jewish people requires. However, dialogue that aims at nothing more than mutual understanding fails to fulfil the Christian obligation to make disciples of all people, including Jews. Both classical Judaism and classical Christianity make truth claims. The Jewish scholar Jon D. Levenson points this out. He thinks, for example, that *Dabru Emet* suffers from one of the great pitfalls of interfaith dialogue over the past several decades, because people have attempted "to avoid any candid discussion of fundamental beliefs and to adopt instead the model of conflict resolutions or diplomatic negotiation." He maintains:

> The easygoing relativism profoundly impedes any sophisticated understanding of the two millennia of Jewish-Christian dialogue and dispute over the meaning of Scripture. A more accurate statement would note that it is precisely the points of commonality that make disputation over the differences inevitable – at least within communities committed to the idea of religious truth and not simply to the theological equivalent of "I'm, OK,

you're OK."

Levenson further adds: "Participants in Jewish-Christian dialogue often speak as if Jews and Christians agreed about God but disagreed about Jesus. They have forgotten that in a very real sense, orthodox Christians believe Jesus *is* God."[16]

(b) In Denial: "Jews Do Not Believe in Jesus"

In recent years, some Christians have entered into interfaith dialogue with Jewish leaders, being willing to accept the condition that Jewish believers in Jesus are excluded even when they are qualified to participate. Christian scholar Wolfhart Pannenberg, professor emeritus of Systematic Theology from Munich, criticises this viewpoint in a response to *Dabru Emet*, Pannenberg states:

> One of the new developments made possible by the reestablishment of a Jewish state in Palestine has been the emergence of groups of "messianic Jews" within Israel, Jews who confess their faith in Jesus the Messiah without leaving the Jewish community and a Jewish way of life. Since the end of the Jewish congregation of Jerusalem in the first century, this is the first time that a Jewish-Christian church reemerges so that a Jew need not turn to a gentile church when he or she comes to believe in Jesus the Christ. The "messianic Jews" intend to remain Jews while professing Jesus to be the Messiah. Sooner or later Christian-Jewish dialogue will have to take notice of this fact ...[17]

Rabbi Barry Cytron, Director of Jay Phillips Center for Jewish-Christian Learning, comments on this by saying:

> In his remarks on "messianic Jews," Prof. Pannenberg touches on a sensitive, hurtful area in interfaith relationships. To many in the Jewish community, the tactics employed by "messianic Jews" to spread their beliefs are often unseemly. Several recent books have documented these efforts at conversion and the ill-will that lingers from such attempts. The guidelines of the Evangelical Lutheran Church in America on Jewish-Christian relationships forthrightly address this issue: "Groups such as 'Jews for Jesus' or 'Messianic Jews' consist of persons from a Jewish background who have converted to Christianity and who wish to retain their Jewish heritage and identity. Lutherans should be aware that most Jews regard such persons as having forsaken Judaism, and consider efforts to maintain otherwise to be deceptive."[18]

Unable to disprove the unique identity of Jewish believers in Jesus, Cytron attacks only their methods of evangelism.

(c) Anti-Semitism

Despite the presence of Jewish believers in Jesus in the church throughout the centuries, ecclesiastical and civil authorities often persecuted Jews. Because attacks against the Jewish people during the crusades, inquisitions, and pogroms were committed against the Jewish people in the name of Christ, it is little wonder that Jews have associated the good news of Jesus with bad news for the Jews.

Not all Christians or churches were responsible for such anti-Semitic acts. Yet the perception among Jewry at the start of the twenty-first century is that both Christians and the message of Christianity are responsible for the wrongs of the past. Whilst that misimpression is an obstacle to Jewish evangelism, it does not justify its curtailment. Those who conducted such hateful acts in the name of Jesus will be held to account by God. Vengeance is His alone. The gospel is no less true.

The teaching that the New Testament itself is anti-Semitic is to be rejected. Indeed, there have been terrible anti-Semitic misuses of the New Testament within church history. However, taking the New Testament scriptures out of their biblical and historical contexts to support anti-Semitic hatred does not make the word of God anti-Jewish.

The harsh words found in the Gospels against the Jewish people reflect the internal debate among Jews at the time about the Jew Jesus. They are similar to the unflattering intramural depictions of a disobedient Jewish people in the Old Testament that were uttered by Moses or the prophets. Whilst strongly expressed, the Gospel challenges are to be seen in the context of God's covenant faithfulness to His people and His longing for their repentance, as well as in Jesus' love for His people.

It should be categorically denied that the Jewish people alone were to blame for the death of Jesus. They were no more responsible for His crucifixion than were all humanity. So who is to blame and who is without guilt? Since all have sinned and fall short of the glory of God, then all bear guilt for the death of Jesus. Yet, God in His loving grace made the death of His Son possible, in His wisdom and love, to save the lost, both Jew and gentile alike.

(d) Modern Marcionism

Marcion, a theologian of the second century, denied that the heavenly Father of Jesus was the same as the God of Israel as portrayed in the Hebrew Scriptures. He believed that the Old Testament God was an evil God of wrath, while the Father of Jesus was a good God of love.

The early church rightly declared Marcion a heretic. Nevertheless, a modern Marcionism exists in the church today. It is right to combat the false notion today that the God of the Old Testament is a wrathful God and the God of the New Testament is a God of love.

The starting point for biblical theology is the unity of the Scriptures. The one true God is revealed throughout the entire Bible. That God is a God of righteousness, exhibiting wrath at times. He is also the God of grace, extending loyal loving kindness, pouring out His mercy and goodness with infinite measure. The God of Israel in the Old Testament is the same heavenly Father of Jesus in the New Testament. Christians are called on here to reject and correct popular notions that reflect modern Marcionism. Such false ideas can hinder Jewish people from understanding the true nature of God as rightly found throughout the Bible.

(e) Eschatology

Evangelicals have different interpretations of Old and New Testament prophetic texts concerning the Jewish people and the land of Israel. Some are hesitant to speak about the fulfilment of specific prophecies with regard to the establishment of the present-day state of Israel. Others are not. Some await further fulfilment of prophecy in the spiritual restoration of ethnic Israel and the coming of the Messianic kingdom. Others do not apply these prophetic texts exclusively either to ethnic Israel or to the church. This view does not detract from the reality of the promises, but is open to how they will be fulfilled, either to the church or to the Jewish people in their homeland.

Christians must note that the land promised to Abraham is today the home for both Jewish and Arab peoples. Any view of future outcomes that does not respect the present inhabitants, or fails to see them as precious in the sight of God is at risk of being unchristian. The love of Christ is available for all and forever. Enthusiasm for the potential fulfilment of prophecies associated with the state of Israel must not overshadow or miss the centrality of the crucified and resurrected Christ. The present return of Jewish people to the land and the rebirth of Israel as a gathered nation are evidence of God's faithfulness. If God's loyal love to Israel endures, then surely likewise His love for all in Christ is secure.

Indeed, expectation of the imminent return of Christ should be a strong inspiration for the task of Jewish evangelism. He will return in glory and power to fulfil His purposes of judgement and salvation. Before that day, the gospel must first go out to all nations and to all Israel. This glorious future hope should guide all Christians in setting evangelism as their priority both now, and until the Lord returns in glory.

(f) Reconciliation

The promised land of the Bible is the home today of both Jews and Arabs. The continuing tension between Israeli and Palestinian people is tragic. Christians everywhere cannot allow themselves the luxury of a dispassionate regard for the suffering of all peoples in that land.

Christians, wherever they are, must guard their hearts against the pressures of nationalism and the urge to take sides in the political disputes raging in the State of Israel and the Occupied Territories. Christians must pray for and support their Palestinian and Jewish brothers and sisters in Christ as they are engaged in the pursuit of a just peace.

It must be remembered that God's loving grace extends to all the descendants of Abraham. Therefore, Christians should pray for God's work of salvation and reconciliation though His Spirit among the peoples of the land of Israel and its neighbours.

The Lord is growing His church among Israelis and Palestinians, some of whom are worshipping together in local congregations. The Lord Jesus alone is the one who can bring a true and lasting peace into the hearts of the people in His land.

(g) Jewish and Muslim Evangelism

There are many parallels and similarities between Jewish and Muslim evangelism. The church has much to gain in sharing the common challenges they present and learning from both. A commitment to both outreaches prevents polarisation within the body of Christ.

Those involved in Christian-Muslim dialogue often encounter similar opposition to that experienced by those engaged in Jewish-Christian dialogue. The Islamic faith in the one God and Muslim identity as descendants of Abraham are often presented in such a way as to exclude any need for their salvation in Jesus Christ. Once again, the key theological issue is the uniqueness of Christ for salvation as the ultimate expression of the loving God.

Baptised Jewish believers in Jesus, along with Muslims who come to faith in Christ and are baptised, are often ostracised from their respective communities. Even worse, many that publicly identify themselves risk martyrdom for their Christian faith. Today, the church can support Jews and Muslims who come to Christ by advocating strongly for their religious freedom as brother and sister believers in their home communities. In addition, the Christian church can do more to encourage contextualised expressions of Jewish or Arab Christian identity among their respective people groups. These new believers should be encouraged to develop appropriate cultural identities and practices as followers of Jesus within the body of Christ.

5. CASE STUDIES: STRATEGIES AND INITIATIVES IN JEWISH EVANGELISM

Good things are happening globally in the field of Jewish evangelism. Following is a selection of current and prospective Jewish evangelism initiatives that are encouraging. It should be remembered that each of these initiatives needs the ongoing support of the body of Christ, through prayer, finances, and volunteer help. These case studies, strategies, programmes, and plans are signs for us that God is still at work among Jewish people and they are hearing and receiving the good news of Messiah Jesus. The continued involvement of Jewish people in Jewish evangelism is living testimony that God is faithful to His plan to make Israel a light to the nations.

(a) Jewish Evangelism at the Local Level
(i) City-wide Evangelistic Campaigns

Jewish mission strategists realise that Jewish people rarely seek out the truth about Jesus on their own. Jewish missionaries must go out and actively seek to engage people who may be open to the gospel. Since many Jewish people tend to gravitate towards urban centres, these locations become prime areas for direct outreach.

For several years, various Jewish evangelistic agencies have conducted outreach campaigns in urban centres. In 2001, the Jews for Jesus organisation launched Operation Behold Your God (BYG). It is a focused, long-range initiative to conduct a significant evangelistic outreach in every city of the world, outside of Israel, with a Jewish population of 25,000 or more before summer, 2006. Campaigns are composed of a combination of Jews for Jesus staff, co-operating with other mission agencies and teams of well-trained volunteers from local churches and Messianic congregations. They engage in evangelistic literature distribution, phone calling, door-to-door witnessing, multimedia outreach and special events. BYG campaigns have required the development of new evangelism strategies for cities that present special city-specific opportunities and unique problems such as government regulations that are resistant to gospel penetration. Each campaign is less than a month in duration and includes a follow-up programme with trained local co-ordinators for continued discipleship ministry. Outcomes have been tracked, with more than 700 Jews and over 2700 gentiles making professions of faith by 2004.

(ii) Holiday Outreaches

Jewish mission agencies and Messianic congregations conduct outreaches during the Jewish High Holy days. Constituents and congregational members are encouraged to bring Jewish friends and family to Rosh HaShanah (New Year) and Yom Kippur (Day of Atonement) services. These are often worship services with evangelistic emphasis.

Light of Messiah Ministries in Atlanta, Georgia, developed a creative initiative involving local churches in outreach to their Jewish communities during Jewish holidays. Christians are invited to sponsor food gift baskets for their Jewish friends.

They are then hand-delivered by Jewish believers to the homes of Jewish families as a way of wishing a "Sweet New Year" or a "Happy Passover." An opportunity is presented to share the gospel.

(iii) Direct Mail to Jewish Homes

Direct mail to Jewish people is an important component of Jewish evangelism. During evangelistic campaigns, mailers are sent out to Jewish homes, offering a free book or multimedia presentation or an invitation to attend an event like an apologetics debate or a holy day service. Most of the missions publish newsletters that address subjects of interest to Jewish people from a Messianic Jewish perspective.

Shema Yisrael, a ministry near Detroit, Michigan, sends out regular evangelistic mailings to Jewish homes in their area. They partner with local churches, which help provide postage and people to address and stuff envelopes. Postcards are also mailed with a brief message appealing to anyone who might be interested in knowing why some Jews believe in Jesus. The cards offer a free book or video and contact information to reach the congregation. Mailing responses include phone calls and people who visit their congregation as a result.

(b) Reaching Specific Jewish Groups

Diversity of Jewish communities and culture requires development of different methods to reach specific segments of Jewry. Following are examples of some strategies for reaching sub-groups of world Jewish population with the gospel of Jesus.

(i) Reaching "Generation J"

Mainstream Judaism wrestles with the question of how to reach the younger Jewish generation. Jewish missions face the same challenge. Materials are being developed for younger Jewish people today, referred to as "Generation J," but there is still much more to be done. This age group is uniquely caught in the modern to post-modern paradigm shift. Some ideas that are been tried are "web-zines," outreaches to Jewish college students over school holiday periods, and evangelistic nightclub outreaches. Campus ministry is a vital component to reach "Generation J."

Hope of David, a Messianic congregation in Atlanta, Georgia, conducted a significant outreach from 1999 to 2002 at the University of Georgia, where 1,000 out of 30,000 students declare themselves Jewish. The outreach strategy used four methods: literature distribution, public lectures, information displays in the student square, and a student-led organisation that partnered campus Christian groups and Messianic Jews. To form on-campus ministry, most American public universities require that initiatives come from registered students rather than outside agents. Hope of David began by enlisting the co-operation of Christian student organisations that already existed. Once the required minimum number of students had signed up, the group could distribute literature advertising public lectures on subjects with controversial twists in order to draw students. Topics included: "A Jewish Perspective on the Resurrection of Jesus," "Astrology and the

Birth of Messiah," and "A Jewish Christmas." The student-led organisation met weekly for Bible study and worship. Volunteers ran information tables and distributed literature, helping to develop crowds for the public lectures. Hope of David found the college age group ideal for reaching young Jewish adults who were in the process of making their own decisions about new ideas. Jewish students are not easily introduced to the gospel. It is therefore important to keep proclaiming and keep learning more effective ways to reach "Generation J."

(ii) Ministry to Jewish "New Agers", "JuBus" and "HinJus"

New Age and Eastern religions and practices are filling a spiritual vacuum among Jewish people. Reaching JuBus (Jewish Buddhists) and HinJus (Jewish Hindus) and the practitioners of New Age Judaism requires unique approaches to these worldviews. However, specialised training and materials are available.

This area is an especially important outreach for Israeli Jews. Many young Israelis are turning to Eastern and New Age religions. After serving their term of service in the Israeli army, many choose to sojourn to India to explore these beliefs. At the same time, some of these young people are open to the gospel. A joint initiative through the co-operation of the Caspari Center in Israel and the Danish Israel Mission seeks to minister to Israeli people via short-term mission programmes. Teams of Israeli Jewish Believers with volunteers and staff from Jewish mission agencies undergo a month-long orientation, coinciding with New Age Festivals taking place in Israel. Teams then spend three months in India ministering to Israeli New Agers who are also open to the gospel.

(iii) Reaching the Intermarried

Demographic evidence points to an increasing population of Jewish-gentile couples and indicates a community that is already experiencing cultural change. That phenomenon is an opportunity for appropriate Christian evangelistic efforts. While Jewish communities tend to view intermarriage as a threat to Jewish survival, no similar alarm is sounded in the Christian church. Hence, the overwhelming response to the needs of dating, cohabiting, and intermarried Jewish-gentile couples and their families has come from traditional Jewish agencies. Christian churches should become alert to this ministry opportunity in their area and mobilise for outreach to a segment of Jewish people that is ready to respond to a hope for spiritual harmony.

The single greatest challenge expressed by Jewish-gentile couples is the struggle to find spiritual harmony.[19] The Christian message offers couples the means to know the one true God without obliterating the ethnic distinctions of the partners. Sensitivity to provide the accurate gospel message must consider the different cultural perceptions of Jewish-gentile partners. Already, a few Messianic congregations have effectively responded to the opportunity by providing specific ministry for the Jewish-gentile intermarried couples. See Appendix D for more.

(iv) Reaching Israelis in Bolivia

A missionary couple with Avant Ministries, based in Cochabamba, Bolivia, and working with the Yuquis Indians, also has an unusual opportunity for evangelistic ministry to Israelis. Their region is a popular destination for Israeli backpackers who stumbled upon the mission station, noted the gracious hospitality and wrote them up for an Israeli travel guidebook. Israelis subsequently came to their home intentionally. The mission family now regularly receives Israeli visitors. A typical visit includes a tour of the mission facility, a slide show of the Yuqui mission work, and an Israeli meal. Hebrew Bibles, including New Testaments, are distributed. Discussions about the Christian mission and true Christian beliefs take place over a typical Israeli dinner. Thus far, their mission has been a witnessing hub to over eight thousand Israelis.

(v) Strategy for Hassidic Jews

Hasidic Outreach Partnership for Evangelism (HOPE) is an outreach to Hassidic, ultra-orthodox Jews who live in a very closed community. They are among the most difficult Jews to reach. The aim of HOPE is to network ministries and workers from around the world to concentrate resources and prayer in reaching these people for Christ. Other Jewish ministries, while not specifically targeting any one Hassidic community, conduct outreach to Hassidic Jews. Staff members of Jewish evangelistic ministries with offices in metropolitan centres like New York or London, for instance, meet with inquiring Hassidic Jews from time to time.

(vi) Reaching Post-modern Jewish People

The profound cultural change that has occurred in the past few decades as a result of post-modern thinking has impacted Western Jewry. One aspect of post-modern thought rejects the notion of objective truth claims and instead maintains that each person's story and experience is valid and deserves to be heard as truth. Many Jews are therefore open to new narratives about spirituality. Mission efforts must prepare to interact with post-modern thinking Jewish people.

One resource grappling with post-moderns is "The Y Course," co-authored by London-based Jewish believer Joseph Steinberg. It is an eight-week series on DVD that is based on the book *Beyond Belief?* The Y Course confronts the reality that post-modern society, including Jewish people, does not know who Jesus is, what he did, or what he said. The course distinctively explores life, rather than religion. It tells the story of Jesus, rather than studying Christian discipleship subjects like prayer or healing. It examines real life questions like suffering, the validity of other religions, and life after death. It gives people time to process what they discover. The Y Course uses relevant illustrations and stories that relate to the culture and experience of the post-modern audience. It is one more resource for churches that are using seeker-based evangelism courses to reach out to Jewish and gentile post-moderns.

(vii) Ministry to Children

Reaching Jewish children directly with the gospel poses ethical concerns. Evangelism among Jewish children often occurs in the context of ministry to Jewish believing children.

Club Maccabee in Chicago recognises the need of Messianic Jewish children for regular Bible instruction and fellowship with other Jewish children. The Club programme is structured into 25 weekly sessions. Both believing and non-believing Jewish children take part. Parental permission is a prerequisite for participation. Children receive Jewish education, Holy Day instruction, Hebrew language lessons, and teaching from the scriptures reflecting a Jewish perspective. In four years Club Maccabee has developed an organised programme which is now being used by several Messianic congregations in America, Argentina, and in the Former Soviet Union. The club in Chicago has grown, expanding from primary grades into high school programmes.

Backyard bible clubs and summer camps are also offered for Jewish children. Extensive mission and congregational programmes are functioning in the United States and in Israel.

(c) Media Evangelism

One of the most exciting resources that Jewish missions have at their disposal is the media. Knowing how to effectively utilise the media in all its aspects is crucial for those in Jewish evangelism.

(i) Cyber Evangelism

The World Wide Web has become the internet street corner, coffee shop, or marketplace for witnessing and religious discourse around the world today. A wide selection of apologetic materials are available online to answer the questions Jewish people are asking. Bulletin or message boards are available for individuals to express their thoughts and interact with others. Perhaps the most exciting salon for electronic communication is with internet chat rooms. PALtalk and webcams enable text conversations to take on tone and texture.[20]

(ii) Timely Response to Events

Contemporary culture requires that those engaged in Jewish evangelism be ready to respond immediately to current events in a manner that is relevant to Jewish community interests. One example was the phenomenon around the film "The Passion of the Christ."

Mel Gibson's movie, and the controversy surrounding it, provided opportunities for gospel proclamation to Jewish people. Jews were already talking about the implications of the film, so it was not missiologically difficult for mission agencies to enter the conversation, focusing on the message of Jesus. Several ministries immediately produced literature to answer questions raised by the film, and that addressed the message of the "Passion" and Christ's passion depicted in the Bible. Chosen People Ministries maintained prayer stations on the film's opening night to engage people before and after the film. Jews for Jesus ran full-page ads in *Variety* and the *New York Times* entitled, "An Open Letter to Mel Gibson from a Jew for Jesus." They created opportunities for more coverage and additional discussion of the subject through subsequent media interviews and articles. The church and

those involved in Jewish evangelism must be as media savvy and culturally aware as is the Jewish audience that is available for the gospel.

(iii) Radio and Television Ministries

Radio and television programmes that feature Messianic Jews are developing as interest in Jewish influences on Christianity and Jewish evangelism continues to grow. Some of the more widely known US television programmes are "Zola Levitt Presents," "Jewish Voice Today," "Sid Roth's Messianic Vision," "Jewish Jewels," and elements of "Middle East TV" broadcasting into Israel. Shows focus on educating Christians about Jews and Jewish evangelism, while reaching an over-heard audience of interested Jewish people. The increasing popularity of radio via Internet has enabled radio efforts such as Messianic Bureau International's "Messianic Jewish Radio" and "Messianic Minutes." Programmes typically feature testimonies of Jewish believers in Jesus, Messianic music, and Bible teaching.

(iv) The Power of Story in Jewish Evangelism

Testimonies through suffering: "Survivor Stories" is a video project featuring seven poignant testimonies of Jewish Holocaust survivors who have come to faith in Christ. They make a powerful case for the gospel. It has been shown to seekers in secular venues in the US, France, Ukraine, Russia, England, Brazil, and Canada. Evangelistic newspaper ads, billboards, and radio spots have offered seekers a study guide or a free copy. They can learn about the power to forgive and overcome hatred through the Messiah Jesus. Over 21,000 copies of the video have been distributed in this manner. In light of the atrocities committed in a Christianised Europe, this film offers an opportunity to present the loving Jesus of the Bible to a hurting segment of the Jewish community.

Testimonies through conflict: "Forbidden Peace" is a documentary video of Muslim background Palestinians and Israeli Jews who share their stories of faith in Christ. Beginning with their need to be reconciled to God, they take their stories further to their need to be reconciled to one another. The message of the video is that the only hope for true and lasting peace in the Middle East, or anywhere, is in Jesus. This film has been used on college campuses, with the sponsorship of campus Christian ministries. Often, after it was shown, a team of a believing Arab and Jew field questions. A follow-up survey for further information is offered along with a study guide for post viewing consideration.

Testimonies of the self-sufficient: Jews are thought of, for the most part, as well educated and fulfilled with material satisfactions. So, stories of Jews who are successful by the world's standards, yet recognise their spiritual poverty, are powerful evangelistic tools. The account told by a successful Jewish businessman, Stan Telchin, in *Betrayed,* has been translated into over 30 languages. Hundreds of Jewish readers of his story have come to faith in Christ. It is listed in the bibliography section, along with other testimonies of Jewish believers who are physicians, law-

yers, or concert pianists.

A media savvy missionary: Secular radio, television, print, and Internet media outlets can be valuable resources for communicating the gospel in public discourse. It is therefore necessary that the church and Jewish missions develop and maintain strategies for encouraging media opportunities locally, nationally and internationally. That includes knowing how and when to write attention-grabbing press releases, cultivating media contacts, making the most of a story, and being ready to comment on current events that pertain to Jews around the globe. It is more than five years since a well-known Jewish mission leader (along with two rabbis and a Christian educator) was a guest on "Larry King Live" via CNN in the US. Yet that show has been re-run in Israel and North America with responses still coming from hearts that have been spiritually moved. The church needs to know what to say and when to say it in developing media as an evangelistic resource.

(d) Training and Education

Leadership training and education of Jewish missionaries and church mission workers is a long-term investment in the field of Jewish evangelism. A vision for more is needed.

(i) Jewish Evangelism in Bible Colleges and Seminaries

Many Bible colleges and seminaries offer opportunities to study in Israel. A few, like Nyack College in New York, Philadelphia Biblical University, and Moody Bible Institute in Chicago, have chosen to emphasise Jewish evangelism.

By and large, the task of generating excitement about Jewish missions is left to Jewish mission agencies. Finding a platform to encourage Jewish evangelism on some Bible college campuses can be difficult. So Jewish missions often have to find creative means of informing Christian students about short-term evangelism opportunities, internships, and the possibility of serving in the field. To increase awareness and enthusiasm for Jewish evangelism, mission programmes may include discussions, lectures, and missions courses for Jewish studies on Bible College and Seminary campuses.

(ii) Training for Leadership in Jewish Evangelism

Leadership training for the twenty-first century missionary in Jewish evangelism needs specialised preparation to meet emerging trends in the field. Graduate level programmes are being developed to equip Jewish mission leaders to meet sociological trends such as intermarriage and youth work. There is also a need for more active mentoring programmes.

(iii) Opportunities for Teen and College-age Jewish Believers

Young Jewish believers in Jesus are interested in Jewish evangelism. To foster that enthusiasm, Jewish mission agencies must develop appropriate entry-level programmes. For instance, Jews for Jesus offers *Halutzim*, a study-tour for 16-18 year old Jewish believers. They travel to a major cities, like New York, to engage in street evangelism training and experiences. They also get a taste of Jewish New York, time to fellowship with local Jewish believers in the same age group, and time for Bible study to seek God's direction for their lives.

College-age Jewish believers can also engage in *Project Joshua*, two weeks for training in evangelism in the land and with the people of Israel. *Project Joshua* takes place during the December school break, beginning in New York with lectures and basic training for outreach in Israel. Students are equipped with gospel tracts and Hebrew New Testaments. They evangelise through tract distribution and one-on-one conversations on the streets in Jerusalem, Haifa, and Tel Aviv. They also receive instruction in biblical and historical geography. Besides exploring Israel they meet with Israeli Jewish and Arab college students. Chosen People Ministries also offers *eXperience Israel*, a two-week mission and training trip to Israel for those between 18 and 30 years of age, and *Teen STEP*, a one-week mission trip to New York City for younger people between 14 and 17 years old.

Youth camp programmes in the US are featured divisions of the Messianic Jewish Alliance of America (MJAA), the Union of Messianic Jewish Congregations (UMJC), and the Jews for Jesus' *Camp Gilgal*. The latter now operates four regional camps for youth through college age Jewish believers and unsaved Jewish young people in the US. A variety of youth camps and conferences have already been mentioned as functioning in Israel under the aegis of congregations and mission agencies.

Younger Jewish believers need opportunities for discipleship and outreach ministry to others their own age. The church and mission strategists can help by encouraging younger Jewish believers to invest their lives in reaching other Jewish youth with the gospel. Many young people who participate in the programmes above continue in the field of Jewish evangelism.

(e) Co-operation and Networking: Jewish Missions and the Church

Jewish mission societies seek to facilitate co-operation with one another and with the church as much as possible. In many ways, this is already happening. That gives hope for further partnerships, which are surely needed in an increasingly globalised mission world.

(i) Networking among Jewish Missions

The Lausanne Consultation on Jewish Evangelism (LCJE) is a network of mission agencies and individuals that are committed to partnership and co-operation in evangelism. The conference statement from the LCJE international conference in Helsinki 2003: "Jesus and His People" reads, "We call on one another, as those involved in the ministries of evangelism, teaching, and congregational planting, to work in cooperation to bring *Jesus and His People* together."[21] The unique purposes of the LCJE include sharing information and resources with other workers in the field of Jewish evangelism. Partnerships and co-operative evangelistic efforts encourage efficient use of God's resources for the cause of Jewish evangelism. Appendix A has more information.

(ii) Financial Accountability to the Christian Community

Jewish mission efforts are a sort of "niche" ministry with a target population of only fourteen million people spread all over the globe. They face many unique challenges. One involves reports and accountability to Christian supporters. The question is often posed, "How many Jewish people came to Christ this year?" The answer is not particularly impressive in most cases. Jewish evangelism has rarely seen responses like those of a Billy Graham crusade. It is more like a handpicked harvest, with fruit collected one by one. Yet, ministries feel pressure to put their best foot forward when it comes to reporting results. They are tempted to trumpet successes and downplay failures. Hence, some reports are vague and unspecific regarding ministry efforts. To quote the late Menahem Benhayim, a pioneering Messianic leader in Israel,

> The lack of hard information has often led to wild estimates and misleading publicity about the size and the scope of the movement. Much of the information promulgated was fueled by anti-mission extremists and sometimes by well-meaning Christian and Messianic enthusiasts to encourage friends and supporters about the movement's growth and impact upon the Jewish community in Israel; and there have also been outright liars who have provided their supporters with fabricated tales of success.[22]

Some mission leaders fear that if people knew the numbers they might feel less inclined to support the efforts. Still, even those who do report specific statistics can be misleading. Occasionally, anti-missionaries take annual mission income and divide that by the number of Jewish people reported to have made professions of faith. They use the figures to equate each "convert" as a per dollar ratio. It is a method that is intended to discourage Christians from supporting Jewish evangelism. Opposition to Jewish evangelism wants the church to believe that they can "get more for their money" by shopping elsewhere, since Jewish souls are no bargain for the mission budget! However, accountability between Jewish missions and the churches that support them only encourages partnership in a difficult field and the need and value of support.

(iii) Co-operation with the Church in Prayer/Intercession

The Apostle Paul offered these words, *"Brethren, my heart's desire and prayer to God for Israel is that they may be saved"* (Romans 10:1). Passion in proclamation of the gospel must be undergirded with the fervency of intercessory prayer as the priestly ministry of evangelism. The church can further the work of Jewish evangelism by including the salvation of Jews on the prayer agenda. Parachurch groups, like Watchmen on the Wall, consider prayer for Jewish people and Israel as their chief ministry. These groups are known for conducting all-night prayer vigils on behalf of Jewish people and Israel.

(iv) Cooperation through Compassion Ministries

Jewish people are generally regarded as being philanthropic. It is fitting that ministries to Jewish people are seeking to help Jews in need. There are a number of compassion ministries, many helping Jewish people in Israel, the Former Soviet Union, and Ethiopia.

For example, the Messianic Jewish Alliance of America sponsors the *Joseph Project*. It supplies food, clothing, basic toiletries, medical supplies, toys, building materials, and other necessities to impoverished people in Israel. *The Russian Emergency Aliyah Relief Fund* helps Russian Jews immigrate to Israel. The *Messianic Jewish Israel Fund* helps meet the financial needs of Messianic Jews in Israel and *Operation Tikvah* helps Jews in Ethiopia. Many of these efforts involve short-term mission projects to deliver aid and comfort. Gentile Christians who have a heart for Jewish people and specifically Israel have formed agencies such as Christian Friends of Israel. Compassion ministries in the body of Christ make a proper methodological connection between their relief efforts and gospel proclamation.

(v) The South - Majority Church and Jewish Evangelism

Extraordinary growth is occurring in the church of the "majority world." Most of Asia, Africa, and Latin America have small Jewish populations. Nevertheless, churches in these regions have the same obligation to pray for Jewish people and encourage witness to them, as do churches everywhere else.

A helpful model is seen in the LCJE Japan network. Through the efforts of LCJE Japan, guest speakers from the Jewish mission world are brought to Japan to teach and inspire local church groups. The Japan network of agencies also organises local prayer groups, arranges for biblical study tours to Israel, and produces appropriate literature. Majority world leaders can connect with missions, with a special calling to Jewish evangelism, to building bridges of encouragement, prayer support, and sharing for mutual benefit.

Following are some practical suggestions to enable the church in the majority world to be a vital part of the Jewish evangelism effort:

1. 1. Pray that God will send missionaries to the Jewish people.
2. 2. Christian world organisations in the west might raise scholarship funds to enable majority world pastors and Bible teachers to study in Israel, learning about Jewish evangelism and the Jewish roots of the Christian faith.
3. 3. Pray faithfully for the salvation of Jewish people.
4. 4. See to it that libraries at theological institutions in the global south have literature and journals on the subject of Jewish evangelism.

6. TODAY WE PRAY: OUR FATHER IN HEAVEN

During the 2004 Forum for World Evangelization we have asked ourselves what God is saying to the church. What does the word of God say about the Jewish people and sharing the good news with them? Today we pray:

– Lord, give your church *a new heart* for the Jewish people, a heart which is rooted in your love for them, and which blesses this people and prays for their peace and salvation.
– Lord, give your church *a new vision,* a vision which appreciates today the presence of Jewish believers in your church, and which hopes for the ingathering of a full number from the Jewish people and the nations.
– Lord, give your church *a renewed call* to share the good news in word and deed with Jewish people everywhere and to live out your great commission from Jerusalem and to the ends of the world.

Our Father in heaven,
hallowed be your name,
your kingdom come,
your will be done
on earth as it is in heaven.
Give us today our daily bread.
Forgive us our debts,
as we also forgive our debtors.
And lead us not into temptation,
but deliver us from the evil one.
For yours is the kingdom and the power
and the glory forever.
Amen.

APPENDIX A
Lausanne Consultation on Jewish Evangelism (LCJE)

LCJE is the only global organisation today in which people involved in the field of Jewish evangelism can come together and . . .

- Share information and resources
- Study current trends
- Stimulate one another's thinking on theological and missiological issues
- Strategize on a global level so that more Jewish people will hear and consider the good news of Jesus
- Arrange consultations that will be useful to those engaged in Jewish evangelism

How did it begin?

In 1980, the Lausanne Committee for World Evangelization (LCWE) sponsored the Consultation on World Evangelization (COWE) in Pattaya, Thailand. "Reaching Jews" was one of 17 mini-consultation groups at that event. This group has continued as a task force, now called the Lausanne Consultation on Jewish Evangelism (LCJE).

What has happened since?

LCJE has met for international consultations every 3-4 years and more often on a regional basis. There are chapters in North America, South America, Europe, Israel, South Africa, Australia, and Japan. In Germany and Finland there are local LCJE groups.

The *LCJE Bulletin* is published quarterly to keep its members abreast of what is happening between international conferences. Over the years a lot of written resource material has been collected: reports on Jewish mission work from different parts of the world, history of Jewish believers, theological issues, etc. Some of the material from more recent conferences can be found online: www.lcje.net

Who can join LCJE?

Jewish evangelism agencies, congregations engaged in Jewish evangelism, scholars and writers in the field, individual agency workers, and congregational leaders.

Membership is open to any agency, congregation, or individual that is recommended by two other members. All members need to be in substantial agreement with the Lausanne Covenant. Online: http://www.lausanne.org.

International Coordinating Committee (ICC) – 2003-2007

> Tuvya Zaretsky, USA (President)
> Kai Kjær-Hansen, Denmark (International Co-ordinator)
> Derek Leman, USA (Committee Member)
> Lisa Loden, Israel (Committee Member)

International address

> LCJE, Ellebækvej 5, Box 11,
> DK-8520 Lystrup, Denmark
> E-mail: lcje-int@skjern-net.dk
> Homepage: www.lcje.net

APPENDIX B
LCWE Statements in Support of Jewish Evangelism
Christian Witness to the Jewish People (1980)

Drafted by members of the "Mini-Consultation on Reaching Jewish People" in Pattaya, Thailand in 1980 and sponsored by LCWE. Online: http://www.Gospelcom.net/lcwe/LOP/lop07.htm

The last paragraph of the report reads

> Including Jewish people is a test of our willingness to be involved in world evangelisation. It is a test of our faith in the one exclusive way of salvation and of our proclamation of Christ as an adequate Saviour for those who are apparently adequate so far as worldly righteousness is concerned.

The Willowbank Declaration on the Christian Gospel and the Jewish People (1989)

The *Declaration* came out of a theo-logical consultation held at Willowbank, Bermuda, that was sponsored by the World Evangelical Fellowship (WEF) and supported by the Lausanne Committee for World Evangelization (LCWE) in 1989. Online: www.lcje.net

The following is taken from the Preamble,

> In recent years, "messianic" Jewish believers in Jesus, who as Christians celebrate and maximize their Jewish identity, have emerged as active evangelists to the Jewish community. Jewish leaders often accused them of deception on the grounds that one cannot be both a Jew and a Christian. While these criticisms may reflect Judaism's current effort to define itself as a distinct religion in opposition to Christianity, they have led to much bewilderment and some misunderstanding and mistrust.

Manila Manifesto (1989)

This document was released by LCWE at the Second International Congress on World Evangelization in Manila. Online: http://www.Gospelcom.net/lcwe/statements/manila.html

The following paragraph is from a section on the uniqueness of Jesus Christ for salvation,

> It is sometimes held that in virtue of God's covenant with Abraham, Jewish people do not need to acknowledge Jesus as their Messiah. We affirm, that they need Him as much as anyone else, that it would be a form for anti-Semitism, as well as being disloyal to Christ, to depart from the New Testament pattern of

taking the Gospel to "the Jew first..." We therefore reject the thesis that Jews have their own covenant which renders faith in Jesus unnecessary.

APPENDIX C
Jewish Population
Countries with the largest Jewish population in the Diaspora:[23]

United States	5,800,000
Israel	5,094,200
France	498,000
Canada	370,500
United Kingdom	300,000
Russia	252,000
Argentina	187,000
Germany	108,000
Australia	100,000
Brazil	97,000
Ukraine	95,000
South Africa	75,000
Hungary	50,000
Mexico	40,000
Belgium	31,400

Metropolitan areas with largest core Jewish populations (outside of Israel):

New York, USA	2,051,000
Los Angeles, USA	668,000
South Florida, USA	498,000
Philadelphia, USA	285,000
Paris, France	284,000
Chicago, USA	265,000
Boston, USA	254,000
San Francisco, USA	218,000
London, UK	195,000
Toronto, Canada	175,000
Buenos Aires, ARG	168,000
Washington, DC	166,000

APPENDIX D
Intermarriage Ministry

Increasing numbers of mixed couples in the Jewish communities of the world present a significant missiological opportunity, especially in America. Sociological studies indicate that exogamous marriages are at a higher risk of ending in divorce than where the partners' ethnicity and religion are the same. Therefore, a growing number of Jewish-gentile couples are seeking resources for preserving cross-cultural spousal relationships and for raising bi-cultural children.

Evangelicals ought to see intermarriage as a missiological opportunity. Recent research indicates that one of the most significant challenges reported by Jewish-gentile couples in America is the longing for spiritual harmony.[24] It is possible to introduce these culturally mixed couples to spiritual unity through sensitive presentation of the good news in Jesus Christ.

The American Jewish community is undergoing a dramatic cultural shift with intermarriage rates in the last fifteen years in excess of 50%. Interfaith couples often describe feeling as if they are on the fringe of their respective Christian and Jewish communities. American missiologist Paul E. Pierson observed that "movements of renewal and mission have normally risen on the periphery of the broader church and usually existed in some tension with it."[25] Here, then, is a place to work and pray for a fresh initiative of the Holy Spirit among Jews and Gentiles.

Christian churches generally do not have a special evangelistic ministry for the Jewish spouses of their intermarried gentile members. Christian clergy are not concerned about communal survival in the face of intermarriage, as is the case with the Jewish community. The percentage of Christians who intermarry is comparatively insignificant compared to the ratio of Jewish people who marry "out" of their community. So Christians have not felt the same urgency for dramatic action, as have American Jewish leaders. A few Messianic congregations have focused on ministry to Jewish-gentile couples, but much more could be done.

Pastor Scott Brown and the Son of David congregation in Rockville, Maryland, dedicated themselves in particular to embrace Jewish-Gentile couples. They also proclaim the Messiahship of Jesus without embarrassment about the cause of Jewish evangelism.[26]

Another resource for ministry to intermarried couples is a video project of Chosen People Productions in New York. "Joined Together?" was professionally produced in 2002. The forty-five minute video offers testimonies for "discovering a spiritual basis for unity in your interfaith marriage."

Intermarriage Ministry: Case Study

The following case study is offered as an illustration of effective practice in ministry with a Jewish-gentile couple on the West Coast of the United States. (The names "Marc" and "Sharon" are pseudonyms):

Marc was raised in New York, the son of Holocaust survivors and an observant Jew. When I first met him, he was dying of abdominal cancer. At the time of our first visit, he was living with Sharon. She was a Christian who had not been walking with the Lord for several years. It was Marc's diagnosis of a terminal illness that rekindled her desire for the Lord. It also compelled her to find a way to share the hope of eternal life with Marc.

He was culturally disposed to reject the Christian message. We met to discuss the biblical basis of marriage, not how he could find the Messiah. However, as he engaged with the Bible, his curiosity about the living God grew. Ultimately, Marc wanted to know what Sharon believed that was giving her peace in the face of their dawning separation in death.

Eventually, Marc found spiritual harmony with Sharon, through the gospel. He came to faith just nine months before he died from his long battle with cancer. Through their faith in the salvation of Jesus, he and Sharon found a basis on which to share their life together that was previously impossible.

At Marc's request I officiated at his funeral. He gave specific instructions to tell his Jewish family about Jesus. Marc found peace in knowing the Messiah of Israel during his last months of life with Sharon, but the hope for others lives on in their testimony.

By Tuvya Zaretsky
Jews for Jesus, Los Angeles

ENDNOTES

1 For a huge collection of documents, see (1) Rolf Rendtorff and Hans Herman Henrix, eds., *Die Kirchen und das Judentum: Dokumente von 1945 bis 1985*, (Paderborn/München: Bonifatius Verlag/Christian Kaiser, 1988). (2) Hans Herman Henrix and Wolfgang Kraus, eds., *Die Kirchen und das Judentum: Dokumente von 1986 bis 2000*, (Paderborn: Gütersloher Verlagshaus/ Christian Kaiser/Bonifatius Verlag, 2001).

2 Cf. Kai Kjær-Hansen, "The Problem of the Two-Covenant Theology" in *Mishkan* 21 (1994), 56-57.

3 *Dabru Emet*, (September, 2000). Online: www.jcrelations.net Books sympathetic to *Dabru Emet* include (1) Tikva Frymer-Kensky and David Novak, Peter Ochs, David Fox Sandmel and Michael Signer, eds., *Christianity in Jewish Terms*, (Boulder, Colorado/Oxford: Westview Press, 2000). (2) Carl E. Braaten, Robert W. Jenson, eds., *Jews and Christians: People of God*, (Grand Rapids/Cambridge: Eerdmans, 2003).

4 Cf. Nahum N. Glatzer, *Franz Rosenzweig: His Life and Thought*, (New York: Schocken Books, 1953), 341.

5 Jon D. Levenson, "How Not to Conduct Jewish-Christian Dialogue" in *Commentary* (December, 2001), 31-37.

6 Arthur A. Cohen, *The Myth of the Judeo-Christian Tradition*, (New York: Schocken Books, 1971), 216-217.

7 Sergio DellaPergola, Uzi Rebhun and Mark Tolts, "Prospecting the Jewish future: population projections, 2000-2080" in David Singer and Lawrence Grossman, eds., *American Jewish Year Book, 2000* (New York: American Jewish Committee, 2000).

8 Patrick Johnstone and Jason Mandryk, (21st edition) *Operation World: When We Pray God Works*, (London: Paternoster Press Publishing, 2001), 362.

9 See Jews for Judaism web site: www.jewsforjudaism.org/web/mainpages/missionary_cult_challenge.html

10 Moishe Rosen, "The Fact of Failure" in *LCJE Helsinki, Finland 2003*, (Århus: LCJE, 2003), 297-298.

11 See e.g. www.jbuff.com

12 In this report we use the term "Messianic Jew" in the broadest sense to refer to all Jewish believers in Jesus. Other terms are also used and no one term has met with universal acceptance. See chapter 3 for further discussion under "What's in a Name?"

13 See Kjær-Hansen and Skjøtt, *Facts & Myths*, (1999), (cf. Bibliography).

14 See United States Conference of Catholic Bishops' website August 12, 2002, "Reflections on Covenant and Mission." At http://www.usccb.org/comm/archives/2002/02-154.htm

15 See *Mishkan* 39 (2003). This issue of *Mishkan* is devoted to the topic "The Divinity of Messiah".

16 Jon D. Levenson, (cf. note 5), 33, 35, 37.

17 Wolfhart Pannenberg in *Jews and Christians: People of God*, (cf. note 3), 185.

18 Barry Cytron in *Jews and Christians: People of God*, (cf. note 3), 193.

19 See Wan and Zaretsky, *Jewish-Gentile Couples*, (2004), (cf. Bibliography).

20 See Rich Robinson, "Using the Internet in Evangelism" in *LCJE Bulletin* 69 (August, 2002), 10-14. Online: www.lcje.net

21 *LCJE Bulletin*, 73 (September, 2003), 5. Online: www.lcje.net

22 Cf. Lisa Loden, "Facts & Myths: A Selective Evaluation" in *Mishkan* 32 (2000), 11.

23 See David Singer and Lawrence Grossman, eds., *2003 American Jewish Year Book: the Annual Record of Jewish Civilization, 103*, (New York:

The American Jewish Committee, 2003).

24 See Wan and Zaretsky, *Jewish-Gentile Couples*, (2004), 98, (cf. Bibliography).

25 Pierson, Paul E, *Emerging Streams of Church and Mission*, (Pattaya: Forum for World Evangelization, 2004), 1-3.

26 See web site at www.sonofdavid.org

BIBLIOGRAPHY

History and Theology: Jewish Believers in Jesus and Missions

Ariel, Yaacov. *Evangelizing the Chosen People: Missions to the Jews in America, 1880-2000*. Chapel Hill, NC: University of North Carolina Press, 2000.

A comprehensive survey of the history of modern Jewish evangelism in the US written by a non-Jesus believing Jew.

Cohn-Sherbok, Dan. *Messianic Judaism*. New York: Cassell, 2000.

A non-Jesus believing rabbi describes the history and beliefs of the modern messianic movement, arguing for the authenticity of Messianic Judaism as a legitimate branch of Judaism within a pluralist model.

Crombie, Kelvin. *For the Love of Zion*. London: Hodder & Stoughton, 1991.

On Christian witness, the restoration of Israel and the history behind the ministry of Christ Church in Jerusalem.

Fruchtenbaum, Arnold. *Hebrew Christianity: Its Theology, History and Philosophy*. Tustin, CA: Ariel Ministries Press, 1983.

Gives the theological basis for Hebrew Christianity and practical suggestions for Hebrew Christian identity and practice.

Gundry, Stanley N. & Louis Goldberg, eds. *How Jewish is Christianity: Two Views on the Messianic Movement*. Grand Rapids: Zondervan, 2003.

A discussion of the rationale, biblical basis and practice of Messianic faith and Messianic Judaism.

Kjær-Hansen, Kai and Bodil F. Skjøtt. *Facts & Myths About the Messianic Congregations in Israel*. Jerusalem: United Christian Council in Israel & Caspari Center for Biblical and Jewish Studies, 1999. (= *Mishkan* 30-31, 1999).

Detailed figures are given for membership, attendance, leadership qualifications and theological distinctives for 81 Messianic Jewish congregations and groups.

Kjær-Hansen, Kai, *Joseph Rabinowitz and the Messianic Movement*. Grand Rapids: Eerdmans, 1995.

Detailed study of an important pioneer of the contemporary Messianic movement, considering mission strategy, theology, relationship to mission agencies and church denominations.

Maoz, Baruch. *Judaism is Not Jewish: A Friendly Critique of the Messianic Movement*. UK: Mentor: Christian Focus Publications and Christian Witness to Israel, 2003.

A critical survey of the theology and practice of the Messianic movement in Israel and the US.

Pritz, Ray. *Nazarene Jewish Christianity: From the End of the New Testament Period Until Its Disappearance in the Fourth Century*. Leiden: E.J. Brill, 1988.

An important historical study of Jewish Christians in the early centuries.

Sevener, Harold A. *A Rabbi's Vision: A Century of Proclaiming Messiah, A History of Chosen People Ministries.* Charlotte, NC: Chosen People Ministries, 1994.

> *A venerable history of one of the older US Jewish missions.*

Skarsaune, Oskar. *In the Shadow of the Temple: Jewish Influences on Early Christianity.* Downers Grove, IL: InterVarsity Press, 2002.

> *A new perspective on the development of the early church and the interaction between the church and the ancient synagogue.*

Stern, David H. *Messianic Jewish Manifesto.* Jerusalem: Jewish New Testament Publications, 1988.

> *A key programmatic text for the theological development of Messianic Judaism.*

Tucker, Ruth A. *Not Ashamed: The Story of Jews for Jesus.* Sisters, OR: Multnomah Publishers, 1999.

> *A Missiologist and historian provides background and analysis of the people and methods used in the first twenty-five years of this Jewish mission.*

Biographies and Testimonies

Bernstein, A. *Some Jewish Witnesses for Christ.* London: Operative Jewish Christian Institution, 1909. Reprinted Jerusalem: Yanetz Publishers, 2001.

> *An older survey of individual testimonies of Jewish believers, most of who entered mission service.*

Cohen, Steve. *Disowned.* San Francisco: Purple Pomegranate Productions, 1995.

> *The testimony of the current director of the Apple of His Eye, US Jewish mission society of the Lutheran Church Missouri Synod.*

Guinness, Michelle. *Child of the Covenant.* London: Hodder and Stoughton, 1985.

> *With insight and humour a well-known writer and broadcaster in the UK, married to a family famous for both missionary work and brewing, tells her story of coming to faith and her marriage to an Anglican clergyman.*

Rosen, Ruth. *Jesus for Jews.* San Francisco: A Messianic Jewish Perspective, 1987.

> *Testimonies of Jews who came to faith in Jesus from a variety of backgrounds.*

——. *Jewish Doctors Meet the Great Physician.* San Francisco: Purple Pomegranate Productions, 1988.

> *Testimonies of Jewish doctors who came to faith in Jesus.*

Runge, Albert. *A Brooklyn Jew Meets Jesus.* Camp Hill, PA: Christian Publications, 2001.

> *A Chosen People Ministries mission worker tells his own story of coming to faith in spite of traditional Jewish objections.*

Telchin, Stan. *Betrayed.* Grand Rapids: Chosen Books, 1981.

> *A prosperous insurance executive and synagogue leader's journey to faith in Jesus.*

Tools for Jewish Ministry

Brown, Michael L. *Answering Jewish Objections to Jesus.* Grand Rapids: Baker Books. 2000, 2003.

> *3 volumes of thorough and up-to-date apologetic information.*

Cohen, Steve. *Beginning from Jerusalem.* St. Louis: Apple of His Eye Mission Society, 2001.

> *A Jewish believer in Jesus and mission leader offers insights about Jewish evangelism especially for American Lutherans.*

Goldberg, Louis. *Our Jewish Friends.* Neptune, NJ: Loizeaux Brothers, 1977.

> *Advice on Jewish evangelism from a Jewish believer in Jesus, scholar and former professor of Jewish Studies at the Moody Bible Institute, Chicago.*

Leman, Derek. *Jesus Didn't Have Blue Eyes: Reclaiming Our Jewish Messiah.* Stone Mountain, GA: Mt. Olives Press, 2004.

> *A brief account of the Jewishness of Jesus.*

Rosen, Moishe and Ceil. *Witnessing to Jews.* San Francisco: Purple Pomegranate Productions, 1998.
> *A practical handbook of creative lessons on Jewish evangelism written for Christians by a modern missionary pioneer, statesman and his wife.*

Wan, Enoch and Tuvya Zaretsky. *Jewish-Gentile Couples: Trends, Challenges and Hopes.* Pasadena: William Carey Library. 2004.
> *Research into the difficulties encountered by Jewish-gentile couples with insight and some practical strategies for ministry to them.*

Media: Videos and CD

Forbidden Peace: The Story Behind the Headlines. San Francisco: Purple Pomegranate Productions, 2004, VHS and DVD.
> *Several Israelis and Palestinians share first-person accounts of how they have been reconciled to God through Jesus and how they have found true peace with one another.*

Joined Together? New York: Chosen People Productions, 2002.
> *A forty-five minute video provides testimonies for discovering a spiritual basis for unity in interfaith marriage.*

Survivor Stories: Finding hope from an unlikely source. San Francisco: Purple Pomegranate Productions, 2001, 2004, VHS and DVD.
> *Jewish Holocaust survivors tell how they endured a "living hell" to become believers in Jesus.*

Academic Journals

Mishkan. Jerusalem: Caspari Center for Biblical and Jewish Studies.
> *A journal dedicated to biblical and theological thinking on issues related to Jewish evangelism, Hebrew-Christian/Messianic-Jewish identity, and Jewish-Christian relations.*

Kesher. Albuquerque, NM: Union of Messianic Jewish Congregations.
> *A journal of Messianic Judaism which provides a forum to address the issues, that face contemporary Messianic Judaism.*

Libraries

Several mission organisations have compiled resource libraries. The largest, comprised of some 6,000 volumes is currently maintained at the international headquarters of the Jews for Jesus ministry in San Francisco, California.

Resources Produced by LCJE

LCJE Bulletin, Issue 77 was published in August 2004. Recent issues can be found online at www.lcje.net

Proceedings of the International LCJE conference material:

LCJE Zeists 91, Fourth International Conference 1991, vol. 1-4.

LCJE Jerusalem 95, Fifth International Conference 1995, vol. 1-5.

LCJE New York 99, Sixth International Conference 1999, vol. 1-5.

LCJE Helsinki, Finland 2003, Seventh International Conference, vol. 1-5.

Papers from LCJE-North America conferences; see www.lcje.net

Information on magazines and newsletters published by LCJE member ministries can be found at www.lcje.net

Jewish Missions History Project, see www.lcje.net/history. An on-line digital library of primary source documents from the history of Jewish missions, particularly those prior to 1945.

* * *

Scripture quotations are from the New International Version of the Bible

CONCLUSION TO THE LOP COMPENDIUM

By Greg H. Parsons

Global Strategist for the Lausanne Committee for World Evangelization

General Director, U.S. Center for World Mission, Pasadena, Calif., U.S.A.

CONCULSION TO THE LOP COMPENDIUM

By Greg H. Parsons
Global Strategist for the Lausanne Committee for World Evangelization
General Director, U.S. Center for World Mission, Pasadena, Calif., U.S.A.

INTRODUCTION

A number of years ago, a man in California was released from prison, having served some 15 years for a crime he didn't commit. When he got out, he was amazed by the choices he had to make. Things in the world had changed and options had multiplied. Just selecting a toothbrush from dozens of brands, multiple sizes, harnesses and features was overwhelming. Then he had to choose toothpaste!

This could be the reaction to you as you read these volumes and trying to get a sense for what happened in Thailand in the fall of 2004. Where do we fit in what God is doing? How can we choose what to do as we put our hands to the plow of advancing God's Kingdom in our world?

Looking through at the LCWE compendiums and Occasional Papers recently, including those being written from the Issue Groups (IGs) from the 2004 Lausanne Forum, I was reminded that the spirit of Lausanne is one of grand breadth and depth. The idea of connecting people with a common vision is compelling and—most importantly—produces unity that has changed the world. The central issue in the name itself—that of *world evangelization*—is common among evangelicals like few other things. Recently, TIME magazine noted this is "the life-blood of evangelicals"[1]—we feel a burden to reach the lost.

LEADERSHIP

Lausanne has also given leadership to the global evangelical church. Leadership has been defined as the ability to rally people to change something for a better future. Leaders have a dissatisfaction with the status quo.

We are not compelled by or dependent on human effort and vision. The interesting fact is that this task is not really even ours—it is His. Jesus said that all authority was given to Him. Behind Jesus' authority on earth is a God of purpose. John Stott noted years ago that the living God is a missionary God.[2] Henry Blackaby speaks of God on mission—that He initiates His work and we join Him in it.[3] Thus, Jesus earthly ministry is not merely a model for what we do—He is at work today.

ISSUE GROUP PAPERS

The 31 IGs produced as a result of the LCWE 2004 Forum seek to continue the LCWE tradition and expand it. They include a vast breadth of interests, thinking, planning, action steps, and hands-on involvement. Many IGs worked prior to the meetings and processed a great deal of information. Some have had subsequent meetings—face-to-face or electronically. Many and varied ministries, innovative ideas, and case studies are described. It is truly amazing what God has done and is doing.

While there were some IGs that had brief cross-over meetings with other IGs during the gathering in Thailand, they were not able to read papers from the others groups and thus not able to revise their own work with the insights of others. Yet, as you read through the papers, you see that there are only a few variations in the suggested action steps. The steps often include researching, informing, mobilizing, and training believers such as pastors, leaders, and ordinary believers so they would understand the issue better and act differently—thus reaching out to focus on

the need of that issue.

But the effectiveness of these action steps seemed to boil down to two core requirements: (1) growing, active, multiplying churches or fellowships and (2) committed, involved believers.

Almost every IG saw these two needs and commented that this is core to advancing that issue. But two related issues rose from my experience in Thailand and my reading of the IG papers:

- How do we see the church established and multiplying in *every* culture, region, nation—especially where it is not present? and,

- How do we help believers truly live out their faith in their day-to-day lives—from Monday to Saturday—in the midst of their life, family, work, and business.

The variety of the IGs demonstrate that there are many additional types of ministry or outreach that God is calling His church to engage in and recruit others toward, in order to reach more deeply into a culture, region, or nation and bring transformation. Historically, we have seen that strong fellowships of believers are the necessary ingredient to be the catalyst for that transformation. That is why some have focused on the establishment of the church among every people as a prior requirement. Without this foundation, the deeper work represented in the many of the IGs will not be built in most situations. The establishment of the church in a new culture is the bedrock to which that we connect other kinds of ministry.

Hence, some are called to pioneer the church where it is not present. That is the rallying cry of Ralph Winter's presentation in 1974, "Cross-Cultural Evangelism: The Task of Highest Priority."[4]

This doesn't mean that Muslims, Hindus, or Buddhists unreached people groups are more important. The issue of priority in the title of that presentation merely points to the need of churches, in order to have the capacity, for example, for broad outreach to the disabled. Without the church being present, there won't be as many honest businesses, or ministry to victims of AIDS or prostitutes, or.... Usually, it is committed believers who seek to be a positive influence in their world and initial ministries represented by many IGs.

Once the church is established (and sometimes as it is being planted), some are called to multiply it in the local context, others focus on nurturing those churches—a role most pastors serve. Still others are called to begin or further specific ministries to target specific kinds of needs that arise during different times in history. These are the mobilizers, and they usually work *with* churches or seek to encourage the church's deeper involvement in specific ministry. Most of us tend to mobilize people in areas of ministry for which we have a passion.

Reading these papers reminds us of the crucial role of local churches. We are either starting them up so there are people to mobilize and organize for ministry, or we are helping them to grow into new areas of ministry to which the Lord is call-

ing them.

This could be illustrated in the distinction between IG #6, which was called the "Hidden and Forgotten People Groups" Issue Group. The leaders guiding this IG saw the need early on to split the group into two. One focused on unreached people groups, and the other focused on the disabled people in every people group. The first was seeking to the church established in new cultures, so that there is a *base* of outreach to the disabled and others. Some in the LCWE leadership have proposed splitting this group into two in the future.

I believe it may also be helpful to break down—in our minds if not in actual lists—the different IGs according to whether they primarily serve in (1) the establishment of the church, or (2) the mobilization of believers in local ministry, or (3) foundational issues and service by undergirding the church with theology, prayer, or hands-on ministry. Perhaps we should have divided the chapters of the Compendium in this way, rather than in number order.

A WORD OF CAUTION

Finally, a word of caution on two fronts:

First, since God is at work all around the globe and we are desiring to join that work, we must move away from using guilt as a motivation to the reality of knowing that God at work—He is advancing His purposes and glory. We are not involved in competing issues or strategies or ministries, they are complementary. Just because one of them happens before another doesn't make one calling more important than another. Guilt, if it is from God, may be in the picture, and He will bring that when He desires. Guilt, and other motivations brought on by man, do not continue to motivate for the long run, when the pressures of life and ministry increase.

The second area of concern is that of loose definitions and terminology. One example of this can be found in several IG papers, where a broad redefinition of the term "unreached people" (or "unreached people group") is used to mean any non-believer.[5] Many use this phrase—for whatever reason—in ways that show they may not fully understand how it (and other terms) have been defined. This not only shows that we haven't done our homework but that we are trying to sound trendy—using a popular but often misunderstood phrase to make our area look cutting edge. Certainly we want to attract people to that which we are called, but not in a way that will produce competition between groups, make one seem more important than another, or create confusion.

Finally, there were a few things the reader might have hoped would be reflected in the IG papers. I would propose these be a part of the future work of each the IGs.

Family

While several IGs talk about the family from various angles, or make passing reference, I suggest that the family is cen-tral both to the stability of a culture as well as to outreach. It is often also the backbone of business and commerce.

It is not just something to reach out to in ministry, but it should be central to our outreach and ministry strategy.

Granted the idea of family will take various shapes, and the word will conjure up different pictures for different people, but it was Abraham's "family" that was called out, and it was called to bless the families or clans or people groups of the earth. Most of us have heard stories of multi-generational families in ministry situations around the world who had a greater impact than the usual couple or small nuclear family that is often sent out. Right now, we have a multi-generational family on our staff in Asia and doors of opportunity are opening all around them. Let's explore this issue more deeply in the future.

Satan

Only twelve of the IGs actually mention Satan, or the "evil one," or the "devil." It is as if he is in the background, almost a distant character at times. While we don't want to be overly focused on him and his on-going destructive work, we must not fail to remember he is on the prowl—and increasingly so where the Lord is working more visibly.

I would like to see the different IGs explore and suggest how Satan may be seeking to tamper with or otherwise thwart our efforts in each area. How is he attacking those who seek to work with street children, or plant churches, or the disabled. We must seek to understand and emulate what the apostle Paul said in 2 Corinthians 2:11, "...so that we may not be exploited by Satan—for we are not ignorant of his schemes." Are we exploited or ignorant? What should we do about it?

Communication to the World

There is also the need to consider who might see what we write in our IG papers or what we say in our gatherings. What if a Muslim or Hindu radical read these volumes? Would you want your name connected with it? I'm suggesting we back down on what we believe, but about *how* we say it.

We should be able to communicate our message to (1) believers, (2) those from other religious blocs—especially from the non-believing group we may be working with, and (3) the secular media. How would any given IG paper or section of it be different if we wrote with that in mind? Can we rethink our "Christianese" and state things in a fresh way? The Scriptures talk about singing a new song as one expression of creativity. Can we explain and extol Christ in new ways that demonstrate the broad depth and breadth of who He is and how He is at work?

CONCLUSION

God is raising up those who will lead in the future. The current LCWE leadership noted that God seems to be raising up

"unknowns" around a vision heading in the direction in world evangelization. Many of us have seen that in other networks and ministries as well.

In various ways the IG papers in these volumes are broad and overlapping. In a way, that is the beauty of LCWE. Yet to really give leadership at this time, Lausanne needs to give a clear focus. What are the issues that are core to what it means to be an evangelical[6] and to be salt and light in the world?

Clearly, the establishment of believing fellowships of those who seek and serve Christ is foundational to our seeing the kind of transformation we want God to accomplish. Then we can build on those fellowships a broad range of ministries and service to the watching world, and get more fully engaged in what God is doing and wants to see happen.

We as evangelicals do care about the lost—reaching them is our passion. There is a task remaining, and yet it is not one that God has given to us as if He is no longer involved. Jesus is moving today. He is advancing His Kingdom. We are not involved because *we* happen to see a need that must be met in the world. We are involved because *He* gives us a part in His task. It brings Him glory as we obey Him, and He empowers us that we might see world evangelization advance.

ENDNOTES

1 "The 25 Most Influential Evangelicals in America," David Van Biema et al., TIME (U.S. Edition), Vol. 165, No. 6; Feb. 7, 2005, page 42.

2 Found in *Perspectives on the World Christian Movement*, ed. Ralph D. Winter and Hawthorne (Pasadena: William Carey Library, 1999), page 3.

3 *Experiencing God: Knowing and Doing the Will of God*, Henry T. Blackaby and Claude V. King, (Nashville: Lifeway Press. 1990). Also summarized in *Perspectives on the World Christian Movement*, ed. Winter and Hawthorne. (Pasadena: William Carey Library. 1999), page 55.

4 From LCWE 1974 compendium, *Let the Earth Hear His Voice*, ed. John Stott (Wm. B. Eerdmans Publishing Company, 1996).

5 An unreached people group has been broadly agreed upon to be: a people group within which there is no indigenous community of believing Christians able to evangelize this people group.

6 I use this word realizing that we may have lost it to the media or secular world's definition years ago. It is fast becoming similar to "Christian," which is now so broad as to be singularly unhelpful.

APPENDIX A

SPECIAL ISSUE GROUPS FOR
SENIOR PASTORS, SENIORADVISORS, AND
EXECUTIVES OF INTERNATIONAL EVANGELISTIC
ORGANISATIONS

Each section of this paper was prepared by the Convenor of the Issue Group
in fellowship with the participants

CONTENTS

PASTORS, MISSION PASTORS, AND CHURCH LEADERS
Chaired by Eu Yat Wan

We Affirm:

Recognition and appreciation of the issues of the strategic thinking of Lausanne in dealing with issues that affect missions and the local church.

The realization of Mission as transformation and proclamation, and the need for ongoing discussion and prayer.

The centrality of the local church.

Discipling nations as the unifying theme of the church.

The shift of the missionary movement to the 2/3 world has resulted in the internationalization of missions requiring greater networking and the building of relationships.

The affirmation of the call and clarification of the role of the Mission Pastor.

Develop tools to equip and empower the vast majority of churches who do not have a full time Mission Pastor.

The greatest need for the world is hope in Jesus.

The greatest carrier to meet this need is the church.

The greatest call for the church is for leadership

The highest priority for leadership development is discipleship and mentoring. In making this affirmation, we note that discipleship is sharing the gospel with the end result being that the disciple becoming a discipler. Mentoring is on the job training towards the objective of becoming a leader to many and a mentor to potential leaders.

We affirm the key findings of the 2004 Forum and pray that these may be announced to the church around the world so that every congregation is strengthened in its resolve to be obedient to the Great Commission.

Action Points:

Encourage churches within our spheres of influence to utilize the resources of the Lausanne Issue Groups.

Establish a network of Mission Pastors around the world under the auspices of Lausanne for ongoing synergy.

Strengthen the mission vision and effectiveness of the vast majority of churches that are under 300 members through research, networking, and development of resources.

Every Senior Pastor to be asked to partner in prayer with at least one other Senior Pastor from another people group with a view to praying that the Commission be fulfilled.

Every Senior Pastor in every church be encouraged and assisted in attending and observing a church in a different country to broaden their awareness that they become global Christians.

Recommendations:

1. That the centrality of the local church in the task of mission be emphasized more extensively within the Lausanne movement. This would be reflected in future programs that are generated within the movement

2. That Lausanne affirms the continued development of Regional and International networks of Missions Pastors.

3. That the Lausanne movement invest resources for missions leaders of the vast majority of local churches around the world that have less than 300 members.

4. Develop bases of cooperation between local churches, theological and missionary training structures and mission agencies to enhance the effectiveness of the local church and maintain focus on the achievement of the task.

5. Encourage synergistic cooperation between North-South, East-West bodies.

PARTICIPANTS IN THE PASTORS/ CHURCH LEADERS' GROUP

Gary Barnes, Convener,	USA
Yatwan Eu, Co-Convener	Singapore/Australia
Phitsanunart Joseph Srithawong	Thailand
Carol Childress	USA
Alan Ellard	Thailand
Monnie Brewer	USA
William L. Flanagan	USA
David Gibson	USA
Sundar Thapa,	Nepal
Liz/Elizabeth Gold	USA
Frank Gregory	USA
James W. Gustafson	USA
Kevin Hovey	Australia
Bruce Huseby	USA
Sang (Sabastian) Huynh	USA
Daniel Fish	Maynmar
Thakaen Langkulasane	Thailand
Patricia Larson	USA
Harry Larson	USA
Mel Loucks	USA
Paulo Moreira	Brazil
Shelby Neese	USA
John Nordlander	USA
Chris Alexander	USA
Sherman Pemberton	USA
Sirirat Pusurimkham	Thailand
Jeff Relth	USA
Mossee Shah	Bangladesh
Gary Stubblefield	USA
Teresa Tay	Singapore

Timothy Tay	Singapore
Chee Min Then	Singapore
George Verwer	England
Richard E. Waldrop	USA
Fritz Wuerschum	Germany
David S. K. Yoo	South Korea
Anne Zimmerman,	USA

SENIOR ADVISORS TO THE LAUSANNE MOVEMENT
Chaired by Paul Cedar

The Senior Advisors Group for the 2004 Forum on World Evangelization was comprised of some 25 experienced Missions/Evangelism leaders from around the world. The major purpose of this group of world-class Christian leaders was to serve as advisors and consultants to the various Issue Groups involved in the 2004 Forum on World Evangelization.

This group met twice during the Forum for an extended period of time. The first meeting was one of orientation for the Senior Advisors to prepare them for their important advisory role. They were informed that they were free to attend any of the Issue Groups. They were encouraged not to dominate or interfere with the flow and leadership of the meeting. However, they could participate in the discussions and were to make themselves available to consult and advise the group leaders if requested to do so. The Senior Advisors were encouraged also to report back to the chairman if they encountered any major difficulties or if they discerned that any of the Issue Groups were straying off course or were facing major challenges or difficulties. The "good news" is that none of them had to make such a report. Instead, virtually all of the Issue Groups functioned very well.

The second meeting of the Senior Advisors Group took place on the concluding day of the 2004 Forum. At the time, the various Senior Advisors shared a brief report of their involvement and activities. About half of them reported that they had spent the majority of their time involved in one of the Issue Groups which particularly attracted their interest.

The other half of the Senior Advisors reported that they found it both enjoyable and beneficial to participate in a number of the Issue Groups during the days of the Forum. Most reported, also, that they felt that they were able to make some significant contributions to the groups in which they had become involved.

In addition, many of the Issue Group leaders reported that the Senior Advisors had been a source of help and encouragement to them and to their Issue Groups.

None of the leaders expressed criticism or disappointment with the participation of the Senior Advisors that had participated in their groups. As we met together for the closing session of the Senior Advisors, we received reports from each of them. We concluded that the Senior Advisors had fulfilled their purposes well and that the Lord had used them in significant ways to enrich the important work of the Issue Groups. We extend our deep gratefulness to each of the Senior Advisors who served so faithfully and effectively loving servants of our Lord Jesus Christ.

THOSE WHO SERVED AS SENIOR ADVISORS INCLUDES THE FOLLOWING:

Dr. Peter Brierley	England
Mrs Vonnette Bright	USA
Russell Brown	USA
Dr. Luis Bush	Argentina/USA
Dr. Paul Cedar	USA
Dr. Robert Coleman	USA
Dr. Todd Johnson	USA
Dr. John Kao	Canada
Pastor Kosse Kuzuli	Congo
Dr. Paul Larsen	USA
Dr. Rochunga Pudaite	India
Dr. Sunil Sudar	Egypt
Dr. Viggo Sogaard	Denmark/USA
Dr. Valdir Steuernagel	Brazil
Dr. Ralph and Barbara Winter	USA
Dr. Chris Wright	England
John Sorensen,	U.S.A.
Steve Strauss,	U.S.A.
Ola Tulluan,	Norway
Joshua Wathanga,	United Kingdom
Jerry White,	U.S.A.

CEOS OF INTERNATIONAL EVANGELISTIC ORGANISATIONS
Chaired by H. Eddie Fox

We had an excellent group of CEOs. We met together every time the Issue Groups were in session, and the attendance continued fully each time we met. We had about 40 persons participating throughout the Forum. We had a sharing time and a provocative discussion together as CEOs. It was a unique fellowship that was fully participative by all those involved.

Four people were asked to share regarding their ministry and reflect on the following themes:

(i) The Core Values of your ministry in announcing the gospel, particularly as it relates to the Lausanne Covenant.

(ii) How you live out those core values in spreading the good news of Christ.

(iii) Specific strategies of the ministry.

(iv) Why it is important to be in this kind of fellowship.

I asked the International Bible Society, the Navigators, the Mennonite Board of Mission, and the Norwegian Lutheran Board of Mission to share more fully with the group. This was a distinctive group of agencies, as they are parachurch, and yet they are also representative of church agencies. Everyone shared with the group during the time we met.

The group expressed gratitude for the Lausanne movement and its leadership in world evangelism. The group also expressed interest in continuing the fellowship established in the CEO group and also the desire to impact the work of world evangelism together.

The group of about 40 persons contributed to the overall forum and were energized by the "common table" around which we gathered for prayer, insight, sharing, and encouragement for the ministry of spreading the gospel of the Lord Jesus Christ around the whole world.

CEO PARTICIPANTS

Kjetil Aano,	Norway
F. Douglas Armstrong,	Canada
Peter Bradley,	USA
Arthur Brown,	USA
Jeff Chadwick,	USA
Charles Davis	USA
Trevor Durston,	United Kingdom
Ron Ensminger,	USA
H. Eddie Fox,	USA
Marshall R. Gillam,	USA
David Guiles,	USA
Gary Hipp,	USA
Margaret Jacobs,	Western Australia
Roberto Laver,	USA
Steve Moore,	USA
Doug Nichols,	USA
Emmanuel Oladipo,	United Kingdom
Clive J. Pritchard,	United Kingdom
Don Schmierer,	USA
Richard Showalter,	USA

APPENDIX B

EVANGELICALS IN THE WORLD OF THE 21ST CENTURY

by Dr Peter Brierley

APPENDIX B

EVANGELICALS IN THE WORLD OF THE 21ST CENTURY

by Dr Peter Brierley, Senior Lausanne Associate for Research

"Facts are the fingers of God. To know the facts is the necessary condition of intelligent interest. Knowledge does not always kindle zeal, but zeal is 'according to knowledge' and will not exist without it. A fire may be fanned with wind, but it must be fed with fuel; and facts are the fuel of this sacred flame, to be gathered, then kindled, by God's Spirit, and then scattered as burning brands, to be as live coals elsewhere."[1]

Prepare for a revolution! Two major changes have been in progress in world Christianity across the 20th century which will create a big impact on the 21st century church:

The progress towards a Third World domination of Christianity, and

The progress towards a world Christianity dominated by evangelicals.

These two trends are of course related to each other and impact upon each other. They cannot be separated and in order to examine the second (the prime purpose of this paper) the first may not be ignored.

This paper has been produced at the request of the Administration Committee of the Lausanne Committee for World Evangelisation [LCWE] as it prepares for the 2004 Forum on World Evangelisation. It is intended to give some of the background to the work of the Forum, and is primarily a statistical paper as this is that which I am best able to produce.

INTRODUCTION
Background

The basis of the trends set out here is Dr David Barrett's hugely valuable *World Christian Encyclopedia* [WCE], the second edition of which was published in two volumes by Oxford University Press in 2001.[2]

The importance of the WCE is that for every country in the world it gives a breakdown of the number of adherents of each religion, with a total which adds up to the full population. So it is easy to calculate the proportions of Christians or Muslims, for example, in a particular country.[3] This information is given for the years 1900, 1970, 1990, 1995, 2000 and 2025. For the overall world total the numbers are also projected to 2050.

In this context "Christians" are defined as:

Followers of Jesus Christ as Lord, of all kinds, all traditions and confessions, and all degrees of commitment.

To distinguish this term from others commonly used, some would refer to these numbers as Christian "adherents" or the Christian "community", and recognise sub-groups, especially of membership and attendance, within this broad terminology. The following diagram (not drawn to scale) illustrates the sub-groups, which overlap:

The three circles in this diagram – the outer circle, and the two overlapping circles inside it – represent three ways of measuring people attached to the church.

The outer circle represents all those who call themselves "Christian" whether or not they belong to a church or go to church. This group includes those who have a firm faith as well as those who may not; people who believe in God, agree with the Ten Commandments or do not support either. They simply wish for whatever reason to call themselves "Christian", and are those which the various national Population Censuses measure.

The two inner circles represent those who are church members and those who are church attenders. They overlap because obviously many churchgoers are also members and vice versa. The diagram shows that there are some members who do not attend church and some churchgoers who are not members. The WCE does give the number of adult members in each country for 1970 and 1995, but these are not used in this paper because forecasts of future trends need to be based on more than two measurements.

There are several other ways of defining groups within the Christian community. Three used by David Barrett, the totals of which tally to the overall total, are:

By their "profession": This has two categories – "crypto-Christians" [secret believers, hidden Christians, usually known to churches but not to state or secular or non-Christian religious society] and "professing Christians" [all the rest]. This classification is noted, but not used in this paper.

By their "affiliation": Also made up of two categories – "unaffiliated Christians" [people who profess allegiance and commitment to Christ but who have no church affiliation] and "affiliated Christians" [all the rest]. The "affiliated" Christians are further broken down by denomination. This classification is used when denominational breakdowns of numbers are given.

By their "belief system": David Barrett calls these "trans-megabloc groupings". They are: Evangelicals (with a capital 'E'),[4] Pentecostals/Charismatics, and Great Commission Christians.

This third category is the most useful for this paper, because of our focus on evangelicals. In fact, the last group in this category is also defined as "evangelical" (with a small 'e') as follows:

Church members of evangelical conviction, involved with Christ's mission on earth; synonymous with

believers in Jesus Christ who are aware of the implications of Christ's Great Commission, who have accepted its personal challenge in their lives and ministries, are attempting to obey his commands and mandates, and who are seeking to influence the body of Christ to implement it.

This "evangelical" (or "Great Commission") group is closest to those who follow the Lausanne Covenant and is therefore especially used in the rest of this paper. Apart from *Operation World*,[5] the WCE is the only publication known to the author which gives such numbers for every country in the world.

Problems with the figures

David Barrett's comprehensive analysis is very valuable. However, we need to be aware that not everyone agrees with some of his numbers. Professor Philip Jenkins, for example, in his book *The Next Christendom*,[6] disagrees with some of the estimates. In an article he wrote:

"To take a major example, the *Encyclopaedia* gives India's current Christian population as 62 million, around 6% of the whole. This includes 41 million 'professing Christians' and 21 million 'crypto-Christians.' This overall number is far higher than that reported by Indian census data, which are the figures used by the US government. The CIA *Factbook* says there are around 24 million Indian Christians, and this number is reproduced by the US State Department. Undoubtedly, Indian census counts discriminate against religions held by the underclass, which results in an undercounting of Christian strength. It is far from clear, though whether that undercount can explain the huge discrepancy (almost 40 million people!) that separates our sources here."[7]

Philip Jenkins has also criticised the number of Christians in China (90 million in the WCE) as too high, and the number in Egypt (15 million in WCE) as three times the normally accepted number. Others have also criticised the numbers in the WCE.[8]

One of the reasons behind these criticisms is that David Barrett includes what some call "non-Trinitarians" in his figures for Christians – Jehovah's Witnesses, Mormons, etc. He also includes a sizeable group (about 6% of the total) who are "unaffiliated", Christians. These have no church affiliation, which seems almost a contradiction in basic terminology, and raises questions of how these could have been measured.

However, it is perhaps generally accepted that, even if the numbers are sometimes too great, the *broad distribution* of them across the world, and especially the *trends* in them, are likely to be as accurate as any other estimates. In any case, there are no others available in such detail. We need to remember these criticisms, and balance them against the fact that there is no alternative but to use them!

Annual updates are published by David Barrett giving his figures for the latest year.[9] In these continental and denominational breakdowns he excludes the unaffiliated, so we have to be careful to compare the correct numbers!

Years used

David Barrett gives figures for both 1970 and 1990 for every country. This period of 20 years is important for us as both the large Lausanne Congresses were held during that period; in 1974 in Lausanne, Switzerland and in Manila in the Philippines, in 1989. I had the personal privilege of being present at both.

The change in the Christian scene around the world between these dates is usually attributed to the acceptance of many evangelicals of social action as part of the Gospel. This is strongly emphasised in the Lausanne Covenant, a key result of Lausanne I, largely crafted by Rev John Stott, the fifth section of which declares "evangelism and sociol-political involvement are both part of our Christian duty".[10]

A second key change among evangelicals in this period was the expansion on their emphasis on reaching "unreached peoples". This also may be attributed to Lausanne I. Peter Wagner was initially appointed as Chair of the Lausanne Strategy Working Group in 1975, but after a few years resigned and Edward Dayton became Chair.[11] As head of MARC, a division of World Vision international, Edward Dayton produced a series of annual "Unreached Peoples Directories" from 1979 to 1984, focussing on the strategic implications of these in a book in 1985.[12] David Barrett contributed to the series with a 1986 volume.[13]

The 2004 Forum is designed to look ahead. As 1970-1990 is a 20 year period, for ease of comparison we have taken the year 2010 as our second date, 20 years on from 1990, based on the estimates made by David Barrett for 1995, 2000 and 2025 (using linear regression, or a straight line fit, as the main estimation method). Further projections again use a 20 year interval to 2030, with a third 20 year period taking us to David Barrett's final 2050 forecast.

World Christianity compared to the population

It may be helpful to look at the overall population of the world first and to see how this divides into the Third World and what, for simplicity of comparison, I am calling here the First World.[14] This is given in the following Table:

Table 1: Population of the world and the Christian Community, 1970-2050

Year/ Period	Population in millions			Christians in millions			% Christians are of Population		
	First World	Third World	TOTAL	First World	Third World	TOTAL	First World	Third World	TOTAL
1970	907	2,789	3,696	722	514	1,236	*80*	*18*	*33*
1990	1,030	4,236	5,266	813	934	1,747	*79*	*22*	*33*
2010	1,284	5,467	6,751	855	1,390	2,245	*67*	*25*	*33*
2030	1,462	6,646	8,108	887	1,836	2,723	*61*	*28*	*34*
2050	1,546	7,363	8,909	876	2,176	3,052	*57*	*30*	*34*
Daily increase in thousands									
1970-1990	17	198	215	13	57	70	*76*	*29*	*33*
1990-2010	35	168	203	6	62	68	*17*	*37*	*33*
2010-2030	24	162	186	4	61	65	*17*	*38*	*35*
2030-2050	11	99	110	-2	47	45	*-18*	*47*	*41*

The top half of Table 1 shows the population of the world, broken down into its two main components, First World and Third World. These figures are all in millions of people. The second broad vertical band of three columns gives the number of Christians as given by David Barrett in the WCE, or as estimated for the intervening years. They show how the Third World has not only exceeded the First World in total numbers of Christians (fewer in 1970, more in 1990) but is rapidly increasing being almost three times as large by 2050. These numbers are graphed in Figure 1. The third band of columns in Table 1 expresses the Christian numbers as a percentage of the total. These columns show that while the Christian proportion of the world remains static at 33% or 34%, the reality is of a steadily increasing proportion of the Third World who are Christian, and a fast decreasing proportion of the First World. The rise in the Third World percentage is fairly uniform; however, the percentage who are Christian in the First World decreases especially in the period 1990-2010, that is, the twenty year period we are currently living in. We meet for the 2004 Forum at a time when the Christian proportion of the First World is declining quite rapidly.

The bottom part of Table 1 shows how large that decline is, as it translates the figures in the top portion into the change that is taking place on a daily basis. These figures are in thousands. So, for example, between 1970 and 1990 the world's population increased at the rate of 215,000 people per day. This is a *net* figure; the number of births would be much greater than this, but these are offset by the number of deaths. A positive figure

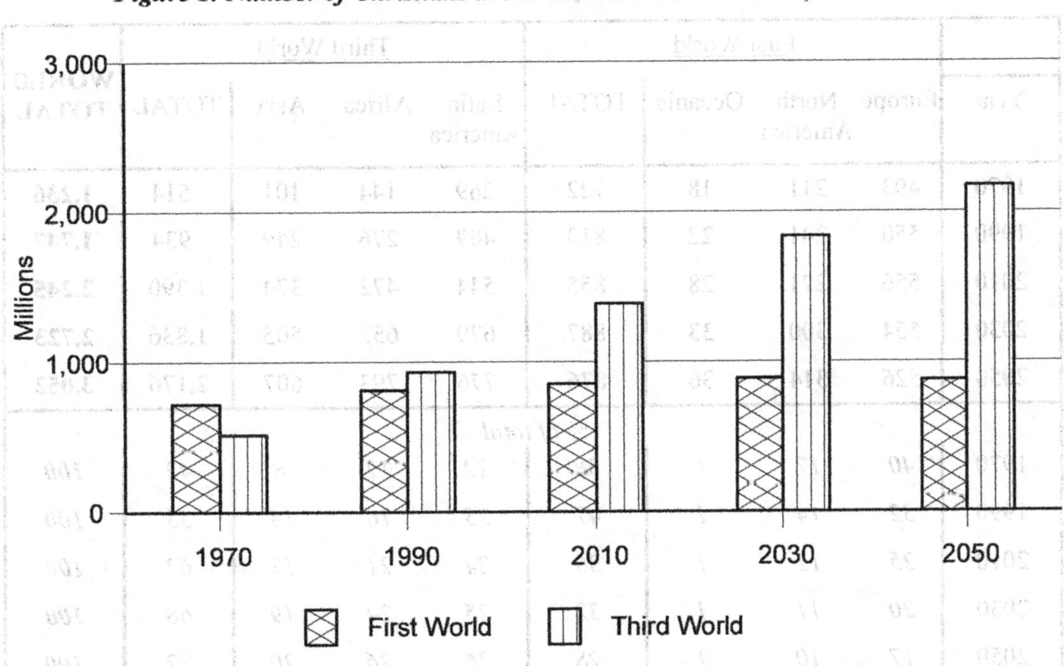

Figure 1: Number of Christians in the First and Third Worlds, 1970-2050

simply shows that there are many more births than deaths.

Of this 215,000 daily increase, 70,000 or 33% were of Christian people. Again this is a *net* figure, looking at those who are born into Christian families as well as conversions, offset by those who die and those who drop out of the faith for whatever reason. The 1970 to 1990 years saw a much greater Christian proportion of the daily increase in world population than has happened since.

However, it is expected to rise again between 2010 and 2030, especially in the Third World, but then fall away after 2030. The expected decline in later years is mainly because the United Nations demographers (whose population figures are used here) believe the European population will begin to decline then. With many European countries having so few children (and some with very high abortion rates), this is quite possible.

CHANGE NO 1: THIRD WORLD DOMINATION OF CHRISTIANITY

At the beginning of this paper two major changes in world Christianity were indicated. Let us look in more detail at the first, progress towards a Third World domination of Christianity. If you think of European Christianity as one side of a set of scales and Asian and African Christianity on the other, the scales are tipping towards Asia and Africa. In 1900 they had only 6% of the world's Christians. During the 20th century that grew to 31% (at 2000), and is now growing so quickly that by 2010, only 10 years later, it is expected to be 42%. In other words, in 6 years time, 3 out of every 7 Christians will live in Asia or Africa.

Table 2: Christian community in millions by continent, 1970-2050

| Year | First World | | | | Third World | | | | WORLD TOTAL |
	Europe	North America	Oceania	TOTAL	Latin America	Africa	Asia	TOTAL	
1970	493	211	18	722	269	144	101	514	**1,236**
1990	550	241	22	813	409	276	249	934	**1,747**
2010	556	271	28	855	544	472	374	1,390	**2,245**
2030	554	300	33	887	679	652	505	1,836	**2,723**
2050	526	314	36	876	776	793	607	2,176	**3,052**
% of total									
1970	*40*	*17*	*1*	*58*	*22*	*12*	*8*	*42*	*100*
1990	*32*	*14*	*1*	*47*	*23*	*16*	*14*	*53*	*100*
2010	*25*	*12*	*1*	*38*	*24*	*21*	*17*	*62*	*100*
2030	*20*	*11*	*1*	*32*	*25*	*24*	*19*	*68*	*100*
2050	*17*	*10*	*1*	*28*	*26*	*26*	*20*	*72*	*100*

Figure 2: Continental proportions in World Christianity, 1970-2050

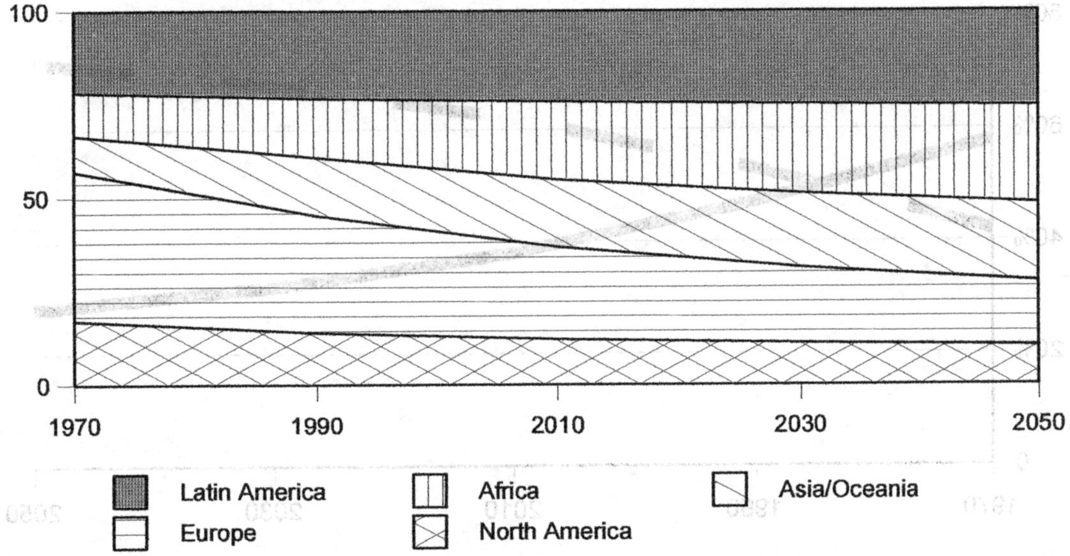

Table 2 breaks down the middle segment of Table 1 by individual continent, and these are then graphed in Figure 2. The Third World was already over 50% of the world's Christians by 1990 (53%), and by 2010 will be 62%. By 2050, if present trends continue, they will total 72%, nearly three-quarters of Christendom. Figure 3 plots the total percentages for the First and Third Worlds, the First being defined for this purpose as Europe, North America and Oceania.

The story in the bottom half of Table 2, and shown in Figure 2, is that the proportions of Christians in both North and Latin America are changing relatively slowly, while the proportions in Europe, Asia and Africa are changing extremely rapidly. This simple graph hides something important. The difference between the two percentages (Third and First World) in 1970 was 16% (seen also in

Table 2). In 1990 the difference was 6%, and by 2010 it will be 24%. In 2030 and 2050 it will be 36% and 48% respectively. The *differences* between these percentages 1970 to 1990 is 10%. Between 1990 and 2010 it is 24%, and then between 2010 and 2030 and 2030 and 2050 it is 12% each. The largest of these differences, 24%, is between 1990 and 2010. This is the period when the change between First and Third World is happening most quickly.

That period is *now, this decade and the one before*. This is the time when the First World must recognise the pre-eminence of the Third World. The change that is happening must be matched by changing resources, methods of working, responsibilities, training and ideas, as well as leadership of our ministries and organisations.

Figure 3: Proportions of First and Third World Christianity, 1970-2050

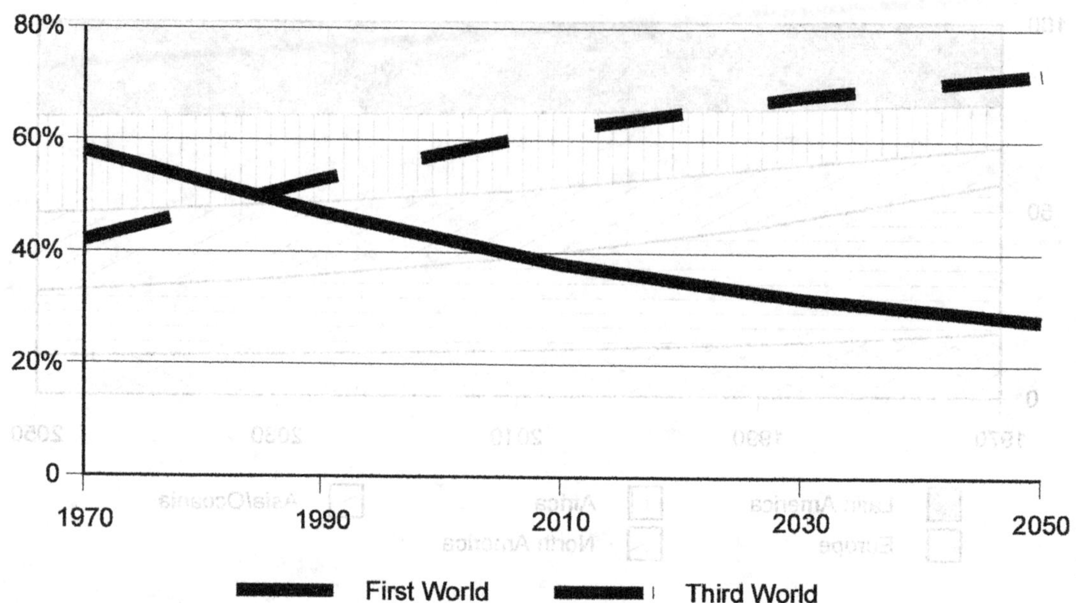

The dominance of the Third World in world Christianity will continue to increase after 2010, but at a slower pace. The rate of that change is greatest today, which is why the revolution is happening, indeed has already happened! That is why this Forum takes place at such an important time; it is vital to develop strategies and structures which are appropriate for the people movement that has already taken place.

World Christianity – by denomination

The move to Third World domination of Christianity is seen not only when you look at the world by continents but also by denomination. This is given in Table 3, and illustrated in Figure 4.

Figure 4 shows:

- The increasing proportion of Christians in the Independent churches across the world,

- The slowly declining proportion of the Roman Catholic Church, and

- The total of the other five groups (Protestant, Orthodox, Anglican, Marginal and Unaffiliated) keep about the same position.

To find the reasons for these changes we have to look at the denominations which are not growing. They are nearly all institutional groups, and such churches have a number of problems:

- They find it hard to change quickly and so cannot easily adapt to changes in society such as post-modernism.

- They have local structures which have been established for hundreds of years, and which cannot therefore be altered easily.

- Their buildings or other property may be legally registered in a way which

Table 3: Christian community in millions by denomination, 1970-2050

Year	Anglican	Independent	Orthodox	Protestant	Roman Catholic	Marginal	Unaffiliated	WORLD TOTAL
1970	48	96	140	211	624	11	106	1,236
1990	68	302	204	296	753	22	102	1,747
2010	97	460	226	399	910	36	117	2,245
2030	123	627	258	496	1,046	49	124	2,723
2050	146	753	267	574	1,125	62	125	3,052
% of total								
1970	*4*	*8*	*11*	*17*	*50*	*1*	*9*	*100*
1990	*4*	*17*	*12*	*17*	*43*	*1*	*6*	*100*
2010	*4*	*20*	*10*	*18*	*41*	*2*	*5*	*100*
2030	*5*	*23*	*9*	*18*	*38*	*2*	*5*	*100*
2050	*5*	*25*	*9*	*19*	*37*	*2*	*4*	*100*

Figure 4: World Christianity by denomination, 1970-2050

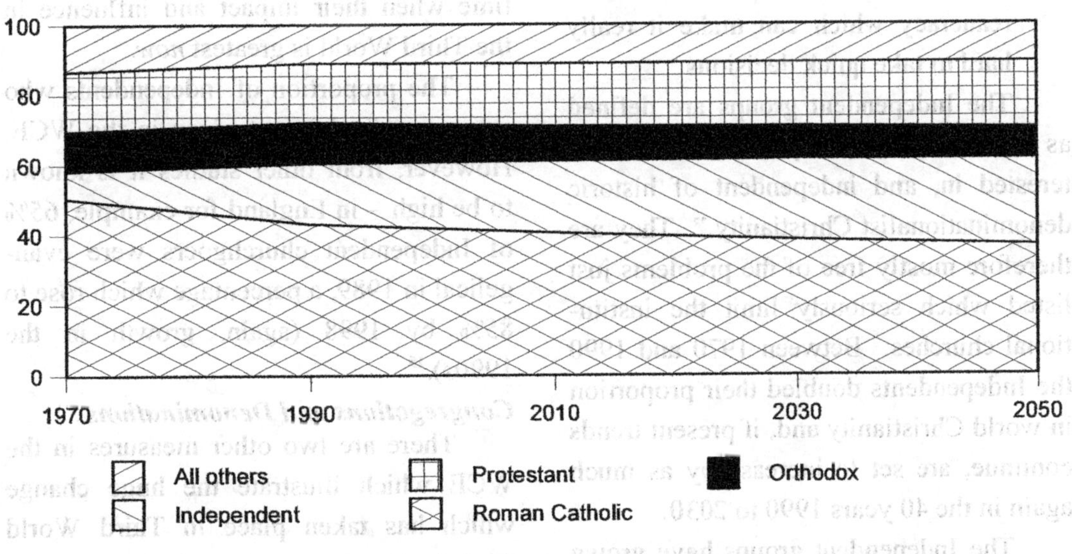

makes it very difficult to alter them, sell them, or use them for other purposes.

- In many cases they are State churches, and their legal responsibilities cannot be dropped or amended without lengthy discussions. There may be financial responsibilities as with many of the Lutheran State churches.

- They are more likely to see themselves as guardians of the Christian heritage. This sometimes means leaders who are more comfortable looking back to the past rather than forward to the future, though but this is less true than it used to be.

- They are usually broader theologically than the non-institutional churches, and therefore are accountable to a wider range of people for any change.

- Most of them have a hierarchical bureaucracy which can make it really hard to take quick decisions.

The Independent groups are defined as those which are "separated from, uninterested in, and independent of historic denominationalist Christianity." They are therefore mostly free of the problems just listed which seriously limit the institutional churches. Between 1970 and 1990 the Independents doubled their proportion in world Christianity and, if present trends continue, are set to increase by as much again in the 40 years 1990 to 2030.

The Independent groups have grown most in the Third World, moving from 9% of the total in 1970 to 22% in 1990, a percentage projected to grow much more slowly to 29% in 2050. In Africa, for example, they were 12% of the Christian community in 1970, but 23% by 1990; in Asia, they were 21% in 1970 but 46% in 1990.

In the First World, the Independent groups were 6% of the total in 1970, rising to 11% in 1990, forecast to grow steadily to a projected 21% by 2050. In Europe, for example, they were just 2% of the Christian community in 1970, but 4% by 1990.

Figure 5 shows the proportion that Independent groups were of the Christian community in the First and Third Worlds since 1970. The greatest difference between the two percentages, 11%, is between 1990 and 2010; before and after that period, the difference is smaller. In other words it is in exactly this same period of 20 years that the Independent churches have grown. It means that the time when their impact and influence in the Third World is greatest *now*.

The proportion of Independents who are evangelical is not given in the WCE. However, from other studies it is known to be high – in England for example, 65% of Independent churchgoers were evangelical in 1989, a percentage which rose to 85% by 1998 (again, growth in the 1990s).[15]

Congregations and Denominations

There are two other measures in the WCE which illustrate the huge change which has taken place in Third World Christianity: the number of congregations and denominations. These are both

Figure 5: Proportion of Independents in First and Third World Christianity, 1970-2050

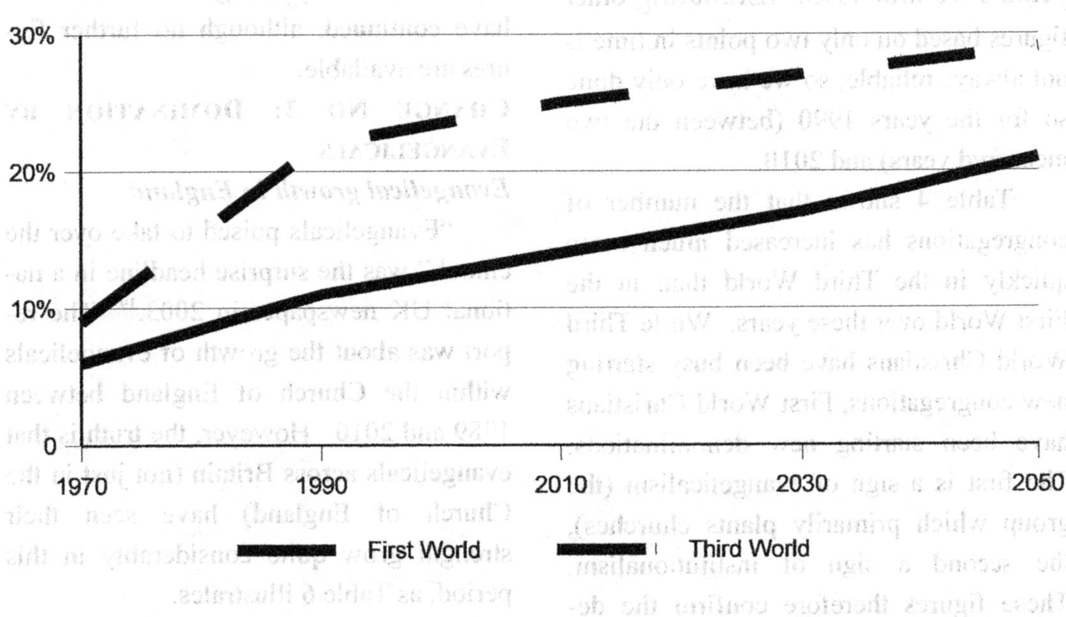

***Table 4: Number of Congregations and Denominations
in the First and Third Worlds, 1970-2010***

Year	First World				Third World			
	Europe	North America	Pacific	TOTAL	Africa	Asia	Latin America	TOTAL
1990	19,915	64,378	6,211	90,504	12,829	23,958	4,744	41,531
2000	22,897	71,088	9,452	103,437	12,442	69,203	10,192	91,837
% increase 1990-2000	*+15*	*+10*	*+52*	*+14*	*-3*	*+189*	*+115*	*+121*

given by continent, but only for the years 1970 and 1995. Estimating other figures based on only two points in time is not always reliable, so we have only done so for the years 1990 (between the two measured years) and 2010.

Table 4 shows that the number of congregations has increased much more quickly in the Third World than in the First World over these years. While Third World Christians have been busy starting new congregations, First World Christians have been starting new denominations. The first is a sign of evangelicalism (the group which primarily plants churches), the second a sign of institutionalism. These figures therefore confirm the denominational figures we have just considered.

Mission workers

In *Operation World*,[16] Patrick Johnstone gives details of the number of Protestant, Independent and Anglican mission workers, both going to and serving from the various continents. Table 5 compares the number of expatriate or national workers[17] sent from one country to work in another, for the years 1990[18] and 2000.

There has been an explosion of Third World mission workers in the 1990s, doubling the number in 1990 and almost equalling the First World total. This is especially seen in Asia, where two-thirds of mission workers serve within or are sent from India, a quadrupling of their numbers over the decade. South Korea also tripled their number.

Note again that the major rise is in the Third World, and that this spectacular increase occurred during the 1990s. There is no reason why the growth should not have continued, although no further figures are available.

CHANGE NO 2: DOMINATION BY EVANGELICALS

Evangelical growth in England

"Evangelicals poised to take over the church" was the surprise headline in a national UK newspaper in 2003.[19] The report was about the growth of evangelicals within the Church of England between 1989 and 2010. However, the truth is that evangelicals across Britain (not just in the Church of England) have seen their strength grow quite considerably in this period, as Table 6 illustrates.

Table 6 shows that the proportion of evangelicals is growing within all denominations, whether you look at churches or people.[20] It is likely such growth will continue beyond 2010. It also shows that the average congregation is larger in evangelical churches (except for Roman Catholics in 1989), and that this trend is likely to get more pronounced as time moves on.

However, even though the proportion of evangelicals is growing in England, the majority of their congregations are seeing their average numbers decrease, as are non-evangelicals. With decreasing numbers (and presumably also fewer people in the congregation willing to take leadership roles), churches are likely to have to cut back their activities. Even more disastrous is that vision for growth and change is also very likely to decrease.

How typical of the rest of the world is the evangelical growth in England?

Table 6: Percentage of churches and churchgoers in England which are evangelical, by denomination, 1989-2010

		Church of England			Roman Catholics		
		1989	1998	2010	1989	1998	2010
	Churches	*18%*	*22%*	*29%*	*1%*	*3%*	*5%*
	Churchgoers	*26%*	*35%*	*50%*	*a%*	*4%*	*14%*
Average congregation	Evangelicals	115	95	75	150	430	600
	Non-evangelicals	70	50	30	450	320	190
		All others			TOTAL		
	Churches	*58%*	*61%*	*63%*	*35%*	*38%*	*42%*
	Churchgoers	*62%*	*66%*	*74%*	*30%*	*37%*	*50%*
Average congregation	Evangelicals	100	95	85	105	95	90
	Non-evangelicals	85	75	50	135	10065	

Evangelicals in the world

David Barrett's figures for evangelicals are summarised in Table 7, projected forward for the same years we have used before.

The trends in this Table are very similar to those in Table 2. Africa and Asia's proportion increases, Asia's more than Africa's (the opposite of Table 2), but Europe and North America's proportions drop.

The one continent which is different is Latin America, where the proportion of evangelicals is slowly growing, but it is only a third of the proportion Latin America has of the Christian community. Pentecostalism is growing in Latin America but it has a long way to go before it seriously displaces the huge size of the Roman Catholic Church in that continent.

Figure 6 illustrates the figures in Table 7, and may be compared with Figure 2. It shows the increasing importance of Asian evangelicalism, moving from a sixth of the world in 1970 to over a third if current trends continue by 2050.

Table 7: Evangelical Christians in millions by continent, 1970-2050

| Year | First World | | | | Third World | | | | WORLD TOTAL |
	Europe	North America	Oceania	TOTAL	Latin America	Africa	Asia	TOTAL	
1970	129	52	4	185	19	30	43	92	**277**
1990	185	99	8	292	44	68	157	269	**561**
2010	201	119	10	330	62	120	217	399	**729**
2030	211	146	12	369	81	167	310	558	**927**
2050	226	168	15	409	99	207	382	688	**1,097**
% of total									
1970	*47*	*19*	*1*	*67*	*7*	*11*	*15*	*33*	*100*
1990	*33*	*18*	*1*	*52*	*8*	*12*	*28*	*48*	*100*
2010	*27*	*16*	*1*	*44*	*9*	*17*	*30*	*56*	*100*
2030	*23*	*16*	*1*	*40*	*9*	*18*	*33*	*60*	*100*
2050	*21*	*15*	*1*	*37*	*9*	*19*	*35*	*63*	*100*

Figure 6: Continental breakdown of Evangelical Christianity, 1970-2050

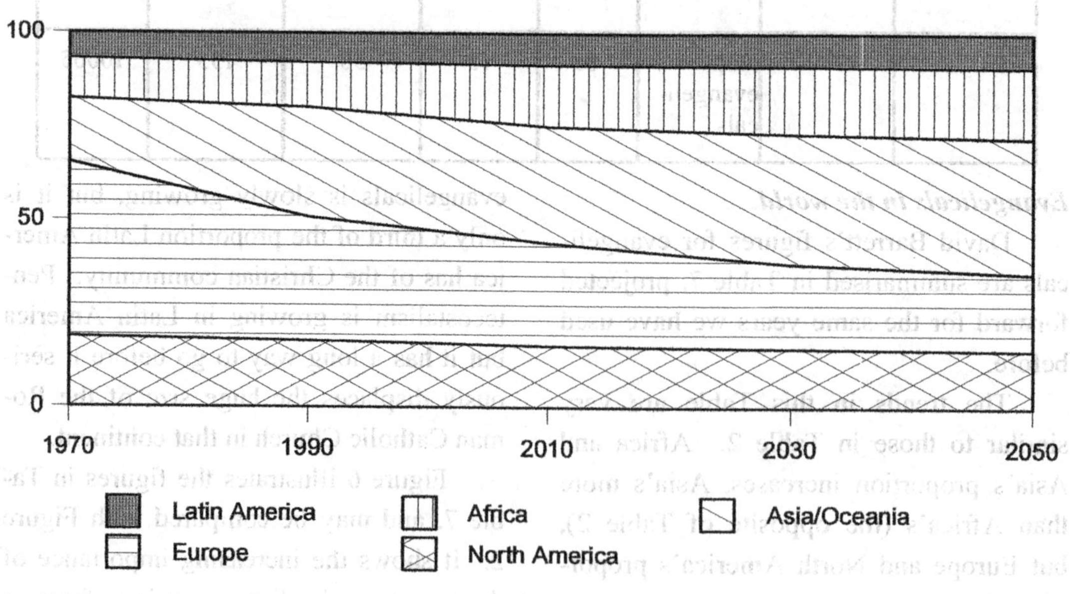

Figure 7: Proportions of First and Third World evangelicals, 1970-2050

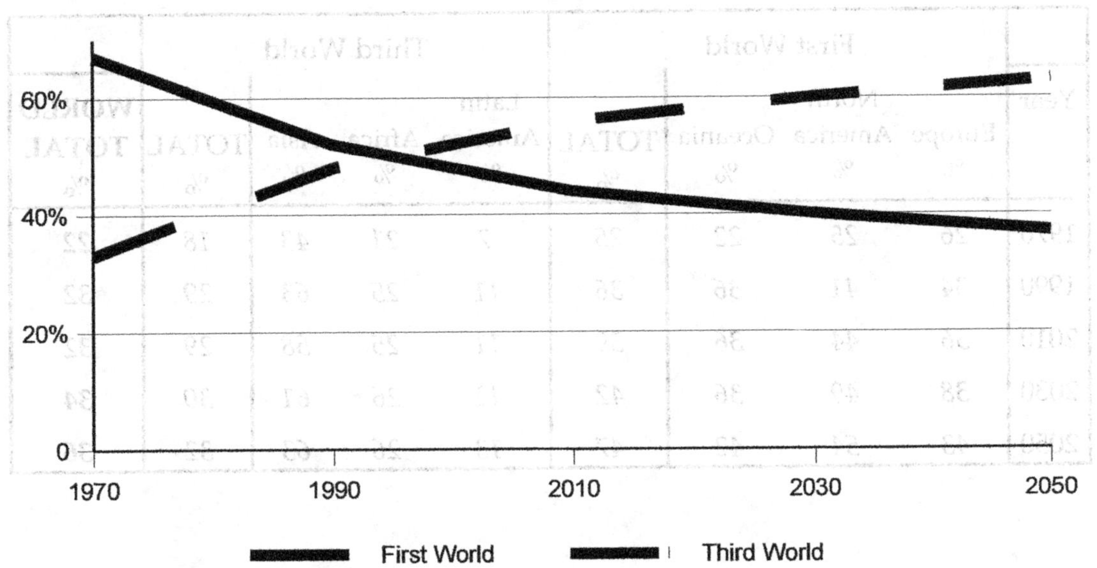

The proportions relating to the First and Third World are graphed in Figure 7 in a similar way to Figure 3. There is a difference, however. The proportion of evangelicals did not reach dominance in the Third World as quickly as the Christian community generally. The lines in this graph crossed in 1995, 10 years after the lines for the community in Figure 3.

This graph shows that Third World evangelicalism really grew rapidly between 1970 and 1990. Could that have had some relation to the social work emphasis enshrined in the Lausanne Covenant produced at the 1974 gathering? Others might see it as the long term results of the impetus given to evangelicalism by Billy Graham from the 1950s onwards.

Evangelical growth across the world

The figures in Table 7 may be used in another way. The number of evangelicals as a percentage of the Christian commu-

nity in a particular continent for a given year is shown in Table 8.

Table 8 shows that the proportion of evangelicals among Christian people has been growing since 1970. The proportion was just over a fifth, 22%, in 1970, and if present trends continue, is likely to be more than a third, 34%, in 2030. The big increase, as already noted, took place between 1970 and 1990.

However, Table 8 shows that evangelicalism in the Third World is growing quite slowly while in the First World it is growing quickly. Figure 8 graphs the proportion of the community that is evangelical

This graph shows that the proportion of evangelicals has been higher in the First World than in the Third World over this whole 80 year period, and will continue to be, if present trends continue. The "rapid growth" between 1970 and 1990 happened

Table 8: Percentage of evangelicals in the Christian community by continent 1970-2050

Year	First World				Third World				WORLD TOTAL %
	Europe %	North America %	Oceania %	TOTAL %	Latin America %	Africa %	Asia %	TOTAL %	
1970	26	25	22	25	7	21	43	18	22
1990	34	41	36	36	11	25	63	29	32
2010	36	44	36	39	11	25	58	29	32
2030	38	49	36	42	12	26	61	30	34
2050	43	54	42	47	13	26	63	32	36

Figure 8: Percentage of the community who are evangelical in the First and Third World, 1970-2050

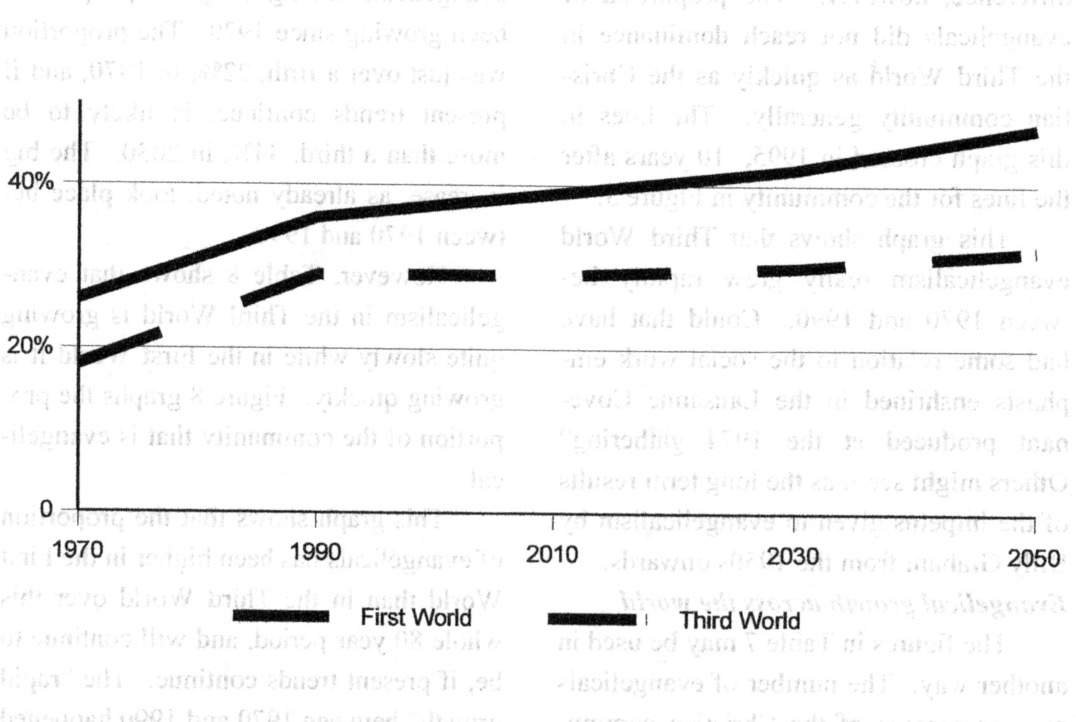

the proportions relating to the First and Third World as graphed in Figure 7 in a similar way. To Figure 7 difference, however. The proportion of evangelicals did not reach dominance in the Third World as quickly as the Christian community generally. The lines in this graph refer to 1995, 10 years after the lines for the community in Figure 6.

This graph shows that Third World evangelicalism nearly grew rapidly between 1970 and 1990. Could that have had some relation to the social work emphasis enshrined in the Lausanne Covenant produced at the 1974 gathering? Others might see this as the long term results of the impetus given to evangelicalism by the Billy Graham from the 1950s onwards.

Evangelical growth across the world The figures in Table 7 may be used in another way. The number of evangelicals as a percentage of the Christian commun-

ity in a particular continent. For a given year, the lines show that the proportion of evangelicals among Christian people has been growing since 1970. The proportion was just over a fifth, 22%, in 1970, and if present trends continue, is likely to be more than a third, 35%, in 2050. The big increase, as already noted, took place between 1970 and 1990.

Evangelicalism in the Third World is growing quite slowly while in the First World it is growing quickly. Figure 8 graphs the proportion of the community that is evangelical.

The graph shows that the proportion of evangelicals has been higher in the First World than in the Third World over this whole 80 year period, and will continue to be, if present trends continue. The rapid growth between 1970 and 1990 happened in both the First and Third Worlds, but since 1990 the percentage has hardly changed in the Third World (about a third of the total), but has been steadily growing in the First World and will reach almost half, 47%, by 2050.

Evangelical and Pentecostal?

These proportions are all based on the WCE figures, and the period of greatest growth, 1970 to 1990, is taken directly from the *Encyclopedia*. There is other evidence that can be compared with the WCE data. Writers such as David Martin in his excellent assessment of Pentecostalism in Latin America, *Forbidden Revolutions*,[21] give a picture of an ever-increasing evangelicalism. He says it is growing in numbers in Latin America from 44 million in 1990 to 52 million 10 years later, but as a proportion of the total Christian community it remains at 11%.

This needs to be put into context. The World Evangelical Alliance "is in contact with two million local churches with up to 400 million members in 123 countries".[22] The General Secretary, Gary Edmonds, says the "fastest growth is hap-

pening in Latin America. Each year millions of Catholics join Pentecostal and Charismatic churches. In some regions of Brazil, evangelicals account for 40% of the population."[23] Perhaps the difference is partly one of definition: the WCE counted 80 million Pentecostals in Brazil in 2000, 47% of the population, and 51% of the Christian community, but numbered only 24 million evangelicals.

In Latin America as a whole in 2000 David Barrett records 52 million evangelicals but 141 million Pentecostals/ Charismatics. In Africa there were 91 million evangelicals in 2000 according to Barrett but 126 million Pentecostals. In the other four continents the number of evangelicals is greater than his number of Pentecostals/Charismatics.

If we use the number of Pentecostals/ Charismatics for Africa and Latin America (assuming that most Pentecostals are evangelical), but the larger evangelical number for the other continents, the percentages in Table 8 change to the following:

Table 9: Percentage of evangelicals or Pentecostals/Charismatics in the Christian community by continent 1970-2050

| Year | First World | | | | Third World | | | | WORLD TOTAL % |
	Europe %	North America %	Oceania %	TOTAL %	Latin America %	Africa %	Asia %	TOTAL %	
1970	26	25	22	25	4	12	43	14	21
1990	34	41	36	36	29	34	63	40	38
2010	36	44	36	39	31	36	58	41	39
2030	38	49	36	42	35	38	61	43	43
2050	43	54	42	47	39	40	63	46	46

Using these figures gives a steep rise in the first half of the 21st century, with almost half, 46%, of the Christian community either evangelical or Pentecostal by 2050 if these trends continue. The period we are now in, between 1990 and 2010, sees little change. It is only after 2010 that the proportions are expected to grow considerably.[24] There is also an even bigger rise in the percentages between 1970 and 1990.

These percentages would change the graph given in Figure 9 below.

On these figures, First World experience is very similar to that of the Third World, indicating that the Christian community is indeed becoming more evangelical/Pentecostal in the 21st century. Unlike the previous revolution, however, this one doesn't really begin for another 15 years!

Evangelical v non-evangelical

David Barrett gives one further piece of information in the WCE which is important to us. He breaks down the change in the number of adherents in the last decade in the 20th century between natural (or 'biological') growth and 'conversion' growth. Thus the number of Christians increased from 1,747.5 million in 1990 to 1,999.6 million in 2000. He estimates this increase of 252 million people was made of 227 million biological increase and 25 million conversion increase. These numbers may be expressed as percentages, shown in Table 10 respectively as 1.29% and 1.04%. Table 10 does two things – it breaks these percentages down between First and Third World, and between evangelicals and non-evangelicals; it also compares them with the overall population.

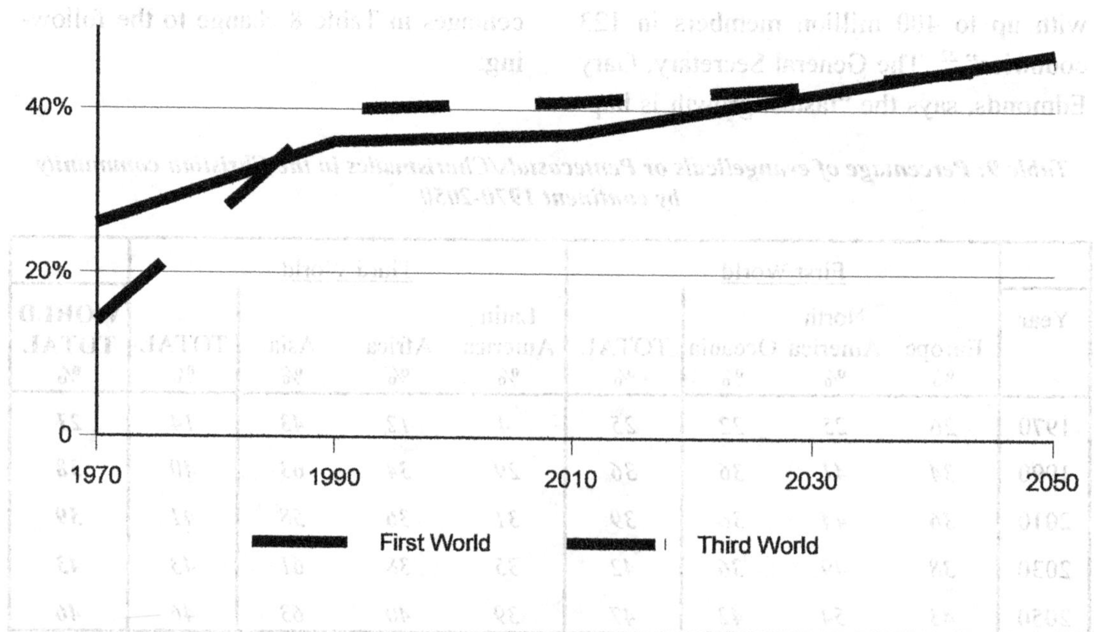

Figure 9: Percentage of the community who are evangelical or Pentecostal/Charismatic in the First and Third World, 1970-2050

Table 10: Types of Christian growth

Group	Total World			First World			Third World		
	Biological growth rate %	Conversion growth rate %	TOTAL in millions in 2000	Biological growth rate %	Conversion growth rate %	TOTAL in millions in 2000	Biological growth rate %	Conversion growth rate %	TOTAL in millions in 2000
Evangelicals	1.27	1.16	648	1.17	1.09	376	1.34	1.22	271
Non-evangelicals	1.30	-0.08	1,352	1.14	-1.04	469	1.36	1.01	883
Total Christians	1.29	1.04	2,000	1.15	-0.77	845	1.35	1.11	1,154
Total population	1.31	n/a	6,055	1.09	n/a	1,054	1.33	n/a	5,001

The Table shows that the Christian population is increasing annually faster than the world population in both the First and Third Worlds (1.15% is greater than 1.09% in the First World and 1.36% is greater than 1.33% in the Third World). However the overall rate of increase of Christians compared to the world population is *slower* because there is a negative conversion rate in the First World, that is, people are leaving the Christian faith faster than they are joining it. This loss is sufficiently large to cancel out the overall increase of Christians from biological growth compared to the population generally.

The difference in birth rates between Christians and non-Christians is however very finely balanced, and this is also true between evangelicals and non-evangelicals. Overall, non-evangelicals have slightly more children than evangelicals, but this is because there are more non-evangelical births in the Third World proportionately than evangelical births. In the First World there are slightly more evangelical births than non-evangelical, but because the numbers in the Third World are greater the overall balance goes the Third World way.

The evangelical conversion rate, however, is positive in the First World and even greater in the Third World. The First World's problem is the non-evangelicals who are leaving, whereas in the Third World the non-evangelicals have a positive conversion rate, though lower than that of evangelicals.

What this all means therefore is that evangelicals are growing across the world, both because of conversions and because of children being born into evangelical families. Of these two causes for growth, the family numbers are slightly greater in both First and Third World.

Non-evangelicals are also growing, biologically far faster than through conversion, and in the First World the numbers leaving the faith are greater than those joining it by conversion. So many are leaving in the First World that they cancel out conversion gains in the Third World. Therefore, across the world as a whole, non-evangelicals are leaving the faith rather than joining it.

Evangelical conversions however are sufficient to outnumber the non-evangelical losses, so that Christianity grows worldwide primarily through children being born into Christian families, but also because overall there is a positive conversion rate.

COMPARING THE TWO CHANGES

We have seen that the same kind of trend is happening in both of the major axes of change. Such uniformity happens in other aspects of global life also. David Smith says it "has led sociologists to employ the term *glocalisation* in order to describe the complex inter-relation ... of both the increasing uniformity of institutions and behaviour around the world *and* the appearance and growth of rediscovered local identities, cultures and religions."[25]

The danger is that the similarities in the trends lead to the conclusion that the Western, First World, model will dominate. Not at all! The first revolution described in this paper is of an increasing *Third* World Christianity. First World Christianity has enormous problems which the Third World must try to avoid. These problems are explained further by David Smith: "Western Christians need to experience a mental, conceptual and spiritual transformation. ... Received ideas concerning evangelism, which are based on Christendom assumptions that the church and the world share a basically common world-view, simply will no longer do."[26] He quotes the European theologian Hoekendijk:

"There is nothing left that can be called into memory, nothing that can be awakened."[27]

The idea of memory has been taken further by Grace Davie in one of her books on European Christianity.[28]

This argues for a radical approach to church life in the First World, looking for "mission-shaped" churches, or "missional churches" as Professor Eddie Gibbs calls them.[29] There are many books urging radical and strategic thinking.[30] The management guru Tom Peters urges First World Christians to "eradicate 'change' from our vocabulary, and substitute 'revolution'".[31]

Evangelicals are not the only growing body

David Watson, the British evangelist, once wrote, "the real contest today is between Third World Christianity and Islam."[32] Figure 10 shows how the different religions of the world are changing. It is apparent that Islam faster than the general population increase while the proportion who are Christian remains static at 33%.

Figure 10: The world's religions in millions, 1970-2050

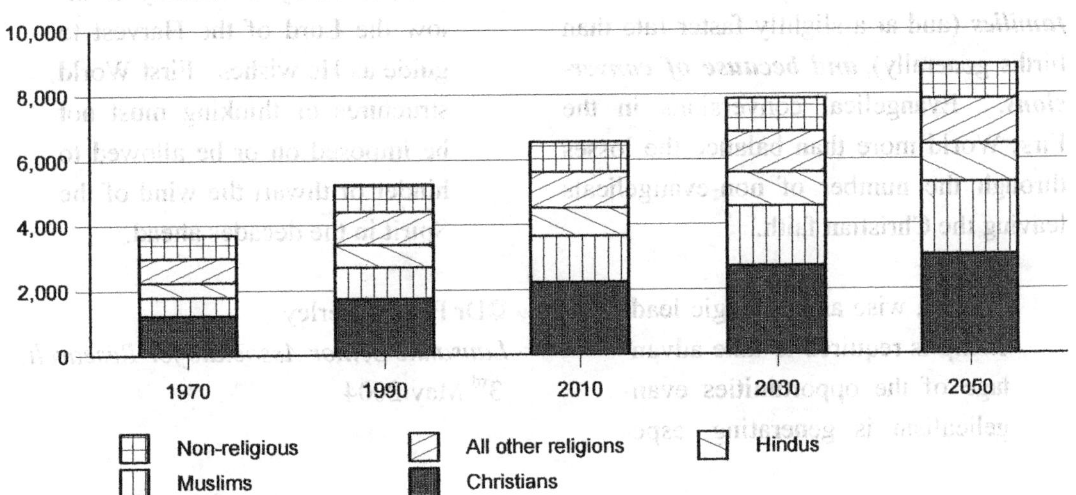

CONCLUSIONS

This paper has demonstrated seven factors which the Lausanne Forum 2004 needs to take seriously:

1) ***Third World Christianity is growing strongly***, and is doing so especially at this present time. In contrast, First World Christianity is declining significantly at present. These two movements counterbalance each other to keep the proportion of the world's population which is Christian the same percentage, 33%.

2) ***The groups that are growing especially are the non-institutional Independent churches***, many of whom are Pentecostal and Charismatic. There are more Independent churches in the Third World than in the First.

3) This Third World growth is supported by a much greater ***increase in the number of congregations, denominations and mission workers*** than in the First World, all of which are closely linked to Independent and evangelical practice.

4) Careful measurement of evangelical growth in England has shown this is beginning to accelerate. It seems likely that ***similar evangelical growth*** could occur also in the world church, especially in the decade or two after 2010.

5) The growth is particularly strong in Asia and Africa, and much less so in Latin America. However measuring the evangelical growth is difficult because David Barrett does not always classify Pentecostals as evangelicals. Including his Pentecostal figures for Asia and Latin America shows an acceleration, indeed an ***explosion, of evangelical growth***.

6) It is important on the one hand that ***world leadership reflects this Third World evangelicalism***, but at the same time, continued experimentation and variety must be encouraged. There would be nothing worse than a new kind of evangelical institutionalism because of success in certain areas.

7) ***Evangelical growth occurs because of children born into Christian families*** (and at a slightly faster rate than births generally), ***and because of conversions***. Evangelical conversions in the First World more than balance the losses through the number of non-evangelicals leaving the Christian faith.

Careful, wise and strategic leadership is required to take advantage of the opportunities evangelicalism is generating, especially in the Third World, accompanied by a humility to allow the Lord of the Harvest to guide as He wishes. First World structures or thinking must not be imposed on or be allowed to hinder or thwart the wind of the Spirit in the decades ahead.

©Dr Peter Brierley
Lausanne Senior Associate for Research
3rd May 2004

ENDNOTES

1 A T Pierson, editor *Missionary Review of the World*, Minister of Spurgeon's Tabernacle 1891-3, leader in the Student Volunteer Movement, and much else, in his book *The Crisis of Missions*.

2 A third volume was subsequently published by the William Carey Library the same year. Both publications were co-edited by Todd Johnson.

3 In fact the *Encyclopedia* does it for you.

4 These are defined as "A subdivision mainly of Protestants consisting of all affiliated church members calling themselves Evangelicals, or all persons belonging to Evangelical congregations, churches or denominations; characterised by commitment to personal religion."

5 An incredible prayer diary for the world, *Operation World*, 21st century edition, is edited by Patrick Johnstone and Jason Mandryk, and published by WEC International, London, and Paternoster Lifestyle, Carlisle, UK also in 2001. It used the same basic database as the WCE.

6 *The Next Christendom*, Professor Philip Jenkins, Oxford University Press, Oxford, UK, 2002.

7 Article "After *The Next Christendom*" in the *International Bulletin of Missionary Research*, OMSC, Connecticut, USA, Volume 28, Number 1, January 2004, Page 21.

8 So, for example, *Future Church*, Dr Peter Brierley, Monarch Publications, Crowborough, East Sussex, UK, 1998, Page 32.

9 In the January issue of the *International Bulletin of Missionary Research*, OMSC, Connecticut, USA.

10 *New Issues Facing Christians Today*, Rev John Stott, Marshall Pickering, London, UK, 1999, Page 12.

11 *On the Crest of the Wave*, Becoming a World Christian, Professor C Peter Wagner, Regal Books, Ventura, California, USA, 1983, Page 18.

12 *The Future of World Evangelization*, Edward Dayton & Sam Wilson, MARC Europe, London, UK, 1985.

13 *Clarifying the Task*, Unreached Peoples Directory 1986, Harley Schreck and Dr David Barrett, MARC Publications, Monrovia, California, USA, 1987.

14 Essentially the "First World" is the same as the Western World, consisting essentially of Europe (the European Union countries and the neutral countries not part of the EU) and North America. The "Second World" was the name given to the Communistic bloc before the USSR fell in 1989, and is not now used.

15 *The Tide is Running Out*, Dr Peter Brierley, Christian Research, London, UK, 2000, Page 150.

16 Op cit (Item 5: *Operation World*), Page 747.

17 National mission workers are defined as those "working within their own home country. This includes field missionaries and also those in a supportive role, but with missionary status."

18 1990 figures come from *Operation World*, Patrick Johnstone, OM Publishing, Carlisle, and WEC International, Gerrards Cross, Bucks, UK, 1993, Page 643.

19 *Daily Telegraph*, 25th August 2003.

20 And in actual numbers of churches.

21 *Forbidden Revolutions*, Pentecostalism in Latin America, Catholicism in Eastern Europe, Prof David Martin, Gospel & Culture, SPCK, 1996.

22 Report in *idea*, German Evangelical News Agency, English Edition, Volume 3, Number 4, 2nd December 2003, Page 1.

23 Ibid.

24 The actual figures would be, respectively for Africa, Latin America and Total: 1970 – 17, 12 and 257; 1990 – 94, 119 and 662; 2010 – 168, 168 and 883; 2030 – 245, 235 and 1,159; and 2050 – 321, 302 and 1,414. All figures in millions.

25 *Mission After Christendom*, David Smith, Darton, Longman and Todd, London, UK, 2003, Page 99.

26 Ibid., Page 123.

27 *The Church Inside Out*, J C Hoekendijk, SCM Press, London, UK, 1967.

28 *Religion in Modern Europe*, The Putative Memory, Dr Grace Davie, Oxford University Press, Oxford, UK, 2000.

29 *ChurchNext*, Professor Eddie Gibbs and Rev Dr Ian Coffey, IVP, Nottingham, UK, 2000, Page 225.

30 Including *Coming Up Trumps!*, Four ways into the Future, Dr Peter Brierley, Authentic Media, Carlisle, and Christian Research, London, UK, 2004.

31 Article "Proven Principles for Change Leaders and Managers" by Dr Larry Johnston, in McConkey/Johnston, Inc. Newsletter, Fall 2003, Page 2.

32 *Sex and the City of God*, Gordon Preece, Zadok Paper S125, Winter 2003, Zadok Institute for Christianity and Society, Fitzroy, Australia, Page 11.